THE
PHILOSOPHY OF
HEGEL

MODERN LIBRARY COLLEGE EDITIONS

THE
PHILOSOPHY OF
HEGEL

Edited by
CARL J. FRIEDRICH
Harvard University

THE MODERN LIBRARY • New York

"The Phenomenology of the Spirit," translated by J. B. Baillie, and "Logic," translated by W. H. Johnston and L. G. Struthers, are reprinted by permission of George Allen and Unwin Ltd.

The selection from "Lectures on Aesthetics," translated by B. Bosanquet and W. M. Bryant, is reprinted by permission of Routledge & Kegan Paul Ltd.

The selections from the Introduction to "The Philosophy of History" are given in a new translation by Carl J. Friedrich based upon the text as edited by Georg Lasson with the kind permission of the publisher Felix Meiner now at Hamburg.

Library of Congress Catalog Card Number: 54-13055

Manufactured in the United States of America

TO PAUL WILLIAM FRIEDRICH

When a man has finally reached the point where he does not think he knows it better than others, that is when he has become indifferent to what they have done badly and he is interested only in what they have done right, then peace and affirmation have come to him.

> HEGEL, *in one of the casual notes preserved at Widener in his own hand.*

CONTENTS

vii

PREFACE

Someone who knows my other work may well be surprised to find me dealing with Hegel. For the philosophy of Hegel has always seemed to me fundamentally wrong. Perhaps this very prejudice is responsible for my undertaking this re-evaluation. As a student of the history of political thought I have been increasingly impressed with the vast scope of Hegel's influence: Communism and Fascism, pragmatism and existentialism, to name only the most outstanding movements in politics and philosophy, are incomprehensible without Hegel's philosophy. Contemporary social science, especially in America, bears the impact of Hegelian thinking to an extraordinary degree. Cultural anthropology and social psychology, especially of the psycho-analytic and *Gestalt* variety, and much of present-day sociology, whether inspired by Veblen or Max Weber, are more Hegelian than they would like to admit or do acknowledge.

Thus regardless of how one may personally assess these movements and patterns of thought—and I confess to much doubt and perplexity—they call for a more thorough knowledge of Hegel, based upon a reading of some of the original texts, than is now generally found among American scholars and interested laymen alike. Such knowledge and reading is greatly obstructed by the available translations of Hegel's work in English. Far be it from me to claim any satisfaction with what little improvement I have been able to accomplish in the revisions of such classics as Baillie's *Phenomenology* and Sibree's *Philosophy of History*. But I hope that they will prove somewhat more comprehensible—in so far as Hegel can be comprehended—to the contemporary American reader. There is also the problem of what to select.

The tendency of the past has been to choose the (usually very abstract) introductions to Hegel's great systematic treatises, like the *Philosophy of History*. By this procedure one of Hegel's most significant traits as a thinker, namely, an avid interest in and concern with concrete detail of historical and social significance, of human life and activity, is submerged. In these selections, we have tried, hard as it is, to show Hegel as the mind trying to distill "concrete conceptions" (Max Weber's "ideal types") which are closely related to "actual reality" and yet are not "abstracted" from that reality, but are the result of a process of intuitional ratiocination. This process is at once the source of Hegel's most striking suggestiveness and of his most dangerous errors. The matter is made manifest in that touchstone of philosophical speculation: war.

Strictly speaking, war is neither glorified (as by Nietzsche) nor sanctified (as in *justum bellum* theories); for either view Hegel would have had little more than contempt. His deep-felt preference for Periclean Athens as contrasted with Sparta or Rome, on both of which he is rather harsh, shows that. Yet as linked to the decisive events in world history, as one idea and one national spirit triumphs over the other, there is no appreciation for the poignant value of the lost cause, and while the view is a highly intellectualist one, it still is in the last analysis a "success philosophy"—as are pragmatism, Communism and Fascism. I frankly admit that I do not like it. Ultimately, maybe, every philosophy has to be a "success philosophy," unless it is willing to accept chaos as the basic principle of the universe; but there are great differences of degree. Battles do not decide the truth of an idea or the value of the human beings engaged in them, and wars even less so. World history may well be the world court, but if it is, we finite mortals are not invited to the judgment table.

The strident rationalism, the gigantic *superbia cognoscendi* or conceit of knowledge which underlies his outlook revolves around three central concepts of Hegel's philosophy which are closely related to each other: reality, spirit and dialectics. Characteristically, one cannot be comprehended without the other; yet one has to begin somewhere. The Introduction seeks to help the reader unravel these conceptions and their interrelationships. But in so doing, it to some extent is itself caught in the web of their interdependent difficulties. Do not, dear reader, get too discouraged after the first ten pages; they will seem clearer at the end. Clearer, but not clear.

It is the task of the historian, I believe, to portray a man's thought as he finds it and not to simplify and clarify it, until it is no longer the great vision of an individual human being, but a textbook. Professor Montagu in his *Great Visions of Philosophy* has described Hegel's vision as an 'optimistic" one which sees the world as objectified reason. There is much to this interpretation, but it is too simple and too clear. It neglects the deep pessimism of the man who saw himself as summing up a world upon which the sun of the spirit was setting, as the dusk was falling fast: the world of Christian civilization. It neglects the perplexing mysticism of a man who referred all arguments ultimately to a God the existence of whom might be "proved" by exploring the manifestations of his spirit in history. Hegel's vision as a whole is a vast and inclusive structure, full of contradictions and cross-currents. These contradictions and cross-currents have been the starting point of all the different Hegelians, Neo-Hegelians and Crypto-Hegelians who have enlivened the intellectual landscape of Western culture since his day.

In preparing these selections, I have been given kind help by a number of people. Saxe Commins of Random House, Ernest W. Hocking of New Freedom, N.H., and Walter Kaufmann of Princeton have cheered me along, when the spirit began to lag. The Introduction has been read and helpfully criticized by Theodore S. Baer, Henry Kissinger and Herbert Shyer of Harvard, by John Ladd of Brown University and by Paul W. Friedrich of Yale University. The publishers of the earlier translations were kind enough to grant permission to use them. Friends too numerous to mention listened to my stewings and stormings regarding various points of interpretation. Finally, I must thank Mrs. Clacia Healy for the devotion and industry she brought to the exasperating task of copying the Hegelian texts and helping in the editorial work.

CARL J. FRIEDRICH

Cambridge, Mass.
April, 1953

INTRODUCTION

by CARL J. FRIEDRICH

I

The Problem of Hegel Today

Anyone who undertakes to deal with Hegel in pragmatic, positivistic America today is running the risk of being immediately set down as a hopeless obscurantist. For if the problematic and the logical approach to philosophical problems is generally acknowledged to make sense, the dialectical approach is considered dubious, to say the least. In spite of the popularity of Marx and Marxism among the more advanced intellectuals, Hegel remained "in the doghouse," a victim of the "revolt against idealism" and of the antagonism to all things German caused by the National Socialist dictatorship and more particularly by Hitler. It soon became the fashion to talk about Hegel as if he had practically written *Mein Kampf.* The writer of these pages himself shared to a considerable extent these feelings and animosities. And, philosophically speaking, he considers himself as anti-Hegelian as ever. But Hegel came increasingly to interest him as a historical phenomenon. This towering figure, dominating the thought of the Western world in so many different ways, seemed to him too little known, both to himself and to others. The palpable absurdity of making him at the same time the philosopher of Fascism and Communism appeared counterbalanced by the obvious links his philosophy has with both. Only a study of what he actually has to say would be a real remedy for the existing confusions.

Georg Wilhelm Friedrich Hegel was born on August 27, 1770, at Stuttgart, and died on November 14, 1831. His life therefore parallels that of Goethe, although he was twenty-two years his junior. He had a deep admiration for Goethe's universal genius, though the gulf between the two men is in some respects very great. What bridged it was a humanism rooted in an abiding enthusiasm for classical and, more particularly, Greek antiquity, and a dislike for the more conventional forms of church life. Indeed Hegel's thought sprang from and continued to revolve around the problem of how an ethical community could be organized, how the national state might be made into the all-engulfing, loyalty-inspiring community which the Greek polis had been. In a very special sense, Hegel was *the* philosopher of the national state. His youthful idea of a *Volksreligion,* a religion deeply embedded in and expressive of a particular nation's spirit, was conceived in these terms and in opposition to the conventional Protestant theology taught at the famous seminary attached to the University of Tübingen where he studied together with Friedrich Hölderlin and Schelling. Together, these three poet-philosophers formed one of the fountains of the romantic stream. Hegel was a romantic, in his original approaches, and the rise and spread of the movement fills his lifetime. He, however, turned against many of its more significant aspects.

Hegel was a Suabian, and the son of a government official. Suabia has been the cradle of more thinkers and poets than any other German region, and the mystic strain of self-centered religiosity is proverbial for its inhabitants. Their capacity to combine this spiritual intensity with an exceptional shrewdness and practical sense of business is equally well known. The curious combination of elevated highmindedness and loving attention to concrete detail which is a peculiarity of Hegel's thought may thus be seen as a projection of a distinctive feature of the folkways from which he sprang. Suabia is also the corner of Germany in which the constitutional tradition of government by consent is firmly entrenched. This is not so much a matter of "democracy" as it is akin to the older English tradition of government according to law and participation of at least a substantial portion of the people in the making of it. But this kind of government did not preclude a strong sense of obligation toward and acceptance of the authority of those entrusted with the enforcement of the law. Indeed, a near religious reverence for authority was readily accepted as part of this tradition. The setting of Hegel's boyhood was precisely the kind of conventional bourgeois officialdom against which the youthful Schiller revolted when he wrote his *Die Räuber*

Nonetheless, Hegel was caught in the revolutionary enthusiasm which swept Germany in the wake of the French Revolution. Henceforth, freedom remained a central value never to be surrendered, though recurrently reinterpreted. And though Hegel, then a young tutor in Switzerland—unlike his great countryman Immanuel Kant—soon turned against the French Revolution, he nonetheless became the philosopher of the French revolutionary goals of a secular national state in which the citizen is the loyal participant. For Hegel, even more than Kant, was a philosopher who spun his subtle threads of logic and metaphysic in response to a deep and abiding political drive. In a letter, he once told a friend that he had always had a strong inclination toward politics. If Hegel insisted that thought had to be fed by passion to be significant, his own work is a striking illustration of such passion-fed philosophizing. This also no doubt serves to explain the extraordinary influence of Hegel's thought. He has dominated the century since his death, and the force of his impact is anything but spent, considering that both Marxism and Fascism are incomprehensible without an understanding of Hegel.

Before sketching in somewhat greater detail Hegel's life and work, it may be well to consider the violent controversy which has raged regarding him all these years. Everyone knows about the shower of invectives against Hegel with which Schopenhauer has adorned his philosophical writings. "Charlatan" was his favorite term for speaking of his great contemporary. In recent years, the tradition has been revived by at least one writer.[1] On the other hand, no less a philosophic critic than Morris Cohen has called Hegel the greatest philosopher of the nineteenth century, and when I asked a brilliant French critic of the Hegelian system[2] about this remark, he replied: "Which other is there?" A number of very important studies of Hegel have appeared in recent years, and there was a regular rebirth of Hegel among German professional philosophers who had pretty much relegated him to limbo by the end of the nineteenth century.[3] Considering the importance of Hegel for Marx and Marxism, this was natural enough as a sequel of the revolution of 1917. Did not Marx down to the end of his life acknowledge his profound admiration for Hegel, indeed express his contempt for the small minds that criticized him without understanding him? [4]

When republishing Rudolf Haym's famous critique of the Hegelian system, Hans Rosenberg in 1927 added an essay on the history of Hegel interpretations which he begins with the following broad assessment:

As the great completer of a period of philosophical and speculative thought Hegel is a unique figure. With near gigantic power his universal mind joined the spiritual and historical reality and the mass of thought of thousands of years . . . a synthesis of antiquity and Christianity beyond anything attempted so far. Not only because of its encyclopedic universalism and the architectonic marvel of its structure but even more by the richness of original, profound, elevated and grandiose ideas and by the extraordinary effect which it has exercised, the system of Hegel will forever occupy a pre-eminent position . . . Hegel has exercised a profound and lasting influence upon learning and especially the sciences of man, upon political thought and upon life itself up to the very present.[5]

It is indeed startling to reflect upon the fact that Hegel has been credited with and discredited by his evident connection with Communism and Fascism, with the moderate socialism of a T. H. Green, or the conservative constitutionalism of a Hocking. The cultural anthropologists of contemporary America are as much indebted to him as are the philosophers of history in the style of Toynbee. Northrop has suggested [6] that the Hegelian heritage is the peculiar and distinguishing feature of the East (in the sense of the countries east of the Rhine); but surely the impact of Hegel in the work of the Neo-Hegelians in England and the Hegelians of Italy, notably Benedetto Croce, makes such a construction more than doubtful. Hegel's influence on existentialism, on Kierkegaard and Jaspers, on Heidegger and Sartre, is tremendous. His influence on Dewey is well known; it is less generally appreciated that as the first philosopher stressing process, he must be seen as the precursor not only of Dewey, but also of Bergson and Whitehead. His viewpoint antedated and reinforced the impact of Darwin and Darwinism. As an "anti-reductionist," he sought to build defenses against subjectivism and materialism which link him with modern philosophers. All of historicism's world-wide sweep traces to the impact of the Hegelian concern with history as the concretization of what he epitomized as the world spirit. We may be critically inclined toward this Hegelian heritage, as the writer certainly is, but we cannot gainsay its universal significance. No one interested in the clash of ideas that is rending the world today can afford to neglect the work of Hegel.

The problem which Hegel sought to answer is the problem of man's destiny, the problem of the meaning of his existence. It is a problem arising from the disintegration of Christian faith, as manifested in the French Revolution, and Hegel struggled to offer an answer in secular terms. When he turned back to the Greeks for help, he did so in spite of his keen awareness that the world of the Greeks was dead and gone. Yet in his youth, he cherished a dream, shared with his friend Hölderlin, that somehow Greece might be revived. On one of the loose leaves which are preserved at Widener Library, Hegel has put in a flowing hand: *"Auferstehen, ja auferstehen wirst Du, mein Griechenland!"* (You will, yes, you will be resurrected, my Greece!) In his *Philosophy of History*, probably the most moving passages are those contained in his treatment of Greece, offered below. Yet, the entire *Philosophy of History* is a farewell to any such illusions. Hegel as a thinker was profoundly convinced that all he could adequately comprise within his thought was what was past. The very central role which *becoming* occupies in his philosophy meant that he could only know that which *had* unfolded, not that which might yet come. Here lies one of the most fertile sources of error in the interpretation of Hegel as a philosopher. Hegel was very insistent that he could not speak about the future, that all he was able to analyze was the past (see below pp. liii).

It is generally assumed that Hegel is extremely abstract, and it must indeed be admitted that many passages of his main works are very difficult to understand. But Hegel shares with Aristotle—to whom he is related by many important bonds—

the capacity for distilling the general from the concrete detail in such a way that for him it remains concrete. Indeed, Hegel was highly polemical in his vigorous opposition to all "abstract" thought. To him, any thought that was not taking account of the fullness of things was abstract, and his mocking brief essay on *Who Thinks Abstractly?* is a straightforward exposition of this central thought. His notion of the concrete is closely linked to his belief in the organic wholes of which the spirit is the most comprehensive. Georg Lasson has put emphatically the close kinship between Hegel and Aristotle in this respect:

In Aristotle Hegel encountered a kindred spirit. The sober sense for the actually real (*Wirkliche*), the skillful manysidedness of the reflexion, the cautious weighing of aspects of a concept and the elevated conception of the living spiritual unity of the universe were as peculiar for one as for the other. The way in which Aristotle used the development of Greek philosophy as a premise for his system by summing it up and concluding it, corresponds to Hegel's understanding of the interrelations in the history of philosophy. . . . Upon this model Hegel has perfected his method to its mastery. It is the dialectics of the concept which enables him to recognize true being in the concrete single thing or event in which the general gives itself its particular form (*Gestalt*), rather than in the abstracting of the general and the juxtaposition of the particular things which results from it . . . the more comprehensive methodical context (we find in Hegel) shows, as in Aristotle, the pattern of a *spiritual organism* . . . The naturally organic is, therefore, the first and immediate appearance of the concept in reality (actuality—*Wirklichkeit*).

Very significant is Hegel's contrasting of Plato and Aristotle, in his *History of Philosophy*. He says there: "Aristotle is the most worthy to be studied among the ancients . . . In Plato we have the general in a rather abstract form as a principle; a basis has been laid. In Aristotle thought has become concrete; it is no longer the motionless, abstract idea, but rather the idea taken as concrete in its working." [7]

Concretization is, thus, for Hegel not the process by which a general or abstract concept or thought is manifested in a particular thing or event (*Dingheit*) but the process by which thought takes hold of any real something, no matter how spiritual or general. It is motion, a continuous weaving back and forth.[8] Abstraction is by contrast the process by which the concept is separated from the world of being as a subjective thought—a contrast which can be understood particularly well, through reading Hegel's discussion of the Stoic philosophy, or rather its basic principle.

This basic position is bound up with Hegel's linking of the world spirit with God. In his *History of Philosophy* he suggests several times that all philosophy is pantheistic. In the *Phenomenology of the Spirit* Hegel concludes his discussion of the absolute knowledge with the proposition that such knowledge is the spirit which knows itself to be spirit, and he adds that the way to arrive at such knowledge is to recall the spirits (of the successive stages in the development of the spirit) and thus to see how they bring about the organization of their realm. This can be done, because these spirits have been preserved in a double aspect. One is history, free existence appearing in the form of something accidental, the other is the aspect of organization which is the science of knowledge as it appears. The two together, history and the philosophical mastery of the organizations or patterns which it produces, or what Hegel calls comprehended history (*begriffene Geschichte*), constitute remembrance of the absolute spirit, the reality, the truth and the certainty of its rule (*Thron*) and thereby the knowledge of God Himself. Without such knowledge, he adds, the absolute spirit would be lifeless and alone. Clearly, then, concretization in the sense of a historical unfolding is the only way in which the spirit can be conceived as existing.

As has recently been said by one of the most extraordinary Swiss students of German intellectual history, Hegel is "that melting together (never before seen in the history of philosophy) of the lyrical, the poetical, the visionary, of the vitally concrete with the most disciplined conceptualization . . . It is a melting together which is the sign of old age . . ."[9] And while many who speak of political matters today do not realize that they are moving within the charmed circle of Hegel's spiritualistic philosophy of success, the prevailing mood of both East and West, of the Totalitarians *and* of the Constitutionalists, is that somehow such a projection is justified, and that God is on their side and will give them victory through the realization of their aims in concrete history.

II

Hegel's Youth and Beginnings

Hegel studied at the famous theological seminary at the University of Tübingen from 1788 to 1793. As already noted, two fellow seminarians were to be among the great of the romantic movement, the poet Friedrich Hölderlin (1770–1843) and the philosopher F. W. J. Schelling (1775–1854), the arch transcendentalist who inspired Ralph Waldo Emerson and David Henry Thoreau. With Hölderlin and Schelling he read and discussed enthusiastically the works of Rousseau and Schiller, started an exploration of Kant and more especially immersed himself in the study of Greek poetry and philosophy which led him to his idea of a folk religion which, far removed from formal theology and ritual, is the ever-present form of a people's life and ethics.

The most striking feature of the re-evaluation of Hegel in recent years is the greatly changed view of Hegel's early work. Wilhelm Dilthey explored with great care the manuscripts of what Hegel had written in the years before the *Phenomenology of the Spirit,* the first of his mature writings (see below). In a now famous study, *Die Jugendgeschichte Hegels*[10] Dilthey undertook to show how central for the development of Hegel's philosophy were the theological studies of his youth. While he was a tutor at Berne (1791–96) and at Frankfurt (1796–1800), Hegel was centrally concerned with two issues, namely, how to overcome his theological antecedents and how to transcend the heritage of Kant. This effort found expression in a number of unpublished writings which enable us to understand better the origin of Hegel's central concept of the spirit, of *Geist*. In it, Christian notions combined with ideas of the French Revolution tracing back to Montesquieu which were given by Hegel a universal application. It has been maintained that "the deepest root of Hegel's system was a personal religious experience." Certainly his effort at re-interpreting Christianity in terms of Kantian ethics must have seemed unsatisfying, to say the least. Hegel's *Life of Jesus* as well as his *Positivity of Christianity*[11] were way-stations in this curious evolution which culminated in his *The Spirit of Christianity*. There is a startling change involved in this culmination: in *The Spirit of Christianity* Hegel speaks as a mystic who has had a vision which he seeks to express in philosophical or rather in metaphysical terms. The earlier antipathy to Christianity which stemmed from his love of the Greeks and his admiration of Kant's ethical philosophy is now resolved into a higher unity (a typically Hegelian process). Richard Kroner rightly comments that "this essay shows how the fusion of Greek soul and Kantian Reason . . . permitted Hegel to rise to the plane on which he could understand the message of Jesus."

This development raises the issue of the relation between Kant and Hegel. That Kant exercised a profound influence upon the youthful Hegel there can be no doubt. But are we therefore justified in saying that Hegel was a Kantian? One does not have to minimize Kant's influence to deny such a proposition. To claim that Hegel remained a Kantian, "no matter how much he disputed many of Kant's doctrines and even his fundamental position," as one writer does, is to make nonsense out of the history of thought and of ideas. Aristotle is not a Platonist, because he started from Plato, since he made it his task to transcend the Platonic philosophy, and succeeded in doing so. And the distance between Kant and Hegel is considerably greater than that between Plato and Aristotle. In the vital matter of politics, Plato and Aristotle are both elitists, inclined toward aristocratic patterns of government and society. They accepted slavery and war as natural. Hegel and Kant are diametrically opposed to each other on a number of vital issues of this type. To be sure, Hegel would never have found his dialectical method without the transcendental dialectic delineated in Kant's *Critique of Pure Reason*.

Such links are the rule in the history of philosophic thought;

similar ties bind Hobbes and Spinoza to Descartes, Kant to Hume, Marx to Hegel, etc. But they do not establish identities; indeed they are often the crux of the most vital antitheses. Anyone familiar with the Hegelian dialectics would feel particularly insistent upon this point, I should think. No, Hegel is the most radical opposite to all that Kant desired to prove in his critical philosophy. Its key position was to deny the possibility of metaphysical dogmatism, and to outline a critical, that is to say, a hypothetical approach to the problem of truth. There is little doubt in my mind that Kant would have criticized even more sharply the work of Hegel than he did that of Herder and Fichte who clearly stand in a similar relation to Kant as does Hegel.[12]

As I have pointed out elsewhere, Kant is the philosopher of peace and international constitutional order, whereas Hegel is the philosopher of war and of the national authoritarian state. Authoritarian, but not totalitarian, Hegel is as emphatic in his rejection of the despotic rule of one, as he is of the corrupt rule of the few, and the demagogic rule of the many. His thought seems to resemble closely that of Plato and Aristotle; like them he lays great stress upon the importance of law and justice as the touchstone of sound government. But there is a difference hidden here, which to Hegel at least seemed basic. His ever-repeated conviction that the Greeks lacked a full grasp of the meaning of freedom (see, e.g., the discussion in his *Philosophy of History* below p. 65) for otherwise they could not have accepted slavery, is for Hegel summed up in their failure to understand that man is intended to be free as man, that freedom is involved in the very idea of man. The authoritarian government he believes in is a constitutional monarchy of the type English Tories favored before the nineteenth century, where the classes or estates, as he calls them, each fulfill their appointed role, where each citizen has some share in the shaping of law, but where the mainstay of the government is a strong monarchy, firmly attached to the law, and ready to restrict itself to the main tasks of government, including, above all, defense.

Those who include Hegel among the believers in the regimented society should read carefully his explicit rejection of such theories, not only in the *Constitution of Germany* (1802), but the relevant passages in his other works, more especially the *Philosophy of Right and Law* (1821) (see below § 189, p. 273 and § 261, p. 285). One of his main objections to the French revolutionary movement, as it actually developed, was that it swept away the many intermediary civic bodies and institutions of local government. Here, as in so many other matters, Hegel remained close to the thought of Montesquieu whose view on the importance of intermediary powers he fully accepts. Interestingly enough, he also cherished the political thought of Henry Benjamin Constant (1767–1830). As one of his most learned interpreters, Georg Lasson, has remarked: "Hegel began reading Benjamin Constant [at Berne] to whom he gave attention to the very end of his life and to whom he owes a good part of his monarchical liberalism." [13] To those who incline to interpret Hegel in a sharply anti-liberal fashion, these ties to Montesquieu and Benjamin Constant ought to give pause.

Hegel's study of the German constitution belongs already to his years of being a professor at the University of Jena (1801–6) as do a work on natural law and a system of ethics. These legal and political efforts, when taken together with the earlier sharp critique of the constitution of Württemberg (now largely lost) show Hegel's other side: the hard-headed realist interested in the concrete detail of practical politics. We can only include a few brief extracts which offer glimpses of this side of Hegel's interests. Only a close study of these works, as well as the later ones, giving an evaluation of the sessions of the Diet of Württemberg (1817) and of the English Parliamentary Reform Bill (1832) will provide an adequate basis for a considered judgment.

It was in Jena that Hegel closely co-operated with, but also came to break away from, his friend Wilhelm Schelling. It is in these critical years that Hegel came fully to work out his central concept of the spirit and to this decisive topic we must now turn.

III

The Discovery of the Geist

Recent research has suggested that the discovery of the spirit was not a sudden one, but germinated slowly over the years beginning with Hegel's early efforts to grapple with the problems of religion.[14] When he finally came to write his first major work, his dislike of the "emptiness" of Schelling's absolute and his even stronger dislike of Fichte's subjectivism caused him to focus upon his great metaphysical construct, the spirit seen as a real, concrete and objective force. There is a tie here to Montesquieu of whose work Hegel spoke with great respect to the end of his life; but of course in Montesquieu the idea of "spirit" is devoid of the metaphysical and religious connotation given it by Hegel.[15]

The Phenomenology of the Spirit has been extravagantly praised and violently condemned.[16] It is a work of vast scope. Upon the basis of its extraordinary analysis of the consciousness of the self * it identifies the spirit as the final given which it posits as the essence of man and his history. It therefore proceeds to trace through the course of human history the unfolding of this spirit, in order to discover how far the development of the spirit could be "verified" in its manifestations in actual history. The result has been sharply attacked as being a most unfortunate mixture of history and psychology: a psychology confused by history and a history ruined by psychology.[17] Truly, the work is neither history nor psychology in the accepted sense of either term. It makes use of such materials as either of them offer, but it is itself philosophy, indeed metaphysics, pure and simple. Or rather, it was intended as the first part of

---

* The term "self-consciousness" used by professional philosophers ought to be guarded against, since it carries a totally different psychological connotation in English than Selbstbewusstsein—a connotation which is curiously at opposite poles to the German analogue. For the German adjective selbstbewusst when not used in a philosophical, but a psychological sense, means confident, even high-spirited, as contrasted with the implication of the English self-conscious, as timid, worried, tormented.

Hegel's system of metaphysics, of which the second part was to be his system of Logic. He afterwards abandoned this scheme (see below p. xxxix) and the *Phenomenology* thus contains most of the ideas later spelled out in his *Philosophy of Right and Law,* and his great series of Lectures, notably those on religion, aesthetics, and the philosophy of history.

Although some very deep students of Hegel, especially in the tradition of the English Neo-Hegelians, have been inclined to speak of this work as the *Phenomenology of the Mind,* notably Baillie whose translation we in part have used, the word "mind" does not render the personalized character of the spirit which seems to me essential to Hegel's conception. Indeed, it is unfortunate that the English "spirit" is a neuter, whereas the German is a masculine noun. For example, *"der wirkende Geist"* conjures up the notion of a person actually and creatively at work, whereas the working spirit lacks some of this activist implication, while the working mind would suggest something quite different. While calculated to eliminate some of the more extraordinary, not to say odd, features of Hegel's philosophy, "mind" injects at the same time a subjectivist aspect which is certainly alien to Hegel's most insistent intention. He was intensely concerned with substituting an *objective,* for a *subjective* philosophy, such as he conceived Fichte's and even Schelling's to be. Anyone looking at Hegel's work from a psychological standpoint may well feel that this is a vain pretense, and that Hegel carries subjectivism to an extreme by proclaiming the most subjective to be the most objective. But as a historian one has to acknowledge that for Hegel the spirit was a personalized entity, and the most objective entity at that, completely outside the self, as well as inside it.

Hegel gave to this work the subtitle: "Science of the Experience of the Consciousness." He believed, in other words, that consciousness makes numerous experiences, aside from the sense experiences which sensationalism and eighteenth-century empiricism had so exclusively stressed, and that of these experiences there could be had an objective scientific knowledge, demonstrable and of the broadest significance. Indeed, these experiences are of greater significance than ordinary sense experience which is the "most abstract" [18] whereas these experiences lead the mind to ever greater concreteness. We have already commented upon Hegel's unusual use of these words; it can now be seen that concreteness arises from the completeness of the conceptual framework. The mind proceeds from the this-and-here of the given thing to the grasp of all the concepts that are involved in its being what it is, and only when it is so "understood" does it possess the concreteness which we attribute to it "by itself," yet even its very unity as a thing is nothing sensuous, but is a universal. "Immediate certainty does not take hold of the truth by itself, for its truth is general, whereas such certainty wants to take hold of a particular something." [19] In short, experience is that aspect in the life of the spirit by which the spirit becomes conscious of itself. It is the task of the *Phenomenology* to illumine the process by which this happens. Kuno Fischer has, in his celebrated analysis of the *Phenomenology*, put the matter thus: "Since consciousness relates to the objects as well as differentiates itself from them, the things and the self itself are the themes of the first two main stages: the first is the consciousness of things, the second that of the consciousness of the self. . . . The conciousness of things and the consciousness of self are related like the objects and the self, like the objective and the subjective [given] the unity and identity of which is, according to the doctrine of identity, reason: hence reason is the theme of the third main stage which may be designated as that of consciousness of reason. But reason is, according to Hegel and to express it in Hegelian terms, not a substance, but a subject, i.e. it is reason conscious of itself or *spirit;* the revelation of the spirit is the world order and its highest stage the idea of God in the world, that is the representation of the divine (absolute) or *religion* which is perfected in the true knowledge of God. The true knowledge of God is the *absolute knowledge.* Thus the *Phenomenology* distinguishes between the second and the last stage, between the consciousness of the self and absolute knowledge three main stages: *"reason," "spirit"* and *"religion."* [20]

Since there has been a good deal of dispute among learned men concerning what the purpose of the *Phenomenology* is, it may be well at this point to state this purpose in Hegel's own terms. Philosophy, Hegel agrees with many others, seeks true knowledge. This task obliges philosophy to examine critically the several sciences to see how much truth they contain. These sciences are, since they exist in the phenomenal world, themselves appearance. But they claim to be giving the truth; consequently philosophy must examine them critically. "For that reason, we are undertaking a presentation of knowledge as it appears (phenomenal knowledge)."

Thus all knowledge commences with experience, but it does not flow from it. The higher knowledge of philosophy has to be applied to it as a measuring rod. The effective matching of the two sets the stage for the final and conclusive effort: the totality of being is comprehended as the spirit which posits and reveals itself. This spirit creates both the world of thought and the world of actual reality (*Wirklichkeit*) and takes it back into itself. Thus the first part of Hegel's philosophical system consists in a philosophic comprehension of the existing knowledge, of experience and of actuality. The three are one for Hegel's philosophical approach.[21] The world of the actual consciousness *is* the world of the known actuality or reality. That is why the *Phenomenology* treats of the different modes of the spirit as it appears. Thus it does not treat existing knowledge by taking up one field of knowledge after another, but by taking up each kind of relation of the consciousness to the total reality so that the entire reality is always being under consideration at each stage of the inquiry. But of course the inquiry must therefore be limited to the most important relations and hence some of the transitions in the *Phenomenology* are very startling. It is revealing that in thus approaching the world through the consciousness Hegel places a very much greater emphasis upon the realm which in German is designated as *Geisteswissenschaften*—clearly a term of Hegelian derivation, only roughly equivalent with the social sciences and the humanities —rather than that of *Naturwissenschaften*. But the most revealing of all is Hegel's almost complete lack of interest in the field of mathematics which to him appears empty and devoid of any true relation to actuality. (This lack is incidentally one of the great differences between Hegel and Kant; it is a difference of persistent significance, as suggested by pairing Plato and Aristotle, Descartes and Hobbes, Leibnitz and Spinoza.) It is interesting to hear Hegel himself on mathematics: "The evidentness of this defective kind of knowledge upon which mathematics prides itself . . . results from the poverty of its purpose and the defectiveness of its material; it is therefore of a kind which philosophy must reject. The purpose or concept of mathematics is quantity. This is precisely the non-essential, non-conceptual relationship. The activity of this kind of knowledge occurs on the surface, does not touch the thing itself, nor the essence nor the concept, and therefore it gives no comprehension. The material about which mathematics offers a nice treasure of truths is space and unity (*das Eins*). . . . But the actually real is not something spatial as considered in mathematics; with such unreality (*Unwirklichkeit*) as the entities of mathematics neither the concrete sensuous intuition nor philosophy is concerned." [22]

It is the history of man in all its manifold and variegated manifestations that constitutes the core of the reality Hegel is primarily concerned with. Society and state, religion and ethics, art and music and literature, they all are brilliantly commented upon, as forms of the objective spirit as it realizes itself.

Philosophy, in Hegel's view, is not concerned then with the abstract and the non-real; its element, its content is the actually real, that which posits itself and lives in itself, that is to say has existence in its very concept. Philosophy therefore is the process which creates its different stages as it passes through them. This activity constitutes its "truth." Truth thus includes the negative, that is to say, that which it negates. This negated aspect could be called error, Hegel says, if it could be looked upon as something absolutely wrong. What Hegel has in mind is that each stage in the forward movement of the mind negates the preceding stage, yet could not exist without its having that preceding stage to reject; it is built upon its antecedent. That which vanishes in the process must itself be looked upon as essential, yet not as something fixed which is cut off from what *is* true, as something outside. Nor is the true to be looked upon as something similarly static, dead and only positive. What appears is the becoming and the passing away which itself does not become or pass away. This process of becoming and passing away truly exists, is in itself, and constitutes the actual reality and the active life of the truth. In these memorable phrases, Hegel indicates his basic conception of the dialectic process. To clinch the argument, to make doubly sure that the clearly vitalistic conception of truth and thought is fully grasped by the reader, Hegel adds that "truth is a Bacchantic ecstasy wherein every member is drunk." Yet this truth is, because all such motion eventually is dissolved, also lucid, it is simple rest. This Hegelian conception of philosophy is therefore thoroughly "historicist" or "relativistic" as we have become accustomed to say; like much modern anthropology and sociology it sees truths but no truth, as it looks back. And yet Hegel rises above this Bacchantic ecstasy when he has truth recognize itself as such, and to appreciate that what truly is always true is that all is in flux, and that therefore the truth-seeker ought properly to address himself to the study of this life process of truth seeking itself. In the judging of this movement, Hegel says, the particular configurations of the spirit and the specific thoughts do not endure, but they are as positively necessary aspects as they are negative and vanishing aspects. The movement as a whole is thus conceived as something that has its essence in remaining movement, and in it the various spiritual configurations recall their antecedents and preserve them.

This brings us to a concluding problem, at once philosophical and linguistic, in the Hegelian analysis, and more especially in the *Phenomenology*. It is the concept of how the negative, that which is being negated in the dialectical process is at once superseded and preserved. The German word for both processes is *Aufhebung,* the verb *aufheben,* the participle *aufgehoben.* Hegel was quite aware of the fact that he was in a sense playing upon a word, when he suggested the use of this one word in both connotations, and there is therefore no particular reason for or sense in trying to find an English equivalent which does not exist. The proper solution is to speak of this process as **we** have as one of both superseding and preserving. More precisely it is a matter really of suspending rather than superseding; the word supersede almost carries the connotation of preserving that which is being replaced. It has often been alleged that there is also a third meaning, namely to elevate or even to transcend, but the German word for these processes is *empor-heben*.[23] The word "transcend" is particularly objectionable in this connection, because of its associations with "transcendental"; for it is precisely the knowledge as it appears in the historical process of progressing thought to which this idea of the simultaneous suspending and preserving applies, as contrasted with the transcendent knowledge that is "absolute."

These very general notions which are basic for all of Hegel's work become more tangible in a number of more specific fields to which we expect to turn presently, but in none more so than his treatment of the history of his own proper field, philosophy. It is one of those works known to us only through the editorial and critical labor bestowed upon his lectures. Still, among Hegel's more revealing, as well as more readable, works, the *History of Philosophy* is outstanding. It too consists mostly of lecture notes, but these have through the devoted labors of Professor Hoffmeister been so carefully collated that a reasonably clear view of Hegel's own position at least as far as the general introduction is concerned can be formed. More especially do we now know which passages of the original edition by Michelet were based upon Hegel's own manuscript. Among these, the so-called Berlin preface is probably the most significant. In any case, we have chosen this rather extended preface as the basis of our selection, with a few additions from such passages as, in the opinion of Hoffmeister, are clearly based upon Hegel's own writing.

The key thought of Hegel's *History of Philosophy* is that this history reveals the gradual unfolding of the truth, that in it the dialectic of the spirit is explicitly working out its themes, that philosophy is one aspect of the general spirit at work in history. This last position is stated pointedly:

The essential category is unity, the inner nexus of all the different configurations [of the spirit]. It must be maintained that it is only *one* spirit, *one* principle which expresses itself in the political state just as much as in religion, art, ethics, manners, commerce and industry. These are merely branches of a main stem. This is the main point. The spirit is only one, it is the substantive spirit of an epoch, of a nation, of a period which forms itself in many ways . . . One ought not to imagine that politics, the constitutions, the religions, etc., are the roots or the cause of philosophy or *vice versa* that philosophy is the basis of these other forms. All these aspects have *one* character . . .[24]

Thus, the unity of culture and cultural expressions which has become so central a tenet of much modern work in history and the social sciences is firmly stated. Since philosophy is the field in which the spirit becomes conscious of itself, the forward movement of the spirit can be most clearly seen here. It is evident that the Hegelian insistence upon the unity of all culture is a principle which underlies the work of cultural historians and anthropologists alike. In present-day America the viewpoint of Hegel is now so widely accepted that it is difficult to believe that it once was a revolutionary principle.[25] Hence it is very important for a full understanding of Hegel's viewpoint to bear in mind that it was during the very time of the writing of the *Phenomenology* that Hegel lectured for the first time on the history of philosophy (1805–6). As Rosenkranz comments: "Now he became most explicitly conscious of the unity of philosophy in all philosophies as a continuum within a great context. Now he for the first time worked through world history from the standpoint of absolute knowledge."[26]

IV

Religion

It has become increasingly fashionable to interpret Hegel as primarily a religious thinker, rather than a philosopher. Titles such as "The Philosophy of Hegel [seen] as a contemplative doctrine of God"[27] are characteristic for a tendency to stress throughout Hegel's work the strand which Dilthey had elaborated regarding his youthful work, as has already been pointed out. I believe that there can be little question that Hegel himself would be very much puzzled, if not provoked, by such an interpretation. In his later years, to be sure, he is reported to have grumbled, in reply to such questions, that he had been born a Lutheran and that he proposed to remain one. The remark is curious in view of his unquestioned pantheistic tendency which is sharply at variance with the orthodox Lutheran position, of course. But a philosophic enterprise that may seem strongly religious in its overtones to a completely agnostic age may well have been a liberating force from the fetters of established orthodoxy at the time it was written. Hegel is somewhat in this position. But in view of this re-evaluation, Hegel's philosophy of religion is now assigned a more central place, and must definitely be considered a part of the living Hegel. How closely this religious element in Hegel is tied to his idea of the spirit and the place of logic in discovering it— an aspect of Hegel's philosophy which has understandably but not very adequately been dubbed "panlogism"—may be seen from a passage in his *Logic,* at the end of his discussion of Kant:

According to Kant, the things that we know about are to us appearances only, and we can never know their essential nature, which belongs to another world which we cannot approach. Plain minds have not unreasonably taken exception to this subjective idealism with its reduction of the facts of consciousness to a purely personal world, created by ourselves alone. For the true statement of the case is rather as follows. The things of which we have direct consciousness are mere phenomena, not for us only, but in their own nature; and the true and proper case of these things, finite as they are, is to have their existence founded not in themselves but in the universal divine Idea. This view of things, it is true, is as idealist as Kant's; but in contradistinction to the subjective idealism of the critical philosophy should be termed absolute idealism. Absolute idealism, however, though it is far in advance of vulgar realism, is by no means restricted to philosophy. It lies at the root of all religion; for religion too believes the actual world we see, the sum total of existence, to be created and governed by God.[28]

And in the very beginning of this basic work, Hegel suggests that "the objects of philosophy, it is true, are on the whole the same as those of religion. In both the object is truth." In keeping with this outlook, Hegel's *Phenomenology* culminates in a moving discourse on the several kinds of religion, capped by his chapter on "absolute knowledge"; for through such absolute knowledge, the end of both philosophy and religion is united and realized.[29]

Even R. Haym, in his critical lectures on Hegel, remarked that theology was the cradle of Hegel's philosophy. And he added that Hegel's interest was essentially a religious one; that not only the shadow of dogma, but the solid body of pious reverential sentiment were originally the object of his reflection. It seems very clear that for Hegel all knowledge ultimately and in the last analysis is derived from the depth of religious experience, and culminates in it. But Haym at the same time suggested that the Hegelian philosophy eventually lost contact with this basic religious experience and knows it only through its transformation into the process of the thinking spirit and of the logical concept.

On the whole, Hegel's philosophy of religion, at the time of his lectures on the subject, "construes orthodoxy instead of religion . . . and becomes modern scholasticism." [30] It may well be doubted whether this is a wholly just approach to the matter; it is motivated by a dislike for the particular philosophical positions at which Hegel arrived and which seemed at variance with certain dominant Protestant views (themselves orthodoxies). If one considers certain key statements of Hegel this will become clear.

In the introduction to the *Philosophy of Religion*, Hegel remarks: "Spirit, in so far as it is the Spirit of God, is not a spirit beyond the stars, beyond the world. On the contrary, God is present, omnipresent, and exists as spirit in all spirits. God is a living God, who is acting and working. Religion is a product of the Divine Spirit; it is not a discovery of man, but a work of divine operation and creation in him." [31] There follows the characteristic Hegelian argument that the development of reason is in no sense opposed to this religion, this feeling for and faith in the existence of God as living and working here and now, but is itself the most intense expression of this living and working God. "For it, namely reason, is itself the essential fact, the spirit, the Divine Spirit." And he mocks the "proud irony" of the theologians who are inclined to take it amiss that their doctrine is made reasonable. This approach is made even more explicit in the beginning of Hegel's *Proofs of the Existence of God* (left ready for the printer in 1829). He here recognizes that these proofs have come to be looked upon as a barren, antiquated "desert" from which "we have escaped and brought ourselves back to a living faith"; he speaks of the "warm feeling of religion" and of the tendency to look upon a search for a rational proof as "irreligious." From his standpoint, where logic is the quintessence of the divine spirit by which God is present in the world, nay indeed through which he works and creates the world, such proofs are a direct sign of the religious experience itself; they are nourished and maintained by it, as they nourish and maintain it in turn. "For the nature of proof . . . is only the consciousness of the proper movement of the object in itself." But in doing this, Hegel once again proceeded to undertake by rational means what Kant had shown to be beyond the ken of rational analysis and knowledge. And the mere assertion that reason and understanding are the highest, the most intense form of the divine in the world did not, of course, prove anything about their ability to cope with the essentially religious realm. Yet Hegel is most explicit and doctrinally firm about this key point. "The lifting of the spirit to God occurs in the innermost regions of the spirit upon the basis of thought; religion as the innermost affair of man has here its center and the root of its life; God is in his very essence thought and thinking, however his image and configuration be determined otherwise."

It has rightly been observed that this notion that religion is thought is most clearly evident in Hegel's approach to the proofs of the existence of God. Kant had disposed of the older syllogistic proofs by showing their inadequacy. Hegel brings forward dialectic proofs which frankly introduce the religious element into the very thought pattern. The true proving of the existence of God consists in this dialectic imitating of the dynamics of religious experience. But this involves the danger that the experience itself is diluted as it becomes reflected in dialectic patterns. I wish that space had permitted us to include some part of these proofs, because, written by Hegel for publication, they are evidently the part of his philosophy of religion which he himself considered most crucial. Man's lifting his heart to God and discovering him in this process is a "lifting into the realm of thought," dialectic thought, of course, which is dynamic and full of vitality. It is clear that Hegel appears to be the super-rationalist. He thunders against mysticism which seeks to avoid the glaring light of rational, albeit dialectic, discourse. Philosophy of religion has therefore the one basic task of understanding the religion which is. Its highest form is Christianity. Its distinguishing feature is that the nature of God is seen as love, limitless love, and that means spirit. The evident, revealed religion is the religion of the spirit. "Man knows about God only in so far as God knows about himself in man; this knowledge is self-consciousness of God, but this knowledge is at the same time God's knowledge of man, and this God's knowledge of man is man's knowledge of God; the spirit of man knowing God is only God's own spirit." Here we have a most extreme formulation of the principle of identity which informs the entire dialectic; the antitheses are at once suspended and preserved.

Hegel does at times speak of himself as a pantheist; yet at others, as we have noted, he is most insistent that he continues in the Protestant orthodoxy of his family tradition. There can be little doubt that Hegel at times uses formulas that indicate ideas customarily associated with pantheism.[32] The very fact that Hegel at times seems to identify God with the world would seem to point in this direction. But it is impossible to stop here. Because only if the world is seen in its usual meaning as an outside, as something existing materially and autonomously, can God be said to be truly dispersed throughout the world through such identifications. But in Hegel, the phenomenal world is no world at all; the true world is that of the spirit and this spirit is a personalized being through which God actualizes himself. Thus God himself remains a personal being. One may well object that this makes no sense; the only reply can be that Hegel does say these things and that it is here that the limits of his system's meaning are reached, which a word like "absolute idealism" symbolizes. Hegel's extraordinary notion that true understanding only results from contemplating (*Schauen*) the active spirit at work in all its multiform ways is here centrally involved. This process of thinking which is seeing at the same time, which is experiencing at the same time [for the contemplation encompasses, must encompass all the different realms of human experience: observation (nature), feeling (religion), willing (law and ethics), interpreting (history), comprehending (philosophy) and creating and re-creating (art, etc.)]—this process discloses the world at the same time that it discloses the existence of God and his working.[33] Hegel's whole system may be interpreted in a sense in terms of the basic metaphor of the incarnation, that is to say, the union of God and man. This is a very singular sort of pantheism: Hegel's acceptance of the doctrine that Christ is both God and man at the same time, and being the one just as much as the other obliges him to formulate his doctrine of the spirit in terms of "levels of reality," the higher ones being seen as more real and more spiritual.

This sense of concrete actualization is built upon a keen interest in development. As we showed in discussing the spirit, Hegel's idealism is distinctly dynamic. This dynamism of Hegel's approach is vividly reflected in his treatment of religion. Absolute spirit appears as religion; for religion is the knowledge of this absolute spirit. This knowledge is, however, not a static matter, but itself passes through several stages. The three main stages are those of the natural religion, of the artistic religion and of the revealed or spiritual religion. The old Orient brought forward the first, Greece the second and Christianity embodies the third. The extraordinary combination of abstract conception and concrete imagery may be seen in the selections from the *Phenomenology* (below pp. 399). It is evident that the evolution of the religious experience of

mankind is for Hegel of central importance. It is in parallelism
to this evolution that the evolution of history, of art and literature and of the state and its constitution as well as ethics are
seen: the history of philosophy, more particularly, provides the
rational mirror in which the unfolding of the spirit in these
various concretizations may be watched and comprehended.

Clearly, for Hegel Christianity was the fulfillment of the
spirit's inner destiny, as Hegel saw it. More especially, its
Protestant form was for him the necessary basis of the "absolute knowledge" for which he strove and which he conceived to
be the culmination of religious development. The fact that
God became man, the incarnation, is the decisive event, as
contrasted with the deification of man, the apotheosis which
the Greeks and Romans believed in. As he put it in the *Phenomenology*: "It is the faith of the world that the spirit is present as a real man, that is a self-consciousness . . . that the conscious which believes, *sees and feels and hears* this divinity.
Thus it is not imagined, but *it is really so*." And the true community—a concept closely akin to the traditional "invisible
church"—is by Hegel seen as the "general divine man" which
comes into existence as the incarnation is believed in. "Just as
the individual divine man has a father existing in himself and
an actual mother, so the general divine man, the community,
has its own deed and knowledge for its father, but for its
mother it has eternal love . . ." [34] Characteristically, in an
early letter exchange with his friend Schelling, he replied to
the latter's general exclamation: "We do not want to stay behind!" by this revealing remark: "Reason and liberty remain
our key-words. Our point of unity the invisible church." Upon
this original ground of the *corpus mysticum* and its true faith
the absolute knowledge becomes possible which consists in the
spirit knowing itself.

Hegel's basic notions were thus worked out when he completed the *Phenomenology* in 1805, and the extended *Lectures
on the Philosophy of Religion*, published after his death on
the basis of notes by his students, merely elaborated this basic
theme. But Hegel was not permitted to continue his academic
work at Jena; as a sequel to the victory of Napoleon, the uni-

versity fell upon evil days. Hegel went to Bavaria, first to edit a newspaper, in Bamberg, the *Bamberger Zeitung*, from 1807–8, but he found this work a hard "yoke" and a "galley" slavery. Therefore his friend Niethammer, a high official in the educational system of Bavaria who had just succeeded in putting through a reform of the Bavarian high schools, secured for him the post as professor of philosophical propaedeutics and as rector (principal) of the Latin School (Gymnasium) at Nürnberg (1808); Hegel was very happy and relieved. For although he hoped for a university chair, he was ever a modest and contented man, and when he heard the good news, he wrote (Oct. 28, 1808) to Niethammer: "The love of my friends is, next to my scientific work . . . the happiness of my life . . ." It was in this post that Hegel found the time to work out his basic work, the *Logic*.

But before we turn to the *Logic*, brief mention should be made of Hegel's marriage in 1811. For unlike so many of his predecessors, he (and Fichte) married. Thus the long line of bachelors, extending from Descartes to Hume and Kant, was broken. Is this marriage of Hegel's symbolic of the turn from radical individualism to a broader social view of man? Should the "rediscovery of the community" which has been dated from Rousseau have something to do with it? Or is it a matter of the expanding bourgeois culture bringing in its train a fuller recognition of the value of the intellectual and a securer place for him in the social order? Certainly Hegel's stress on the organic and full life reveals itself here as rooted in a fuller, more vital personality structure than was possessed by some of his eminent predecessors. For this marriage, entered into at full maturity, but preceded by several solid friendships, was no expedient or calculated proposition, but an ardent affair of the heart.

A charming beauty of the ancient family of the Nürnberg Tuckers, Marie embodied the best traditions of the Western German patriciate. Her rare education and charm made her an independent and at times vividly opposing companion, different from Hegel in many important traits. His courtship was so deeply felt that he burst several times into romantic poetry. Hegel's biographer, Rosenkranz, gives a lively account of Hegel in this period, including a sharp quarrel. In the course of it Hegel once appealed to his fair friend to remember that "in all not superficial minds a sense of sadness is linked with all sense of happiness." And he reminded her that she had promised to reconcile his true inner being with the way he often behaves, and that he had confidence in her ability to do this, that this indeed must be the strength of their love. In any case, his love had been deepened by his discovery of how deeply she cared. A happy marriage of twenty years followed, with children and the stability of a simple but comfortable domestic establishment. Hegel, unlike some others, did not disdain the details of domestic management; he was a good father and husband. I believe that it is quite important to consider his thought in terms of such personal solidity and bourgeois "virtue." As Rosenkranz observes: "The reverence of Hegel for marriage and the happiness which he found in it were religious in the strictest sense." [35]

V

Logic

Hegel's *The Science of Logic* was published in 1812 and 1816 (2-half) and is known as the large *Logic* (in contrast with the small one contained in the *Encyclopedia* and published in 1817). It is generally acknowledged to be the culmination of his philosophical system. It is a vast structure and unsuited for inclusion—in whole or in part—in a set of selections intended to introduce the interested reader to Hegel's philosophy. It deserves to be read in its entirety, *after* the implications of Hegel's challenge have prepared one for the "problems" which it is intended to "solve." Its vast structure defies all easy condensations. And yet, something of the central problem is so vital to the Hegelian pattern of thought that a very general sketch must be attempted.

It has been claimed by devoted Hegelians that Hegel's *Science of Logic* compares with Kant's *Critique of Pure Reason* like the "ripe fruit with the much-promising bud." [36] Such a comparison is conceivable only from the vantage point of Hegel himself; to Kant's many followers it is as wrong as it is historically misleading. For the *Logic* of Hegel radically transcends, indeed it repudiates the very "limits" within which Kant had hoped to confine "any future metaphysic." It is rationalistic ontological speculation of the very sort which Kant had hoped to have banished from the history of philosophy forever. *The Science of Logic* is no logic in the traditional sense at all, and Hegel took great pride in the fact that it was not. For this traditional logic was concerned with what Hegel considered "abstractions" and lifeless ratiocination concerning such abstractions. The true logic is concerned with the *ground of being*, the beginning and the end of all philosophy. In short, it is ontology.

Traditional logic is based upon the law of contradiction, according to which A is not non-A. Hegel's entire *Logic* is built upon an ontological repudiation of this principle. He does not repudiate it for "abstract thought," that is to say, for ordinary scientific thought. But he does reject it for philosophical and dialectical purposes. The repudiation takes the form of dialectic. This dialectic is the celebrated core of Hegel's philosophical method, the procedure upon which he based his proud claim of having "completed" the task of the spirit as manifest in philosophy. "I know," Hegel says in his Introduction to the *Logic*, "that my method is the one and only true one." And the reason he thought so was the dialectic which enabled him, he thought, to grasp the object as it is in itself. This dialectic method is nothing separate and apart from its content or object; it is at work in the object and "moves it along." [37]

In order to appreciate what Hegel is getting at it is necessary to realize that the dialectical process is not a type of deduction. It is common to associate with the notion of dialectic some idea of *a priori* reasoning. In Hegel's view this is entirely inadmissible. Dialectics is descriptive: descriptive of the process of thought which one must have experienced in order to be able to understand it. Dialectic in this sense shares something of the intuitive quality of all direct experience.

The central experience with which dialectic struggles is the inadequacy of all concepts. Hence Hegel insists that such concepts must be made to correspond to the fluidity and richness of what is being seen when life in its fullness is beheld. We have therefore considered it desirable to render the specific Hegelian *Begriff* as conception rather than concept;[38] for it is intended to be something broader, more comprehensive and lacking logical precision in the traditional sense. As Hartman says: "The result is a new concept of the concept." [39] Besides first the object with which the conception is concerned and second the conceiver, one other persistent core of so fluid a conception remains: its various aspects form a unique system, and through this interrelationship all the conceptions in turn form a system.

If the conception thus only emerges in the process of reasoning, if it involves "hard work" as Hegel in typical German fashion likes to insist, then the dialectic is this "movement of the conceptions," this dynamic process by which they are distilled, not as something static and fixed, but as something forever evolving and achieving new forms as the perspectives change through the relation with other conceptions.

The law of dialectic is probably the best-known and at the same time the least understood aspect of Hegel's philosophy. The thesis-antithesis-synthesis triad has an arid and formal ring, especially when associated with some of the later notions of the materialist interpretation of history. In point of fact, we are here confronted with something very much more perplexing, more rich and yet at the same time more confused than the simple logical triad suggests. We have already discussed the notion, so central to Hegel's dialectic, that both antithesis and synthesis preserve, as well as suspend the antecedent conception. We have also mentioned the related notion that the synthesis "elevates" the two antecedent conceptions; it is through such synthesis that the conceptions reach ever new "levels of discourse." And it is Hegel's contention that this dialectic process is not something he invented, not a new-fangled notion at all, but a sound and objective description of what has actually occurred in the history of the spirit as manifest in the development of philosophy.

The "vast power of negation" which fascinated Hegel is the

originator of ever-new thought. Hegel does not pretend to understand how this can be; all he knows is that it is so. Philosophical thought records and analyzes the experiences which it has made; that is all. Hence the somewhat stereotype character of this dialectic. No synthesis, no matter how unique, can help arousing this power of negation, can help eliciting a contradiction and thus starting the process all over again. In terms of abstract logic, the Hegelian position amounts to claiming that: A is non-A. This formidable challenge to established logical principles is rooted in an ontological, that is to say, metaphysical assumption. This metaphysical assumption is the core of the Hegelian philosophy: the absolute is reason. Hence Hegel can assert that dialectic is God's thinking himself in man or, to put it another way, dialectic is eternal reason realizing itself in man's thought. The whole argument of *The Science of Logic* stands and falls with this metaphysical basis which shows that its problem is derivative of the more basic problems of religion and politics outlined above.

One of the difficult, if not unresolvable, problems of Hegel's dialectic approach is that of where to begin. He chooses, rather surprisingly, the conception of being (*Sein*). But in order to understand this, one has to remember that the entire *Phenomenology of the Spirit* is a kind of prolegomena for the *Logic*. What is most immediately given is being, but being without reference to any particular thing, indeterminate being. This at once posits the negation of being: the absence of all determination suggests non-being, or the nothing (*Nichts*). We have here the contradiction of the non-being being—a basic dialectic issue in Plato's *Parmenides*. But whereas in Plato the static eternity of the ideas stands in the way of a resolution, Hegel dialectically resolves, that is to say, suspends and preserves, the antithetical paradox by suggesting that both being and non-being—or rather nothingness—are superseded by the higher synthesis of becoming (*Werden*). The truth of both being and non-being is to be found in their actual coexistence in "becoming" which constitutes "the identity of their identity and their non-identity." As Hegel puts it in the *Logic*, the truth is "each immediately disappears in its opposite." [40]

The category of becoming is extremely important for Hegel; all higher being is movement, development, action, history. Hence God, too, is essentially becoming. God as merely being is lifeless, an abstraction, a motionless substance. For Hegel, God is active, a spiritual being full of life and unfolding in accordance with His inner nature. But the process does not stop at becoming; as becoming is actualization, it becomes something. The being here and now (*Dasein*) is definite, is a settled something that has ceased to become. Thus it is, according to Hegel, that becoming (*Werden*) suspends itself, as it suspends being and nothingness or non being, and becomes something actually existent here-and-now (*Dasein*). But as always it at the same time also preserves itself as well as being and nothingness in this being here-and-now. As being and nothingness disappear into becoming, so becoming disappears, because that which is disappearing, disappears itself. "Becoming is an untamed restlessness (*haltungslose Unruhe*) which coalesces into a result that rests." [41]

One could go on now to pursue the meandering course of dialectic through its complex unfolding in the *Logic;* enough has perhaps been said to indicate, if ever so briefly, just how the dialectic proceeds and how extraordinarily obscure much of its reasoning appears. One might well exclaim with Wagner in Goethe's *Faust:* "I am as dazed by all this as if a millstone were going around in my head." Finiteness and infinity, quantity and measure, being for and by itself, reflection and essence, phenomenal and actual world, conception, subjectivity, and objectivity, and finally the idea—these and many other minor categories are treated in the same extraordinary way, their interrelationship being traced as one vast system of contradictions, with the conceptions containing these contradictions.

This may be illustrated once more in the concept of freedom, so central to the entire Hegelian philosophy. Hegel does not identify freedom with freedom of the will, or freedom from the operation of causality. Freedom is the activation of one's own inner tendency; it is an unfolding of oneself; it is self-realization. The teleological, Aristotelian matrix is clearly apparent here, and its inherent contradiction is comprehended in its very conception; without such contradiction it would not be actual in any true sense. True freedom is true necessity, is true cause, because it is true inner law and hence true substance.

To know and understand (in so far as it can be understood) this metaphysical conception of freedom as meaningful destiny through self-fulfillment is vital for a grasp of Hegel's thought on right, law and history. The essential systematic connection of his entire philosophy is nowhere more apparent. *The Science of Logic* is providing the conceptions for an understanding of the working of the objective spirit in its various fields; but it is equally true that an intense, ever-moving, concrete vision of the work which the objective spirit has accomplished throughout the ages is essential to an understanding of the conceptions with which *The Science of Logic* deals. We therefore now turn to these concrete manifestations of the living spirit as it unfolds.

VI

Law and Ethics

Hegel's view of law and ethics, involving as it does also his view on politics and history, is basically at variance with prevailing views, the concept of the state being that of a community rather than of an institution (*Anstalt*). The failure to grasp this divergence of the concept of the state, as Hegel uses it, has been the source of most of the misunderstandings. For if the prevailing modern concept of the state as primarily a government, an institutional manifold comprising those who exercise command functions *in* the community is substituted for Hegel's essentially Aristotelian conception of the state as the highest community, there arise immediately authoritarian, not to say totalitarian implications which are far removed from the essential liberalism of Hegel's conception.* For the monarchical

---

* The most recent instance of this kind of misunderstanding among serious writers (for the propagandists talking in some such terms are legion) is Sir Ernest Barker who in his *Political and Social Theory*

predilection of Hegel is in line with the liberal thought not only in Germany, but in England (Burke, Macaulay) and France (de Tocqueville, Benjamin Constant) as well. Hegel's real appreciation of Victor Cousin[42] for whom he strongly exerted himself before the Prussian authorities and got released from jail is further evidence of this approach which also expresses itself fully in the comments on the Reform Bill. But it was a conservative liberalism which, inspired by a sense of history and hence of growth, was nonetheless anxious to avoid radical change and above all revolutionary upheavals. In this respect, Hegel's *Philosophy of Right and Law* is, as the date of its publication, 1821, would suggest, essentially a restoration philosophy, not very far removed from de Tocqueville whose approach to America he shares.[43]

Hegel's approach to law is closely tied to his central concern with religion. Ethics (*Sittlichkeit*) is the concrete ethical world of social life. For Hegel, it is a higher form which he contrasts with the "abstract subjectivity" of mere morality. Mere morality constitutes the sphere within which the will operates as an "independent identity"; the person becomes a subject (see below p. 252 § 105). Ethics is more concrete, precisely because it is more objective, but for its actualization it requires the state. Hegel adduces an anecdote: "To a father who asked how he might best bring up his son, a Pythagorean answered: 'By making him the *citizen of a state with good laws.*'" This anecdote is very revealing about Hegel himself; for the state that the Greek had in mind (as Hegel knew very well) was the *polis*, the highest community, which to Hegel is the objective realization of any genuine freedom. Individuals

---

(1951) claims that Hegel did not differentiate between state and society. But this is precisely the point at which Hegel deviates from the notions of Aristotle and he is quite explicit about it. Barker also writes as if Hegel shared the romantic and reactionary views of men like von Haller whose views Hegel actually criticized sharply, as in the famous footnote (see below p. 282) on von Haller. His pointed remarks about the state not invading the private sphere (see below p. 285) are in line with this general outlook. Barker's views appear in fact very similar to those of the true Hegel, once account is taken of certain divergencies in terminology.

have an ethical being only in so far as they belong to this ethical sphere which is the state. As Hegel puts it quite simply: "The state is the actual reality (*Wirklichkeit*) of the ethical *Idea*." This may be and, in my opinion, is a most unfortunate way of defining the state. But whether we like it or not, let us only be sure that we do not make the crucial mistake of assuming that Hegel means the state as ordinarily conceived, that is to say the state as an institution engaged in law enforcement, or a state as a configuration of power, etc. For this is not the entity about which Hegel is making his assertions.[44] If one is to understand this proposition, it is necessary to read it the other way around as well: "The ethical idea is actualized (*verwirklicht*) in the state." Only in so far as the community through its organization realizes the ethical idea can it be said to be a state. "The state has its immediate existence in the ethical habits (*Sitte*) of the individual and in his self-consciousness." Self-realization is possible for the individual in the state only, because that is what the state consists of.

In a sense, these are elaborate tautologies, or, more precisely, identifications. But such identifications have a most important practical implication, as is immediately apparent, if we consider Hegel's notion that it is the highest duty of the individual to be "a member of the state." What this means is not some kind of totalitarian destruction of the individual, but an insistence that it is the duty of the individual to realize the ethical idea by participating in the community which is dedicated to this task. From the point of view of those who would insist on the state's being an institution for issuing commands, or a configuration of power, such a position may well be considered as destructive of the state's most essential characteristic and hence subversive. Haller's notion that the state is power and that the most powerful must rule, Hegel rightly characterizes as the notion that the state and its power are phenomena of nature and hence a denial of the state's true concern with the just and the ethical, a denial, that is, of the state as based upon law. Characteristically, and rather dramatically, Hegel takes Haller to task for belittling Magna Charta and similar enactments; in Hegel's view they are basic law and "contribute to every piece of bread that the citizens eat." Hegel's rather difficult language has kept obscure his central position in the *Philosophy of Right and Law*, namely that "it is the hardest thing which can happen to a man, to be alienated from thought and reasonableness, from reverence for the laws and from the knowledge of how infinitely important, even divine, it is that the duties of the state and the rights of the citizens, as well as the rights of the state and the duties of the citizens be determined by law." In short, Hegel's approach is in line with, but makes metaphysically an earnest effort to buttress philosophically, the proposition in favor of a "government of laws and not of men."

If any test of this side of the matter is needed, all that is necessary is for the reader to turn to Hegel's views on Church and State (see below pp. 289–91). Only in its outward manifestations, its ownership of property and the like, is a church obliged to acknowledge "a limited subjection to the police power." When it comes to matters of doctrine, it is "a matter of conscience and part of the subjective freedom—the sphere of the inner life which is not the concern of the state." How is this view to be reconciled with the idea then that the state is the actualization of the ethical idea? "The ethical truth exists as law," Hegel answers, and the doctrine of the state is embodied in this attachment of the citizens to principles of law. What constitutes the essential difference is what is involved in the difference between the religion as revealed truth, and philosophy as rational truth. To restate a position previously discussed, we might cite a passage in which the Russian writer and man of affairs, Baron Boris d'Yxkull, a friend and student of Hegel's, has described the main theme of their conversations during long walks: "Religion is the anticipated (*geahnte*) philosophy, philosophy nothing but conscious religion; both seek, but by different paths, the same, namely God." [45]

This rationality of the state as the embodiment of ethics gives it a kinship to science and scholarship. After noting the church's inclination to resist rational, scientific inquiry and mentioning Bruno and Galileo, Hegel concludes the argument by rejecting the view of those who would consider the separation of church and state as a misfortune (as De Maistre and other restoration reactionaries had done) and asserts that "only through this separation has the state been able to become what it was intended to be: the self-conscious rationality and ethics." But Hegel insists likewise that this separation is most fortunate for the churches, since it enables them to concentrate upon their essential task which, as we already know, is in Hegel's view the highest there is, namely to provide the community in which man can become certain of God.

Anyone who takes the foregoing principles seriously will not be surprised to find Hegel display a positive appreciation of public opinion which he links with sound common sense (below pp. 317 ff, § 316–19). Yet, he has no illusions, but appreciates the curious intermingling of truth and error in public opinion and he therefore suggests that it deserves "as much to be respected as to be despised." So one must rise above public opinion to accomplish something great and truly significant "He who says and accomplishes what his time wants and desires is the great man of that time." In keeping with these views, freedom of speech and of the press receive the kind of limited support from Hegel which is still characteristic of English and Continental law.

So far, so good. But the discussion of the state is concluded by Hegel's defense of war. He remarks rightly that in all that has been said there is involved an "ethical aspect of war." War, he asserts, is not to be looked upon as an absolute evil, resulting from accidental causes, such as the whims of princes, the interests of particular persons, etc. No, war is also the way in which a state's ethical reality asserts itself against others. Eternal peace, he says, would produce a situation as foul as that of a sea never whipped by gales, and through war "the ethical health of nations is maintained." The notions here involved are related to those underlying William James's celebrated essay on "The Moral Equivalent of War," although James puts the idea more in terms of individual ethical health.[46] There is a fierce and cynical ring, though, to certain phrases which occur in this connection, such as that about the cavalry with bare sabers (below pp. 321 ff, § 324). "Wars take place where they are rooted in the nature of things; afterwards the seed sprouts again . . ." Yet, much of the sentiment behind the crusades and wars, cold and hot, in defense of ideals or for their propagation, is in actual fact very close to the Hegelian viewpoint. For it is always the state as an ideal entity, as a community engaged in realizing the ideal and hence manifesting the dynamics of the world spirit that is meant by Hegel. Here we come upon the celebrated dictum of Hegel that world history is the world court which must be assessed in terms of Hegel's philosophy of history to which we shall turn presently.*

It has at times been suggested that Hegel developed these ideas, including more particularly the views on war, in response and with conscious adaptation to the Prussian tradition, after his arrival in Berlin. Actually, none of the ideas are in any sense novel for him. His ideas were distorted as we noted by substituting the existent Prussian "state" for the "state" of Hegel's ethical radicalism. But we find not only the sharp distinction of state and society, as already noted, but all those points which are in keeping with his ideas on ethical autonomy. To make the state the kind of ethical community which Hegel postulated—that is, participate effectively in law-making—a people must give themselves laws. Hegel thought it ridiculous to suggest that the people are not mature enough for that. By the same token he demanded the trial by jury, *public* judicial trials, local self-government for towns and other corporate entities. We have already noted his spirited defense of Magna Carta, and his positive although moderate inclination to support freedom of the press. How clearly Hegel embraced these notions at a much earlier date, his early constitutional writings (see below) as well as his study on natural law will show. Hegel evidently thought that the Prussia of Hardenberg was the embodiment of these requirements; one could say that he

---

* How far Hegel is from the modern totalitarians, and how close to traditional views, may be seen from his insistence upon the civilized nature of modern warfare. How far are even so-called "peace-loving" states from Hegel's belief that "war therefore contains the norm of internal law that the possibility of peace should be maintained . . . war is not conducted against the internal institutions nor against the peaceful life of family and private persons." (See below pp. 328 ff, § 338.

"idealized" the Prussian state rather than "Prussianized" his idea of the state.[47] As his biographer noted, the government had not yet organized reaction and few doubted that soon a popular representation would be set up for all of Germany.

Upon the publication of the *Philosophy of Right and Law*, Hegel found himself the target of sharp criticism. His intemperate remarks against the more radical elements of the national democratic movement were bitterly resented, more especially his attack against his fellow philosopher Fries. And since Hegel was in the strong position of professor at Berlin (where he had gone in 1818), his comments do indeed seem to be "kicking the underdog," an unattractive behavior which is adversely commented upon even by such admirers as Rosenkranz. There was a political element involved here, and, as Rosenkranz remarks, Hegel had to pay heavily for this intemperate remark, for it caused quite a few to suspect him of a change of heart, of a rather obsequious adaptation to the Prussian bureaucracy, and a general sympathy with reactionary trends. These suspicions were reinforced by Hegel's including in the preface the words: "What is rational, that is actually real (*wirklich*), and what is actually real (*wirklich*), that is rational." This proposition seemed to many a formula of complete quietism, especially when it came as the culmination of an argument violently condemning revolutionary, nay even progressively reformatory ideas as "empty abstractions."

Hegel undertook to answer the argument in the Introduction to the revised *Encyclopedia* which he had first published in Heidelberg in 1817 as an introduction to his system. He starts by remarking (§ 6) that it is decisive to realize that the content of philosophy is *Wirklichkeit*, the true or actual reality which is the living spirit which has created itself and become the world—the world of the external and internal consciousness. This consciousness of the world we call experience. Then, after quoting the sentence, Hegel rather bitterly remarks:

These simple sentences have seemed to some extraordinary and have been attacked, even by those who would not deny that they believe in philosophy and religion. It is unnecessary to deal with religion, since its doctrines about God's government of the world clearly enunciate these propositions. What concerns the philosophical meaning, one ought to presuppose sufficient education in these people for them to know not only that God is actually real (*wirklich*), but that He is the most real (*wirklich*), that He alone is truly real, but also formally speaking that what is here-and-now (*Dasein*) is partly phenomenal, and only partly real. In ordinary life one calls every notion, error, the evil and all that goes with it, as well as everything, be it ever so deformed and transitory, something real. . . . I have dealt with all this in a lengthy *Logic* where I treat of actual reality (*Wirklichkeit*) and have distinguished it not merely from the accidental which has also existence, but also from being-here-and-now (*Dasein*), from existence and other terms.

Hegel then elaborates again his insistence that norms are indeed valid, where they are directed toward changing that which is contingent, but that they are "empty abstractions" when they seek to change that which is truly actual and real, in the sense of being a manifestation of the spirit and of the idea. The meaning and limits of this conception are made more concrete by Hegel's philosophy of history. How much Hegel was basically in line with Christian tradition can be seen in Richard Hooker's discussion of Goodness: "Because there is not in the world any thing whereby another may not some way be made the perfecter, therefore all things that are, are good."[47a]

VII

History and the Arts

In Hegel's conception of the world, of man and his God, history occupies a very special place. For it is in history that the whole of his gigantic conception is, in a sense, *validated*. This validation is, of course, not carried out with the detachment of a scientific observer who is ready to revise his general hypotheses in the light of his findings, who treats them merely as working hypotheses employed for the ordering of the facts which "speak louder." Not at all. Hegel leaves no doubt that the idea is superior to what would appear to others as empirical fact, and these facts are devalued as only phenomenal appearances without true reality such as Hegel vindicates for his concrete visions, his conceptions of the higher logic of dialectic understanding. In the Introduction to *The History of Philosophy* (see below pp. 163–164) as well as elsewhere he makes this amply clear. But oddly enough, such low esteem for mere facts does not induce in Hegel any lack of interest in what these facts are. All his works are alive with concrete detail, and *The Philosophy of History* more especially teems with historical fact. Nor are these details in any sense irrelevant. In keeping with Hegel's cherished principle that everything, no matter how intrinsically unimportant and deceptive, partakes in some small way in the truth and is suspended and preserved in the higher, more comprehensive being, he dwells with the loving attention of the would-be historian upon many specific items, and the whole of his historical construct has a grand sweep and a magnificent intensity of interpretative unity to it.

In our time, when we have become less stridently confident regarding a "scientific" history that could tell just how things have happened (*wie es wirklich gewesen ist*), when confronted with a multiplicity of interpretative views thoughtful historians have gone so far as to propose that everyone be his own historian,[48] even so sweeping a construction as that of Hegel has lost some of its terror. Tolerantly considered, Hegel's structure appears no more daring than those of a Toynbee or a Spengler, perhaps not even quite as willful. For surely the carefully elaborated underlying conceptions of Hegelian rationalism, his cogently, if unconvincingly argued dialectic, his basically Christian teleology in terms of one loving God are a more impressive pattern than the bald generalities of biological analogy and of cultural discreteness in Spengler, or the mechanistic notions of challenge and response or the unexplained assumptions of some kind of ascent in Toynbee. The latter require less philosophical insight and thereby recommend themselves to the layman, but they can hardly be proclaimed as intrinsically more convincing, when offered as interpretative principles of universal validity.[49]

It has been said so often as to have become almost a common-place that Hegel looked upon his philosophy of history as an eschatological design, or, as one recent writer has put it, as prophecy. The prophetic proclamations of Marx and Engels, linked as they were by their authors to Hegel's thought, have served to reinforce this notion and to rivet upon it the sanction of self-evident obviousness. But a reading not only of the Introduction, but of *The Philosophy of History* as a whole (or at least in such substantial additions of its concrete substance as we are here offering) reveals Hegel as essentially looking backward and assessing the way we have come, rather than the road ahead. In a famous sentence from the preface of the *Philosophy of Right and Law* (see below p. 227) Hegel suggests that "the owl of Minerva begins its flight when dusk is falling." This poetic simile is intended to reinforce Hegel's carefully elaborated notion that man can perceive the conception of actuality, the divine essence, only when the actuality has already been fully unfolded and indeed has become cut and dried. Philosophy to him "paints gray in gray" because the essence which it understands is a form of life that has grown old. Applied to history seen as the unfolding of freedom, this suggests that Hegel would feel himself to be at the end rather than at the beginning of a period. And he says quite specifically that "what happens in the future, does not concern us." What Hegel is referring to is on one hand the Slavic world, which he explicitly excludes from his consideration, because it is something in between the West and Asia and has not so far appeared as an autonomous stage of the configurations of the spirit.

On the other hand, the American reader might be particularly interested in what Hegel says about America. "America is therefore the land of the future in which in times to come . . . world history shall reveal itself. . . . But what has so far happened there is only an echo of the old world and an expression of an alien aliveness, and as the country of the future it does not concern us here. For in history our concern must be with what has been and with what is." [50] It is evident that Hegel does not flatter himself to have found in his philosophy of history, any more than in his dialectic, a key to the future. His sense of the real, his *Wirklichkeitssinn*, obliged him to view the future as a closed book. This did not keep him from throwing out a guess as to one important aspect of American life, its frontier. As part of a highly realistic appraisal of the differences not only between North America and Europe, but also between South America and North America, Hegel wrote: "Concerning politics in North America the need of a firm cohesion is not yet present, for a real state and a real government only develop when there is a difference of classes, when riches and poverty become very large and a situation arises where a great number of people can no longer satisfy its needs in the accustomed way. But America does not yet approach this tension . . . For a state to become a state it is necessaary that the citizen cannot continually think of emigrating, but that the class of cultivators, no longer able to push to the outside, presses upon itself and is gathered into cities and urban professions. Only then can a civic system develop and that is the condition for an organized state." Hegel elaborates this further in his effort to show that America and Europe cannot be compared, and that the conditions in America do not prove that a republican system is capable of survival. Sure, America is an independent and powerful state, but only when the entire land will be settled and occupied will a fixed order of things emerge. And what it will be. Hegel does not profess to know. It is likely to be a new configuration of the world spirit. Until now America has been an annex of Europe. What it eventually will be is no concern of his.[51]

But beyond this history which for Hegel includes the past up to the present, there is philosophy. Philosophy's task is concerned neither with what has been nor with what will be, but with what is and is eternally so. This presumably also holds for the philosophy of history. At the very end of his survey of the concrete history, Hegel observes that the history of the world, all the changing scenes which it presents, is the process of the development and of the realization of the spirit. He therefore claims this interpretation of history to be the true theodicy, the justification of God in history. And he feels that only this insight can reconcile the spirit with world history, that what has happened is not only not without God, but is essentially his work. In a letter to a Russian friend, Hegel suggested that Russia possessed an enormous possibility through the developing of its intensive nature, and it is not unreasonable to maintain that Hegel reluctantly admitted to himself that a new dichotomy, a new antithesis might well be in the making. But as to its substance, his philosophy condemned him to silence.

We have included enough of Hegel's *Philosophy of History* to make it unnecessary to give a summary here. That he sees it as the history of freedom, as the self-realization of the spirit, our preceding analysis has made clear, anyhow. It only remains to say a word about our inclusion of so much of Hegel's actual treatment of history, rather than the Introduction which is the part of Hegel's philosophy of history mostly studied today. It seemed essential to do so, if the true view of Hegel is to emerge. Hegel was, as we have seen, very deeply concerned over "concreteness," and this concreteness is a matter of envisaging actual reality in all its many different facets. Only by studying how Hegel links his vast generalities with the concrete detail of historical data—even including geographical data—can one see how he meant them. To be sure, many of these facts are now obsolete; modern scholarship has put in critical perspective most of the writers upon whose work Hegel based his interpretation. But there is enough of a common core left to allow one to see how Hegel selected and organized his facts to provide suitable validation for his conception of the march of history.

Hegel's *Philosophy of History* consists of lecture notes, collated and edited after his death; only the main part of the introduction has been published, by modern scholars, in accordance with Hegel's own manuscript. The same is, of course, true of his *Philosophy of Religion* and his philosophy of art as embodied in the *Lectures on Aesthetics*. There has been a good deal of learned discussion as to how far one might go in accepting these lectures as authentic. There can be little question that the works written and published by Hegel himself, like the *Phenomenology,* the *Philosophy of Right and Law,* the *Logic* and the *Encyclopedia,* have a superior claim, when it comes to controversial points. At the same time, one sympathizes with Kuno Fischer, when he insists that the philosopher owes a great and permanent gratitude to the devoted labors of these pupils of Hegel who compared different sets of notes and tried to present a generally faithful portrait of these lectures. There were, of course, individual variations, and perhaps the most careful of the editors was the man who prepared the *Lectures on Aesthetics,* Heinrich Gustav Hotho. He has also left us a very vivid account of Hegel as a lecturer:

Tired, sullen, he sat crumpled up and with head hanging down and constantly looked through his long lecture notes, while continuing to talk, going through them backward and forward, looking now at the top of the page, now at the bottom. His constant hemming and coughing disturbed the flow of speech, each sentence stood by itself and emerged after an effort, and disjointed and disorganized; every word, every syllable seemed reluctant to part from him, while it received from the unmetallic voice enunciating in broad Suabian dialect a curiously thorough emphasis, as if each were the most important. In spite of all, the whole appearance imposed such a deep respect, such a sense of dignity, and attracted by the genuineness of the deepest earnestness, I found myself inescapably fascinated, even though I understood little of what was being said. But no sooner had I become accustomed to this external aspect of his lecturing, through eager persistence, than the inner advantages of it struck me more and more forcibly and combined in fact with those faults into a whole which had in itself the measure of its perfection.[52]

Hotho wisely comments that in his opinion the reason for this extraordinary effect was that Hegel had to produce anew each time, even though he had thought about the matter for years, each of his powerful thoughts, "to bring them up from the deepest bottom of things." He also remarks upon the fact that Hegel seemed completely absorbed in the matter at hand, oblivious of his listeners, almost, yet he seemed to have a "paternal care" for making the matter as clear as possible.

One is reminded of a letter he had written many years before Hotho heard him, to his Dutch friend van Ghert who had mentioned complaints about Hegel's incomprehensibility among his friends:

I am sorry that there are complaints about the difficulty of the presentation. The nature of such abstract matters brings it about that one cannot give to them the easiness of an ordinary book. Truly speculative philosophy cannot either be given the form and the style of Locke's writings or of the ordinary French philosophy.[53]

Actually, Hegel is quite readable, once he gets away from the profundities of metaphysics and dialectics. This is not only clearly indicated in the descriptive parts of the *Lectures on the Philosophy of History* (and other works), but also in those on *Aesthetics,* or as he himself would prefer to say, the philosophy of art (*Kunst* taken in the broadest meaning). Art, together with religion and philosophy, is for Hegel absolute spirit, and he relates all art to the idea of which it is an expression. Thus the content of art is emphasized, but it is a highly spiritual content. And while the particular formulations of Hegel have lost much of their significance, the basic approach is one which has come to dominate the field of the history and interpretation of the arts to an ever-increasing extent. Thus, we find in Hegel a sharp rejection of all utilitarian, moralistic or sententious approaches to art. Art is called upon to reveal the truth in the form of a sensuous creation, and has its end in itself. Other purposes, like "teaching, purifying, improving," do not concern the work of art.[54] In short, Hegel is almost ready to pronounce the later dictum: *l'art pour l'art.* What keeps him from going quite that far is that he relates art, as just mentioned, to the absolute spirit, to the idea, to truth. Yet, Hegel's approach to art was rooted in vital personal experience. He spent a great deal of time in art galleries; during his Berlin professorship, he made three long trips, to the Low Countries and Brussels, 1822, to Austria and Vienna, 1824, and to France and Paris, 1827, and perhaps their main purpose was to see the great works of art and architecture.[55] While in Vienna, he was enchanted with Italian opera, and his letters to his wife were expressing not only general joy, but detailed appreciation. When Mendelssohn produced, for the first time after generations, Bach's Passion according to St. Matthew in Berlin, Hegel was greatly impressed.[56] His taste in music, contrary to Schopenhauer's, was altogether of a high order.

Within the general framework of his philosophy, Hegel expounds the basic distinction between the *Kunstschöne* and the *Naturschöne,* the beautiful in art and the beautiful in nature. His aesthetics is only concerned with the beautiful in art; obviously because only this kind of beauty is clearly partaking of the idea. Beauty in art developed, according to Hegel, in three broad stages or phases: symbolic art, classic art, and "romantic" art. Roughly, these three phases correspond to the oriental, the Graeco-Roman and the Western Christian periods. It can be seen at once that the parallelism with the phases in the history of freedom is close. Indeed, these stages in the history of the world spirit obviously served to provide the framework of the Hegelian aesthetics. It is a developmental philosophy of art in which the succeeding modes of expression are correlated with the dialectic in the unfolding of the spirit and its consciousness. That is why we are offering some substantial selections from *The Phenomenology of the Spirit,* bearing on this aspect of Hegel's thought, in addition to brief excerpts from the *Lectures on Aesthetics;* they show how Hegel's thought on art is embodied in the dialectics of the spirit.

Hegel undertook to establish a link also between these phases and the several fields of artistic endeavor. Thus architecture is the art form most suited to the symbolic phase, sculpture to the classic, while painting and music are best adapted to the "romantic" stage. This is in part due to their being progressively more suited to expressing a state of subjective self-consciousness. It does not, of course, mean that the others are not also present in some way in each phase, but they are less significant, and Hegel feels that they merely implement the main forms. But this highly constructivist pattern still leaves out poetry. Now poetry, for Hegel, is the highest of all art forms. This is due to its being most akin to thought (which somewhat

tends to interfere with the artistic immediacy, Hegel admits).
Poetry's kinship to thought makes it a significant art form in
all the successive phases or stages, unfolding in its epic, lyric
and dramatic forms in characteristic creations. Hegel's lectures
contain long and penetrating observations on specific works of
classic and Western literature; it is evident that most of them
are based upon personal reading. He places dramatic poetry in
the front as the highest form of poetry, and shows a marked
preference for the work of Shakespeare. Shakespeare thereby
appears to be the very pinnacle of asethetic achievement, once
again demonstrating Hegel's inclination toward English modes
of thought and value judgment.

It is evident that this whole structure is a veritable bed of
Procrustes. Not only is there a lack of some of the most vital
differentiations, such as the familiar style concepts of Gothic,
Renaissance, Baroque and so forth, but an almost complete
failure to see the development of the arts in terms of their
proper techniques and means of expression. Nor is the interrelationship of the several arts seen as constituting a harmonious whole. And yet, in spite of these evident shortcomings,
Hegel's *Aesthetics* was a trail-blazer. Building upon the views
Kant had offered in his *Critique of Judgment,* Hegel was the
first of the great modern philosophers to outline a philosophy
of the beautiful in art; what is more, he was the first to try to
work out an over-all developmental pattern. And while many,
if not most of his specific suggestions have now been rejected,
the attentive reader soon discovers a substantial sediment of
ideas originally suggested by Hegel in contemporary works
on the history and philosophy of art and culture.

Hegel's lectures on the beautiful conclude with a rather
touching note of emotion. "In this way, we have arranged
every essential aspect of the beautiful and of artistic creation
philosophically into a wreath the binding of which belongs
among the most worthy tasks of philosophical science. For in
art we are dealing not with a merely agreeable or useful toy,
but with the liberation of the spirit from the finite forms and
content, with the presence and the reconciliation of the absolute in the sensuous and the phenomenal, with the unfolding

of truth . . . which reveals itself as world history of which it
is itself the most beautiful part and hence provides the best
reward for the hard work involved in dealing with actual
reality and its knowledge . . . If I have succeeded . . . my
last wish is that a higher and indestructible bond of the idea
of the beautiful and the true may have been tied which will
keep us forever firmly united." [57]

Hegel died, rather unexpectedly, on November 14, 1831,
after contracting cholera. His fame had been steadily mounting
during the preceding years, and toward the end of his life he
reigned supreme as the philosophical "pope" of Berlin, his influence radiating throughout the German universities. Yet,
within a relatively short period, his influence began to decline
and by the middle of the century was being superseded by
Schopenhauer and a revival of Kant's philosophy which he
had labored so hard to prove "abstract" and "subjectivist." By
the end of the century, Hegel was all but dead, especially in
German universities, except for the very significant development of Neo-Hegelianism in British thought. Hegel's significance has been best stated by an English philosopher in
terms that would have pleased Hegel:

The philosophy of Hegel is not something simple invented out of
nothing by himself and flung at random into an astonished world.
. . . It is not the pet theory of some erratic genius, nor is it
merely one theory among many rivals. The true author of it is, not
so much Hegel, as the toiling and thinking human spirit, the universal spirit of humanity getting itself uttered through this individual. It is the work of ages. It has its roots deep in the past. It
is the accumulated wisdom of the years, the last phase of the one
"universal philosophy." For the truth is, to use a phrase of Hegel's,
neither new nor old, but permanent. Yet Hegel, too, is profoundly
original. . . . It recognizes all past truth, absorbs it into itself *and
advances.*[58]

We are more inclined to see it in terms of its historical implications. It was a great, a bold, and an enormously influential
philosophy. But in spite of all of Hegel's protestations about the
future, it proved a seed of dragon's teeth. His refusal to

acknowledge the limits of the human mind, his confusing notion that his dialectics had made obsolete the law of contradiction, and his consequent tendency to obscure the difference between fact and norm, they all and other related features of his system contributed to the cultural and political crisis in which civilization finds itself today.

VIII

Hegel's Influence

But this decline of philosophical interest in Hegel soon after his death is no measure of the influence of the Hegelian philosophy. This, indeed, has been so all-engulfing that a tracing of his influence would fall little short of an intellectual history of the hundred-odd years since his death. We indicated something of that in our introductory remarks. Marxism and Fascism, especially in its Italian form, no less than existentialism and pragmatism are clearly unthinkable without Hegel. This does not mean that they are Hegelian, nor even less, as latter-day propagandists are fond of insisting, that Hegel is to be held responsible for them—anyone acquainted with Hegel's work could write out the kind of biting critique of each one of these movements which Hegel would himself make of them.

But it does mean that a knowledge of Hegel is perhaps more essential than that of any philosopher of the past for anyone who wishes to understand the intellectual crisis of our time. Hegel himself would, no doubt, feel that the crisis was the result of the failure of those who followed to heed his teachings. But he would not be surprised; as we have seen, his sense of standing at the end of a great historical cycle was profound. He knew that the dusk was falling upon Christian culture, and if he had the abiding faith that the world spirit would shape its next incarnation, he did not at all profess to know what it might be. This kind of resignation lends itself to being superseded by eager followers who wish to project the master's thought.

The crop of Hegel's followers, among whom Marx was to become the most famous, eagerly undertook to devise such projections. The so-called Young Hegelians, radicals of the left with more or less advanced views, undertook to elaborate various distinct elements in Hegel's philosophy: Hartmann the self-conscious, Feuerbach the progressive, Strauss and Bruno Bauer the pantheistic and critical, Kierkegaard later the religious and mystical. Each one, in doing so, rejected some distinctive and vital element in the Hegelian synthesis. Among these, the most famous is, of course, the substitution of the materialist for the idealist position by Feuerbach, which was followed out by Ruge and Marx. The latter's argument was based upon Hegel's radical rationalism and proclaimed that since the Prussian and all other contemporary states were not rational, they were not truly real and hence were bound to go. Transforming Feuerbach's speculative materialism into an economic "materialism" which actually stresses organization (the pattern of control of the means of production), Hegel's dialectic became in the hands of Marx a proposition to the effect that every economic system contains the antithesis of another which will supersede it—a travesty of Hegel's sophisticated dialectic, to be sure, but of enormous political effect.[59]

But apart from these philosophical and political impacts of the broadest and most comprehensive sort, Hegel's influence has flown through many smaller channels to shape the thought of a large part of the social sciences, not only in Germany, but throughout Europe and especially in the United States.

In an interesting recent American study, we read: "Although you may never encounter a person who calls himself a Hegelian, Hegel's influence survives in many places. Anyone who talks about the main trends of history as if wisdom might be gained through historical studies is quite possibly affected by Hegel's thinking. At the least, he is raising the kind of questions that Hegel boldly explored." [60] It is manifestly impossible to do more than make a few hints. For example, Max Weber's crucial categories of "understanding" and of "ideal types," derived from the methodological work of Rickert and Windelband,[61] are Hegelian, especially in their teleological implications. Similarly, the work of Toynbee is rooted in Hegel's philosophy of history, and indeed closer to Hegel than some of the intervening work in this field because of its matrix of Christian eschatology, and its stress upon the religious factor, though of course very timid in making explicit its framework of general ideas transcending historical relativity. Finally, the work of the cultural anthropologists, such as Ruth Benedict, is derived from Hegel's philosophy. To be sure, in so far as theirs is frank cultural relativity without any broader universal framework, it is a denial of Hegel's central insistence upon reason and the idea as absolute truth. But as we have seen, much of Hegel's significance lies not in this central insistence but much more in the fact that he interpreted these "absolutes" in developmental, teleological terms, saw them as unfolding in history, and assigned to particular nations (or in fact cultures, as we would nowadays say, since the Orient, Antiquity and the West are his main constituents throughout) relative and yet quite distinctive tasks. The list could be much further extended. In consent and in dissent, and often in absorbing while rejecting, the modern social sciences carry a heavy and in many ways fateful Hegelian heritage. When Benedetto Croce made his famous assessment of *What Is Alive and What Is Dead in Hegel's Philosophy*[62] there had as yet been no Communist revolution, no Fascism, no existentialism. His was the estimate of a nineteenth-century liberal which showed how difficult it is to evaluate a thinker's vitality. For better or worse, much of Hegel's most potent thought still awaits effective transcendence in a higher and more convincing philosophy. Until now, the best and not wholly satisfactory answer is still to be found in the philosophy of Immanuel Kant.

After reading Hegel, Walt Whitman burst into a stanza which shows a strikingly deeper comprehension of Hegel than most:

Roaming in thought over the Universe, I saw the little that is
    Good steadily hastening towards immortality
And the vast all that is called Evil I saw hastening to merge
    itself and become lost and dead.

The romantic, the visionary and the mystic in a world view that is completely dynamic caught this seer of the democratic enthusiasm and fired him to project the American role which Hegel himself had refused to discuss. In *Democratic Vistas*, Walt Whitman was even more explicit in taking up the Hegelian challenge:

In the future of these States there must arise poets immenser far . . . I have eulogized Homer, the sacred bards of Jewry, Aeschylus, Juvenal, Shakespeare . . . But I say there must, for future and democratic purposes, appear poets . . . of higher class than any of those poets not only possessed of the religious fire and abandon of Isaiah, luxurious in the epic talent of Homer, or for proud characters in Shakespeare, but consistent with the Hegelian formula, and consistent with modern science.

The cosmic purposes of a universal meaning, read in the mind of man—such was the bold challenge of Hegel. Marx mocked at it: "The ideal is nothing else than the material world reflected by the human mind, and translated into forms of thought." Marx's materialist dialectic confronts us today in the power of the Soviet Union. Hegel is no answer. Yet much of the Western response is at best Hegelian. The reiteration of outworn formulas is no substitute for the challenge of ideas. What Hegel teaches us, if he teaches us anything, is that a vital body of thought must be fresh and must transcend what has gone before. But what Hegel also teaches us, if we search with care, is that there must be immortal ideas, lasting truths, a perennial philosophy. This perennial philosophy no one can be sure of; it is the common core of succeeding efforts at stating the lasting truth; it remains as a task.

Selections from

THE PHILOSOPHY OF HISTORY

Translated by
Carl J. and Paul W. Friedrich

Note on the Text

The translation here presented is composed of two parts. The selections from the Introduction—translated by Carl J. Friedrich from Georg Lasson's second edition (1920), for which the kind permission of Felix Meiner Verlag was granted —constitute the first part. This section concludes with Hegel's own statement of the different kinds of history, as contained in a manuscript published by Lasson in the edition just mentioned. The second part, from page 43 on, consists of selections from the main body of the work; these translations are by Paul W. Friedrich, as revised by the editor, and are based upon Sibree's old translation which followed the German of Karl Hegel. The reason for this combination is that the original is available in three different versions, all of them resulting from the editing of notes and manuscript material left after Hegel's death. Lasson discovered an actual manuscript, and the selections from the Introduction are almost entirely taken from this authentic Hegelian text. It was the original intention to use Sibree much more extensively than was actually found wise; in fact, his translation, while providing the starting point, is all but gone. Still, there is enough of a relation to enable the student who wishes to go further than the present selections to turn to Sibree for additional detail.

INTRODUCTION

THE SUBJECT OF THESE LECTURES IS THE PHILOSOPHY OF world history. What history—world history—is I need not explain. The general notion of it is sufficient and we largely agree on it.* But what may strike you in the title of these lectures and what may seem to call for an explanation or justification is that we propose to consider a philosophy of history, that we propose to treat history philosophically.

The philosophy of history is nothing else but the thinking, the reflecting upon history. We humans cannot avoid thinking about things, for man is thinking; that is what differentiates him from the animal. All that is human—feeling, knowledge and insight, desire and will—all these contain thinking, if they are human and not animal. The same is true of all concern with history. But such reference to the general share of thinking in all human affairs as in history may seem inadequate, because we maintain that thinking is subordinate to being, to that which is given, that thinking has being as its basis and is guided by it. To philosophy, on the other hand, are attributed its own thoughts, which speculation evolves out of itself without regard to that which is and which it then applies to history, thus treating history as material, not leaving it as it is but arranging it according to its thoughts; that is, it constructs a history a priori.

History has only to grasp clearly what is and what has been, the events and the deeds. History is the more true, the more it sticks to what is given and has as its objective that which has happened, though this is not readily at hand and calls for manifold researches connected with thinking. The task of philosophy seems to be in contradiction to this objective, and it is with this contradiction I wish to deal in my introduction—with the reproach made to philosophy because of the thoughts it

---

* But see the further discussion, in the fragment reprinted below, on the different kinds of history writing, pp. 35 et seq.

brings into history and according to which it treats history. That is to say, the general purpose of the philosophy of world history must first be stated and the immediate consequences which result must be noted. The relation of thoughts and events will thereby automatically be clarified. Therefore—and to avoid becoming too prolix in this introduction, rich material awaiting us in the world history itself—it seems unnecessary to enter into refutations and corrections of the many more special false ideas and reflections current concerning the viewpoints, principles, and notions about the purpose and the sense of treating history, and, more particularly, concerning the relation of concepts and philosophy to historical matters. (Each new preface to a history and, in turn, each preface to a review of such a history presents a new theory.) I shall pass these over or, in some cases, recall them.

1. THE RATIONAL VIEW OF WORLD HISTORY

First of all, let me remark concerning the preliminary concept of a philosophy of world history that, as I have said, one accuses philosophy of approaching history with thoughts and of looking at history in terms of thoughts. But the only thought philosophy brings along is the very simple thought of reason, namely that reason rules the world and that things have happened reasonably (according to reason) in world history. This conviction and this insight is a presupposition in regard to history as such. In philosophy itself this is no presupposition or assumption; in philosophy speculative knowledge proves that reason—we can limit ourselves to this term without discussing the relation to God—is the substance as well as the infinite power, that it is the infinite stuff of all natural and spiritual life as well as the infinite form, the activation of this being its content. It is the substance, that through which and in which all actual reality (*Wirklichkeit*) has its being and existence. It is the infinite power, in the sense that reason is not so powerless as to achieve merely ideal existence—merely an ought— and hence exist only apart from actual reality, who knows where, perhaps only in the heads of a few men. It is the infinite content, all essence and truth, and hence its own stuff which it gives its activity to work on. Reason does not need, like finite action, conditioning materials or given means from which it might receive nourishment by way of objects for its activity; reason feeds upon itself and is itself the material which it works upon. Just as reason is only its own premise and presupposition, just as its end is the absolute and final end (*Endzweck*), so reason is also the activation and production (of this end) from inside itself into the phenomena not only of the natural universe but of the spiritual as well, in world history. It is this which, as noted, is proved in philosophy and is presupposed here as so proved: that this idea (of reason) is the true, the eternal, the absolutely potent, that it reveals itself in the world, and that nothing is revealed in the world except this idea, its grandeur and its honor.

Those who are not familiar with philosophy I could ask perhaps to approach the exposition of world history with the faith in reason and with the thirst for its understanding. It is indeed the desire for rational insight and for knowledge, rather than merely for a collection of bits of information, which may be presupposed as the subjective desire involved in the study of the sciences. In fact, I do not have to ask for such faith in advance. What I have so far said and will say hereafter is not merely a presupposition . . . but a summary of the whole undertaking, the result of the reflections we are engaged in, a result which is known to me because the whole is known to me. It has been and is being concluded from the contemplation of world history itself that things happened according to reason, that this history is the rational and necessary way of the world spirit which is the substance of history, the one spirit whose nature is one and always the same and which explicates its one nature in the world's existence. (The world spirit is the spirit altogether.) This must be, as noted, the result of history itself. But we must take history as it is; we must proceed historically, empirically. Among other things, we must not allow ourselves to be seduced by professional historians; for at least among German historians, even those of great authority who are proud of their study of the sources, there are those who do precisely what they reproach the philosophers with, namely, the imparting of a priori inventions to history. To give an example, it is a very widespread invention that there existed a first and most ancient people which, directly instructed by God, lived in perfect understanding and wisdom, and possessed a penetrating knowledge of all natural laws and of intellectual truth; or that there have existed such and such priestly nations; or, to be more specific, that there existed a Roman epic poem from which the Roman historians have derived their older history, etc. Such a priori statements we shall leave to the brilliant professional historians, among whom they are not unusual.

As the first condition we can therefore say that we seek to comprehend the historical data truly. But there is an equivocation involved in such general terms as "truly" or "comprehend." For the average and mediocre historical writer who thinks and claims to be merely receptive, to be dedicated to what is given, is not actually passive in his thinking. He brings along his categories and he sees what is there through them. The true (interpretation) does not lie on the surface; in all science reason cannot sleep but must think. He who looks at the world according to reason is viewed by the world according to reason too. The two are in a mutual relationship.

But it is not our business here to treat of the different ways of thinking, of the viewpoints, of judgment, even of so basic a matter as the importance or unimportance of information and what needs to be emphasized in the vast material before us.

I shall recall here only two forms of the general conviction that reason rules the world and therefore also world history, because they offer an opportunity to touch upon the main point which causes the difficulties. . . . The first is the historical view of the Greek Anaxagoras that *Nous,* the general intellect or reason, rules the world, but not an intelligence seen as self-conscious reason, not a spirit as such; this distinction is important. The motions of the solar system occur according to unalterable laws; these laws are the reason of the system. But neither the sun nor the planets which rotate according to these laws has a consciousness of these laws. Only man distills these laws from existence and knows them.

This thought that reason is in nature, that it is ruled by general laws unalterably, does not startle us; . . . we are accustomed to it and do not stress it. I have mentioned it partly in order to indicate that history shows us that views we consider commonplace have not always been in the world, but rather that such a thought once marked the beginning of an epoch in the history of the human spirit. Aristotle says of Anaxagoras that as the originator of this thought he appeared like a sober man among drunks.

Socrates took this thought over from Anaxagoras, and it then became dominant among philosophers, with the exception of Epicurus who attributed all events to chance. We shall see later in which other religions and among which other peoples the same thought appeared. Plato then lets Socrates say (in *Phaedo* 97/98) concerning this discovery that thought—not conscious thought, but at first indeterminedly a reason which is neither conscious nor unconscious—rules the world: "I was happy about it and hoped to find a teacher who could interpret nature according to reason and who could demonstrate the particular end in the particular thing and the general end, the final end, the good in the whole. I would not have given up this hope for anything. But," Socrates continues, "how disillusioned I was when I started to work on the writings of Anaxagoras and I found that he mentioned only external causes—air, ether, water and the like—instead of reason." It is evident that what Socrates found unsatisfactory about the principle of Anaxagoras was not the principle itself but the failure to apply it to concrete nature. Nature was not conceived or understood in terms of this principle. The principle remained abstract or, to be more precise, nature was not conceived as a development of this principle or as an organization produced by reason as its principle.

I want to call attention right here at the outset to this difference between stating a proposition, a principle, a truth only abstractly and proceeding to a more definite determination and a concrete development. This difference is decisive and, among other things, we shall encounter this issue at the end of our world history, when interpreting the newest political situation.*

I have mentioned this first appearance of the thought that reason rules the world, and the shortcomings of this thought, because it finds its application in another form which is well known to us and of which we have a strong conviction: the religious truth that the world does not result from chance and external, accidental causes, but that providence rules the world. I mentioned a moment ago that I did not want to demand that one believe in this principle, but I might appeal to the belief in this religious form, were it not the peculiarity of the science of philosophy to deny the validity of such presuppositions. To put it another way, the science we are proposing to deal with ought itself to produce the evidence, if not for the truth, for the correctness of this principle by showing its concreteness. The truth that a divine providence prevails in the events of this world corresponds to this principle, for divine providence is the wisdom based on infinite power which realizes its ends, that is, the absolute, rational final end of the world; reason is thinking which determines itself in complete freedom: *Nous.*

Yet, the difference—indeed the contradiction—between this belief and our principle presents itself in the same way as between Anaxagoras and Socrates in connection with the principle of Anaxagoras. For that belief is also indeterminate; it is a belief in providence in general and does not proceed to the definite, to the application for the whole (of world history), to the all-inclusive sequence of world events. Instead of this application, natural explanations have been put forward: the passions of men, the stronger army, talent or genius of this or that individual, or the absence of such in a particular state. These are so-called natural, accidental causes such as Socrates criticized in Anaxagoras. Interpretation stops with abstract notions and the idea of providence remains quite general. The definite aspect of providence, its specific action, is called the

* See below, pp. 523-545. For an explanation of this Hegelian insistence upon concreteness, see the Introduction above, pp. xvii-xviii.

plan of providence (the end and the means for this destiny, these plans.) This plan is said to be hidden from our view; indeed it is said to be arrogant to want to know and understand it. The ignorance of Anaxagoras as to how reason is revealed in actual reality was naïve; thought, in the sense of consciousness of thought, had not yet progressed further either in him or in the rest of Greece. He therefore was not able to apply the general principle to the concrete facts, to know and understand these facts in terms of it. A first step in the direction of recognizing the unity of the concrete and the general was made by Socrates, but only in one-sided, subjective terms; Socrates was therefore not opposed to such application. But the aforementioned belief in providence is opposed to its application on a large scale, to the understanding of the plan of providence. In particulars one is willing to admit providence, and pious souls recognize in many particular events, where others see only accidents, decrees not only of God but of His providence. But it happens only in particular situations, as when help has come unexpectedly to a particular individual in need . . .

In world history the individuals we deal with are nations and the wholes that are states. We cannot therefore stop with these lesser matters in believing in providence, nor can we stop with the abstract and indeterminate belief which merely sees the general proposition that there is a providence in the world. Rather we must make an earnest effort to understand the concrete as the means and ways of providence which are spread out openly before us as the phenomena of history. All we have to do is relate them to this general principle.

But in mentioning the understanding of the plan of divine providence I have recalled a question which is of prime importance in our time, namely, the possibility of knowing and understanding God—or rather, since it has ceased to be a question, the doctrine which has become a prejudice that it is impossible to know and understand God, a doctrine which is contrary to Holy Writ where it is commanded as the highest duty not only to love God but to know Him. It is likewise denied—this is also stated in Holy Writ—that it is the spirit which leads us to the truth, that the spirit knows and understands all things, and that it permeates the depths of the Deity. I could have omitted this reference . . . but I wanted to recall these religious truths. . . . We have reached the point where philosophy must guard religion against certain kinds of theology.

In the Christian religion God has revealed Himself, giving to men the knowledge of what He is so that He is no longer secluded and secret. With this possibility of knowing Him God has imposed upon us the duty to so know Him. The development of the thinking spirit, which has started from this basis, from the revelation of the Divine Being, must at last progress to the point where what was at first presented to the spirit in feeling and imagination is comprehended by thought. Whether the time has come to achieve this knowledge depends upon whether the final end of the world has at last entered into actual reality in a generally valid and conscious manner.

It must now at last be the right time to comprehend this rich production of creative reason which is world history. Our effort to know aims at gaining the insight that what was intended by the eternal wisdom has actually come to pass, not only in the realm of nature, but in the realm of the spirit which is actual and active in the world. Our contemplation of history is in this sense a theodicy, a justification of God. Leibnitz attempted it metaphysically, in his way, in abstract, indefinite categories: the wrongs in the world, including the evil, were to be understood and the thinking spirit was to be reconciled with the negative aspects. In world history the whole mass of concrete wrongs is laid before our eyes. . . . Such reconciliation can only be achieved by knowing and understanding the affirmative aspects in which the negative aspects disappear as something subordinate and overpowered. It can be achieved only through becoming conscious, on one hand, of what is in truth the final end of the world and, on the other (through becoming conscious), that this final end has been realized in the world and that the evil alongside it has not become valid and effective (*geltend*).

Reason, which it has been said rules the world, is as

indefinite a word as providence. One speaks of this reason without being able to state what is its meaning, what is its content, and what is the criterion by which we may determine whether something is in accord with reason or not. Reason comprehended in its determination, this only is the heart of the matter; the other viewpoint, which stops with reason in general, is nothing but words. We now turn to the second aspect which we propose to consider in this introduction.

II. THE IDEA OF HISTORY AND ITS REALIZATION

The destination[*] of reason in itself and its relation to the world raises the same question as that which will exist after the final end of the world. It ought to be realized, to be actualized. Two aspects must therefore be considered: the content of this final end, the destiny in itself and as such, and the realization thereof.

Our subject, world history, occurs in the field of the spirit. The world comprises both physical and psychic nature. The physical nature affects world history . . . but the spirit and the course of its development is its substance. . . . The first thing, therefore, which we must do is abstractly to determine the spirit. (The spirit is not an abstraction; it is not abstracted from human nature but individual, active, completely alive. It is consciousness, but also its object. It is the nature of the spirit to have itself as its object.)[†] . . .

In the light of this discussion it can be said of world history that it is the description of the spirit as it works out the knowledge of that which it is in itself. The Orientals do not know that the spirit is free in itself, or that man is free in

---

[*] The German term "Bestimmung" usually translated as "determination" also means "destination" or "destiny." This meaning is implied here.

[†] These parenthetic sentences are inserted from the lecture notes, as given by Lasson, op. cit., p. 31. Hereafter Hegel develops the idea of the spirit much in the same terms as in the Phenomenology of the Spirit, for which see pp. 410 ff. below.

himself. Because they do not know it, they are not free. They only know that "one" is free; therefore such freedom is only arbitrariness, ferocity, obtuseness of passion or—by contrast—mildness and gentleness, which itself is merely accident or arbitrament. This "one" is therefore a despot, not a free man, not a man.

The consciousness of freedom arose among the Greeks, and therefore they were free; but they, like the Romans, knew only that a few are free, and not man as such. Neither Plato nor Aristotle knew it. Therefore the Greeks not only had slaves to whom their lives and their beautiful freedom was tied, but their freedom was itself only an accidental or contingent, undeveloped, passing and limited flower, involving a harsh servitude of the human and humanitarian sentiments.

Only the Germanic nations have in and through Christianity achieved the consciousness that man *qua* man is free and that freedom of the spirit constitutes his very nature. This consciousness arose first in religion, in the innermost region of the spirit. But to extend this principle to the secular realm was a further task, the solution and execution of which required a difficult and long labor, a civilizing process (*Bildung*). Slavery, for example, did not cease immediately upon the conversion to Christianity; even less did freedom immediately become dominant in (Christian) states, nor were governments and constitutions organized according to reason and based upon the principle of freedom. The application of the principle to secular matters, the permeation and transformation of the secular state by this principle, constitutes the course of history. I remarked before upon the difference between the principle and its application. . . . World History is the progress in the consciousness of freedom, a progress which we must know and understand in its (inherent) necessity. . . .

Hence, what constitutes the reason of the spirit in its determination (that is, its destination), . . . what constitutes the final end of the world we claim to be the spirit's consciousness of its freedom and thus the actualization (*Wirklichkeit*) of its freedom. That this (concept of) freedom is still indeterminate and ambiguous in definition; that freedom, being the highest (good) implies infinitely many misunderstandings, confusions, and errors; that it involves all kinds of commotions—this one has never known better nor experienced more clearly than in our time. But right now we shall be content with the general notion, just the same. . . .

[Further observations in line with the *Phenomenology of the Spirit,* etc., follow here.]

The immediate question can only be: which means does freedom employ? . . . This question of the means . . . leads into history and its phenomena. If freedom as such is the internal conception, the means are something external—the phenomena which present themselves in history as it occurs before our eyes. The most obvious view of history shows us the actions of men which emanate from their needs, their passions, their interests, and the ideas and purposes shaped by them, from their character and talents. In this drama of activity only the needs, passions, interests, etc., appear as the springs of action. The individuals do, perhaps in part, will more general ends, something truly good, but they will it in such a way that it is limited in nature, e.g., noble love of country may be directed toward a country which is insignificant in the world and in relation to the world's general end; the same may be said of love of one's family, friends—honesty generally. In short, all virtues belong here. In them we can perceive the destination of all these persons and their spheres of work toward reason. But they are single individuals, small in comparison to the mass of mankind . . . the circumference of existence of their virtues is of relatively small scope. In part the passions, the purposes of particular interest, the satisfaction of egotism and selfishness are the most potent. Their force lies in the fact that they respect no limits which law and morality wish to set, and that the natural force of passion is more immediate and closer to man than the artificial and lengthy discipline which leads to order and moderation, to law and morality.

When we contemplate this drama of passions and the consequences of their violence, of the unwisdom which is associated not only with them but with good intentions as well, when we keep before our eyes how in history evil has triumphed and the most flourishing empires have been brought low by human beings, when we look upon these individuals with deepest sympathy in their unspeakable woe, we can end up by feeling sorrow for this vainglory and an indignation of the good spirit (if such be in us) since this destruction is not simply the work of nature, but of men. . . .

In looking upon history as this butchery, . . . the thought naturally arises: for what final end have all these sacrifices been made? . . . We propose to see all these events as means toward the final end which we believe to be the true result of world history, its substantive destination, its absolute final end. We refuse to reflect upon these events in terms of direct reflection and leave to others the sentimental contemplation of them. . . .

First of all, we note that what we have called principle, final end, destination, or what we have called the spirit in itself, its nature, its conception, is merely something general and abstract. A principle, a maxim or a law is something general and inward which as such, be it ever so true, is not fully actually real. Purposes, principles and the like are in our thoughts only in our inward intention or in books; they are not yet in actual reality (*Wirklichkeit*). What is by itself, is only a possibility, a potentiality, but it has not yet emerged into full existence. A second element must be added to make it actually real, which is its activation, or actualization, and the principle of this is the will and the activity of men in the world. Only by this activity are those conceptions and determinations (destinations?) realized and actualized.

The laws and principles do not live, are not enforced by themselves. The activity which gives them existence and works them out is the needs and desires of man, his inclinations and his passions. To bring something into existence by deed, I must be concerned with it. I want to be in on it, I want to be satisfied by carrying it out—in short, it must be of interest to me. "Interest" means to be in, to be part of something. A purpose for which I am to be active must in some way be my own purpose. I must be able to satisfy my own purpose even though this other purpose or end may have many other aspects which do not concern me. This is the infinite right of the subject, the second essential aspect of freedom, that such a subject finds itself satisfied in some activity or work . . . It is important to avoid a misunderstanding here. It is often said that someone is only interested in the sense of seeking only his own private gain, without conviction . . . But he who is interested in something is always himself a part of it. . . . Nothing happens, nothing is achieved but that the individuals who are involved also are satisfied, in their own particular interests . . . these interests may be those of needs and wants, but they may be those of insight, conviction or at least of opinion or prejudice, whenever the need of arguing, of intellect and reason have been awakened. Human beings demand that what they are to be active for be acceptable to them . . . This is especially true of course in our own time, when men are not drawn to action by loyalty and authority, but wish to determine for themselves the share they have in something and to do so by their own intelligence, their autonomous conviction or belief.

Thus we say that altogether nothing has ever come into being without the interest of those whose activity was involved. We may further call an interest a passion. And (in view of what happens) when an individual, by relegating all his other interests and purposes, . . . with all his innate capacity of will immerses himself wholly in something, concentrates all his resources and powers upon this one purpose, we are obliged to state that nothing great happens in the world without passion. Passion, to be sure, is the subjective and hence formal aspect of the energy of will and of activity, while its content or purpose is still indeterminate. The same is true in connection with convictions, one's insight and conscience. . . .

From this elucidation of the second essential aspect of historical reality of a purpose it follows parenthetically regarding the state, that a state will be well-organized and strong in itself if its general end is joined to the private interests of its citizens, the one is satisfied and realized through the other—a very important proposition in itself. Yet within a state many arrangements are needed, many inventions of useful institutions, involving long struggles of the understanding, until what is most appropriate to its purpose becomes conscious. Also (there will have to take place) struggles with the particular interests and the long and difficult disciplining of the passions, before such a conjunction of the general and the particular interests is achieved. The time of such a conjunction constitutes in the history of a state the period of its flowering, of its virtue, of its power and its happiness. But world history does not begin with some such conscious purpose or end. . . . The history of the world starts with its general end, namely to satisfy the desire of the spirit to conceive itself (*dass der Begriff des Geistes befriedigt werde*), only by itself, that is to say as nature; it is the innermost and unconscious drive, and the whole business of world history is the work of bringing it into consciousness. . . . The infinite mass of wills, interests and activities are the tools and means of the world spirit to accomplish its end . . . to come to itself and to contemplate itself as actual reality. That those living processes of individuals and nations, by seeking and satisfying their own limited ends, serve at the same time as the means and tools of something higher of which they know nothing and which they therefore accomplish unconsciously—this could be questioned, and has been questioned, has been many times denied, and has been ridiculed and despised as a dream, as philosophy. As against this, I have proclaimed at the outset that reason rules the world, and I have stated this as our presupposition and faith. . . . This reason is immanent in historical existence and it realizes itself in and through it. . . . The speculative truth of this proposition is treated in the *Logic*.* . . . Hence I cannot prove it here, but I can illustrate it by examples in this philosophy of history.

What is involved here is that in world history something else results from the actions of men than what they intend and achieve, something else than they know or want. They accomplish their interest; but something else is accomplished, which was implied in it, but which was not in the conscious-

---

* See below, pp. 177 ff.

ness and the intention of the actors. To give an analogy, a man may set fire to the house of another out of revenge which may indeed be justified; . . . the immediate action is to hold a small flame to a small part of a beam. What had not been immediately involved follows: the part of the beam is joined to the rest, to other beams of the house, and those in turn to other houses; hence a vast conflagration develops which destroys the property and perhaps the lives of many human beings who were not the object of the revenge. This result was neither part of the primary deed nor the intention of him who commenced it. Hence this action is more generally determined; though in intention it was only an act of revenge against an individual, it was also a crime . . . and implies therefore a penalty. This example merely shows that in the immediate action something else may be implied than is consciously willed by the actor. . . .

But let me give another example which contains this conjunction of the particular and the general. . . . When Caesar was in danger of losing the position, not yet of predominance, but of equality besides the other men who stood at the head of the state and of succumbing to them who were about to become his enemies—and who had at the same time on their side and in support of their interests the formal constitution and the power of legal form—he fought these men in his own interest of maintaining his position, his honor and his security. His victory over them, since their power consisted in rule over the provinces of the Roman empire, thus became the conquest of this entire empire. Caesar thereby became, though the formal constitution remained, the individual ruler of the state. What the execution of his purely negative, defensive purpose thus secured for him—namely, the monocratic rule over Rome—was at the same time a necessary destination of Rome in the history of the world. Hence his work not only brought him particular gain but instinctively accomplished what was timely in and by itself. Such are the great men in history whose own particular purposes contain the substantial task which is the will of the world spirit. This substance is their true power and strength, for it is at work in the general, unconscious instinct of their contemporaries. They are inwardly driven to it and have no resistance against him who has undertaken the execution of such a purpose in his own interest. Rather, nations gather around his banner. He shows them and executes what is their own immanent drive.

[Hereafter Hegel's lectures dwelt, according to the various reports we have, upon the role of the ordinary men who sustain social life (*die erhaltenden Individuen*) as well as the role of the world historical individuals who initiate major changes. In this connection, a sentence from his own MS may be quoted: "If we cast a glance at the destiny of these world historical individuals, they have had the good luck to be the executioners of a purpose which forms a stage in the forward march of the general spirit." He then turns to the value of the individual.]

If we must therefore accept the proposition that the individuals, their purposes and their satisfactions are sacrificed, . . . and they are seen as means to an end,* there nonetheless is in every individual a side which we hesitate to view this way, even in relation to the highest (namely, reason and the world spirit), because it is something absolutely not subordinate but something intrinsically eternal and divine in them. This is their morality, their ethics, their religiosity.† . . . When we speak of a means we initially think of it as something extrinsic to the end which has no share in it (the means). In fact even natural things—the most ordinary lifeless things employed as means—must have the quality of corresponding to the purpose, must have something in them which they have in common with the purpose or end. Human beings are hardly ever external means to the rational end. Not only do they satisfy together with this end . . . their own and different particular purposes, but they share in the rational end itself and thereby

---

* This phrasing which recurs in Hegel is presumably chosen to counteract and contradict Kant's categorical imperative which forbids us to treat human beings as means and hence concludes "there shall not be war." Hegel expounds the opposite. See above, pp. xlviii-ix.
† See below, pp. 252 ff. and 260 ff.—Ed.

remain autonomous or final ends (*Selbstzwecke*), not only formally . . . but materially (*dem Inhalte nach*). In this sphere belongs what we wish to see removed from the category of means, namely morality, ethics and religion. Man is only an end in himself (or final end) through what is divine in him—by what has from the beginning been called reason and, insofar as it is active in itself, what has been called freedom. Without entering into further detail, we may say that religion, ethics, etc., have their basis and source in this autonomy and through it are elevated above external necessity and contingency. But we must not forget that we speak of human beings in this sense only, when and insofar as these elements (morals, ethics, religion) exist within them—in other words insofar as they partake of individual freedom. Considering this destiny, religious and ethical decline, corruption and loss become the guilt of the individuals (in history).

This is the seal of man's high absolute destiny, that he knows what is good and evil and he can therefore will either the good or the evil—in short, that he can become guilty, guilty not only of evil but of the good as well, guilty not of this or that or everything in which he is and which is in him but guilty of what belongs (in the sphere) of his individual freedom, its good and evil. Only an animal is truly and completely innocent. But to exclude all misunderstandings . . . would lead far afield. . . .*

But in considering the fate which befalls virtue, ethics and religiosity in history, we must not yield to the laments that the good and pious often are badly off while the evil and bad ones are well off. This "being well off" covers many things, like wealth, honor and the like, but such "being well off" cannot be made a criterion when we are dealing with an autonomous or final end in a rational world order. We can with more right demand that good, moral, legal ends secure their execution within the framework of a world end. . . . What troubles people and makes them discontent—and they pride themselves on this discontent—is that more general ends which they

---

* Cf. what Hegel has to say on the subject of guilt below, pp. 257 ff.

consider good and right, more particularly ideals of political institutions, are found to be not realized at present (they like to invent such ideals and to get enthusiastic about them). They juxtapose what is right to what are their notions of what ought to be. In these cases it is not the particular interest, the passion which desires to be satisfied, but reason, right and freedom. Armed with these titles, these demands are proudly proclaimed and cause people to be not only discontent with the state of the world and its events but highly indignant. In order to do justice to such views one would have to enter into an examination of the demands thus presented, of the very assertive views and insights. At no time have more pretentious ideas been presented. If history in the past presents itself primarily as a struggle of the passions, history in our time shows itself predominantly as a struggle of justified ideas, partly as a struggle of passions and interests disguised behind such higher claims . . .

We shall presently turn to the state. As to the violation and disappearance of religious, moral and ethical purposes and conditions, we must admit right now (we shall return to it later) that these spiritual forces are absolutely justified. But their configurations, their content and development in actuality may be of a limited sort (what is general in them is infinite) and hence may be subject to natural causes and contingencies. To this extent these forces are transitory, exposed to decline and violation. . . . The religion, the ethics of a restricted life, the life of a shepherd or of a peasant has infinite value in its concentrated intensity and in its limitation to a few and very simple aspects of life. It has the same value as the religiosity and the ethics of someone of highly developed knowledge and of an existence rich in extent and activity. This inward center, this simple sphere of the right of subjective freedom—the source of will, decision and action, the abstract content of his conscience, that wherein guilt and value of the individual, his everlasting court, are comprised—remains untouched by the loud noise of world history. It remains apart not only from the external and temporal changes but also from those which the absolute necessity of the concept of freedom implies. . . .

This may suffice concerning the means which the world spirit employs for the realization of its conception. . . .

[Here follows an extended discussion of the state, of law, of the state and religion, of culture and of the constitution, which is very vital for Hegel's argument but which is here omitted because it parallels what is given below, and in greater detail, in our selections from *The Philosophy of Right and Law*, pp. 272-329.]

III. THE MARCH OF WORLD HISTORY

1. *The Concept of Development*. The abstract change which occurs in history has long since been interpreted in such a way as to contain a progression to the better, the more perfect. The changes in nature show only a cyclical movement. . . . Only in the changes which occur in the field of the spirit does the novel occur. This aspect of the life of the spirit long ago led to seeing man as destined for something different than the merely natural things, . . . a capacity for genuine change for the better, the more perfect, a drive toward perfection, as we have said. This principle which makes change itself something lawful has been ill received by those religions, like the Catholic one, and those states which claim to be static or at least stable as a matter of right. And even if generally the changeability of secular things, such as the state, is admitted, religion *qua* religious truth is excepted therefrom, or the changes, revolutions, the destruction of the rightful one are attributed to accidents or maladroitness or, more particularly, to the irresponsibility, corruption and evil passions of men. And, indeed, perfectibility is almost as indeterminate as all change; it is without purpose or goal; the better or more perfect which it is supposed to aim at is quite vague.

The principle of development contains further the notion that an inner destiny or determination, some kind of presupposition is at the base of it and is brought into existence. This formal determination is essential. The spirit which has world history as its stage, its property and its field of actualization is not such as would move aimlessly about in a game of external accidents, but is instead the absolutely determining factor. The peculiar destiny or determination of the spirit is completely fixed as against the contingencies which it employs for its purposes and which it dominates. But there is also an evolution of the organic things in nature; their existence is not merely changed directly and from the outside, but this change results from within, from an inward and immutable principle, from a simple essence whose existence is at first very simple, when it is a germ, but which brings into being a differentiation which becomes involved with other things and then undergoes a continuous process of alteration which again is turned into the reverse, namely, the preservation of the organic principle and its configuration (that is to say, a new seed and germ). Thus the organic individual produces itself; it makes itself into that which it is in itself. Thus the spirit is only what it makes itself, and it makes itself into what it is in itself.* But natural evolution occurs in a direct, unhindered way, and without contradiction . . . It is different in the case of the spirit. The transition from the spirit's destination to its realization is mediated by consciousness and will. . . . The object and purpose are primarily the natural destination itself and as such. This destination is of infinite strength and richness, has an infinite claim, because the spirit animates it. Thus the spirit is within itself opposed to itself; it has to overcome itself as the genuinely hostile obstacle of its end. The development which as such is a steady evolution—for it expresses itself as something which remains itself—is a hard and never-ending struggle of the spirit against itself within itself. What the spirit wants is to achieve its own conception, but it hides this conception from itself and is proud and joyful in this alienation. . . .

There are several great periods in world history which have passed without seeming to have continued, at the end of

---

* In passages such as these, the neutral gender of the word "spirit" makes itself felt most disadvantageously. In German the spirit makes *himself* what *he* is *him*self. The central position of the organic analogy is very striking in this statement.—Ed.

which the entire vast gain of culture was destroyed and one had to begin anew in order to achieve, perhaps with the help of a few remains of former treasures, those levels of culture which had been achieved long before. . . . But there exist also continuing developments, rich and highly elaborated structures and systems of culture with unique aspects. The formal principle of development cannot suggest a preference of one of these developmental models nor can it make comprehensible the purpose of the decline of those older periods. It has to look upon these events and, more especially, the relapses as external accidents. It can judge the respective merits only according to rather indefinite standards which are relative and not absolute ends, since the evolution itself is the final (term of reference).

World history presents therefore the stages in the development of the principle whose meaning (*Gehalt*) is the consciousness of freedom. The development occurs in stages not only because the spirit does not act directly, mediately by and through itself, but because it is differentiated by the dividing, the differentiating of the spirit within itself. The more detailed determination of these stages is in its general nature logical, but in its more concrete form it belongs to the philosophy of the spirit.* Of this abstract dimension we remark here only upon the following: The first stage is the immediate one where, as already noted, the spirit is embodied in naturalness, in which it is only in unfree isolation (one is free). The second stage is that in which the spirit emerges into a consciousness of its freedom. But this first emergence (*Losreissen*) is imperfect and partial (some are free); it emerges from the immediate naturalness, is related to it and hence is still affected by it as an aspect. The third stage is the rising from this particular freedom into the pure and general freedom (man is free *qua* man); that is, the spirit rises to the self-confidence and self-consciousness of the essence of freedom.

These stages are the basic principles of the general process. How each of them is in turn a process of molding it and what

---

* Presumably this is a reference to *The Phenomenology of the Spirit;* see below, pp. 399 ff.

is the dialectics of their transition, this must be reserved to the explication.*

[Hegel concludes the section with stress again on the organic view according to which the whole being is contained in the seed, and he reminds the reader of the Aristotelian *dynamis* which is *potentia,* that is force and power.]

The imperfect seen thus as the opposite of something contained within itself is the contradiction which does indeed exist but which must be superseded and preserved (*aufgehoben*), must be resolved; it is the drive, the impulse of the life of the spirit within itself to break through the bonds, the shell of naturalness, of sensuousness, of estrangement from itself and to arrive at the light of consciousness, that is of itself.

2. *The Beginning of History.* In general, the beginning of history has been conceived in terms of a state of nature in which freedom and right and law existed in perfection. But this was merely a hypothetical reflection . . . A rather different presumption . . . alleged to be a historical fact has lately been put into circulation, . . . namely, the existence of a primitive people from which all knowledge, science and art has been handed down (Schelling; Schlegel's *Sprache und Weisheit der Inder*). . . . The high authority put behind this assumption is the Bible story (of Adam and Eve). This story presents the primitive stage, however, partly in the few and well known features, partly as a radical change in man or in Adam as one person. . . . There is no justification here for imagining a people and a historical state which existed in such primitive form, nor do we have here a pure knowledge of God and nature. Nature, so it is invented, originally stood open and clear like a bright mirror before the eyes of man (Schlegel's *Philosophie der Geschichte*, I, 44), and divine truth was equally apparent. . . . From this state all religions started, but they soiled and covered this first truth with errors and confusions. But in all these erroneous mythologies, so it is alleged, traces

---

* See below, pp. 43 ff.

of the origin and of those first religious doctrines of truth exist and can be recognized. Hence the main interest attributed to the study of these ancient peoples is to go to the point where such fragments of the first revealed truth can still be encountered in their greater purity.* We owe much to the interest in these researches, but the results of the research are witness against the thesis. . . . That the knowledge of God or the knowledge of other scientific and astronomical knowledge† characterized the beginning of world history, that the religions of the various peoples have traditionally started from such knowledge and that they resulted from a degeneration and corruption of it . . . all these are assumptions which have neither a historical foundation, nor can they, if we oppose a philosophical conception to mere guesswork, ever achieve it.

The only procedure proper and worthy of philosophical contemplation is to begin history where reasonableness enters into the world's existence . . . where there is a state in which such reason manifests itself in consciousness, will and deed. The unorganic existence of the spirit . . . is not a subject of history. The natural and therefore religious ethics is the piety in the family. Ethics in such a society consists in this, that the members do not behave toward each other as individuals with a free will, they do not act as persons. The family is therefore outside the development which becomes history. But if unity of the spirit goes beyond this circle of sentiment and natural love (which is the family) and if it reaches the consciousness of personality, then the dark and brittle center develops in which neither nature nor spirit is open and clear. Nature and spirit can become open and clear only through the work of later, indeed very late, culture of that spirit which has become conscious of itself. For consciousness alone is open and hence that to which God or indeed anything can be revealed . . . Freedom is merely to know and understand such general and substantial matters as law and right, to will them and to create a reality which suits them—the state.

* Hegel here cites Lamennais, Abel Remusat, Saint Martin and Baron von Eckstein.
† Hegel here refers to J. S. Bailly, but very disparagingly.—Ed.

Peoples can lead and have led a long life without a state, before they reach the point where they achieve their destiny—they may even have reached a significant development in certain directions. But such pre-history lies outside our task; there may have followed a real history or these peoples may never have arrived at the formation of a state.

[Hegel then comments upon the discovery of the interrelation of the Aryan languages and admits that it is very exciting, but it has nothing to do with what he is concerned with; its "falls outside history."]

History unites, as we use the term, the objective and the subjective aspects. It designates the *historiam rerum gestarum* as well as the *res gestas* themselves, the telling of the history as well as the deeds and events themselves. This joining of the two meanings we must consider as something more than external accident. We must assume that the telling of history appears contemporaneously with the historical deeds and events. It is an inward and common foundation from which they both spring. Family memories, patriarchal traditions have an interest within the family, the tribe. The uniform course of their situation is no object for memory, but distinguishing deeds or turns of fate may stimulate memory (*Mnemosyne*) into shaping pictures such as love and religious sentiment demand of the imagination . . . But only the state produces the kind of content which is not only suitable for the prose of history but which creates it. Instead of merely subjective governing commands which suit the particular moment, a consolidating community which is raising itself into a state requires laws, general and generally valid determinations. It thus produces a record (*Vortrag*) as well as an interest in rational deeds and events which have permanent results. Memory (*Mnemosyne*) is driven to add the permanence of memory to the present configuration and organization of the state in order to serve the perennial purpose of the state. Deep sentiments, like love, and the religious imagination and its products are in themselves entirely present and satisfactory. But the extraneous existence of the state is, in spite of its rational laws and customs, an incomplete presence the comprehension of which requires the consciousness of the past for its integration.

The periods, whether of hundreds or of thousands of years, which passed before the writing of history and which are filled with revolutions, migrations and the wildest changes are without objective history because they had no subjective writing of history. This did not happen accidentally; such writing does not exist because it could not. Only in a state in which law becomes conscious are there clear deeds and, with them, clarity of the conscious mind which gives the capacity as well as the ability to preserve them. It is striking to anyone who becomes acquainted with the treasures of Indian literature that this country which is so rich in spiritual productions that go very deep has no history and thereby contrasts sharply with China which possesses an admirable set of historical chronicles going back to the most ancient times. India has, besides its ancient religious and brilliant poetical works, ancient law books which are needed for the shaping of history, but it has no history. But in that country the differentiation and beginning organization of society became ossified into castes; therefore the laws regulate the civil (private) rights but make them at the same time dependent upon those allegedly natural differentiations, and hence primarily fix the competencies (not the rights but the non-rights) of these castes toward each other, that is, the higher toward the lower. Thereby ethics was banned from the Indian realms and from Indian life, despite its brilliance. As a result of this un-freedom of a naturally fixed caste order, all other cohesion of society is wild arbitrament, passing drift, raging without final end of progression or development. Thus no object is there for memory and a wild though deep imagination wanders about in a field which ought to have a firm goal and thus become capable of history. . . .

Because of such conditions it could happen that the rich, indeed immeasurable growth of families into tribes, of tribes into nations . . . and therefore also the spread and development of the world of human language, remained silent and occurred in a quiet and gradual way. It is a fact resulting from these circumstances that the languages were highly developed in the uncultured state of the peoples who spoke them, that the mind flung itself into this theoretical field, in a significant evolution.

The extended and coherent grammar is the work of thinking which thus explicates its categories. It is a further fact that with the progress of civilization in society and state this systematic expression of the mind is polished and that language becomes poorer and less explict (*ungebildet*)—(it is) a curious phenomenon that the progress (of language), as it becomes more intellectual and makes reason more explicit, neglects that thoughtful elaborateness and precision, finds it a hindrance and no longer needed. Language is the deed of the theoretical intelligence in the specific sense, for it is the expression of it. The activities of memory and imagination without language are purely inward expression (incommunicable?). But this theoretical deed . . . is wrapped in the mist of a silent past. . . . It has achieved no history. . . . The advance of language and the forward movement and division of the nations reaches the point where it is of interest and significance for the concrete reason only when in contact with existing states or leading to the formation of states.

3. *The Course of Development.* We must now sketch the march of history, but only from the formal side. . . . The indication of the concrete content will be given in the periodization.*

World history constitutes, as previously determined, the development of the spirit's consciousness of its freedom and of the resulting actualization . . . there are stages . . . The logical and even more the dialectical nature of a concept, which is that it determines (*bestimmt*) itself, that it posits determination (*Bestimmungen*) and that it suspends these in turn and, by this suspension (and preservation), gains an affirmative and indeed richer and more concrete determination—this inherent necessity and the necessary succession of pure abstract

---

* This periodization is omitted here; the interested reader will find it in Sibree, *op. cit.,* pp. 163 ff. and in the original, ed. Lasson, pp. 232 ff. It is easily perceivable from the division of the work itself.—Ed.

conceptual determinations is a subject of the *Logic*.* Here we need only remark that each stage as distinguished from the others has its determinate and peculiar principle. Such a principle becomes in history the determinate spirit of a people or nation. In it the spirit expresses concretely all aspects of its will and of its consciousness, of its entire actuality. It is the common impress of its religion, its political constitution, its ethics, its legal system, its customs and culture, as well as of its science and scholarship, of its art and techniques, of the direction of its crafts and commerce. The special peculiarities must be understood in terms of its general nature, the particular principle of a people, just as conversely the factual historical details will reveal the general idea that is peculiar to them. It must be shown empirically and in a historical fashion that a definite particularity is in fact the peculiar principle of a people. To achieve this presupposes not only skill in abstracting but a familiarity with the ideas; . . . we must know them a priori, just as the greatest scientist in this type of inquiry, Kepler, had to be familiar with curves, cubes and squares and their relations a priori, before he could invent (sic! *erfinden*, not *entdecken*) his immortal laws which constitute determinations taken from that group of ideas. He who is ignorant of these matters of the elementary (mathematical) determinants cannot comprehend those laws any more than he could invent them, no matter how long he may look at the sky and its stars. It is from this lack of acquaintance with the thoughts on the developing forms of freedom that there flows at least some of the reproaches made to a philosophical contemplation of an otherwise empirical science (history) on account of the so-called a priori character of ideas which are being brought to the material (of history). Such determinants of thought thus appear as something alien to the subject itself. . . . Consequently it is said that philosophy does not understand such sciences. And it must be admitted that philosophy does not have the kind of knowledge which prevails in these fields but proceeds according to categories of reason, knowing the mind, its value and its standpoint.

* See below, pp. 175 ff.

In such scientific work it is important to distinguish the essential from the unessential and to emphasize it. But in order to do this it is necessary to know the essential. This essential aspect is, when one considers world history as a whole, as previously noted, the consciousness of freedom . . . Direction toward these categories constitutes direction toward the truly essential.

[After a paragraph in which Hegel discusses the parallel problem in the natural science fields, by suggesting that there are aberrations, such as miscreances which do not disprove orderly evolution, he continues:]

Similarly one proceeds when one says rightly that genius, talent, moral virtues and sentiments, piety may appear in all regions and under all constitutions and political arrangements; there are plenty of examples. But if this is intended to prove that the difference which is related to the self-consciousness of freedom is unimportant and unessential as compared to these qualities, then such reflections remain abstract categories, and avoid establishing a definite content for which there is (to be found) no principle in these abstract categories. The state of scholarship which moves within such formal views offers a vast field for acute questions, learned arguments, startling comparisons, deep-seeming reflections and declamations which will seem the more brilliant the more uncertain they are, so that they can continually be renewed and altered . . . In this sense the Indic epic poems may be compared with the Homeric ones and put above them because presumably the range of imagination is what matters. . . . In the same sense, Chinese philosophy has been represented as the same as Eleatic philosophy or the system of Spinoza because it is based upon the One. . . . Examples of courage, of nobility and the like . . . are made the ground for asserting that nations where these occur are as ethical and moral as the most cultured Christian nations. One has finally raised the question as to whether man has become better as history has progressed and, with it, culture, education and the rest . . .

We may be excused if we do not further elucidate the formalism and error of such views and do not set forth the true principles of morality, or rather of ethics against such false moralizing. For world history moves upon a higher plane than that upon which morality has its peculiar place; for morality is the private conviction of the individuals, their particular will and mode of action: these have their value, their reward and punishment. But what the final end of the spirit requires and accomplishes—this end being in and by itself—what providence does, all that lies beyond the obligations, cannot be imputed to nor expected of individuals in regard to their ethics. Those who have resisted what was made necessary by the progression of the idea of the spirit, who have done so out of ethical considerations and hence noble conviction, are morally superior to those whose crimes were converted by a higher order into means for carrying out the will of this higher order. But in revolutions of this kind both parties to the conflict are really placed within the same sphere of disaster; it is only a formal right which has already been abandoned by the living spirit and God that these defend who are by law entitled to do so. The deeds of the great men who are world historical individuals thus appear justified not only in their inner (and to them unknown) meaning, but also from the world standpoint. From this standpoint moral circles ought not to object to world historical deeds and to those who accomplish them . . . The litany of private virtues, such as modesty, humane love and gentleness ought not to be raised against them. World history could dispense entirely with the sphere to which morality and the oft-discussed conflict between morals and politics belongs, not only by abstaining from such (moral) judgments . . . but by omitting altogether reference to individuals. For what world history is reporting are the deeds of the spirit of the nations, while the individual configurations which occurred in the field of extraneous reality might be left to history proper.

A formalism similar to the moral one plays around with such indefinite notions as genius, poetry, even philosophy, and discovers these everywhere. They are products of the reflecting thought which emphasizes and denotes important differences, without going down into the true depth of the matter. To move about among these with facility is (part of) being educated. But such education is something formal . . .

[Here follow further observations repeating what Hegel has said above and in many other places about the nature of the formal, and the abstract kind of analytical thought to which he objects.]

Just as reflection produces the general notions about genius, talent, art, science and so forth and proceeds to equally general observations concerning them, so evidently formal education and culture (*Bildung*) can at every stage of the configurations of the spirit emerge, grow and flourish—indeed not only can but must do so. At such a stage a state will be developed and upon this basis of civilization the development will go forward to rational reflection and thus to laws and others forms of generality. In the life of the state the necessity as such of formal education (*Bildung*) is implied, hence the development of the sciences and of a cultured poetry and art. The arts known as the fine (*bildenden*)* ones anyhow call because of their technical requirements for man's civilized living together. Poetry which has less need for external means since it is directly produced by the spirit, since the voice is its material, emerges boldly and in a cultured (*gebildet*) form when a people has not as yet achieved a legally organized life. This is so because, as previously remarked, language by itself and apart from civilization reaches a high stage of intellectual development (*Verstandesbildung*).

Philosophy, too, must appear in the life of a state, since philosophy is merely the consciousness of a particular form of thought . . . the thought about thought. Hence the characteristic material for the system of philosophy has been prepared

---

* The term *bildende Kuenste* for fine arts literally calls for a synonym which does not exist in English. It is evident that the German term, meaning to suggest that these arts are arts which handle and shape some material (architecture, sculpture, painting), allows for a word play according to which these arts would also be "educating" "civilizing" arts.—Ed.

by the general culture (*Bildung*). In the development of the state there occur, however, periods when either the spirit of nobler men is driven to flee from the present into the regions of the ideal in order to find reconciliation with themselves which they can no longer find in a reality filled with conflict (*entzweit*). Or after the analytic intellect has attacked all that is sacred and profound and that was embedded naïvely in the religion, the laws and customs of a people, and has transformed these (*credenda* and *miranda*) into shallow and superficial, abstract and godless generalities, then thought is driven to thinking reason and must seek to restore in its own field what has been corrupted.

There exist therefore in all world historical peoples poetry, fine arts, science and philosophy. But not only are tone, style and general direction different, but even more the meaning (*Gehalt*). This meaning concerns the most important difference, that of the degree of reason. It will not do that a pretentious aesthetic criticism demands that stuff, the substance of the content (of works of poetry and art) ought not to determine our judgment, that it insists that the beautiful form as such, the range of imagination and such like are the purpose of art and alone should be given attention and enjoyed by a liberal mind and a cultured spirit. If the meaning (of the work of art) is itself insignificant or wild and fantastic or meaningless, the common sense of mankind refuses to abstract from this (lack of meaning) and to enjoy such works. If one thus wishes to equate the Indic epic poetry with the Homeric on account of a number of formal qualities, such as range of invention and imagination, vividness of the symbols and sentiments, beauty of the diction and so forth, the difference in meaning remains. Hence the substantial interest of reason remains infinitely different, since that interest is concerned with the consciousness of freedom and the development of this conception in the individuals. There exists not only a classical form but also a classical content. Furthermore, form and content are so closely linked in a work of art that one can be classical only if the other is too. For a fantastic, limitless content the form too becomes limitless and misshapen or mean and pedantic, for that is reasonable which has moderation and a (defined) purpose.

Likewise Chinese, Indic, Eleatic, Pythagorean, Spinozistic, indeed all modern metaphysics may be treated as parallels since all start from the One, or from unity, the very abstract and general. But such a comparison or equation is very superficial. For in doing this, one overlooks that which alone matters here, namely, what such unity is determined to be. It makes a vital difference whether that unity is conceived of as abstract or as concrete—concrete to the point where it is unity in itself, i.e., Spirit. Such equating (of these philosophies) proves therefore that he (who undertakes it) knows only of abstract unity, and in judging thus of philosophy, he is ignorant of what constitutes the interest of philosophy.

[Hegel then stresses once again the importance of freedom in his developmental view, and proceeds to illustrate the point with reference to the Chinese and Indians. See also below, pp. 43 ff. For the distinctive aspects of morals see below, pp. 252 ff.]

Chinese morality has earned the highest praise since the Europeans have become acquainted with it and with the writings of Confucius; its high quality has been readily recognized by those who are acquainted with Christian morality. Similarly the grandeur of Indian religion and poetry, as well as Indian philosophy have been acknowledged especially in their rejection and sacrifice of the senses. Both these nations lack, however, and one must say completely, the essential consciousness of the conception of freedom. For the Chinese, their moral rules are like laws of nature, extraneous positive rules, obligatory rights and duties and rules of etiquette toward each other. Freedom, through which alone the substantive regulations of reason become an ethical conviction, is lacking; morals are a matter for the state and are attended to by officials and courts. Their works, when not law codes of the state but directed toward the subjective will and conviction (*Gesinnung*), read like a list of commandments which are needed for happiness, thus resembling the writings of the Stoics. Opposed to them appears to be arbitrariness which may decide to obey such commandments or not. Accordingly, the idea of an abstract subject, the wise man, stands at the head of such doctrines, both in the Chinese and the Stoic moralists. Likewise in the Indic doctrine of abandoning sensuousness, lusts and earthly interests the goal and end is not an affirmative, ethical freedom, but nothingness as far as consciousness is concerned and spiritual as well as even physical extinction.

Of the different kinds of History Writing*

[There are three ways of looking at history: the original, the reflective and the philosophical one.

As far as the first is concerned, I think some names may give an impression, e.g., Herodotus, Thucydides and others like them. They lived in the climate of the events which they described, were part of it. They transformed by the spirit, into the realm of imagination the happenings, the deeds, the occurrences and situations which they had in front of themselves. They bring it about that that which has passed, which is living in memory, achieves everlasting duration. They bind together what rushed by fleetingly and deposit it in the temple of Memory (*Mnemosyne*), for all eternity. To be sure, these writers of immediate history used reports and tales of others, for it is not possible for one man to see everything himself, but this is nothing different than the use the poet makes of the developed language to which he also owes so much. The poet too works out his material for the imagination. The main work is his; it is his creation. It is the same with the writers of history. (After some further remarks about poetry which repeat previous observations, Hegel continues:) Here we are con-

* The discussion of this topic, usually constituting the first part of the so-called "special introduction" and based on the lecture notes—see, e.g., Lasson's ed. as cited, pp. 167-177—is here offered in the form in which Lasson published it on the basis of a manuscript written by Hegel himself and included as an appendix in the Lasson edition as cited, pp. 248-259. However, since the MS obviously lacks the first page or two, we are giving the beginning of the discussion in the form in which it is found in the lecture notes, as noted above, pp. 167-9 (abbreviated), but enclose it in brackets.

cerned with peoples which were fully developed and who had a consciousness of what they were and what they wanted. The real history of a people begins with its developing this consciousness . . .

The histories (of these original historians) cannot be very long; note Herodotus, Thucydides, Guicciardini; what is present and vivid in their environment constitutes their essential material. . . . The writer describes what he has himself participated in, lived with. The periods are short, (comprising) individual configurations of men and events. He gathers the individual, unreflected aspects into a portrait in order to transmit this picture to posterity as sharply defined as he had it in front of himself, looking at it or hearing about it. His culture and that of the events which he describes, the spirit of the writer and the spirit of the actions which he tells are one and the same. . . .

(Hegel then repeats what he said above concerning the historian who is also an actor upon the scene, a statesman or soldier, above pp. 35, and then queries whether the speeches Thucydides composed speak against this interpretation.)

But we must remember that the actions themselves are transformed into speech in order to affect the imagination.]

Speeches are actions of men, indeed very essential and effective actions. Often it is said, they are *only* speeches. But speeches in a nation, as action between nations or princes, are an essential topic of history, especially of the more ancient history. . . .

Thus a writer's own reflections do not explain and describe the consciousness of a people or of a nation. He has to let persons and nations say themselves what they want. . . . The motives and feelings he need not explain on his own account nor does he need to make them conscious within himself. He does not impute to them alien speeches made by himself. Even if he elaborates them, their content, that is to say, this culture and this consciousness are the consciousness of those whom he makes deliver these speeches. Thus we read in Thucydides the speeches of Pericles, the most educated, most genuine and most noble statesman as well as those of other orators, ambassadors, etc. In these speeches those human beings pronounced the maxims of their people, of their own personality, (they set forth) the knowledge of their political situation and moral and spiritual condition, their nature, the principles of their objectives and actions. The historian has little or nothing left for his own reflection and whatever he lets those (whom he describes) say is not an alien and imputed consciousness but their own. If one wants to study the substance of history, the spirit of nations, if one wants to live in and with them one must study historians of this kind and linger over them. Indeed one cannot study them long enough for in them one has the history of a people or a government vividly, freshly and at first hand. Whoever wishes to enjoy history rather than become a learned historian can largely study these writers.

From these historians must be distinguished the bibles of the nations. Every people has such a basic book, a bible or a Homer.

This kind of historian is not as frequent as one might think. In order that there appear such historians it is not only necessary that the culture of a people have reached a high stage but also that it be not isolated in a priesthood or among scholars but that it have molded political and military leaders. There have been enough naïve chroniclers like the monks of the Middle Ages but they were not at the same time statesmen who stood in the center of historical and political events though there were a few learned bishops. Statesmen then had not developed a political consciousness.

Such a historian is Herodotus, the father that is to say of the writers of history and the originator of history; then there is Thucydides; Xenephon's *Retreat of the 10,000* is a similarly original work; Caesar's *Commentaries* are the master work, a simple direct work of a great spirit.

But these writers are not peculiar to the ancients. In more modern times the situation has not much altered. Our culture records and transforms immediately all events into reports; we have in more recent times received admirably simple, definitive and yet brilliant reports about events, about war and peace. These reports can be appreciated alongside the commentaries of Caesar because of the wealth of their content; in the definiteness with which they describe measures and conditions they are even more instructive. Many French memoirs should be included here. . . . While quite a few deal with small matters and anecdotes, they are as often written by brilliant minds and concern a larger and more interesting subject. Such a chef d'oeuvre are the memoirs of Cardinal Retz. In Germany such writings of masters who have themselves been part of the events are rare. A noteworthy exception is the *Histoire de Mon Temps de Frédéric II*. It is not sufficient to have been a contemporary of such events nor to have been nearby in the position to receive good information about it. The writer must himself have the status and be in the circle of the actors; he must share their views and thoughts and their education. If one thus stands on top of the events one can see everything in place. That is not the case when one looks at events through some kind of moralizing goggles or judges them by one's own wisdom. In our times it is the more necessary to listen to those who by right govern and have the power to do so and to stay clear of the limited view of the estates (parliamentarians) which are excluded from the immediate political participation and which therefore cheer themselves with moral principles and thereby try to transcend the higher orders, in short who are not within the immediate circle of political observation and life.

The second kind of history writing we may call the reflective kind of history, history which goes beyond what is present to the writer. Here matters are not present in time but present in the spirit. Such history has to do with that which is explicitly and completely past. There are a number of different kinds of this history.

Original history always comprises a short period. The desire for surveying a larger whole produces reflective history. Many of the writers who are generally called historians belong in this category. Digesting the historical matter becomes the main task, which the worker approaches with his own spirit which is different from the spirit of the matter he deals with. Hence the maxims, the ideas, the principles, become important which the historian adopts regarding the nature and the purpose of the actions and events as well as concerning historical method. Among us Germans this kind of reflection and cleverness is very varied. Each historian has his own method and way, insisting upon his particular approach. The English and French generally know how one should write history; they remain within the ideas of a common culture. With us everybody thinks up something special. The English and French therefore have admirable historians. But in Germany, as one looks over the critical reviews of the last ten or twenty years one finds that practically every review begins with a new theory about the way history should be written, a theory which is opposite to the book reviewed. We are, in short, constantly striving to determine how history should be written.

There is a need for having surveys of the entire history of a people, of a country and of the whole world and it is necessary to write history like that. Such history books are put together out of original historians as well as out of separate reports, informations and the like. This kind of reflective history is similar to the preceding as it has no other purpose than to describe the entire history of a country or of the world. . . . The writers of such history like to present their story vividly so that the reader has the impression of listening to contemporaries, an eye-witness to the events, but the effort usually fails. The whole work usually has a particular flavor; there is an individual with a particular education who is the author but the times which such a work traverses are of very different education and culture, as are the original writers whom the author can use. Hence the spirit which animates such a history is different from the spirit of the times it deals with. The historian wants to describe the spirit of the times but it usually is the spirit of the gentleman himself.*

Thus Livius lets the ancient kings of Rome, the consuls and army leaders of old times make speeches of a kind which only

---

* This is an obvious reference to Goethe's well-known lines in *Faust*.—Ed.

a clever lawyer of the time of Livius could make. They contrast most sharply with such genuine speeches as the fable
Menenius Agrippa tells of the stomach and the intestines.
Similarly, Livius gives details and elaborate descriptions of the
battle and other events with a succinctness and attention to
detail which could not have been attempted in the period when
these events occurred. He writes as if he had actually witnessed
these events . . . their definiteness usually contrasts with the
lack of cohesion and sequence which mars Livius' description
of the march of main events. One can see most readily the
difference between such a compiler and an original historian
if one compares Polybius himself with the way in which Livius
uses, selects from and abbreviates the history of the period for
which we have the work of Polybius . . . How could it be
possible, even if one wanted to, to enter completely into the life
of Greece which in so many and most important respects
appeals to us but, in the most important, is neither sympathetic
nor natural to us? We may have the greatest interest in Athens
and the actions which occurred there. It was the fatherland
indeed, the most noble fatherland of a highly cultivated people.
Yet we cannot sympathize with the Athenians when they
prostrate themselves before Zeus and Minerva, trouble themselves with sacrifice on the day of battle and engage in
slavery . . .

Any such history as seeks to cover long periods of the entire
history of the world must give up the individualizing description of what actually happened and must take refuge in abstractions. Such history must epitomize, must abbreviate. This
means not only that many events and actions are left out but
also that thought or intellect is the most potent epitomizer.
For example, a battle has been fought and a great victory won;
a city has been besieged in vain; battle, victory, siege—all these
are general ideas which contrast and extend and individualize
a whole into a simple idea. If we recount that at the beginning
of the Peloponnesian war Plataea was for a long time besieged
by the Spartans, that after a part of the inhabitants had fled
the city was taken and the remaining citizens executed—such
a tale briefly states what Thucydides describes with so much

interesting detail. It would be the same if we said that an expedition of the Athenians to Sicily had turned out badly, but for a survey this (sort of observation) is necessary. What matters is that not only is the content quantitatively reduced but by reflection it is reduced to general ideas. Of course such a tale becomes drier. Who cares about it when Livius tells a hundred times of a hundred wars: this year the Romans successfully made war upon the Volsci or the Fidenates. This way of writing history is dull. The form of abstract ideas renders it dry. Writers try to cope with this by helping the mind through clearly relating the individual traits. They collect such traits from everywhere. A variegated mass of detail, of picayune interests, of intrigues and military deeds, private matters which do not have any influence for political interest, thus displaying an inability to produce a whole, like a novel by Walter Scott . . . It would be much better to leave this sort of thing to Walter Scott, who knows how to depict in detail the deeds and fortunes of a single individual, for this does not provide a portrait of high interests of state. The particular traits ought to be characteristic, indicative of the spirit of the time . . .

A second kind of reflective history is the pragmatic one. There is really no sense in this term, for pragmatic history is what the writer of history generally intends: a well informed and clear presentation of the march of history and its life—a totality which we no longer have in front of us, a reflected world, a past world. Such history writing springs from the needs of the present and the mind is aware of this present. In short, there is a need for understanding history. The whole congeries of interests such as the whole of a state, epoch-making events is the subject matter here. Here, too, the interest is a present one in its very individual quality, but the historian has resigned himself (to his inability of reproducing) the sense of immediacy in expressing the sense of tangible vividness of the circumstances and fortunes of the several private individuals. What he is concerned with is the meaning of the events, their purpose, the state, the fatherland and their inner cohesion. It is the general relations, which are lasting and valid now as formerly and always, with which the activity of the mind is concerned. Such pragmatic reflections even though they be very abstract indicate in fact the present interest which is to give life to the tale of the past and relate it to present living. But whether such reflections are in fact interesting and enlivening depends upon the mind of the writer. The worst manner of pragmatic history writing is the mean, psychologizing approach which traces the speculations, inclinations and passions as the motivations of men and therefore does not see their task as the driving force. This is the moralizing kind of history writing . . . which attacks events and persons from time to time with a moral judgment, with pious Christian reflections and intersperses the tale with all kinds of observations, exclamations or doctrines. . . .

THE PHILOSOPHY OF HISTORY

[*main part*]

THE ORIENTAL WORLD

We have to begin with the Oriental World, but not before the period in which we discover states in it. The diffusion of language and the formation of races lie beyond the limits of history. History is prose, and myths fall short of history. The consciousness of external definite existence only arises in connection with the power to form abstract distinctions and assign abstract predicates. The ability to comprehend objects in an unpoetical form manifests itself in proportion as a capacity for the expression of law is acquired. The prehistorical is that which precedes political life; it also lies beyond self-cognizant life. Surmises and suppositions may be entertained respecting the prehistorical period, but these do not amount to facts. The inherent and distinctive principle of the Oriental World is the substantiveness of ethics and morality. We have the first example of a subjugation of the mere arbitrary will, which is submerged in this substantiveness. Moral distinctions and requirements are expressed as laws, but so that the subjective will is governed by these laws as by an external force. Nothing subjective is recognized, in the form of conviction, conscience or formal freedom. Justice is administered only on the basis of external morality, and government exists only as the prerogative of compulsion. Our own civil law contains, it is true, some purely compulsory ordinances. I can be compelled to give up another man's property, or to keep an agreement which I have made; but we do not posit the moral in the mere compulsion of the subjects, but rather in their disposition, their sympathy with the requirements of the law. Morality is the subject of

positive legislation in the East; but although their moral pre-
scriptions (the substance of their ethics) may be perfect, what
should be internal subjective sentiment is made a matter of
external arrangement. There is no want of a will to command
moral actions, but there is lacking the kind of will to perform them which would result from their being commanded
from within. Since the spirit has not yet turned inward, it
appears as natural spirituality. The external and internal, law
and moral sense, are not yet distinguished and still form an
undivided unity; the same is true of religion and the state.
The constitution is generally a theocracy, and the Kingdom of
God is a secular kingdom in the same way that a secular
kingdom is also divine. What we call God has not been realized
in consciousness in the East, for our idea of God involves the
lifting of the soul to the supernatural. We obey because what
we are required to do is confirmed by an internal sanction,
while in the East the law is regarded as inherently valid without requiring a subjective confirmation. In such law men do
not recognize their own will, but one which is entirely foreign
to them.

Of the several parts of Asia, we have already eliminated
Upper Asia and Siberia as unhistorical. The rest of the Asiatic
World is divided into four areas: first, the river-plains, formed
by the Yellow and the Blue Rivers and the uplands of Far East
Asia—China and the Mongols. Secondly, the valley of the
Ganges and that of the Indus. The third theater of history is
formed by the river-plains of the Oxus and Jaxartes, the uplands of Persia, and the other valley-plains of the Tigris and
the Euphrates, to which the Near East is attached. The river-
plain of the Nile is the fourth area of the Oriental World.

History begins with China and the Mongols, the realm of
theocratic rule. Both rest upon the patriarchal principle; this
is so modified in China as to admit the development of an
organized system of secular polity, while among the Mongols
it limits itself to the simple form of a spiritual religious realm

(*Reich*). The monarch is chief as patriarch in China. The laws of the state are partly legal, partly moral; so that the internal law is the subject of an external legal command. By the internal law I mean an individual's knowledge of the content of his will, his own inwardness. The sphere of inwardness does not, then, attain maturity here, since moral laws are treated as legislative enactments, and laws on their part are given an ethical aspect. All that we call subjectivity (subjective responsibility) is concentrated in the supreme head of the state, who in all his legislation has an eye to the health, wealth and benefit of the whole. This secular empire is confronted by the spiritual realm of the Mongols at the head of which stands the Lama, who is honored as God. No secular political life can be developed in this spiritual empire.

The second configuration (*Gestalt*) is the Indian realm. Here we observe the dissolution of the unity of political organization, of a perfect civil machinery such as exists in China. The particular forces of society appear as unfettered and free in relation to each other. To be sure, the different castes are fixed; but, in view of the religious doctrine that established them, they appear like natural distinctions. Individuals are thereby still more devoid of self, although it might seem as if they would gain (in self-identity) from the development of the social distinctions in question. For since we find the organization of the state no longer, as in China, determined and arranged by the one substantial subject, the distinctions that exist are attributed to nature, and so become differences of caste. The unity in which these divisions must finally meet is a religious one; and thus arises theocratic aristocracy and its despotism. Here begins, therefore, the distinction between spiritual consciousness and worldly conditions; but as the unfettering of the distinct forces is the main point, so we also find in the religion of the Indians the principle of the isolation of the constituent elements of the Idea. The principle of the Indians posits the harshest antithesis: the conception of the purely abstract unity of God, and of the general sensual powers of nature. The only connection between the two is one of constant change, a restless rushing from one extreme to the other, a wild ecstasy without consequence, which must appear as madness to a disciplined, intelligent consciousness.

The third important configuration is the Persian realm, which steps upon the scene in contrast to the immovable unity of China and the wild and turbulent unrest of India. China is quite peculiarly oriental; we might put India into parallel with Greece, and Persia with Rome. For in Persia the theocracy appears as monarchy. Now monarchy is the kind of constitution which does indeed unite the members of the body politic in the head of the government as in a point; but it regards that head neither as the general determinator nor as the arbitrary ruler, but as a power whose will is a kind of legality which it shares with the subjects. We thus have a general principle, a law, which is at the basis of the whole, but which, since it is natural, is affected by a contradiction. Therefore the image which the spirit has of itself is at this stage of progress a purely natural one, namely light. This universal principle is as much a regulative one for the monarch as for each of his subjects, and the Persian spirit is accordingly a clear, luminous spirit which lives in the idea of a people in pure morality, as in a sacred community. But on the one hand this community contains the contradiction unresolved since it is a natural one. Its sanctity is determined in its norms (from the outside). On the other hand this contradiction is manifest in Persia as a rule over hostile peoples and the union of the most widely differing nations. The Persian unity is not the abstract one of the Chinese Empire; it is meant to rule over many and various nationalities, which it unites under the mild force of its universality just like a beneficial sun shining over all, awakening and warming them. This universality is like a root; it allows the particular to grow freely and to expand and ramify as it wishes. The various principles and forms of life have full play and continue to exist together in the organization of these several peoples. We find roving nomads among this multitude of nations; in Babylonia and Syria we see commerce and industrial pursuits in full vigor, the wildest sensuality and uncontrolled turbulence. The coasts make possible a relation with foreign lands. In the midst of this confusion we encounter the spiritual God of the Jews who, like Brahma, exists only in thought, and yet is jealous and excludes from his being all particular distinctions, such as is freely allowed in other religions. The Persian Empire, then, since it can tolerate these several principles, exhibits the contradiction in a lively, active form. It is not, like China and India, abstract and calm, and stable within itself. It therefore provides a real transition in the history of the world.

If Persia forms the external transition to Greek life, the internal transition is mediated by Egypt. Here the contradictions in their abstract form are made to interact; this interaction brings about their resolution. This seeming reconciliation presents a struggle of the most contradictory principles, which are not yet capable of harmonizing themselves, but which, positing the birth of this harmony as a task, make themselves a riddle for themselves and for others. The solution of it is the Greek world.

If we compare these various kingdoms in the light of their various fates, we find the empire of the two Chinese rivers the only durable realm in the world. Conquests cannot affect such an empire. The world of the Ganges and the Indus has also been preserved; such thoughtlessness is also not transitory, but it is destined to be disturbed, conquered, and subjugated. While these two realms have remained till the present day, nothing remains of the empire of the Ganges and the Euphrates except, at most, a heap of bricks; for the Persian realm, as the exposed realm of transition, is by nature transitory, and the kingdoms of the Caspian Sea are exposed to the ancient struggle of Iran and Turan. The empire of the one

Nile is only present beneath the ground, in its silent dead—
now being dragged away to the four corners of the earth—and
in their majestic habitations; for what remains above the
ground is nothing but such splendid tombs.

[Here follows a more detailed elaboration of the general principles
set out above; Hegel deals with each civilization in turn, but the
progress of critical scholarship has what he has to say so far
removed from historical reality that we decided to omit most of
these sections; only a brief general statement on Persia and the
section on Judaea are included as showing against what background
Hegel saw the Greeks.]

PERSIA

With the Persian Empire we first enter into the continuity
of history. The Persians are the first historical people; Persia
was the first empire that passed away. While China and India
remain stationary and perpetuate a natural vegetative existence
even to the present time, Persia has been subject to those
developments and revolutions which alone suggest a state of
history. . . . The light which shines and illumines what sur-
rounds it, first rises in Persia. For Zoroaster's light belongs to
the world of consciousness, to spirit as a relation to something
distinct from itself. In the Persian world we see a pure exalted
unity as the substance which leaves free the special existences
with substance in it. This unity is free as the light . . . it
governs individuals only to excite them to become strong in
themselves, to develop and assert their individuality. Light
makes no distinctions. The sun shines on the righteous and the
unrighteous, on high and low, and confers on all the same
benefit and prosperity. Light is vitalizing only in so far as it is
brought to bear on something distinct from itself, operating on
it and developing it. It poses the contradiction to darkness,
and thus opens up the principle of activity and life. The prin-

ciple of development begins with the history of Persia. It therefore constitutes strictly the beginning of world history. The general interest of the spirit in history is to attain an unlimited immanence of subjectivity, to attain a reconciliation by an absolute contradiction.

Thus the transition which we have to make is only in the sphere of the idea and not in an external historical connection. The principle of this transition is that the general, which we recognized in Brahma, now becomes conscious, becomes an object and acquires an affirmative significance for man. Brahma is not worshipped by the Hindus. He is nothing more than a state of mind of the individual, a religious feeling, a nonobjective existence, a relation which annihilates concrete aliveness. But this general [being] acquires an affirmative nature in becoming an object. Man becomes free and confronts the highest being, which is now objective for him. We see this generality emerging in Persia, involving a distinction of man from the general [being], at the same time the individual identifies himself with the general [being]. This distinction was not made in the Chinese and Indian principle.

[After repeating what was said above, pp. 44–46, Hegel continues:]

Unity first elevates itself, and distinguishes itself from the merely natural in the Persian principle. It is the negation of that unreflecting relation which allowed no exercise of mind to intervene between the mandate and its adoption by the will. This unity is in the Persian principle represented as light— not simply light as such, the most general physical element, but light as the purity of spirit, the good. The particular, the involvement in limited nature is thus abolished. Light therefore, in a spiritual and physical sense, means elevation, freedom from the merely natural. Man acquires a relation to light, to the abstract good, as to something objective which is voluntarily acknowledged, revered, and put to work.

JUDAEA

The other (besides the Syrian) people living on the coast of the Mediterranean Sea and belonging to the Persian Empire is the Jewish. Here we also find a basic book, the *Old Testament,* in which the views of these people are exhibited. . . . We find that the spiritual is entirely purified in the case of the Jews. The pure product of thought, which is conceiving of oneself in thought, becomes conscious, and the spiritual develops itself with radical definitions against nature or any union with nature. It is true that we observed the pure Brahma at an earlier stage, but only as the general natural being, and with the limitation that Brahma does not himself become an object of consciousness. We saw this abstraction become an object of the consciousness among the Persians, but it was looked at as something sensuous, as light. But light now becomes Jehovah, the pure One. This conception forms the break between the East and the West; spirit descends into itself and recognizes the spiritual as the abstract fundamental principle. Nature, which is the primary and fundamental thing in the East, is now reduced to the condition of a mere creature, and spirit now occupies the first place. God is known as the creator of all men, as he is of all nature; he is known as absolute activity generally. But this great principle of the Jews, as further determined, is an exclusive unity. This Jewish religion must necessarily possess the element of exclusiveness, which consists essentially in the belief that only the One People which adopts it recognizes the One God and is acknowledged by him. The God of the Jewish people is the God only of Abraham and of his seed: national individuality and a special local worship are involved in such a conception of deity. All other gods are false before the One God; moreover, the distinction between the true and the false is quite abstract, for, as regards the false gods, not a ray of the divine is supposed to shine upon them. But every spiritual activity and, the more so, every religion is of such a nature that, whatever be its peculiar character, an affirmative element is necessarily contained in it. However erroneous a religion may be, it possesses some truth, although in a mutilated way. There is a divine presence and a divine relevance in every religion, and a philosophy of history has to discover a spiritual element even in the most imperfect forms. But it does not follow that because it is a religion, it is therefore good. We must not fall into the lax conception that the content is of no importance, but only the form. The Jewish religion does not admit such slack tolerance, being absolutely exclusive.

The spiritual here directly renounces the sensuous, and nature is reduced to something merely external and divine. This is actually true of nature at this stage; for only later can the idea be reconciled with this its externality. The first utterance of the idea will be in opposition to nature; for the spirit, which had been humiliated until then, only now attains its true dignity, while nature resumes its proper position. Nature is external to itself, it is something posited, created; and this idea, that God is the Lord and creator of nature, leads men to regard God as the exalted One, while the whole of nature is only his robe of glory, to be employed in his service. Compared to this exalted being, the Indian idea is only that of an unrestrained nature. The sensuous and immoral are no longer sanctioned by spiritual value, but disparaged as the divine. Only the One, the spirit, the non-sensuous, is the truth; thought exists free for itself, and true morality and righteousness can now appear; for God is honored by righteousness, and right-doing is "walking in the way of the Lord." Happiness, life and temporal prosperity are conjoined with this as its reward, for it is said: "that thou mayest live long in the land." Here (within such a view) we have also the possibility of a historical perspective; for here the prosaic intellect can put the limited and circumscribed in its proper place, and comprehend it as the proper form for finite existence. Men are regarded as individuals, not as incarnations of God; sun is seen as sun, mountains as mountains, not as possessing spirit and will.

We observe among this people a severe religious ceremonial, expressing a relation to pure thought. The concrete individual does not become free, because the absolute itself is not comprehended as concrete spirit; since spirit still appears posited as non-spiritual. True, the inwardness is manifest—the pure heart, repentance, devotion; but the particular concrete subject has not yet become objective for itself in the absolute. The subject therefore remains closely bound to the observance of ceremonies and the law, the basis of which latter is pure freedom in its abstract form. The Jews possess that which makes them what they are through the One: consequently the subject has no freedom for himself. Spinoza regards the code of Moses as having been given the Jews for punishment, a rod of correction. The subject, or individual, person, never achieves the consciousness of independence; on that account we do not find among the Jews any belief in the immortality of the soul; for individuality does not exist in and for itself. But in Judaism the family is autonomous, although the individual subject is valueless; for the worship of Jehovah is attached to the family, which is thus the substantial being. But the state is not appropriate to the Judaic principle, and it is alien to the legislation of Moses. Jewish history on the whole exhibits remarkable features, but it is disfigured by sanctifying the exclusion of the spirits of other nations (liquidation of the inhabitants of Canaan being even commanded), by a want of culture generally, and by the superstition arising from the idea of the high value of their peculiar nationality. Miracles also disturb us in this history, when seen as history; for as far as the concrete consciousness is not free, concrete insight is also not free. Nature is undeified by the Jews, but it is not yet understood.

The family became a great nation, through the conquest of

Canaan; it took possession of a whole country and erected a public temple in Jerusalem. But the bond of statehood, properly speaking, did not exist. Heroes arose in cases of danger and placed themselves at the head of armed hosts. Yet the nation was for the most part subjugated. Kings were chosen later on, and it was they who first rendered the Jews independent. David even made conquests. Originally the legislation was adapted to a family only, yet the need for a king is already foreseen in the books of Moses. The priests are to choose this king, he is not to be a foreigner, not to have horsemen in large numbers, and he is to have few wives. This kingdom fell apart after a short period of glory and was divided. Since there was only one tribe of Levites and only one temple in Jerusalem, idolatry resulted from this division. The One God could not be honored in different temples, and there could not be two kingdoms attached to one religion. The honor rendered to God, the subjective side of religion, was still very limited and unspiritual in character, however spiritual the objective conception of Him may have been.

THE GREEK WORLD

The Forms of Beautiful Individuality

Man, due to his needs, maintains a practical relation to external nature; in making nature satisfy his desires, he has recourse to a system of means. For natural objects offer resistance in various ways. In order to subdue them, man employs other natural agents; he thus turns nature against itself, and invents instruments for this purpose. These human inventions belong to the world of the spirit; such an instrument is therefore to be respected more than a mere natural object. The Greeks were accustomed to set an especial value upon them; for man's delight in these inventions appears in a very striking way in Homer. The making of Agamemnon's scepter is given in detail, and mention is made of doors that turn on hinges and of accouterments and furniture in a way that expresses delight. The honor of human inventions subjugating nature is ascribed to the gods.

But on the other hand, man uses nature for ornament, which is intended only as a token of wealth and of that which man has made for himself. We find ornament already very much developed among the Homeric Greeks. It is true that both barbarians and civilized nations adorn themselves: but barbarians content themselves with mere ornament, they want their persons to be pleasing because of an external addition. But ornament by its very nature is destined to beautify something other than itself, the human body. It is the human body in which the human being finds himself and which, in common with nature at large, he has to transform. The spiritual interest of primary importance is, therefore, the development of the body to a perfect organ for the will. This adaptation may on the one hand be the means for ulterior objects, and, on the other hand, appear as an object in itself. Thus among the Greeks we find this boundless impulse of individuals to display themselves, and to find enjoyment in doing so. The Greeks are too strongly stirred, too much bent upon developing their individuality, to venerate nature simply as it is, in its power and goodness. That peaceful condition which followed upon the giving up of a predatory life, when generous nature afforded security and leisure, turned their energies in the direction of self-reliance, the effort to dignify themselves. But while on the one hand they have too much personal independence to be dominated by superstition, this did not go to the length of making them vain. . . . The exhilarating sense of personality, in contrast with sensuous subjection to nature, and the need not of mere pleasure, but of the display of individual powers, in order to gain special distinctions and consequent enjoyment, constitute therefore the chief characteristic and principal occupation of the Greeks. Free as the bird singing in the sky, the individual only expresses what lies in his untrammeled human nature, in order to have his importance recognized. This is the subjective beginning of Greek art, in which the human being elaborates into a work of art his physical freedom, his beautiful movement and agile vigor. The Greeks began by training their own bodies to be beautiful before they attempted the expression of such in marble and paintings. The innocuous contest in games, in which everyone exhibits his powers, is of very ancient date. Homer gives a noble description of the games conducted by Achilles in honor of Patroclus. . . . These games and aesthetic displays, with the pleasures and honors that accompanied them, were only private at the outset, occasioned by particular events; but in the sequel they became an affair of the nation, and were fixed for certain times at appointed places. . . . If we look at the inner nature of these sports, we observe first how sport itself is opposed to serious business, to dependence and need. This wrestling, running, contending was no serious affair; it *bespoke no obligation* of defense, no necessity of combat. Serious occupation is labor that has reference to some need. Man or nature must succumb; if the one is to live, the other must fall. In contrast with this kind of seriousness, sport presents the higher seriousness; for in it nature is wrought into spirit. In this exercise of physical powers, man shows his freedom, he shows that he has transformed his body into an organ of spirit, even though in these contests he has not advanced to the highest grade of serious thought.

Man has also his voice, which admits and requires a more extensive purport than the mere sensuous present. We have seen how song is united with dance and ministers to it, but subsequently song makes itself independent and calls for musical instruments to accompany it; it then ceases to be unmeaningful, like the modulations of a bird, which may indeed express emotion, but have no objective significance. Song requires meaning created by imagination and spirit, which is then further formed into an objective work of art.

The Objective Work of Art

If it is asked what is the subject of song as thus developed among the Greeks, we should answer that its essential and absolute meaning is religious. We have examined the idea embodied in the Greek spirit; Greek religion is nothing else than this idea made objective as the essence of being. According to this idea, the godly and divine contains within itself the powers of nature, but only as an element undergoing a process of transformation into spiritual power. Nothing remains of the origins of this natural element but the analogies involved in the representations which the Greeks formed of spiritual power; for the Greeks worshipped God as spiritual. We cannot, therefore, regard the Greek gods as similar to the Indian, as some power of nature for which the human shape supplies only the outward form. The essence of the Greek gods is the spiritual itself, and the natural is only the point of departure. But on the other hand it must be observed that the divine beings of the Greeks are not yet the absolute free spirit, but spirit in a particular mode, fettered by the limitations of humanity, still dependent as a determinate individuality on external conditions. The gods of the Greeks are objectively beautiful individualities. The divine spirit is here so conditioned as to be not yet regarded as abstract spirit, but as a specialized existence. It continued to manifest itself in sense, but so that the sensuous is not its substance, but only an aspect of its manifestation. This must be our leading idea in the consideration of Greek mythology. . . .

In the idea of the Greek spirit, then, we find the two elements, nature and spirit, in such a relation to each other that nature forms merely the point of departure. This degradation of nature is the major turning point in Greek mythology, expressed as the war of the gods, the overthrow of the Titans therein represented, for the Titans are the merely physical and natural beings from whose grasp supremacy is wrested. It is true that they continued to be venerated, but not as governing powers, for they are relegated to the verge and limbus of the world. . . . The second point is that the new divinities retain natural elements, and consequently in themselves a determinate relation to the powers of nature. Zeus has his lightnings and clouds. . . . Should it be said that this change of the natural into the spiritual is due to our allegorizing, or that of the later Greeks, we would reply that this transformation of the natural into the spiritual is the Greek spirit itself. The epigrams of the Greeks exhibit such advances from the sensuous to the spiritual. This blending of the natural with the spiritual cannot be understood by abstract analytical thought.

It must be further observed that the Greek gods are to be regarded as individualities, not as abstractions, like knowledge, unity, time, heaven and necessity. Such abstractions do not form the substance of these divinities; they are not allegories, not abstract beings to which various attributes may be attached. . . . Nor are the divinities symbols, for a symbol is only a sign, a signification of something else. The Greek gods themselves express what they are. . . . Since the whole range of spiritual and moral qualities was appropriated by the gods, the unity above them all remained abstract; it was formless and meaningless fate, necessity, whose grievous character arises from the absence of the spiritual. The gods have by contrast a friendly relation to men, for men are themselves spiritual beings. The higher thought, embodied in the knowledge of unity as God, as the one spirit, lay beyond the level of thought attained by the Greeks. The question also arises, where the external origin of the special and adventitious aspects of the Greek gods is to be looked for. It arises partly from local characteristics, the scattered settlement of the Greeks at the commencement of their national life, fixed at certain points, and consequently introducing local ideas. The Greeks told very lively and most attractive stories of their gods, in endless variety, since rich new fancies were continually gushing forth in the living spirit of the Greeks. A second source from which special characteristics in their conception of the gods arose, is the worship of nature, of which images retain a place in the Greeks' myths, as certainly as they appear there in a regenerated and transfigured form. The preservation of the original myths opens up the famous chapter on the mysteries, already mentioned. These mysteries of the Greeks, because unknown, have attracted the curiosity ever since; it is often supposed that they contain profound wisdom. But it must first be remarked that their unique and primary character, in virtue of its very antiquity, shows them destitute of excellence and inferior. The more refined truths are not expressed in these mysteries, and the view many have entertained that the unity of God was taught in them, in opposition to polytheism, is incorrect. The mysteries were rather antique rituals, and it is as unhistorical as it is foolish to assume that profound philosophical truths are to be found there. On the contrary, only natural ideas, ruder conceptions of the metamorphoses occurring everywhere in nature and of the vital principle that pervades it, were the subjects of those mysteries. If we put together all the historical data available on the question, the result we shall inevitably arrive at will be that the mysteries did not constitute a system of doctrines, but were sensuous ceremonies and exhibitions consisting of symbols of the universal operation of nature, as, for example, the relation of the earth to celestial phenomena. The chief basis of the representations of Ceres and Proserpine, Bacchus and his train, was the universal principle of nature; and the accompanying details were obscure stories and representations, mainly bearing on the universal vital force and its metamorphoses.

Spirit has to undergo a process analogous to that of nature, for it must be twice-born, abnegate itself. Thus the representations given in the mysteries called attention, though only feebly, to the nature of spirit. In the Greeks they produced an emotion of shuddering awe; for an instinctive dread comes over men when they perceive the significance of a form, which as a sensuous phenomenon does not express that significance, and which therefore both repels and attracts, causes surmises by the meaning that reverberates through the whole, but at the same time awakes a disturbing dread at the repellent form. . . .

The Greeks received most of their gods from foreign lands, as Herodotus expressly states with regard to Egypt, but these exotic myths were transformed and spiritualized by the Greeks. Thus the brutes which continued to rank as gods among the Egyptians were degraded to external symbols, accompanying the spiritual god. The Greek gods, while they are represented as human, each have an individual character; this anthropomorphism has been described as a defect. Quite on the contrary, man as a spiritual being constitutes the element of truth in the Greek gods which rendered them superior to all other natural deities, and superior also to all mere abstractions of the one and highest essence. It may be posited as an advantage of the Greek gods that they are represented as men, as is supposed not to be the case with the Christian God. Schiller says:

> While the gods remained more human,
> The men were more divine.

But the Greek gods must not be regarded as being more human than the Christian God. Christ is much more a man: he lives, dies, suffers death on the Cross, which is infinitely more human than the humanity of the Greek idea of the beautiful. But in referring to this common element of the Greek and Christian religion, it must be said of both that if a manifestation of God is to be supposed at all, his natural form must be that of the spirit, which for sense conception is essentially human; for no other form can lay claim to spirituality. God appears indeed in the sun, in the mountains, in the trees, in everything that has life, but a natural manifestation of this kind is not the form proper to spirit.

But if the question were asked: does God necessarily mani-

fest himself? the question must be answered in the affirmative.
There is no essential existence which does not manifest itself.
The real defect of the Greek as compared with the Christian
religion is, therefore, that in the former the manifestation constitutes the highest mode in which the divine being is conceived to exist; it constitutes the sum and substance of divinity.
In the Christian religion, on the other hand, the manifestation
is regarded only as a temporary phase of the divine. Here the
manifested God dies and elevates himself to glory; only after
his death is Christ represented as sitting at the right hand of
God. The Greek god, on the contrary, exists for his worshippers
perennially in the manifestation, in marble, metal or wood,
or as shaped by the imagination. But why did God not appear
to the Greeks in the flesh? Because man only had worth, honor
and dignity in so far as he elaborated and developed himself in
response to the freedom of the beautiful manifestation in hand;
the form, the shaping of the divinity remained the product of
the particular individual. One aspect of the spirit is that it
produces itself, makes itself what it is. The other aspect is that
it is originally free, that freedom is its nature and its idea. But
the Greeks, since they had not attained an intellectual conception of themselves, did not yet realize spirit in its universality.
They did not have the idea of man and the essential unity of
the divine and human nature which accords with the Christian view. . . .

True reconciliation of the ideal-real and phenomenal was
not attained by the Greek spirit, since subjectivity was not
comprehended in all its depth; the human spirit did not yet
assert its true position. This defect showed itself in the fact
of fate as pure subjectivity appearing superior to the gods. It
also shows itself in the fact that men take their resolves from
oracles, and not yet out of themselves. Neither human nor
divine subjectivity, recognized as infinite, has absolute decisive
authority as yet.

The Political Work of Art

The state unites the two phases just considered, the subjective and the objective work of art. In the state, the spirit is not a mere divine object, nor is it merely subjectively developed to a beautiful physique. It is here a living, general spirit, which is at the same time the self-conscious spirit of the individuals composing the community.

Only the democratic constitution was suited to this spirit and this state. In the Orient, we saw despotism in magnificent development, as a form of government strictly appropriate to the Orient. The democratic form in Greece is no less well adapted to its place in world history. In Greece we find the freedom of the individual, but it has not yet advanced to such a degree of abstraction that the subjective unit is conscious of direct dependence on the substantial, the state as such. At the Greek level of freedom, the individual will is unfettered in the entire range of its vitality, and embodies the substantial being [the state] according to its particular nature. In Rome, on the other hand, we shall observe the harsh rule over the individual members of the state. Finally, in the Germanic realm, we shall observe monarchy, in which the individual is connected with and shares work not only with the monarch, but with the whole monarchical organization.

The democratic state is not patriarchal. It does not rest on an as yet uneducated confidence. It implies laws, with the consciousness of their being based on an equitable and moral basis; it also implies that these laws are known as positive. . . . The first lawgivers are known under the name of The Seven Sages. This title did not imply that they were sophists, that is, teachers of wisdom, proclaiming the right and the true. The Seven Sages were merely thoughtful men, whose thought had not advanced to the point of science proper. They were practical political men. . . . Thus Solon was commissioned by the Athenians to give them laws, since the existing ones were no longer adequate. Solon gave the Athenians a constitution by which all obtained equal rights, yet not so as to render the democracy a quite abstract one. The main aspect of a democracy is an ethical conviction of its citizens. Virtue is the basis of democracy, says Montesquieu; this sentiment is as important as it is true with reference to the notion of democracy commonly entertained. To the individual citizen in a democracy, the essential is the substance of justice, public affairs and the general interest; but they are thus essential only as ethical usage in the form of objective will. Morality proper, the inward conviction and intention, is not yet there. Law exists and is, in point of substance, the law of freedom. It is valid directly because it is law. In this ethics, laws exist like natural necessities, just as in beauty the natural aspect, its appeal to the senses, is present. The Greeks remain in the intermediate stage, that of beauty, because they have not yet attained the higher standpoint of truth. While ethical custom and wont is the form in which the right is willed and done, the form is a stable one. Such ethics does not yet involve reflection and subjectivity of will, which are the foes of genuineness. The interests of the community may, therefore, be intrusted to the will and decision of the citizens. This must be the basis of the Greek constitution; for no principle yet existed which could oppose such ethical usage when wished, and hinder its actually realizing itself. The democratic constitution is here the only possible one: the citizens are still unconscious of particular interests, and therefore of evil; the objective will is undivided in the Greeks. Athene the goddess is Athens itself, the actually real and concrete spirit of the citizens. The divinity only ceases to inspire them when the will has retreated within itself, into the inner sanctum of knowledge and conscience, and has posited the infinite separation of the subjective and the objective. This constitutes the true position of the democratic constitution; its justification and absolute necessity rests on this still imminent objective ethics. The same justification cannot be pleaded for the modern conceptions of democracy. These provide that the interests of the community, the public affairs, shall be discussed and decided by the people; that the individual members of the community shall deliberate, present their respective opinions, and give their votes, and this on the ground that the interests of the state and public affairs are the interests of these members. All this is quite true. But the essential condition and distinction lies in: who are these members? They have an absolute right only in as far as their will is still the *objective* will, and not one that wishes this or that, not mere *good* will. For the good will is something particular. It rests on the morality of individuals, on their conviction and inwardness.* That very subjective freedom which constitutes the principle and the peculiar form of freedom in our world and which forms the absolute basis of our political and religious life, could appear only as a disaster. Inwardness was akin to the Greek spirit, and it was to reach it soon, but it plunged the Greek world into ruin. . . . We may assert that the Greeks, living in the first and genuine form of their freedom, had no conscience. The habit of living for their fatherland without further reflection prevailed among them. They did not know the abstraction of a "state" which to our mind is the essential point. Their end was their living fatherland, this actual Athens, this Sparta, these temples, these altars, this form of social life, this group of fellow citizens, these mores and habits. To the Greek his fatherland was a necessity, without which he could not live. It was the sophists, the teachers of wisdom, who first introduced subjective reflection and the new doctrine that each man should act according to his own conviction. Once reflection comes into play, each man has his own opinion and inquires as to whether the principles of right and law cannot be improved. Instead of sticking to an

---

* This discussion is clearly inspired by Rousseau, whose ethics rest upon the proposition that "The only absolute good is a good will."—Ed.

existing state of things, inward conviction is discovered; and thus begins a subjective independent freedom in which the individual is capable of bringing everything to the test of his own conscience, even in contravention of the existing constitution. Each individual has his principles, and he regards as the best his own views, which ought therefore to be realized in practice. This decay is noted already by Thucydides, when he speaks of everyone's thinking that things are going badly when he is not present.

Confidence in great men is antagonistic to this state of things, in which everyone presumes to have a judgment of his own. It is evidently not supposed that the people think that they know best what is right when, in earlier times, the Athenians commission Solon to give them laws, or when Lycurgus appears at Sparta as lawgiver and regulator of the state. At a later time, too, the people placed their confidence in great plastic personages: Cleisthenes, Miltiades, Themistocles, and Pericles, the great pinnacle of Athens. But envy appeared as soon as any of these men had performed what was needed; the sentiment of equality asserted itself against conspicuous talent, and the man was either imprisoned or exiled. Finally the sycophants arose among the people, who reviled all individual greatness, and all those who took a lead in public affairs.

But there are three other points in regard to the Greek republics that must be particularly emphasized:

1. With the democracy as it existed only in Greece, oracles are intimately connected. For an independent decision, a consolidated subjectivity of the will, based upon prevailing reasons, is necessary, but the Greeks did not yet have such strength and vigor of subjective will. The oracles were consulted when a colony was to be founded, when an alien god was to be adopted, or when a general was about to give battle to the enemy [here follow examples]. In their private affairs, too, the Greeks made decisions not so much by themselves; they took

the decision from someone else. However, with the advance of democracy we find that the oracles are no longer consulted on the most important matters, but the particular views of popular orators are put forward and decide the situation. Just as at this time Socrates relied on his demon, so the popular leaders and the people derived their decisions by themselves. But ruin, corruption, and constant changes in the constitution occurred at the same time.

2. Slavery is another circumstance that demands special attention. This was the necessary condition of a democracy of beauty, where it was the right and duty of every citizen to deliver speeches respecting the management of the state, or to listen to them, in the public assembly; to take part in the exercises in the gymnasium, and to join in the celebration of festivals. It was a necessary condition of such occupations that the citizen be free from handicraft work, and that what is performed among us by free citizens, the work of daily life, should be done by slaves. The equality of the citizens entailed the exclusion of the slaves. Slavery does not cease until the will has been completely reflected within itself, until right and law are conceived as appertaining to every freeman, and the freeman is simply man in his general nature as endowed with reason. But the Greeks still occupied the standpoint of ethics as mere mores and wont. . . .

3. It must be remarked, thirdly, that such democratic constitutions are possible only in small states, states which do not much exceed the size of a city. The whole state of the Athenians is united in the one city of Athens. Tradition says that Theseus united the scattered villages into an integral whole. The entire population of Athenian territory took refuge in the city in the time of Pericles, at the beginning of the Peloponnesian War, when the Spartans were marching upon Attica. In such cities only can the interests of all be the same; in large realms, on the contrary, diverse and conflicting interests are

sure to be found. The living together in one city and the fact that the inhabitants see each other daily makes possible a common culture and a living democratic polity. The main point in a democracy is that the character of the citizens must be plastic and all of one piece. The citizen must be present at the critical stages of public business. He must take part in the decisions, not merely with his vote, but by being agitated and agitating, putting the passion and interest of the whole man into the affair, so that the warmth of a resolution is present in the entire proceeding. That insight which all are to reach must be produced in the individuals by oratory. No general fervor would be excited among the individuals if this were attempted by writing, which is an abstract and lifeless way; and the greater the number, the less weight would each individual vote have. In a large realm a general inquiry might be made, votes might be gathered in the several communities, and the result counted, as was done by the French Convention. But this is a dead affair, and the world is thereby already broken up and dissolved into a paper world. In the French Revolution, therefore, the republican constitution never actually became a democracy: tyranny, despotism raised their voice under the mask of freedom and equality.

We now come to the *second period* of Greek history. In the first period, the Greek spirit attained its strength and maturity. The second period shows the Greek spirit *manifesting* itself and appearing in its full glory, producing a work for the world, justifying its principle in the struggle, and triumphantly maintaining itself against attack.

The Wars with the Persians

The period of contact with preceding world-historical people is generally regarded as the second in the history of any nation. The world-historical contact of the Greeks was with the Persians; in this contact, Greece showed itself in its most glorious qualities. The occasion of the Median Wars was the revolt of the Ionian cities against the Persians, in which the Athenians and Eretrians assisted them. The circumstance which in particular induced the Athenians to take part in this revolt was that the son of Pisistratus, after his attempts at regaining sovereignty in Athens had failed, had gone to the king of the Persians. The Father of History, Herodotus, has given us a brilliant description of these Median Wars, and for our present purpose we need not dwell upon them. . . .

Greece was thus freed from the pressure that threatened to overwhelm it. Greater battles have unquestionably been fought; but these battles of the Greeks are not only immortal in the historical records of nations, but also in those of science and art, of the noble and the moral generally. They were world historical victories. They were the salvation of culture and of spiritual vigor, and they rendered the Asiatic principle powerless. How often, on other occasions, have not men sacrificed everything for one grand object! How often have not warriors fallen for duty and for country! But here we are called upon to admire not only valor, genius and spirit, but the purport of the conflict, the effect, the result, which are unique in their way. In all other battles a particular interest is predominant. But the immortal fame of the Greeks is none other than their due, considering the noble cause which was then saved. In world history, it is the importance of the cause itself that will decide the fame of the achievement, not the formal valor that has been displayed. In the case before us, world history hung trembling in the balance. Oriental despotism, a world united under one lord and sovereign, on the one side, stood facing separate states, insignificant in extent and resources but animated by free individuality. Never in history was the superiority of spiritual power over material bulk made so gloriously manifest. This war, and the subsequent development of the leading states is the most brilliant period of Greece. . . .

Athens

[After some introductory remarks about Athenian constitutional history, Hegel writes:]

As a general principle, the democratic constitution affords the widest scope for the development of great political personalities, for it, above all other forms of government, not only allows, but encourages the display of the individual's powers. At the same time, no member of the community can obtain influence unless he has the power of satisfying the spirit and opinions as well as the passions and levity of a cultivated people.

A lively freedom existed in Athens, and a live equality of manners and spiritual culture. If inequality of property could not be avoided, it did not become extreme. Alongside this equality, and within this freedom, all inequality of character and talent and all difference of individuals could express itself most freely and find the most abundant stimulus to development in its environment. For, generally speaking, the key aspects of Athenian character were the independence of the individual and a culture animated by the spirit of beauty. It was Pericles who instituted the production of those eternal monuments of sculpture whose scanty remains astonish posterity. It was before these people that the dramas of Aeschylus and Sophocles were performed, and later on those of Euripides which, however, do not exhibit the same plastic ethical character, and in which the principle of corruption is more manifest. The orations of Pericles were addressed to this same people. From it came a group of men whose genius has become classical for all centuries; for to this number belong, besides those already named, Thucydides, Socrates, Plato and Aristophanes—Aristophanes, who preserved the political seriousness of his people at the time when it was being corrupted and who, animated by this seriousness, wrote his poetry for his country's benefit. We recognize in the Athenians great active-ness and open-mindedness, and the development of individuality within the sphere of an ethical spirit. The reproach which we find in Xenophon and Plato refers rather to the later period when misfortune and the corruption of the democracy were present. But we must not turn to Xenophon, or even to Plato, if we wish to find the verdict of the ancients on the political life of Athens, but to those who had a thorough knowledge of the state in its full vigor, who managed its affairs and have been considered its greatest leaders. Among these, Pericles is the Zeus of the human pantheon of Athens. Thucydides puts into his mouth the most thorough description of Athens, on the occasion of the funeral ceremonies for the warriors who had fallen in the year of the Peloponnesian War. He says he wants to show for what city and in the support of what interests they had died. Thus the speaker turns immediately to the essential. He paints the character of Athens, and what he says is most profoundly thoughtful as well as most right and true. "We love the beautiful," he says, "but without ostentation or extravagance; we philosophize without being seduced thereby into effeminacy and inactivity; for when men give themselves up to thought they get further and further away from the practical, from activity for the public, the general. We are bold and daring, but with this courage, we give an account of what we undertake; we have a consciousness of it. Among other nations, on the contrary, courage is caused by lack of culture. We know best how to distinguish between the agreeable and the hard way, yet we do not shrink from perils." * Thus Athens offered the drama of a state which lived primarily for the purpose of beauty, and which yet had a fully developed consciousness of the seriousness of public affairs and of the interests of man's spirit and life; it combined these with bold courage and practical good sense.

---

* Hegel does not actually insert quotation marks, but quotes freely from memory, as was his wont, even with poetry.—Ed.

Sparta

Here we see, by contrast, rigid abstract virtue, a life devoted to the state, but in such a way that freedom and individuality are pushed back. The polity of Sparta is based on institutions which are fully in line with the interest of the state, but whose object is an unspiritual equality, and not free movement. The very beginnings of Sparta are very different from those of Athens. The Spartans were Dorians, the Athenians Ionians; and this national difference had an influence on their constitution also. As far as the inception of Sparta is concerned, the Dorians invaded the Peloponnesus with the Heracleidae, subdued the indigenous tribes and condemned them to slavery; for the Helots were doubtless aborigines. The fate that had befallen the Helots was suffered at a later date by the Messenians; for such inhuman severity was innate in Spartan character. While the Athenians had a family life, and the slaves among them shared the fellowship of the house, the relation of the Spartans to a subjugated race was one of even greater harshness than that of the Turks to the Greeks; a state of war was constant in Lacedaemon. In entering upon their office, the Ephors made a complete declaration of war upon the Helots, and the latter were habitually sacrificed to the young Spartans for their military exercises. The Helots were set free on some occasions, and fought against the enemy. Moreover, they displayed extraordinary valor in the ranks of the Spartans, but on their return they were butchered in the most cowardly and insidious way. As in a slave-ship, the crew are constantly armed, and the greatest care is taken to prevent an insurrection, so the Spartans were constantly on the alert regarding the Helots, and were always in a state of war, as of against enemies.

Property in land was divided into equal parts, according to the constitution of Lycurgus, of which 9,000 only belonged to the Spartans, and 30,000 to the Lacedaemonians or Perioeci. At the same time, in order to maintain this equality, no real estate was allowed to be sold. But with how little success this arrangement was made is proved by the fact that in the sequel Lacedaemon declined chiefly as a result of the inequality of property. Since daughters inherited, many estates had come by marriage into the hands of a few families, and at last all the property was in the hands of a limited number. This occurred as if to show how foolish it is to try to force equality, an attempt which, while ineffective in realizing its professed object, also destroys the most essential liberty, namely the free disposition of property. Another remarkable feature in the legislation of Lycurgus is his forbidding all money except that made of iron, an enactment which necessarily brought about the cessation of all business and traffic. The Spartans, moreover, had no naval force, a thing indispensable to the support and furtherance of commerce. On the occasions when such a force was required, they had to apply to the Persians for it.

With an especial view to support in the interest of common manners and a more intimate acquaintance of the citizens with each other, the Spartans had their meals in common. But such a community disparaged family life, for eating and drinking is a private affair and consequently belongs to the inside of the home. It was so among the Athenians; with them communication was not material but spiritual, and even their banquets, as we see from Xenophon and Plato, had a spiritual quality. Among the Spartans, on the other hand, the costs of the common meal were met by the contributions of the several members, and he who was too poor to offer such a contribution was consequently excluded.

As to the political constitution of Sparta, its basis may be called democratic, but with considerable modifications which made it almost into an aristocracy and oligarchy. At the head of the state were two kings, at whose side was a senate, chosen from among the best men. The senate also performed the functions of a court of justice, deciding rather in accordance with ethical and legal customs than with enacted law. It was also the highest state council, the Council of the Kings regulating the most important affairs. Finally there were the Ephors, one of the highest magistracies; we have no definite information respecting their election. Aristotle says that the mode of election was exceedingly childish. We learn from Aristotle that even persons without nobility or property could attain this dignity. The Ephors had full authority to convoke popular assemblies, to call for the vote, and to propose laws, almost in the same way as the people's tribunes in Rome. Their power became tyrannical, almost like that which Robespierre and his party exercised for a time in France.

While the Spartans directed their entire attention to the state, culture, art and science were not native to them. Spartans appeared to the rest of the Greeks to be stiff, awkward, coarse beings who could not transact more intricate business, or at least did it very clumsily. Thucydides has the Athenians say to the Spartans: "You have laws and customs which have nothing in common with those of others: and besides this when you go into other countries you proceed in accordance neither with these nor with the traditional usages of Hellas." They were, on the whole, honorable in their intercourse at home; but as regarded their conduct toward other nations, they themselves plainly declared that they held the arbitrary commendable, and the useful right. It is well known that in Sparta . . . the stealing of what one needed was permitted under certain conditions; only the thief must not allow himself to be discovered. Thus the two states, Athens and Sparta, confront each other. The ethics of Sparta is rigidly directed toward the state; we find a similar ethical relation in Athens, but with a developed consciousness and boundless activity in the creation of the beautiful, and subsequently of the true also.

This Greek ethics, though extremely beautiful, attractive and interesting in its manifestations, is not the highest point of spiritual self-consciousness. It lacks the form of infinity, the reflection of thought within itself. It lacks emancipation from the natural element, the sensuous that is involved in the very nature of beauty and divinity, and from the immediacy of Greek ethics. Infinity of self-consciousness and self-comprehension on the part of thought is wanting; these states of mind require that what is regarded as right and moral by a man should be confirmed by him by the testimony of his own spirit; it requires that the beautiful in sense perception also become the true, may become an inward supersensuous world.

The position occupied by that aesthetic spiritual unity which we have just described could not long remain a place of spirit. Further advance, as well as corruption, started from subjectivity, inward morality, individual reflection and an inner life generally. The perfect bloom of Greek life lasted only about sixty years, from the Median Wars, 492 B.C., to the Peloponnesian War, 431 B.C. Then the principle of [subjective] morality which was bound to enter became the germ of corruption which, however, showed itself in a different form in Athens from that which it assumed in Sparta. In Athens, it was evident levity, in Sparta, private deprivation of morals. In their fall the Athenians showed themselves not only amiable, but great and noble, in a way which makes us lament their passing away. Among the Spartans, on the contrary, the principle of subjectivity progresses into vulgar greed and issues in vulgar ruin.

The Peloponnesian War

The principle of corruption displayed itself first in the external political developments, in the contest of the states of Greece with each other, and the struggle of factions within the cities themselves. Greek ethics made Hellas unfit to form one common state. For the necessary condition of that degree of freedom which the Greeks achieved was the existence of many small states separate from one another, and the concentration of life in the cities where the interest and spiritual culture pervading the whole could be the same for all. Only a passing unification occurred in the Trojan War, and union could not be achieved even in the Median Wars. Although the tendency toward such a union is discernible, it was weak and endangered by jealousy, and the contest for hegemony set the states against each other. A general outbreak of hostilities occurred in the Peloponnesian War. [Here follow some several statements about this war, based essentially on Thucydides.]

We have now to understand the *corruption* of the Greek world in its deeper meaning, and we may note the principle of that corruption as inwardness becoming free in and by itself. We see this inwardness arising in various ways. Thought, the inward and general, menaces the beautiful Greek religion, while the passions and caprice of individuals menace the political constitutions and laws. Subjectivity, comprehending and manifesting itself in everything, threatens the entire, immediate, existing state of things. Thought therefore appears here as the principle of decay, the decay of substantial ethics, for it introduces an antithesis and asserts essentially rational principles. For the concrete vitality found among the Greeks is a kind of ethics, a life for religion, for the state, without further reflection and without general propositions, which lead away from the concrete configuration and must oppose it. The law exists and the spirit exists within it. But as soon as thought arises, it investigates the various political constitutions. It discovers what is best and demands that this recognized best should take the place of things as they are.

The self-emancipation of thought is involved in the principle of Greek freedom, inasmuch as it is freedom. With the sophists began the process of reflection on the existing state of things, and of ratiocination. The very busyness and activity which we observed among the Greeks in their practical life and in their practice of the arts showed itself also in the turns and windings which these ideas took. As material things are changed, worked up and used for other than their original purposes, similarly the content of the mind, what is thought and known, is being agitated; it is made an object about which the mind can employ itself, and this occupation becomes an interest in and for itself. The movement of thought, and what goes on within it, this careless play of ideas now becomes an interest. The educated sophists, not erudite or scientific men, but masters of subtle turns of thought, astounded the Greeks. They had an answer for all questions. They had a general viewpoint on all religious or political interests. In the ultimate further development of their art they claimed the ability to prove anything, to discover a justifiable side in every position. In a democracy it is a matter of first importance to be able to speak in popular assemblies, to urge one's opinions in public matters. This demands the capacity for duly presenting before the people that point of view which we desire then to regard as essential. Intellectual culture is required for such a purpose. The Greeks acquired this discipline under their sophists. This intellectual culture then became the means, in the hands of those who possessed it, of putting over views and interests on the people. The expert sophist knew how to turn the subject of the discussion this way or that way at pleasure, and thus were the doors thrown open to all human passions. A leading principle of the sophists was that "Man is the measure of all things"; but in this, as in all their sayings, an ambiguity is contained, since "Man" may be the spirit in its depth and truth, or merely a capricious and private individual. The sophists meant the merely subjective Man and thus declared mere arbitrary will and pleasure the principle of right, and the individual's utility as the final ground of appeal. This sophistic principle appears again and again, though under different forms, in various periods of history. Thus subjective opinion of what is right, mere feeling, is made again the ultimate ground of decision in our own times.

In beauty, as the principle of the Greeks, the concrete unity of spirit was conjoined with reality, with country and with family, etc. Within this unity no fixed point of view had as yet been adopted within the spirit itself. Thought, as far as it transcended this unity, was still determined by accident. The beautiful conducted men in the path of ethical propriety, but apart from this they had no firm abstract principle of truth and virtue. But already Anaxagoras had taught that thought itself was the absolute essence of the world. Socrates, at the beginning of the Peloponnesian War, first freely expressed the principle of inwardness, of the absolute independence of thought in itself. He taught that man has to discover and recognize in himself what is the right and the good, and that this right and good is in its nature universal. Socrates is celebrated as a teacher of morality, but we should rather call him the *inventor* of morality. The Greeks had ethics, but Socrates undertook to teach them what moral virtues and duties, etc., were. The moral man is not he who merely wills and does that which is right, not the naïve man, but he who has the consciousness of what he is doing.

Socrates, by assigning the determination of men's actions to insight and conviction, posited the individual as capable of a final moral decision, even of one opposed to his country and its mores. He thus made himself an oracle in the Greek sense. He said he had a demon or voice within him which counseled him what to do, and which revealed to him what was advantageous to his friends. The rise of the inner world of subjectivity was the rupture of the existing reality. Though Socrates himself continued to perform his duties as a citizen, it was not the actual state and its religion, but the world of thought that was his true home. Now the question of the existence and the nature of the gods began to be discussed. Plato, the disciple of Socrates, banished from his ideal state Homer and Hesiod, who had been the originators of Greek religious ideas, and demanded a higher conception, consonant with thought, of what was to be revered as divine. Many citizens now left the practical and political life in order to live in the ideal world. The principle of Socrates is revolutionary toward the Athenian state;

for the peculiarity of this state was that mores were the form of its existence, that is to say, thought could not be separated from actual life. When Socrates wishes to make his friends reflect, the discourse always is negative; he makes them conscious that they do not know what is right. But when Socrates was condemned to death because he uttered the necessarily emerging principle of subjective consciousness, there is, on the one hand, high justice, inasmuch as the Athenian people condemn their deadliest foe; on the other hand, there is also high tragedy, since the Athenians had to make the discovery that what they had damned in Socrates had already struck firm root among themselves, and that they must be pronounced guilty or innocent along with him. Feeling thus, they condemned the accusers of Socrates and declared him without guilt. In Athens, hereafter, that higher principle which proved the ruin of the Athenian state developed steadily. Spirit had acquired the propensity to satisfy itself, to reflect. The spirit of Athens appears majestic even in decay, because it manifests itself as the free and the liberal, presenting its successive phases in their pure particularity, in that form in which they really exist. Lovable and serene even in the midst of tragedy is the lightheartedness and nonchalance with which the Athenians accompany their ethics to its grave. We recognize the higher interest of the new outlook in the fact that the people made merry over their own follies, and found great entertainment in the comedies of Aristophanes, which contain the severest satire even while they bear the stamp of the most unbridled mirth.

The same corruption is introduced in Sparta, when the individual seeks to assert his individuality against the moral life of the community. But in Sparta we merely see the separate side of particular subjectivity, corruption in its undisguised form, blank immorality, vulgar selfishness, rapacity and venality. All these passions manifest themselves in Sparta, especially in the persons of its generals, who, for the most part living at a distance from their country, obtain an opportunity of securing advantages at the expense of their own state as well as of those to whose assistance they are sent.

The Macedonian Empire

Alexander had been educated by the profoundest and also the most comprehensive thinker of antiquity, *Aristotle,* and the education was worthy of the man who had undertaken it. Alexander was initiated into the profoundest metaphysics: thereby his nature was thoroughly refined and liberated from the customary bonds of mere opinion, crudities and idle fancies. Aristotle left this grand nature as genuine as it was before his instructions commenced, but he impressed upon it a deep consciousness of the truthful, and he formed the spirit full of genius into a plastic being. . . .

[Here follows a brief and very laudatory summary of Alexander's career.]

Alexander had the good fortune to die at the proper time. It may be called good fortune, but it is rather necessity. An early death had to hurry him away, that he might stand before [the eyes of] posterity as a youth. Achilles, as remarked above, begins the Greek world, and Alexander concludes it: these youths not only give a fairest sight of themselves, but at the same time provide a complete and perfect image of the Greek essence. Alexander finished his work and completed his image, and thus bequeathed to the world one of the noblest and most beautiful of visions, which our poor reflections only serve to obscure. The modern standard applied by recent philistines among historians, that of virtue or morality, does not suit the world-historical figure of Alexander.

The Decline of the Greek Spirit

In the internal condition of the Greek states which were broken up into factions, enervated by selfishness and debauchery, the point of interest is no longer the fate of these states,

but the great individuals who arise amid the general corruption and honorably devote themselves to their country. They
appear as great tragic characters who with their genius and
the most intense exertion are yet unable to extirpate the evils
in question. They perish in the struggle without having had
the satisfaction of restoring repose, order and freedom to their
fatherland, nay, without even having secured a reputation with
posterity free from all stain. Livy says in his prefatory remarks:
"In our times we can neither endure our faults nor the means
of correcting them." And this is quite as applicable to these last
of the Greeks, who began an undertaking which was as honorable and noble as it was doomed to frustration. Agis and
Cleomenes, Aratus and Philopoemen thus sank under the
struggle for the good of their nation. Plutarch characterizes
these times very well in sketching us a picture of them. He
gives us a conception of the meanings of the individuals of
this period.

The third period in the history of the Greeks brings us to
their contact with the people which was to play the next role on
the theater of the world's history. The chief excuse for this
contact was . . . the liberation of Greece. After Perseus, the
last Macedonian king, had been conquered in the year 168
B.C. and brought in triumph to Rome, the Achaean league
was attacked and broken up, and Corinth was finally destroyed
in the year 146 B.C. Looking at Greece as Polybius describes
it, we see how a noble nature such as his has nothing left but
to despair at the state of affairs and retreat into philosophy. If
such a nature attempts to act, it can only die in the struggle. In
deadly juxtaposition to the multiform variety of passion which
Greece presents, that distracted condition which mixes good
and evil in one common ruin, there stands, like a blind fate,
an iron power ready to reveal that degraded condition in all
its weakness, and to smash it to pieces in miserable ruin; for
cure, amendment and consolation are impossible. This crushing
fate is the Romans.

THE ROMAN WORLD

Napoleon, in a conversation with Goethe on the nature of tragedy, expressed the opinion that modern tragedy differed essentially from the ancient, because we no longer had a fate which overwhelmed men; politics had taken the place of the ancient fate. Therefore he thought that the irresistible power of circumstances to which the individual must bend should be used as the modern form of fate in tragedy. The *Roman world* is such a power, chosen for the very purpose of casting the ethical individual into bonds, as also of collecting all deities and spirits into the pantheon of world dominion in order to mold them into an abstract generality. This precisely is the difference between the Roman and Persian principle: that the former stifles all lively spirit, while the latter allowed of its existence in the fullest measure. The world sank into sorrow and grief because it was the end of the state that the individuals and their moral life should be sacrificed to it. The heart of the world was broken and it was all over with the genuineness of spirit, which had arrived at a feeling of fatality. Yet the supersensuous free spirit of Christianity could arise only from this feeling.

In the Greek principle we have seen the spiritual existence in its exhilaration, its serenity and enjoyment. Spirit had not yet retired into abstraction. It was still involved with the natural element, the particularity of individuals, on which account the virtues of individuals themselves became ethical works of art. Abstract general personality had not yet appeared, for spirit first had to develop itself to that form of abstract generality which has exercised such a severe discipline over humanity. Here then in Rome we find that free general outlook, that abstract freedom, which on the one hand places an abstract state, a political constitution and power, over the concrete individual, and subordinates it completely, on the other hand creates a personality in juxtaposition to that generality—the freedom of the ego, which must be distinguished from individuality. For such a personality constitutes the fundamental conception of law and right. It appears primarily in the category of property, but it is indifferent to the concrete characteristics of the living spirit with which individuality is concerned. These two elements which constitute Rome, political universality on the one hand, and the abstract freedom of the individual on the other, appear in the form of inwardness or subjectivity (*Innerlichkeit*) in the first instance. This subjectivity, this retreating into oneself which we observed as the corruption of the Greek spirit, here became the ground on which a new side of the world's history arises. In considering the Roman world, we are not dealing with a concretely spiritual life, rich in itself. The world-historical element in the Roman world is the abstraction of universality, pursued with soulless and heartless severity, in order to validate that abstraction, the purpose of which is mere dominion or rule.

Democracy was the fundamental condition of political life in Greece, as despotism was in the East. In Rome, it is the aristocracy, rigid and opposed to the people. The democracy was also rent asunder in Greece, but only by factions. In Rome it is principles that keep the entire community in a divided state; they struggle and occupy a hostile position toward one another. First the aristocracy struggles with the kings, then the plebs with the aristocracy, till democracy gets the upper hand; then arise the factions from which arose the later aristocracy of commanding individuals which subjugated the world. It is this dualism that, properly speaking, marks Rome's inmost being.

Erudition has regarded Roman history from various points of view and has adopted very different and opposing opinions. This is especially the case with the more ancient part of the history, which has been taken up by three different classes of scholars—historians, philologists and jurists. The historians hold to the main features and show respect for the history as such, so that we may get oriented best under their guidance, since they allow the validity of the records in the case of the leading events. It is otherwise with the philologists, by whom generally received traditions are less regarded, and who devote more attention to various details which can be combined in various ways. These combinations first gain a footing as historical hypotheses, but are soon after claimed as established facts. The jurists in Roman law have instituted the minutest examination and mixed their inferences with hypotheses to the same degree as the philologists have in their department. The result is that the most ancient part of Roman history has been declared to be nothing but a fable, so that this department of inquiry is brought entirely within the province of learned criticism, which always finds the most to do where the least is to be got for the labor. While on the one side the poetry and the myths of the Greeks are said to contain profound historical truths, and are thus transmuted into history, the Romans are made to have myths and poetical views. Epic poetry is affirmed to be the basis of what has hitherto been taken for prosaic and historical fact.

[After a simple description of the geography of Italy, Hegel continues:]

We noted that subjective inwardness is the general principle of the Roman world. The course of Roman history therefore involves the progress of inward seclusion, of certainty of oneself toward an external reality. The principle of subjective inwardness in the first place only receives positive fulfillment and content from without, through the particular will to rule, to govern, etc. The development consists in the purification of inwardness into abstract personality; which gives itself reality in the existence of private property; the rigid persons can then be held together only by despotic force.

This is the general course of the Roman world: to proceed from the inner sanctum of subjectivity to its direct opposite. The development here is not of the same kind as that of Greece, the unfolding and expanding of its own content on the part of the principle. It is rather the transition of the principle to its opposite, which does not appear as an element of corruption, but is demanded and posited by the principle itself.

The common division of the particular sections of Roman history is that of the monarchy, the republic and the empire, as if different principles had made their appearance in these forms. But the fact of the matter is that the same principle, that of the Roman spirit, underlies all of this development. In our division, we must rather keep in view the course of world history. The annals of every world-historical people were divided above into three periods, and the statement must prove true in this case also. The first period comprehends the rudiments of Rome, in which the elements which are essentially opposed still repose in calm unity; until the contrarieties have acquired strength and the unity of the state becomes powerful, because it has produced and maintained this contrast within itself. In this vigorous condition the state directs its forces outward, that is, in the second period, and makes its debut on the theater of world history. This is the most beautiful period of Rome, that of the Punic Wars and the contact with the antecedent world-historical people. A wider stage is opened toward the East. The history of the epoch of this contact has been treated by the noble Polybius. The Roman Empire now acquired that world-conquering extension which paved the way for its fall. Internal corrosion occurred, while the contrast was developing into a self-contradiction and utter incompatibility. The Roman world closes with despotism, which marks the third period. The Roman power here appears in its pomp and splendor, but it is at the same time profoundly ruptured within itself. The Christian religion, which began with the imperial dominion, receives a great extension. The third period comprises the contact of Rome with the North and the Germanic peoples, whose turn then comes to play their part in world history.

[We selected one more brief passage from Hegel's treatment, entitled:]

The Elements of the Roman Spirit

Before we come to Roman history, we have to consider the elements of the Roman spirit in general and mention and investigate the origin of Rome with reference to them.

To the unfree, non-spiritual and unfeeling intelligence of the Roman world we owe the origin and development of positive law. We saw above how, in the East, relations in their very nature belonging to the sphere of outward and inward mores were made legal commands. Mores were also juristic law among the Greeks, and on that very account the constitution was entirely dependent on mores and loyalty and had not yet a fixity of principle within it to counterbalance the mutability of men's inner life and individual subjectivity. It was the Romans who then succeeded in establishing this important separation and discovered a principle of law and right which is external, one not dependent on conviction and sentiment. While they have thus bestowed a valuable gift upon us in point of form, we may use and enjoy it without becoming victims of that sterile intellect, in other words, without regarding it as the *ne plus ultra* of wisdom and reason. The Romans were the victims of this principle, living beneath its sway; but they thereby secured freedom of spirit for others, that inward freedom which has consequently become emancipated from the sphere of the limited and external. Spirit, soul, conviction and religion have now no longer to fear being involved with that abstract juristical understanding.

We thus see the Romans fettered by the abstract and finite intellect. This is their highest destiny, and hence also their highest consciousness, in *religion*. For it was the very religion of the Romans to be thus constrained, while the religion of the Greeks was the serenity of free imagination. We are in the habit of looking upon Greek and Roman religion as the same. . . . This may do in so far as the Greek gods were more or less introduced by the Romans, but the Roman religion is not the Greek. It has been said that in Greek religion the awe of nature has been developed into something spiritual, a spiritual figure of the imagination, that the Greek spirit did not stop at the inner anxiety, but made the relation to nature one of freedom and serenity. The Romans, however, stopped at this silent and dull inwardness. The Roman spirit thus remaining inward became constrained and dependent as the word *religio* (from *ligare*) suggests.

[A very extensive treatment of Roman history follows which undertakes to show in detail how the general propositions we have given work out in the concrete unfolding of the Roman world. It is with regret that one omits these discussions which contain many an acute observation. Towards the end, the coming of Christianity is discussed and we offer a brief excerpt from that section.]

Christianity

At the beginning of the rule of the emperors, the principle of which we have comprehended as a finite and particular subjectivity raised to infinite scope, the salvation of the world was born within the same principle of subjectivity; namely, as *this* particular man, in abstract subjectivity, but in reverse, namely thus that finiteness is merely the form of his appearance, while its essence is infinity, the absolute being by and for itself. The Roman world, as we have described it, in its perplexity and in its sorrow of being abandoned by God, caused a breach with reality and a general longing for a pacification which could only be achieved inwardly and by the spirit; it thus prepared the ground for a higher spiritual world. The Roman world was the fate which crushed the Greek gods and the serene life in their service. . . . Its sorrow is like the birth pangs of another higher spirit which was revealed by the *Christian religion.* This higher spirit contains the reconciliation and the liberation of the spirit, because man now becomes conscious of the spirit in its universality and infinity. . . .

God is understood as spirit only by being known as the Trinity. This new principle is the hub around which world history revolves. History is divided by going forward to this point, and starting from it. "When the time was fulfilled, God sent his son . . ." it says in the Bible. That saying means that the self-consciousness had risen to those aspects which belong to the conception of the spirit, and to a desire of comprehending these aspects in an absolute manner.

[Then, after resuming once more what he had said about the spirit of the Greeks and the Romans, the natural spirit and its inwardness, Hegel continues:]

Here we see the world-historical importance and significance of the Jewish people; for from it has sprung the higher development by which the spirit arrived at absolute self-consciousness. . . . We find this destiny of the Jewish people most beautifully and purely expressed in the Psalms and the books of the Prophets; for here the thirst of the soul for God, the deepest sorrow of the soul about its faults, the desire for justice and piety constitute the content. The mythical description of this spirit is found at the very beginning of the books [of the Old Testament] in the story of the *fall.* Man, created in the image of God, so the tale goes, had lost his absolute contentment, because he had eaten of the tree of knowledge of good and evil. Sin is here the knowledge: by knowledge man has destroyed his natural happiness. This is a deep truth that evil results from consciousness; animals are neither good nor bad, and similarly the merely natural man. Only consciousness produces the splitting of the ego, according to the infinite freedom of arbitrary will, and the pure content of the will which is the good.

[After stating his general views on this subject at greater length, Hegel continues:]

Sin is knowledge of good and evil, separating them; but knowledge also heals this old break and is the fountain of the infinite reconciliation. For knowledge also means to destroy the external and alien elements of the consciousness and is thus the return of subjectivity to itself. To posit this in the actual consciousness of the world means the *reconciliation of the world*. The identity of the subject and God entered the world when *the time was fulfilled;* the consciousness of this identity is the knowledge of God as He truly is. The content of the truth is the *spirit* itself, the living movement within itself. The nature of God of being pure spirit is *revealed to man in the Christian religion*. And what is the spirit? He (it) is the One, the infinite consistent within Himself (itself), the pure identity. . . . It is part of the appearance of the Christian God that it is unique in its way; it can happen only once, for God is subject and as an appearing subjectivity only one individual. . . . Furthermore, the sense existence in which the spirit appears, is only a passing aspect. Christ is dead; but only when dead is He raised to heaven and sits at the right of God; only thus is He spirit. He himself says: *When I am no longer among you, the spirit will lead you to all the truth*. Only on Pentecost the disciples were filled with the Holy Spirit. When he was alive, Christ was not for his disciples what he became later as spirit of the community. . . . It is not right to think of Christ only as a past historical person. If one asks: what are the circumstances of his birth, of his father and mother, of his education, of his miracles, it all means [asking] what is He considered unspiritually? For if one considers Him only according to His talents, character and morality, as a teacher and the like, one places Him on the same level with Socrates, and others, even if one puts his morals higher. . . . If Christ is merely a splendid, even a sinless individual . . . the notion of the speculative idea, of absolute truth is being denied. But this is what matters and we must start from it. You can make by exegesis, criticism and historical research anything you want, you may show, if you wish, that the doctrines of the church have been created at some council by the interest and the passion of the bishops . . . all such circumstances may be what they will. All that matters is what the idea or truth is in and by and for itself.

[Hegel elaborates this central theme by further detailed analysis and by quotation from the Bible, with special reference, of course, to St. John, and the doctrine of the visible and the invisible church; but he concludes with his central tenet of the consonance of reason and religion:]

Often one has tried to establish a conflict between *reason* and *religion,* just as between *religion* and *world;* but when studied more closely, this is merely a distinction. Reason, generally speaking, is the essence of the spirit, the divine as well as the human. The difference between religion and world is merely this, that religion is reason in mind and heart, that it is a temple of imagined truth and freedom in God; the state according to this same reason is a temple of human freedom in the knowledge of and the will for the actual reality, the content of which may itself be called divine. Thus freedom in the state is confirmed and substantiated by religion, because ethical law in the state is merely the execution of what is the basic principle of religion.

[The tasks here involved Hegel believes to have been assigned to the Germanic peoples.]

THE GERMANIC WORLD

The Germanic spirit is the spirit of the new world. Its end is the realization of absolute truth as the unlimited self-determination of freedom, that freedom which has its own absolute form as its content. The destiny of the Germanic peoples is to be the bearers of the Christian principle. The principle of spiritual freedom, of reconciliation and harmony (of the objective and the subjective), was introduced into the still simple, unformed minds of these peoples. The part assigned to them in the service of the world spirit was that of not merely possessing the idea of freedom as the substratum of their religious conceptions, but of producing it in free and spontaneous developments from their subjective self-consciousness.

In entering on the task of dividing the Germanic world into its natural periods, we must remark that we cannot relate it externally to an earlier world-historical people, nor forward to a later one. History shows that the process of development among the peoples now under consideration was an altogether different one. The Greeks and Romans had reached inner maturity before they directed their energies outward. The Germanic peoples, on the contrary, began with self-diffusion, deluging the world, and overpowering in their course the inwardly rotten, hollow political fabric of the civilized nations. Only then did their development begin, kindled by a foreign culture, a foreign religion, polity and legislation. The process of culture formation they underwent consisted in taking over foreign elements and transcending them. Their history presents a turning inward and a relating of these alien elements to themselves. In the Crusades, indeed, and in the discovery of America, the Western world directed its energies outward. But it was not thus brought in contact with a world-historical people that preceded it; it did not displace a principle that had previously governed the world. Relation to an external principle here only accompanies, but does not constitute the history; the relation does not bring with it essential changes in the nature of those conditions which characterize the people in question, but rather it wears the stamp of an internal revolution. The relation to other countries is therefore quite different from that sustained by the Greeks and the Romans. For the Christian world is the world of perfection; the principle is being fulfilled and consequently the end of our days is fully come. The idea can discover no point in the aspirations of the spirit that is not satisfied in Christianity. For its individual members, the church is, it is true, the preparation for an eternal state to be realized in the future, since the separate individuals who compose it, in their several isolated capacities, occupy a position of particularity. But the church also has the spirit of God actually present in it, it forgives the sinner and is a present kingdom of heaven. Thus the Christian world has no absolute existence outside its sphere, but only a relative one which is already implicitly vanquished. . . . Hence it follows that an external reference ceases to be the characteristic element determining the epochs of the modern world. We have therefore to look for another principle of division.

The Germanic world took up Roman culture and religion in their completed form. There was indeed a Germanic and Northern religion, but it had by no means taken deep root in the soul. Tacitus therefore calls the Germanic tribes: *"Securi adversus deos"* (secure against the Roman gods). The Christian religion which they adopted had received from the Councils and the Fathers of the Church, who possessed the whole culture and, in particular, the philosophy of the Greek and Roman worlds, a perfected dogmatic system. The Church likewise juxtaposed a fully developed language, Latin, to the native tongue of the Germanic peoples. A similar alien influence predominated in art and philosophy. What of Alexandrian and of formal Aristotelian philosophy was still preserved in the writings of Boethius and elsewhere, became the fixed basis of speculative thought in the West for many centuries. The same principle holds in regard to the form of secular rule. Gothic and other chiefs gave themselves the name of Roman Patricians, and the Roman Empire was restored at a later date. Thus the Germanic world appears, superficially, to be only a continuation of the Roman. But an entirely new spirit lived in it, through which the world was to be regenerated, that of the free spirit which rests on itself, the absolute self-determination (*Eigensinn*) of subjectivity. To this inner spirit (*Innigkeit*) is juxtaposed the content as something absolutely different. The distinction and antithesis which evolved from these principles is that of church and state. On the one hand, the Church develops itself as the embodiment of absolute truth; for it is the consciousness of this truth, and at the same time it works to make the individual correspond to it. On the other side stands secular consciousness, which, with its ends, occupies the world of the finite—the state, proceeding from the emotions, from faith and from subjectivity generally. European history presents the development of each of these principles by itself, in church and state; it also presents the antithesis of the two, not only against each other, but within each of them, since each of them is itself the totality. European history finally presents the reconciliation of this conflict and antithesis.

The three periods of this world will have to be treated accordingly.

The first begins with the appearance of the Germanic nations in the Roman Empire, with the first development of these peoples, which as Christians have now taken possession of the West. Because of the barbarous and simple character of these peoples, this initial period does not possess any great interest. The Christian world presents itself at this time as Christendom, one mass in which the spiritual and the secular are only different aspects. This epoch extends to Charlemagne.

The second period develops the two sides to a logically consequential independence and opposition, with the Church by itself as a theocracy, and the state by itself as a feudal monarchy. Charlemagne had formed an alliance with the Holy See against the Lombards and the factions of the nobles in Rome. A union thus arose between the spiritual and secular power, and a kingdom of heaven on earth promised to follow in the wake of this conciliation. But just at this time, instead of a spiritual kingdom of heaven, the inwardness of the Christian principle has the appearance of being altogether directed outward and of leaving its proper sphere. Christian freedom is perverted to its very opposite, both in the religious and the secular respect; on the one hand to the severest bondage, on the other hand to the most immoral excess, and to the crudity of every passion. Two aspects of society should be especially noted in this period. The first is the formation of states, which present themselves as a regulated subordination, so that every relation becomes a firmly fixed private right, excluding a sense of universality. This regulated subordination appears in the feudal system. The second aspect presents the contrast of church and state. This conflict exists solely because the Church, to whose management the spiritual was committed, itself descends into every kind of worldliness, a worldliness which appears only the more detestable because all passions assume the sanction of religion.

The time of Charles the Fifth's reign, the first half of the sixteenth century, forms the end of the second, and likewise the beginning of the third period. Secularity appears now as gaining a consciousness of its own in the morality, rectitude, probity and activity of man. The consciousness of independent validity is aroused through the restoration of Christian freedom. The Christian religion has now passed through the terrible discipline of being shaped (*Bildung*), and it first attains truth and actual reality through the reformation. This third period of the Germanic world extends from the Reformation to our own times. The principle of free spirit is here made the banner of the world, and from this principle are evolved the universal axioms of reason. Formal thought, the intellect, had already been developed; but thought first received its true meaning with the Reformation, through the reviving concrete conciousness of the free spirit. From that epoch thought began to gain a shape properly its own: principles were derived from it which were to be the norm for the constitution of the state.

Political life was now to be consciously regulated by reason. Customary morality and traditional usage lost their validity. The various rights had to prove that their legitimacy was based on rational principles. Only then is the freedom of spirit realized.

We may distinguish these periods as realms of the Father, the Son and the Spirit (Holy Ghost). The realm of the Father is the substantive, undifferentiated mass, merely changing, like the rule of Saturn who devours his children. The realm of the Son is the appearance of God merely in relation to secular existence, illuminating it like an alien object. The realm of the Spirit is the reconciliation.

These epochs may also be compared with the earlier world empires; for since the Germanic realm is the realm of totality, we see the distinction of the earlier epochs. Charlemagne's time may be compared with the Persian Empire; it is the period of substantial unity, this unity having its foundation in the emotions and feelings of the inner man, still abiding in its simplicity both in the spiritual and the secular.

The time preceding Charles the Fifth answers to the Greek world and its merely ideal unity; real unity no longer exists because particular powers have become fixed in privileges and particular rights. Just as the different estates with their rights are isolated within the states themselves, so do the various states maintain a merely external relation to one another abroad. A diplomacy arises which leagues the states with and against each other in the interest of a European balance of power. It is the time in which the world becomes known (discovery of America). Consciousness likewise becomes clear within the world above the senses. Substantive, real religion achieves clearness in the sphere of the senses (Christian art in the age of Pope Leo), and also becomes clear to itself in the sphere of innermost truth. We may compare this time with that of Pericles. The turning inward of the spirit begins (Socrates—Luther), though Pericles is wanting in this epoch.

Charles the Fifth possesses enormous possibilities through outward means and appears absolute in his power; but he lacks
the inner spirit of Pericles, and therefore the absolute means
of establishing a free rule. This is the epoch when spirit becomes clear to itself through real divisions. Now the differences
within the Germanic world appear and manifest their essential
nature.

The third epoch may be compared with the Roman world.
The unity of a general principle is here quite as decidedly present, yet not as the unity of abstract world rule, but as the
hegemony of self-conscious thought. Rational purpose counts
now, and privileges and particularities melt away before the
common end of the state. People want right and law in and for
itself; not only particular treaties are valid, but principles enter
into diplomacy. Nor can religion maintain itself apart from
thought, but either advances to the conception [the comprehension of the idea], or, compelled by thought itself, becomes
intensive belief, or lastly, in despair over thought it retreats
into superstition.

The Barbarian Migrations

We have on the whole little to say respecting this first
period, for it affords us comparatively slight materials for reflection. We will not follow the Germanic peoples back into
their forests, nor investigate the origins of their migrations.
Those forests of theirs have always passed for the abodes of
free peoples, and Tacitus sketched his famous picture of Germania with a certain love and longing, contrasting it with the
corruption and artificiality of that world to which he himself
belonged. But we must not on this account regard such a
state of wildness as an exalted one, and perchance fall into
some such error as Rousseau's, who represents the condition of
the American savages as one in which man is in possession
of true freedom. There is certainly an immense amount of
sorrow and misfortune of which the savage knows nothing;

but this is a merely negative advantage, while freedom is essentially affirmative. Only the blessings of affirmative freedom are those of the highest consciousness. . . .

[Here follow some more detailed comments on the several Germanic tribes.]

We find, moreover, a great Slavic nation in the East of Europe, whose settlements in the West extended along the Elbe down to the Danube. The Magyars settled in between them. In Moldavia, Wallachia and northern Greece appear the Bulgarians, Serbians and Albanians, likewise of Asiatic origin, left behind as broken barbarian remains in the shocks and counter-shocks of the advancing hordes. These people did indeed found kingdoms and sustain spirited conflicts with the various nations that came across their path. Sometimes, as an advanced guard, an intermediate nationality, they took part in the struggle between Christian Europe and unchristian Asia. The Poles even liberated beleaguered Vienna from the Turks; and a part of the Slavs were conquered by Western reason. Yet this entire body of peoples remains excluded from our consideration, because hitherto it has not appeared as an independent phase in the series of configurations of reason in the world. Whether it will happen hereafter does not concern us here; for in history we have to do with the past.

The Germanic nation was characterized by a sense of natural totality, and we may call this *Gemüt*,* or a "feeling mind." *Gemüt* is that enveloped, indeterminate totality of the spirit in reference to the will, in which man's satisfaction is attained in a correspondingly general and indeterminate way. Character is a particular form of will and interest asserting itself; but *Gemütlichkeit* has no particular aim such as riches or honor;

---

* The term *"Gemüt,"* when used thus specifically, is untranslatable, but after Hegel characterizes it, it is clear that he has reference to a certain state of mind in which feeling is very much a part. Perhaps some such word as heartfulness might do, but we prefer to leave it untranslated.—Ed.

in fact does not relate to an objective condition, but to the entire condition, a general sense of enjoyment. It contains will purely as formal will and its purely subjective freedom as a sense of self. For *Gemütlichkeit,* every particular object is important because the *Gemüt* surrenders itself entirely to each. But since it is not interested in the particular ends as such, it does not become isolated in vile or evil passions, or evil, generally speaking. The *Gemüt,* or feeling mind, does not thus divide itself; it looks, on the whole, more like benevolence. Character is its direct opposite.

This is the abstract principle innate in the Germanic peoples, and the subjective side as compared with the objective one in Christianity. The *Gemüt* has no particular content; Christianity, on the other hand, is especially concerned with content as an object. The *Gemüt* involves the desire to be satisfied in a general way; and it is exactly that which we found to be the content in the principle of Christianity. The indefinite as substance, objectivity, is the purely universal, is God; but that the individual be received in grace by God is the complementary aspect of Christian concrete unity. The absolutely universal is that which contains in it all particulars, and hence is itself indefinite. The subject is the definite, yet both are identical. This was shown above as the content in Christianity; here we find it subjectively as *Gemüt* or feeling mind. The individual subject must now also gain an objective form, that is, unfold into an object. It is necessary that, for the vague feeling of the *Gemüt,* the absolute should become an object, in order that man may achieve a consciousness of his unity with that object. But this calls for the purification of the subject, requires that it become a real, concrete subject, that it, as a secular subject, share in general interests, that it act in accordance with general ends, that it know of the law, and that it find satisfaction in it. Thus these two principles correspond with each other, and the Germanic peoples, as we have said, have the capacity to be the bearers of this higher principle of spirit.

Next, we consider the Germanic principle in the primary phase of its existence, that is, the earliest historical condition of the Germanic nations. Their *Gemütlichkeit* is in its first appearance quite abstract, undeveloped and without particular content; for no substantial ends are found in the *Gemüt* as such. Where the *Gemütlich* is the only form of a state of mind, it seems without character and merely dull. *Gemüt*, when abstract, is dullness; thus we see a barbarian dullness, confusion and vagueness in the original condition of the Germanics.

We know little of the *religion* of the Germanic peoples. The Druids belonged to Gaul and were extirpated by the Romans. There was indeed a peculiar northern mythology, but how slight a hold the religion of the Germanic peoples had upon their hearts has already been remarked upon, and it is also evident from the fact that Germanic people were easily converted to Christianity. The Saxons, it is true, offered considerable resistance to Charlemagne; but this was directed not so much against the religion he brought with him as against oppression itself. Their religion did not have profundity, and the same may be said of their *conceptions of law*. Murder was not regarded and punished as a crime; it was expiated by a pecuniary fine. This indicates a lack of depth of sentiment, the *Gemüt* is not divided against itself, which leads them to regard it only as an injury to the community when one of its members is killed, and nothing more. The blood revenge of the Arabs is based on the feeling that the honor of the family has been injured. Among the Germanics, the community had no dominion over the individual, for freedom is their first consideration when they unite into a social relationship. The ancient Germans were famed for their love of freedom; the Romans from the very first formed a correct idea of them in this particular. Freedom has been the watchword in Germany down to the most recent times, and even the league of the princes under Frederick II had its origin in the love of liberty. This element of freedom, when developing into a social relationship, can establish only popular communities. These communities constitute a whole, and every member of the community, as such, is a free man. Homicide could be settled by a fine because the free man was regarded as sacred, permanently and inviola· bly, whatever he might have done. This absolute validity of the individual constitutes a main feature, as Tacitus already observed. The community or its presiding officer, with the assistance of members of the community, delivered judgment in affairs of private law with a view to the protection of person and property. The whole community had to be consulted for affairs affecting the body politic at large, for wars and the like.

The second aspect is that social nuclei were formed by free association, or fellowship, and by voluntary attachment to military leaders and princes. The link in this case was that of loyalty, for loyalty is the second watchword of the Germanic peoples, as freedom was the first. Individuals freely attach themselves to an individual and make this relation an inviolable one. We do not find this with the Greeks and Romans. The German associations or fellowships are not only related to an objective thing, but to the spiritual self, the subjective inmost personality. Heart, *Gemüt*, the entire concrete subjectivity, which does not abstract from content, but regards it as a condition of attachment, making itself dependent on both the person and the thing, makes this relation a compound of loyalty to a person and obedience to a principle.

The union of the two relations, of individual freedom in the community and of the bond implied in the association, is the main point in the formation of the state. In this, duties and rights are no longer left to arbitrary choice, but are fixed as legal relations. But it works this way: the state is the soul of the whole and remains its lord, and from it are derived definite aims and the authorization both of political acts and powers, the generic character and interests of the community constituting the basis of the whole. Here we have the peculiarity of the Germanic states, that, contrariwise, social relations do not assume the character of general terminations and laws, but are entirely split up into private rights and private obligations. . . . Thus the state is compounded of private rights, and a sensible political life emerges only rather late from wearisome struggles and convulsions.

We have said that the Germanic nations were predestined to be the bearers of the Christian principle, and to carry out the idea as the absolutely rational end. At the beginning, there is only dull volition, in the background of which lies the true and the infinite. The true is present only as a task, for their *Gemüt* is not yet purified. A long process is required to complete this purification so as to realize concrete spirit. Religion comes forward with a challenge to the violence of the passions and rouses them to furor. The power of the passions is embittered by a bad conscience and heightened to an insane rate. . . . We behold the terrible spectacle of the most fearful extravagance of passion in all the royal houses of that period. Clovis, the founder of the Frankish Monarchy, is stained with the blackest of crimes. Harshness and cruelty characterize all the succeeding Merovingians; the same spectacle is repeated in the Thuringian and other royal houses. The Christian principle is, to be sure, the task for their souls, but these souls are still rather crude. The will, potentially truthful, mistakes itself and separates itself from the true and proper end by particular, limited ends. Yet the will realizes involuntarily in this struggle with itself what it wants [i.e., what it is meant to will]; it fights what it truly wants, and yet achieves it; for basically and itself, it is reconciled. The spirit of God lives in the community; it is the inward propelling spirit. But it is in the world that the spirit is to be realized, in a material not yet brought into harmony with it. Now this material is the subjective will, which thus has a contradiction within itself. We often observe a change of this kind on the religious side: a man who has been fighting and hacking away at actuality all his life, who has struggled and reveled in secular occupations with all the strength of character and passion, will on a sudden repudiate it all and go into religious seclusion. But secular business cannot be thus repudiated in the world; it calls for completion and the discovery is ultimately made that spirit finds the end of its struggle, and contentment in that very sphere which it made the object of its resistance—it finds that secular pursuits are a spiritual occupation.

We thus observe that individuals and peoples regard that which is their misfortune as their greatest happiness and, conversely, struggle against their happiness as their greatest misery. *La vérité, en la repoussant, on l'embrace.* Europe arrives at the truth since and in so far as it has rejected the truth.

While, therefore, this long process is commencing in the West, a process in the world's history necessary to that purification by which spirit in the concrete is realized, the purification necessary for developing spirit in the abstract, which we see carried on contemporaneously in the East, is more quickly accomplished. The latter does not need a long process, and we see it produced rapidly, even suddenly, in the first half of the seventh century, in Mohammedanism.

[Here follows an extended discussion of Mohammedanism.]

The Middle Ages

While the first period of the Germanic world ends brilliantly with a mighty empire, the second commences with a reaction resulting from the contradiction occasioned by that infinite falsehood which rules the Middle Ages and constitutes their life and spirit. This reaction is first that of the particular nations against the universal rule of the Frankish Empire, manifesting itself in the splitting up of that great empire. The second reaction is that of individuals against legal authority and the state's power, against subordination and the military and judicial arrangements. This produced the isolation and therefore the defenselessness of individuals. The universality of the power of the state disappeared through this reaction: individuals sought protection with the powerful, and the latter became oppressors. Thus a system of general dependence was gradually introduced, and this relationship of protection was then systematized into the feudal system. The third reaction is that of the Church, the reaction of the spiritual element against the existing order of things. Secular wildness was repressed and kept in check by the Church, but the latter was itself secularized in the process, and abandoned its proper position. From that moment begins the introversion of the secular principle. These relations and reactions all go to constitute the history of the Middle Ages, and the culminating point of this period is the Crusades; for with them arises a universal instability, but one through which the [separate] states first attain internal and external independence.

Feudality and the Hierarchy

Thus these three peoples (the Normans, Magyars and Saracens) invaded the empire from all sides in great masses and almost clashed with each other in their devastating marches. France was devastated by the Normans as far as the Jura, the Hungarians reached Switzerland and the Saracens Valaise. Calling to mind the existing military organization, and considering also this miserable state of things, we cannot fail to be struck with the inefficiency of all those far-famed institutions, which ought to have shown themselves most effective at such a juncture. We might be inclined to regard the picture of the noble and rational constitution of the Frankish Monarchy under Charlemagne as an empty dream, although it appeared to be strong, comprehensive and well-ordered, internally and externally. Yet it actually existed; the entire political system being held together only by the strength, the greatness, the noble soul of this one man; it was not based on the spirit of the people, nor had it entered into it. The constitution was superimposed *a priori*, like that which Napoleon gave to Spain, and which disappeared immediately with the physical power which had maintained it. But what gives a constitution reality is that it exists as objective freedom, as a substantial way of willing, as duty and obligation acknowledged by the subjects themselves. But obligation was not yet recognized by the Germanic spirit, which hitherto showed itself only as *Gemüt* and arbitrary subjective will. For the Germanic spirit there was as yet no inwardness involving unity, but only an inwardness of an indifferent, superficial "being by itself." Thus that constitution was without firm bond . . . for in fact no constitution was as yet possible.

This leads us to the second reaction, that of individuals against the authority of the law. The capacity of appreciating legal order and the common weal is altogether absent, has no vital existence among the peoples themselves. The duties of every free citizen, the authority of the judge to give judicial decisions, that of the count to hold his court, and interest in the laws as such, show themselves as weals as soon as the strong hand from above ceases to hold the reins. The brilliant administration of Charlemagne had vanished without leaving a trace and the immediate consequence was the general need of the individuals for protection. A certain need for protection is sure to be felt to some degree in every well-organized state; each citizen knows his rights and also knows that the social state is absolutely necessary for the security of private property. Barbarians do not know this sense of need, they want of protection by others. They look upon it as a limitation of their freedom if their rights must be guaranteed by others. Hence, the impulse toward a firm organization did not exist. Men had to be placed in a defenseless position before they felt the necessity of the organization of a state. The forming of states had to start afresh. The commonwealth as then organized had no validity or firmness at all either in itself or in the minds of the people; and its weakness manifested itself in the fact that it was unable to give protection to its individual members. As observed above, the sense of obligation was not present in the spirit of the Germanic peoples; it had to be created. At the start, the will could be disciplined only regarding the externals of possession. As people experienced the importance of the protection of the state, they were forcibly brought out of their dullness and impelled by necessity to seek union and a social condition. Individuals were therefore obliged to look out for themselves by taking refuge with individuals, and by submitting to the authority of certain powerful men who had made a private possession and personal rule out of that authority which formerly belonged to the commonwealth. . . . This is the constitution of the feudal system. *"Feudum"* is connected with *"fides"*; the fidelity or loyalty implied in this case is a bond established on unjust principles, a relation that does indeed aim at something legitimate, but which has the unjust as its content; for the loyalty of vassals is not an obligation to the commonwealth, but a private one and therefore by this very fact subject to the sway of chance, caprice and violence. General injustice, general lawlessness is transformed into a system of dependence on and obligation to private individuals, so that the mere formal side of the matter, the mere fact of compact, constitutes its sole connection with the principle of right and law. . . .

[Hegel then proceeds to describe the further development of feudalism and sums it up:]

Thus all right and law vanished before particular might; for equality of rights and rational legislation, where the interests of the whole, of the state, are the end, had no existence. The third reaction, noted above, was that of the element

of universality against the real world as split up into particularity. This reaction proceeded upwards from below, from
that isolated possession itself, and was then promoted chiefly
by the Church. A general sense of the nothingness of its con·
dition seized on the world. In that condition of utter isolation,
where only the might of the powerful had any validity, men
could find no repose and Christendom was, so to speak,
agitated by the tremor of an evil conscience. In the eleventh
century, the fear of the approaching final judgment and the
belief in the speedy end of the world spread through all
Europe. This inner anxiety impelled men to the most absurd
actions. Some bestowed the whole of their possessions on the
Church, and passed their lives in continual penance; the
majority dissipated their worldly possessions in riotous debauchery. The Church alone increased its riches through
donations and bequests. About the same time, too, terrible
famines swept people away; human flesh was sold in open
market. During this state of things, lawlessness, brutal lust,
and the most coarse caprice, deceit and cunning were common. Italy, the center of Christendom, presented the most
revolting view. All virtue was alien to these times, and consequently the word *virtue* lost its proper meaning; in common usage it denoted only violence and oppression, sometimes
even rape. The clergy was equally corrupt. Their baliffs and
stewards had made themselves masters of the ecclesiastical
possessions, and ran them quite at their own pleasure, restricting the monks and clergy to a scanty pittance. Monasteries
that refused to accept such stewards were compelled to do so,
the neighboring lords taking the office on themselves or giving
it to their sons. Only bishops and abbots maintained themselves in possession, being able to protect themselves partly
by their own power, partly by means of their retainers, since
these higher clerics were, for the most part, of noble families.
The bishoprics being secular fiefs, their occupants were
bound to the performance of imperial and feudal service. The

investiture of the bishops belonged to the kings, and it was to their interest that these ecclesiastics should be attached to them. Whoever desired a bishopric, therefore, had to make application to the king, and thus a regular trade was carried on in bishoprics and abbacies. Usurers who had loaned money to the king thus received compensation; the worst of men came into possession of spiritual offices. There could be no question that the clergy ought to have been chosen by the religious community, and there were always some persons who had the right of electing them, who were influential; but the king compelled them to yield to his orders. Things were little better as far as the Holy See was concerned. This situation got too awful ... Gregory VII ... sought to protect the independence of the Church in this terrible situation by two measures. First, he enforced the *celibacy of the clergy*. ... The second measure was directed against *simony*, that is to say the selling and arbitrary filling of bishoprics, or even the papacy. ... By these two big measures Gregory VII intended to free the Church of its dependence and its violence. But Gregory made still further demands upon the secular power; all benefices should only be assigned to an incumbent after ordination by his superior, and only the Pope should dispose of the Church's vast possessions. The Church aimed as a divine power to rule the secular, on the abstract principle that the divine is higher than the secular ... whole communities became vassals of the Church. ...

We have then to consider the spiritual element in the Church—the form of its power. The essence of the Christian principles has already been shown; it is the principle of mediation. Man realizes his spiritual essence only when he conquers his natural being. This conquest is possible only on the supposition that the human and the divine nature are essentially one, and that man, so far as he is spirit, also possesses the essentiality and the substantiality that belong to the idea of God. The mediation is conditioned by the consciousness of this unity; to see this unity was given to man in Christ. The main thing is, therefore, that man should lay hold on this consciousness, and that it should be continually awakened in him. This was the design of the Mass: in the host Christ is presented as actually present; the piece of bread consecrated by the priest is the present God, who is thus seen and offered up ever and anon. And it is true that the sacrifice of Christ is an actual and eternal happening, Christ being not a mere sensuous and single, but a completely universal, i.e., divine, individual. But it is wrong to isolate the sensuous aspect, and to have the host adored, even apart from its being taken, and thus not to make the presence of Christ essentially one of spiritual vision. Rightly, therefore, did the Lutheran Reformation particularly attack this dogma. Luther proclaimed the great doctrine that the host had spiritual value and Christ was received only on the condition of faith in him; apart from this, the host, he affirmed, was a mere external thing, possessed of no greater value than any other thing. But the Catholic kneels before the host, and thus the merely outward is made into something holy. The Holy as a mere thing has a character of externality; thus it is capable of being taken possession of by another to my exclusion. It may come into an alien hand, since the process of appropriating it is not one that takes place in spirit, but is conditioned by its quality as an external object, by its quality of thingness. The highest of human blessings is in the hands of others. A distinction arises here between those who possess this blessing and those who have to receive it from others, between the clergy and the laity. The divine is foreign to the laity. This is the absolute schism in which the Church in the Middle Ages was involved: it arose from the recognition of the Holy as something external. The clergy imposed certain conditions to which the laity had to conform if they would be partakers of the Holy. The entire development of doctrine, spiritual insight and the knowledge of divine things, belonged exclusively to the Church. The Church has to ordain and the laity have simply to believe. Obedience is their duty, the obedience of faith, without insight on their part. This condition of things rendered faith a matter of external legislation, and resulted in compulsion and the stake.

As men are thus cut off from the Church, so are they from the Holy in every form. For on the same principle as that by which the clergy are the mediators between man and Christ, as well as God, the layman cannot turn directly to the Divine Being in his prayers, but only through mediators: the saints, who—dead and perfect—conciliate God for him. Thus originated the adoration of the saints, and with it that conglomeration of fables and lies concerning the saints and their lives. The worship of images had for a long time been popular in the East and had, after protracted arguments, been retained. An image, a picture, though sensuous, still appeals rather to the imagination; but the coarser natures of the West desired something more immediate to look at, and thus arose the worship of relics. The consequence was a kind of resurrection of the dead in the medieval period; every pious Christian wished to be in possession of such sacred earthly remains. The chief object of adoration among the saints was the *Virgin Mary*. She is certainly the beautiful image of pure love, a mother's love. But spirit and thought stand higher than even this; and in the worship of this image that of God in spirit was lost, and Christ himself was put to one side. The element of mediation between God and man was thus conceived and held as something external. And thus absolute un-freedom became the established law through the perversion of the principle of freedom. . . . The individual has to confess, is bound to expose all the particulars of his life and conduct to the view of the confessor, and is then informed what to do. . . . Thus the Church took the place of *conscience*: it put men into apron strings like children and told them that man could not be freed from the torments which his sins had merited by any self-improvement, but only by outward actions; actions not of his own good will, but performed by command of the ministers of the Church. They consisted of hearing Mass, doing penance, going through a certain number of prayers, and undertaking pilgrimages, for example, actions which are unspiritual, stupefy the soul, and which are not only mere external ceremonies, but are such as can be even in one's stead performed by others. One could even buy some of the extra good works ascribed to the saints and thus secure salvation earned by them. An utter derangement of all that is recognized as good and moral in the Christian Church was thus produced; only external requirements are insisted upon, and these can be complied with in a merely external way. A condition of absolute un-freedom is injected into the very principle of freedom.

The absolute separation of the spiritual from the secular principle generally is connected with this perversion. There are two divine realms, the intellectual one in the *Gemüt* and knowledge, and the ethical one whose material and ground is secular existence. It is science alone which can comprehend the kingdom of God and the time has worked toward realizing this unity. But piety as such has nothing to do with the secular; it may appear in the way of charity, but this is not yet legally ethical, is not yet freedom. Piety is outside of history, and has no history; for history is rather the realm of spirit present to itself in its subjective freedom as the ethical realm of the state. In the Middle Ages, the realization of the Divine in actual life was wanting; the contradiction was not yet harmonized. The ethical was represented as worthless, and that in its three most essential particulars.

One aspect of ethics is that connected with love, with the emotions in the marital relation. It need not say that celibacy is contrary to nature, but that it is contrary to ethics. Marriage was indeed reckoned among the sacraments by the Church; but nonetheless, it was degraded inasmuch as celibacy was reckoned as the more holy state. A second aspect of ethics is presented in activity, in the work a man has to perform for his subsistence. His honor consists in his depending entirely on his industry, conduct and intelligence for the supply of his wants. On the contrary in the Middle Ages, poverty, laziness and inactivity were regarded as nobler, and the un-ethical thus was consecrated as holy. A third aspect of ethics is that *obedience* be rendered to the ethical and the rational as an obedience to laws which I know to be right; that it be not that blind and unconditional compliance which does not know what it is doing and whose action is a mere groping about without consciousness or knowledge. But it was exactly this latter kind of obedience that passed for the most pleasing to God. Thus the obedience of un-freedom, imposed by the arbitrary will of the Church, was put above the true obedience of freedom.

In this way the three vows of chastity, poverty and obedi-ence turned out the very opposite of what they ought to be, and in them all, social morality was degraded. The Church was no longer a spiritual (*geistige*) power, but an ecclesiastical (*geistliche*) one; and the secular world maintained to it an unspiritual, automatic and uncomprehending relation. As the consequence of this we see everywhere vice, unscrupulousness, shamelessness, and a distracted state of things of which the entire history of the period offers a detailed picture.

According to the above, the Church of the Middle Ages exhibits itself as a manifold self-contradiction. For subjective spirit, although testifying of the absolute, is at the same time a finite spirit, existing as intelligence and will. Its finiteness begins in its being split by this distinction; here begins at once the contradiction and the self-alienation; for the intelli-gence and will are not permeated by the truth, which is for them something given. . . .

The second form of the contradiction has to do with the relation within the Church itself The true spirit exists in man, is *his* spirit; the individual achieves for himself the certainty of this identity with the absolute in the religious worship or cult, the Church occupying merely the position of a teacher and a director of this cult. But here in the medieval church, on the contrary, the ecclesiastical profession, like the Brahmins in India, are in possession of the truth, not indeed by birth, but by virtue of knowledge, doctrine and practice, but with the further proviso that these alone are not sufficient, and that only an external form, an unspiritual title, constitutes the actual possession of the truth. This outward form is ordination, whose nature is such that the consecration imparted inheres essentially like a sensuous quality to the individual whatever the character of his soul, be he irreligious, immoral or absolutely ignorant. The third kind of contradiction is involved in the Church's acquisition of possessions and an enormous property, a state of things which is none other than a lie since, in truth, the Church despises or ought to despise riches.

The state of the Middle Ages is, as we saw, similarly involved in contradictions. We spoke above of an imperial rule recognized as assisting the Church and constituting its secular arm. But the power thus acknowledged contains the contradiction that this imperial rule is an empty honor, not serious in the eyes of the emperor himself, or of those who wish to make him the instrument of their ambitious aims. Passion and physical force exist by themselves and are not subject to any control by that merely abstract image. Secondly, the bond of union which holds the medieval state together and which we call loyalty is left to the arbitrary choice of men's feeling (*Gemüt*), which recognizes no objective duties. Consequently, this loyalty is the most disloyal. German probity in the Middle Ages has become proverbial; but examined more closely in history, we find a veritable Carthaginian or Greek loyalty; for the princes and vassals of the emperor are loyal and dependable only for their selfish ends, individual advantages and

passions, but utterly disloyal to the empire and the emperor
. . . the state is not organized as an ethical whole. A third
contradiction presents itself within the individuals exhibiting,
on one side, piety and the most beautiful and intense devotion, and on the other hand, a barbarous intelligence and will.
We find an acquaintance with general truth and yet the
most uncultured, the rudest ideas of the secular and the
spiritual: a brutal show of passion along with a Christian
sanctity which renounces all that is worldly and devotes itself
entirely to holiness. So self-contradictory, so deceptive is this
medieval period, and it is a fad of our time to make its
excellence a slogan. Primitive barbarism, rudeness of manners
and childish fancy are not revolting, but simply regrettable.
But the highest purity of soul defiled by the most horrible
barbarity; the known truth degraded to a mere tool by lies
and self-seeking; that which is most irrational, coarse and
vile, justified and strengthened by the religious—this is the
most disgusting and revolting spectacle that was ever witnessed, and which only philosophy can comprehend and
justify. For such a contradiction must arise in man's consciousness of the Holy while this consciousness still remains
primitive and immediate. The profounder the truth with
which spirit comes into an implicit relation, while it has
not yet become aware of its own presence in that profound
truth, so much the more alien is it to itself in this its unknown
form; but only as the result of this alienation does it attain
its true reconciliation.

[After summing up the argument, and remarking upon the growth
of cities, Hegel continues:]

The principle of free property, however, began to develop
from the protective relation of feudal protection; that is, freedom originated from un-freedom. The feudal lords and barons
enjoyed, properly speaking, no free or absolute property, any
more than their subjects; they had great power over the latter,

but at the same time they were also the vassals of princes higher and mightier than themselves and to whom they were under obligations which, to be sure, they only fulfilled when compelled to do so. The ancient Germanics had known of none other than free property; but this principle had been perverted to its complete opposite, and it is now for the first time in the later Middle Ages that we notice a few feeble beginnings of a reviving sense of freedom. Individuals brought into closer relation by the soil which they cultivated formed among themselves a kind of union or confederation.

[Hegel then describes the development of guilds, and freer institutions in the cities, as the other power opposing the growing dynastic power. There follows a section on the Crusades, which he views primarily as a religious, yet as a forlorn enterprise. "Christendom found the empty grave, and not the linking of the worldly and the eternal, and hence it lost the Holy Land." After this disappointment, the searching spirit turned to the founding of knightly and monastic orders. With this he links the development of science and of abstract thought.]

Transition from Feudalism to Monarchy

The tendencies in the direction of the general were partly of a subjective, partly of a theoretical, order. But we must now give particular attention to the practical political movements in the state. The advance which that period witnessed presents a "negative" aspect in so far as it involves the termination of subjective caprice and the fragmentation of power. Its affirmative aspect is the emergence of a supreme authority which is to all a state power properly so called, whose subjects enjoy an equality of rights, and in which the particular will is subordinated to the substantial end, the common interest. This is the progress from feudalism to *monarchy*. The principle of feudal rule is the external force of individuals, of princes and liege lords; it is a force destitute of a principle

of right and law. The monarchial principle also implies a
supreme authority, but it is an authority over persons possessing no independent power to exercise their arbitrary will.
Arbitrary will is no longer opposed to arbitrary will, for the
supreme power in a monarchy is essentially the power of the
state directed toward the substantial legal end. Feudal rule is
a polyarchy: there are many lords and servants. In a monarchy, on the contrary, there is one lord and no servant, for
servitude is abrogated by it and in it right and law are valid.
Monarchy is the source of real freedom. Thus in monarchy
the arbitrary will of individuals is suppressed and a commonwealth of rule is established. It seems doubtful whether the
desire for law, or arbitrary will, is the impelling motive in
the suppression of the fragmented powers, as well as in the
resistance to that suppression. Resistance to royal authority is
called liberty, and is praised as legitimate and noble when the
idea of arbitrary will is associated with that authority. But it
is by the arbitrary will of an individual that a commonwealth
is formed; and comparing this state of things with that in
which every point is a center of arbitrary violence, we find
a much smaller number of points suffering such violence. The
great extent of such a realm necessitates general arrangements
for the purpose of cohesion, and those who govern in accordance with those arrangements are at the same time, in virtue
of their office itself, essentially obedient to the state. Vassals
become officials of the state whose duty it is to execute the laws
by which the state is ordered. But since this monarchy is
developed from feudalism, it bears at first the stamp of the
system from which it sprang. Individuals . . . become members of estates and corporations; the vassals are powerful only
by sticking together as an estate; facing them the cities constitute a power in the commonwealth. Thus the power of the
ruler can no longer be merely arbitrary. The consent of the
estates and the corporations is essential. If the prince wishes

to have that consent, he must will what is just and reasonable.

We now see a development of states, while feudal rule knows no states. The transition from feudalism to monarchy occurs in three ways:

1. Sometimes the lord gains mastery over his independent vassals by subjugating their particular power, thus making himself sole ruler.

2. Sometimes the princes free themselves from the feudal relation altogether and become the territorial rulers of their own states.

3. Sometimes the lord unites in a more peaceful way the particular lordships with his own, and thus becomes ruler of the whole.

These processes do not indeed present themselves in history in that pure and abstract form in which they are presented here. We often find more than one mode appearing together; but one or the other always predominates. The cardinal consideration is that the basis and essential condition of this formation of states is to be looked for in the *particular nations* in which it had its birth. Europe is composed of particular nations, each constituting a unity in its very nature, and having the absolute tendency to form a state. All did not succeed in attaining this political unity. . . .

[Here follows a brief discussion of each of the main nations, as they emerged.]

Humanity has now attained the consciousness of a real reconciliation of spirit within itself, and a good conscience in regard to actuality, to secular existence. The human spirit has come to stand on its own feet. There is no revolt against the divine in this new-won sense of self, but rather a manifestation of that better subjectivity which recognizes the divine in its own being, which is permeated by what is genuine, and which directs its activities to general objects, both of rationality and beauty.

Art and Science at the End of the Middle Ages

The heaven of the spirit is clearing for humankind. With that tranquil settling down of the world into the political order of the state which we have reviewed, there was joined a wider, a more concrete progress of the spirit to a nobler humanness. The grave, the dead of the spirit, and the other-worldly, were given up. The principle . . .* which drove the world into the Crusades now rather developed in the secular sphere by itself. . . . The Church, however, remained, and retained the principle in question, but not externally and in its immediacy; it was transfigured by art. Art gives spirit and soul the merely external object of the senses by giving it a form which expresses soul, feeling, spirit. Thus a devotional exercise confronts not merely something for the senses, and is pious toward a mere thing, but toward its higher aspect, that expressive form with which spirit has invested it. It is one thing for the mind to have before it a mere thing, such as the host in itself, or a piece of stone, wood, or a bad picture. It is quite another thing for it to contemplate a painting, full of spirit, or a beautiful work of sculpture, wherein soul holds converse with soul, and spirit with spirit. In the former case, spirit is outside itself, bound to something utterly alien to it, the sensuous, the non-spiritual. In the latter, the sensuous object is a beautiful one, and the spiritual form gives it a soul, being true within itself. But, on the other hand, since religion is supposed to be dependence upon some other external being, a something, that kind of religion does not find its satisfaction in being brought into relation to the beautiful: the worst, ugliest, most ordinary representations will suit its purposes equally well, perhaps better. Accordingly real master-pieces such as Raphael's Madonnas do not enjoy the amount of veneration or elicit the amount of offerings which inferior

---

* Hegel says: "Das Prinzip des Dieses"—the meaning being quite obscure. See below, the excerpt of the *Logic,* for elucidation.—Ed.

images receive which are more usually visited and are made the object of greater devotion and generosity. Piety passes by the former for the very reason that were it to linger it would feel an inward stimulus and attraction; but such appeals are something alien, where all that is wanted is a sense of self-less bondage and dependent dullness. Thus art in its very nature transcended the principle of the Church. But as art offers only sensuous representations, it is at first regarded as a harmless and indifferent matter. The Church, therefore, continued to go along with art but broke with the free spirit in which art had originated when this free spirit advanced to thought and science.

For art received a further support and experienced an elevating influence as a result of the study of antiquity; through such study the West became acquainted with the true and eternal aspects of man's activities. . . .

[After some further general remarks, including a brief discussion of the invention of printing, Hegel concludes:]

These three events, the so-called revival of learning, the flourishing of the fine arts, and the discovery of America and of the passage to India by the Cape, may be compared with that golden dawn which after long storms betokens the return of a bright and glorious day. This day is the day of a general culture, which breaks on the world after the long, eventful and terrible night of the Middle Ages, a day which is distinguished by science, art and inventive impulse, that is, by the highest and noblest which the human spirit, freed by Christianity and emancipated by the Church, presents as its eternal and veritable content.

Modern Times

We have now arrived at the third period of the Germanic world, and thus enter upon the period of spirit conscious that it is free, inasmuch as it wills the true, the eternal, that which is in and for itself universal.

In this third period, also, three divisions may be made. First we have to consider the Reformation, the all-enlightening sun following on that golden dawn which we observed at the end of the medieval period; next, the unfolding of the post-Reformation state of things; and lastly, the modern times, dating from the end of the last century.

The Reformation

The Reformation resulted from the corruption of the Church. That corruption was not an accidental phenomenon; it was not the mere abuse of power and dominion. A corrupt state of things is very frequently represented as an abuse; it is taken for granted that the foundation was good, the system, the institution itself, faultless, but that the passion, the subjective interest, in short the arbitrary will of men, has made use of that which in itself was good to further its own selfish ends, and that all that is required is to remove these contingencies. On this showing, the case can be saved, and the evil that disfigures it appears as something foreign. But when accidental abuse of a good thing really occurs, it is limited to particulars. A great and general corruption affecting a body of such large and comprehensive scope as a church is quite another thing.

The corruption of the Church developed from within itself (see above pp. 105–110). Henceforth it falls behind the world spirit; it has gone further, for it has become capable of recognizing the sensuous as sensuous, the merely outward as the merely outward. It had learned to work within the finite in a finite way, and in this very activity to maintain an independent and confident position as a rightful valid subjectivity.

There is superstition in this ecclesiastical piety; the mind is fettered to a sensuous object, a mere ordinary thing in its most varied forms. This was slavish deference to authority, for the spirit, in this case having renounced its proper nature in its most essential quality, is un-free, and is held in bondage. This constituted a belief in miracles of the most absurd and childish sort; for the divine was supposed to manifest itself in a quite disconnected and finite way for purely finite and particular purposes. Lastly, lust of power, riotous debauchery, all forms of barbarous and vulgar corruption, hypocrisy and deception manifested themselves in the Church, for in fact the sensuous in it is not subjugated and trained by the mind; it has become free, but only in a rough and barbarous way. On the other hand the virtue of the Church was but abstractly negative, since it was negative only in opposition to sensuous appetite. This virtue does not know how to be ethical in sensuous existence; it merely flees from, renounces, but does not live in actual reality.

These contrasts within the Church—barbarous vice and lust on the one hand, and an all-sacrificing elevation of soul on the other—became still wider in consequence of the energetic position which man is sensible of occupying in his subjective power over outward and material things in the natural world, in which he feels himself free, so gaining for himself an absolute right. The Church, whose office it was to save souls from damnation, made this salvation itself a mere external means, and then became degraded so far as to perform this office in a merely external fashion. The remission of sins, the highest satisfaction which the soul craves, the certainty of its peace with God, that which concerns man's deepest and most inmost nature, is offered to man in the most grossly superficial and easy-going fashion, to be purchased for mere money. At the same time, it was done for purely material purposes: display. One of the objects of this sale was indeed the building of St. Peter's, the most marvelous building of Christianity [erected] in the metropolis of religion. But, as that paragon of works of art, the Athene and her temple-citadel at Athens, was built with the money of the allies and resulted in the loss of both allies and power, so the completion of this Church of St. Peter and Michelangelo's *Last Judgment* in the Sistine Chapel were the last judgment and ruin of this proud spiritual edifice.

The ancient and ever-preserved inwardness of the German people had to effect this revolution out of the simple, modest heart. While the rest of the world was sailing to India, to America, to gain wealth and acquire a secular dominion to encompass the globe, and on which the sun shall never set, we find a simple monk looking for that specific embodiment of deity which Christendom had formerly sought in an earthly grave of stone, in the deeper grave of absolute ideality of all that is sensuous and external, and finding it in the spirit and the heart—the heart, which, wounded immeasurably by the offer of the most external to satisfy the inmost and deepest cravings, now detects the perversion of the absolute relation of truth in its various features, pursues it and destroys it. Luther's simple doctrine is that this specific embodiment of deity, infinite subjectivity, that is true spirituality, Christ, is in no way present and actual in an outward form. It is obtained in its essential spiritual form only in being reconciled to God, in *faith* and *spiritual consummation*. These two terms express everything. It is not the consciousness of a sensuous thing as God, nor even of something merely conceived, and which is not actual or present, but of a reality that is not sensuous. This elimination of the external reconstructs all the doctrines and reforms all the superstition into which the Church consistently wandered off. This change especially affects the doctrine of works. Works include what may be performed in any way, not necessarily in faith, in one's own soul, but as mere external observances prescribed by authority. Faith is by no means merely a certainty respecting mere finite things, a certainty which belongs only to a finite subject, such, for example, as the belief that such or such a person existed and said this or that, or that the children of Israel passed dryshod through the Red Sea, or that the trumpets before the walls of Jericho worked like our cannons. If nothing of all this had been related to us, our knowledge of God would be none the less complete. In fact it is not a belief in something absent, past and gone, but the subjective certainty of the eternal, of absolute truth, the truth of God. The Lutheran Church affirms that the Holy Spirit alone produces this certainty. The individual attains this certainty not in virtue of his particular but of his essential being. The Lutheran doctrine is therefore altogether the Catholic doctrine, with the exception of all that flows from that element of externality, in so far as the Catholic Church asserts this external aspect. Luther therefore could not do otherwise than refuse to yield an iota in regard to that doctrine of the Eucharist in which the whole question is concentrated. He could not concede to the "reformed" church that Christ is a mere memory, a reminiscence. Thus he agreed with the Catholic Church, that Christ is actually present, but in faith, in the spirit. He maintained that the spirit of Christ really fills the human heart, that Christ therefore is not to be regarded as a merely historical person, but that man has an *immediate relation to him in spirit*.

Since, then, the individual knows that he is filled with the divine spirit, all the relations of externality are eliminated. There is no longer a distinction between priests and laymen. We no longer find one class in possession of the substance of the truth, as of all the spiritual and temporal treasures of the Church. The heart, the feeling spirituality of man can and ought to come into possession of the truth; and this subjectivity is the common property of all mankind. Each man has to accomplish the work of reconciliation in his own soul. The subjective spirit has to receive the spirit of truth into itself and give it a dwelling place there. Thus that absolute

THE PHILOSOPHY OF HISTORY   121

intense inwardness of the soul which pertains to religion itself
and freedom in the Church are both secured. Subjectivity now
appropriates the objective content of Christianity, that is, the
doctrine of the Church. In the Lutheran Church the subjectivity and the certainty of the individual are just as necessary
as the objectivity of the truth. Truth with Lutherans is not a
prepared thing; the individual himself must become truthful,
surrendering his particular being in exchange for the substantial truth, and making that truth his own. Thus the subjective spirit becomes free in (and through) the truth, negates
its particularity and comes to itself in realizing its truth.
Thus Christian freedom became actually real. If subjectivity
be placed in feeling only, without that objective side, we have
the standpoint of the merely natural will.*

In this proclamation of these principles is unfurled the new,
the last banner round which the peoples rally, the flag of the
free spirit, which is by itself in the truth, and only so [find-
ing its life in the truth, and only enjoying independence in
it]. This is the banner under which we serve, and which we
bear. Time, since that epoch, has had no other work to do
than to shape the world in accordance with this principle;
thus the reconciliation and the truth become objective in
form. Culture is essentially concerned with form. The work
of culture is the production of the form of universality, which
is none other than thought. Consequently law, property,
ethics, government, constitutions, and the like, must be worked
out in a general way in order that they may accord with the
idea of free will and be rational. Thus only can the spirit
of truth manifest itself in subjective will, in the particular
activities of the will. Objective spirit can appear when the
intensity of the subjective free spirit arrives at the form of
universality. This is the sense in which we must understand

* This aside of Hegel's is, like a number of similar comments, made
against the "subjective" religiosity, bent on feeling, as expounded by
Jacobi and Schleiermacher.—Ed.

the state to be based on religion. States and laws are nothing else than religion manifesting itself in the relations of the actual world.

This is the essence of the Reformation: man is in his very nature destined to be free.

At its commencement the Reformation concerned itself only with particular aspects of the corruption of the Catholic Church. Luther wished to act in union with the whole Catholic world and demanded general councils. His theses found supporters in every country. In answer, Luther and the Protestants are reproached for exaggerating, even misrepresenting, the corruption of the Church in their descriptions. All one needs to do is to consult the statements of the Catholics themselves, bearing upon this point, and particularly the official proceedings of the ecclesiastical councils. But Luther's challenge, which was at first limited to particular points, was soon extended to the doctrines of the Church. Leaving individuals, he attacked institutions at large—the life in the monasteries, the secular rule of the bishops, etc. His writings challenged not merely specific dicta of the Pope and the councils, but the very way of making such decisions; finally, the authority of the Church itself. Luther rejected that authority and set up in its stead the Bible and the testimony of the human spirit. And it is a fact of the greatest importance that the Bible became the basis of the Christian church. Thenceforth each individual should instruct himself from it and direct his conscience in accordance with it. This is the vast change in the principle by which man's religious life is guided. The entire tradition and the whole fabric of the Church becomes problematical and the principle of its authority is subverted. Luther's translation of the Bible has been of incalculable value to the German people. It has given them a book for all the people such as no nation in the Catholic world has; for though they have a vast number of prayer-books, they have no basic text for popular instruction.

In spite of this, one has argued in modern times whether it is judicious to place the Bible in the hands of the people. Yet the few disadvantages thus entailed are far more than counterbalanced by the enormous benefits. Casual narratives which might be offensive to the heart and understanding are readily recognized for what they are by the religious sense, which, holding fast to the substantial truth, easily vanquishes any such difficulties. . . .

The denial of the authority of the Church necessarily led to a separation. The Council of Trent fixed once more the principles of the Catholic Church. After this Council there could be no question of reuniting the church. Leibnitz later discussed the question of the reunification of the churches with Bishop Bossuet; the Council of Trent remained the insurmountable obstacle. The churches became hostile parties, for a striking difference manifested itself even in respect to secular arrangements. In the non-Catholic countries, monasteries and episcopacies were suspended and the right of propriety was not recognized. Education was reorganized, the fasts and holy days were abolished. Thus there was a secular reform, in regard to the external state of things. A rebellion occurred against the secular authorities in many places. In Münster the Anabaptists expelled the bishop and established a government of their own, and the peasant masses arose to emancipate themselves from the burden weighing upon them. But the world was not yet ripe for a political transformation as a consequence of ecclesiastical reformation.

The Catholic was thus essentially influenced by the Reformation. The reins of discipline were drawn tighter and the greatest occasions of scandal, the most crying abuses were abated. Much of the intellectual life that lay outside its sphere, but with which it had previously maintained friendly relations, it now repudiated. The Church came to a dead stop, "hitherto and no further!" It severed itself from advancing science, from philosophy and humanistic literature, and an occasion soon offered itself of declaring its hostility to scientific pursuits. The celebrated Copernicus had discovered that the earth and the planets revolve around the sun, but the Church declared against this forward step. Galileo, who had explained in the form of a dialogue the evidence for and against the Copernican theory (declaring, indeed, himself in favor of it), was forced to ask forgiveness for this crime on his knees. Greek literature was not made the basis of culture; education was intrusted to the Jesuits. Thus the spirit of the Catholic world in general fell behind the spirit of the age.

Here an important question must be answered: why was the Reformation limited to *certain nations,* and why did it not permeate the whole Catholic world? The Reformation originated in Germany and struck root only in the purely Germanic nations. Outside of Germany itself, it established itself in Scandinavia and England. But the Romanic and Slavic nations kept decidedly aloof from it. Even Southern Germany has only partially adopted the Reformation; the general situation there was a mixed one. In Swabia, Franconia and the Rhine region there were many monasteries and bishoprics, and many free imperial towns, and the reception or rejection of the Reformation very much depended on the influences which these ecclesiastical and civil bodies exercised. We have already noted that the Reformation was a change influencing the political life of the age. Furthermore, authority is much more important than people are inclined to believe. There are certain premises which men are in the habit of accepting on the strength of authority, and it was thus mere authority which often decided for or against the adoption of the Reformation. In Austria, Bavaria and Bohemia the Reformation had already made great progress; and though it is commonly said that when truth has once entered men's souls, it cannot be rooted out again, it was nonetheless stifled in the countries in question, by force of arms, by stratagem, or by persuasion.

The Slavic nations were agricultural. This condition of life brings with it the relation of lord and servant. The work of nature predominates in agriculture; human industry and subjective activity are on the whole less brought into play in such work. The Slavic peoples did not therefore arrive so quickly or readily as other nations at the fundamental sense of subjective self, at the consciousness of a general interest, nor at political power (state); hence they could not participate in the emerging freedom.

But neither did the Reformation permeate the Romanic nations: Italy, Spain, Portugal, and in part France. Physical force perhaps did much to repress it; yet this alone would not be sufficient to explain the fact, for when the spirit of a nation demands anything no force can subdue it. Nor can it be said that these nations were lacking in culture; on the contrary, they were rather in advance of the Germans in this respect. It was rather owing to the fundamental character of these nations that they did not adopt the Reformation. But what is this peculiarity of character which was such a hindrance to the freedom of spirit? The pure, tender inwardness of the Germanic nations was the proper soil for the emancipation of spirit. The Romanic nations, on the contrary, have maintained in the very depth of their soul, in their spiritual consciousness, the disunion and estrangement; they are a product of the fusion of Roman and Germanic blood, and still retain this heterogeneous heritage. The German cannot deny that the French, the Italians and the Spaniards possess a more finite character, that they pursue a settled end (even though it may have a fixed idea for its object) with perfectly clear consciousness and the greatest attention, that they carry out a plan with great circumspection and that they exhibit the greatest determination in regard to specific objects. The French call the Germans "entiers," entire, that is, stubborn; they are also strangers to the whimsical originality of the English. The Englishman has his sense of freedom in relation to the specific; he does not trouble himself about the intellect, but on the contrary feels himself so much the more free, the more what he does or may do is contrary to reason, i.e., to general principles. But among the Romanic peoples we immediately encounter that internal division, that holding fast to an abstract principle, and [as the counterpart of this] an absence of the totality of spirit and sentiment which we call *Gemüt* (feeling mind):* there is none of that meditation of the spirit about itself. In their inmost beings these people may be said to be alienated from themselves. The inner life is a region whose depth they do not appreciate, for it is absorbed in particular interests, and the infinity of the spirit is not there. Their inmost being is not their own. They leave it "over there" and are glad to have its concerns settled for them by another. That other to which they leave it is the Church. They have indeed something to do with it themselves; but since that which they have to do is not self-originated and self-prescribed, not their very own, they attend to it in a superficial way. *"Eh, bien,"* said Napoleon, "We shall go to Mass again, and my comrades will say: 'That is the word of the command!'" This is the leading feature in the character of these nations—the separation of the religious from the secular interest, as the special sense of self. The ground of this disunion lies in their inmost soul, which has lost that collectedness, its profoundest unity. Catholicism does not claim the essential direction of the secular; religion remains an indifferent matter on the one side, while the other side of life is different from it, and by itself. Cultivated Frenchmen therefore feel an antipathy to Protestantism because it seems to them something pedantic, sad, and meanly moral. It requires that spirit and thought should be directly involved with religion. In attending Mass and other ceremonies, on the contrary, it is not necessary to think; one has an imposing sensuous spectacle before one's eyes, during which one reiterates words without much attention, while yet the necessary is being done.

---

* See above p. 95.

We spoke above of the relation of the new church to secular life, and now we have only to give further detail. The development and advance of spirit from the time of the Reformation onward consists in this, that spirit, having now gained the consciousness of its freedom, through the process of mediation which takes place between man and God . . . now takes it up and follows it out in shaping the secular existence. Through this reconciliation man becomes conscious that the secular is capable of embodying the truth, whereas it had been formerly regarded as an evil only, as incapable of good, which remained other-worldly. It is now known that the ethic and law in the state are also divine and commanded by God, and that content-wise there is nothing higher or more sacred. It follows that marriage is no longer deemed less holy than celibacy. Luther took a wife to show that he respected marriage, not fearing the calumnies to which he exposed himself by such a step. It was his duty to do so, as it was also his to eat meat on Fridays in order to prove that such things are permitted and right, in opposition to the imagined superior value of abstinence. Man, through the family, enters the community, as he does the relation of interdependence in society. This is an ethical union. The monks, on the other hand, separated as they were from the ethical society, formed as it were the standing army of the Pope, like the Janizaries who formed the basis of Turkish power. The marriage of the priests lets the outward distinction between laity and clergy disappear.

Unemployment no longer was seen as something saintly; it was acknowledged to be better to make oneself independent by activity, intelligence and industry. It is considered more honest that he who has money should spend it even on un-urgent needs than that he should give it away to idlers and beggars; for he gives it to an equal number of persons, and these must at any rate have worked for it. Industry, crafts and trades now have become ethical, and the obstacles which the Church had erected to their recognition have vanished. For the Church had pronounced it a sin to lend money on interest: but the necessity of doing so led to the opposite, the direct violation of her injunctions. The Lombards and particularly the house of Medici, advanced money to princes in every part of Europe.

The third aspect of sanctity in the Catholic Church, blind obedience, was also suspended. Obedience to the laws of the state, the reason in will and action, was made the principle of human conduct.* In this obedience man is free, for the particular obeys the general. Man himself has a conscience; therefore he is free to obey. This involves the possibility of a development of reason and freedom, and of their introduction into human relations; and what is reason, now also are the divine commands. The rational no longer meets with objections from the religious conscience; it can develop steadily in its own sphere, without having to resort to force against an adverse power.

This reconciliation of church and state occurred immediately. We have, as yet, no reconstruction of the state, of the system of law, and the like, for thought must first discover the essential principles of right. The laws of freedom had first to be developed into a system of what is right in and by itself. The spirit does not appear in such perfection right away; the Reformation limits itself at first to direct and simple changes, such as the secularization of monasteries, bishoprics, etc. The reconciliation between God and the world was at first developed in an abstract form, and was not yet expanded into a system of an ethical world.

In the first instance this reconciliation must take place in the individual soul, must be realized by conscious sentiment; the individual must gain the assurance that the spirit dwells within him, that, in the language of the Church, a brokenness of heart has been experienced, and that divine grace has en-

---

* This point is well illustrated by the legislation on supremacy in England in the reign of Henry VIII and Elizabeth I.

tered into the heart. By nature man is not what he ought to be; only through a transforming process does he arrive at truth. This, then, is the general and speculative aspect of the matter, that the human heart is not what it should be. It has been asked of the individual that he become conscious of what he is in himself. Dogmatism insisted upon man's knowing that he is evil. But the individual is evil only when the natural manifests itself in mere sensual desire, when an unrighteous will exists untrained, untamed, violent. And yet it is asked that such a person know that he is depraved, and that the good spirit dwells in him. He thus is required to have and to experience in a direct way what is, in a speculative way, by itself. Reconciliation having, then, assumed this abstract form, men tormented themselves with a view to force upon their souls the consciousness of their sinfulness and to know themselves as evil. The most simple souls, the most innocent natures followed broodingly the most secret workings of the heart, in order to observe them. With this duty was linked the opposite one that man should know that the good spirit dwells in him, that divine grace has entered his soul.

The important distinction between the knowledge of abstract truth and the knowledge of what has actual existence was neglected. Men became the victims of a tormenting uncertainty as to whether the good spirit has an abode in man, and it was deemed indispensable that the entire process of spiritual transformation should become perceptible to the individual himself. An echo of these torments may still be traced in many of the chorals of that time; the Psalms of David which exhibit a similar character were at that time introduced as church hymns. Protestantism took this turn of pedantic pondering and was for a long time characterized by a self-tormenting disposition and spiritual wretchedness. This has at present induced many people to enter the Catholic Church, that they might exchange this inward uncertainty for a formal broad certainty based on the imposing totality of the Church. Yet, into the Catholic Church too there entered some elaborate reflection upon the character of human actions The Jesuits pondered the first beginnings of volition as elaborately as the Protestant; but they had a casuistry which enabled them to discover a good reason for everything, and so get rid of evil, i.e., the burden of guilt.

Another remarkable phenomenon was connected with this, common to the Catholic and the Protestant world. The human mind was driven into the inward, the abstract, and the religious element was regarded as different from the secular. That lively consciousness of his subjective life and of the inward origin of his will which had been awakened in man brought with it the belief in evil as a vast power in the secular world. This belief presents a parallelism with the view in which the sale of indulgences originated. Just as eternal salvation could be bought by money, it was now believed that by paying the price of one's salvation by a compact with the devil the riches of the world and the unlimited gratification of desires and passions could be secured. Thus arose that famous legend of Faust, who, in disgust at the unsatisfying character of theoretical science, is said to have plunged into the world and purchased all its glory at the expense of his salvation. Faust, if one may trust the poet, had in exchange the enjoyment of all that the world could give. But those poor women who were called witches were reputed to get nothing more by the bargain than the gratification of a petty revenge by making the neighbor's cow go dry or by making a child get sick. But in dealing out punishment it was not the magnitude of the injury, the loss of milk or the sickness of child, that was considered; it was the abstract power of evil in them which was persecuted. The belief in this abstract, special power whose dominion is the world, in the devil and his devices, occasioned an incalculable number of trials for witchcraft both in Catholic and Protestant countries. It was impossible to prove the guilt of the accused. They were only suspected. It was therefore only an immediate conviction on which this fury against the evil was based. One felt indeed compelled to have recourse to proofs, but the basis of these judicial processes was simply the belief that certain individuals were possessed by the power of evil. This delusion raged among the nations in the sixteenth century with the fury of a pestilence. The main impulse was suspicion. The principle of suspicion assumed a comparable terrible form under the Roman Emperors, and under Robespierre's reign of terror, when mere conviction was punished. . . .

Influence of the Reformation on Political Development

In tracing the course of the political development of the period, we observe in the first place the consolidation of the monarchy, and the monarch invested with the authority of the state. We have earlier the incipient stage in the rise of royal power, and the beginning unity of the states of Europe. The entire body of private obligations and rights which had been handed down from the Middle Ages still retained validity. Infinitely important is this form of private rights, which the constituents of the state's power have assumed. At their apex we find something very positive—the exclusive right of one family to the possession of the throne, and the hereditary succession of sovereigns further restricted by the law of primogeniture. This gives the state an immovable center. The fact that Germany was an elective empire prevented its being consolidated into one state. Poland has vanished from the family of independent states for the same reason. The state must have a final decisive will: and if an individual is to be the final deciding power, he must be determined in a direct and natural way, not by election, wisdom, etc. Even among the free Greeks the oracle was the external power which decided their policy on critical occasions. Here birth was the oracle, something independent of any arbitrary will. But the circumstance that the highest position in a monarchy is assigned to a family seems to indicate that the dominion is the private property of the family. As such dominion would seem to be divisible, and since the idea of the division of power is opposed to the principle of the state, the rights of the monarch and his family needed to be more strictly defined. Domains do not belong alone to the individual ruler, but are assigned to the dynastic family as a trust. The estates of the realm possess a control; for they have to guard the unity of the body politic. The royal power thus no longer denotes a kind of private property, private possession of estates, demesnes, jurisdiction, etc. It has become a property of the state, a function pertaining to the state.

Equally important, and connected with that just noted, is the transformation into state property of the executive powers, functions, duties and rights, which naturally belong to the state, but which had become private property and private contracts and obligations. The rights of seigneurs and barons were annulled, and they were obliged to content themselves with official positions in the state. This transformation of the rights of vassals into official functions took place in different ways in the several kingdoms. In France the great barons, who were governors of the provinces, who could claim such offices as matters of right, and who, like the Turkish Pashas, maintained with the revenues from such offices a body of troops which they might bring into the field against the king at any moment, were reduced to a position of mere landed proprietors or court nobility. Their governorships became offices held under the government. The nobility were employed as officers, generals in an army belonging to the state. Because of this, the rise of standing armies is so important. For these armies supply the monarchy with an independent force and are as necessary for the security of the central authority against the rebellion of the subject individuals as for the defense of the state against foreign enemies. Fiscal organization indeed had not as yet assumed a systematic character, the revenue being derived from customs, taxes and tolls in countless variety, besides the subsidies and contributions paid by the estates of the realm. In

return for these payments the right of presenting a statement
of grievances was conceded to them.

[Here follows a similar discussion of Spain.]

It would lead us too far to pursue in detail the process of the
suppression of the aristocracy in the several states of Europe.
The main purpose of this process was, as already stated, the
curtailment of the private rights of the feudal nobility and the
transformation of their seigneurial authority into an official
position in connection with the state. This change was in the
interest of both the king and the people. The powerful barons
seemed to constitute an intermediate body charged with the
defense of liberty; but, properly speaking, it was only their
own privileges which they maintained against the royal power
on the one hand and the citizens on the other. The barons of
England won Magna Carta from the king, but the citizens
gained nothing from it; on the contrary, they remained in
their former position. Polish liberty, too, meant nothing more
than the freedom of the barons in contraposition to the king,
the nation being reduced to a state of absolute subordination.
When liberty is mentioned, we must always be careful to
observe whether it is not really private interests which are
being discussed. For although the nobility were deprived of
their sovereign power, the people were still oppressed in consequence of their absolute dependence, their serfdom, and subjection to aristocratic jurisdiction. They were partly declared
utterly incapable of possessing property, partly subjected to a
condition of bond service which did not permit their freely
selling the products of their industry. The supreme interest
of emancipation from this condition concerned the power of
the state as well as the subjects. This emancipation was to
give them as citizens the character of free individuals, and
determined that what was to be performed for the general good
should be a matter of justice and not mere chance. The aristocracy of possession maintains possession against both the power

of the state at large and against individuals. The aristocracy should fulfill their true task, to support the throne, to be occupied and active on behalf of the state and the general good, and at the same time to maintain the freedom of the citizens. This in fact is the advantage of that class which forms the link between ruler and the people, that they undertake to know and to be active for that is intrinsically rational and general. This knowledge of and concern for the general must take the place of positive personal right.

There now first appears a system of states and a relation of states to each other. They became involved in various wars. The kings, having enlarged their political authority, turned their attention to foreign lands, insisting on claims of all kinds. Conquest was invariably the end and real interest of the wars of the period.

Italy especially had become an object of such conquest, and was a prey to the rapacity of the French, the Spaniards, and, at a later date, of the Austrians. In fact absolute isolation and dismemberment has always been an essential feature of the character of the Italians in ancient as well as in modern times. Their stubborn individuality was united. But the original character reappeared in full sharpness as soon as the bond was broken. In later times the Italians attained a joy in the fine arts, as bond of union, after having escaped from the selfishness of the most monstrous order which displayed its perverse nature in crimes of every description. Thus their culture, the mitigation of their selfishness, reached only beauty but not rationality, the higher unity of thought. The Italian nature is different from ours even in poetry and song. The Italians are ready improvisers; they pour out their very souls in art and the ecstatic enjoyment of it. For such an artistic character, the state must be casual.

The wars in which Germany engaged were not yielding her much honor. She allowed Burgundy, Alsace, Lorraine, and other parts of the empire to be wrested from it.

Common interests arose from these wars between the various political powers. The object of this community of interest was the maintenance of the status quo, the preservation of the independence of the several states, in fact, the balance of power. The motivation for this was of a decidedly practical kind, that is, the protection of the several states from conquest. The alliance of the states of Europe as a means of shielding individual states from the violence of the powerful, the preservation of this balance of power took the place of that general aim of former times, the defense of Christendom, whose center was the papacy. This new political motive was necessarily accompanied by a diplomatic relation, by which all the members of the great European system, however distant, felt what happened to any one of them. Diplomacy had been brought to the greatest refinement in Italy, and it was thence transferred to Europe at large.

Several princes in succession seemed to threaten the balance of power in Europe. Charles V was aiming at universal monarchy at the very beginning of the state system. He was at the same time emperor of Germany and king of Spain. The Netherlands and Italy were his, and the whole wealth of America flowed into his coffers. With this enormous power, which, like the contingencies of fortune in the case of private property, had been accumulated by the most felicitous combinations of political dexterity—marriage among other things—but which lacked inner, true cohesion, he was nevertheless successful against France, or even against the German princes; nay, he was even compelled to a peace by Maurice of Saxony. His whole life was spent in quelling disturbances in all parts of his empire and in conducting foreign wars.

The balance of power in Europe was similarly threatened by Louis the Fourteenth. He had become absolute ruler by the suppression of the grandees of his kingdom which Richelieu and after him Mazarin had accomplished. Besides, France had the consciousness of its intellectual superiority in a refinement of culture in advance of anything in the rest of Europe. The pretensions of Louis were founded not on extent of dominion (as was the case with Charles V) so much as on that culture which distinguished his people, and which at that time was received and admired everywhere together, with the language that embodied it. The French could therefore plead a higher justification than the Emperor Charles V. But the very rock on which the vast military resources of Philip II had already foundered—the heroic resistance of the Dutch—also proved fatal to the ambitious schemes of Louis. . . .

[There follow some brief remarks on Charles VII of Sweden and on the Turks. Then Hegel continues:]

An event of special importance following in the train of the Reformation was the struggle of the Protestant church for political existence. The Protestant church, even in its original appearance, was too intimately affecting secular interests not to occasion secular complications and political contentions respecting political possession. The subjects of Catholic princes became Protestants, they had and made claims to ecclesiastical property, changed the nature of the tenure and repudiated or declined the discharge of those ecclesiastical functions to whose due performance the emoluments were attached. Moreover, a Catholic government is bound to be the secular arm of the Church. The Inquisition, for example, never put a man to death, but, acting as a kind of jury, simply declared him a heretic. He was then punished according to civil laws. Again, innumerable occasions of offense and irritation originated with the processions and feasts, the carrying of the host through the streets, withdrawals from convents, etc. Still more excitement would be felt when an archbishop of Cologne attempted to make his archbishopric a secular principality for himself and his family. Their confessors made it a matter of conscience with Catholic princes to wrest estates that had been the property of the Church from the hands of the heretics. In Germany, however, the condition of things was favorable to Protestantism since several territories which had been imperial fiefs had become autonomous principalities. But in countries like Austria the princes were indifferent to Protestants or hostile to them. In France they were not safe in the exercise of their religion except as protected by fortresses. Without war the existence of the Protestants could not be secured. The question was not one of simple conscience, but involved decisions respecting public and private property which had been taken possession of in contravention of the rights of the Church, and whose restitution the Church demanded. A condition of absolute mistrust developed; absolute because mistrust bound up with the religious conscience was its root. The Protestant princes and towns formed a feeble union at that time and the defensive operations they conducted were much feebler still. After they had been worsted, Maurice the Elector of Saxony, by an utterly unexpected and adventurous piece of daring, extorted an equivocal peace, which left the deep sources of hate altogether untouched. It was necessary basically to fight out the issue. This took place in the Thirty Years' War, in which first Denmark and then Sweden took over the cause of freedom. The former was soon compelled to quit the field, but Sweden, under Gustavus Adolphus, that hero of the North of glorious memory, played a part which was so much the more brilliant inasmuch as she began to wage war against the vast force of the Catholics, alone, without the help of the Protestant estates of the Empire. All the powers of Europe, with a few exceptions, now fell upon Germany, flowing back toward it as the fountain from which they had originally started, and where now the right of religious inwardness and that of internal separateness were to be fought out. The struggle ended without an idea being discovered, without having gained a principle or an intellectual concept. The struggle ended in the exhaustion of all parties, in a scene of utter desolation, where all the contending forces had been wrecked. It ended with letting parties simply take their course and maintain their existence on the basis of external power. The issue is in fact of an exclusively political nature. In England too separateness was established by war. The struggle was directed in this case against the kings, who were secretly attached to Catholicism because they found the principle of absolute and arbitrary rule confirmed by its doctrines. The fanaticized people rebelled against the assertion of absolute power according to which kings are obliged to render account to God alone (that is, to the Father Confessor), and, in opposition to Catholic external-ity, achieved the extreme of inwardness in Puritanism, which, when developing in the real world, appears partly fanatically elevated, partly ridiculous. The fanatics of England, like those of Münster, wanted to govern the state directly by the fear of God. The soldiery sharing the same fanatical views prayed while they fought for the cause they had espoused. But a mili-tary leader now had the physical force of the country and consequently the government in his hands. In the state there must be government, and Cromwell knew what governing is. He therefore made himself ruler and sent that praying parlia-ment about their business. His right to authority, however, vanished with his death, and the old dynasty gained possession of the throne. Catholicism, we may observe, is commended to the support of princes as promoting the security of their gov-ernment particularly if the Inquisition be connected with the government; the former constituting the bulwark of the latter. But such a security is based on a servile religious obedience and is only present when the constitution and the law of the state still rest upon actual positive possession. But if the constitu-tion and laws are to be founded on a veritable eternal right, then security is to be found only in the Protestant religion, in whose principle rational subjective freedom also attains de-velopment. The Catholic principle was fought especially by the Dutch as bound up with Spanish rule. Belgium was still attached to the Catholic religion and remained subject to

Spain. The northern part of the Netherlands, Holland, on the contrary, stood its ground with heroic valor against its oppressors. The trading class and the guilds and companies of marksmen formed a militia whose heroic courage was more than a match for the then famous Spanish infantry. The trading cities held out against disciplined troops, just as the Swiss peasants had resisted the Knights of Austria. During this struggle on the continent itself, the Dutch fitted out fleets and deprived the Spaniards of a part of their colonial possessions, from which all their wealth was derived. As independence was secured for Holland in its holding to the Protestant principle, so that of Poland was lost through its endeavor to suppress that principle in the case of dissidents.

The Protestant church had been acknowledged as independent by the Peace of Westphalia, to the vast dishonor and humiliation of Catholicism. This peace has often passed for the palladium of Germany, as having established its political constitution. But this constitution was in fact a confirmation of the particular rights of the countries into which Germany had been broken up. It involved no thought, no conception of the proper end of a state. One must read *Hyppolytus à Lapide* (a book which, written before the conclusion of the peace, had a great influence on the relations within the Empire) if one wants to become acquainted with the character of that German freedom of which so much is made. In this peace the establishment of a complete particularity, the determination of all relations on the principle of private right is proclaimed. This peace is constituted anarchy such as the world had never seen before. Guaranteed and secured by the most inviolable sanctions was the proposition that the Empire is properly a unity, a whole, a state, while yet all relations are determined so exclusively on the principle of private right that the interest of all the constituent parts is to act for themselves contrary to the interest of the whole, or to neglect that which its interest demands, even if required by law. It was shown immediately after this settlement what the German Empire was as a state in relation to other states. It waged ignominious wars with the Turks, from whom Vienna had to be liberated by the Poles. Still more ignominious was its relation to France, which in time of peace took possession of free cities, the bulwarks of Germany, and of flourishing provinces, and retained them undisturbed.

This constitution, which completely terminated the career of Germany as an Empire, was chiefly the work of Richelieu, by whose assistance, Roman cardinal though he was, religious freedom in Germany was saved. Richelieu, with a view to further the interests of the state whose affairs he superintended, adopted for it the exact opposite of the policy which he promoted in the case of his enemies; for he reduced the latter to political impotence by establishing the political independence of the several parts, while at home he destroyed the autonomy of the Protestant party. His fate was that of many great statesmen: he was cursed by his countrymen, while his enemies looked upon the work by which he ruined them as the most sacred goal of their desires, the consummation of their rights and liberties.

The Protestant church later perfected the guarantee of its political existence by the fact that one of the states which had adopted the principles of the Reformation raised itself to the position of an independent European power. This power was bound to come into existence with Protestantism: Prussia, which made its appearance at the end of the seventeenth century, found in Frederick the Great, if not its founder, yet certainly the consolidator of its strength. The Seven Years' War was the struggle by which that consolidation was accomplished. Frederick II demonstrated the independent vigor of his power by resisting almost all of Europe—an alliance of its leading states. He appeared as the hero of Protestantism, and that not merely as an individual, like Gustavus Adolphus, but as the ruler of a state. The Seven Years' War was indeed itself not a war of religion; but it was such in view of its ultimate issues, and in the conviction of the soldiers as well as of the powers. The Pope consecrated the sword of Field-Marshal Daun, General of Maria Theresa of Hapsburg, and the chief object of the allied powers was the crushing of Prussia as the bulwark of the Protestant church. But Frederick the Great not only made Prussia one of the great powers of Europe as a Protestant power, but was also a philosophical king, an altogether peculiar and unique phenomenon in modern times. There had been English kings who were subtle theologians, contending for the principle of absolutism. Frederick on the contrary took up the Protestant principle in its secular aspect. Being disinclined toward religious controversies he did not side with this or that opinion, yet he had the consciousness of general aims, which is the profoundest depth to which spirit can attain, and which is thought conscious of its own inherent power.

The Enlightenment and the Revolution

Protestantism had introduced the principle of inwardness, together with religious emancipation and contentment with oneself, but accompanying this with the belief in the inward as evil and in the power of the worldly. Within the Catholic Church, too, the casuistry of the Jesuits introduced interminable inquiries, as protracted and subtle as those of scholastic theology, respecting the inward aspect of the will and the motives that affect it.

This dialectic, which unsettled all particular judgments and opinions, transforming the good into evil and the evil into good, left at last nothing remaining but the pure activity of inwardness itself, the abstract element of the spirit—thought. Thought contemplates everything in general form and is consequently the activity and the production of the general. In the older scholastic theology the real subject-matter, the doctrine of the Church, remained something beyond.* Protestant theology, too, retained the relation of the spirit to the other world; for on the one hand there remains the will of the individual, the spirit of man, I myself, and on the other hand the grace of God, the Holy Ghost, and likewise (in evil means) the devil. But in thought, the self is present to itself and its content, its objects are just as absolutely present to it. For in thinking I must elevate the object and see it as something general. This is simply the absolute freedom, for the pure ego, like pure light, is simply by itself. Thus what is different, sensuous or spiritual, no longer presents an object of dread, for in contemplating such diversity it is inwardly free and can freely confront it. A practical interest makes use of and consumes the objects offered to it. A theoretical interest contemplates them, assured that they in themselves present no alien element. Consequently, the furthest reach of inwardness, of subjectivity, is thought. Man is not free when he is not thinking; for then he is related to the world around him as to another. This comprehension, the reaching of the ego beyond other forms of being with the most profound self-certainty, directly contains the reconciliation of the opposites. For it must be observed that the unity of thought with its object is already implicitly present, for reason is the substantial basis of the consciousness as well as of the external and natural. Thus that which presents itself as the object of thought is no longer something beyond (*ein Jenseits*),* not of another substantial nature.

The spirit has now advanced to the level of thought. It involves the reconciliation in its completely pure essence, challenging the external world to exhibit the same reason which the subject possesses. The spirit perceives that nature, the world, must also be an embodiment of reason, for God created it rationally. A general interest in the observation and compre-

---

* Something beyond = *jenseits,* meaning beyond the subject and its reasoning.—Ed.

hension of the present world developed. The general in nature is nothing other than species, genera, force, gravitation, etc., phenomenally presented. Thus experience became the science of the world, for experience involves on the one hand the observation of phenomena, on the other hand, also, the discovery of a law, of what is inside, the hidden force that causes those phenomena, thus reducing to their simple principles the data supplied by observation.

The consciousness of thinking was first elevated from that sophistry of thought which unsettles everything, by Descartes. As it was the purely Germanic nations among whom the principle of spirit first manifested itself, so it was by the Latin nations that the abstract was first comprehended. . . . Experimental science therefore very soon made its way among the French, in common with the Protestant English, and among the Italians. It seemed to men as if God had just created the moon and the stars, plants and animals, as if the laws of the universe were now established for the first time. For they only felt a real interest in the universe when they recognized their own reason in its reason. The human eye became clear, perception quick, thought active and interpretative. The discovery of the laws of nature enabled men to contend against the monstrous superstition of the time, as also against all notions of mighty alien powers which magic alone could conquer. Men said, and Catholics no less than Protestants, that the external with which the Church wanted to associate superhuman virtue was external and material, and nothing more, that the host was simply dough, the relics of the saints mere bones. The independent authority of the subject was maintained against belief founded on authority and the laws of nature were recognized as the only bond connecting the external with the external. Thus all miracles were objected to, for nature is now a system of known and recognized laws. Man is at home in it, and only that passes for truth in which he finds himself at home; he is free through the knowledge of nature. Thought was also directed to the spiritual side of things. Right and morality came to be looked upon as having their foundation in the present will of man, whereas formerly it was referred only to the command of God enjoined from without. . . . What the nations acknowledge as international law was deduced empirically from observation (as in the work of Grotius). The source of the existing civil and constitutional laws was looked for, after Cicero's fashion, in those instincts of men which nature has planted in their hearts, e.g., the social instinct. It was also looked for in the principle of security of the person and property of the citizens and in the principle of the general good, of reason of state. On the basis of these principles private rights were on the one hand despotically disregarded but on the other hand the general objectives of the state were carried through in opposition to mere positive or prescriptive claims. Frederick II may be mentioned as the ruler with whom the new epoch enters actual reality, in which the real interest of the state achieves general recognition and highest justification. Frederick II merits especial notice, because he comprehended in thought the general end of the state, and because he was the first ruler who kept the general interest of the state steadily in view, and refused to admit the validity of any particular interests when they stood in the way of the end of the state. His immortal work is a native code, the Prussian common law. How the head of a household energetically provides and governs with a view to the welfare of the household and of his dependents, of this Frederick has given a unique example.

These general conceptions, deduced from the present consciousness, the laws of nature and the content of what is right and good, have been called *reason*. The recognition of the validity of these laws was called the *Enlightenment*. From France it passed over to Germany and a new world of ideas arose. The absolute criterion against all authority based on religious belief and positive laws and right, especially political right, is the verdict passed by spirit itself on the character of that which is to be believed or obeyed. Luther secured spiritual freedom to mankind and the reconciliation in the concrete. He triumphantly established the position that man's eternal destiny must be worked out in himself. But the content of what is to take place within him, what truth is to become vital in him, was taken for granted by Luther as something already given, something revealed by religion. In the Enlightenment the principle was established that this content must be capable of actual investigation, something of which I can gain an inward conviction, and that every dogma must be referred to this ground of inward conviction.

This principle of thought appears at first in a general and abstract form, and is based on the principle of contradiction and of identity. The results of thought are thus posited as finite. The Enlightenment utterly banished from things human and divine and extirpated all that was speculative. Yet while it is extremely important that the multiform complex of things should be reduced to its simplest definition, and brought into the form of universality, this still abstract principle does not satisfy the living spirit, the concrete human soul.

This formally absolute principle brings us to the last stage in history, to our world, to our own time.

Secular life is the positive and definite embodiment of the spiritual kingdom, the kingdom of the will manifesting itself in outward existence. Feeling, sense and impulse are also forms in which the inner life realizes itself. But these things are transient and disconnected. They are the ever-changing content of will. But that which is just and moral belongs to the essential, independent and intrinsically general will. If we would know what right really is, we must abstract from inclination, impulse and desire as the particular. We must know what the will is in itself. For benevolent, charitable and social impulses remain impulses to which other impulses are opposed. What the will is in itself must be differentiated from these specific and contradictory impulses. Until then will remains abstract will. The will is free only when it does not will anything alien, extrinsic, foreign to itself (for as long as it does so, it is dependent), but wills itself alone, wills the will. The absolute will is the will to be free. Will making itself its own object is the basis of all right and law and obligation and consequently of all statutory laws, commands and duty and imposed obligations. The freedom of the will itself, as such is itself absolute, inherently eternal right and law and the supreme right in comparison with other rights; nay, it is even that by which man becomes man, and is therefore the fundamental principle of the spirit.

But the next question is: how does will assume a definite form? For in willing itself, it is nothing but an identical reference to itself. In point of fact, however, it wills something specific. There are, we know, distinct and special duties and rights. A particular content, a definite form of will is demanded; for pure will is its own object, its own content, which is no content. In fact, this form is nothing more than formal will. But this is not the place to discuss how a definite form of freedom and rights and duties is evolved from this simple will. It may, however, be remarked that the same principle was theoretically formulated in Germany by the Kantian philosophy. According to it the simple unity of self-consciousness, the ego, constitutes the impenetrable and absolutely independent freedom and is the fountain of all general conceptions, of all conceptions elaborated by thought, of theoretical reason. And likewise the highest of all practical conceptions, practical reason, is free and pure and will. Rationality of will is nothing else than maintaining oneself in pure freedom, willing this and this alone, right purely for the sake of right, duty purely for the sake of duty. This remained calm theory among the Germans, but the French wished to give it practical effect. Two questions therefore suggest themselves: why did this principle of freedom remain merely formal? and why did the

French alone, and not the Germans, set about to realize it? ... The principle remains formal because it originated in abstract thought, in the intellect, which is primarily the self-consciousness of pure reason, and being immediate it is abstract. Nothing further is developed from it as yet, for it still remains in a contrary position to religion, that is, to the concrete absolute content of the world.

As to the second question, why the French immediately passed over from the theoretical to the practical, while the Germans contented themselves with theoretical abstraction, it might be said that the French are hot-headed (*ils ont la têtc près du bonnet*); but the reason lies deeper. The fact is that the formal principle of philosophy in Germany encounters a concrete real world in which spirit finds inward satisfaction and in which the conscience is at rest. For, on the one hand, it was the Protestant world which advanced so far in thought as to realize the absolute culmination of self-consciousness. On the other hand, Protestantism enjoys, with respect to the moral and legal relations of the real world, a quiet confidence in the moral conviction of men. Such conviction, at one with religion, is the fountain of all lawful arrangements in private and constitutional law. The Enlightenment was on the same side as theology in Germany. In France it immediately took up a position of hostility toward the Church. In Germany the entire secular relations had already been improved by the Reformation; those pernicious institutes of celibacy, poverty and laziness had already been abolished. There was no deadweight of enormous wealth attached to the Church, and no constraint was put upon ethics, a constraint which is the source and cause of vices. There was not that unspeakable iniquity which arises from the interference of spiritual power with secular law, not that other of the sanctified legitimacy of kings, the doctrine that the arbitrary will of princes is divine and holy in virtue of their being "the Lord's Anointed." On the contrary, their will is regarded as deserving of respect only so far as it wisely wills right and law, justice and the common good. The principle of thought, therefore, had so far been reconciled already. Moreover the Protestant world had a conviction that the principle which would result in a further development of law was already present in the reconciliation which had been evolved previously.

A consciousness which is abstractly developed and sensible can be indifferent to religion, but religion is the general form in which truth exists for the non-abstract consciousness. The Protestant religion does not admit of two kinds of conscience, while in the Catholic world the Holy stands on the one side and on the other side abstraction opposed to religion, to its superstition and its truth. This formal, individual will is now made the basis of general propositions. Right in society is that which the law wills, and the will exists as an isolated one. Thus the state, as an aggregate of many individuals, is not a substantial unity in and by itself. It is not the truth of right and law in and by itself, to which the will of its individual members ought to be conformed in order to be true free will. On the contrary, atoms of the will are made the starting point, and each will is represented as absolute.

A principle was thus discovered to serve as the rational basis for the state, which does not, like previous principles, belong to the sphere of opinion, such as the social impulse, the desire for security of property, and the like. Nor does this principle owe its origin to piety, as does that of the divine appointment of the governing power. Rather, it is a principle of certainty, resulting from the recognition of identity with my self-consciousness; but it is not yet the principle of truth which needs to be distinguished from it. This is a vast discovery with regard to the most inward and freedom. The consciousness of the spiritual is now the foundation of the political society, and philosophy has thereby become dominant. It has been said that the French Revolution resulted from philosophy, and it is not without reason that philosophy has been called world wisdom. For it is not only truth in and by itself, as the pure essence of things, but also truth as it is alive in the world. We should not, therefore, contradict the assertion that the Revolution received its first impulse from philosophy. But this philosophy was only abstract thought in the first instance, not the concrete comprehension of absolute truth—an immeasurable difference.

[After elaborating these thoughts further, Hegel states:]

The two following points must now occupy our attention: first, the course which the Revolution in France took; second, how that Revolution became world-historical. 1) Freedom presents two aspects. The one concerns its content, its objectivity, the thing itself. The other relates to the form of freedom, involving consciousness on the part of the individual of his own activity. For freedom demands that the individual recognize himself in these acts, and that they should invariably be his, it being in his interest that the desired result be attained. The three elements and powers of the living state must be considered according to the above analysis, their examination in detail being referred to the *Philosophy of Right and Law*.

[What follows here closely parallels what may be found in the selections from that work, below § 273 ff; p. 293.]

In view then of these main considerations we have to trace the course of the French Revolution and the remodeling of the state in accordance with the idea of right. Purely abstract philosophical principles were set up at first. Conviction and religion were not taken into account. The first constitutional form of government in France was one which recognized royalty. The monarch was to stand at the head of the state, and on him, in conjunction with his ministers, was to devolve the executive power; the legislative body, on the other hand, was to make the laws. But this constitution involved an internal contradiction from the very first, for the legislature absorbed the whole power of the administration. The budget, affairs of war and peace, and the levying of the armed forces were in the hands of the legislative chamber. The budget, however, is in its nature something different from law, for it is annually renewed, and the power to which it properly belongs is that of the executive. With this, moreover, is connected the indirect nomination of the ministry and officers of state. The executive was thus transferred to the legislative chamber, as it was to the parliament in England. This constitution was also vitiated by the existence of absolute mistrust. The royal family lay under suspicion because it had lost the power it formerly enjoyed, and the priests refused the oath. Neither government nor constitution could be maintained on this footing, and the ruin of both was the result. A government of some kind, however, is always in existence. The question presents itself, then, whence did it emanate? Theoretically, it proceeded from the people, really and truly from the National Convention and its Committees. The forces now dominant were the abstract principles, freedom, and, in so far as it exists within the limits of the subjective will, virtue. This virtue had now to conduct the government in opposition to the many, who had been rendered unfaithful to virtue through their corruption and attachment to old interests, or a liberty that had degenerated into license, or through the violence of their passions. Virtue is here a simple abstract principle and distinguishes the citizens into two classes only, those who are favorably disposed and those who are not. But conviction can only be recognized and judged of by conviction. Suspicion therefore prevailed. But virtue, as soon as it is suspect, is already condemned. Suspicion attained a terrible power and brought to the scaffold the monarch, whose subjective will was in fact the Catholic religious conscience. Robespierre set up the principle of virtue as supreme, and it may be said that he was serious about virtue. Virtue and terror were the order of the day; for subjective virtue, which governs on the basis of conviction only, brings with it the most fearful tyranny. It exercises its power without judicial formalities, and the punishment it inflicts is equally simple—death. Such a tyranny could not last, for all inclinations, all interest, reason itself revolted against this terribly inconsistent liberty which was so fanatical in its concentration. An organized executive government was introduced, analogous to the one that had been displaced. Its chief and monarch was a changeable Directory of Five who might form a moral, but did not have an individual unity. Suspicion continued to prevail, and the government was in the hands of the legislative assemblies. This constitution therefore had the same fate as its predecessor, for the absolute necessity of a governmental power had been proven. Napoleon restored it as military authority and followed up this step by establishing himself as an individual will at the head of the state. He knew how to rule and soon settled the affairs of France. He scattered the barristers, the ideologues and the abstract-principle men who were still around. Mistrust no longer prevailed but respect and fear. He then, with the vast might of his personality, turned his attention to foreign relations, subjected all Europe and diffused his liberal institutions everywhere. Greater victories were never gained, expeditions displaying greater genius were never conducted, but never was the powerlessness of victory exhibited in a clearer light. The conviction of the peoples, both religious and national, ultimately overthrew this colossus. Constitutional monarchy was restored in France with the "Charte" as its basis. But here again the antithesis of conviction and mistrust appeared. The French were lying to one another when they issued addresses full of devotion and love for the monarchy and loading it with benediction. For fifteen years a farce was played. For although the "Charte" was the standard under which all were enrolled, and though both parties had sworn to it, yet the ruling conviction was a Catholic one which regarded it as a matter of conscience to destroy the existing institutions. Another breach therefore took place and the government was overturned. At length, after forty years of indescribable war and confusion, a weary heart might well congratulate itself on seeing a termination and pacification of all these disturbances. But although one main point is set at rest, there remains on the one hand that rupture which the Catholic principle inevitably occasions, on the other hand that which has to do with man's subjective will. The main one-sidedness consists in this, that the [ideal] general will should also be the empirically general, that is, that the individuals as such should rule or at any rate take part in the executive government. Not satisfied with the establishment of rights, with freedom of person and property, with the existence of a political organization in which are to be found various circles of civil life, each having its own functions to perform, and with that influence over the people which is exercised by the intelligent members of the community, and the confidence that is felt in them, liberalism sets up in opposition to all this the atomistic principle of individual wills. It maintains that all should emanate from their express power and have their express sanction. Asserting this formal side of freedom, this abstraction, the Liberals allow no political organization to be firmly established. The particular orders of the government are forthwith opposed by the advocates of liberty as the mandates of a particular will, and are branded as the displays of arbitrary power. The will of the many expels the ministry from power, and the opposition steps in. But the latter, having now become the government, have the many against them. Thus are agitation and unrest perpetuated. This collision, this knot, this problem, is that with which history is now occupied, and whose solution it has to work out in the future.

2) We have next to consider the French Revolution, for the event is world-historical in its significance, and that contest of formalism which we discussed in the last paragraph must be properly distinguished from its wider bearings. As regards

outward diffusion, the principle of the French Revolution permeated almost all the modern states, either through conquest or by express introduction into their political life. Particularly all the Latin nations, and specially the Catholic world, France, Italy, Spain, fell under the dominion of liberalism. But it became bankrupt everywhere; first, the grand firm in France, then its branches in Spain and Italy; twice, in fact, in the two states into which it had been introduced. This was the case in Spain where it was first brought in by the Napoleonic constitution, then by that which the Cortes adopted. This happened first in Piedmont when it was incorporated into the French Empire, and a second time as a result of internal insurrection. A liberal constitution was also set up twice in Rome and Naples. Thus liberalism traversed the Latin world as an abstraction emanating from France; but religious subjection held that world in the fetters of political servitude. For it is a false principle that the shackles which bind right and freedom can be broken without the emancipation of the conscience, that there can be a Revolution without a Reformation. Therefore these countries sank back into their old condition, with some modifications of the outward political condition in Italy; Venice and Genoa, those ancient aristocracies, which could at least boast of legitimacy, vanished like rotten despotisms. Material superiority in power can achieve no enduring results: Napoleon could no more coerce Spain into freedom than Philip II could force Holland into slavery. Contrasted with these Latin nations we observe another development in the other powers of Europe, especially the Protestant nations. Austria and England were not drawn into the vortex of internal agitation and exhibited great proofs of their internal solidity. Austria is not a kingdom but an empire, an aggregate of many political organizations. The inhabitants of its chief provinces are not German in origin and character and have remained unaffected by ideas. Elevated neither by education nor religion, the lower classes in some districts have remained in a condition of serfdom, and the nobility have been kept down, as in Bohemia. In other regions, while the former have continued the same, the barons have maintained their despotism as in Hungary. Austria has surrendered that more intimate connection with Germany which was derived from the imperial dignity. It has renounced its numerous possessions and rights in Germany and the Netherlands. It now takes its place in Europe as a distinct power, involved with no other.

England by great exertions maintained itself on its old foundations. The English constitution remained intact amid the general convulsion, though it seemed so much more liable to be affected by it. As a public parliament, that habit of assembling in public meeting which was common to all the orders of the state, as well as the free press, offered singular facilities for introducing the French principles of liberty and equality among all the classes of the people. Was the English nation too backward in point of culture to apprehend these general principles? In no country has the question of liberty been more frequently a subject of reflection and public discussion. Or was the English constitution so entirely a free constitution, had those principles already been so completely realized in it that they could no longer excite opposition or even interest? The English nation certainly applauded the emancipation of France, but it proudly relied on its own constitution and freedom, and instead of imitating the example of the foreigners, it displayed its ancient hostility to its rival and was soon involved in a popular war with France. The constitution of England is a complex of mere particular rights and particular privileges. The government is essentially administrative, that is, it conserves the interests of all particular classes and orders. Each particular church, parochial district, county, society, takes care of itself, so that the government, strictly speaking, has nowhere less to do than in England. This is the leading feature of what the English call their liberty and is the antithesis of such a centralized administration as exists in France, where down to the last village the *maire* is named by the ministry or their agents. Nowhere can a people less tolerate free action on the part of others than in France. There the Ministry combines in itself all administrative power, to which on the other hand, every parish, every subordinate division and association has a part of its own to perform. Thus the common interest is concrete and particular interests are taken cognizance of and determined in view of that common interest. These arrangements, based on particular interest, render a general system impossible. Abstract and general principles consequently have no attraction for Englishmen, addressed as they are to inattentive ears. The particular interests above referred to have positive rights attached to them which date from the ancient times of feudal law and which have been preserved more in England than in any other country. By an inconsistency of the most startling kind, we find them contravening equity most grossly. There are nowhere fewer institutions characterized by real freedom than in England. In point of private right and freedom of possession they present an incredible deficiency. Sufficient proof of this has been afforded by the rights of primogeniture, involving the necessity of purchasing or otherwise providing military or ecclesiastical appointments for the younger members of the aristocracy. The parliament governs, although Englishmen are unwilling to allow that such is the case. It is noteworthy that what has always been regarded as the corruption of a republican people presents itself here; there is election to seats in parliament by means of bribery. But they also call this freedom, the power to sell one's vote and to purchase a seat in parliament. This utterly inconsistent and corrupt state of things nevertheless has one advantage in that it provides for the possibility of government. It introduces a majority of men into parliament who are statesmen, who from their very youth have devoted themselves to political business and have worked and lived in it. And the nation has the correct conviction and conception that there must be a government, and is therefore willing to give its confidence to a body of men who have had experience in governing. . . . This is quite different from appreciation of principles and abstract views which everyone can understand at once, and which are besides to be found in constitutions and charters. It is a question whether the reform in parliament now under consideration will, when consistently carried out, leave the possibility of a government. The material existence of England is based on commerce and industry, and the English have undertaken the weighty responsibility of being the missionaries of civilization to the world. For their commercial spirit makes them traverse every land and sea, to form connections with barbarous peoples, to create wants and stimulate industry, and first and foremost to establish among these peoples the respect for property, civility to strangers, conditions necessary to commerce, that is, the relinquishment of a life of lawless violence. Germany was overrun by the victorious French hosts, but the German people delivered it from this yoke. One of the leading features in the political condition of Germany is that code of law which was certainly occasioned by French occupation, since this was the especial means of bringing to light the deficiencies of the old system. The fiction of an empire has utterly vanished. The empire has been broken up into sovereign states. Feudal obligations have been abolished, for freedom of property and of person have been recognized as fundamental principles. Offices of state are open to every citizen, talent and aptitude being of course the necessary prerequisite. The executive government is focused upon administration and the personal decision of the monarch constitutes its apex. A final decision is absolutely necessary, as was remarked above. Yet with firmly established laws and a settled organization of the state, what is left to the sole arbitrament of the monarch is, in point of substance, no great matter. It is certainly very fortunate for a nation when a sovereign of noble character is its lot. Yet in a great state even this is of small moment, since its strength lies in the reason incorporated in it. Minor states have their existence and tranquillity secured to them more or less by their neighbors. They are, therefore, properly speaking, not independent and have not the fiery trial of war to endure. As has been remarked, a share in the government may be obtained by everyone who possesses competent knowledge, experience, and a morally disciplined will. Those who know ought to govern; knowledge, not ignorance and the presumptuous conceit of knowing better. Lastly, as to conviction, we have already remarked that in the Protestant church the reconciliation of religion with legal right has taken place. In the Protestant world there is no sacred, no religious conscience in a state of separation from, or perhaps even hostility to, secular right. This is the point which consciousness has attained, and these are the principal bases of that form in which the principle of freedom has realized itself. For the history of the world is nothing but the development of the idea of freedom.

Objective freedom, the laws of real freedom, demand the subjugation of the mere contingent will, for this is completely formal. If the objective is rational in itself, human conviction and insight must correspond with the reason which it embodies, and then we have the other essential element, subjective freedom, also realized. We have confined ourselves to the consideration of that progress of the idea and have been obliged to forego the pleasure of giving a detailed picture of the prosperity, the periods of glory that have distinguished the rise and fall of nations, the beauty and the grandeur of the character of individuals, and the interest attaching to their fate. Philosophy concerns itself only with the glory of the idea mirroring itself in the history of the world. Philosophy escapes from the weary strife of the passions that agitate the surface of society into the calm region of contemplation. That which interests it is the recognition of the process of development which the idea has passed through in realizing itself, the idea of freedom, whose reality is the consciousness of freedom and nothing short of it. World history, with all the changing drama of its histories, is this process of the development and realization of the spirit. It is the true theodicy, the justification of God in history. Only this insight can reconcile the spirit with world history and the actual reality, that what has happened, and is happening every day, is not only not "without God," but is essentially the work of God.

Selections from

THE HISTORY OF PHILOSOPHY

Translated by Carl J. Friedrich*

* This translation is based upon the critical edition of the Introduction, made by Professor J. Hoffmeister, and published by Felix Meiner Verlag who kindly consented to its use.—Ed.

LECTURES ON THE HISTORY
OF PHILOSOPHY

[In Michelet's edition, Hegel offers some introductory remarks about the difficulty of dealing with the history of philosophy, because its subject (*Gegenstand*) is controversial, and notes that many voluminous and learned works in this field are worthless, because the authors do not know what philosophy is. Hegel then observes that nevertheless no definition of philosophy can be given at the outset, because the history of philosophy itself must reveal what it is. "Its concept must be found." Hence the "Introduction" from which most of the selections are presumably taken assumes the concept of philosophy as a science.*]

Introduction to the History of Philosophy †

. . . The history of philosophy presents and describes the line of noble spirits, the gallery of heroes of reflecting reason who have penetrated by virtue of this reason into the essence of things, of nature and of the spirit, into the essence of God. They have created for us the greatest treasure, the treasure of rational knowledge. What we and the present world possess of self-conscious rationality is not . . . grown from the soil of the present; it is essentially a heritage and the result of the labor of all the preceding generations of mankind . . . What we are in philosophy (as indeed in other fields of knowledge) we owe largely to tradition which binds

---

* Hegel's use of the word "science" in connection with philosophy is of Greek origin and the German term *Wissenschaft* or field of knowledge is more appropriate than the English "science" with its overtones of a more specialized method.—Ed.

† From the Berlin MS. of the Introduction—Hoffmeister, pp. 21 ff. Subdivision designations, such as I. or a) have been omitted, in order to avoid confusion.—Ed.

with a sacred chain all that is past, and which has preserved and transmitted to us what the *Vorwelt* has brought forward . . .

The content of this tradition is of a spiritual nature. This general spirit does not stand still. . . . The spirit of the world does not sink into indifferent rest. This is due to its basic nature. Its life is action. Such deed presupposes some existing material to which it is directed and which it shapes and remolds. Thus what each generation has brought forward as knowledge and spiritual creation, the next generation inherits. This inheritance constitutes its soul, its spiritual substance, something one has become accustomed to, its principles, its prejudices and its riches. At the same time it is a received inheritance, (and hence) existing material. And since each generation has (its own) spiritual activity and vitality, it works upon what it has received and the material thus worked upon becomes richer. Our position is the same: to grasp the knowledge which is at hand, to appropriate it, and then to mold it. What we produce, presupposes something already there; what our philosophy is exists essentially only in such a context and has of necessity grown from it. History is what shows us our growth, the growth of our science, not the growth of something alien.

The more detailed explanation of this proposition will constitute the Introduction to this history of philosophy . . . Philosophy is the science of necessary thoughts, of their essential connection and system, the knowledge of what is true and therefore eternal and imperishable; history on the other hand is concerned in the common view with past events, that is, with accidental, passing and past affairs. . . .*

---

* In Michelet's edition there follow here some elaborations which connect the very dogmatic statement in the text with other ideas of Hegel. "It is an old prejudice that it is thought by which man differs from animals. Let us retain it . . . All that is human, whatever it may look like, is only human because thought is at work in it or has been so. But thought, though it is the essential, the substantial, the active

[After outlining the proposed introduction, and making some general remarks about false approaches to history in general and to the history of philosophy in particular, Hegel continues:]

Nonetheless, it is a well-established fact that different philosophies exist and have existed. The truth is one, however. The instinct of reason has an inescapable sense of or faith in this [proposition]. Hence only one philosophy can be the true one. And since they are so different, the others must, one concludes, be erroneous. Yet, each philosophy asserts, argues and proves to be this one true one. . . . However, different as are these philosophies, they have this in common that they are philosophy . . . it is essential to achieve a deeper insight into why the philosophical systems are different. The philosophical understanding of what is truth and philosophy enables one to understand this difference as such in quite another sense than that suggested by the abstract antithesis of truth and error. . . .

It is necessary to speak of the nature of truth from its idea and to state a number of propositions concerning truth which cannot here be proved. It is only possible to make them clear and comprehensible. . . . The first of these is the proposition, already stated, that the truth is only one. To know this one truth is the starting point and the end of philosophy: to understand it as the fountain from which all other laws of nature, all phenomena of nature and consciousness spring.

However, this proposition that truth is only one is itself merely abstract and formal. It is most essential to understand

---

is occupied with many things. The most excellent of these things must be that wherein thought is not occupied with something extraneous, but only with itself which is the most noble, therein thought has searched for and found itself. The history with which we are concerned is the history of thought finding itself. Thought only finds itself by creating itself—indeed it only exists and is actual (wirklich) by finding itself. These creations are the philosophies. And the sequence of these creations, of these discoveries which thought aims at . . . are the work of three and a half thousand years."—Ed.

that this one truth is not merely a simple abstract throught or proposition. Rather this truth is something concrete in itself. It is a common prejudice to think that the science of philosophy deals only with abstractions, with empty generalities. By contrast, what we observe, our empirical self-consciousness, our self as felt, the sense of life are thought to be that which is concrete, which is determined in itself, which is rich. In fact, philosophy does work in the realm of thought, it deals with generalities, its content is abstract, but only formally. But in itself the idea is essentially concrete, the unity of distinct particulars. Thus knowledge based on reason (rational knowledge) is differentiated from knowledge based on intellect (intellectual knowledge), and it is the business of philosophy to show that by contrast with intellect the truth, the idea, does not consist in empty generalities, but in something general that is in and by itself, the particular and the definite. . . .

. . . The truth so understood has a tendency to develop. Only the living, the spiritual moves, agitates within itself, develops itself. The idea is, therefore, concrete in itself and unfolding itself, an organic system, a totality, which contains a rich set of levels and aspects.

Philosophy is the understanding of this development and is at the same time itself this thought development, since it is the thought which understands. The further this development has gone, the more perfect has philosophy become.

This development does not move outward as if into externality; rather this development as it unfolds is moving inward, that is, the general idea remains the basis and the all-inclusive and unchanging. . . . Thus the general idea is made more distinct. A further development of the idea or its greater distinctness are one and the same. The most extensive is at once also the most intensive.

These are the abstract propositions concerning the nature of the idea and its development. For this is what a fully developed philosophy is like in itself. It is one idea, in its entirety and in all its branches, just as in a living individual one life, one pulse beats in all its members. All the parts of philosophy as they appear and their systematization arise from the one idea. All these particular systems are only mirrors and images of this one living being. They have their actuality (*Wirklichkeit*) only in this unity, and their differences, their different definite positions are together only its expression and the form which is contained in the idea. This, the idea, is the center . . .

Thus philosophy is a system in its unfolding. The same is true of the history of philosophy, and this is the central point, the basic conception which this treatment of the history of philosophy will deal with. . . .

The one way of dealing with this development, the deducing of the several forms, the presentation of the necessity of their determinations, is the task and the business of philosophy itself. And since this concerns the pure idea . . . it is the task and business of logic.

The other way shows the different stages and developmental aspects in time, how they occurred and at these particular places, within one nation or another, under such and such political circumstances and complications, that is, under this empirical form. This is the drama which the history of philosophy presents to us.

This view is the only one worthy of this science . . . according to this idea I now am ready to assert that the sequence of the systems of philosophy in history is the same as the sequence in the logical deduction of the concepts as determined by the idea. I assert that if one treats the basic concepts of the systems which have appeared in history purely and stripped of what is their external configuration, their application to particular situations and the like, he arrives at the different levels of the determination of the idea in its logical content. . . . From this it follows that the study of

the history of philosophy is the study of philosophy itself . . .
But in order to recognize the progress in the development of
the idea in the empirical form and appearance in which philosophy presents itself in history, one must to be sure to bring
along the knowledge of the idea, just as one must bring along
the concept of what is right and proper, if he is to judge
human conduct.

[Hegel sets forth in the following paragraphs his views of what
he calls the metaphysics of time; he insists upon the developmental
significance of the being-in-time (see for that below, *The Phenomenology of the Spirit*) and then turns to "The Conception of
Philosophy." In this connection he develops his notion that a particular philosophy is the expression of a particular nation's spirit.]

The definite form (*Gestalt*) of a philosophy is not only
contemporaneous with the definite form (*Gestalt*) of the nation within which it appears, with its constitution and form
of government, its ethics, its social life, aptitudes, customs and
forms of leisure, with its efforts and labors in art and science,
with its religions, with its belligerent and other external relations, with the decline of states, in which this particular principle had asserted itself, and finally with the origin
and emergence of new views in which a higher principle is
created and developed. Rather the spirit works and spreads
out the principle of this stage of its self-consciousness into
the entire wealth of its many-sidedness. It is a rich spirit, the
spirit of a people, an organization—a cathedral which has
many vaults, passages, columnades, halls, and other subdi-
visions; it all has been created as one whole, with one purpose
or end. Of these many aspects of the spirit philosophy is one
form, but which one? Philosophy is the finest flower, it is
the conception (*Begriff*) of its whole forms (*Gestalt*), it is
the consciousness and the spiritual essence of the whole situation, the spirit of the time, present as the spirit comprehending
itself. The multiform whole of the spirit reflects itself in

philosophy as the simple focal point, which is the conception which knows itself.

A certain stage of spiritual development must be reached, before man philosophizes. After providing for the necessities of life, man began to philosophize, Aristotle said. Philosophy is a free, not an egotistical activity. A free one, because the anxiety of lust has disappeared . . . a kind of luxury, since the term luxury designates those pleasures and occupations which do not relate to external needs. . . . One could say that when a nation has gone beyond its concrete life . . . it is approaching its decline. Indifference toward its living existence and dissatisfaction appear; because of them such a people must escape into the realms of thought. Socrates, Plato felt no joy in connection with Athenian political life. . . . In Rome philosophy and Christian religion spread under the Roman emperors during a time of unhappiness in this world, of the decline of political life. Again modern science and philosophy appeared in the fifteenth and sixteenth century, during the decline of medieval life when Christian religion, political and private life had been in harmony.

But not only does the time as such arrive when man philosophizes, but in a particular people a particular philosophy appears. . . . The relation of political history to philosophy is not this, however, that it be its cause. There exists a distinct being, which permeates all aspects and which presents itself in the political as well as in the other aspects. . . .

[Hegel then proceeds to discuss the interrelation between philosophy and the other spiritual manifestations, more especially the sciences, art and religion; the last is of especial concern to Hegel and we give a brief excerpt.]

In their religions, the nations have set down what they imagine the essence of the world, the substance of nature and spirit to be, and how man is related to them. The absolute essence is here the subject of their consciousness . . . In devotional exercise and in cult man transcends (*aufhebt*) the contradiction [between the here and the beyond] and raises himself to the consciousness of being united with the essence [of the world], a sense of confidence in the grace of God. . . . This essence is altogether the reason which is in and by itself, the general and yet concrete substance, the spirit of which the basic ground (*Urgrund*) exists objectively in consciousness . . . Like philosophy so religion must be understood first, that is, religion must be recognized as rational. For religion is the work of reason as it reveals itself, indeed it is reason's highest and most rational work. It is absurd to maintain that priests have thought up religion for the people as a fraud for their own benefit. . . . Religion has often been abused—a chance which results from external circumstances and its temporal existence . . . But this region of the spirit is the sacred temple of truth itself, the temple wherein the deception of the senses, of the finite notions and purposes is gone. . . .

This rational essential content of religion could, it seems, be isolated, presented and set forth as a historical sequence of philosophical positions. But the form in which this content is present in religion is different from the one present in philosophy, and therefore the history of philosophy is different from the history of religion. Since both are so closely related, it is an old tradition to speak of a Persian, an Indian philosophy. . . . But in this oriental antiquity, religion and philosophy are looked upon as not separate from each other. . . . But the form by which the content which is general in and by itself becomes part of philosophy is the form of thinking, the form of the general itself. In religion this content presents itself through art, presents itself to the immediate external view, also to the imagination and the feeling. The meaning is present to the reflective mind; it is the testimony of the spirit which comprehends such a content. . . .

The consciousness of this religion is the product of the

thinking imagination (*Phantasie*), or of the thought which only comprehends through the imagination and which expresses itself through the work of the imagination. Therefore, although in true religion infinite thought and the absolute spirit have been and are revealed . . . religion must, just because it is religion, address itself explicitly to the heart and to sentiment (*Gemüt*). It thus enters the sphere of the subjective, and thus the area of finite ways of representation. . . .

[After further elaboration of this view of religion, Hegel points out that this world of cult and visible representation has not only given rise to fraud, but has also misled people into thinking that to point out such fraud is an adequate explanation of religion. Anticipating Marx's dictum that religion is the opium of the people (which was a commonplace in eighteenth-century rationalism), he repudiates it. This side of religion, its anthropomorphism, had aroused the ire of philosophers since the days of Xenophanes and Plato, until they came to realize that this is a "wrapping" hiding the true content. In this connection, Hegel comments on the myths in Plato which he believes to be attempts by Plato to make his deeper meaning more apparent, to "unwrap it," as it were, and expresses the view that these myths eventually, like the religious ones, become obscure and call for explanations which show that they are not suitable modes of philosophical expression. He continues:]

After having indicated the general basis, the development of philosophy in time, we are confronted with the notion that since true philosophy is contemplation, thought and knowledge, it exists beyond time, and not within history. Such a view is contrary to the nature of spirit, of knowledge. The original oneness with nature is nothing but dull perception (*Anschauung*), concentrated consciousness, which for that very reason is abstract, and not organic in itself. Life, God should be concrete, and they are concrete in one's feeling, but nothing is differentiated. . . . What matters [in philosophy] is that the infinite wealth of a world view (*Weltanschauung*) be organized and that it replace that dull perception . . . The vision of God by the pious soul (*Gemüt*) is something quite different from the intelligible view of the nature of the spirit . . . Thinking is an introspection (*Insichgehen*) of the spirit and therefore is a process by which the spirit makes what it is intuitively seen to be an object [of rational discourse] . . . it sets itself off from itself.

[Here follow some of the familiar formulas of Hegel about the spirit; see, e.g., above, Introduction to *The Philosophy of History*.]

[This process takes] a long time, and the length of time it has taken the spirit to work out philosophy may surprise some. I have already said that our present philosphy is the result of the work of all the centuries [preceding]. . . . Concerning this slowness of the world spirit, one should consider that it is in no hurry, it has plenty of time—thousands of years are to you like a day. The spirit has plenty of time precisely because it is outside of time, it is eternal. . . . It has not only plenty of time; for it is not only time that is required in working out a [new] concept; much else is needed. It does not care that this process consumes so many generations of human beings, that it entails such a tremendous expense of becoming and passing away. It is rich enough for such expense. It works in the grand manner. It has plenty of nations and individuals to expend. . . .*

To illustrate the slowness and the immense expense and labor of the spirit involved in comprehending itself, a concrete example may be cited, the concept of its freedom—a major concept. The Greeks and Romans—let alone the Asiatics —knew nothing of this concept that man as man is born

---

* In a passage such as this, the fact that the English "spirit" must be treated as a neuter deprives one of the more dramatic personalized effect of Hegel's spirit which as a masculine being does all these things, like God.

free, that he is free. Plato and Aristotle, Cicero and the Roman jurists did not possess this concept, although it is the fountain of the law. Their peoples knew it even less. They knew indeed that an Athenian, a Roman citizen . . . is free, that there are free and unfree. Just because of that they did not know that man is free as man—man as man, that is, man in general, such as thought comprehends him and as he himself comprehends himself [in thought]. With the Christian religion the doctrine arose that all men are free before God, that Christ has freed men, has made them equal before God, and freed them for Christian freedom. These notions made freedom independent of birth, class, education, etc., and this means immense progress. But these notions are still [short of and] different from the view that the concept of man *implies* that he is free . . . it has taken centuries . . . this insight, this knowledge is not very old, though we assume it, as if it were a matter of course. Man should not be a slave; it does not [nowadays] occur to any people, to any government to wage war in order to acquire slaves. . . .

[After reiterating the importance of effort, of hard work involved in the unfolding of the spirit, and the fact that each time has its particular task in this work of the generations, a basic necessity, Hegel arrives at the final conclusions to be drawn for the treatment of the history of philosophy.]

From this necessity it follows that the beginning [of philosophy] is the least formed, distinct and developed, that it is rather the poorest, the most abstract, and that therefore the first philosophy consists of very general, indistinct thought, that it is the most simple philosophy, whereas the most recent philosophy is the most concrete and the deepest. One must know this in order not to look for more in the old philosophies than is contained in them, not to seek in them the satisfaction of spiritual needs which did not exist at the time [they were developed] and which belong to a more advanced period. . . .

[Hegel then proceeds to illustrate this idea briefly by reference to Thales. After criticizing some existing histories of philosophy for imputing to the ancients ideas which they did not and could not have, Hegel returns to the theme that the newest philosophy is the most developed, the richest and the most profound:]

In this latest philosophy all that appears at first as past must be preserved and contained: it must be a mirror of the entire history [of philosophy]. The last form which results from such progress as a progressive explication is the most concrete.

[Here follow some snide remarks about those who detract from the importance of new work in philosophy by talking about "fashionable" philosophy, citing in support a distichon of Schiller and Goethe.]

I have said that the philosophy of a period contains the preceding one, since it results from it. It is a basic aspect of development that one and the same idea—there is only one truth—is at the bottom of all philosophy, and that each succeeding one contains the preceding ones . . . Consequently in dealing with the history of philosophy, we are not dealing with what has passed [away]. The content of this history are the scientific products of reason (rationality? *Vernünftigkeit*), and these are not something perishable. What has been worked out in this field is the truth, and the truth is eternal, existing at one time and no longer at another. The bodies of the spirits who are the heroes of this history, their temporal life may have passed, but their works have not followed them. For the content of their work is the rational, which they have not imagined, dreamed up, or merely opined, and their deed is only this, that they have brought what is in itself rational out of the mine of the spirit where it lay as a substance, as its inner essence, into the light of day, into the consciousness, and made it knowledge. These deeds therefore are not only deposited in the temple of memory, like images of something dead and gone, but they are now just as present and alive as when they first appeared. They are results and works which have not been suspended and destroyed by those which followed; they do not have canvas, nor marble, nor paper, nor yet imagination and memory as their element in which they are preserved—elements which are themselves perishable . . . Rather they have [as their element] thought, the imperishable essence of the spirit which neither moths nor thieves can touch. The conquests of thought . . . constitute the very being of the spirit . . . the history of philosophy deals with what does not age but is presently alive and living.

But for this very reason, the spirit is not satisfied with a former philosophy since there lives in it a deep, yet distinct concept. What it wants to discover is this concept which constitutes its inner destiny and the root of its existence . . . it will understand and comprehend itself. . . . Hence the philosophy of Plato and Aristotle, e.g., live and are present, but philosophy is no longer at that stage. There cannot be today Platonists, Aristotelians, Stoics, Epicureans, etc. To try to resurrect them . . . is as impossible, as silly, as if a man would try to be a youth, a youth to be a child, even though man, youth and child are one and the same individual. . . . Mummies brought among the living cannot stand up; the spirit has long . . . acquired a deeper conception of itself. . . . Such a warming over must be seen therefore as passing through a learning process, a belated wandering through necessary stages of development. . . . One must know what he is looking for in the ancient philosophers and in the philosophy of every other period, or at least one must know that he confronts at each such stage, as they are made conscious, only those forms and needs of the spirit which lie within the limits of that stage. In the spirit of the modern age deeper ideas are dormant which in order to awaken and know themselves call for a different environment from those abstract, unclear and gray thoughts of the past.

Selections from

THE SCIENCE OF LOGIC

Translated by W. H. Johnston and L. G. Struthers[*]

[*] Reprinted with the permission of George Allen and Unwin Ltd.

THE SCIENCE OF LOGIC

INTRODUCTION

General Concept of Logic

THE NEED TO BEGIN WITH THE SUBJECT ITSELF, WITHOUT preliminary observations, is felt nowhere more strongly than in the science of logic. In every other science, the subject dealt with, and the method of the science, are distinguished from one another; and further the subject is not absolutely original, but depends upon other concepts, and is connected in all directions with other material. It is therefore granted to these other sciences to regard both their principles (with the connections of these) and also their method, as starting from assumptions—to begin with applying forms of definition and so on, which are presupposed as known and accepted, and to make use of familiar forms of reasoning for the establishment of their general concepts and fundamental determinations.

Logic on the other hand cannot take for granted any of these forms of reflection or rules and laws of thought, for these are a part of the very fabric of logic, and must be demonstrated within the boundaries of the science itself. But not only the scheme of philosophic method, but also the very concept of philosophy in general belongs to the content of logic and in fact constitutes its final result; what Logic is, cannot be set out beforehand—on the contrary this knowledge of what Logic is can only be reached as the end and consummation of the whole treatment of the subject. Moreover the subject of logic (thinking, or more precisely conceptual thinking) is really treated of within the boundaries of the science itself; the concept of this thinking is engendered in the course of development of the science, and therefore cannot precede it. Therefore what is set forth in a preliminary way in this Introduction does not aim at establishing the concept of logic at all, or at justifying beforehand its substance and method scientifically, but—by help of some reasoned and historical explanations and reflections—at bringing more clearly before the mind the point of view from which this science is to be regarded.

When logic is taken as the science of thinking in general, it is understood that this thinking constitutes the *bare form* of cognition, that logic abstracts from all *content*, and that the (so-called) other *constituent* of a cognition—that is, its *matter*—must come from a different source; that thus logic—as something of which this matter is wholly and entirely independent—can provide only the formal conditions of true knowledge, and cannot, in and by itself, contain real truth, nor even be the path to real truth, because just that which is the essence of truth—that is, its content—lies outside logic.

But in the first place it is most inept to say that Logic abstracts from all *content*, that it teaches only the rules of thinking without going into what is thought or being able to consider its nature. For since thinking and the rules of thinking are the subject of logic, logic has directly in them its own peculiar content—has in them that second constituent of cognition—its matter—about the structure of which it concerns itself.

But secondly, the ideas upon which the concept of logic has hitherto rested have partly died out already, and, for the rest, it is time that they should disappear altogether, and that this science should be taken from a higher point of view, and should receive an entirely different structure.

The hitherto accepted concept of logic rests upon the assumed separation of the *content* of knowledge and the *form* of knowledge (or *truth* and *certainty*)—a separation that is assumed once for all in ordinary consciousness. First, it is assumed that the material of knowledge is present in and for itself in the shape of a finished world apart from thinking, that thinking is in itself empty, and comes to that world from outside as form to matter, fills itself therewith, and only thus gets a content, and thereby becomes real knowing.

Next, these two constituents—for it is supposed that they have the reciprocal relation of constituents, and cognition is constructed out of them in a mechanical or at best a chemical fashion—these constituents are placed in an order of merit in which the object is regarded as something in itself finished and complete, something which, as far as its reality is concerned, could entirely dispense with thought, while on the other hand, thought is something incomplete which has to seek completion by means of some material, and indeed has to adapt itself to its material as if it were a form in itself pliable and undetermined. Truth is supposed to be the agreement of thought with its object, and in order to bring about this agreement (for the agreement is not there by itself) thinking must accommodate and adapt itself to its object.

Thirdly, when the difference of matter and form, of object and thought, is not left thus nebulous and undetermined, but is taken more definitely, each is regarded as a sphere separated from the other. Thus thought in its reception and formation of material is supposed not to go beyond itself—its reception of material and accommodation thereto is still regarded as a modification of self by which thought is not transformed into its other; moreover, self-conscious determination is held to belong to thought alone; thus thought in its relation to the object of thought does not go out of itself to the object, while the object, as a thing in itself, simply remains a something beyond thought.

These views concerning the relation to one another of subject and object express the determinations which constitute the nature of our ordinary consciousness just as it appears; but these prejudices, translated into the sphere of reason—as if the same relationship held there or had any truth by itself—are errors, the refutations of which throughout all departments of the spiritual and physical world is philosophy itself; or rather, since these errors bar the way, they must be renounced at the very threshold of philosophy.

The older metaphysic had in this respect a loftier conception of thought than that which has become current in more modern times. For the older metaphysic laid down as fundamental that that which by thinking is known of and in things, that alone is what is really true in them; that what is really true is not things in their immediacy, but only things when they have been taken up into the form of thought, as conceptions. Thus this older metaphysic stands for the view that thinking and the determinations of thinking are not something foreign to the objects of thought, but are rather of the very essence of those objects; in other words that *things* and the *thinking* of them are in harmony in and for themselves—indeed language itself expresses an affinity between them—that thought in its immanent determinations, and the true nature of things, are one and the same content.

But *reflective* understanding assumed possession of philosophy. We must learn precisely what is meant by this expression, which indeed is frequently used as a catchword; by it is to be understood generally the abstracting and separating intelligence which clings tenaciously to the separations which it has made. Directed against reason, this intelligence behaves as *crude common sense* and maintains the view that truth rests upon sense-reality, that thoughts are *only* thoughts, meaning that it is sense-perception that first endows them with substance and reality, that reason—in as far as it is merely reason—can spin nothing but idle fancies. In this renunciation of reason by itself, the concept of truth is lost; it is restricted to the cognition of merely subjective truth; of mere appearance of something to which the nature of the thing itself does not correspond; *knowing* falls back into *opinion*.

But this turn which cognition takes, and which has the air of being a loss and a retrogression, has something deeper behind it—something upon which the uplifting of reason to the loftier spirit of the newer philosophy chiefly depends. That is, the ground of this now everywhere prevalent idea is to be sought in a perception of the *necessary conflict* with each other of the determinations of understanding. The reflection already mentioned is this, that the immediate concrete must be transcended, and must undergo determination and abstraction. But reflection must, just as much, transcend these its own separate determinations, and forthwith relate them to each other. Then at the standpoint of this relating, the conflict emerges. This relating activity of reflection belongs in itself to reason; that transcending of these determinations which attains to a perception of their conflict, is the great negative step toward the true concept of reason. But this perception, being merely partial, falls into the error of fancying that it is reason which is in contradiction with itself, and does not recognize that the contradiction is just the lifting of reason above the limitations of understanding, and the dissolution of these. Instead of starting from this point to make the final step upwards, knowledge, recognizing the unsatisfactory nature of the determinations of understanding, flies straight back to sensible existence, thinking to find therein stability and unity. But on the other hand, since this knowledge knows itself to be knowledge only of appearances, its insufficiency is confessed, yet at the same time it is supposed that things, though not rightly known in themselves, still are rightly known within the sphere of appearances; as though only the *kinds of objects* were different, and the one kind, namely things in themselves, did not fall within knowledge, and the other kind, namely appearances, did so fall. It is as though accurate perception were attributed to a man, with the proviso that he yet could not perceive truth but only untruth. Absurd as this would be, a true knowledge which did not know the object of knowledge, as it is in itself, would be equally absurd.

The *criticism of the forms of common understanding* has had the result (mentioned above) that these forms have no *applicability to things in themselves.* This can have no other meaning than that the Forms are in themselves something untrue. But if they are allowed to remain as valid for subjective reason and for experience, then criticism has made no change in them, but leaves them in the same attitude toward the subject of knowledge, as they formerly had toward the object of knowledge. But if they do not suffice for the Thing in itself, then still less should common understanding, to which they are supposed to belong, put up with them and be content with them. If they cannot be determinations of the *thing in itself,* they can still less be determinations of understanding, to which we must allow at the very least the dignity of a thing in itself. The determinations of finite and infinite are similarly in conflict—whether they are applied to the world, to time and space, or are determinations within the mind; just as black and white produce gray whether they are mixed on a canvas or on the palette; so if our world-representation is dissolved by having the determinations of finite and infinite transferred to it, still more must the mind itself, which contains them both, be something self-contradictory and self-dissolving. It is not the constitution of the matter or object to which they are applied or in which they occur, that can make the difference, for the object contains the contradiction only through these determinations and in accordance with them.

Thus this criticism has only separated the forms of objective thinking from the thing, and left them, as it found them, in the subject of thought. For in doing so, it has not regarded these forms in and for themselves, according to their characteristic content, but has simply taken them up as a corollary from subjective logic; so that it was not a question of the deduction of them in themselves, nor of a deduction of them as subjective-logical forms, and still less a question of the dialectical consideration of them.

Transcendental idealism, carried more consistently to its logical conclusion, has recognized the emptiness of that specter of the *thing-in-itself* which the critical philosophy left over—an abstract shadow, detached from all content—and had it in view to demolish it altogether. Also this philosophy made a beginning of letting reason produce its own determinations out of itself. But the subjective attitude of this attempt did not admit of its being carried to completion. Henceforth this attitude—and with it that beginning, and the development of pure philosophy—was given up.

But that which has commonly been understood by logic is considered without any reference to metaphysical import. In its present condition, this science has indeed no content of such a kind that it be regarded by ordinary consciousness as reality and truth. But logic is not on this account a mere formal science, destitute of significant truth. In any case, the province of truth is not to be looked for in that subject-matter which is lacking in logic, and to the want of which the inadequacy of the science is commonly attributed: the emptiness and worthlessness of the logical forms reside solely in the way in which they have been considered and treated. While as fixed determinations they fall apart and cannot be held together in organic unity, they are mere dead forms, and have not dwelling in them the spirit which is their living concrete unity. Thus they are destitute of solid content and substantial filling. The content which we miss in the logical forms, is nothing other than a solid foundation and concreting of those abstract forms, and it is customary to seek this substantial essence for them, from outside. But it is just logical reason which is that substantial or real, which holds together in itself all abstract determinations, and is their solid absolutely concrete unity. Thus we do not need to seek far afield for what is usually regarded as a filling or content; it is not the fault of the subject-matter of logic if it is supposed to be without content or filling, but of the way in which logic is conceived.

This reflection leads us nearer to the problem of the point of view from which logic is to be regarded; how it is distinguished from the mode of treatment which this science has hitherto received, and to what extent it is the only true point of view upon which logic is in the future to be permanently based.

In the *Phenomenology of Spirit* (Bamberg and Würzburg, 1807) I have set forth the movement of consciousness, from the first crude opposition between itself and the object, up to absolute knowledge. This process goes through all the forms of the *relation of thought to its object*, and reaches the *concept of science* as its result. Thus this concept (apart from the fact that it arises within the boundaries of logic) needs here no justification, having already received its justification in that place; the concept is incapable of any other justification than just this production by consciousness; for to consciousness, all its forms are resolved into this concept, as into the truth. A reasoned deduction or elucidation of the concept of science can at best render this service, that by it the concept is presented to the mind, and a historical knowledge of it is produced; but a definition of science, or—more precisely— of logic, has its evidence solely in the inevitableness (already referred to) of its origin. The definition with which any science makes an absolute beginning can contain nothing other than the precise and correct expression of that which is presented to one's mind *as the accepted and recognized* subject-matter and purpose of the science. That exactly this or that is thus presented is a historical asseveration, in respect of which one may indeed appeal to certain facts as commonly accepted; or rather the request can be made that certain facts may be granted as accepted. And still we find that one man here and another there will bring forward, here a case and there an instance, according to which something more and other is to be understood by various expressions, into the definition of which therefore a narrower or more general determination is to be admitted, and in accordance with which the science is to be arranged. It further depends upon argument *what* should be admitted or excluded, and within what limit and scope; and there stand open to argument the most manifold and varied opinions, among which only arbitrary choice can make a fixed and final decision. In this mode or procedure, of beginning a science with its definition, nothing is said of the need that the *inevitableness* of the *subject-matter,* and therefore of the science itself, should be demonstrated.

The concept of pure science, and the deduction of it, are assumed in the present treatise so far as this, that the *Phenomenology of Spirit* is nothing other than the deduction of this concept. Absolute knowledge is the truth of all modes of *consciousness,* because according to the process of knowledge, it is only when absolute knowledge has been reached that the separation of the *object of knowledge* from *subjective certainty* is completely resolved, and truth equated to this certainty, and this certainty equated to truth.

So pure science presupposes deliverance from the opposition of consciousness. Pure science includes *thought in so far as it is just as much the thing in itself as it is thought,* or *the thing in itself in so far as it is just as much pure thought as it is the thing in itself.* Truth, as *science,* is pure self-consciousness unfolding itself, and it has the form of self in that what exists in and for itself is the known concept, while the concept as such is that which exists in and for itself.

This objective thinking is then the content of the pure science. Hence logic is so little merely formal, so little destitute of the matter necessary for real and true knowledge, that on the contrary its content is the only absolutely true, or (if we wish still to employ the word *matter*) is the true genuine matter—a matter, however, to which form is not external, since this matter is in fact pure thought, and thus Absolute form itself. Logic is consequently to be understood as the system of pure reason, as the Realm of pure thought. *This realm is the truth as it is, without husk in and for itself.* One may therefore express it thus: that this content *shows forth God as He is in His eternal essence before the creation of nature and of a finite spirit.*

Anaxagoras is praised as the man who first gave voice to the idea that we ought to lay down, as the world-principle, *Nous,* that is thought, and thought as the world-essence. He thus laid the foundation of an intellectualist view of the universe, and of this view logic must be the pure form. In it we are not concerned with thinking *about* something lying outside thought, as the basis of thought, nor with forms which serve merely as *signs* of truth; on the contrary, the necessary forms and characteristic determinations of thought are the content and the supreme truth itself.

In order that we may at least envisage this we must put aside the opinion that truth is something tangible. Such tangibility has for example been imported even into the Platonic ideas, which are in the thought of God, as though they were things existing, but existing in a world or region outside the world of reality, a world other than that of those ideas, and only having real substantiality in virtue of this otherness. The Platonic idea is nothing other than the universal, or more precisely the concept of an object of thought; it is only in its concept that anything has actuality; in so far as it is other than its concept, it ceases to be actual and is a non-entity; the aspect of tangibility and of sensuous externality to self belongs to that non-entical aspect. From the other side, however, one can refer to the characteristic ideas of ordinary logic; for it is assumed that, for instance, definitions comprise not determinations which belong only to the cognizing subject, but determinations which belong to the object, and constitute its most essential and inmost nature. Again, when from given determinations we conclude to others, it is assumed that what is concluded is not something external to the object and foreign to it, but that it belongs to the object—that being corresponds to thought. Speaking generally, it lies at the very basis of our use of the forms of concept, judgment, inference, definition, division, and so on, that they are forms not merely of self-conscious thinking but also of the objective understanding. *To think* is an expression which attributes especially to consciousness the determination which it contains. But in as far as it is allowed that *understanding, and reason, are of the world of objects,* that spirit and nature have general laws in accordance with which their life and their mutations are governed, in so far is it admitted that the determinations of thought also have objective validity and existence.

The critical philosophy has indeed turned metaphysics into logic, but—as already mentioned—like the later idealism it shied at the object, and gave to logical determinations an essentially subjective signification; thus both the critical philosophy and the later idealism remained saddled with the Object which they shunned, and for Kant a "thing-in-itself," for Fichte an abiding "resistance-principle," was left over as an unconquerable other. But that freedom from the opposition of consciousness, which logic must be able to assume, lifts these thought-determinations above such a timid and incomplete point of view, and requires that those determinations should be considered not with any such limitation and reference, but as they are in and for themselves, as logic, as pure reason.

Kant considers that logic—that is, the aggregate of definitions and propositions which are called logic in the ordinary sense—is fortunate in that it has fallen to its lot to attain so early to completion, before the other sciences; for Logic has not taken any step backwards since Aristotle—but also it has taken no step forward—the latter because to all appearance it was already finished and complete. If logic has undergone no change since Aristotle—and in fact when one looks at modern compendiums of logic the changes consist to a large extent merely in omissions—what is rather to be inferred from this is that logic is all the more in need of a thorough overhaul; for when spirit has worked on for two thousand years, it must have reached a better reflective consciousness of its own thought and its own unadulterated essence. A comparison of the forms to which spirit has risen in the worlds of practice and religion, and of science in every department of knowledge, positive and speculative—a comparison of these with the form which logic—that is, spirit's knowledge of its own pure essence —has attained, shows such a glaring discrepancy that it cannot fail to strike the most superficial observer that the latter is inadequate to the lofty development of the former, and unworthy of it.

As a matter of fact, the need of a transformation of logic has long been felt. It may be said that, both in form and in content, as exhibited in textbooks, logic has become contemptible. It is still trailed along rather with a feeling that one cannot do without logic altogether, and from a surviving adherence to the tradition of its importance, than from any conviction that that familiar content, and occupation with those empty forms, can be valuable and useful.

The additions—psychological, educational, even physiological—which logic received during a certain period were, later, almost universally recognized as disfigurements. In themselves, a great part of these psychological, educational, and physiological observations, laws, and rules, must appear very trivial and futile, whether they occur in Logic or anywhere else. Besides, such rules as for instance that one should think out and test what one reads in books or hears by word of mouth, that when one does not see well, one should use spectacles to help one's eyes—rules which in textbooks on so-called applied logic are put forward with great seriousness and formality to help us to attain to truth—these must appear to all the world to be superfluous—except indeed to the writer or teacher who is at his wits' end to know how to piece out the inadequate lifeless content of his logic.*

As to this content, we have given above the reason why it is so empty and lifeless. Its determinations are assumed to stand immovably rigid and are brought into a merely external relation with one another. Because in the operations of judgment and syllogism it is chiefly their quantitative element that is referred to and built upon; everything rests on an external difference, on mere comparison, and becomes a wholly analytic procedure, a matter of merely mechanical calculation. The deduction of the so-called rules and laws (especially of syllogism) is not much better than a manipulation of rods of unequal length in order to sort and arrange them according to size—like the child's game of trying to fit into their right places the various pieces of a picture puzzle. Not without reason, therefore, has this thinking been identified with reckoning, and reckoning with this thinking. In arithmetic the numbers are taken as non-significant, as something that, except for equality or inequality—that is, except for quite external relations—has no significance—that contains no thought, either in itself or in its relations. When it is worked out in a mechanical way that three-fourths multiplied by two-thirds make a half, this operation involves about as much or as little thought as the calculation whether in any figure of syllogism this or that mood is admissible.

In order that these dead bones of logic may be revivified

---

* *Observation in first edition.* A work on this science which has recently appeared, *System of Logic* by Fries, returns to the anthropological foundations. The ideas and opinions on which it is based are so shallow in themselves and in their development that I am saved the trouble of having to take any notice of this insignificant performance.

by mind, and endowed with content and coherence, its method must be that by means of which alone logic is capable of becoming a pure science. In the present condition of logic, hardly a suspicion of scientific Method is to be recognized. It has very nearly the structure of merely empirical science. For attaining their purpose, empirical sciences have hit upon a characteristic method of defining and classifying their material as best they can. Pure mathematics again has its own method, which suits its abstract objects and the quantitative determinations with which alone it is concerned. I have in the preface to the *Phenomenology of Spirit* said what is essential concerning this method and especially concerning the subordinate nature of such science as can find a place in mathematics; but it will also be more closely considered within the bounds of logic itself. Spinoza, Wolf, and others, have allowed themselves to be misled into applying this method in philosophy, and identifying the external process of conceptless quantity with the conceptual process, which is self-contradictory. Hitherto philosophy had not discovered its own method; it regarded with an envious eye the systematic structure of mathematics and, as already remarked, borrowed this, or sought help in the method of sciences which are only a medley of given material and empirical maxims and ideas— or took refuge in a crude rejection of all method. But the exposition of that which alone is capable of being the true method of philosophic science belongs to logic itself; since method is the consciousness of the form taken by the inner spontaneous movement of the content of Logic. In the *Phenomenology of Spirit* I have set out an example of this method as applied to a more concrete object, namely, to consciousness.* We have here modes of consciousness each of which in realizing itself abolishes itself, has its own negation as its result—and thus passes over into a higher mode. The one and

---

* And later as applied to other concrete objects, and corresponding departments of Philosophy.

only thing *for securing scientific progress* (and for quite *simple* insight into which, it is essential to strive) is knowledge of the logical precept that negation is just as much affirmation as negation, or that what is self-contradictory resolves itself not into nullity, into abstract nothingness, but essentially only into the negation of its *particular* content, that such negation is not an all-embracing negation, but is *the negation of a definite somewhat* which abolishes itself, and thus is a definite negation; and that thus the result contains in essence that from which it results—which is indeed a tautology, for otherwise it would be something immediate and not a result. Since what results, the negation, is a *definite* negation, it has a *content*. It is a new concept, but a higher, richer concept than that which preceded; for it has been enriched by the negation or opposite of that preceding concept, and thus contains it, but contains also more than it, and is the unity of it and its opposite. On these lines the system of concepts has broadly to be constructed, and to go on to completion in a resistless course, free from all foreign elements, admitting nothing from outside.

I could not of course imagine that the method which in the system of logic I have followed—or rather which this system follows of itself—is not capable of much improvement, of much elaboration in detail, but at the same time I know that it is the only true method. This is already evident from the fact that the method is in no way different from its object and content; for it is the content in itself, *the dialectic which it has in itself*, that moves it on. It is clear that no expositions can be regarded as scientific which do not follow the course of this method, and which are not conformable to its simple rhythm, for that is the course of the thing itself.

In accordance with this method I would observe that the divisions and headings of the books, sections, and chapters which are given in the work, as well as to some extent the explanations connected with them, were made for the purposes of a preliminary survey, and that in fact they have only a *historical* value. They do not belong to the content and body of the science, but are compiled by external reflection, which has already run through the whole of the scheme, and hence knows and indicates in advance the sequence of its phases, before these introduce themselves in the subject itself.

In the other sciences, too, such preliminary definitions and divisions are in themselves no other than such external specifications; but even within each science they are not raised above this status. Even in logic, for example, we may be told that "logic has two principal parts, (1) the Doctrine of Elements and (2) Methodology"; then under the first head we forthwith find, perhaps, the superscription: *Laws of Thought;* and then: *Chapter I—Concepts. First Section: Of the Clearness of Concepts*—and so on. These determinations and divisions, made without any deduction or justification, furnish the systematic framework and the whole bond of connection of such sciences. Such a logic regards it as its business to say that concepts and truths must be *derived* from principles; but in what this logic calls method, derivation is the last thing that is thought of. The procedure consists, it may be, in grouping together what is similar, in putting what is simpler before what is compound, and other external considerations. But as for any inner necessary connection, this goes no further than the list of sections, and the transition consists merely in saying *Chapter II;* or *We now come to judgment,* and the like.

The headings and divisions which occur in this system too are designed in themselves to have no other significance than that of a table of contents. But in addition to this the *necessity of connection* and the *immanent origination* of distinctions must show themselves in the discussion of the subject matter, for they are part of the self-development of the concept.

That by means of which the concept forges ahead is the above-mentioned negative which it carries within itself; it is this that constitutes the genuine dialectical procedure. *Dialectic*—which has been regarded as an isolated part of logic, and which as regards its purpose and standpoint has, one may aver, been entirely misunderstood—is thus put in quite a different position. The Platonic dialectic too, even in the *Parmenides* (and still more directly in other places), is sometimes intended merely to dispose of and to refute through themselves limited assertions, and sometimes again has nullity for its result. Dialectic is generally regarded as an external and negative procedure, that does not pertain to the subject matter, that is based on a mere idle subjective craving to disturb and unsettle what is fixed and true, or that at best leads to nothing except the futility of the dialectically treated matter.

Kant set dialectic higher, and this part of his work is among the greatest of his merits, for he freed dialectic from the semblance of arbitrariness attributed to it in ordinary thought, and set it forth as *a necessary procedure of reason.* Since dialectic was regarded merely as the art of producing deceptions and bringing about illusions, it was straightway assumed that it played a cheating game, and that its whole power depended solely on concealment of the fraud; that its results were reached surreptitiously, and were a mere subjective illusion. When Kant's dialectical expositions in the *Antinomies of Pure Reason* are looked at closely (as they will be more at large in the course of this work) it will be seen that they are not indeed deserving of any great praise; but the general idea upon which he builds and which he has vindicated is the *objectivity of appearance* and the *necessity of contradiction* which belong to the very nature of thought-determinations; primarily indeed in so far as these determinations are applied by reason to *things in themselves;* but further, just what these determinations are *in reason* and *in respect of that which is self-existent*—just this it is which is their own nature. This result, *grasped on its positive side,* is nothing other than the inherent negativity of these thought-determinations, their self-moving soul, the principle of all physical and spiritual life. But if people stop short at the abstract-negative aspect of the dailectic, they reach only the familiar result that reason is incapable of cognition of the infinite; a strange result, for —since the infinite is the reasonable—it amounts to saying that reason is incapable of cognizing that which is reasonable.

It is in this dialectic (as here understood) and in the comprehension of the unity of opposites, or of the positive in the negative, that *speculative knowledge* consists. This is the most important aspect of the dialectic, but for thought that is as yet unpracticed and unfree, it is the most difficult. If thought is still in the process of cutting itself loose from concrete sense-presentation and from syllogizing (*Räsonnieren*), it must first practice abstract thinking, and learn to hold fast concepts in their definiteness and to recognize by means of them. An exposition of Logic with this in view must, in its method, follow the division above mentioned, and with regard to the more detailed content must hold to the determinations of the particular concepts without embarking upon the dialectic. As far as external structure is concerned, this logic would be similar to the usual presentation of the science, but as regards content would be distinct from it, and still would serve for practice in abstract thinking, though not in speculative thinking (a purpose which could not be in any degree fulfilled by the Logic which has become popular by means of psychological and anthropological trappings). It would present to the mind the picture of a methodically ordered whole, although the soul of the structure, the method itself (which lives in dialectic), would not be apparent in it.

As regards *education and the relation of the individual to logic,* I observe in conclusion that this science, like grammar, has two different aspects or values. It is one thing to him who approaches logic and the sciences in general for the first time, and another thing to him who comes back from the sciences to logic. He who begins to learn grammar, finds in its forms and laws dry abstractions, contingent rules, briefly an isolated multitude of determinations which only indicate the worth and significance of their face-value. At first, knowledge recognizes in them nothing whatever but barely themselves. On the other hand, if anyone has mastered a language, and has also a comparative knowledge of other languages, he and he only is capable of discerning the spirit and the culture of a people in the grammar of their language. Those same dry rules and forms have now for him a full and living value. Through grammar he can recognize the expression of mind in general— that is, logic. Thus he who approaches logic finds in the science at first an isolated system of abstractions that is self-contained and does not reach out to other knowledges and sciences. On the contrary, contrasted with the wealth of our world-presentations and the apparently real content of the other sciences, and compared with the promise of absolute science to unfold the essential character of this wealth, the *inner nature* of spirit and of the world, and to unveil *the truth*, this science—in its abstract form in the colorless cold simplicity of its purely formal determinations—looks, rather, as if the last thing to be expected from it were the fulfillment of such a promise, and as if it would stand empty in face of that wealth. On a first acquaintance, the significance of logic is limited to itself; its content is regarded as only an isolated occupation with thought-determinations, *alongside of* which other scientific activities have their own material and their own intrinsic worth, upon which logic may perhaps have some formal influence which it seems to exercise spontaneously, and for which logical structure and logical study can certainly be dispensed with at need. The other Sciences have mostly rejected the regular Method, of a connected series of definitions, axioms, theorems and their proofs, and so forth; while so-called natural logic plays its part automatically in such series, and works of its own motion, without any special knowledge having thought itself for its object. Above all, the matter and content of these sciences keeps entirely independent of logic, and altogether makes its appeal more to our senses, feeling, impressions, and practical interests.

Thus then logic must certainly be learnt, at first, as something of which one has indeed perception and understanding, but which seems at the beginning to lack scope, profundity, and wider significance. It is only through a profounder acquaintance with other sciences that logic discovers itself to subjective thought as not a mere abstract universal, but as a universal which comprises in itself the full wealth of particulars; just as a proverb, in the mouth of a youth who understands it quite accurately, yet fails of the significance and scope which it has in the mind of a man of years and experience, for whom it expresses the full force of its content. Thus the value of logic only receives due appreciation when it is seen to result from knowledge of the particular sciences; so regarded, it presents itself to the mind as universal truth, not as a *particular* department of knowledge *alongside of* other departments and other realities, but as the very essence of all these other contents.

Now though when one begins to study it, logic is not present to the mind in all this recognized power, yet nonetheless the mind of the student conceives from it a power, which will lead him into all truth. The system of logic is the realm of shades, a world of simple essentialities freed from all concretion of sense. To study this science, to dwell and labor in this shadow-realm, is a perfect training and discipline of consciousness. In this realm the mind carries on a business which is far removed from the intuitions and aims of sense, from emotions, from ideas which are a mere matter of opinion. Regarded on its negative side, the work consists in holding at bay the accidentals of syllogizing thought and the arbitrary preference and acceptance from among opposing arguments.

But above all, thought wins thus self-reliance and independence. It becomes at home in the region of the abstract and in progression by means of concepts which have no substratum of sensation, it develops an unconscious power of taking up into the forms of reason the multiplicity of all other knowledge and science, comprehending and holding fast what is essential therein, stripping off externalities and in this way extracting what is logical, or, which is the same thing, filling with the content of all truth the abstract outline of logic acquired by study, and giving it the value of a universal, which no longer appears as a particular side by side with other particulars, but reaches out beyond all this, and is the essential nature thereof—that is, the absolute truth.

General Classification of Logic

In what has been said of the concept of this science, and the direction which its justification must take, it is implied that a general classification can at this point be only provisional, and hence can be indicated only so far as the author already knows the science and is thus in a position to present here, historically and in a preliminary fashion, the principal forms in which the concept will manifest itself in the course of its development.

A provisional attempt can, however, be made to render generally intelligible what is required for such a classification, although in doing so one must employ a method that will only receive its full elucidation and justification within the precincts of the science itself. First, then, it is to be remembered that we here presuppose that the classification must harmonize with the concept, or rather must be immanent in it. The concept is not indeterminate; it is determinate in itself; and the classification is the developed expression of this its determinateness. It is the fundamental and significant classification* of the concept; not of anything taken from without, but the fundamental classification, that is, the determination of the concept by itself. The quality of being right-angled,

---

* German, *Urteil.*—Trans.

acute-angled, or equilateral, the determinations according to which triangles are classified, are not contained in the determinateness of the triangle itself; that is, they are not contained in what we are accustomed to call the concept of the triangle, any more than the commonly admitted concept of animal in general, or of mammal, bird, and so forth contains the determinations by which animals are classified into mammals, birds, and so on, and these classes are subdivided into further genera. Such determinations are obtained otherwise, that is, from empirical contemplation; they come to these so-called concepts from without; but in the philosophical treatment of classification, it must be shown that the classification has its origin in the concept itself.

But in the Introduction the concept of logic itself is stated to be the result of a science which lies outside logic, and thus this concept too is here presupposed. Logic was there found to determine itself as the science of pure thought, having pure knowledge as its principle, which is not abstract, but a concrete living unity; for in it the opposition in consciousness between a subjective entity existing for itself, and another similar objective entity, is known to be overcome, and existence is known as pure concept in itself, and the pure concept known as true existence. These are then the two *moments* which are contained in logic. But they are now known as existing inseparably, and not as in consciousness each existing for itself; it is only because they are known as distinct and yet not merely self-existent that their unity is not abstract, dead, and immobile, but concrete.

This unity constitutes an element of the logical principle, so that the development of the distinction which is immediately latent within it takes place only within this element. We have said that the classification is the fundamental classification of the concept, the positioning of the determination immanent in it and thus of its distinction; hence this positing is not to be understood as resolving that concrete unity back into its determinations regarded as self-existent entities, which here would be mere retrogression to the former position, namely, the opposition of consciousness. This opposition, on the contrary, has vanished, and that unity remains the element, beyond which the distinctions which occur in the classification and the development generally, do not pass. And thus determinations (such as the subjective and the objective, thought and being, concept and reality, whatever the respect in which they were determined)—determinations which, at an earlier point on the road to truth, were self-existing, are now, in their unity (which constitutes their truth), degraded to the rank of forms. In their distinction they therefore remain, in themselves, the whole concept, and this is placed under its own determinations in the classification.

Thus the whole concept is to be considered, first as existent concept, secondly merely as concept; in the former case it is merely the *concept in itself*, the concept of reality or being; in the latter, it is the concept as such existing for itself (as it is found, to give a concrete example, in thinking man, and even in the sentient animal and in organic individuality in general, though there it is not conscious, still less known: *concept in itself* it is only in inorganic nature). Logic is accordingly to be divided into the Logic of the concept as Being, and of the concept as concept; or, to employ terms more habitual though least definite and therefore most ambiguous, into *objective* and *subjective* logic.

The basic element, then, is the unity of the concept in itself, and the inseparable nature of its determinations; these, therefore, in so far as they are distinct, and the concept is posited in their distinctness, must at least be somehow related. There results a sphere of mediation—the concept as a system of *determinations of reflection*, that is, of being in transition to the being-in-self of the concept; thus the concept is not yet posited as such for itself; immediate being, as something external, still cleaves to it. This is the doctrine of essence, which is intermediate between the doctrine of being and that of the notion. In the general classification of this logical work it has been placed under objective logic, since, though essence already is the inward, the character of subject has been expressly reserved for the notion.

In recent times Kant* has opposed to what is commonly called Logic yet another, namely *Transcendental Logic*. What has here been called objective logic would partly correspond to what is transcendental logic with him. He distinguishes it from what he calls general logic because (a) it considers concepts which refer *a priori* to objects and thus does not abstract from the entire content of objective cognition—in other words it contains the rules of pure thinking about an object; and (b) because it further considers the origin of our cognition, so far as this cannot be ascribed to the objects. It is on the second of these two aspects that the philosophic interest of Kant is exclusively directed. His chief aim is to claim the categories for self-consciousness, for the subjective ego. By virtue of this de-

---

* It is to be remembered that I frequently take the Kantian philosophy into consideration in this work (superfluous though this may seem to some), because, however its detailed determinations and the individual parts of its development may be regarded in this work and elsewhere, It still remains the basis and beginning of modern German philosophy; whatever faults we may find with it, this must be set down undiminished to its credit. And further, objective Logic must frequently refer to it for this other reason, that it treats important definite aspects of Logic in greater detail, whereas later philosophical expositions have either neglected these, or else displayed a mere crude contempt for them; which has not, however, remained unavenged. The philosophies which are most widely diffused among us did not get beyond the Kantian results, that reason can cognize no valid content, and with regard to absolute truth must be referred to faith. Kant's *results* are made the immediate *beginning* of these philosophies, so that the preceding exposition, from which those results are derived, and which is philosophic cognition, is cut away beforehand. Thus the Kantian philosophy becomes a pillow for the intellectual sloth, which soothes itself with the idea that everything has been already proved and done with. Those who look for knowledge and a definite content of thought, which are not to be found in this dry and sterile acquiescence, must turn to that preceding exposition.

termination, his point of view remains within the boundaries of consciousness and its opposition, and there is a surplus, beyond the data of sensation and intuition, which is not posited and determined by thinking self-consciousness and is foreign and external to thought, namely, the thing-in-itself; though it is easy to perceive that such an abstraction as the thing-in-itself is itself only a product of thought, namely, of purely abstracting thought. Other disciples of Kant have expressed themselves concerning the determination of the object through the ego in this sense, that the objectifying of the ego is to be considered as an original and necessary activity of consciousness, so that this original activity does not yet contain the idea of the ego itself; this latter being the consciousness, or even the objectifying, *of* such consciousness. On such a view, this objectifying activity, freed from the opposition of consciousness, is just that which can, generally, be called *thought* as such.* But this activity should no longer be called consciousness: consciousness comprehends within it that opposition of ego and object which does not exist in this original activity. The name of consciousness gives a greater appearance of subjectivity to it than the expression "thought," which, however, is here to be taken in the absolute sense as thought *infinite* and untainted by the finitude of consciousness: briefly, as thought as such.

Kant's philosophy then, directing its interest on the so-called transcendental element of the determinations of thought, the treatment of these received no attention: it has not considered what they are in themselves apart from the abstract relation to the ego common to all, or what are their reciprocal deter-

---

* If the expression "objectifying activity of the ego" appears to suggest other productions of Spirit, e.g., imagination, it is to be remembered that we are speaking of a determining of an object in so far as the moments of its content do not belong to sensation and intuition. Such an object is a thought: to determine it means, partly, first to produce it, partly, in so far as it is already posited, to have further thoughts about it, further to develop it by thought.

minations and relations. Hence this philosophy has in no way contributed to knowledge of their natures. The only interesting matter bearing upon the point occurs in the *Critique of Ideas*. But for the real progress of philosophy it was necessary that the interest of thought should be directed upon the formal side, the ego, consciousness as such, that is, the abstract relation of subjective knowledge to an object; and that the cognition of infinite form, that is, of the concept, should be introduced in this manner. But in order that this cognition may be reached, that finite determination, in which the form still is ego, or consciousness, has still to be cast off. The form, thus developed into purity by thought, will then have in itself the capacity of self-determination, that is, of giving itself content, and that a necessary content, in the shape of a system of determinations of thought.

Objective logic then takes the place of the former metaphysic considered as the scientific reconstruction of the world, which was to be built of thoughts alone. If we refer to the last stage in the evolution of this science, we find, first and immediately, that it is ontology whose place is taken by objective logic—that part of this metaphysic which is to investigate the nature of *ens* in general—*ens* comprehending both being and essence, a distinction for which the German language has fortunately preserved different terms. Secondly, objective logic also comprises the rest of metaphysics, in so far as the latter attempted to comprehend with the pure forms of thought certain substrata primarily taken from sensuous representation, such as soul, world, God; and the determinations of thought constituted what was essential in the method of contemplation. Logic, however, considers these forms detached from such substrata, which are the subjects of sensuous representation; it considers their nature and value in themselves. The old metaphysic neglected this, and thus earned the just reproach of having used these forms uncritically, without a preliminary investigation as to whether and how far they were capable of being determinations of the thing-in-itself, to use the Kantian expression, or, to put it better, determinations of the rational. Objective Logic thus is their true critique, a critique which considers the forms of thought not under the abstract form of apriority as opposed to the *a posteriori*, but considers each according to its particular content.

Subjective logic is the logic of the notion, of essence which has transcended its relation to any mere being, real or apparent, and in its determination is no longer external, but is the free, independent, and self-determining Subjective, or rather the Subject itself. Since the subjective involves the misconception of the contingent and arbitrary, and, more generally, of determinations belonging to the form of consciousness, no special weight is to be attached to the distinction between the Subjective and the Objective, which will develop itself more clearly within the body of the Logic.

Thus logic is divided broadly into objective and subjective logic; more definitely, it has three parts, namely—

1. The Logic of Being,
2. The Logic of Essence, and
3. The Logic of the Notion.

BOOK I

THE DOCTRINE OF BEING

With What Must the Science Begin?

It has only recently been felt that there is a difficulty in finding a beginning in philosophy, and the reason for this difficulty, as well as the possibility of solving it, has been much discussed. The beginning of philosophy must be either mediate or immediate, and it is easy to show that it can be neither the one nor the other: so that either method of beginning is refuted.

It is true that the principle of any philosophy also expresses a beginning, but this beginning is objective and not subjective; it is the beginning of all things. The principle is a content somehow determined—water, the one, *nous*, idea—substance, monad, and so forth; or, where it relates to the nature of cognition and so is designed rather to be a criterion than an objective determination (like thought, intuition, sensation, ego, or subjectivity itself), it is still the determination of the content to which interest is directed. On the other hand, the beginning as such, considered as something subjective in the sense of some contingent way of introducing the exposition, remains neglected and indifferent; and so the need of the question, with what we are to begin, still seems unimportant compared with the need of a principle, which alone seems to contain the interest of the matter—the interest as to what is the truth and the absolute basis of all things.

The modern embarrassment about a beginning arises from yet another need with which those are unacquainted who, as dogmatists, seek a demonstration of the principle, or who, as skeptics, seek a subjective criterion with which to meet dogmatic philosophy—a need which, finally, is entirely denied by those who begin with explosive abruptness from their inner revelation, faith, intellectual intuition, and so forth, and desire to dispense with method and logic. If thought at first is abstract and concerns itself merely with the principle regarded as content, but in the progress of its evolution is forced to regard also the other side, the behavior of cognition, then subjective activity is perceived as an essential moment of objective truth, and the need arises of uniting method with content and form with principle. The principle is to be the beginning, and the actual *"prius"* for thought is also to be first in the logical thought-process.

We have here only to consider how the logical beginning

appears; the two aspects in which it can be taken, mediately as a result or immediately as a beginning proper, have already been named. The question which seems so important to contemporary Thought, whether knowledge of the truth is immediate and simply begins, whether it is an act of faith, or a mediated knowledge, is not to be discussed here. In so far as such consideration can be undertaken preliminarily, this has been done in another (in my *Encyclopedia of the Philosophical Sciences*, 3rd Edn. *Vorbegriff*, §§ 61 ff.) work. We need only quote here that there is nothing in Heaven, Nature, Spirit, or anywhere else, which does not contain immediacy as well as mediacy, so that these two determinations are seen to be unseparated and inseparable, and the opposition between them null. As regards philosophical discussion, the determinations of mediacy and immediacy, and hence the discussion of their opposition and truth, occur in every logical proposition. With regard to thought, knowledge, and cognition, this opposition receives the more concrete shape of knowledge mediate or immediate; and the nature of cognition is considered within the science of logic itself, in so far as cognition, in its wider and concrete form, falls within the science of spirit and the phenomenology of spirit. But to ask for clearness about cognition before the beginning of the science, is to demand that it shall be discussed outside its precincts; but outside the precincts of Science this cannot be done—at least not in a scientific manner, and such a manner alone is here in question.

The beginning is logical in that it is to be made within the sphere of thought existing freely for itself, in other words, in pure knowledge; its mediacy here arises from the fact that pure knowledge is consciousness in its last and absolute truth. We have remarked in the introduction that the "Phenomenology of Spirit" is the science of consciousness, demonstrating that consciousness has for result the concept of Science, that is, pure knowledge. The science of manifested spirit, which involves and demonstrates the necessity, and hence the proof, together with the mediation in general, of that standpoint which is pure knowledge, is thus presupposed by logic. In this science of manifested spirit we start from empirical and sensuous consciousness; this is immediate knowledge proper, and in the work mentioned its validity is discussed. Other kinds of consciousness, such as faith in divine truths, inner experience, knowledge through inner revelations, and so on, are shown on slight reflection to be very inappropriate as instances of immediate knowledge. In the treatise referred to, immediate consciousness is also the first and immediate element in the science, and therefore the presupposition: in the logic, that is, presupposition which appeared as the result of those reflections —namely, the idea as pure knowledge. Logic is pure science, that is, pure knowledge in the whole extent of its development. In its result, this idea has determined itself to be certainty become truth; certainty which in one aspect is no longer over against the object, but has incorporated it with itself and knows it to be itself; and, from another aspect, has given up its conviction that it is opposed to and destructive of the object: it has renounced this subjectivity and is one with this renunciation.

Starting from this determination of pure knowledge, the beginning of the science of knowledge is to remain immanent; and in order to effect this, no more is requisite than that we must contemplate, or rather, putting aside all reflections and opinions otherwise held, we must just absorb that which is presented.

Pure knowledge, taken as shrunk into this unity, has transcended all reference to an other and to mediation; it is the undifferentiated, and as such ceases to be knowledge; nothing is there but simple immediacy.

Simple immediacy is itself an expression of reflection, and refers to its distinction from the mediated: properly expressed, this simple immediacy is therefore pure being. Just as pure knowledge is to mean nothing except purely abstract knowing as such, so pure being is to mean nothing except being in general; being and nothing else, without any further determination or filling.

Being is here the beginning represented as arising from mediation, a mediation which transcends itself; it being assumed that pure knowledge is the result of finite knowledge, of consciousness. If no assumption is to be made, and the beginning is to be taken immediately, it determines itself only this way, that it is to be the beginning of logic, of independent thought. Nothing is there except the decision (which might appear arbitrary) to consider thought as such. The beginning must be an absolute, or, what here is equivalent, an abstract beginning: it must presuppose nothing, must be mediated by nothing, must have no foundation: itself is to be the foundation of the whole science. It must therefore just be something immediate, or rather the immediate itself. As it cannot have any determination relatively to Other, so also it cannot hold in itself any determination or content; for this would be differentiation and mutual relation of distincts, and thus mediation. The beginning therefore is pure being.

To this simple exposition of what is proper to the subject of the perfectly simple, which is the logical beginning, the following further reflections may be added; their function however cannot be to elucidate or confirm this exposition, which is complete in itself, since they are rather the result of ideas and reflections which, though they may come in our way at the outset, must, like every other preliminary prejudice, be disposed of within the science itself; so that really they should be made to await such disposal.

It has already been perceived that the absolutely true must be a result, and that, conversely, a result presupposes some primary truth; which, however, because it is primary, is not necessary, considered objectively, and, from the subjective side, is not known. Consequently the idea has arisen in recent times that the truth with which philosophy begins must be hypothetical or problematical, and that hence philosophy at first must be mere seeking. This view, frequently urged by Reinhold in the later period of his philosophy, must in justice be allowed to be based on a genuine interest regarding the speculative nature of the beginning in philosophy. The analysis of this view is also an occasion for commencing a preliminary understanding of the meaning of logical progress; for the view in question immediately implies a reference to progress. Progress in philosophy, in this view, is in fact retrogression and justification, the result of which is to show that the beginning was not taken arbitrarily, but is, indeed, partly the truth, partly the primary truth.

If it is considered that progress is a return to the foundation, to that origin and truth on which depends and indeed by which is produced that with which the beginning was made, then it must be admitted that this consideration is of essential importance; and it will be more clearly evident in the logic itself. Thus consciousness is led back on its road from immediacy, with which it begins, to absolute knowledge as its inmost truth; and the first term, which entered the stage as the immediate, arises, precisely, from this last term, the foundation. Still further, we see that absolute spirit, which is found to be the concrete, last, and highest truth of all being, at the end of its evolution freely passes beyond itself and lapses into the shape of an immediate being; it resolves itself to the creation of a world which contains everything included in the evolution preceding that result; all of which, by reason of this inverted position, is changed, together with its beginning, into something dependent on the result, for the result is the principle. What is essential for the science is not so much that a pure immediate is the beginning, but that itself in its totality forms a cycle returning upon itself, wherein the first is also last, and the last first.

Hence it equally results on the other hand that we must regard as result that to which the movement returns as into its foundation. From this point of view the first is equally the foundation, and the last derived: it is a result, in so far as we start from the first and reach the last (the foundation) by a series of correct conclusions. And further, the movement away from the beginning is to be considered merely as a further determination of it, so that the beginning remains the foundation of all that follows without disappearing from it. The movement does not consist in the derivation of an other, or in a transition into something veritably other; in so far as such a transition occurs, it cancels itself again. Thus the beginning of philosophy, the basis which is present and preserves itself in all the developments which follow, remains a something immanent throughout its further determinations.

What is one-sided in the beginning, owing to its general determination as something abstract and immediate, is lost in this movement: it becomes mediated, and the line of scientific advance becomes a circle. It also follows that the constituents of the beginning, since at that point they are undeveloped and without content, are not truly understood at the beginning; only the science itself fully developed is an understanding of it, complete, significant, and based on truth.

Now precisely because the result stands out as the absolute foundation, the advance of this knowledge is not something provisional, problematical, or hypothetical; it must be determined by the nature of the subject and the content. This beginning is not arbitrary nor temporarily accepted, nor is it something which, appearing arbitrary and assumed under correction, in the event turns out rightly to have been made the beginning. (The case is not that of the construction we are directed to make in order to prove a theorem in geometry, where it is only the proof which shows that we did right to draw just these lines, and then, in the proof itself, to begin with comparisons of just those lines or angles. For itself, the drawing of such lines and making of such comparisons does not render the proof self-evident.)

In this way the reason why in the pure science we begin from pure being was above indicated immediately in the science itself. This pure being is the unity into which pure knowledge returns, or, if pure knowledge as form is to be kept separate from its unity, then pure being is the content of pure knowledge. It is in this respect that pure being, the absolutely immediate, is also absolutely mediated. But it is equally essential to take it one-sidedly as pure immediacy, just because it is here taken as the beginning. Were it not to be taken as this pure indeterminateness, then, in so far as it were determinate, it would be taken as mediated and as thus already carried a step further; for what is determinate contains an other for a first element. It is therefore in the nature of the beginning to be being and nothing else. For entering into philosophy there is therefore no further need of preparations, nor of other considerations or connections.

We cannot extract any closer determination or positive content for the beginning from the fact that it is the beginning of philosophy. For here at the beginning, where there is as yet no philosophy, philosophy is an empty word, or an idea taken at random and not justified. Pure knowledge affords only this negative determination, that the beginning must be the abstract beginning. In so far as pure being is taken as the content of pure knowledge, the latter must draw back from its content and leave it to itself without further determining it. Or again, if pure being is to be regarded as the unity into which knowledge has collapsed at the point where its union with the object is consummated, then knowledge has disappeared into this unity, leaving no distinction from it, and hence no determination for it. Nor is there any other something, nor any content, which could be used to make a more closely determined beginning.

But even the determination of being, which has been accepted so far as beginning, could be omitted, so that the only requirement would be to make a pure beginning. There would then be nothing but the beginning itself, and it would remain to be seen what that is. This position might be used to pacify those who partly will not be satisfied because we begin with being (from whatever considerations), still less with the resulting transition of being into nothing, partly know no better than that in any science a beginning is made by presupposing some idea—such idea being next analyzed, so that it is only the result of this analysis which affords the first definite concept of the science. Were we too to observe this procedure we should have no particular object before us, because the beginning, as being the beginning of thought, must be perfectly abstract and general, pure form quite without content; we should have nothing but the idea of a bare beginning as such. It remains to be seen what we possess in this idea.

So far, there is nothing: something is to become. The beginning is not pure nothing, but a nothing from which something is to proceed; so that being is already contained in the beginning. The beginning thus contains both, being and nothing; it is the unity of being and nothing, or is not-being which is being, and being which is also not-being.

Further, being and nothing are present in the beginning as distinct from one another: for the beginning points forward to something other; it is a not-being related to being as to an other: that which *is-beginning*, as yet *is* not: it is advancing toward being. The beginning therefore contains being as having this characteristic, that it flies from and transcends not-being, as its opposite.

And further, that which is-beginning, already is, and equally, as yet, is not. The opposites being and not-being are therefore in immediate union in it: in other words, it is the undifferentiated unity of the two.

The analysis of the beginning thus yields the concept of the unity of being and not-being, or (in a more reflected form) the unity of the state of being differentiated, and of being undifferentiated, or the identity of identity and non-identity

This concept might be considered as the first or purest (that is, most abstract) definition of the absolute; which in fact it would be were we concerned with the forms of definitions and the name of the absolute. In this sense, this abstract concept would be the first definition of the absolute, and all further determinations and developments would be richer and more closely determinate definitions of it. Being may be rejected as a beginning by some because of its transition to nothing and the resulting unity of being and nothing: let these see whether their beginning, which starts with the idea of the beginning, and the analysis of this (which, though doubtless correct, also leads to the unity of being and nothing), will turn out more satisfactory than the method by which being is made the beginning.

But there is yet a further observation to be made on this method. This analysis presupposes as already known the idea of the beginning: it has therefore copied the methods of other sciences. These presuppose their object, and take leave to assume that everyone has the same idea of it, and is likely to discover in it roughly the same determinations that they themselves indicate and extract from the object in various ways by analysis, comparison, and other forms of reasoning. But that which constitutes the absolute beginning must likewise be something otherwise known; now if it is something concrete, and therefore contains a multiplicity of determinations within itself, then this relation, which it is in itself, is assumed as something known: it is asserted to be something immediate, and this it is not; for it is merely a relation of distincts, and therefore contains mediation. Further, in the concrete the contingency and arbitrariness proper to analysis and to varying determination begin to operate. The determinations which are extracted depend on what each individual finds given in his own immediate and contingent idea. The relation contained in a concrete, that is, a synthetic unity, is necessary only in so far as it is not a datum, but is produced by the inherent movement of the moments tending back into this unity—a movement which is the opposite of the analytic method, which is an activity belonging to the object and external to the object.

What has been said implies this further point, that that with which we must begin, cannot be something concrete, something containing a relation within itself. For such presupposes a mediation and a transition within itself from a first to an other, of which process the concrete, now reduced to simplicity, would be the result. But the beginning must not be a first *and* an other: in a thing which in itself is first *and* an other, progress has already advanced a step. That which constitutes the beginning (and that is, the very beginning itself) must therefore be taken, in its simple immediacy without content, as something not admitting analysis, hence as pure vacuity, as Being.

If anyone, impatient of the consideration of the abstract beginning, should demand that we begin, not with the beginning, but directly with the matter itself, the answer is that the matter is just this empty being: it is in the course of the science that we are to discover what the matter is; the science must not therefore presuppose this as known.

If any form is taken for the beginning in preference to empty being, then the beginning suffers from the flaws mentioned. Those who remain dissatisfied with this beginning are asked to set themselves the task of beginning differently in order to avoid these faults.

There is however one novel beginning in philosophy, which recently has become famous and cannot be passed over without mention, namely that which begins with the ego. It arose partly from the reflection that all that follows must be derived from the first truth, partly from the need that the first truth should be something known and, even more, something immediately certain. Such a beginning generally is not a contingent idea which can take a different form in different subjects. For, the ego, this immediate consciousness of self, first manifests itself partly as something immediate, partly as something known in a far higher sense than any other idea; things otherwise known, though they belong to the ego, are a content distinct from it and therefore contingent, whereas the ego is simple certainty of itself. But the ego in general is also something concrete, or rather the most concrete of all things—consciousness of self as of a world infinitely complex. In order to make ego the beginning and basis of philosophy, this concrete element must be removed by an absolute act by which the ego is purged of itself and is presented to its own consciousness as abstract ego. But this pure ego is now no longer immediate, nor is it the known and ordinary ego of our consciousness, to which the science was to be linked immediately and equally for all. Such an act would really be an exaltation to the standpoint of pure knowledge, where the distinction between subjective and objective has disappeared. But as this elevation is demanded immediately, it is a subjective postulate: in order to prove itself a legitimate demand the movement of the concrete ego from immediate consciousness to pure knowledge would have to be proved and demonstrated upon itself from inner necessity. Without this objective movement pure knowledge, even when defined as "intellectual intuition," appears as an arbitrary standpoint, or even as one of the empirical conditions of consciousness, with regard to which all depends on whether one individual finds it within himself or can produce it, and another not. But this pure ego must be pure essential knowledge, and pure knowledge is posited in the individual consciousness only through the absolute act of self-exaltation—it is not present immediately in consciousness; and it is just in this respect that the advantage is lost which is to arise from this beginning of philosophy, namely that it is something thoroughly well known which everyone finds immediately within himself as the starting point of further reflection. Rather, in its abstract essential nature this pure ego is something quite unknown to ordinary consciousness, some-thing which it does not find in itself. And here, on the contrary, there sets in the disadvantage of the illusion that we are speaking of something known, namely the ego of empirical self-consciousness, whereas in fact we are speaking of something remote from this consciousness. The determina-tion of pure knowledge as ego involves a permanent recollec-tion of the subjective ego, the barriers of which are to be forgotten, and preserves the idea that the propositions and relations yielded in the further development of the ego occur or are found in ordinary consciousness, since it is this of which they are asserted. This confusion, instead of immediate illumination, produces so much the more glaring complications and indeed a total loss of direction; among laymen especially it has led to the crudest misunderstandings.

Next, as regards the fact that the ego in general is deter-mined as subjective, it is true that pure knowledge clears the ego of its limited meaning, according to which the object presents to it an insuperable opposition. But for this very reason it would at least be superfluous to retain this subjective attitude and the determination of pure essence as ego. Such a determination, however, not only involves this disturbing am-biguity, but, more closely regarded, it still remains a subjective ego. The actual development of the science which starts from the ego shows that the object there persists in having and retaining its determination as *other* relatively to the ego, so that this ego from which we start is not pure knowledge which has veritably overcome the opposition of consciousness, but is still imprisoned in the sphere of appearance.

This further essential observation must here be made: it is true that the ego in itself can be defined as pure knowledge or intellectual intuition, and asserted as a beginning; but in philosophy what matters is not that which is there already in itself, or internally, but the present *in thought* of the internal element and the determinateness in which the latter thus presents itself. Whatever element of intellectual intuition is present at the beginning of the science, it cannot be anything but primary, immediate, and simple determination; or, if the object of such intuition is called the eternal or the divine or the absolute, the same applies to whatever of these elements is present in the beginning. Whatever name be applied of richer content than that expressed by mere being, the only matter for consideration is how such an absolute enters into thinking knowledge and the expression of this. True, intellectual intuition is the forcible rejection of mediation and of demonstrative external reflection. But if it asserts more than simple immediacy, it asserts something concrete, something containing distinct determinations. But it has already been remarked that to express and represent such a thing is a mediating movement, which begins with one of the determinations and proceeds to the other, even although the latter returns to the former; and further, such a movement must not be arbitrary nor assertory. Hence in such a representation a beginning is not made with the concrete, but with the simple immediate whence the movement starts. Further, if a concrete thing is taken as the beginning, there is lacking the proof which is demanded by the complex of determinations contained in the concrete.

The expression of the absolute, the eternal, or God (and God has the most undisputed right that the beginning should be made with Him), or the contemplation or thought of these, may contain more than pure Being: if that is so, such content has yet to manifest itself to thinking (and not to presentational) knowledge; for, however rich this content, the first determination which emerges into knowledge is something simple, for it is only the simple which does not contain something more than pure beginning: the immediate alone is simple, for there only no transition has taken place from one to an other. If these richer forms of presentation, such as the Absolute, or God, express or contain anything beyond being, then this is, in the beginning, but an empty word and mere being; so that this simple vacancy without further meaning is, absolutely, the beginning of philosophy.

This consideration is so simple that the beginning as such requires no preparation nor further introduction; and this preliminary discussion was not so much intended to deduce it as to remove all preliminaries.

Selections from

PHILOSOPHY OF RIGHT AND LAW

Translated by J. M. Sterrett (§§ 34–157) and C. J. Friedrich
(§§ 257–340); also connecting summaries by C.J.F.

PHILOSOPHY OF RIGHT AND LAW

Preface

THE IMMEDIATE OCCASION FOR PUBLISHING THIS OUTLINE IS the need to offer to my listeners a guide for the lectures which I am giving on the philosophy of right and law. This textbook is a broader and especially a more systematic development of the same basic concepts which are contained in the *Encyclopedia of the Philosophical Sciences* (1817) which are likewise intended as texts for my lectures.

But since it is appearing in print and therefore will reach a larger public, I am inclined to elaborate the *notes* which are intended briefly to mention related or divergent views, the further implications and the like. . . . However, this outline differs from an ordinary textbook by virtue of its method which is decisive. For it is presupposed that the philosophical way of proceeding from one matter to another and of scientific proof, that this speculative manner of knowing differs essentially from other modes of knowing. . . . The nature of such speculative knowledge I have developed fully in my *Science of Logic;* in this outline only here and there an explanation has been added concerning its elaboration and method. In view of the concrete and so very diverse quality of the subject we have abstained from proving and stressing the logical derivation in all detail—the whole as well as the development of its parts rests upon the logical spirit. I wish the study would be primarily understood and judged from this standpoint. For what we are here concerned with is *science,* and in science content is essentially tied to form.

[Hegel then speaks of the two predominant tendencies of either repeating the old trash or setting forth vague new generalities. Against both, science of the philosophical kind must be worked out.]

Anyhow, *the truth* concerning *right, ethics, and the state* is *very old*, just as it is *publicly declared and known in public laws, public morals and religion*. What more does this truth require, in case the thinking spirit is not content to possess it in this simple form, but to *comprehend* it and to find a rational form for this content which is in itself rational? For then such truth would appear justified to free thought which does not stop with what is given, whether it be given by the external and positive authority of the state or the consensus of mankind, or by the authority of inner feeling of the heart and of the immediately consenting testimony of the spirit, but which starts in itself and thus demands to know itself united with truth in the innermost sense.

The simple tendency of the naïve mind is to accept with trustful conviction the truth which is publicly known and to build upon this firm foundation its behavior and firm position in life.

[Hegel then points out that even this naïve attitude has difficulties, resulting from the many different opinions, but more important is the difficulty which arises from man's seeking freedom and a basis for his ethical behavior by thinking. This basic right is perverted when only what diverges from established right is recognized as thought. This is particularly noticeable with reference to the state where hostility against what is publicly accepted was presumed to be the only basis of theory. Hegel ironically remarks that one gets the impression that there never had been any state or constitution that was any good and that therefore it is necessary to start from scratch. This he contrasts with the study of nature where it is agreed that one must find out "how it is . . . that it is rational in itself" and that science is to discover this rationality as an "eternal harmony," its immanent law. By contrast, in the world of ethics and of the state which is rational to start with, reason is not supposed to be involved. In a longish footnote, Hegel develops the contrast between laws of nature and laws based upon right (*Rechtsgesetze*). These latter laws are therefore subject to further evaluation which opens the door to purely subjective opinions. But the truth is nothing subjective, he says, but is here too the very conception of the thing (*der Begriff der Sache selbst*). And such conception does not come to us naturally, but must be worked out by great scientific, i.e., philosophical effort. Truth is not merely a problem; it can be found. And it is important to find it, for the subjective opinions discredit philosophy with all those who are attached to the state. Hegel then criticizes the Kantian critical standpoint (without naming him) as one who claims that "the truth cannot be known" and that therefore the truth is "what each and every one may *lift from his heart, his sentiment and enthusiasm* concerning ethical subjects, especially the state, government and the constitution." Hegel bitterly turns against the romantic movement, and more especially Fries whom he calls the "leader of all this superficiality." For him the ethical world and more particularly the state is "the architectonics of rationality" which clearly differentiate the various aspects of public life, of each and every one's rights and duties, and which by such severe measure where every pillar, arch and vault is held in balance makes the strength of the whole result from the harmony of its parts. To substitute feeling for the work of reason and intellect of several thousand years is too easy. Hegel quotes Goethe's *Faust*, where Mephistopheles says, "Despise the mind and scientific work, the highest gifts of all mankind, and you have surrendered to the Devil and must go to destruction." Hegel then mentions that this sentimental agitation has also adopted the cloak of piety and claims the Bible as authority for its contempt for the law. True religion brings "from its inner service of God reverence for the laws of a truth which is in and of itself and above the subjective feeling."

After some more bitter words about those who refuse to study and recognize the inner rationality of law and right, Hegel alludes to the fact that as a result sound men get restless when anyone begins to speak philosophically about the state. Superficial approaches lead to the principles of the sophists who, as Plato has shown, "ground the principles of law and right upon *subjective purposes and opinions,* upon the *subjective feeling and the particular conviction*." From such views there results not only "the destruction of public order and laws, but also that of ethics, of affection and right among private persons." Hegel criticizes the governments for even protecting and promoting such views as these in which "*reason*, and again *reason*, and in endless repetition *reason* is accused, belittled and condemned." After elaborating this complaint, Hegel concludes:]

It is, therefore, to be considered an advantage for science—and it is in fact as mentioned the result of the inner necessity of the subject—that the former philosophizing which kept evolving within itself as an academic wisdom has been put into close contact with reality where the principles of rights and duties are serious. . . . It is precisely this *relation of philosophy to reality* which is involved in these misunderstandings, and I am therefore now returning to what I have mentioned before. Philosophy is, because it is the *exploration of the rational*, by that very fact the *prehension of the present and the actual (Wirklichen)*, and not the construction of something *otherworldly* that might be God knows where. . . . In the course of the following study I noted that even the Platonic Republic which is proverbially taken to be an *empty ideal* has essentially taken up nothing else but the nature of Greek ethics. When faced with the challenge of the deeper principle of the free and limitless personality, which to Greek ethics directly could appear only as an unsatisfied longing and hence as a disaster, *Plato* tried to aid Greek ethics against this challenge. But he could try to do this only in an outward and particular form of that Greek ethics by which he hoped to cope with the disaster, and in doing so he violated most deeply its deeper impulse, namely, the free and limitless personality. Yet he showed himself to be a great spirit in that the very principle around which his particular idea revolved was the axis around which the impending revolution of the world was revolving.

> The rational is actual;
> And the actual is rational.

Upon this conviction rests all naïve consciousness, as does philosophy, and philosophy starts from it in considering the *spiritual* universe as well as the *natural* one. If reflection, sentiment or whatever form subjective consciousness may have, looks upon the *present* as something *vain,* transcends it and knows it better, such subjective consciousness is itself vanity, since it has reality only in the present. If correspondingly the *idea* is seen as merely just an idea, an opinionated notion, philosophy by contrast offers the insight that nothing is actual but the idea. Hence what matters is to recognize and know the substance which is immanent and the eternal which is present beneath the temporal and passing which appears.* For the rational which is synonymous with the idea appears (by entering through its actuality into an outward existence) in a limitless wealth of forms, appearances and configurations, and thus encloses its kernel with a variegated rind. Consciousness at the outset lives in this rind, but the conception permeates it in search of the inner pulse which beats in the outer configurations. These endlessly manifold relations, this endless material and its regularities are not the subject of philosophy. It would mix in matters which do not concern it; it may save itself the trouble to offer good counsel in such matters. Plato could have omitted recommending to the nurses not to stand still with their children, always to rock them in their arms, likewise Fichte could have omitted perfecting the passport police to the point of suggesting that not only the description of suspects be entered in their passport, but a picture. In such elaborations there is no longer any philosophy and philosophy may omit such matters the more readily as it ought to be most liberal (tolerant) in all such endless details. . . .

Therefore, this treatise in so far as it contains political science is intended to be nothing else but an attempt *to understand the state as something rational in itself and so to describe it.* As a philosophical study it ought to be furthest from con-

---

* This elaboration shows that what Hegel means with his usually misquoted statement is that "the rational is the idea and the idea is rational," certainly less objectionable an expression of radical idealism.—Ed.

structing a *state as it ought to be*. The instruction which it may be able to impart cannot be directed toward telling the state how it ought to be but rather how the state is to be recognized and known as the ethical universe. *Hic Rhodus, hic salta.* . . .

To understand that which exists is the task of philosophy; for what exists is reason. As to the individual, everyone is the *son of his time,* and therefore philosophy is *its time comprehended in thought.* It is as silly to imagine that any philosophy could transcend its own time as that an individual could jump out of his time, jump beyond Rhodes. If a man's theory goes beyond its time, if it builds a world *as it ought to be,* it may exist, but only in his opinion. . . .

With a little change, that saying might be: here is the rose, dance here. Whatever lies between reason as self-conscious spirit and reason as existing actuality, whatever separates that reason from this one and prevents it from being satisfied with it, is the fetter of some kind of abstraction which has not been set free as a conception. To recognize and know reason as the rose within the cross of the present and thus to enjoy this present, this sort of rational insight is the *reconciliation* with actuality which philosophy provides for those who have received the inner demand to understand. Such men then are able to maintain subjective freedom in what is substantial. . . .

It is this which constitutes the more concrete meaning for what we designated above as the *unity of form and content;* for form in its most concrete meaning is reason as understanding knowledge, while content is reason as the substantial essence of ethical and natural actuality; the conscious identity of the two is the philosophical idea. It is a great willfulness, but a willfulness which does man honor, not to be willing to recognize anything that has not been justified in thought— this willfulness is the characteristic feature of modern times, and in any case the particular principle of Protestantism.

What Luther began through faith, felt and witnessed in spirit, is the very same thing which the more mature spirit seeks to comprehend in a *conception*, and thus to free itself in the present and to find itself. It is a famous saying that half a philosophy leads you away from God . . . whereas the true philosophy leads you to Him. It is the same with the state. Reason does not content itself with an approximation which is neither cold nor warm and is therefore spit out; nor does it content itself with the cold desperation which admits that in this temporal existence things go badly or at best "fair to middling" and that . . . therefore one better keep one's peace with reality. It is a warmer peace with reality which knowledge provides.

To say one more word about preaching what the world ought to be like, philosophy arrives always too late for that. As *thought* of the world it appears at a time when actuality has completed its developmental process and is finished. What the conception teaches, history also shows as necessary, namely, that only in a maturing actuality the ideal appears and confronts the real. It is then that the ideal rebuilds for itself this same world in the shape of an intellectual realm, comprehending this world in its substance. When philosophy paints its gray in gray, a form of life has become old, and this gray in gray cannot rejuvenate it, only understand it. The owl of Minerva begins its flight when dusk is falling.

But it is time to close this preface. As a preface it could only speak extraneously and subjectively of the standpoint of the writing which it precedes. To speak philosophically of a subject, it admits only a scientific and objective treatment. Therefore to the author any objection of a different sort from a scientific treatment of the subject itself must appear as a subjective epilogue and chance assertion and hence must be indifferent to him.

Berlin, June 25, 1820.

Introduction

1. *The philosophical science of law and right has as its subject the idea of law and right,* the conception of law and right and their actualization (realization—*Verwirklichung.*) . . . The unity of being and of the conception, of body and soul is the idea. It is not merely harmony, but complete fusion. Nothing lives which is not in some way idea. The idea of law and right is freedom, and in order to be truly comprehended, it must be recognizable (knowable) in its actual being.

2. The science of law and right is a *part of philosophy*. It must develop the *idea* which is the rational in a thing from its conception, or to observe the thing's own, immanent development (which amounts to the same). As a part it has a definite *starting point* which is the true *result* of what *precedes* it and which constitutes the so-called *proof* of it. The conception of law and right lies, therefore, outside the science of law and right, as far as its *development* is concerned, its deduction is here presupposed and its conception is to be treated as a *given*.

3. Law and right are *positive*, generally speaking, a) by virtue of its *form*, to be valid in a state; this legal authority is the principle for knowing law and right, it is the *positive science of law*. b) In relation to its *content*, such law receives a positive element 1) by the particular *national character* of a people, the stage of its *historical* development and the interrelation of all those conditions which belong to *natural necessity*, 2) by virtue of the necessity that a system of legal right must contain the *application* of the general conception to the particular and external quality of things and cases—an application which is no longer speculative thought and development of the conception, but a matter of subsuming such things under the

concept by understanding; 3) by the *final* determinations which are required for actual *decisions*.

[Here follows a long discourse against the romantic inclination to plead the sentiments of the heart against such hard thinking as is involved in the philosophy of law and right. What he has said about the limits of such a philosophy is merely intended to forestall the expectation that actual laws can be derived from such a philosophy. "To pervert the proposition that the law of nature or philosophical law and right is different from positive law into one which maintains that they are opposed to and in conflict with each other," this Hegel would consider a great misunderstanding.

Hegel then refers to Montesquieu and praises him as the expounder of the "truly historical view" which is also the "genuinely philosophical standpoint" according to which law is not seen in isolation, abstractly, but as part of a totality and "related to all the other aspects of a nation and a period," for only thus do they receive their true significance and their justification.

Hegel then states with appreciation the position of the historical school of law which he thinks very worthwhile, provided they do not confuse "the development in terms of history" with the "development from the conception." He sharply rejects the tendency of this school to convert a "historical justification" into "a justification valid in and by itself," and illustrates this point by reference to certain institutions of the Roman law, such as the *potestas* of the father, or Roman matrimony. The historical tracing out and "justifying" does not reach the "conception" which is the "truly essential." The point itself, as well as its insistent elaboration, show Hegel's animosity to the position of historical relativism which is so often imputed to him in our day. Speaking specifically of a newly published textbook, he remarks that the author forgets "to state whether the Roman law satisfied the highest demands of reason." And after citing the author's comparison of these Roman jurists with mathematicians (and Kant), Hegel characteristically comments: "But this intellectual rigor has nothing to do with the demands of reason and with philosophical science." Hegel even praises the Roman jurists for their lack of rigor and their escape into silly fictions, in order to deviate from unjust and repulsive institutions like slavery.]

4. The basis of law and right is altogether the *spiritual*, its
starting point the *will* which is *free*. Freedom constitutes
its substance and its end, and the legal system is the realm
of actualized freedom, the world of the spirit created by
the spirit as its second nature.

5. The will contains first the element of *pure indeterminacy*
or the pure reflection of the ego in itself by which every
kind of limitation, that is, every given and definite content,
is dissolved, be such content given by nature, needs, passions or impulses or immediately present. This indeterminacy is the limitless infinity of *absolute abstraction* or
generality, the pure *thought* of itself.

[Hegel then sharply criticizes as people "who know nothing about
will" those who would distinguish thinking and willing as different capacities. For the freedom of the will cannot be conceived
except as freedom of thought. Such thoughtless "will" is the basis
for destructive revolutionary action, the "spirit of negation."]

6. Secondly, the *ego* is the transition from such undifferentiated indeterminacy to differentiation, to the *determining
and positing* of a definite content and object. Such content may be given by nature or created by the conception
of the spirit. By this positing of itself as a *determinate* one
the *ego* enters into *existence*. We have here the aspect of
finiteness or *particularity* of the ego.

  This second aspect of the *determination* is likewise
negative; it too is suspension, namely the suspension of the
first and abstract negation. Like the particular altogether
in the general, this second aspect is contained in the first
and merely the positing of what the first is already in
itself . . .

[There follows here a critique of Fichte (and by implication of
Kant) as philosophers who stopped with the positive in the ego.
"The next step was to comprehend the negation which is immanent
in the general, as it is in the ego. . ."]

7. Thirdly, the will is the unity of these two aspects: the *particularity* which is reflected in itself and thereby is carried back to *generality*. . . . The Ego determines itself in so far as it is the relation of the negation to itself. Being this relation to itself, the ego is indifferent toward this determinacy, knows it as its own and as ideal, as a mere potentiality by which it is not bound, but in which it is merely because it posits itself in this determinacy. This is the freedom of the will which constitutes its conception or substantiality, its weight, in the same way as weight constitutes the substantiality of the body.

All self-consciousness knows itself as something general —as the potentiality of abstracting from all particulars— and also as a particular something having a definite object, content, end. But these two aspects are merely abstractions; the concrete and true (and everything true is concrete) is the general.

[Hegel here elaborates in terms of his general logic and refers to the Encyclopedia 112–114.]

11. The will which is merely free in itself is the *immediate or natural will*. The determining factors are . . . the *impulses, passions, propensities* by which the will finds itself determined by nature. This content . . . derives from the rationality of the will and is therefore rational in itself . . . but it is not yet in the form of rationality. This content is, to be sure, *my will for myself*; but form and content are still different and the will is thus a *finite will in itself*.

Empirical psychology recounts and describes these impulses and propensities and the needs which spring from them, as it finds them by experience and seeks to classify this material in the usual way. . . .

13. By the deciding the will posits itself as the will of a particular individual and as one which is differentiated from

others. But apart from its *finiteness* as consciousness, the immediate will is *formal* because of the difference of form and content; to such will belongs only the *abstract decision* as such; its content is not yet the content and the work of its freedom. . . .

14. The finite will stands above the content, the different impulses, as an *infinite ego*. It is at the same time *bound,* since it is only formally infinite, to this content which constitutes its particular nature and its external actuality . . . This content is therefore as far as the reflection of the ego in itself is concerned only a potential one . . . the ego the potentiality of becoming this content or another— to choose among these extraneous determinations . . .

15. The freedom of the will is according to this definition *arbitrary*. In such arbitrariness these two aspects are contained: the free reflection which abstracts from all content and the dependence upon the internally and externally given content and material. Because this content which is in itself necessary as an end is as far as reflection is concerned seen as potential, arbitrariness is *contingency* understood as being will.

[Hegel elaborates this thought by pointing out that it had been rightly objected to abstract rationalism and its self-determination that there are external circumstances which compel; hence the notion of arbitrary will may be called a deception, if it is identified with freedom, as is the case (according to Hegel) in Kantian and Friesian philosophy.]

16. That which the will has chosen in its decision, it can reject again later. But by this potentiality of *ad infinitum* going beyond this and any other content it might put in its place the will does not get beyond the finiteness. For every such content is something different from the form and hence something finite. . . .

17. The contradiction which the arbitrary will is (§ 15) *appears,* since it is the dialectics of the impulses and propen-

sities, as a mutual interference of these impulses; the satisfaction of one requires the subordination or sacrifice of another, etc. For since an impulse points simply in its predetermined direction and has no moderation in itself, the subordinating and sacrificing determination is the contingent decision of the arbitrary will. It does not matter whether this arbitrary will proceeds with calculating intellect or in some other way.

18. Concerning the *evaluation* of the impulses, this dialectic lets the decisions of the immediate will appear *immanent*, hence *positive* and hence *good; man* is called *by nature good*. But in so far as these impulses are *determined by nature*, and are hence opposed to freedom and the concept of the spirit and are *negative*, they must be *eradicated*; man is then called by nature evil. . . .

Supplement. The Christian doctrine that man is by nature evil is superior to the other which considers him good . . . The doctrine of original sin without which Christianity would not be the religion of freedom has that significance.

19. The demand for *purifying* the impulses contains the general notion that they ought to be freed of their immediate naturalness and of the subjective and accidental content, that they should be brought back to their substantial essence. The truth contained in this indefinite demand is this: the impulses should provide the rational system for the determination of the will; to thus conceive them through the conception of the will is the content of the philosophical science of right and law.

The content of this science can be presented in accordance with its several aspects, such as right, property, morality, family, state, etc., in this form, that man has by nature an impulse for justice, for property, for morality, also the impulse for sexual love, for sociability, etc. . . .

20. The reflections concerning the impulses which compares

them and their means, their consequences and relates them to the total satisfaction—*happiness*—*generalize* this material from a *formal* standpoint and purify this material by ridding it of its external crudeness and barbarity. This generalizing thought constitutes the absolute value of *education* (see § 187 below).

21. The truth, however, of this formal universality which is by itself indeterminate and receives its determination from each material to which it is applied consists in a *universality which determines itself, which is the will, is freedom*. Since this will has the universality, has it itself as the infinite form, as its content, its object and its end, it is not only the will which is free in itself, but also the will which is free for itself—the true idea.

The self-consciousness of the will determined by passion and impulse is *sensuous* . . . The *reflecting* will has the two aspects: the sensuous and general thought; the will which is in and for itself has as its object will itself, and therefore has will in its pure universality as its object . . . The immediateness of naturalness and its particularity . . . is suspended (and preserved) in this universality. But this suspension and preservation which involves elevation to the general is that which we call the activity of *thought*. The self-consciousness which purifies and elevates its object, content and end to this level of generality, accomplishes this as thought which *realizes itself through will*. Here is the point at which it becomes clear that the will is truly free will only as *thinking* intelligence. Those who speak philosophically of right, morality and ethics and yet wish to exclude thought and refer one to sentiment, to the heart, to enthusiasm, thus pronounce the deepest contempt for thought and science . . .

22. The will which is free in and for itself is truly infinite, because its object is this will itself. Hence its object is for this will not something else nor yet a limit; the will has

rather returned merely into itself. Furthermore, it is not mere potentiality, capacity, potency (*potentia*), but the actually infinite (*infinitum actu*); for the existence of the concept, its objective externality is inwardness is itself.

[In this paragraph, Hegel develops in very general terms the idea of the objective and the subjective will which he really does not clearly differentiate. As he himself says in a supplementary remark: "Usually one believes the subjective and the objective as firmly opposed to each other. But this is not the case here, since they merge into each other. Objective and subjective are not abstract terms, like negative and positive, but have a more concrete meaning." He then elaborates the several meanings of subjective and objective, but reaches no conclusion as to which to adopt. One wonders why he did not drop the distinction altogether.]

27. . . . the abstract conception of the idea of the will is *the free will which wills the free will.*

28. The activity of the will to resolve the contradiction of subjectivity and objectivity and to transform its ends from the subjective into the objective . . . constitutes the essential development of the substantial content of the idea (§ 21). . . .

29. Right and law, then, result from the fact that any human existence is an existence of free willing beings. Right and law are altogether freedom, as an idea.

[Here follows a critique of the Kantian proposition that law consists in limiting one's own freedom so that it may coexist with everyone else's freedom. Hegel claims that in part it is merely negative, and in part nothing more than an empty formalism. Hegel further claims that since Rousseau there has been this tendency to think of will not as rational will, but as the individual's particular arbitrary will. Once this is taken as the point of departure, the rational can only be seen as a limit for the will and its freedom.]

30. Law and right are *altogether* something *sacred* only because they make present the absolute conception, the self-conscious freedom. The *formalism* of law (and of duty,

too) results from the divergent development of the conception of freedom. The more concrete and richer general idea of law and right has a higher claim than the more formal, more abstract and therefore more limited law . . .

Each stage in the development of the idea of freedom has its own particular law and right, because they are the embodiment of freedom in one of its particular forms. If one speaks of the conflict between morality, ethics and law and right, this can happen only because by right is meant only the formal right of abstract personality. Morality, ethics and the state's interest each have their peculiar law and right, because each of these configurations is a determination and embodiment of *freedom*. . . .

31.

[In this paragraph Hegel indicates that he presupposes the knowledge of the method developed in the *Logic* by which the immanent unfolding of a conception is studied by means of the *dialectic*. "This dialectic is not some external activity of subjective thought, but is the very soul of the content which organically puts forward its branches and fruits." He repeats what he has said in so many other places that for him a rational consideration of an object is not reasoning about such an object, but realizing the rationality inherent in the object. "Science has only the task to make conscious this inherent rationality of the objects." § 32 elaborates upon this theme.]

33.

[In this paragraph Hegel outlines once again his system, as here presented. He relates the stages in the development of the free will to the different forms of law, as he sees them: the abstract and formal to the immediate will, the sphere of morality to the reflected will of the individual subject, ethics to the unity of these two aspects, to freedom as the actualized idea. The latter stage, Hegel further subdivides into what he calls that of the "natural spirit" to which corresponds the family; that of the spirit divided in itself to which corresponds the civil society, and finally that of the general and objective freedom to which corresponds the state. He adds that "this actual and organic spirit of a people becomes through the relation of the particular national spirits in world history actual as world spirit and reveals itself as such: the right of this world spirit is the highest."]

FIRST PART: *Abstract Right*

34. The absolutely free will, if we consider it according to its abstract *concept* (*Begriff*) is in its most undeveloped and unreal form—that of mere immediacy. Considered in this most imperfect form it is only abstract actuality (i.e., mere potentiality) relating merely to itself and negative in regard to all reality. It exists thus in itself as *particular will* of a *subject*. According to the phase of *particularity* the will has a further content of definite aims. But, as excluding individuality, it has this content at the same time as an external and immediately present world that happens to be before it.

Supplement. When it is said that the absolutely free will, as it exists in its merely abstract *concept,* is in the form of immediacy it must be understood in the following way. The fully perfected *Idea* (*Idee*) of the will would be the condition in which the *concept* would have fully realized itself, and in which its determinate being (*Dasein*) would be nothing other than its own development. At first, however, the *concept* is abstract, containing all sorts of definite contents. But these contents are as yet merely potential and undeveloped. If I say "I am free" the "I" which is free, is simply this oppositionless potential being, whereas in morality there is actual opposition. On the one hand I am an individual will, and on the other is the good or the universal even though it be in myself. Thus in morality the will already contains the distinctions of individuality and universality and is thus rendered definite. But primarily no such distinction is present. For in the first abstract unity there is neither progress nor mediation. The will is thus simply in the form of immediacy, or of mere being (*Sein*). The essential insight to be reached here is that this lack of determinateness or characterization is itself a sort of determination of the will. For it consists in the lack, as yet, of any difference between the will and its content. But this, being opposed to characterization, brings itself to the character of being a determined thing. This characterization is here simply that of abstract identity. The will becomes thereby individual will—the person.

·5. The universality of this for itself free will is merely formal relation to its own self. This is indeed a self-conscious though contentless relation. The subject is thus far person. The conception of personality implies that I as person, perfect in every way (in subjective willfulness, instinct, desire as well as in respect to my merely external existence), am determined and finite, and yet that I am absolute relation to myself. Thus I know myself, in finite conditions, as infinite, universal and free.

Personality first begins here, in so far as the subject has not merely self-consciousness in the sense of conscious relation to external things but where he has consciousness of himself as perfect though abstract *ego*, which negates all concrete limitations and validity. Thus there is in personality the knowledge of self as object, but as a purely self-identical object raised through thought into simple infinitude. Individuals and peoples alike lack personality in so far as they have not yet attained to this pure thought and knowledge of self. . . .

Supplement. It is the merely *abstractly* independent will that we call person. In one sense it is rightly held that the highest destiny of man is that of being person. In spite of this, however, we sometimes use this term person in a despicable sense. Person, however, is essentially different from subject; for the term subject expresses only the potentiality of personality. In this way, we might speak of every kind of living being as subject. Person,* however, is the subject, for whom subjectivity is consciously a possession; for, as person, I am absolutely for myself. Person is the individuality of freedom in pure self-acquired being. As such a person, I know myself as free in myself, and can abstract myself from every condition and circumstance, as there is naught but pure personality before me; and yet I am, as such, an entirely determined form of being. I am so old, so large, in this place, etc. Personality is thus at once lofty and lowly. It contains the unity of the finite and the infinite, of the boundless and the definitely bounded. It is the very loftiness of personality that it can sustain this contradiction, which could neither contain nor endure anything purely natural.

36. (1) Personality, in general, contains the capacity of rights, and constitutes the concept and the abstract foundation of merely formal right. Hence, the precept of merely abstract right is this: Be a person, and respect others as persons.

37. (2) Particularity of will is indeed a phase of total consciousness of will; but it is not yet explicitly present in abstract personality as such. It is present only as different from personality, the characteristic of freedom; it is present only as desire, need, instinct, accidental liking, etc. Thus, in formal rights, there is no question concerning particular interests—one's own gains or welfare, nor concerning the particular ground or motive of one's will, nor concerning insight and intention.

Supplement. The element of particularity not yet being present in the person in the form of freedom, we have, at this stage, no concern with anything relating to it. Where the person has no other interests than his formal

---

* Compare with Hegel's use of the term "Subject" in the higher sense, in § 105.—Ed.

rights, he is likely to make these a matter of caprice, especially if he be of narrow mind and heart. It is chiefly the rough, uncultivated man who stands for his rights, while the magnanimous man considers the many different interests involved along with his own. Thus, abstract right is at first merely potential, and thus quite formal in regard to the whole circle of interests involved. Therefore, the legal right affords a warrant, which, however, it is not necessary for a cultured man to pursue, because it represents only one side of the whole context; for potentiality is the sort of being which has also the significance of not being.

38. In relation to the concrete activity of moral and ethical (*sittlich*) relations, we may say that abstract right is only a potentiality, and legal right thus only a permission or warrant. The necessity of this sort of right limits itself, by reason of its abstractness, to the negative form of preserving personality and all its results from injury. Hence, there are only legal prohibitions. Even the positive form of legal injunctions has only prohibition at its basis.

39. (3) The specific and immediate individuality of the person is related to a world of nature, over against which the personality of the will stands as something subjective. But the limitation of subjectivity to this personality as something universal and infinite, is something quite contradictory and futile. Personality is itself the activity which abrogates this contradiction and gives itself reality, or what is the same, posits that world of nature as being its own.

40. Rights are primarily, the immediate form of determinate being which freedom proposes to itself:

(a) *Possession and Property.* Freedom is here that of abstract will as such, or of a single individual as a self-relating personality.

(b) The person distinguishing himself from himself, relates himself to another person, both having definite existence for each other only so far as they both are owners of property. There is here an implicit identity which gains definite form through the transference of property of one to the other. This involves a common will and the maintenance of rights. This is the sphere of *Wrong* and *Crime*.

. . . Here it is evident that the right to things belongs only to personality as such. The so-called *rights of person* among the Romans implied a man's having the *status* of being a legal person. Personality was thus only a *status* as opposed to slavery. . . . Hence, such rights were not the rights of a person as such. We shall see later on that the family relation involves, as its essential condition, rather the giving up of personality, or of the strict legal rights of person. Hence, it is not the place to treat of the rights of definite concrete personality before treating of those of abstract personality. . . .

FIRST SECTION: *Property*

41. In order that a person be a fully developed and independent organism, it is necessary that he find or make some external sphere for his freedom. Because the person as absolutely existing, infinite will is, as yet, in this entirely abstract form, we find that this external sphere which is essential to constitute his freedom, is designated as being equally something distinct and separable from himself.

Supplement. The rationality of property does not lie in its satisfaction of wants, but in its abrogation of the mere subjectivity of personality. It is in property that person primarily exists as reason. Although the primitive reality of my freedom in an external thing be a bad form of reality, still abstract personality in its immediate form can have no other sort of real existence.

42. That which is thus immediately distinct from the free spirit, is for this free spirit, as well as in its own nature,

something external, unfree, impersonal and rightless. . . .
Supplement. As this thing lacks subjectivity, it is something external not only to the subject but also to itself. Thus space and time are external and I, as a sensuous being, am myself external, spatial and temporal. The sensuous perceptions I may have are of something which is external even to itself. The animal may have sensuous perceptions, but its soul does not have its soul, its own very self, for object, but some external thing.

43. As immediate concept and thus as a single individual, person has a natural form of existence.

This physical form of being belongs to a person partly as an independent physical organism and partly through his relation to his body as an external thing. We are here speaking of person in relation to immediate forms of external existence, his body among others, rather than in his relation to them as developed into more definite things through the mediation of the will. . . .

44. As a person, I have the right to put my will into everything, which thereby becomes *mine.* The thing has no substantial end of its own, but only attains this quality by being related to my will. That is, mankind has the right of absolute proprietorship.

The so-called philosophy which ascribes independent reality to immediate individual impersonal things, as well as the philosophy which assures us that the spirit cannot recognize the truth or know what the thing in itself is— all such philosophy is immediately refuted by the conduct of free will toward these things. If, perchance, such things have for sensuous perception and representation the appearance of independent reality, we find that on the other hand the free will is the idealism, the real truth of such apparent reality.

Supplement. All things are capable of being made the property of man, because he is free will and as such in and for himself, while everything else lacks this quality. Every man, therefore, has the right to put his will into things that is, to annul them and make them his own. For they, as external, have no self-aim; they are not that infinite reference of self to self, as subject, but are even externalities to themselves. Every living thing (the animal) is such an externality and thus a thing. Only the will is infinite, absolute in reference to all else, which in turn is only relative. To make such things *mine* is really only to manifest the dignity of my will in comparison with them, and to demonstrate that they are not independent and do not have any self-end. This manifestation is made through my putting in the thing another end than that which it immediately had. I give the living thing, the animal, as my property, another soul, I give it my soul. Thus the free will is the idealism which preserves things, but not as they are immediately, while realism holds them as being in and of themselves absolute and real, though they are finite. Animals themselves do not have this realistic philosophy as to things. For they eat things up, thereby proving that they are not absolute and independent.

45. Possession is constituted by my having anything merely within my own external power. The special interest in possession comes from my having made some element of natural want, desire or caprice my own. The side of this activity of possession, which brings out my free and actual will, is the positive and legal side, or the characteristic of *property*.

In respect to want, which appears as the primary phase, property seems to be means. But the true position from the standpoint of freedom is that which regards property in its first definite form as essentially an end for freedom itself.

46. In *property* my will becomes personal to me, hence objective as the will of the individual. Thus property receives

the character of private property and also that of common property, which according to its nature can be possessed as parceled out among many individuals. Here we have the characteristic of a potentially dissolvable community or partnership, it being a matter of caprice whether or not I shall let my portion remain in the common property. . . . *Supplement.* In saying that the will becomes personal in property, it is to be noted that person is here used in the sense of particular being, so that property becomes personal property. As I give to my will this form of externality, it is essential that property have the definite character of being mine in particular. This is the important doctrine of the necessity of private property. Any restriction made to it must be made solely by the State. Frequently indeed, especially in our times, private property has been restored by the State. Many states have rightly enough abolished cloisters, because ultimately a community has no such right to property as the person.

47. As person I am to possess my own life and body as I do other things just in so far as I put my will into them. . . . The souls of the animals possess their bodies indeed, but they have no right to their life because they do not put their will into it.

48. The body, in so far as it is an uncultivated piece of external existence, is inadequate to the spirit. The spirit must first take possession of it in order to make it its animated tool. But in reference to other people I am essentially free even as to my body. . . . It is but a vain sophistry which says that the real person—the soul—cannot be injured by maltreatment offered to one's body. . . . Violence done to my body is really done to me.

49. It is the rational thing then for me, in relation to external things, to possess property. But the particular form or amount of property possessed depends upon subjective

aims, needs, caprice, talents and external circumstances. Moreover, such possession, in this sphere of abstract personality, is not yet explicitly set forth as identical with freedom. Hence it is a matter of mere legal contingency as to the kind and quantity of property that I possess.

All persons are equal in this abstract sphere, if indeed we can here speak of many persons. This is but a tautological proposition. For person is yet abstract and unparticularized. Equality is identity of the understanding. This is the standpoint first taken by reflective thought and mediocrity of spirit, when the relation of unity and difference first occurs to it. Here then we have only the abstract equality of abstract persons. Outside of this, that is, in every particular form of possession, there is really inequality. The demand sometimes made for an equal division of lands or possessions can only be made by a very superficial understanding. For in the sphere of actual particular possessions there falls not only the contingency of external nature, but also the whole of the spiritual nature with its infinite number of differences and its developed organic form of reason. We cannot speak of an injustice of nature in an unequal partition of possessions and means, for nature is not free and so neither just nor unjust. That all men should have a competency for their needs is a well-meant moral desire, but without any objective reality. Then, too, it is to be noted that what we call a competency is something different from possessions and belongs to the later stage, *Civil Society*.

Supplement. The equality which one might introduce in regard to the partition of goods would, in any event, be destroyed in a short time, since property depends upon industry. The impossibility of such an equal distribution should prevent all attempts to secure it. . . . It is wrong to maintain that justice demands that each one should have an equal amount of property. For the demand is only that each should have property. It is then rather true that equality of possessions would be unjust in the sphere of particularity, which is the sphere of inequality. . . .

50. A thing belongs to the accidental first comer who gets it, because a second comer cannot take possession of what is already the property of another. The first comer is not legal owner by virtue of his being the first comer, but because he is free will. He becomes first comer only by the accidental fact that another one comes after him.

51. * * *

Supplement. The primary concept of property is that one puts his will into a thing. The fuller concept involves the full realization of the idea of property. It is necessary that the inner act of the will by which I say that something is mine, be made cognizable by others. In really making a thing my own, I give it the power of manifesting this in external form. It must not remain mine simply in my inner will. Children sometimes cry out against others taking possession of a thing, that they had wished it first. But such wishing is inadequate for grown-up people. The form of subjectivity must be worked out into objectivity.

52. Taking possession of the material of a thing makes it my property, as it does not belong to itself. . . .

53. Property has its proximate characteristic determinations in the relation of the will to the thing. This gives us,

(A) Immediate *Possession* in so far as the will has its objective reality in the thing as a positive existence,

(B) *Use* or *Consumption* in so far as the will has its objective reality in negating the thing possessed,

(C) *Relinquishment* of property, as the return of the will into itself out of the thing. These three phases are the positive, the negative, and the infinite judgment of the will in relation to the thing.

A. *Possession*

54. Possession arises (a) partly from the mere *corporeal seizure* of a thing, (b) partly from the expenditure of *formative work upon it* and (c) partly from mere designation, or putting the sign of ownership upon it.

55. * * *

    (a) *Supplement*. The hand is the chief organ of corporeal possession. This no beast possesses. And what I grasp with the hand becomes in turn the means of grasping more.

56. (b) Through the expenditure of formative work upon a thing possessed, it comes to have a sort of independent existence and ceases to be limited to actual present corporeal seizure as the condition of possession. . . .

57. Man is, primarily, a natural sort of existence, external to his essential being. It is only through the culture of his body and spirit, especially through the apprehension of his freedom through self-consciousness, that he takes possession of himself and becomes his own owner. This act may also be called that of actualizing his *concept* or of developing his potentiality, faculties, talents. Through such act the natural man becomes positively his own and truly objective. He is thus distinguished from simple self-consciousness and becomes capable of maintaining the proper form of manhood.

[In the remainder of this paragraph Hegel shows at some length, that the only justification that can be offered of slavery and of mere lordship over men comes from considering man as a merely natural form of existence. On the other hand, the absolute wrong of slavery can only be maintained by considering man as he is ideally, as having all his potentialities developed, that is, as free, independent, cultured and spiritual. This, too, is an abstract and one-sided view, identifying immediately the merely natural man with the spiritual man. The truth is that man by nature as a mere natural being is unfree, and that man by nature as fully developed man is free. But man has such a spiritual nature, not in the state of nature but in the state of an ethical, civilized community. The blame of slavery really lies upon the will of the enslaved man or people, rather than upon those who enslave them. The enslaved has not said, give me liberty or death, but rather, give me life even at the expense of liberty.

Historically, slavery occurs in the transition from the state of mere nature to the state of grace, in the concrete social relations of the civilized community. It occurs in that stage of human development where a wrong is still right. At such a stage, the wrong is of real worth and its place can be justified.]

58. * * *

(c) *Supplement.* Possession by means of designation or sign of ownership is the most perfect form, for the other kinds of it have more or less the effect of a sign. When I seize or when I form a thing, the ultimate significance is always that of a sign to others that I put my will in the thing so as to exclude their possessing it. The concept of a sign is that a thing does not stand for what it is, but for what it signifies. A cockade, for example, signifies citizenship in a state, though the color has no connection whatever with the nation, and represents not itself but the nation. Man shows his sovereignty over things by being able to give a sign and thus acquire possession.

B. *Use or Consumption*

59. Use is the satisfaction of my want through the alteration, destruction, or consumption of the thing, the selflessness of whose nature is thus made evident, and its real destiny accomplished.

Supplement. The thing is reduced to a means of satisfying my needs. In any struggle for existence between a person and a thing, one of them must lose its own being in order for there to be unity; but, in such a conflict, the I is the vital, willing, the real affirmative, while the thing is merely a thing. It must perish and I preserve myself, such being the rational prerogative of that which is organic.

61. * * *

Supplement. The relation of *use* to *property* is that of substance to quality, of potential to actual power. The field is only a field in so far as it produces a harvest. He who has the whole use of a field is the real owner, and it is an empty abstraction to recognize any other property in it.

62. Partial, or temporary use, or possession of a thing is, however, to be distinguished from ownership. It is only the complete and permanent use of a thing that constitutes me owner of that whose abstract title may belong to another. Only in so far as I permeate the thing throughout with my will, thus making it impermeable by others, is it truly mine. It is thus the essential nature of proprietorship that it be free and complete. . . .

It is more than fifteen hundred years since, under the influence of Christianity, personal freedom began to flourish, and became, at least for a small part of the human race, recognized as a universal principle. But the freedom of ownership has only since yesterday, we may say, been recognized here and there as principle. This is an example from universal history of the length of time required by Spirit for its advance into self-consciousness; also, an illustration against the impatience of mere opinion.

63 * * *

Supplement. We find, however, that the qualitative form of the use passes over into quantitative. . . . This last takes the form of *value*. . . . Money is the abstract form of value. Gold represents everything except the human wants; hence, it is itself ruled by the conception of specific value. A man can, in a way, be the owner of a thing without being the possessor of its real worth. A family which has possessions which it can neither sell nor spend, is not owner of their worth.

64. Giving form, and putting one's mark upon a thing, are, however, external circumstances, needing continually the presence of the active subjective will to give them meaning and value. This presence is manifested through *Use* and *Consumption,* which must be continuous to avail. Without this active presence of will in them, things are deserted—become masterless; hence, property may be lost or acquired by *prescription.* . . . *Prescription* is founded upon the very character of property, namely, upon the actual manifestation of the will to possess something. Public monuments are national property, so long as they are of worth through the indwelling soul of national honor and traditions. Deprived of this national spirit, they become masterless, and are thus the fair booty of any individual who chooses to take them, e.g., the Grecian and Egyptian works of art in Turkey. So, too, the extinction of copyright in the family of an author rests upon the same principle. Literary works become masterless (though in just the opposite way), like national monuments; that is, they become universal property as to their worth, instead of being private property. So, the mere land of unused cemeteries, or that which is otherwise consecrated to eternal non-use, implies merely a non-present, arbitrary will, through the infringement of which no real interest is injured. Sacred respect for all such unused land cannot be guaranteed.

C. *The Relinquishment of Property*

65. I can relinquish my property, because it is mine only in so far as I put my will into it. I can give up (*derelinquere*) my lordship over anything that is mine, or I can deliver it over to another will for possession. But this refers only to such things as are by their very nature external.

Supplement. Such a true alienation is a direct declaration of the will, in contrast with alienation by prescription. In fact, when the whole process of property is looked at, we see its relinquishment to be a genuine act of taking possession. The first phase of property is the immediate taking possession of a thing. Then further ownership is acquired through use, while taking possession through the voluntary relinquishment of ownership is the last and fullest sort of ownership.

SECOND SECTION: *Contract*

72. Property, even as an external form of existence, is merely a thing. As property, the thing has been permeated by human will. In contract, we have the process which represents and resolves the contradiction that I am and remain independent exclusive proprietor, so far as I, in a will identical with the other will, cease to be proprietor.

73. I can alienate property not only as an external thing, but it also belongs to its very concept that I dispose of it as property, in order that my will stand over against me as some definite objective affair. But my will, as thus parted with, is another will. This process, accordingly, wherein that necessity of the concept is real, is the unity of different wills, in which their differences and peculiarities are annulled. But in this identity of will there is, at this stage, implied that each will, as not identical with the other, is and remains explicitly particular will.

75. As both of the contracting parties are related to each other as independent persons, we have

(a) Contract proceeding from the arbitrary choice of the parties.

(b) The common will expressed in the contract is only common and not a genuine universal.

(c) The subject matter of contract is only a particular

external thing, as only such can be relinquished at the arbitrary choice of the individual.

[Hegel then decries the subsumption of *marriage* under contract, notes that Kant does so and remarks that it is a shame. Nor can the State be related to a contract, whether this be a contract of all with all or one of all with the prince, or the government. He comments that great confusions have resulted from this contractual theory. He states that this results in misinterpreting public as private law and right and refers to his treatment of the matter further on.]

SECOND PART: *Morality*

105. The moral standpoint is that of the will in so far as it is infinite, not merely in an abstract and potential form, as actually thus infinite for itself. This reflection of the will into itself and its independent identity, as opposed to merely implicit being, and the immediacy and the self-developing determinations in this latter, constitutes the *person a subject.*

106. Since subjectivity now constitutes the characteristic of the *concept,* and is different from the concept in the form of implicitly existent will, and, indeed, as subjectivity is at the same time the will of the subject as an independent individual which still contains the element of immediacy, it constitutes the determinate being of the *concept.* Thus subjectivity gives a higher basis for freedom. In reference to the *Idea,* the subjectivity of the will forms the side of existence, its phase of reality. Freedom, or the potential will, can actually exist only in subjective will.

This second sphere, that of morality, represents, therefore, on the whole the real side of the concept of freedom; and the process in this sphere is that of annulling the will which is at first existing only for self, and which is immediately only implicitly identical with the potentially existing universal will, according to that difference in which it becomes profoundly self-involved. The process also includes that of positing the will existing for itself, as identical with the potentially existing will. This process is accordingly the elaboration of this present basis of freedom (of that subjectivity which is at first abstract, that is to say, distinguished from the concept), to equality with the *concept*, which thereby becomes capable of receiving for the *Idea* its true realization. In this process the subjective will determines itself thereby as truly objective and concrete.

Supplement. In treating of strict formal right, we were not concerned with the question as to one's principle or intention. This question concerning the self-determination and motive (*Triebfeder*) of the will, as well as concerning design, enters only here with the moral.

A man desires to be judged according to his own self-determination; he is, in this respect, free, whatever the external conditions may be. One cannot encroach upon this conviction of men; no violence can be done to it, and the moral will is therefore inaccessible. Man's worth is estimated according to his inner action, and hence, the moral standpoint is that of independent freedom.

107. The self-determination of the will is at the same time a phase of its concept, and subjectivity is not only the side of its determinate being, but it is its own determination. The independent free will, defined as subjective, at first as concept, has, itself, determined being in order to exist as *Idea*. The moral standpoint is therefore, as to its form, the right of the subjective will. According to this right, the will recognizes, and is, something only in so far as the right is its own. The will is in this as a subjective thing to itself. . . .

Supplement. The whole determination of the will is again a totality which as subjectivity must also have objectivity. Freedom can realize itself only in the subject, for the subject is the true material for this realization. But this determinate being of the will, which we called subjectivity, is different from the absolutely independent will. The will, in order to become such independent will, must free itself from this other, from the one-sidedness of mere subjectivity. In morality it is the distinct interest of men which comes in question, and this is just the high value of the same, that man knows himself as absolute and that he determines himself. The uncultured man allows himself to be imposed upon by mere brute force and natural laws. Children likewise have no moral will, but permit themselves to be directed by their parents. But the cultured self-developing man desires that he himself be in everything which he does.

108. The subjective will, as immediately for itself and distinguished from the potential will, is hence abstract, limited and formal. But subjectivity is not only formal, but, as the infinite self-determination of the will, it constitutes the formality of the same. As this, in its first appearance as individual will, is not yet posited as identical with the *concept* of the will, we find that the moral standpoint is that of relation, of obligation or requirement. And inasmuch as the element of difference in subjectivity contains just as well determination opposed to objectivity in the form of determinate being, so the standpoint of consciousness is here also attained—or in general, the standpoint of difference, finiteness and phenomenality (*Erscheinung*) of will.

The moral is primarily not yet determined as the opposite of the immoral, as right is not immediately the opposite of wrong; but it is the universal standpoint of the moral as well as of the immoral which is based upon the subjectivity of the will.

Supplement. Self-determination in morality is to be conceived of as the pure restless activity which has not yet attained any definite existence. It is first in the ethical (*Sittlichen*) that the will is identical with the *concept* of the will and has only this latter as its content. In the moral, the will is still related to that which is potential. It is therefore the standpoint of difference, and the process of this standpoint is the identification of the subjective will with the *concept* of the latter. The *ought*, which is the distinguishing element of morality, does not however attain to actual existence, except in concrete social relations of men. This ought to which the subjective will is related is a double thing. It is one time the substantial being of the *concept*, and again the externally existing. Even if the good were posited in the subjective will, it would not yet be thereby executed.

[Hegel in the succeeding paragraphs discusses the proposition that the simple identity of the will transcends the subjective and the objective. This is the meaning of aim or purpose (*Zweck*). After elaborating this problem of the identity of the will, Hegel continues:]

114. The right of moral will has three aspects:

(A) The abstract or formal right of action in such a way that the content of the action, carried out into immediate determinate existence, be mine and represent the purpose of my subjective will.

(B) The special character of the action is its inner content (a) as it is for me, whose universal character is determined by the worth of the action and what it avails for me—that is, inner *intention*— (b) its content as the special aim of my particular subjective being, that is, *individual well-being*.

(C) This inner content in its universality, as elevated into absolute, existing objectivity, is the absolute aim of will as will—that is, the *Good*. This is in the sphere of the reflection with the antithesis of subjective universality, partly of evil, and partly of conscience.

Supplement. In order to be moral, every action must primarily harmonize with my purpose, for the right of the moral will consists in recognizing in any action only that which was internally designed. Purpose thus makes the formal demand that the objective will be also the internal thing willed by me. In the second phase, that of inner *intention*, the question is concerning the relative worth of the action in reference to myself. The third phase concerns not only the relative but the absolute worth of the action, that is, the *Good*. The first breach of the action is between something proposed, and some definite accomplished affair. Then follows the breach between that which is external as universal will and the inner particular character which I give it. Thirdly we have the demand that the intention have universal validity. The *Good* is intention elevated to the concept of the will.

FIRST SECTION: *Purpose and Guilt*

115. The limitation of the subjective will in external action arises from the fact that in all such action there is the presupposition of an external object and its manifold environment. A deed implies the working of a change in this external realm, and the will is culpable in so far as the change thus wrought can be called mine, as being that proposed by me. . . .

Supplement. What was in my purpose can be imputed to me. It is with this proposed deed that we are chiefly concerned when dealing with crime. But in guilt (*Schuld*) there is the merely external judgment as to whether I have done a certain thing or not. Guilt does not primarily imply the quality of imputability.

117. In proposing to work a change in the given external realm, the self-acting will has a general idea of the circumstances. But as these circumstances limit it, the objective phenomenon is accidental and may contain something quite other than one's general idea of it. The subjective will claims as its right that, in any of its deeds, it recognize as its own and be held responsible for only what it proposes to do. The deed can only be imputed to the will, and for this the will demands the right of knowledge. .

118. The action, passing from the internal will into an external realm where external necessity binds all together, is followed by many consequences not calculated upon. In one way, the consequences properly belong to the action, as being what was aimed at. But at the same time the deed passes over into the dominion of external powers which add to it many foreign consequences. It cannot reckon all the consequences as its own, as being aimed at by itself, and so it disclaims responsibility for all consequences not contained in its original design.

It is difficult, however, to distinguish between the accidental and the necessary or proper consequences of one's own action, for the inner purpose or plan is nothing, for others at least, till it enters the objective realm, and, once there, inextricable complication bids defiance to perfectly clear demarkation between the two sorts of consequences. The principle is sometimes announced that in acting we may despise consequences. On the other hand it is proclaimed that actions are to be judged solely by their consequences. Both of these principles are abstract and untrue. . . .

Supplement. This disclaiming responsibility for all consequences not proposed soon leads to the next phase—that of *Intention*. But there are consequences beyond the known and proposed external effects. Although my deed is some one particular thing, it yet contains necessary and universal qualities. I cannot foresee all external effects of a proposed action, but I must know the universal element implicit in every deed. The transition from *Purpose* to *Intention* consists in the recognition that I ought to know the universal element in every action so as to will it, to *intend* it.

141. *Transition from Morality to Ethics (Sittlichkeit).*

The *Good* is as yet abstract. But, as the concrete substance of freedom, it demands determinations or qualities in general, as well as the principle of freedom, as identical with the *Good. Conscience,* which is yet only an abstract principle of determination, likewise demands that its determinations be given universality and objectivity. We have seen how both good and duty, when either of them is raised to independent universality, lack that specific definite character which they ought to have. But the integration of both the *Good* and *Conscience* as relatively independent is potentially accomplished in their organic unity. For we have seen subjectivity vanishing into its own emptiness, already posited (in the form of pure self-certitude or conscience), as identical with the abstract universality of the *Good.* This integration of the *Good* and *Conscience* is the real truth of them both. It is their concrete organic unity. This unity is the sphere of *Ethics,* or the concrete ethical world of social life.

This transition is more scientifically developed in the *Logic.* We are here concerned with its finite abstract side, i.e., with good demanding actualization and with conscience demanding the *Good* for its content. But both of these, as yet partial phases, are not yet explicitly developed into that which they are potentially. This development of both the *Good* and of *Conscience,* so that neither lacks the other, this integration of both into an organic unity, in which each is retained as a member ather than as an independent thing, is the realized *Idea* of the will. In this each one attains its true reality. . . .

We found the first definite characteristic of the determinate being (*Dasein*) of freedom to be that of *Abstract Right*. This, however, passed through the reflection of self-consciousness into the form of the *Good*. Here now we have the truth of abstract right as well as of both the *Good* and *Conscience*. The *Ethical* (*Sittliche*) is subjective disposition of mind, but only in reference to implicit* (*an sich*) rights. That this *Idea* is the truth of the concept of freedom, cannot be merely an accepted presupposition, but must be demonstrated by philosophy. This demonstration is simply that of showing how both *abstract right* and *Conscience* lead back into this organic unity as their truth.

Supplement. Both the standpoints previously considered lack their opposites. Abstract good vanishes into perfect powerlessness, and conscience shrivels into objective insignificance. Hence there may arise a longing for objectivity. A man would sometimes gladly humble himself to slavish dependency in order to escape the torture and emptiness of mere negativity. If recently some Protestants have gone into the Catholic Church, it is because they have found no definite codes and dogmas within their own spirit and have reached out after something stable, after an authority, even if what they obtained did not possess the strength of thought. Ethics (*Sittlichkeit*) or the ethical world of social life, is the absolute unity of subjective and objective good. In this sphere is found the solution of the antinomy in strict accordance with the concept of freedom. *Ethics* is not merely the subjective

---

* It seems that Hegel's thought requires some other term than implicit (*an sich*) here. The ethical in general has to do with the explicit. Hegel's reference to it here as subjective disposition in reference to implicit rights is only made in passing and without further elucidation, and is inexplicable.—Ed.

form and the self-determination of the will, but it has real freedom for its content. Both right and morality need the *ethical*, for their foundation, as without it neither has any actuality. Only the *Idea*, the true infinite is actual. Rights exist only as the branch, or as a plant clinging around a firm tree.

THIRD PART: *Ethics (Sittlichkeit)*

142. Ethics, or the ethical world of concrete social life, is the *Idea* of freedom, as the vital and virile *Good*. It is in self-consciousness that this *Good* attains to its knowledge and volition, and through their activity to its own actualization. On the other hand it is in this ethical substance that self-consciousness has its absolute ground and efficient end. Ethics is the *concept* of freedom, developed into the present existing world and into the nature of self-consciousness.

143. Since this unity of the *concept* of the will and its determinate being (*Dasein*), which is the particular will, is knowing, the consciousness of the difference between these moments of the *Idea* is present, but in such a manner that now each moment by itself is the totality of the *Idea*, and has the *Idea* as ground and contents.

144. (A) The objective ethical (*objektive Sittliche*), which takes the place of abstract good, is substance, *concrete* through its subjectivity as *infinite form*. This substance posits thence *differences* in itself, which thereby are determined by the concept, and through which the ethical concept gains a fixed *content*, which is explicitly necessary and elevated above subjective opinion and inclination. This content consists of the *in and for themselves existing laws* and *institutions*.

Supplement. In all ethics (*Sittlichkeit*) both the objective and the subjective aspects are present; but both are its forms only. The good is here substance, that means the filling up of the objective with subjectivity. When ethics is viewed from the objective standpoint, it may be said that the ethical man is unconscious of himself. In this sense, Antigone declared that no one knew whence the laws had come; that they were eternal: that is to say, they are the absolute independent realities, the determinations proceeding from the nature of the case. But nonetheless this substantial state has also a consciousness, although this consciousness has always, on this standpoint, only the position of a phase.

145. In the fact that the ethical is a *system* of these determinations of the *Idea,* consists its *rationality.* In this manner it becomes freedom, or the in and for itself existing will as the objective, the sphere of necessity, whose moments are the *ethical* powers that rule the lives of individuals and are actualized and revealed in them as their attributes (*Accidenzen*) and conceptions.

Supplement. Since the *concept* of freedom consists in the ethical determinations, these are the substantiality or the universal essence of the individuals, who, consequently, are related to this universal factor as something accidental. Whether the individual exists or not is indifferent to objective ethics, which alone is enduring, and the power through which the lives of individuals are ruled. Hence, ethics, or concrete morality, has been represented to mankind as eternal justice, as gods existing in and for themselves, against whom the vain striving of the individuals becomes only a fluctuating play.

146. (B) The substance is, in this its *actual self-consciousness,* cognizant of itself, and hence object of knowledge. On the one hand, by virtue of the fact that *they exist* in the highest sense of independence, the ethical substance, its laws, and domination, have for the subject an absolute authority and force, infinitely more stable than the mere being (*das Sein*) of nature.

The sun, moon, mountains, rivers, objects of nature in general, *exist;* they have for consciousness the authority not only of mere existence in general, but also of having a particular nature. Consciousness respects this particular nature, and is guided by it when employed with objects of nature. But the authority of ethical nature is infinitely higher, since the things in nature present rationality only in a wholly external (*äusserliche*) and *particular* manner, and conceal this rationality under the form of the contingent.

147. On the other hand, the ethical substance, its laws and authority, are nothing *foreign* to the subject, but they afford the subject the *testimony of the spirit,* as being *of its own essence,* as that in which it feels itself to exist (*Selbstgefühl*), and in which it lives as in its proper element, undifferentiated from itself—a condition that is unmediated and as yet identical, even as *faith* and *trust* are.

Faith and trust belong to incipient reflection, and presuppose a conception and differentiation; as, for example, believing in a heathen religion is different from being a heathen. This relation, or rather relationless identity, in which the ethical is the actual vitality of self-consciousness, can under all circumstances resolve itself into a relation of faith and conviction, and into something mediated by further reflection, into insight founded on reasons. This insight may also begin from any particular aims, interests or considerations, from fear or hope, or from historical antecedents. But its adequate recognition belongs to the thinking concept.

148. For the individual who distinguishes himself from these substantial determinations as the subjective and in himself indeterminate, or as the particularly determined, and to whom they *hence stand in the relation of substance,* these substantial determinations become duties which, in relation to his will, are obligatory.

The ethical *doctrine* of *duties* (that is, as it is *objectively,* and not as conceived according to the empty principle of moral subjectivity, according to which, indeed, nothing determines it, § 134) is, consequently, the systematic development of the sphere of ethical necessity. This forms the content of this *Third Part* of this treatise. The difference of this presentation from the form of a *doctrine of duties* consists in this alone, that, in what follows, the ethical determinations present themselves as necessary relations, without further consequence being added to each of them. *Hence this determination is a duty for man.* A doctrine of duties, when not a philosophical science, takes its subject-matter from conditions and relations contingently presented, and shows their connection with individual conceptions, with those principles and thoughts, aims, motives, feelings, and the like, which are generally entertained, and can add as reasons the further consequence of each duty in reference to other ethical relations, as well as in reference to common welfare and opinion. But an immanent and consistent doctrine of duties can be nothing else but the evolution of *those relations* which become necessary through the *Idea* of freedom, and hence *actual* throughout their whole extent, in the State.

149. Obligatory duty can appear as a *limitation,* only to undetermined subjectivity or abstract freedom, and to the desires of the natural will, or to that moral will which determines its indeterminate good through its own caprice. But the individual has in duty rather his *liberation,* on the one hand, from the dependence imposed on him when under the influence of natural desires alone, as well as from the oppression which he suffers as subjective particularity in the moral reflection as to what ought and what may be done; and, on the other hand, from the undetermined subjectivity which does not express itself

and thus attain the objective characteristics of action, but remains *in itself* as a non-actuality. In duty the individual shakes off subjective fetters and attains substantial freedom.

Supplement. Duty limits only the caprice of subjectivity, and comes in conflict only with the abstract good to which subjectivity clings. When men say, "We wish to be free," this means at first only, "We wish to be free in an abstract sense," i.e., free from objective laws. Hence every determination and organic differentiation in the State is held to be a limitation of this freedom. Duty is not a limitation, or restriction of freedom, but the abstraction of freedom, that is to say, of the opposite to freedom: duty is the arrival of freedom at determinate being, the gaining of affirmative freedom.

150. The ethical, in so far as it reflects itself in the individual character, as such is determined by nature, is *virtue*.

Inasmuch as this shows itself as nothing but the simple conformity of the individual to the duties of the situation in which he finds himself, virtue is *rectitude*.

What man should do, what duties he must fulfill in order to be virtuous, is easily determined in an ethical community. There is nothing else for him to do but that which is prescribed, proclaimed and made known to him in his ethical relations. Rectitude is the universal, that which can be promoted in him partly as the ethical and partly as the legally right. But for the moral standpoint, rectitude easily appears as something subordinate, over and above which one must demand something still more in one's self and others. The desire to be something *particular* is not satisfied with conformity to the universal and objective forms of duty as existing in the current conventional morals. Such a desire finds only in an *exception* the consciousness of the desired peculiarity. The *different sides* of rectitude may just as properly be called virtues, since they are just as much the property (though in the comparison with others, not the particular property) of the individual.

But discourse about virtue borders easily on empty declamation, since it treats only of an abstract and indefinite matter. Such discourse with its reasons and manner of presentation also appeals to the individual, as to a being of caprice and subjective inclination. In an ethical condition of society, whose relations are fully developed and actualized, such peculiar forms of virtue have a place and actuality only in extraordinary circumstances and collisions of these relations—that is, in *actual collisions,* for moral reflection can indeed find collisions under any circumstances, and obtain for itself the consciousness of having made sacrifices and of being something particular and peculiar. For this reason this form of virtue as such occurs oftener in undeveloped states of society and of the community. In such earlier stages the ethical and its actualization is more of an individual choice and a genial nature peculiar to the individual. The ancients, we know, predicated virtue especially of Hercules. In the ancient state however, ethics had not grown to this free system of an independent development and objectivity—thus the deficiency had to be supplied by the geniality of the individual.

The doctrine of virtues, when not simply a doctrine of particular duties, includes the character which is founded in natural determinations. Thus it embraces a *spiritual history* of the nature of man.

Since the virtues are the ethical in reference to the particular, and from this subjective side something undetermined, the quantitative "more" or "less" appears as their determination; and their contemplation brings up the opposite defects as vice. Thus Aristotle determined the correct signification of the particular virtues as the mean between a *too-much* and a *too-little*. The same content which takes the form of duties and then that of virtues, has also the form of impulses. These, also, have the same fundamental content. But since this content of the impulses belongs still to the immediate will and natural sensibilities, and has not been developed to the determination of ethics, the impulses have only the abstract object in common with the content of duties and virtues. But this abstract object, being without determination in itself, does not contain the limits of good and evil in itself. In other words, the impulses are *good* according to the abstraction of the positive, and conversely *bad,* according to the abstraction of the negative (§ 18).

Supplement. Where a person does this or that ethically good act, he is not straightway virtuous, but this he is when ethical behavior is a stable element in his character. Virtue is rather ethical virtuosity. The reason that we do not speak so much of virtue now as formerly, is that ethics is no longer so much some peculiar quality of a particular individual as formerly. The French are, in the main, the people who speak most of virtue, because among them the individual is considered rather as something peculiar, and as having a natural (i.e., not yet ethical) manner of action. The Germans, on the contrary, are more thoughtful, and among them the same content gains the form of universality.

151. But in the simple *identity* with the actuality of individuals, the ethical appears as their common manner of acting, as *custom.* This *habitual* manner of acting becomes a *second nature,* which takes the place of that which at first is simply natural will. It becomes the penetrating soul, meaning, and actuality of its existence, the living and present *spirit* as a world, whose substance first then exists as spirit.

Supplement. As nature has her laws, as the animal, the

trees, the sun, fulfill their law, so also is custom the law belonging to the spirit of freedom. That which legal right and morality have not yet attained, that custom is, namely, spirit. For in legal right the particularity is not yet that of the concept, but only that of the natural will. Likewise at the stage of morality, self-consciousness is not yet spiritual consciousness. The question is, then, only concerning the worth of the subject in himself; that is to say, the subject which determines himself in accordance with the good against the evil, has still the form of arbitrariness. On the other hand, at the ethical stage, the will is the will of the spirit and has a substantial content adequate unto itself. Pedagogy is the art of making men ethical: it considers man as a merely natural being—it shows the way to a new birth, how to convert his first nature into a second spiritual nature, so that this spiritual becomes a *habit* in him. In this habit the opposition of the natural and subjective will disappears and the struggle of the subject is broken. Thus habit belongs to ethics to the same extent as to philosophic thought, for the latter demands that the spirit shall be cultured so as to be opposed to arbitrary notions, and that these shall be crushed and conquered, in order that rational thought have free course.

But man also dies of habit, that is, he is dead when he has fully habituated himself to life, when he has become spiritually and physically obtuse, and when the opposition belonging to subjective consciousness and spiritual activity has disappeared. For man is active only as long as there is something he has not attained, in reference to which he wishes to be productive and effective. When this is accomplished, virile activity and vitality (*Lebendigkeit*) disappear, and the absence of interest that then ensues is spiritual or even physical death.

152. In this manner, *ethical substantiality* comes to its *right* and this right gains its *realization*. For the self-will and

independent conscience of the individual, which existed for itself only and produced an opposition against the concrete ethical life, disappear, when the ethical character recognizes as its motive and end (*bewegende Zweck*) the unmoved universal that has been reduced by its determinations to actual rationality; and when this ethical character recognizes its value, as well as the persistence (*Bestehen*) of particular ends, as being grounded and having its actuality in this determined universal. Subjectivity is the absolute *form* itself and the existing actuality of substance. The distinction of the subject from substance, viewed as the objects, ends, and power of the subject, is nothing but the likewise immediately (*unmittelbar*, i.e., not mediately) vanished distinction of form.

Subjectivity, which is the ground of existence for the concept of freedom (§ 106) and which, on the moral standpoint, is still differentiated from said concept, becomes, in the ethical sphere, the adequate existence of the concept of freedom.

153. The right of individuals to their subjective *determination of freedom* has its realization in the fact that they belong to ethical reality, inasmuch as the *certitude* of their freedom has its *truth* in such objectivity, and they (the individuals) actually possess in the ethical sphere *their essential* being (*Wesen*) and their *inner* universality (§ 147).

To a father who asked how he might best bring up his son, a Pythagorean (it is also attributed to others) answered: "By making him the *citizen of a state with good laws*."

Supplement. The pedagogical attempt to keep pupils away from the common (i.e., communal) life of the present, and to bring them up in the country (Rousseau in *Emile*) has been a vain experiment, for to estrange men from the laws of the world cannot prove a success. Even if youth is educated in solitude, it is certainly unwarranted to think that no fragrant breeze from the spirit world should ever invade this solitude, and that the power of the world spirit is too weak to take possession of this little separated territory. *When he is the citizen of a good state,* the individual first gains his just rights.

The realm of morality (*Sittlichkeit*) is nothing but the absolute spiritual unity of the essence of individuals which exists in their independent reality. . . . This moral substance, looked at abstractly from the mere side of its universality, is the *law* as the expression of such thought. But from another point of view it is also immediate actual self-consciousness as *custom*. On the other hand, the individual consciousness exists as a unitary member of the universal consciousness. Its action and existence are the universal custom (*Sitte*), in which it lives and moves and has its being. . . .

Any merely particular action or business of the individual relates to the needs of himself as a natural being. But these, his commonest functions, are saved from nothingness and given reality solely by the universal maintaining medium, that is, through the power of the whole people of which he is a member. It is this power, too, which gives content as well as form to his actions. What he does is the universal skill and custom of all. Just so far as this content completely individualizes itself, is its reality inwoven with the activity of all. The labor of the individual for his own wants is at the same time a satisfying of the needs of others, and reciprocally the satisfaction of his own needs is attained only through the labor of others. Thus the individual *unconsciously* does a universal work in doing his own individual work. But he also does this *consciously*. The whole, as his object, is that for which he sacrifices himself, and through which sacrifice he fulfills himself. Here there is nothing but what is reciprocal; nothing even in the apparently negative activity of the independent individual but such as enables him to attain the positive significance of independent being. This unity, which throbs through both the negation and the affirmation of the individual, speaks its universal language in the common custom and laws of his people. Yet this unchanging essence—the spirit of his people—is itself simply the expression of the single individuality which seems to be opposed to it. The laws proclaim what each one *is* and does. The individual recognizes this essence as not only his universal outward existence, but also as that which is particularized in his own individuality and in that of fellow-citizens. Hence each one has in this universal spirit nothing else but assurance of himself, and finds in existing reality nothing but himself. In it I behold only independent beings like myself. In them I see the free unity of self with others, which exists through others as it does through me. I see them as myself and myself as them in this free unity or universal substance. Thus reason is realized in truth in the life of a free people. It is present, living spirit, in which the individual not only finds his character, i.e., universal and particular essence, proclaimed and prepared ready to hand, but also finds that he himself is this essence, and has attained his definite character. Hence the wisest men of antiquity have proclaimed the maxim: that wisdom and virtue consist in living in harmony with the (morals) of one's own people.

154. The right of individuals to special characteristics, is contained in ethical substantiality, since particularity is the manner of the external appearance in which the ethical exists.

155. In this identity of the universal and particular will, *duty* and *right* consequently coincide, and man has in the ethical sphere duties to the same extent as rights, and

rights to the same extent as duties. In abstract legal right, the *ego* has the right and another has the duty; in the moral sphere, only the right of my own knowledge and will, together with my welfare united with duty, are demanded.

Supplement. The slave can have no duties, for duties belong to the free man alone. If all rights were on one side and all duties on the other, the whole (*das Ganze*) would dissolve, for identity alone is the foundation which we here must hold fast.

156. The ethical substance, as containing the independent self-consciousness that coincides with its concept, is the *actual spirit* of a family and a people.

Supplement. The ethical is not abstract like the good, but is, in an intensive sense, actual. The spirit has actuality, and individuals are the accidents of this actuality. Consequently, in the ethical sphere, there are only two points of view possible: either to start from substantiality, or to proceed in an atomistic manner and rise from individuality as foundation. But the latter point of view is spiritless, since it leads only to conglomeration; for the spirit is nothing individual, but it is the unity of the individual and universal.

157. The concept of this *Idea* is only spirit, self-knowledge, and actuality, when it is the objectification of itself, the movement through the form of its moments. It is, therefore:

(a) The immediated, or *natural* ethical spirit—the *family*. This substantiality changes at the loss of its unity into that of separation (of the members of the family) and to the standpoint of the relative, thus becoming,

(b) The *civic community*, a union of the members as *independent individuals* (i.e., as private persons) in a formal universality, through their *needs*, and through the *legal constitution* as a means for the safety of persons and property, and through an *external order* for their individual and common interests. This *external state* centers itself together

(c) In the end and actuality of the substantial universal, and of the public life devoted to the common weal—in the *constitution of the State.*

Civil Society

182. The concrete person which is an end for itself as a *particular* person, a totality of needs and a mixture of natural necessity and arbitrary will, is the *one principle* of a civil society. But it is the particular person essentially in its relation to another such particular person, with the result that each makes itself prevail and satisfied only by means of the other. But each must be *mediated by the other principle which is the form of generality.*

183. The selfish end in its actualization, thus conditioned by the generality, causes a system of all-around dependency, so that the subsistence and the welfare of the individual and his legal existence is intertwined with the subsistence, the welfare and the right of all others, is based upon it, and is real and secure only in this interdependence. One may view this system as the *external state,* as the *state based on need and the lower reason (Verstand).*

184. The idea thus divided gives the two aspects their peculiar existence: to the particular the right to develop in all directions and to the general the right to demonstrate itself as the basis and the necessary form of the particular, and hence as power over the particular and as their final end. . . .

[This notion is further developed by Hegel in the following two paragraphs in his usual conceptual form.]

187. The individuals are as citizens of this state *private persons* who have their own interest as their end. Since

this end is mediated by the general which therefore *appears to them as a means,* this end can only be reached by the citizens, if they themselves determined their will, their willing and doing, in a general manner, that is if they make themselves links in the chain of this interdependence. The interest of the idea lies in the process by which the separateness and naturalness of the members of the civil society are elevated—by natural necessity as much as by arbitrary needs—to formal freedom and to the formal *generality of knowing and willing* and thus to educate the subjective being in its particularity.

[In a long note Hegel criticizes the notion that the mores and ethics of an advancing society are inferior to the "state of nature," and explains it by the lack of comprehension for the life of the spirit which must come into conflict with itself, in order to develop. The process by which freedom is achieved means for the individual "the *hard work*" of overcoming mere subjectivity of behavior, the directness of desire, as well as the "subjective vanity of sentiment" and "the arbitrary preference." Because it is such hard work, such self-education is unpopular, but through it "the subjective will gains the *objectivity* by which it becomes worthy and capable of being the *actuality of the idea.* . . .]

188. The civil society contains three aspects:

(a) The mediation of *need* and the satisfaction of the *individual* by its labor and by the labor and the satisfaction of the needs of *all the others*—the *system of needs.*

(b) The actuality of what is contained therein of the general freedom, the protection of property by law.

(c) The protection against the contingency which remains in such systems and the caring for the particular interest as a *common* one, by the *police* and the *corporation.*

[In paragraphs 189–208, Hegel develops his conception of the system of needs—essentially the subject-matter of economics. He refers with interest to the work of Adam Smith, Ricardo and Say as a striking example of how from a multitude of specific detail the scientific understanding can distill "the simple principles" of a thing. Hegel subdivides the discussion into a section dealing with the different kinds of needs, a section on labor, one on the "estate" (*Vermoegen*) which leads him to expound a system of "estates" (*Staende*) or classes which he rather abstractly divides into the "substantial" which cultivates the soil, the "reflecting or formal" which engages in handicraft, manufacture and commerce (hence "indirect") and finally the "general" estate or class which is concerned with the general interest and hence must be maintained by the state. Hegel stresses the fact that in modern society, membership in these professions or classes is voluntary, and that no compulsory system, such as was expounded by Plato, can be considered compatible with freedom. "The recognition that what by reason is necessary in civil society and state, happens as mediated by the arbitrary will of the individual is the closer determination of what is by most people called freedom." (§ 206). This freedom based on property receives its support from law. Hegel therefore turns to the law proper: *Rechtspflege*.]

209. The mutual relation of needs and labor is something relative and as such is reflected or has its *reflection* in the infinite personality which is the (abstract) *law*. It is this sphere of the relative as something which has grown which gives law its *being-here-and-now* or actual existence (*Dasein*). This *actual existence* means that it is something *generally recognized*, something *known and willed* which has validity and objective actual reality as a result of being known and willed.

It is part of education, of thought as a consciousness of the particular in the form of the general, that the ego be conceived as a *general* person so that *all* therein are identical. *Man has rights* (gilt) *because he is a man*, not because he is a Jew, a Catholic, a Protestant, a German, an Italian, etc. The consciousness of this thought is of enormous importance, and is objectionable only if it is opposed to the life of the concrete state in the form of *cosmopolitism.*

210. The objective actual reality of law and right is on the one hand to be for consciousness, to be known altogether, on the other hand to possess the power of actual reality, to be *valid* and therefore to be *known* as something which is *generally valid.*

211. What is in itself *right,* what is made *positive* (*gesetzt*) in its objective being-here-and-now . . . *known* as what is right and law [in the form of] the *statutory enactment* (*Gesetz*). Right and law become through such determination *positive* law.

To posit something *general,* to bring it into consciousness as something general, means, of course, to *think* . . . Whatever is right receives its general form, its true determination only by coming a statutory enactment.

[Hegel then protests against those who would admit that only customary law is true law, and more specifically remarks that the Common Law (*Landrecht*) of England is in part contained in statutes, in part in *written* decisions: "What an enormous confusion results from it in the administration of law . . . experts have often described. More particularly, they comment upon the fact that this so-called unwritten law is contained in the decisions of the courts and judges, and that hence the judges constantly become *law-makers.* . . ." Hegel adds that these judges refer to such previous decisions according to precedent more or less at will, and then recalls that Emperor Justinian to overcome a similar chaos fixed by law the method of citation. "To deny that an educated nation or its lawyers possess the ability to work out a code—since it cannot be a matter of making *new laws,* but to comprehend by thought what exists . . . would be one of the greatest insults that could be inflicted upon such a nation or profession."]

[In paragraphs 212–214, Hegel elaborates his thoughts concerning law as the positive enactment of what is right, and that positive law depends upon such enactments for determining what is right. Ultimately, this is a matter of fitting the particular case; this very specific and determinate decision cannot be worked out by reason, and reason only lays the basis for this sort of positive action and application.]

215. The obligatory nature of law implies, from the standpoint of the right of self-consciousness, that statutory enactments be *generally known*. To suspend these enactments, as Dionysius the tyrant did, in so lofty a place that no one can read them is the same kind of injustice as to bury them in a vast apparatus of learned books, collections of decisions and conflicting judgments and opinions, especially when it is done in a foreign language alluding to the use of Latin in German courts so that the knowledge of valid law is accessible only to those who are learned in it. Those rulers who have given their peoples a digest, even if shapeless like Justinian, or still better a *common law* in the form of a well-arranged and definite code like Frederick the Great and Napoleon became thereby not only the greatest benefactors, but have accomplished a great *act of justice*.

216. For the public code one should demand on the one hand simple general provisions, on the other hand the very nature of this finite material calls for everlasting adjustments. The laws ought to be on one hand a finished and complete whole, but on the other hand there is continuous need of new legal provisions. But this antinomy occurs where the general principles are specified, specifically applied—the principles themselves remain. . . . To demand of a code the kind of perfection which would render it absolutely complete and incapable of further improvement—a demand which is peculiarly a German disease—and then because it cannot be so perfected to reject the incomplete and imperfect, results from not comprehending the nature of finite objects such as private law. In these objects, the so-called perfection is the *perennial* *approximation. . . . Le plus grand ennemi du bien c'est le meilleur* is the expression of true sound common sense.

[In paragraphs 217–218, Hegel discusses the contractual basis of property and the formalities connected with it, and the fact that a crime is never merely the violation of a private right, but endangers the public good.]

[In paragraphs 219–229, Hegel discusses the courts; among other things, he takes a strong stand on behalf of jury trial. We select the following passages:]

224. Just as the making public of statutory enactments is part of the rights of the subjective consciousness, the *realization (Verwirklichung)* of the law in a particular case, the external actions, etc. . . . require that the *administration of law be public.* Deliberations of the members of a court concerning the decision are merely particular opinions and therefore do not require publicity.

225. In the business of adjudication as the application of the statutory enactment to a *particular case* two aspects ought to be distinguished: first the knowledge of the facts of the case in its *immediate particulars,* whether there is a contract extant, whether a certain deed has been committed, etc. . . . and secondly the subsumption of the case under the enactments. . . . These two different decisions involve different functions.

[In paragraphs 226–237, Hegel lays out first the familiar doctrine of the difference between settling points of law and points of fact which serves him as the basis for demanding a jury. To know the facts, or rather to apply judgment in guessing at them "is a knowledge which belongs to every educated person." Lawyers, in Hegel's view, are no better qualified than other persons to deal with such matters. "The right of one's conscious self, the aspect of *subjective* freedom, may be looked upon as the substantial viewpoint when dealing with the question of the necessity of making the administration public, as well as in the matter of jury trials (*Ge-*

schworenengerichte)." Then, after a transitional paragraph, Hegel proceeds to deal with the police and the corporation. One is the arm of the state and its central administration, the other is the realm of independent civic activity. Generally, his viewpoint is that of a conservative liberal who would like to see the police curtailed, but recognizes its importance for order in the state. We select a few paragraphs of particular interest:]

238. The family is the substantial whole which cares for the individual both as concerns his means and aptitudes . . . and his subsistence and support, if he is incapacitated. But civil society tears the individual from this context, alienates the members of the family, and recognizes them as autonomous persons. . . . Thus the individual becomes a *son of civil society*. . . .

239. Civil society thus acquires the character of a *general family*, and as such it has the duty and the right (even contrary to the *arbitrary will* of the *parents*) to *educate* him in so far as such education is related to his becoming a member of society. . . . The boundary between the rights of parents and of civil society is very hard to draw. . . .

242. The purely subjective aspect of poverty, as of all kinds of neediness to which the individual is exposed even in nature, calls for *subjective* aid, not only in regard to the particular circumstances, but also for reasons of *kindness* (*Gemüt*) and *affection*. Here general morality finds much to do. But since such aid depends upon accidents, society will seek to discover the general aspects of neediness and how to meet it, in order to make individual charity less necessary. . . .

243. An active civil society shows *constant progress of population and industry*. The general expansion of the relations of people, their needs and the ways in which means are being provided to meet them, the accumulation of riches increases—for from such duplication great profits

are derived—but on the other hand the atomization and limitation of the particular labor and the resulting dependency and neediness of the class which is tied to such labor is also greatly increased. . . .

244. The fact that a great mass of people sink down below a certain subsistence, and thus suffer a loss of a sense of right and law, of justice and of the honor to exist by one's own activity and labor, produces the proletariat (*Pöbel*) which in turn again further promotes the concentration of riches in a few hands. . . . [The important question of how to reduce poverty is one which particularly agitates and torments modern societies.]

[In paragraphs 245–246 Hegel states that to take the property of the rich to support the poor would violate the principle of self-support of a bourgeois society, while an increase in production would lead to overproduction, a kind of dialectics of wealth which must have strongly appealed to Marx and Engels. To escape from this dilemma, Hegel believes the dialectics of bourgeois society pushes it beyond itself into exporting to less developed peoples.]

[In paragraphs 247-248 Hegel notes that the sea is the natural element of industry; thus remote places are connected—rivers are not natural boundaries, and the oceans connect man with man. He notes the educative force of the sea, pointing to the stupor of the Egyptians and the Indians who refused to go to sea. Colonization fits in here, as a natural projection outward of a thriving civil society. After a transitional paragraph, Hegel turns to the corporation.]

[In paragraphs 250–256, Hegel states his firm conviction of the importance of corporate autonomy:]

252. The corporation has accordingly under the supervision of the government the right to attend to its own interests, to elect members in accordance with their objective qualities, such as aptitude and rectitude, in appropriate num-

bers, to take care of them, to educate them—a kind of second family.

[Hegel is primarily thinking here in terms of traditional craft guilds; but his thought is equally applicable to trade unions and professional associations. He explicitly rejects the closed guild system. His thought is elaborated in the following two paragraphs.]

255. Besides the *family,* the *corporation* constitutes the second *ethical* root of the state which is based upon civil society. . . . Sanctity of marriage and honor of the corporation are the two aspects which the decentralization of civil society involves.

256. The end of the corporation has its truth in spite of its being a limited and finite one . . . in and through a *general end* which is in, by and for itself its absolute actual reality. Thus the sphere of civil society at this point enters the *state.*

[Here follows once again the notion that family and production, country and city, constitute the basis of the state. That there is such a dichotomy, such a division of civil society, proves scientifically Hegel's conception of the state. It appears as a result; but actually the state is *first* and only within it, the family becomes a true civil society.]

The State

257. The state is the actual reality of the ethical *idea;* it is the ethical spirit as the *manifest* (*offenbare*) substantial will that is fully self-cognizant (*sich selbst deutlich*), and that thinks and knows itself and realizes what it knows and in so far as it knows. The state has its immediate existence in the ethical habits (*Sitte*) and in the *self-consciousness* of the individual; in his knowing and doing the state has its mediated existence, just as the individual has his *substantial freedom* in the state as in his own essence, his end and the product of his activity. The *penates* are the intimate, lower gods, the *national spirit*

(*Athene*), the divine essence which *knows* and *wills* itself; reverence is sentiment and an ethical conduct results from it; *political virtue* is the willing of the end which is in and of itself, but has now also become conscious in thought.

258. The state, as the actuality of the substantial *will*—an actuality which it has through the particular self-consciousness when elevated onto a universal level—is that which is in-and-of-itself *rational*. This substantial unity is an absolute, unchanging end-in-itself (*Selbstzweck*) in which freedom gains its supreme right, just as conversely this final end (*Endzweck*) has the highest right *vis-à-vis* the individuals whose *highest duty* it is to be members of the state.

[Hegel elaborates this thought by rejecting all confusion between the state and civil society which would make "the interest of the individuals the final end." Because the state is spirit objectified, the individual can achieve objective truth and ethical quality only through participating in the state. Hegel is clearly adopting the view of classical antiquity, identifying the state with the polis of Plato and Aristotle. Rationality, adds Hegel, consists in the interpenetration of the general (universal) and the special or particular, which in this context means the objective and the subjective freedom. What this means is that rationality consists in acting in accordance with general, that is, thought-out laws and principles.

Hegel then raises the question of the origin of the state, historically, and asserts that the answer is irrelevant to the idea of the state. It is part of the phenomenal world of history. Philosophical reflection has to deal only with the concept and Hegel calls it the great merit of Rousseau that he recognized, as contrasted with all special historical origins, the will as principle of the state, because the will is itself something which in its content is thought. "But Rousseau defined the will only as an individual will in its determined form (like Fichte later) and the general will merely as the *common will*, rather than as that which is rational in the will in-and-of-itself, and the common will as resulting from these individual wills as *conscious* wills. Hence the association of the individuals in the state becomes a *contract* which has their arbitrary decision, opinion and voluntary, explicit consent as a basis. There follow of course the further, merely reasonable consequences which destroy the divine which is in-and-of-itself and its absolute authority and majesty." Hegel feels that these abstractions brought on the first and enormous drama of building the constitution of a great state upon what was believed to be rational while subverting all existing institutions, and since they are mere abstractions the event turned out to be "terrible and shrieking." But Hegel does not wish to be confused with reactionary thought which accepts the given realities, the externalities of appearance as the essence of the state, instead of seeing them as mere aspects of development. He names von Haller's "Restoration of Political Science" as the most blatant attempt to banish reason from the state. He mocks at this effort to interpret the state as mere power bearing no relation to ideas and in a long footnote he elaborates the point that von Haller, in order to combat Rousseau's errors, has gone to the opposite extreme and indulged in a veritable hatred for all legislation, and all formal right. Quoting extensively from the book, he places into the center Haller's proposition that it is the eternal and unalterable order of God that the more powerful rules must rule and always will rule, and comments that it is clear that power or might (Macht) is taken here to mean the accidental power of nature and not the power of the just and the ethical. Hegel's detailed criticism returns again and again to the fact that Haller's is a naturalistic interpretation which completely denies the essence of the state based upon law; he specifically criticizes Haller's belittling Magna Carta and corresponding charters elsewhere as "merely found in books" when as a matter of fact in Hegel's view they as basic laws "contribute to every piece of bread that the citizens eat." He concludes with a memorable passage: "It is the hardest thing which can happen to a man, to be alienated from thought and reasonableness, from reverence for the laws and from the knowledge of how infinitely important, even divine, it is that the duties of the state and the rights of the citizens, as well as the rights of the state and the duties of the citizens be determined by law."]

Supplement. The state in-and-for-itself is the ethical whole, the actualization of freedom. It is the absolute end of reason that freedom be actual. The state is the spirit which dwells in the world and *consciously* realizes itself in the world, whereas in nature it actualizes itself only . . . as a dormant spirit. Only when present as consciousness, knowing itself as existing objectivity, is this spirit the state. When reasoning about freedom one must not start from the individual self-consciousness, but only from the essential nature of self-consciousness, for whether one knows it or not, this essence still realizes itself as an independent power in which the single individuals are only elements: it is the course of God through the world that constitutes the state. Its basis is the force of reason actualizing itself as will. In considering the idea of the state, one must not think of particular states, nor of particular institutions, but one must contemplate the *idea*, this actual God, by itself. Every state, though one may declare it bad according to one's principles, though one may recognize this or that fault, possesses always if it belongs to the developed states of our time the essential elements of its existence. But since it is easier to discover faults than to understand positive characteristics it is easy to fall into the error of overlooking the internal organism of the state itself in dwelling upon particular aspects of it. The state is no work of art, it exists in the world, and hence in the sphere of choice, accident and error. Hence the ill behavior of its members can disfigure it in many ways. But the most deformed human being, the criminal, the invalid and the cripple, are still living human beings: the affirmative, life, exists in spite of the defects, and it is this affirmative side which matters to us here.

259. a) The idea of the state has *immediate* actuality, and is the individual state as a self-related (*sich auf sich beziehender*) organism, it is its constitution or internal public law; b) the idea of the state passes over into the relations of the particular state to other states: external public law (international law); c) the idea of the state is the general idea as

genus and possesses absolute power over individual states; it is the spirit which gives itself its actuality in the process of *world history*.

Supplement. The actual state is essentially an individual state, and still more a particular state. Individuality must be distinguished from particularity. The former is an aspect of the *idea* of the state itself, while particularity belongs to history. The states, as such, are independent of one another and consequently the relation between them can be only external. Hence a third power is needed to unite them. This third power is the spirit which gives itself actuality in world history, and which is the absolute judge over individual states. Several states may, as a federation, establish a court over each other, and combinations of states like the Holy Alliance for example may occur, but these are always only relative and limited, like eternal peace. The only absolute judge who always prevails over the particular is the spirit, being in-and-for-itself which represents itself as the general and as the active factor in world history.

A. *Internal Public (Constitutional) Law*

260. The state is the actuality of concrete freedom. *Concrete freedom* consists in this, that all personal individuality and its particular interests find their complete development and the recognition of their independent rights (as we have seen them in the sphere of the family and of civil society). This occurs partly through these particular interests being transformed into general interests, and partly through individuals recognizing in thought and deed this general interest as being their own *substantial spirit,* and working for it as for their own *final end.* Thus neither is the general valid or realized without the particular interests, knowledge or will of individuals, nor do individuals live only for these particular interests, as private persons, but they have also a share in the general will and an activity conscious of this end. The principle of the modern

state has this enormous strength and depth, that while it allows the principle of subjectivity to evolve itself into the *autonomous extreme* of personal particularity, it at the same time reintegrates all this into *substantial unity;* thus in personal particularity substantial unity is maintained.

[*Supplement.* In this section, Hegel elaborates the point just made, by contrasting the modern state with that of classical antiquity which did not allow the particular individual the freedom to develop his own sphere while at the same time contributing to the general interest. "The general must be active, but the subjective side must likewise be fully and vividly developed. Only if both aspects are present in their full vigor can the state be considered as structured and truly organized."]

[Hegel asserts again in paragraph 261 the idea that private rights and private well-being, in family and civil society, on the one hand require the state as a superior power, but on the other hand the state is also their immanent end. The mutuality of rights and duties (§ 155) flows from it. He recalls that Montesquieu undertook in the *Esprit des Lois* to show how all laws are related to the specific character of a given state. He then elaborates the idea of mutuality in terms of particular general freedom. "The state, as an ethical being, as the interpenetration of the substantial and the particular, implies that a man's obligation toward the substantial is coexistent at the same time with his particular freedom, that is, duty and right are in the state united in one and the same relationship." In spite of this formal identity, right and duty are of course *different in content*. In private law this is not so; here rights are equal for all. But in public law, concretely, "the citizen does not have rights of the same content as his duties toward monarch and government."

Hegel feels that this concept of the combining of right and duty is one of the most important features of a state and determines its inner strength. Duty abstractly considered stops with regarding the particular interest as unessential, unworthy. But the concrete view which is that of considering the idea shows the particular interest as quite essential and its satisfaction as necessary. The fulfillment of one's duty must be in the individual's self-interest, and the general concern of the state also his own proper concern. The individual as citizen fulfilling his duties finds himself protected in his person and property, and he enjoys the consciousness and pride of being a member of such a substantial being, a state.

In a supplementary section, Hegel further elaborates this thought. "Everything depends upon this unity of the general and the particular in the state." Once again he contrasts the polis of ancient Greece with the modern state, declaring that the modern state recognizes the individual's own opinion, will and conscience, whereas in the polis "the subjective end was identical with that of the state." Hegel believes that the ancients accepted the will of the state as final. "Modern man wants to be respected in his inner life." This is what "organizing the concept of freedom" means.]

262. The actualized idea, the spirit, which is differentiated into the two ideal spheres of its concept, the family and the civil society, as its finite aspects, while it is infinite actualized spirit through their ideality, assigns to these spheres the material of this finite actuality, the individuals as a *multitude*. Therefore it appears to be mediated for the individual by circumstances, arbitrary decision and his own choice (§ 185).

Supplement. In the Platonic state, subjective freedom was of no account, since the government assigned to each individual his occupation. In many oriental states this assignment results from birth. The subjective choice which ought to be respected requires free choice by individuals.

[In paragraphs 263–264, Hegel undertakes to reinforce his argument by an organismic analogy according to which the relationship of family, civil society and state corresponds to that between the several aspects of the nervous system. "The laws which govern family and civil society are the rational which illumines them." The individuals are actualized as both private and substantial persons who will both the particular and the general, as previously argued. Thus the "final truth of the institutions of state-made law is the spirit."]

265. These institutions constitute specifically the constitution, i.e., the developed and actualized rationality (or reasonableness), and are therefore the firm basis of the state, as well as the confidence and loyalty of the individuals toward the state. They are the basic pillars of public freedom, because through them the particular freedom is realized and made rational. . . .

[*Supplement*. Hegel reminds the reader that marriage and the other institutions have previously been shown as the basis of the state. He adds: "It has often been said that the end of the state is the happiness of its citizens. This is very true. If they are not well, if their subjective end is not satisfied, if they do not believe that the state secures this freedom, the state stands on a weak foundation.]

266. But the spirit is not only actual and objective unto itself as a realm of appearance and necessity, but also as the inner essence and *ideality* of such phenomena. This substantial generality is object and end *for itself*, but so is that necessity [and object and end for itself] in the form of freedom.

267. The *necessity* in the ideality is the *development* of the idea within itself. It is, as *subjective* substantiality, political *conviction*, while as *objective* substantiality it is the *organism* of the state, that is to say the truly *political* state and its *constitution*.

Supplement. The unity of the freedom that knows and wills itself exists at first as necessity. The substantial here exists as the subjective existence of the individuals. But there is another mode of necessity and that is the organism [of the state], that is to say the spirit is in itself a process, structures itself in itself, establishes distinctions within itself, through which it circulates.

268. Political *loyalty*, or *patriotism* as such, the certainty resting upon *truth*—merely subjective certainty does not result from truth and is mere opinion—and the will which has become *habit* are simply the result of the state's institutions in

which rationality is *actually* present. Such loyalty is exercised by action in conformity with such institutions. This loyalty consists altogether in the confidence which may become a more or less reasoned insight or the consciousness that my substantial and particular interest is conserved and contained in the interest and end of the state . . . whereby the state ceases to be "another" as far as I am concerned and *I* am free in this consciousness.

Usually patriotism is taken to mean merely the readiness to *extraordinary* sacrifices . . . But the conviction is essential. . . . Tested in ordinary civic life and all its relations . . . it justifies the extraordinary effort. . . . Just as men prefer to be generous to being law-abiding, they readily persuade themselves that they possess extraordinary patriotism in order to avoid developing true conviction or loyalty, or to excuse its lack. Nor must it be presumed that you could start with such loyalty based upon subjective notions and thought. . . .

Supplement. Uneducated people take pleasure in arguing and criticizing, because it is easy to do so, but hard to discover the good and to understand its inner necessity. Education begins with criticism, but a fully cultivated person recognizes the positive quality in everything. Similarly in religion one may readily talk of superstition, but it is hard to grasp the truth involved. The apparent loyalty must be distinguished from what people truly want. . . . Men have the confidence that the state must exist, but habit makes it invisible. . . . If someone walks safely at night through the streets, it does not occur to him that it might be otherwise. . . . It is a common notion that the state is held together by force, but it is in fact held together by the basic sense of order which all men have.

269. Loyalty as conviction derives its specific and determined *content* from the different aspects of the *organism* of the state. This organism is (implies) the development of the idea into its distinct parts and their objective actuality. These aspects so distinguished are the *different powers,* their tasks and activi-

ties. Through them the general creates itself continuously and *necessarily* because these powers are determined by the *nature of the concept.* . . . This organism is the *political constitution.*

Supplement. The state is an organism, that is to say a development of the idea into its distinguishing parts. The political constitution continually is created by the state which maintains itself through its constitution. If they fall apart . . . the unity is no longer extant which creates them. [Hegel then elaborates upon the nature of an organism, citing the fable of the stomach.]

[In paragraph 270, Hegel sums up what has gone before: that the state unites the general and the special interests, and that it is thus abstract actuality or substantiality; that its powers are necessarily derived from the distinct aspects of its concept; and that its substantiality is the spirit which has formed itself, knows itself and wills itself. "The state therefore knows what it wants, knows it in its generality as thought, and it acts therefore according to purposes, known principles and laws. . . ."

There follows a long excursus about the relations between the state and religion. He rejects the idea that religion is the basis of the state, as confusing. "The state is divine will, if that will is seen as present spirit which unfolds itself into an actual configuration (*Gestalt*) and into the *organization of a world.*" Hegel argues that those who would juxtapose religion to the state are like those who think that you can achieve knowledge by merely contemplating essence (*Wesen*) and never proceeding to a consideration of existence (*Dasein*). "Religion is the relation to the absolute in the *form of sentiment, imagination and faith.* . . ." Hence religion tends to argue that there needs to be no law for the just man: be pious, and you may do what you will. . . . If such a view does become interested in reality, it becomes *fanaticism* which "like political fanaticism" considers all governmental institutions and legal order as restrictive and would subvert private property, marriage, work and the rest as unworthy of free sentiment. This leads to purely arbitrary decisions "since decisions there must be in actual life. The result is the destruction of all constitutional order which has been developed over many centuries and is the true expression of reason, especially as expressed in laws. The other possibility is escape from the world into a self-righteous seclusion which laments the wickedness of the world. "Instead of mastering mere opinion by the hard work of study and to subjugate his striving by self-discipline and thereby to elevate it into freely willed obedience [to the law], it is the easiest thing to preserve one's self-esteem . . . and to be satisfied with one's piety. . . ."

But if religion recognizes the state, it has its natural place, including its property and the service of the members of its congregation. Since it is the deepest builder of convictional loyalty, the state will require of all its members that they belong to some church—though to which one is a matter of indifference, since the state must not concern itself with these matters of the inner life. The strong state can afford to be very liberal in this respect. It can even afford to tolerate religious bodies which refuse to acknowledge their duty toward the state. (In a remarkable footnote, Hegel mentions the Quakers as members merely of civil society whom one may excuse from oaths, etc. He adds that in spite of formal difficulties, which the emancipation of the Jews may present, those opposed to it overlooked that the Jews are first of all *human beings* who when admitted as fully equal persons in civil society with equal civic rights will adapt themselves in loyalty and general belief to the prevailing convictions; their continued segregation would have isolated them and the state could well be reproached for the resulting evils: the state would have betrayed its own principle of being the objective institution of the spirit.)

Any church, in so far as it owns property, engages in cult observances and the like, enters into the worldly sphere and thus into that of the state. Hence a limited subjection to the police power must be acknowledged. However, the doctrine is a matter of conscience and part of the subjective freedom—the sphere of the inner life which is not the concern of the state. The state itself has a doctrine which manifests itself in the loyalty of its citizens, their convictions and their attachment to principles of law. Hegel sharply rejects those doctrines which would claim all spiritual life for religion and reduce the state to a mechanical framework for unspiritual, external purposes. He notes that similar pretensions may be advanced on behalf of science and learning as concerned with all knowledge. He recognizes that in barbaric times such situations have in fact existed where all spiritual life was in the church. But to proclaim this as the true idea of the state is shallow. Recent developments have shown that "the spirit is free and rational, and thus in itself ethical, and that the true idea is actualized rationality, and that this idea exists as the state." "The ethical truth exists as law. . . ." He further notes that against this rationality religion is based upon the given of revealed truth communicated to the individual through faith. When a church teaches its doctrines, it touches upon matters which are of concern to the state. Since the state is the manifestation of rationality, it was the state which had promoted the freedom of thought and of scientific inquiry; it was a church which burned Giordano Bruno and made Galileo apologize for accepting the Copernican system. Science and the state belong together; for science is directed toward thought, its purpose is knowledge, objective truth and rationality. The state must also resist the abuse of scientific inquiry for the expression of mere opinion; it stands essentially as the mediator between faith and scholarship.

Hegel rejects the idea of the unity of church and state, and asserts on the contrary their separation. Only by such separation can the state fulfill its function above the churches and represent the generality of thought. "It is therefore very wrong to say that the separation of state and church is a misfortune; only through this separation has the state been able to become what it was intended to be: the self-conscious rationality and ethics. Likewise it is the most fortunate thing that could have happened to the churches. . . ." (The supplementary section is merely a restatement of the foregoing.)]

271. The political constitution is *first* of all the organization of the state and the process of its organic life *in relation to itself* in which the state differentiates its several aspects within itself and unfolds them. *Secondly,* the state is as an individuality an *exclusive* single entity which is related to *others* through this individuality, and thus turns its differentiated self toward the *outside* and in accordance with these requirements posits in their ideality the distinctions existing within itself.

[In a supplementary section Hegel notes that the internal and external relations of a state are connected. The internal state which is the civil power and the external direction of it which is the military power ought to be in balance.]

272. The constitution is rational (*vernuenftig*) inasmuch as the state differentiates its operation (*Wirksamkeit*) according to the nature of the concept and likewise determines it. This works as follows: each of the powers is a totality in itself, because it contains the other powers (*Momente*) as effective in itself, yet at the same time they remain part of the state's ideal form by expressing differences of its concept and still constitute only one ideal whole.

[After some critical remarks about the endless talk (*Geschwaetze*) that has been expended upon constitutionalism which has made the concept odious to many, Hegel continues:]

Among current notions, that of the *necessary separation of powers* deserves special mention, for it is a most important provision. If taken in its true meaning, it may rightfully be regarded as the guarantee of public freedom . . . for in this provision the aspect of *rational determination* is contained. . . . But if interpreted too abstractly, it involves on one hand the wrong idea of an absolute autonomy of these powers, and on the other the one-sided conception of them as something negative, as a mutual limitation.* In this view it becomes a hostile relation, a fear of the other (power) and of what evil each may cause for the other, resulting in the provision of opposing it and by such counterbalances to effectuate a general balance, but no living unity. (Against such a view it might be said that) only the concept (of the constitutional state) in itself and for its self-determination contains the absolute origin of the powers as distinguished and not some other ends or utilities. It is on their account alone that the organization of the state

---

* Hegel here is referring to the doctrine of checks and balances, when carried to its abstract, logical extreme.—Ed.

is what is rational in itself and a reflection or image of the eternal reason.

[After repeating his criticism of the negative view and calling it the view of the mob, Hegel continues:]

If the powers called executive and legislative are made autonomous, the state is right away threatened with destruction, or, if the state maintains itself, a struggle ensues by which one power subjugates the other and thus the unity however structured is effected and the existence of state which is the only thing that matters is saved.

Supplement. One should not want to have anything in a state except what is an expression of rationality (*Vernuenftigkeit*). The state is the world which the spirit has created for itself: therefore the state has a definite progress of its own. How often do people talk of the wisdom of God in nature: one ought never to believe that the physical world of nature is something superior to the world of the spirit; for as far above nature as is the spirit, as far above physical life is the state. One should therefore revere the state as something divine upon earth (*irdisch-goettliches*) and realize that if it is hard to understand nature, it is immeasurably more difficult to grasp the state. It is very significant that in recent times definite insights concerning the state in general have been gained, and that one has been occupied so much with the discussing and making of constitutions. But that is not enough. It is necessary that for a rational matter the reasonable way of looking at it (*Vernunft der Anschauung*) be secured, so that one knows what is essential and that not always the most striking is the most essential. The powers of the state should indeed be distinguished, but each must form a whole and contain aspects of the others . . . [Hegel then proceeds to elaborate once more the thought that these powers ought not to be thought of as independent of each other.]

273. The political state is thus divided (*dirimiert sich*) in these substantial differences:

a) the power to determine and constitute or establish the general rules—the *legislative* power,

b) the power to subsume the particular spheres and the individual cases under the general rules—the administrative or *governmental power,*

c) the *monarchical power* as the subjectivity of the final decision of the will, in which the differentiated powers are gathered together into an individual unity and which is there the top and the beginning of the whole, of the *constitutional monarchy.*

The development of the state into a constitutional monarchy is the work of the modern world in which the substantial idea has achieved its infinite form. The *history* of this concentration (*Vertiefung*) of the spirit of the world upon itself is the task of general world history. It amounts to the same thing to speak of this as the free development in the course of which the idea unfolds its aspects—and they are only aspects—in their totality. This unfolding shows that the idea contains them in the ideal unity of the concept in which its real rationality (*Vernuenftigkeit*) consists. It is the history of the true forming of the ethical life.

The old division of constitutions into *monarchy, aristocracy* and *democracy* is based upon the *undifferentiated substantial unity* of its foundation, which has not yet arrived at an *internal differentiation* (a developed organization) and hence not yet at depth and concrete rationality (*Vernuenftigkeit*). From the standpoint of antiquity this classification is true and right. . . . These forms [of government] which belong to different wholes are in the constitutional monarchy reduced to aspects; the monarch is *one;* the governmental (administrative) power calls for *several* and the legislative power for *many.* But such quantitative differences are superficial and do not indicate a true understanding of the matter. . . . [After discussing an erroneous opinion of Fichte, Hegel proceeds:] It is idle to inquire which of these forms of government is the best; such forms can only be discussed historically. In this matter, as in so many others, one should recognize the deep insight of *Montesquieu* when he suggests the now famous principles of these several forms of government, but one must not misunderstand his suggestion. As is known, he suggested *virtue* as the principle of *democracy;* for in truth such a constitution rests upon conviction as the purely substantial form in which the rationality of the will in itself exists in a democracy. But when Montesquieu adds that *England* in the seventeenth century had offered the beautiful drama to demonstrate the efforts of erecting a democracy as hopeless (*unmaechtig*), because virtue had been lacking in the leaders . . . then one should observe that in a fully organized state of society and in the developing and freeing of the *particular* groups (*Maechte der Besonderheit*) the virtue of the heads of the state is insufficient and another form of rational law than that based upon mere conviction is required in order that the whole possess the strength to hold together. . . . Likewise the misunderstanding must be eliminated as if because conviction and virtue are the substantial form of a democratic republic, this conviction be considered not needed or perhaps even absent in a monarchy. It is even more important to avoid the misunderstanding as if virtue and the *legally determined* activity in a *structured* organization were antithetical and incompatible. [After having pointed out that his emphasis upon honor as the principle of monarchy shows that Montesquieu is concerned with *feudal monarchy*, Hegel turns to another question:]

Another question readily presents itself: *who shall make the constitution?* This question seems clear enough, but turns out upon closer inspection to be meaningless. For it presupposes that no constitution exists, but merely an atomistic *mass* of individuals. How such a mass, either by itself or through others, through kindness, thought or violence might arrive at a constitution, one must leave to the mass itself, for the concept of a constitution is not concerned with such a mass. Therefore, if that question presupposes an existing constitution, then the *making* means only a change, and the presupposition of a constitution implies directly itself that the change can happen only by constitutional means. In any case it is absolutely essential that the *constitution*, even though it emerged in time, be not looked upon as *something made;* for it is that which is absolutely of and by itself which must be considered therefore as divine and lasting and above the sphere of that which is made. . . .

274. Since the spirit is actual only as that which it knows itself to be, and since the state, as the spirit of a people is at the same time the law which *permeates all its relations,* its ethics and the consciousness of its individuals, therefore the constitution of a particular people depends upon the kind and formation of its self-consciousness. In this self-consciousness consists its subjective freedom, and therefore the actuality of the constitution.

To want to give to a people *a priori* a constitution which might be more or less rational—this idea overlooks the very aspect through which a constitution is more than a thought or intellectual construct (*Gedankending*). Every people has, therefore, the constitution which is suited for it and which is appropriate to it.

[*Supplement.* After commenting upon Napoleon's unsuccessful attempt at giving the Spaniards a constitution that was rational, Hegel continues: The people must have for its constitution the feeling that it is right and related to its condition, otherwise the constitution may be "there," but it has no significance or value. To be sure, in individuals the desire and the longing for a better constitution may exist, but that the mass of the people be permeated by such an idea is something else again and follows much later. The principle of morality, of the inwardness of Socrates was necessarily created in his time, but it took time until it became the general self-consciousness.]

The Monarchical Power

275. The monarchical power itself contains the three aspects of the totality of the state (§ 272), the *generality* of the constitution and of the laws, the consultation as the relating of the *particular* to the general, and the aspect of the final *decision*. This final decision is the self-determination to which all else refers back and from which its actuality starts. This absolute self-determination constitutes the distinguishing principle of the monarchical power as such . . .

Supplement. The Ego is at the same time the most unique and the most general. In nature, too, there is first of all a single thing, but the reality, the non-ideality, the separateness, is not that which exists by itself (*das Beisichseiende*). Rather the various single things exist side by side. Looked at from the viewpoint of the spirit, all the various different things exist only as something ideal and as a unity. The state seen spiritually is therefore the unfolding of its elements, but the singleness is at the same time what gives it a soul and hence the life-giving principle, sovereignty, which comprises all the differences.

276. The basic feature of the political state is the substantial unity as *ideality* of its elements or aspects. In this *ideality* the particular powers and activities of the state are at the same time dissolved and maintained; yet they are only maintained in this sense, that they possess no independent justification, but only such and going as far as is determined by the idea of the whole; hence they issue from its power and are fluid members of the state which is their own simple self.

Supplement. This ideality of the elements or aspects is like life in an organic body: there is life only in all its parts . . . if separated, each part is dead. It is the same with all separate estates, powers and corporations.

277. The particular business and activities of the state are its essential aspects and hence its own. They are connected with the particular *individuals* by whom they are handled and taken care of only in accordance with their general and objective qualities; they are not related to their particular personalities. . . . The business and the powers of the state can therefore not be *private property*.

Supplement. The activity of the state depends upon individuals; but they are not entitled, by their natural ways, to attend to these affairs, but only by their objective qualification. Ability, aptitude and character belong to the individual's particularity: yet it must be educated and trained for a particular task. Hence no office can be bought, sold or inherited. . . .

278. These two propositions, that the particular business and powers of the state are neither in themselves independent, nor through the will of individuals, but have their root in the unity of the state as their simple self, constitute the *sovereignty* of the state.

[After commenting upon the feudal monarchy of the Middle Ages as a system of government in which there was no internal, if there was external sovereignty (and Hegel is speaking here of internal sovereignty), as being "rather an aggregate" than an "organism," since powers were fragmentized and often private property, Hegel once again repeats his organismic analogy for the "ideal unity of the state." He adds: Since sovereignty is the ideality of all particular rights, the misunderstanding is ready at hand and often occurs, of mistaking sovereignty for mere power and empty arbitrariness, and hence as synonymous with despotism. But despotism signifies a condition of lawlessness, where the particular will of either a monarch or of a people (ochlocracy) prevails as law or rather in lieu of law. Sovereignty, by contrast, signifies the legal, constitutional condition in which sovereignty constitutes the ideality of the particular spheres and activities, so that each sphere . . . is dependent upon and determined by the purpose of the whole. . . . Hegel reinforces this argument by pointing out that in war or civil commotion these particular spheres are all subordinated to the salvation of the state "wherein that idealism arrives at its peculiar actuality."]

279. Sovereignty, taken first as the *general* idea of this ideality, *exists* only as the *subjectivity* which is certain of itself, and as the abstract and in so far as it is abstract uncaused (*grundlos*) *self-determination* of the will in which the final decision rests. This is the individual aspect of the state as such; the state itself is only thereby *one*. Subjectivity can truly be only as a *subject*, personality only as a *person*; in a constitution which has developed to the point of real rationality (*Vernuenftigkeit*) each of the three elements or aspects of the concept has its separate and *by itself actual* configuration. This absolutely decisive aspect of the whole is therefore not individuality in general, but one individual, the *monarch*.

[Hegel elaborates these general propositions along the following lines: Every philosophical field of study (science) is based upon a single concept; in the present case it is "will." The monarch's "I will" personifies the state. Only thus is there truth. Lesser so-called moral persons, like families and villages, may have an "abstract" personality aspect; but personality has not arrived at true existence. All this has been shown before, but to grasp the idea is hard, because reflective rationalizing, so-called rational analysis, stops at particulars, whereas the dignity of a monarch is the *absolute beginning*. Hegel adds some poignant remarks about popular sovereignty. He acknowledges it as meaningful when taken to designate a people's external independence; he also would allow the concept as applying internally, if meant in the broad, just as he spoke himself of the sovereignty of the state. But taken in contrast to the sovereignty of the monarch, which is the usual connotation, it is thoroughly condemned by Hegel as based upon the confused idea of a people as a formless mass. . . . Once the people are seen as an organic whole, sovereignty as the personality of the whole is realized in the person of the monarch (see § 273). Hegel further observes that in the undifferentiated states (Greek polis) where a democracy is possible an individual leader must appear; for "all action and working reality (*Wirklichkeit*) has its beginning and

completion in the decisional unity of a leader." But such leaders remain subordinated to a determining fate; Hegel thinks that the
desire to consult oracles, demons, etc., has its origin here. In the
Demon of Socrates we can see this external will internalized and
recognizing itself as the beginning of self-conscious and hence true
freedom. "This final self-determination can be placed within the
sphere of human freedom only, if it has the position of the end
point, *elevated above all particularities and conditions, and separate
by itself.*

In a supplementary section Hegel restates the same ideas once
more. "The state must be looked upon as a great architectural building, as a hieroglyph of reason which is thus represented in
actuality. All that is related merely to utility, externals, etc., should
be excluded from philosophical consideration."]

280. This final self of the will of the state is in this abstraction
simple and thus *direct* unity. That it should be *natural* unity,
its very concept implies; hence a monarch is essential as being an individual, and hence *this* individual abstracted from
all other content, and as being this individual in a direct,
natural way who is destined by his natural birth for the
dignity of a monarch.

This transition from the concept of pure self-determination
to the immediacy of being and thus to nature is of a purely
speculative kind, and therefore its understanding is a part of
philosophical logic. It is the same kind of transition which is
known as the nature of will altogether: the process by which
to transform into reality some object which is as an imagined
purpose merely subjective.

[Hegel then refers to the analogy of the ontological proof of God's
existence which is no longer understood; truth has been abandoned,
because "only the unity of concept and existence (*Dasein*) is
truth." This failure, Hegel feels, causes men no longer to grasp
and therefore to deny that the possibility of a final decision is *in
and of itself* connected with the nature of the state. In a supplementary section, Hegel raises the familiar issue that the very
natural, human aspect of the monarch seems to make the state

depend upon the *accident* of the monarch's character and rejects this argument as invalid for this reason:]

In a perfect organization all that is required is the end point (*Spitze*) of formal decision-making; as a monarch all that is needed is a man who says "yes" and who puts the dot on the "*i*"; for the end point ought to be such that the peculiarities of character do not matter. Whatever [qualities] the monarch has beyond this last decision-making is something that may be relegated to an indifferent particularity. There may be situations where this particularity asserts itself, but then the state is not yet fully developed or not well-constructed. In a well-ordered monarchy the law alone possesses the objective quality to which the monarch merely adds the "I will it." *

281. Both these elements in their undivided unity, the final groundless self of the will and the equally groundless existence . . . the idea of someone unmoved by *arbitrary* preferences constitutes the *majesty* of the monarch. In this unity is implied (*liegt*) the *true unity* of the state. Only by this its *internal* and *external immediacy* is the unity of the state removed from the possibility of being dragged down into the sphere of the *particular*, its arbitrary purposes and opinions; likewise is it removed from the fight of factions against factions and the weakening and eventual destruction of the state's power.

[Hegel continues with an argument to the effect that birth and inheritance provide the ground of *legitimacy* ideally, and not merely by any positive law. If positive law is made the ground, majesty is dragged down into argument, and instead of being the immanent idea of the state, it becomes something outside the state that might be justified by reference to the well-being of state or people. He ironically remarks that "it is well-known what consequences have

---

* These curious sentences show strikingly that Hegel's concept of monarchy is that of early English constitutionalism as elaborated by Richard Hooker. He himself has made it quite clear that he thought of English monarchy as the Germanic form; see his comments on the Reform Bill, below p. 540 ff.—Ed.

been drawn from such *salut du peuple*." "Hence philosophy may only contemplate this majesty through thinking about it; for every other kind of inquiry than the speculative one of the infinite idea which is based in itself destroys the nature of majesty in and by itself." . . .

Hegel goes on to criticize the idea of elective monarchy, and generally the notion that the monarch is the highest state official, as well as the idea of any sort of contract, because all these notions derive from that of the will as pleasure, opinion and arbitrary preference of the many. This notion seems to him contrary not only to the principle of family and state, but of the idea of ethics itself. The reason is that the *particular* will is thus being made the final arbiter, and this means that the power of the state is dissolved into particular powers which weaken and even destroy its sovereignty.*

In a supplementary note, Hegel once again insists that neither institution by God, nor utility, nor yet positive law are the key to monarchy, but a "felt need of the thing in itself." Monarchs are neither especially strong nor intellectually gifted, but millions accept their rule. Men do not do this contrary to their interest: it is the "inherent power of the idea" which keeps them in this relation. It is different with conquered peoples; revolution here is not treason, for there is no "connection through the idea," no inherent necessity of a constitution.]

282. From the sovereignty of the monarch is derived the right to *pardon* criminals; for it alone can realize this power of the spirit which makes what has happened un-happened, and destroy the crime by forgiving and forgetting it.

The right of pardon is one of the highest recognitions of the majesty of the spirit. . . .

[In spite of these noble propositions, Hegel proceeds to add in a supplementary section that "pardon is the remitting of a penalty which does not suspend the law. The law remains, and

---

* It will be noted how close to the original idea of Bodin Hegel's idea of sovereignty here comes; but like the Elizabethans of Bodin's time he does not really adopt it, because he retains the idea of the supremacy of the law.—Ed.

the pardoned is a criminal, as before; the pardon does not state that he has not committed a crime.]

[In paragraphs 283–286, Hegel reviews the various aspects of monarchical power. He notes, quite in keeping with tradition, the right to appoint officials, especially the high ones, and that these officials, through their "objective" work and counseling, are solely responsible, whereas the peculiar majesty of the monarch, as the "final decisional subjectivity," is above all responsibility for governmental acts. He adds the "in itself general" which is given through the prince's conscience on one hand, and the constitution and the laws on the other. Finally, Hegel returns to the idea that each member or organ of the state has its proper sphere under a free monarchy, and that hereditary descent aids in the maintenance of this constitution. By contrast, feudal and despotic monarchies are afflicted with all kinds of revolutions, violence, civil wars and a resulting general devastation, because the division of governmental business is merely a matter of more or less power. "In an organic relationship in which members, not parts, are related, each maintains the other by fulfilling *its own sphere;* for each member the maintenance of the other members is a substantial purpose and a product of its own self-maintenance. The guarantees . . . are secured through *institutions.* . . . When we speak of a *constitution,* we are talking of objective guarantees, of institutions as aspects which are organically intertwined and mutually conditioned. Thus public liberty and a hereditary throne are mutual guarantees. . . ."]

The Governmental Power

287. Different from the decision is the execution and application of monarchical decisions, and altogether the continuation and maintenance of what has been decided, the existing laws, institutions, etc. This business of *subsuming* in its entirety constitutes the *governmental power* which includes the *judicial* and *police* powers. They are more immediately related to the particular concerns of civil society and assert the general interest regarding these purposes.

288. The common *particular* interests which occur in civil

society and lie outside the general interest of the state are being administered in the corporations of the local communes, of the professions, estates and the like. . . .

Their officials should enjoy the confidence of their equals, but should also be subordinated to the higher interests of the state; hence election with confirmation by higher authorities will be indicated. . . .

[In section 289, Hegel points out that the various corporate bodies, although the carriers of particular interests upon the battlefield of civic society, generate a patriotic sentiment that is loyal to the state, because they each and all depend upon the state. Although such corporate self-administration will often be maladroit, it may be left to constitute a sphere of *formal freedom*. . . . In section 290, Hegel, after pointing out that the division of labor is a feature of governmental administration, notes that the organization is difficult, because at the lower end, where it touches social life, it must be adequate for its concreteness, yet must rise to formal abstraction and eventually be combined into a single whole. He follows this with acute observations about centralization and decentralization, culminating in the remark that one is justified in saying that "in the local communities is rooted the true strength of states." He says this after explicitly rejecting the over-centralization of the French Revolution and Napoleon, recognizing the advantages of "ease, swiftness and efficiency."]

291. Governmental business is *objective*, determined in its substance, and yet to be carried out and executed by *individuals*. There exists no natural link between the two; individuals are therefore not destined for such work by their natural personality or birth. The objective basis of their suitability (*Bestimmung*) for such work is the recognition and proof of their ability—a proof which secures for the state what it needs and at the same time (as its only condition) for each citizen the chance to devote himself to this general profession.

292. The subjective side of choosing such an individual is up to the monarchical as the decisive sovereign power in the state.

It must be chosen among several fairly indeterminate ones, since it is not a matter of genius (as in art, e.g.) and thus the preference is nothing absolutely determinate. . . . It is the linking of two somewhat accidental complements, this combining of an individual with its office.

294. The individual who has by sovereign act been linked to an office is called upon to fulfill his duty as the substance of its relationship and the condition of its being thus linked. He finds in this fulfillment of his duty the opportunity and the secure satisfaction of his special objective (§ 264) and is freed in its external position and official activity from any other subjective dependence and influence.

[After remarking that the state is not interested in casual services, Hegel observes that the public service demands the surrendering of independent subjective objectives; instead, it gives the right to satisfy one's personal desire for self-fulfillment through doing one's duty, not as a mere *servant*. Hegel feels that this linking of the subjective and objective constitutes the inner strength of the state. He adds that the public service is not a contractual relationship or a mandate: "What the public servant has to offer, is a value in itself."]

295. The safeguarding of the state and of the governed against the abuse of power on the part of the authorities and their officials is derived (*liegt*) on one hand directly from the hierarchy and its responsibility,* on the other hand from the right of the communes and corporations to stay the intrusion of subjective arbitrariness of an official in the exercise of his duty, thus supplementing the control from above which may not be adequate.

[The conduct and education of the officials provides the point of contact of the laws and decisions of the government with the particular [interests]. Here is the point, then, on which depends

---

* What Hegel presumably means here is the responsibility toward the superior and eventually, therefore, the prince.—Ed.

the contentedness and confidence of the citizens in their government. . . . Hegel notes that the officials have a way of getting together against the public as well as the monarch, and in such situations the sovereign may have to intervene; at this point he recalls the case of miller Arnold.*]

296. For the conduct of officials to become dispassionate, just and mild as a matter of *habit* depends in part upon the direct *ethical* and *philosophical* education which ought to counterbalance spiritually the purely mechanical aspects of what has to be learned of so-called sciences dealing with the subjects of this work . . . It depends also upon the *size* of the state, because by it the weight of family and other private bonds is weakened and such sentiments as revenge, hatred and other such passions become weaker and duller; for in the occupation with the large interests involved in a large state the subjective aspects are submerged and the habit is created of thinking in terms of large interests, opinions and activities.

297. The members of the government and the officials constitute the largest part of the *middle class* in which the educated intelligence and the consciousness of what is right (*rechtliche Bewusstsein*) of the mass of a people is found. The institution of a sovereign from above and the rights of corporations from below bring it about that this middle class does not assume the isolated position of an aristocracy, and that it does not utilize its education and skill as a means of setting itself up as the arbitrary lord of the rest (*Herrenschaft*). At one time judicial work which should be concerned with the proper interest of the individuals became an instrument of gain and domination, because the knowledge of law was wrapped in learning and a foreign tongue and the knowledge of procedure in a complicated formalism.

---

* A legendary case in which Frederick the Great is supposed to have submitted himself to the law, when as a matter of fact he interfered in too formal an application of law; see the editor's *Constitutional Government and Democracy* (1951, pp. 110 f.), for a convenient reference.

[In a supplementary section, Hegel further emphasizes the importance of the middle class as the true core of a state. "The state in which there exists no middle class has not yet reached a high stage." "That this middle class be formed is a main interest of the state." Hegel opines that this can happen only where distinct spheres of local interest and a civil service representing the general interest mutually check each other.]

The Legislative Power

298. The *legislative power* is concerned with the laws as such in so far as they require further development; it is concerned with these internal affairs which are very general in content. This power is itself a part of the constitution which is above it and thus is in and of itself outside the direct determination by the legislative power; nonetheless, the constitution continues to develop through the development of laws and the progress in general governmental affairs.

Supplement. The constitution must in and of itself be the firm and established ground upon which the legislative power rests; it therefore needs not to be made. The constitution *is there,* but just as essentially it is *becoming,* that is to say it progresses in its development. This progress is an insignificant change which does not have the form of a change. [After giving two medieval examples, Hegel concludes: "Thus the development is an apparently steady and unnoticeable one. After a considerable time the constitution reaches a very different state from its previous one."]

299. The subjects of legislation may be more specifically stated in relation to the individuals in two respects: a) what the state provides for them to enjoy, and b) what they have to contribute. Under a) are comprised all the civil laws, the law of communes and corporations and other general laws and indirectly the entire constitution. The contributions can be determined justly only by reducing them to *money* as the existant general value of things and services. . . .

[Hegel then points out that it is difficult to draw a sharp line between the subject of legislation and administration or execution. Since legislation must try to be specific, and not merely a general command such as "Thou shalt not kill," it tends to approach in content the executive task. "The organic unity of the state must provide one spirit," he insists.

In the remainder of the section, Hegel returns to the subject of why the state contents itself with monetary contributions (military service excepted). He recognizes the impersonal cold quality of such an arrangement, as contrasted with former times, but suggests that this monetary equivalent serves to reinforce the principle of *subjective freedom*, because it leaves it to each individual to decide how he will secure what contribution he has to make. "It is implied in the principle of the modern state that everything the individual does he should do through the intermediary of his own free will. The justice of equality can be realized much more fully through money."]

300. In the legislative power in its totality there are at work first of all the two other powers, the monarchical as the one which has the final decision and the governmental as the one which counsels, because it possesses the concrete knowledge and grasp of the whole in its many aspects and of the needs of the state. But there is also at work the element of the estates.

Supplement. It is part of the false notions of the state to want to exclude the members of the government from the legislative bodies, as was done by the French *Constituante*. In England the ministers must be members of parliament, and this is right, since the members of the government should be connected with and not contrary to the legislative power. The idea of the so-called independence of the power contains the basic error that these independent powers are supposed afterwards to check each other. By such independence the unity of the state is put an end to; yet this unity must be demanded above all else.

301. The element of the *estates* has the purpose of making real . . . the aspect of the state which consists in the sub-

jective *formal freedom,* that is to say in the public consciousness as the *empirical generality* of the opinions and thoughts
of the *many.*

The expression: *the many* signifies the empirical generality
more correctly than the more usual expression: *all.* Children,
women are not meant. . . . There are current so many false
notions and slogans about people, constitution and estates that
it is a useless effort to recite, discuss and correct them. The
notion concerning estates is first of all that the deputies of
the people or even the people themselves will *best understand*
what is best for them, and that they have indubitably the best
will to achieve this best. As regards the first of these notions
it is rather true that the people . . . are that part of the
state *which does not know what it wants.* To know what one
wants, and even more what the will existing in and of itself,
reason, wants is the fruit of deep knowledge and insight which
is not the people's affair. The guarantee which the estates
offer for the realization of the general good and public freedom is not to be found in their particular insight . . . but on
one hand in the deputies' greater insight into the activities of
lower officialdom and into the more pressing and special needs
and faults which they have seen concretely, and on the other
hand in the effect which the possible public criticism of the
many will have in bringing it about that the best knowledge is
employed in the handling of all business and all proposals and
only according to the purest motives—a motivation which also
affects the members of the estates themselves.

[After commenting upon the fact that the estates are tied to
special interests and that it is the view of the mob to suspect the
government of a less good will, Hegel once again sums up his
position by stating that "the peculiar purpose (*Begriffsbestimmung*)
of the state is to be sought in this, that through them the subjective aspect of the general freedom, the proper insight and the
proper will of the sphere we have called civil society comes into
existence in relation to the state."]

Supplement. The attitude of the government toward the estates should not be a basically hostile one; the belief in such a necessity is a sad error. The government is not a party faced by another party, so that both would have to try to gain from the other; if a state gets into such a position it is a misfortune. . . . The true significance of the estates consists in this, that through them the state enters into the subjective consciousness of the people and thus commences to share in it.

302. Considered as a *mediating* organ, the estates stand between the government altogether on one side and the people dissolved into the particular spheres and individuals on the other. Their purpose demands of them as much the *sense* of and the *devotion* to the *state* and the *government,* as to the *interests* of the *particular* groups and *individuals.* This position means that the estates share with the organized governmental power the task of mediation, so that the monarchical power will not be isolated and appear as mere ruling power and arbitrariness, nor the particular interests of the communes, corporations and individuals become isolated, nor the individuals come to be a mere *mass* or *horde* and thus through unorganic opining and willing come to be a massive force against the organic state.

It is one of the most important logical insights to understand that a particular aspect or element which, when standing in opposition to something else, occupies an extreme position ceases to be so placed, when considered as an organic element; for then it is also a middleman or mediator (*Mitte*). [Hegel then states that it is especially important to realize that the estates are in this position, because they have frequently been looked upon as nothing but opposition. In case there were a real opposition of this kind "the state would be in the process of collapse."]

Supplement. The constitution is essentially a system of mediation. In despotic states where there are only prince and people, the latter acts, when it acts, merely as a destructive mass against the organization. But if it enters organically, the mass forces through its interests in a lawful and orderly way. If there is no such method available, the voice of the people will always be a wild one. In despotic states the despot appeases (*schont*) the people and vents his fury upon his entourage. Likewise the people pay only few taxes; in constitutional states the people's own consciousness [of public requirements] increases them. In no country are there so many taxes as in England.

303. . . . in the *estates* as an element of the legislative power the *private "estate"* reaches a *political importance* and effectiveness. But this private estate cannot become operative either as a mere undifferentiated mass, nor as a multitude which is dissolved into its atoms. It must appear as that *which it is,* namely as differentiated into the several estates based upon the particular needs and the work required to meet them (§§ 210 ff.). . . . Only in this way can the particular which is at work in the state be linked with the general.*

What has just been said contradicts another current notion, namely that this private estate, if it is elevated to a participation in general affairs through legislation, must appear in the shape of *individuals,* whether they elect representatives for this function or even everyone exercises his own vote. Such an atomistic, abstract view has no place even in the family or civil society where the individual appears only as a member of a general body. The state is essentially an organization of such members as are *by themselves groups (Kreise). . . . The many* taken as *individuals . . .* are a *togetherness,* but merely as a *multitude*—a formless mass, the movement and action of which would be elementary, devoid of reason, wild and terrible. . . .

[After repeating in general terms what has gone before,

---

* The word *Stand,* here rendered by estate, has a considerably broader meaning in German, including as it does profession, status, even class to some extent in its more fluid connotation. See for this my introduction.—Ed.

Hegel suggests that there is one group or estate which is especially suited to function as a mediator, and that is the landed gentry, because it shares with the monarch the combination of family life and landed possession, an "estate of natural ethics."]

306. This estate is constituted for its political role and importance more especially, because its "estate" or possessions (*Vermoegen*) are equally independent of the state, as of the insecurity of commerce with its search for profit and its instability. It is made secure against the favors of the governmental power and those of the multitude, and even against their own arbitrariness, by the members of this estate foregoing the right (possessed by other citizens) to dispose freely of their property, or to distribute it among their children in accordance with their equal affection. The estate becomes inalienable, subject to entail.

Supplement. This estate has a will of its own. It is usually divided into the educated part and the peasantry. But both of these confront the commercial estate which is dependent upon demand and oriented toward it, and the public estate of the officials which is dependent upon the state. [Hegel tries to justify the entailed estate with its political function: "He who has an independent estate is not hindered by external circumstances, and therefore will act unhindered for the state." Entail makes sure that there is a sufficient number of such persons around.*]

[In paragraph 307, Hegel repeats, in general form, that the "general sacrifices" involved in such handling of landed estates entitle this "substantial estate" to exercise this function without the intermediary of an election.]

308. The other part of the estates is the mobile side of civil society. Externally, the number of its members, essentially

---

* These views of Hegel may well be contrasted with Kant's unqualified condemnation of such privileges as contrary to all justice.

their task and occupation mean that it can enter into public life only through *deputies*. In so far as these are deputed by civil society, it is evident that it does so *as it is*. That is to say not as dissolved atomically into individuals . . . [see above, § 303] but as constituted into fellowships, communes and corporations. . . .

The idea that *all* as individuals should participate in the deliberating and resolving concerning general affairs of state, because they all are members of the state, and its affairs are the affairs of *all* in which to participate with their knowledge and will they all have a *right*—this idea which wanted to introduce the *democratic* element *without any rational form* into the organism of the state (which only through such form is organic) occurs so readily, because it stops at the *abstract* aspect of the individual being a member of the state; superficial thinking clings to such abstractions. The rational view, the consciousness of the idea, is *concrete* and thus coincides with the truly *practical* sense which is indeed nothing else but the rational sense, the sense of the idea . . . The concrete state is a *whole organized into its particular groups or spheres* (*Kreise*) the *member* of a state is the *member* of such an *estate;* only in this its objective meaning it can matter in the state. Such a member contains, generally speaking, the double aspect of being a *private person,* but as a *thinking being* also consciousness and will of the *general;* but this consciousness and will is only then not empty, but *filled* and truly *alive* when it is filled with the particular, too. . . . Its true and alive destination for the general good is first of all achieved in the sphere of the corporation, commune, etc. . . . In the forum of public opinion (§ 316) everyone is free to utter his subjective opinions concerning the general good and to make it prevail.

309. Since the delegation is undertaken for the purpose of deliberating upon and deciding *general* affairs, its meaning is to designate by confidence such individuals as have a better grasp of these affairs than those who delegate them; also they should

assert the general interest and not the particular interest of a commune and corporation against the general interest. They do not stand in the relation of committed or instructed mandatories, since the gathering of these delegates has the purpose of being an animated, mutually informing and persuading assembly of common (joint) deliberation.

Supplement. If representation is introduced, it implies that the consent is no longer directly that of all, but that of authorized agents (plenipotentiaries); for the individual no longer concurs as an infinite person. Representation is based on confidence, and confidence is something else than giving my own vote myself. Majority voting is contrary to the principle that I myself must be present in order to be obliged. To have confidence in a person means that one considers his insight such that he will handle my affairs as his and according to his best knowledge and conscience. The principle of a single subjective will is thereby eliminated; for confidence involves the principles of a man's behavior and action, his concrete conviction altogether. It is a matter of making sure that the person who enters a representative assembly possesses a character, an insight and a will which corresponds to the task of being a participant in general (public) affairs.*

[In paragraph 310, Hegel asserts that the guarantee for such qualifications in a representative is to be found in the experience a man has had in local governmental posts and in the loyalty to and knowledge of the interests and institutions of the state and in the resulting political sense (*Sinn des Staats*). He opines that the mere subjective preference of the people is as inadequate a standard as the possession of an estate; the strictly objective qualifications alone satisfy the state's objective requirements and hence are in keeping with the public interest.]

---

* It should be noted that Hegel's view of delegation and representation is closely akin to that of Burke in its idealistic conception, and that he does not differentiate between delegation and representation.—Ed.

311. Delegation has the further meaning that the delegates are acquainted with the special needs, handicaps and interests of civil society, since they are members thereof. Since such delegation is effectuated by the several corporations in accordance with the nature of civil society (§ 308), (and this simple procedure ought not to be disturbed by abstractions and atomistic notions), such delegation takes care of that. Elections are therefore altogether superfluous or are reduced to a trivial play of arbitrary opinion.

Interest by itself brings it about that among the deputies (delegates) there are men for each major branch of society, e.g., for commerce, for industry, etc., who know this branch well and belong to it; the notion of a free, indeterminate election leaves this vital matter to chance. Each of these branches has the same right as every other to be represented. If the deputies (delegates) are looked upon as *representatives,* this has a rational, organic sense only, if they are not *representatives of individuals,* of a multitude, but representatives of essential *spheres* of society, representatives of its broad interests. Representation thus does not have the meaning that one is *present in place of another,* but that the interest itself is *actually* present, just as the representative is present on behalf of his own objective element. Of elections by the many separate individuals it may be noted further that necessarily and especially in large states the voters become *indifferent* about voting, as insignificant in so large a multitude; hence the voters, no matter how much their right of voting is represented to them as something very important, simply do not appear for it, with the result that this institution is perverted and falls into the hands of a few, of a party, i.e., the particular and accidental interest which was supposed to be neutralized.

[Because the two elements in such an estates' assembly each make their distinct contribution to the deliberations, the assembly is divided into two houses, says Hegel. Such division has the further advantage that several bodies delay and hence make the decision more secure, and as like as not one house may serve to mediate between the government and the other. He further notes that since it is the role of the estates to participate in, rather than to determine themselves the affairs of state, and thus to realize formal freedom (see above § 301), the *general* knowledge is enlarged through *publicity* of their deliberations.]

315. The opening up of such opportunities for better knowledge has the more general aspect that thereby *public opinion* arrives at *true thoughts* and insight into the conditions and idea of the state and its affairs, and thus at the *ability to judge them more rationally* (reasonably). Furthermore, public opinion learns to respect, as well as to know, the activities, talents, virtues and abilities of the authorities and officials of the state. Just as these talents are given by such publicity a powerful opportunity of development and a stage of high honor, this publicity is also an antidote against the vanity of individuals and of the multitude and a means for educating the latter— in fact one of the greatest.

Supplement. The public conduct of the estates' assemblies is a great drama which educates the citizens and the people learn from it their true interests. It is a common notion that all know already what is good for the state and that this knowledge is only enunciated in the assembly. In truth the opposite occurs: only in these assemblies those virtues, talents and aptitudes are developed which can serve as models. Admittedly, such assemblies are burdensome for the ministers who themselves must possess wit and rhetorical talent to counteract the attacks which are leveled at them. Nevertheless, publicity is the greatest means of educating the public about the state's interests. Among a people where such publicity takes place one finds a much more live interest in regard to the state as in places where there is no such assembly or it is conducted without publicity. Only by such publicity of each of their several steps are such chambers linked with *public opinion,* and it becomes clear that there is a difference between what a man figures out for himself at home with his wife or his friends, and what happens in a great assembly where one clever mind devours another.

316. The formal subjective freedom of each individual to have his own judgment, opinion and counsel concerning public affairs and to express it gets its outward manifestation (*Erscheinung*) in the togetherness which is called *public opinion*. The in-and-of-itself general, the *substantial and true*, is in this opinion linked with its opposite, namely the *particular and private opinion* of the many by itself. In thus existing, public opinion is the extant contradiction of itself, knowledge as appearance (*Erscheinung*): the essential just as directly as the non-essential.

Supplement. Public opinion is the unorganic way of making known what a people wants and thinks. What is truly right in a state, must be activated in an organic way and happens through the constitution. But at all times public opinion has been a great power, and it is that more especially in our time when the principle of subjective freedom has acquired such importance and significance. What is now right (*gelten soll*), is so not by force, little by custom and habit, but mostly through insight and reasons.

317. Public opinion contains therefore the eternal, substantial principles of justice, the true content and result of the entire constitution, of legislation and of the general conditions, in the form of *sound common sense*. This common sense constitutes the ethical basis which permeates all in the form of prejudices, as well as the true needs and right tendencies of actual life (*Wirklichkeit*).

[After remarking upon how this basic common sense is falsified by all kinds of peculiar notions and interests, Hegel states that "the bad is what is particular and peculiar, but the rational is what is in-and-of-itself general." Both truth and endless error are combined in public opinion, he claims, and it is hard to decide in earnest. He then comments upon the question whether it is permitted to deceive the people. "A people cannot be deceived about its substantial basis, its essence and the definite character of its spirit; but about how it knows this and how it judges its activities and events, it deceives itself."]

Supplement. The principle of the modern world demands that what a man is to acknowledge should be shown him as rightful. Besides he wishes to have participated in discussing and deliberating upon it. Once he has done this, he will suffer much; his subjective being has been satisfied. . . .

318. Public opinion deserves to be as much *respected* as *despised,* the latter regarding its concrete manifestation and consciousness, the former in regard to its essential basis which, more or less obscured, appears only through the concrete manifestations. And since it does not contain itself the standard of evaluation or the ability to lift its substantial aspect into definite knowledge, independence from this public opinion is the first and formal condition for accomplishing something great and rational—in practical life as well as in science. In doing it, one can be sure that in the sequence public opinion will accept it, recognize it and make it one of its prejudices.

Supplement. In public opinion all falsehood and all truth is contained, but to find the truth is the task of the great man. He who says and accomplishes what his time wants and desires is the great man of that time. He does what is the inner essence of his time, he realizes it, and yet he who does not know how to despise public opinion as one hears it here and there will never accomplish anything great.

[In section 319, Hegel takes up freedom of public opinion, including the press, and remarks that its excesses are prevented by laws and police ordinances, but more importantly by "the rationality of the constitution, the firmness of the government, and the public conduct of representative assemblies." He then continues:]

To define freedom of the press as the freedom to say and to write *what one wants* is parallel to defining freedom altogether as freedom to *do what one wants*. This definition Hegel calls uneducated superficiality, but at the same time admits that it is very difficult to formulate adequate laws, because of the fluidity of the material, and hence judgment becomes highly substantive. Hence all such efforts are subject to objections. More particularly it may be asserted, says Hegel, "that such an expression of opinion is not a deed or action, but merely an *opinion*, a *thought* or a *saying*," and hence that it is unimportant, while at the same time, contrariwise, it is also asserted that such personal opinions are one's most spiritual property and hence deserve respect. The substance of the matter is nevertheless, Hegel continues, that the violation of the honor of individuals, libel and slander, treating with contempt the government, its authorities and officials, and more especially the person of the monarch, ridiculing the laws, inciting to sedition, etc., are crimes or misdemeanors of various gradations. And hence he concludes that the laws must differentiate very carefully by taking into account the situation or setting of such utterances.* The various fields of learning (*Wissenschaften*), based as they are upon truth, do not fall within the category of public opinion. After once again stressing the importance of the situation of concrete *danger* for assessing the limits of freedom of expression, Hegel argues that many such opinions can be left to die of their own lack of weight, and can be treated like the mocking songs the Roman soldiery used to compose in order to avenge itself for the fact that the generals received triumphal arches, whereas they who had done the fighting were not mentioned.

[In paragraph 320 Hegel reverts to his earlier theme that the subjectivity of the monarch, in contrast to the subjective opinion of ordinary individuals, is related to the substantial will and the ideality of the whole state.]

---

* Presumably what Hegel is groping for here is the kind of differentiation which is expressed in the famous formula of "the clear and present danger."—Ed.

II. External Sovereignty

321. *International sovereignty* is such ideality in so far as the elements of the spirit and of its actuality, the state, are unfolded in their *necessity* and *exist* as *members* of the state. But the spirit, having in its freedom an *infinitely negative* relation *to itself*, is essentially a being-by-itself which has *absorbed* the existing difference *into itself*, and thereby is exclusive. The state has in this sense *individuality* which is in its essence an individual, and in the sovereign an actual, immediate individual (§ 279).

322. The individuality, as an exclusive being-in-itself, manifests (*erscheint*) itself in the *relation to other states*, each of which is autonomous toward the others. Since the being-in-itself of the actual spirit has its reality (*Dasein*) in this autonomy, this autonomy is the first freedom and the highest honor of a nation.

Those who talk of the desires of such a totality which constitutes a more or less autonomous state and has its own center, for losing this center and autonomy in order to constitute together with another people another whole, know little of the nature of such a totality and of the pride which a people takes in its independence. . . .

323. This negative relation of the state to itself appears in *reality* as the relation of *one state to another* and as if the negative were something *external*. Existentially, this negative relation has, therefore, the form of a happening or event and the entanglement with accidental events coming from outside. But in fact this negative relation is its most supremely proper aspect, its actual infinity as the ideality of everything finite within it. It is the aspect of the state wherein its substance—the absolute power over everything individual and particular, over life, property and its rights, over the various spheres—renders the unreality of all these other particulars a fact and makes men aware of it.

324. This disposition whereby the interest and the right of individuals are posited as a negligible aspect is at the same time the *positive* aspect of their individuality as it *is in-and-of-itself,* as contrasted with the accidental and changeable aspects. This relationship to the state and their recognition of it is therefore their substantial duty—the duty to maintain the independence and sovereignty of the state, its substantial individuality, by endangering and sacrificing their property and life, as well as their opinions and all that is comprised within one's life.

A very distorted account results, if in connection with this demand for sacrifice the state is looked upon merely as a civil society and its end merely the *security of life and property* of these individuals; for this security is not achieved by sacrificing what is to be made *secure,* on the contrary.

In what has been said is implied the *ethical aspect of war.* War is not to be looked upon as an absolute evil and a purely external accident which has its accidental cause in whatever it may be, in the passions of the rulers, or of the nations, in injustices, etc., that is, in matters which ought not to be. What is by nature accidental, suffers accidents, and this fate is therefore of necessity—generally the concept and philosophy eliminates the purely accidental aspects and recognizes the necessary essence behind this *appearance.* It is *necessary* that the finite, namely, property and life, be *posited* as accidental, because this is the concept of the finite. This necessity has on the one hand the form of the power of nature, as all the finite is mortal and transient. In the ethical being, the state, this power is taken away from nature, and necessity is elevated into a work of freedom, something ethical. The transience of the finite becomes a voluntary passing away, and the underlying negativity becomes the substantial and proper individuality of the ethical being.

War as the state in which the vanity of all earthly goods and things which is often no more than a pious phrase, becomes a deadly serious matter, is therefore the aspect of the state wherein the ideality of the *particular receives* what is *its right* (*Recht*) and becomes actuality. War has the higher meaning that through it, as I have said elsewhere, "the ethical health of nations is maintained, since such health does not require the stabilizing of finite arrangements; just as the motion of the winds keeps the sea from the foulness which a constant calm would produce—so war prevents a corruption of nations which a perpetual, let alone an eternal peace would produce." By the way, this is merely a philosophical idea, or as one sometimes says a justification of providence, and actual wars require still another justification as will be shown below.

[Hegel goes on to argue that the historical observation that successful wars reinforce a state's internal constitutional order shows that the ideality of this internal order and of war are the same. This dubious proposition he follows with the more convincing generalization that people who are dissatisfied with the constitutional order will not make the required effort to maintain their independence: "their freedom died of the fear of death."]

Supplement. In times of peace civil life expands more and more, all the different spheres settle down, and in the long run men sink into corruption; their particularities become more and more fixed and ossified. But health depends upon the unity of the body and if the parts harden, death occurs. Eternal peace is often being demanded as an ideal which mankind must progress toward. Kant proposed a union of princes which would arbitrate the controversies between states, and the Holy Alliance was intended as such an institution. Yet the state as an individual and individuality essentially contains negation. Therefore even if a certain number of states get together into a family, such an association must as an individuality create an antagonism and produce an enemy. Nations do not only emerge from wars stronger, but nations which are quarrelsome within themselves gain by wars some peace within.

To be sure, war brings insecurity of possessions, but this *real* insecurity is nothing but the motion which is needed. One hears a great deal of preaching from the pulpits about the insecurity, vanity and transience of temporal things, but each one thinks as he listens that he will keep what is his. If then this insecurity really appears in the form of cavalry with bare sabers and in earnest, then this sentimental piety, which predicted it all, turns to pronouncing curses upon the conqueror. In spite of it all, wars take place where they are rooted in the nature of things; afterwards, the seed sprouts again and the talk ends about how history repeats itself.

325. Sacrificing oneself for the individuality of the state is the substantial relationship of all the citizens and therefore a *general duty*. Since this relationship is a *single aspect* of the ideality, as contrasted with the reality of particular existence, it becomes itself a particular relationship to which a proper profession (estate), the *vocation of courage,* is dedicated.

326. Conflicts between states may concern a *special* aspect of their relationship; to deal with these is the main task of that *special* part of the state which is dedicated to its defense. But if the state itself, and its autonomy, are in danger, duty calls all its citizens to its defense. If thus the whole has become a force and has been torn from its domestic affairs into the outside world, the defensive war is transformed into a war of conquest.

[That the armed power of a state, its *standing army,* and the particular business of defending it becomes a *vocation or estate* springs from the same necessity by which other special aspects, interests and affairs become the married estate or the vocation (estate) of commerce, public or private business. Hegel adds that there is a lot of argument about standing armies and prevailing sentiment is against it, because the true concept is hard to grasp, and that which is in itself necessarv is harder to appreciate than particular interests.]

327. Courage is in itself a *formal* virtue, because it is the highest abstraction of freedom from all particular purposes, possessions, pleasure, and life. But this negation takes place in an actual, external way, and this alienation is not in itself of a spiritual nature, though it is the fulfillment of courage. The inner conviction of a courageous man may be based upon this or that ground, and its actual result may be beneficial not *for himself* but only for others.

Supplement. The military estate (vocation) is that general estate to which belongs the defense of the state and which has the duty to bring the ideality into existence through itself, that is to say to sacrifice itself. There are different kinds of courage. The courage of an animal, of a robber, on behalf of honor and knighthood, are not yet true courage. The true courage of cultured nations is the readiness to sacrifice oneself in the service of the state . . . not personal courage, but ranging oneself with the general is the important thing. . . .

[In section 328, Hegel elaborates the preceding thought that true courage springs from loyalty toward the state, and in this connection he glorifies the alienation of self involved in subordinating oneself to the *mechanics of an external order and service.* "Complete obedience and relinquishing of one's own opinion and thought and therefore absence of one's own spirit, all that is involved in the most intensive and comprehensive presence of spirit and resolution." He notes that the most hostile, yet most personal action against individuals is combined with a good disposition toward them as individuals. He further notes that to risk one's life is not in itself anything worthwhile, e.g., criminals. It is the higher thought of the general good which has given courage its higher form. He adds that the invention of firearms springs from this more abstract approach which transforms personal bravery into abstract courage.]

329. A state's external relations result from its individuality. Its relation to other states is properly part of the monarchical

power to which therefore immediately and solely falls the task of commanding the armed forces, to maintain relations with other states through ambassadors, etc., to declare war and conclude peace and other treaties.

[Hegel notes that in representative constitutions based upon estates (*staendische*), the question may arise whether war and peace are not to be concluded by them; in any case they retain their influence through the purse. In England, he observes, no unpopular war can be fought. But the notions that princes and cabinets are more prone to go to war is false; whole nations are more apt to get excited. In England the whole people has often demanded war. The popularity of Pitt resulted from it. Only later did the people realize that the war was unnecessary. Finally Hegel mentions in passing that the complexities of relations with many states call for delicate handling; this only the head of the government can do.]

B. *The External Public Law (International Law)*

330. The external public law springs from the relations of autonomous states. What it contains *in-and-of-itself*, possesses *normative* form because it depends for its actuality upon *diverse sovereign wills*.

Supplement. States are not private persons, but completely autonomous totalities in themselves, and hence their relationship is different from a merely moral and legal one. It has often been tried to interpret them thus as legal and moral, but private persons have a court over them which realizes what is law. The relationship between states ought also to be lawful in itself, but in this world that which is in itself must also have power to actualize it. Since there exists no power which can decide against a state what is law (*Recht*) in itself and which might enforce such a decision, the relationship must remain a normative one.

[In section 331, Hegel repeats his view of nation and state as spirit in its substantial rationality and immediate actuality and makes it the basis of sovereignty as he does above (§ 322). This means that his first absolute right is "to be there for another, that is, to be recognized." He continues:

Just as the individual is not an actual person without relation to other persons, so the state is not an actual individual without relation to other states (§ 322). The legitimacy of a state, internally . . . must be *completed* by the recognition of other states. But such recognition requires that it in turn recognizes other states and respects their independence, and therefore it cannot be a matter of indifference to them what happens inside a state. If a people are upon a low cultural level, as, e.g., some nomadic tribes, the question may well arise whether they are truly a state. . . ."]

Supplement. When Napoleon said, before the Peace of Campoformio: "The French Republic requires no recognition, no more than does the sun," these words simply meant that the French Republic was so strong through its mere existence, that recognition was vouchsafed for it, regardless of whether it was pronounced in words.

332. The immediate actuality in which states find themselves with each other develops into manifold relations which are determined by mutual arbitrary decision, and which therefore have the form of *treaties*, generally speaking. The subject-matter of these treaties is, however, of much less great variety than in civil society in which individuals are dependent upon each other in the most varied ways, while autonomous states are largely self-sufficient wholes.

333. The principle of *international law* taken as the *general* norm of what ought to be valid between states as contrasted with the particular content of positive treaties is this, that the treaties *should be honored* since the obligations of states toward each other depend upon them. But because the relation between such states rests upon their sovereignty, they are in a state of nature, so to speak, toward each other and their rights have their actuality not in any general [power] constituted

over them, but in their own free will. The general norm [that treaties are to be observed] remains an *ought* and the actual situation varies in accordance with what is appropriate to their relation, in accordance with treaties that may be suspended.

There is no praetor, at most arbiters and mediators, between states and these latter only in accordance with a particular decision, that is, accidentally. The conception of Kant of an *eternal peace* based upon a federation of states which would arbitrate every conflict and would compose, as a power recognized by the individual state, each trouble, and thus would make a decision by war impossible, presupposes the agreement of the states which would rest upon moral, religious or other grounds and considerations, which would altogether always rest upon the particular sovereign wills and therefore would remain subject to contingency.

334. A conflict between states can therefore when the particular wills do not find any agreement be decided only by *war*. Violations, of which there are many possible in the wide area of the manifold relations of their members, are to be looked upon as a definite breach of a treaty or a violation of their recognition and honor, remain indeterminable. A state may consider any of its special features a significant part of its infinitude and honor. It will be the more inclined to be touchy the more a strong individuality is by long internal peace propelled into seeking and creating a cause for activity abroad.

335. Moreover, a state as a spiritual being cannot stop at regarding merely the *actual* violation; it must also consider the *anticipation* (*Vorstellung*: literally imagination) of such a violation as a danger which *threatens* it from another state, and that means the calculation of changing probabilities, the suspicion of motives, etc., must be added as causes of conflict.

336. Since the states are in the relation of *particular* wills toward each other and the validity of all treaties rests upon it, and since the *particular* will of the whole is concerned with its own well-being, this well-being constitutes the highest law

in its conduct toward others. . . . The primary recognition of states concerns them as concrete wholes.

337. The substantial well-being of the state is its well-being as a *particular* state having its definite interest and condition, its peculiar external circumstances and treaty relations. Its government calls for a *particular wisdom,* and not general providence. Likewise the purpose of the relation with other states and the principle of just wars and treaties is not a general (philanthropic) thought, but the actually infringed or threatened well-being in its definite particularity.

At times, the conflict between morals and politics has been much discussed and the demand made that the latter conform to the former. It is merely pertinent to remark that the well-being of a state has a very different justification from the well-being of an individual, and the ethical substance, the state, has its being (*Dasein*), that is its right to exist not in an abstract, but in concrete existence. Only this concrete existence and not one of the many thoughts which are considered moral norms can be the principle of a state's action and conduct. The notion of the presumed injustice (*Unrecht*) which politics is supposed to imply by this conflict, rests upon the superficiality of the conceptions of morality and ethics, of the nature of the state and its relation to the moral viewpoint.

338. Because states as such recognize each other, a bond remains between them even during a *war,* the state of lawlessness, of violence and contingency. Thus the states are valid in-and-of-themselves for each other so that the war while it lasts is considered as something that ought to pass. War therefore contains the norm of internal law that the possibility of peace should be maintained. Hence ambassadors are respected and generally war is not conducted against the internal institutions nor against the peaceful life of family and private life, nor against private persons.

Supplement. Modern wars are therefore conducted humanely and persons do not hate each other. At most personal hostilities occur among the vanguards of the armies, but in the army as army the hostility is something indefinite which is subordinated to the duty that each respects the other.

339. For the rest, the mutual conduct during war (e.g., that prisoners are taken) and also what in peace time a state concedes to the members of another, etc., depends upon the *customs* of the nations. . . .

Supplement. The European nations form a family according to the general principles of their legislation, their customs, their culture. These modify the conduct according to international law where otherwise the doing of harm would be prevalent. The relation of states is ambiguous: there is no praetor who arbitrates: the higher praetor is alone the universal spirit which is in-and-of-itself, the world spirit.

340. The relation of states toward each other, as particular states, includes the highly animated interplay of their particular passions, interests, purposes, talents and virtues, of force, injustice and vices—their inner life—with the external contingency appearing in its largest dimensions. This interplay exposes the ethical whole itself, the autonomy of the state, to contingency. The principles of the *national spirits* are, because they are particular *existing* individuals having their objective actuality and self-consciousness, altogether limited. Their destinies and actions are in their relation to each other the phenomenal dialectics of the finiteness of these spirits. From this finiteness, the *universal spirit,* the *spirit of the world* which is unlimited creates itself; it is this world spirit which exercises its right over them—and this right is the highest—in world history as the world court.

[Here follows a brief résumé of Hegel's views on world history, which are more fully given in his *Philosophy of History* and which are therefore omitted.—Ed.]

Selections from

LECTURES ON AESTHETICS

Translated in part by
W. M. Bryant
Bernard Bosanquet*

───────────

* The translation by Bosanquet is here reprinted with the permission
of Routledge and Kegan Paul Ltd.

LECTURES ON AESTHETICS

INTRODUCTION

Development of the Ideal in the Special Forms of Art

IN THE FIRST PART OF THIS WORK WE HAVE HAD UNDER CON-
sideration the realization of the idea of the beautiful as constituting the Ideal in art. But, however numerous may be the different phases under which the conception of the ideal is
presented to our view, all these determinations are only related
to the work of art considered in a general way.

Now, the idea of the beautiful as the *absolute idea* contains
a totality of distinct elements, or of *essential moments*, which,
as such, must manifest themselves outwardly and become
realized. Thus are produced what we may call, in general, the
Special Forms of Art.

These must be considered as the development of those ideas
which the conception of the ideal contains within it, and which
art brings to light. Thus its development is not accomplished
by virtue of an external activity, but by the specific force inherent in the idea itself; so that the *Idea*, which develops itself
in a totality of particular forms, is what the world of art presents us.

In the second place, if the forms of art find their principle
in the idea which they manifest, this, on the contrary, is truly
the idea only when it is realized in its appropriate forms. Thus,
to each particular stage which art traverses in its development,
there is immediately joined a real form. It is, then, indifferent
whether we consider the progress as shown in the development
of the idea, or in that of the forms which realize it, since these
two terms are closely united, the one to the other, and since
the perfecting of the idea as *matter* appears no less clearly than
does the perfecting of the *form.*

Hence, imperfection of the artistic form betrays itself also as imperfection of idea. If, then, at the origin of art, we encounter forms which, compared with the true ideal, are inadequate to it, this is not to be understood in the sense in which we are accustomed to say of works of art that they are defective, because they express nothing, or are incapable of attaining to the idea which they ought to express. The idea of each epoch always finds its appropriate and adequate form; and these are what we designate as the special forms of art. The imperfection or the perfection can consist only in the degree of relative truth which belongs to the idea itself; for the matter must first be true, and developed in itself, before it can find a perfectly appropriate form.

We have, in this respect, *three principal forms* to consider:

1. The first is the *Symbolic Form*. Here the idea seeks its true expression in art without finding it; because, being still abstract and indefinite, it cannot create an external manifestation which conforms to its real essence. It finds itself in the presence of the phenomena of nature and of the events of human life, as if confronted by a foreign world. Thus it exhausts itself in useless efforts to produce a complete expression of conceptions vague and ill-defined; it perverts and falsifies the forms of the real world which it seizes in arbitrary relations. Instead of combining and identifying, of blending totally the form and the idea, it arrives only at a superficial and abstract agreement between them. These two terms, thus brought into connection, manifest their disproportion and heterogeneity.

2. But the idea, in virtue of its very nature, cannot remain thus in abstraction and indetermination. As the principle of free activity, it seizes itself in its reality as spirit. The spirit, then, as free subject, is determined by and for itself, and in thus determining itself it finds in its own essence its appropriate outward form. This unity, this perfect harmony between the idea and its external manifestation, constitutes the second form of art—the *Classic Form*.

Here art has attained its perfection, in so far as there is reached a perfect harmony between the idea as spiritual individuality, and the form as sensuous and corporeal reality. All hostility between the two elements has disappeared, in order to give place to a perfect harmony.

3. Nevertheless, spirit cannot rest with this form, which is not its complete realization. To reach this perfect realization, spirit must pass beyond the classic form, must arrive at a pure spirituality, which, returning upon itself, descends into the depths of its own inmost nature. In the classic form, indeed, notwithstanding its generality, spirit reveals itself with a special determinate character; it does not escape from the finite. Its external form, as a form altogether visible, is limited. The matter, the idea itself, because there is perfect fusion, must present the same character. Only the finite spirit is able to unite itself with external manifestation so as to form an indissoluble unity.

When the idea of beauty seizes itself as absolute or infinite Spirit, it also at the same time discovers itself to be no longer completely realized in the forms of the external world; it is only in the internal world of consciousness that it finds, as spirit, its true unity. It breaks up then this unity which forms the basis of Classic Art; it abandons the external world in order to take refuge within itself. This is what furnishes the type of the *Romantic Form*. Sensuous representation, with its images borrowed from the external world, no longer sufficing to express free spirituality, the form becomes foreign and indifferent to the idea. So that Romantic Art thus reproduces the separation of matter and form, but from the side opposite to that from which this separation takes place in Symbolic Art.

As a summary of the foregoing, we may say that Symbolic Art *seeks* this perfect unity of the idea with the external form; Classic Art *finds* it, for the senses and the imagination, in the representation of spiritual individuality; Romantic Art *tran-*

scends it in its infinite spirituality, which rises above the visible world.

Part I

OF THE SYMBOLIC FORM OF ART

I. *Of the Symbol in General*

The symbol, in the sense which we here give to this term, constitutes, according to its very idea, as well as from the epoch of its appearance in history, the *beginning of art.* Thus it ought rather to be considered as the precursor of art. It belongs especially to the *Orient,* and will conduct us, by a multitude of transitions, transformations, and mediations, to the true realization of the ideal under the classic form. We must then distinguish the symbol, properly speaking, as furnishing the type of all the conceptions or representations of art at this epoch, from that species of symbol which, on its own account, is nothing more than a mere unsubstantial, outward form. Where the symbol presents itself under its appropriate and independent form, it exhibits in general the character of *sublimity.* The idea, being vague and indeterminate, incapable of a free and measured development, cannot find in the real world any fixed form which perfectly corresponds to it; in default of which correspondence and proportion, it transcends infinitely its external manifestation. Such is the sublime style, which is rather the immeasurable than the true sublime.

We will first explain what should here be understood by the term symbol.

1. The symbol is a sensuous object, which must not be taken in itself such as it presents itself immediately to us, but in a more extended and more general sense. There are, then, in the symbol two terms to be distinguished: first, the *meaning,* and, secondly, the *expression.* The first is a conception of the

mind; the second, a sensuous phenomenon, an image which addresses itself to the senses.

Thus the symbol is a *sign,* but it is distinguished from the signs of language in this: that, between the image and the idea which it represents, there is a relation which is natural, not arbitrary or conventional. It is thus that the lion is the symbol of courage, the circle of eternity, the triangle of the trinity.

Still, the symbol does not represent the idea perfectly, but only from a single side. The lion is not merely courageous, the fox cunning. Whence it follows that the symbol, having many meanings, is equivocal. This ambiguity ceases only when the two terms are first conceived separately and then in combination; the symbol then gives place to comparison.

Thus conceived, the symbol, with its enigmatical and mysterious character, is peculiarly applicable to a whole epoch of history—to *Oriental art* and its extraordinary creations. It characterizes that order of monuments and emblems by which the peoples of the Orient have sought to express their ideas, but have been able to do so only in an equivocal and obscure fashion. Instead of beauty and regularity, these works of art present a *bizarre,* grandiose, fantastic aspect.

When we find ourselves in this world of symbolic representations and images of ancient Persia, India, and Egypt, all seems strange to us. We feel that we are groping about in the midst of problems. These images do not entertain us of themselves. The spectacle neither pleases nor satisfies us in itself; we must pass beyond the sensuous form in order to penetrate its more extended and more profound meaning. In other productions we see at the first glance that they have nothing serious; that, like the stories of children, they are a simple play of the imagination, which is pleased with accidental and particular associations. But these peoples, although in their infancy, demand a meaning and a truer and more substantial basis of ideas. This, indeed, is what we find among the Indians, the Egyptians, etc., although in these enigmatical figures the meaning may be often very difficult to divine. What part must it play amid this poverty and grossness of conceptions? How far, on the contrary, in the incapability of expressing by purer and more beautiful forms the depth of religious ideas, is it proper to call in the fantastic and the grotesque to the aid of a representation of which the aspiration is not to remain beneath its object? This is a difficult point to decide.

The classic ideal, it is true, presents the same difficulty. Though the idea seized by the mind may here be lodged in an adequate form, the image, beyond this idea of which it serves as the expression, represents other and foreign ideas. Is it possible to see in these representations and these stories only absurd inventions which shock the religious sense—as the amours of Jupiter, etc.? Such stories being related of superior divinities, is it not very probable that they contain a wider and deeper meaning concealed? Whence two different opinions, the one of which regards mythology as a collection of fables unworthy of the idea of God; which present, it is true, much that is interesting and charming, but which cannot furnish a basis for a more serious interpretation. In the other, on the contrary, they pretend that a more general and more profound meaning resides in these fables. To penetrate beneath the veil with which they envelop their mysterious meanings is the task of those who devote themselves to the philosophic study of myths.

All mythology is then conceived as essentially symbolical. This would be to say that myths, as creations of the human spirit, however *bizarre* and grotesque they may appear, contain in themselves a meaning for the reason; general thoughts upon the divine nature—in a word, philosophemes.

From this point of view myths and traditions have their origin in the spirit of man, who can easily make a play of the representation of his gods, but seeks and finds in them also a higher interest, whenever he finds himself unable to set forth his ideas in a more suitable manner. Now, this is the true opinion. Thus, when reason finds again these forms in history, it realizes the necessity of probing their meaning.

If, then, we penetrate to the source of these myths in order to discover there their concealed truth, yet without losing from view the accidental element which belongs to the imagination and to history, we are able thus to justify the different mythologies. And to justify man in the images and the representations which his spirit has created is a noble enterprise, far preferable to that which consists in collecting historical particulars more or less insignificant.

Without doubt, priests and poets have never known under an abstract and general form the thoughts which constitute the basis of mythological representations, and it is not by design that they have been enveloped in a symbolical veil. But it does not follow that their representations cannot be symbols and ought not to be considered as such. Those peoples, at the time when they composed their myths, lived in a state altogether poetic; they expressed their most secret and most profound sentiments, not by abstract formulae, but by the forms of the imagination.

Thus the mythological fables contain a wholly rational basis, and more or less profound religious ideas.

Nor is it less correct to say that for every true work of art there serves as basis a universal thought which, afterward presented under an abstract form, must give the meaning of the work. The critical spirit, or the understanding, hastens on to the symbol or the allegory. Here it separates image from signification, and thus destroys the art-form; to which, indeed, in respect of the symbolic explanation which only brings out the universal as such, no importance attaches.

2. But this mode of extending the symbol to the entire domain of mythology is by no means the method which we are

here to pursue. Our aim is not to discover to what point the representations of art have had a symbolic or allegorical meaning.

On the contrary, we have to inquire how far the symbol, properly speaking, extends as a *special form of art,* while still preserving its appropriate character; and thereby we shall distinguish it in particular from the two other forms, Classic and Romantic.

Now, the *symbol,* in the special sense which we attach to this term, ceases where *free subjectivity* (personality), taking the place of vague and indeterminate conceptions, constitutes the basis of representation in art. Such is the character which the *Greek gods* present us. Greek art represents them as free individuals, independent in themselves; genuine moral persons. Hence we cannot consider them from the symbolic point of view. The acts, for example, of Jupiter, of Apollo, of Minerva, belong only to these divinities themselves; represent only their power and their passions. Should we abstract from these free individualities a general idea and set it up as an explanation, we should abandon and destroy in these figures just that which corresponds to the *i*dea of art. Whence artists have never been satisfied with these symbolic or allegorical explanations applied to works of art and to mythology. If there remains a place for allegory or the symbol, it is in the accessories, in simple attributes, signs—as the eagle by the side of Jupiter, the ox by the side of St. Luke; while the Egyptians saw in the bull Apis a divinity itself.

The difficult point in our investigation is to distinguish whether what are represented as personages in mythology or art possess a real *individuality* or *personality,* or whether they contain but the empty semblance of it, and are only mere *personifications.* This is what constitutes the real problem of the limitation of Symbolic Art.

What interests us here is that we are present at the very origin of art. At the same time we shall observe the progressive advancement of the symbol, the stages by which it proceeds toward genuine art. Whatever may be the narrow line which unites religion and art, we have here to consider the symbol solely from the artistic point of view. We abandon to the history of mythology itself the religious side.

DIVISION.—Many degrees are to be noted in the development of this form of art in the Orient.

But first we must mark its *origin*. This, which is blended with that of art in general, can be explained in the following manner:

The sentiment of art, like the religious sentiment, like scientific curiosity, is born of *wonder*; the man who wonders at nothing lives in a state of imbecility and stupidity. This state ceases when his spirit, disengaging itself from matter and from physical necessities, is struck by the phenomena of nature, and seeks their meaning; when he is impressed by something in them grand and mysterious, a concealed power which reveals itself.

Then he experiences also the need of representing this internal sentiment of a general and universal power. Particular objects—the elements, the sea, the waves, the mountains—lose their immediate meaning and become for the spirit images of this invisible power.

It is then that art appears. It is born of the necessity of representing this idea by sensuous images, which address themselves at once to the senses and to the mind.

In religions, the idea of an absolute power is at first manifested by the worship of physical objects. The divinity is identified with nature itself; but this gross worship cannot last. Instead of seeing the absolute in real objects, man conceives it as a distinct and universal being; he seizes, though very imperfectly, the relation which unites the invisible principle to the objects of nature; he fashions an image, a symbol destined to represent it. Art is then the interpreter of religious ideas.

Such, in its origin, is art, and with it the Symbolic Form is born.

We will attempt, by a precise division, to trace exactly the circle in which the symbol moves.

That which characterizes, in general, Symbolic Art is that it vainly endeavors to find pure conceptions and a mode of representation which is suitable to them. It is a conflict between *matter* and *form,* both imperfect and heterogeneous. Whence the incessant strife between the two elements of art, which seek, uselessly, to place themselves in harmony. The degrees of its development present successive phases or modes of this conflict.

1. At the beginning of art this conflict does not yet exist. The point of departure, at least, is a still undivided *unity,* in the center of which ferments the discord between the two principles. Here, then, the creations of art, little distinguished from objects of nature, are still scarcely symbols.

2. The termination of this epoch is the *disappearance of the symbol,* which takes place by the reflective separation of the two terms, the idea being clearly conceived; the image, on its side, being perceived as distinct from the idea. From their reconciliation (*rapprochment*) is born the reflective symbol or *comparison,* the allegory, etc.

The two extreme points being thus fixed, we may now see, in what follows, the intermediary points or degrees. The general division is this:

I. The true symbol is the *unconscious, irreflective* symbol, the forms of which appear to us in Oriental civilization.

II. Then follows, as a mixed form, or form of transition, the *reflective symbol,* of which the basis is *comparison,* and which marks the close of this epoch.

We have, then, to follow each of these two forms in the successive stages of its development; to mark its steps in the career which it has passed through in the Orient before arriving at the Greek ideal.

Part II

OF THE IDEAL OF CLASSIC ART

I. *The Classic Ideal*

1. The ideal as free creation of the imagination of the artist.—2. The new gods of Classic Art.—3. External character of the representation.

1. As the ideal of Classic Art comes to be realized only by the transformation of preceding elements, the first point to develop consists in making manifest that it is truly sprung from the creative activity of the spirit; that it has found its origin in the inmost and most personal thought of the poet and of the artist.

This seems contradicted by the fact that Greek mythology rests upon ancient traditions, and is related to the religious doctrines of the peoples of the Orient. If we admit all these foreign elements—Asiatic, Pelasgic, Dodonian, Indian, Egyptian, Orphic—how can we say that Hesiod and Homer gave to the Greek gods their names and their form? But these two things—tradition and poetic invention—may be very easily reconciled. Tradition furnishes the materials, but it does not bring with it the precise idea and the form which each god is to represent. This idea these great poets drew from their own genius, and they also discovered the actual forms appropriate to it. Thus were they the creators of the mythology which we admire in Greek art. The Greek gods are for this reason neither a poetic invention nor an artificial creation. They have their root in the spirit and the beliefs of the Greek people—in the very foundation of the national religion; these are the absolute forces and powers, whatever is most elevated in the Greek imagination, inspired in the poet by the muse herself.

With this faculty of free creation, the artist, we have already seen, takes a position altogether different from that which he had in the Orient. The Indian poets and sages have, also, for their point of departure the primitive *data*, consisting of the elements of nature—the sky, animals, the rivers—or the abstract conception of Brahma; but their inspiration is the annihilation of personality. Their spirit loses itself in wishing to represent ideas so foreign to their inner nature, while the imagination, in the absence of rule and of measure, incapable of directing itself, allows itself to wander in the midst of conceptions which have neither the character of freedom nor that of beauty. It is like an architect obliged to accommodate himself to an unequal soil, upon which rise old *debris*, walls half destroyed, hillocks and rocks; forced, besides, to subordinate his plans to particular ends. He can erect only irregular structures which must be wholly irrational and fantastic. Such is not the work of a free imagination, creating according to its own inspirations.

In Classic Art the artists and poets are also prophets and teachers; but their inspiration is personal.

a. At first that which constitutes the essence of their gods is neither a nature foreign to spirit, nor the conception of a single god who admits of no sensuous representation and remains invisible. They borrow their ideas from the human heart, from human life. Thus man recognizes himself in these creations; for what he produces outwardly is the most beautiful manifestation of himself.

b. They are on this account only the more truly *poets*. They fashion at their will the matter and the idea so as to draw from them figures free and original. All these heterogeneous or foreign elements they cast into the crucible of their imagination; but they do not form therein a *bizarre* mixture which suggests the cauldron of the magician. Everything that is confused, material, impure, gross, disordered, is consumed in the flame of their genius. Whence springs a pure and beautiful creation wherein the materials of which it has been formed are scarcely perceptible. In this respect their task consists in despoiling tradition of everything gross, symbolic, ugly, and deformed, and afterward bringing to light the precise idea which they wish to individualize and to represent under an appropriate form. This form is the human form, and it is not employed here as a simple personification of the acts and accidents of life; it appears as the sole reality which corresponds to the idea. True, the artist also finds his images in the real world; but he must remove whatever of accidental or inappropriate they present before they can express the spiritual element of human nature, which, seized in its essence, should represent the everlasting might of the gods. Such is the free, though not arbitrary, manner in which the artist proceeds in the production of his works.

c. As the gods take an active part in human affairs, the task of the poet consists in acknowledging therein their presence and their activity, as well as in signalizing whatever is remarkable in natural events, in human deeds, and in fate—in all in which the divine powers appear to be involved. Thus the poet fulfills in part the role of priest, as well as that of prophet. We moderns, with our prosaic reason, explain physical phenomena by universal laws and forces; human actions, by personal wills. The Greek poets, on the contrary, saw, above all these phenomena, their divine author. In representing human acts as divine acts, they showed the diverse aspects under which the gods reveal their power. Thus a great number of these divine manifestations are only human acts, when such or such divinity intervenes. If we open the poems of Homer, we find there scarcely any important event which may not be explained by the will or the direct influence of the gods. Such interpretations belong to the mode of seeing, to the faith born in the imagination of the poet. Thus, Homer often expresses them in his own name, and places them only in part in the mouth of his personages, whether priests or heroes. Thus, as at the beginning of the Iliad, he has explained the pestilence by the wrath of Apollo; further on he will cause it to be predicted by Calchas. It is the same with the recital of the story of the death of Achilles, in the last canto of the Odyssey. The shades of the lovers, conducted by Hermes to the meadows where blooms the asphodel, there encounter Achilles and other heroes who have battled on the Trojan plain. Agamemnon himself relates to them the death of the young hero: "The Greeks had fought all day; when Jupiter had separated the two armies, they bore the noble body upon vessels and embalmed it, shedding tears. Then they heard coming from above a divine sound, and the Achaians, alarmed, would have rushed to their ships had not an old man, in whom years had ripened experience, arrested them." He explained to them the phenomenon, by saying: "It is the mother of the hero who comes from the depth of the ocean, with the immortal goddesses of the sea, to receive the body of her son." At these words fear abandoned the sage Achaians. From that moment, indeed, there was no longer anything in it strange to them. Something human, a mother, the sorrowful mother of the hero, came before them; Achilles is her son, she mingles her moans with theirs. Afterward Agamemnon, turning to Achilles, continues to describe the general grief: "About thee gathered the daughters of old ocean, uttering cries of grief. They spread over thee vestments, perfumed with ambrosia. The muses also, the nine sisters, caused to be heard, each in her turn, a beautiful song of mourning; and there was not then an Argive there who could restrain his tears, so greatly had the song of the muses melted all hearts."

2. Still, of what nature are the creations which Classic Art produces in following such a method? What are the characteristics of the new gods of Greek art?

a. The most general idea that we should form of them is that of a concentrated individuality, which, freed from the multiplicity of accidents, actions, and particular circumstances of human life, is collected upon itself at the focus of its simple unity. Indeed, what we must first remark is their spiritual and, at the same time, immutable and substantial individuality. Far removed from the world of change and illusion, where want and misery reign, far from the agitation and trouble which attach to the pursuit of human interests, retired within themselves, they rest upon their own universality as upon an everlasting foundation where they find repose and felicity. By this alone the gods appear as imperishable powers, of which the changeless majesty rises above particular existence. Disengaged from all contact with whatever is foreign or external, they manifest themselves uniquely in their immutable and absolute independence.

Yet, above all, these are not simple abstractions—mere spiritual generalities—they are genuine *individuals*. With this claim each appears as an ideal which possesses in itself reality, life; it has, like spirit, a clearly-defined nature, a *character*. Without character there can be no true individuality. In this respect, as we have seen above, the spiritual gods contain, as integrant part of themselves, a definite physical power, with which is established an equally definite moral principle, which assigns to each divinity a limited circle in which his outward activity must be displayed. The attributes, the specific qualities which result therefrom, constitute the distinctive character of each divinity.

Still, in the ideal proper, this definite character must not be limited to the point of exclusive being; it must maintain itself in a just medium, and must return to universality, which is the essence of the divine nature. Thus each god, in so far as he is at once a particular individuality and a general existence, is also, at the same time, both part and whole. He floats in a just medium between pure generality and simple particularity. This is what gives to the true ideal of Classic Art its security and infinite calm, together with a freedom relieved from every obstacle.

b. But, as constituting beauty in Classic Art, the special character of the gods is not purely spiritual; it is disclosed so much the more under an external and corporeal form which addresses itself to the eyes as well as to the spirit. This, we have seen, no longer admits the symbolic element, and should not even pretend to affect the Sublime. Classic beauty causes spiritual individuality to enter into the bosom of sensuous reality. It is born of a harmonious fusion of the outward form with the inward principle which animates it. Whence, for this very reason, the physical form, as well as the spiritual principle, must appear enfranchised from all the accidents which belong to outer existence, from all dependence upon nature, from the miseries inseparable from the finite and transitory world. It must be so purified and ennobled that, between the qualities appropriate to the particular character of the god and the general forms of the human body, there shall be manifest a free accord, a perfect harmony. Every mark of weakness and of dependence has disappeared; all arbitrary particularity which could mar it is canceled or effaced. In its unblemished purity it corresponds to the spiritual principle of which it should be the incarnation.

c. Notwithstanding their particular character the gods preserve also their universal and absolute character. Independence must be revealed, in their representation, under the appearance of calmness and of a changeless serenity. Thus we see, in the figures of the gods, that nobility and that elevation which announces in them that, though clothed in a natural and sensuous form, they have nothing in common with the necessities of finite existence. Absolute existence, if it were pure, freed from all particularity, would conduct to the sublime; but, in the Classic ideal, spirit realizes and manifests itself under a sensuous form, which is its perfect image, and whatever of sublimity it has is shown to be grounded in its beauty, and as having passed wholly into itself. This is what renders necessary, for the representation of the gods, the Classic expression of grandeur and beautiful sublimity.

In their beauty they appear, then, elevated above their own corporeal existence; but there is manifest a disagreement between the happy grandeur which resides in their spirituality and their beauty, which is external and corporeal. Spirit appears to be entirely absorbed in the sensuous form, and yet at the same time, aside from this, to be merged (*plongé*) in itself alone; it is, as it were, the moving presence of a deathless god in the midst of mortal men.

Thus, although this contradiction does not appear as a manifest opposition, the harmonious totality conceals in its indivisible unity a principle of *destruction* which is found there already expressed. This is that sigh of sadness in the midst of grandeur which men full of sagacity have felt in the presence of the images of the ancient gods, notwithstanding their perfect beauty and the charm shed around them. In their calmness and their serenity they cannot permit themselves to indulge in pleasure, in enjoyment, nor in what we especially term satisfaction. The eternal calm must not even extend so far as to admit of a smile nor the pleasing contentment with itself. *Satisfaction*, properly speaking, is the sentiment which is born of the perfect accord of our soul with its present situation. Napoleon, for example, never expressed his satisfaction more profoundly than when he had attained to something with which all the world was dissatisfied; for true satisfaction is nothing else than the inner approbation which the individual gives himself because of his own acts and personal efforts. Its last degree is that commonplace feeling (*bourgeois sentiment, Philisterempfindung*) of contentment which every man can experience. Now, this sentiment and this expression cannot be granted to the immortal gods of Classic Art.

It is this character of universality in the Greek gods which people have intended to indicate by characterizing them as cold. Nevertheless, these figures are cold only in relation to the vivacity of modern sentiment; in themselves they have warmth and life. The divine peace which is reflected in the corporeal form comes from the fact that they are separated from the finite; it is born of their indifference to all that is mortal and transitory. It is an adieu without sadness and without effort, but an adieu to the earth and to this perishable world. In

these divine existences the greater the degree in which seriousness and freedom are outwardly manifested, the more distinctly are we made to feel the contrast between their grandeur
and their corporeal form. These happy divinities deprecate at
once both their felicity and their physical existence. We read
in their lineaments the destiny which weighs upon their heads,
and which, in the measure that its power increases (causing
this contradiction between moral grandeur and sensuous reality
to become more and more pronounced), draws Classic Art
on to its ruin.

3. If we ask what is the outer mode of manifestation suitable
to Classic Art, it needs only to repeat what has already been
said: In the Classic ideal, properly speaking, the spiritual individuality of the gods is represented, not in situations where
they enter into relation one with another, and which might
occasion strifes and conflicts, but in their eternal repose, in
their independence, freed as they are from all species of pain
and suffering—in a word, in their divine calmness and peace.
Their determinate character is not developed so as to excite in
them very lively sentiments and violent passions, or to force
them to pursue particular interests. Freed from all collision,
they are delivered from all embarrassment, exempt from all
care. This perfect calm (wherein appears nothing void, cold,
inanimate, but which is full of life and sensibility), although
unalterable, is to the gods of Classic Art the most appropriate
form of representation. If, then, they take part in the attainment of particular ends, the acts in which they engage must
not be of a nature to engender collisions. Free from offense on
their own part, their felicity must not be troubled by these conflicts. Among the arts it is, therefore, *Sculpture* which more
than the others represents the Classic ideal with that absolute
independence wherein the divine nature preserves its universality united with the particular character. It is, above all,
Ancient Sculpture, of a severer taste, which is strongly attached
to this ideal side. Later it was allowed to be applied to the rep-

resentation of situations and characters of a dramatic vitality.
Poetry, which causes the gods to act, draws them into strife
and conflicts. Otherwise, the calm of the plastic, when it remains in its true domain, is alone capable of expressing the contrast between the greatness of spirit and its finite existence
with that seriousness of sadness to which we have already
referred.

Part III

OF THE ROMANTIC FORM OF ART

Introduction—Of the Romantic in General

1. Principle of inner subjectivity.—2. Of the ideas and forms which
constitute the basis of Romantic Art.—3. Of its special mode of
representation.

As in the preceding parts of our investigation, so now in
Romantic Art, the form is determined by the inner idea of the
content or substance which this art is called upon to represent.
We must, therefore, in the next place, attempt to make clear
the characteristic principle of the new content which, in this
new epoch of the development of human thought, is revealed
to consciousness as the absolute essence of truth, and which
now appears in its appropriate form of art.

At the very origin of art there existed the tendency of the
imagination to struggle upward out of nature into spirituality.
But, as yet, the struggle consisted in nothing more than a
yearning of the spirit, and, in so far as this failed to furnish
a precise content for art, art could really be of service only in
providing external forms for mere natural significations, or
impersonal abstractions of the substantial inner principle which
constitutes the central point of the world.

In Classic Art, however, we find quite the contrary. Here
spirituality, though it is now for the first time able to struggle
into conscious existence through the cancellation or setting

aside of mere natural significations, is nevertheless the basis and principle of the content; it is a natural phenomenon inseparable from the corporeal and sensuous. It is an external form. This form, however, does not, as in the first epoch, remain superficial, indefinite, unpervaded by spirit. On the contrary, the perfection of art is here reached in the very fact that the spiritual completely pervades its outer manifestation, that it idealizes the natural in this beautiful union with it, and rises to the measure of the reality of spirit in its substantial individuality. It is thus that Classic Art constituted the absolutely perfect representation of the ideal, the final completion of the realm of Beauty. There neither is nor can there ever be anything more beautiful.

But there exists something still more elevated than the simply beautiful manifestation of spirit in its immediate sensuous form, even though this form be fashioned by spirit as adequate to itself. For this very union of matter and form, which is thus accomplished in the element of the external, and which thus lifts sensuous reality to an adequate existence, nonetheless contradicts the true conception of spirit which is thus forced out of its reconciliation with the corporeal, back upon itself, and compelled to find its own true reconciliation within itself. The simple, pure totality of the ideal (as found in the Classic) dissolves and falls asunder into the double totality of self-existent subjective substance on the one side, and external manifestation on the other, in order that, through this separation, spirit may arrive at a deeper reconciliation in its own element of the inner or purely spiritual. The very essence of spirit is conformity with itself (self-identity), the oneness of its idea with the realization of the same. It is, then, only in its own world, the spiritual or inner world of the soul, that spirit can find a reality (*Dasein*) which corresponds to spirit. It is, thus, in consciousness that spirit comes to possess its other, its *existence*, as spirit, with and in itself, and so for the first time to enjoy its infinitude and its freedom.

I. Spirit thus rises to itself or attains to self-consciousness, and by this means finds within itself its own objectivity, which it was previously compelled to seek in the outer and sensuous forms of material existence. Henceforth it perceives and knows itself in this its unity with itself; and it is precisely this clear self-consciousness of spirit that constitutes the fundamental principle of Romantic Art. But the necessary consequence is that in this last stage of the development of art the beauty of the Classic ideal, which is beauty under its most perfect form and in its purest essence, can no longer be deemed a finality; for spirit now knows that its true nature is not to be brought into a corporeal form. It comprehends that it belongs to its essence to abandon this external reality in order to return upon itself, and it expressly posits or assumes outer reality to be an existence incapable of fully representing spirit. But if this new content proposes to render itself beautiful, still it is evident that beauty, in the sense in which we have thus far considered it, remains for this content something inferior and subordinate, and develops into the *spiritual* beauty of the essentially internal—into the beauty of that spiritual subjectivity or personality which is in itself (*i.e.*, potentially) infinite.

But in order that spirit may thus realize its infinite nature it is so much the more necessary that it should rise above merely formal and *finite* personality in order to reach the height of the *Absolute*. In other terms, the human soul must bring itself into actual existence as a person (*Subjekt*) possessing self-consciousness and rational will; and this it accomplishes through becoming itself pervaded with the absolutely substantial. On the other hand, the substantial, the true, must not be understood as located outside of humanity, nor must the anthropomorphism of Greek thought be swept away. Rather the human as actual subjectivity or personality must become the principle, and thus, as we have already seen, anthropomorphism for the first time attains to its ultimate fullness and perfection.

II. From the particular elements which are involved in this

fundamental principle we have now in general to develop the circle of objects, as well as the form, whose changed aspect is conditioned by the new content of Romantic Art.

The true content of Romantic thought, then, is absolute internality, the adequate and appropriate form of which is spiritual subjectivity, or conscious personality, as comprehension of its own independence and freedom. Now, that which is in itself infinite and wholly universal is the absolute negativity of all that is finite and particular. It is the simple unity with self which has destroyed all mutually exclusive objects, all processes of nature, with their circle of genesis, decay, and renewal—which, in short, has put an end to all limitation of spiritual existence, and dissolved all particular divinities into pure, infinite identity with itself. In this pantheon all the gods are dethroned. The flame of subjectivity has consumed them. In place of plastic polytheism, art now knows but *one* God, *one* Spirit, one absolute independence, which, as absolute knowing and determining, abides in free unity with itself, and no longer falls asunder into those special characters and functions whose sole bond of unity was the constraint of a mysterious necessity. Absolute subjectivity, or personality as such, however, would escape from art and be accessible only to abstract thought, if, in order to be an actual subjectivity commensurate with its idea, it did not pass into external existence, and again collect itself out of this reality into itself. Now, this element of actuality belongs to the Absolute, for the product of the activity of the Absolute as infinite negativity is the Absolute itself, as simple self-unity of knowing, and, therefore, as *immediacy*. Yet, as regards this immediate existence, which is grounded in the Absolute itself, it does not manifest itself as the one jealous God who dissolves the natural, together with finite human existence, without bringing itself into manifestation as actual divine personality, but the true Absolute reveals itself (*schliesst sich auf*), and thus presents a phase which art is able to comprehend and represent.

But the external existence (*Dasein*) of God is not the natural and sensuous, as such, but the sensuous elevated to the super-sensuous, to spiritual subjectivity, to personality, which, instead of losing the certainty of itself in its outer manifestation, truly for the first time attains to the present actual certainty of itself through its own reality. God in His truth is, therefore, no mere ideal created by the imagination. Rather, He places Himself in the midst of the finitude and outer accidentality of immediate existence, and yet knows Himself in all this as the divine principle (*Subjekt*) which in itself remains infinite and creates for itself this infinitude. Since, therefore, actual subject or person is the manifestation of God, art now acquires the higher right of employing the human form, together with the modes and conditions of externality generally, for the expression of the Absolute. Nevertheless, the new problem for art can consist only in this: that in this form the inner shall not be submerged in outer corporeal existence, but shall, on the contrary, return into itself in order to bring into view the spiritual consciousness of God in the individual (*Subjekt*). The various moments or elements brought to light by the totality of this view of the world as totality of the truth itself, therefore, now find their manifestation in man. And this, in the sense that neither nature as such—as the sun, the sky, the stars, etc.—gives the content and the form, nor does the circle of the divinities of the Greek world of beauty, nor the heroes, nor external deeds in the province of the morality of the family and of political life, attain to infinite value. Rather it is the actual, individual subject or person who acquires this value, since it is in him alone that the eternal moments or elements of absolute truth, which exist actually only as spirit, are multi-fariously individualized and at the same time reduced to a consistent and abiding unity.

If now we compare these characteristics of Romantic Art with the task of Classic Art in its perfect fulfillment in Greek Sculpture, we see that the plastic forms of the gods do not express the movement and activity of spirit which has gone out of its corporeal reality into itself, and has become pervaded by internal independent-being (*Fürsichsein*). The changeable and accidental phases of empirical individuality are indeed effaced in those lofty images of the gods, but what is lacking in them is the actuality of self-existent personality, the essential characteristic of which is self-knowledge and independent will. Externally this defect betrays itself in the fact that in the representations of sculpture the expression of the soul simply as soul—namely, the light of the eye—is wanting. The sublimest works of sculptured art are sightless. Their subtle inner being does not beam forth from them, as a self-knowing internality, in that spiritual concentration of which the eye gives intelligence. The ray of the spirit comes from beyond and meets nothing which gives it a response; it belongs alone to the spectator, who cannot contemplate the forms, so to speak, soul in soul, eye in eye. The god of Romantic Art, on the contrary, makes his appearance as a god who sees, who knows himself, who seizes himself in his own inner personality, and who opens the recesses of his nature to the contemplation of the conscious spirit of man. For infinite negativity, the self-return of the spiritual into itself, cancels this outflow into the corporeal. Subjectivity is spiritual light which shines into itself, into its hitherto dark realm; and while natural light can only shine upon an object, this spiritual light is itself its own ground and object on which it shines, and which it recognizes as being one and the same with itself. But since now the absolute inner or spiritual manifests itself, in its actual outer existence, under the human form, and since the human stands in relation to the entire world, there is thus inseparably joined to this manifestation of the Absolute a vast multiplicity of objects belonging not only to the spiritual and subjective world, but also to the corporeal and objective, and to which the spirit bears relation as to its own.

The thus constituted actuality of absolute subjectivity can have the following forms of content and of manifestation:

1. Our first point of departure we must take from the Absolute itself, which, as actual spirit, gives itself an outer existence (*Dasein*), knows itself and is self-active. Here the human form is so represented that it is recognized at once as having the divine within itself. Man appears, not as man in mere human character, in the constraint of passion, in finite aims and achievements, nor as in the mere consciousness of God, but as the self-knowing one and universal God Himself, in whose life and suffering, birth, death, and resurrection, is now made manifest, also, for the finite consciousness, what spirit, what the eternal and infinite, is in truth. This content Romantic Art sets forth in the history of Christ, of His mother, of His disciples, and even in the history of all those in whom the Holy Spirit is actual, in whom the entire divine nature is present. For, in so far as it is God, who, though in Himself universal, still appears in human form, this reality is, nevertheless, not limited to particular immediate existence in the form of Christ, but unfolds itself in all humanity in which the Divine Spirit becomes ever present, and in this actuality remains one with itself. The spreading abroad [in humanity] of this self-contemplation, of this independent and self-sufficing existence (*In-sich-und-bei-sich-sein*) of the spirit, is the peace, the reconciliation of the spirit with itself in its objectivity. It constitutes a divine world—a kingdom of God—in which the Divine, from the center outward, possesses the reconciliation of its reality with its idea, completes itself in this reconciliation, and thus attains to independent existence.

2. But however fully this identification may seem to be grounded in the essence of the Absolute itself, still, as spiritual freedom and infinitude, it is by no means a reconciliation which is immediate and ready at hand, from the center outward, in mundane, natural, and spiritual actuality. On the contrary, it

attains to completeness only as the elevation of the spirit out of the finitude of its immediate or unrealized existence to its truth, its realized existence. As a consequence of this, the spirit, in order to secure its totality and freedom, separates itself from itself—that is, establishes the distinction between itself, as, on the one hand, a being belonging in part to the realm of nature, in part to that of spirit, but limited in both; and as, on the other hand, a being which is in itself (*i.e.*, potentially) infinite. But with this separation, again, is closely joined the necessity of escaping out of the estrangement from self—in which the finite and natural, the immediacy of existence, the natural heart, is characterized as the negative, the evil, the base—and of entering into the kingdom of truth and contentment by the sole means of subjugating this nugatoriness. Thus, spiritual reconciliation is to be conceived and represented only as an activity, a movement of the spirit—as a process in the course of which there arises a struggle, a conflict; and the pain, the death, the agony of nothingness, the torment of the spirit and of materiality (*Leiblichkeit*) make their appearance as essential moments or elements. For as, in the next place, God separates or distinguishes (*ausscheidet*) finite actuality from Himself, so also finite man, who begins with himself as outside the divine kingdom, assumes the task of elevating himself to God, of freeing himself from the finite, of doing away with nugatoriness, and of becoming, through this sacrifice (*Ertödten*) of his immediate actuality, that which God, in His appearance as man, has made objective as true actuality. The infinite pain attendant upon this sacrifice of the individual's own subjectivity or personality, the suffering and death which were more or less excluded from the representations of Classic Art—or, rather, which appeared there only as natural suffering—attain to the rank of real necessity for the first time in Romantic Art.

It cannot be said that among the Greeks death was comprehended in its essential significance. Neither the natural, as such, nor the immediacy of the spirit in its unity with materiality, appeared to them as anything in itself negative, and to them, therefore, death was only an abstract transition, inspiring neither terror nor fear. It was a cessation with which there were associated no further and immeasurable consequences for the dying. But when personality (*Subjektivität*) in its spiritual self-centered being comes to be of infinite importance, then the negation which death bears within itself is a negation of this so significant and valuable self, and hence becomes fearful. It is a death of the soul, which thus, as itself utterly and completely negative, is excluded forever from all happiness, is absolutely miserable, and may find itself given up to eternal damnation. Greek individuality, on the contrary, did not ascribe to itself this value considered as spiritual personality, and hence ventured to surround death with bright images; for man fears only for that which is to him of great worth. But life has this infinite value for consciousness only when the person, as spiritual and self-conscious, is the sole actuality, and must now, in well-grounded fear, conceive himself as rendered (*gesetzt*) negative through death. On the other hand, however, death does not acquire for Classic Art that *affirmative* signification to which it attains in Romantic Art. That which we call immortality did not attain to the dignity of a serious conception with the Greeks. It is for the later reflection of the subjective consciousness, with Socrates, that immortality for the first time acquires a deeper meaning and satisfies a more advanced requirement. For example (Odyss. XI., v. 482–491), Ulysses in the under world congratulated Achilles as being happier than all others before or after him, because he had formerly been honored as the gods, and now was a ruler among the dead. Achilles, as we know, railed at this happiness, and answered that Ulysses should not utter a word of consolation respecting the dead. Rather would he be a servant of the fields, and, poor himself, serve a poor man for a pittance, than lord it here over all the vanished dead. On the contrary, in Romantic Art death is only an extinction of the natural soul and

of the finite personality; an extinction which operates as negative only against what is in itself negative; which cancels the
nugatory, and thus not only brings about the deliverance of
the spirit from its finitude and state of inner division, but also
secures the spiritual reconciliation of the actual person (*des
Subjekts*) with the absolute or ideal Person. For the Greeks,
that life alone was affirmative which was united with natural,
outer, material existence; and death, therefore, was the mere
negation, the dissolution, of immediate actuality. But in the
Romantic conception of the world it has the significance of
absolute negativity—that is, the negation of the negative; and,
therefore, as the rising of the spirit out of its mere naturalness
and inadequate finitude, turns out to be just as much affirmative as negative. The pain and death of expiring personality
(*Subjektivität*) is reversed into a return to self; into contentment and happiness; into that reconciled affirmative existence
which the spirit can with difficulty secure only through the
destruction of its negative existence, in which, so long as it
remains, it is separated from its own truth and vitality. This
fundamental characteristic, therefore, not only relates to that
form of death which approaches man from the natural side,
but it is also a *process* which the spirit, in order that it may
truly live, must complete within itself independent of this
external negation.

3. The third side of this absolute world of the spirit has its
representative in man, in so far as he neither immediately, in
himself, brings the absolute and divine, *as divine,* into manifestation, nor represents the process of elevation to God, and
reconciliation with God, but remains within the limits of his
own human circle. Here, too, the finite, as such, constitutes
the content, as well from the side of the external affairs of
nature and its realm, together with the most restricted phenomena belonging thereto. For the mode of apprehending this content a twofold attitude presents itself. On the one hand, spirit
—because it has acquired affirmation with itself—announces

itself upon this ground as a self-justified and satisfying element, from which it only puts forth (*herauskehrt*) this positive character and permits itself in its affirmative satisfaction and internality to reflect itself therefrom. On the other hand, this content is reduced to mere accidentality, which can lay claim to no independent validity. For in it spirit does not find its own true being, and therefore can arrive at unity in no other way than by itself, since for itself it dissolves as finite and negative this finite character of spirit and of nature.

III. We have now, finally, to consider somewhat more at length the significance of the relation of this entire content to the mode of its representation.

1. The material of Romantic Art, at least with reference to the divine, is extremely limited. For, in the first place, as we have already pointed out, nature is deprived of its divine attributes; sea, mountain, and valley, streams, springs, time, and night, as well as the universal process of nature, have all lost their value with respect to the representation and content of the Absolute. The images of nature are no longer set forth symbolically. They are stripped of the characteristic which rendered their forms and activities appropriate as traits of a divinity. For all the great questions concerning the origin of the world—concerning the whence, the whither, the wherefore of created nature and humanity, together with all the symbolic and plastic attempts to solve and to represent these problems—have vanished in consequence of the revelation of God in the spirit; and even the gay, thousand-hued earth, with all its classically-figured characters, deeds, and events, is swallowed up in spirit, condensed in the single luminous point of the Absolute and its eternal process of Redemption (*Erlösungsgeschichte*). The entire content, therefore, is thus concentrated upon the internality of the spirit—upon the perception, the imagination, the soul—which strives after unity with the truth, and seeks and struggles to produce and to retain the divine in the individual (*Subjekt*). Thus, though the soul is still destined

to pass through the world, it no longer pursues merely worldly aims and undertakings. Rather, it has for its essential purpose and endeavor the inner struggle of man within himself, and his reconciliation with God, and brings into representation only personality and its conservation, together with appliances for the accomplishment of this end. The heroism which can here make its appearance is by no means a heroism which makes its own law, establishes regulations, creates and transforms conditions, but a heroism of submission, for which everything is settled and determined beforehand, and to which there thenceforth remains only the task of regulating temporal affairs according to it, of applying to the existing world that higher principle which has validity in and for itself, and, finally, of rendering it practically valuable in the affairs of every-day life. But since now this absolute content appears to be concentrated in the spaceless, subjective soul, and thus each and every process comes to be transferred to the inner life of man, the circle of this content is thus again infinitely *extended*. It develops into so much the more unrestrained manifoldness. For though the objective process (of history) to which we have referred does not itself include the substantial character of the soul, still the individual, as subject, penetrates that process from every side, brings to light every point therein, or presents itself in ever newly-developed human inclinations, and is, besides, still able to absorb into itself the whole extent of nature, as mere environment and locality of the spirit, and to assign to it an important purpose. Thus the life (*Geschichte*) of the soul comes to be infinitely rich, and can adapt itself in the most manifold ways to ever-changing circumstances and situations. And if now, for the first time, man steps out of this absolute circle and mingles in worldly affairs, by so much the more immeasurable will be the sphere (*Umfang*) of interests, aims, and inclinations; as the spirit, in accordance with this principle, has become more profound, and has, therefore, unfolded itself in its development to its infinitely enhanced fullness of inner and outer collisions, distractions, progressive stages of passion, and to the most varied degrees of satisfaction. Though the Absolute is in itself completely universal, still, as it makes itself known in mankind especially, it constitutes the inner content of Romantic Art, and thus, indeed, all humanity, with its entire development, forms the immeasurable and legitimate material of that art.

2. It may be, indeed, that Romantic Art, *as art,* does not bring this content into prominence, as was done in great measure in the Symbolic, and, above all, in the Classic, form of Art, with its ideal gods. As we have already seen, this art is not, *as art,* the revealed teaching (*Belehren*) which produces the content of truth directly only in the form of art for the imagination, but the content is already at hand for itself outside the region of art in imagination and sensuous perception. Here, religion, as the universal consciousness of truth in a wholly other sphere (*Grade*), constitutes the essential point of departure for art. It lies quite outside the external modes of manifestation for the actual consciousness, and makes its appearance in sensuous reality as prosaic events belonging to the present. Since, indeed, the content of revelation to the spirit is the eternal, absolute nature of *spirit,* which separates itself from the natural as such and debases it, manifestation in the immediate thus holds such rank (*Stellung*) that this outer, in so far as it subsists and has actual-being (*Dasein*), remains only an incidental world out of which the Absolute takes itself up into the spiritual and inner, and thus for the first time really arrives at the truth. At this stage the outer is looked upon as an indifferent element to which the spirit can no longer give credence, and in which it no longer has an abode. The less worthy the spirit esteems this outer actuality, by so much the less is it possible for the spirit ever to seek its satisfaction therein, or to find itself reconciled through union with the external as with itself.

3. In Romantic Art, therefore, on the side of external mani-

festation, the mode of actual representation in accordance with this principle does not go essentially beyond specific, ordinary actuality, and in nowise fears to take up into itself this real outer existence (*Dasein*) in its finite incompleteness and particularity. Here, again, has vanished that ideal beauty which repudiates the external view of temporality and the traces of transitoriness in order to replace its hitherto imperfect development by the blooming beauty of existence. Romantic Art no longer has for its aim this free vitality of actual existence, in its infinite calmness and submergence of the soul in the corporeal, nor even this *life,* as such, in its most precise significance, but turns its back upon this highest phase of beauty. Indeed, it interweaves its inner being with the accidentality of external organization, and allows unrestricted play room to the marked characteristics of the ugly.

In the Romantic, therefore, we have two worlds. The one is the spiritual realm, which is complete in itself—the soul, which finds its reconciliation within itself, and which now for the first time bends around the otherwise rectilinear repetition of genesis, destruction and renewal, to the true circle, to return-into-self, to the genuine Phoenix-life of the spirit. The other is the realm of the external, as such, which, shut out from a firmly cohering unity with the spirit, now becomes a wholly empirical actuality, respecting whose form the soul is unconcerned. In Classic Art, spirit controlled empirical manifestation and pervaded it completely, because it was that form itself in which spirit was to gain its perfect reality. Now, however, the inner or spiritual is indifferent respecting the mode of manifestation of the immediate or sensuous world, because immediacy is unworthy of the happiness of the soul in itself. The external and phenomenal is no longer able to express internality; and since, indeed, it is no longer called upon to do this, it thus retains the task of proving that the external or sensuous is an incomplete existence, and must refer back to the internal or spiritual, to intellect (*Gemüt*) and sensibility, as to the essential element. But for this very reason Romantic Art allows externality to again appear on its own account, and in this respect permits each and every matter to enter unhindered into the representation. Even flowers, trees, and the most ordinary household furniture are admitted, and this, too, in the natural accidentality of mere present existence. This content, however, bears with it at the same time the characteristic that as mere external matter it is insignificant and low; that it only attains to its true value when it is pervaded by human interest; and that it must express not merely the inner or subjective, but even *internality* or subjectivity itself, which, instead of blending or fusing itself with the outer or material, appears reconciled only in and with itself. Thus driven to extremity, the inner at this point becomes manifestation destitute of externality. It is, as it were, invisible, and comprehended only by itself; a tone, as such without objectivity or form; a wave upon water; a resounding through a world, which in and upon its heterogeneous phenomena can only take up and send back a reflected ray of this independent-being (*Insichseins*) of the soul.

We may now comprise in a single word this relation between content and form as it appears in the Romantic—for here it is that this relation attains to its complete characterization. It is this: just because the ever-increasing universality and restless working depth of the soul constitute the fundamental principle of the Romantic, the keynote thereof is *musical*, and, in connection with the particularized content of the imagination, *lyrical*. For Romantic Art the lyrical is, as it were, the elementary characteristic—a tone which the epic and the drama also strike, and which breathes about the works of the arts of visible representation themselves like a universal, fragrant odor of the soul; for here spirit and soul will speak to spirit and soul through all their images.

DIVISION: We come now to the division necessary to be established for the further and more precisely developing investigation of this third great realm of art. The fundamental idea of the Romantic in its internal unfolding lies in the follow-ing three separate moments or elements:

1. The Religious, as such, constitutes the first circle, of which the central point is given in the history of redemption—in the life, death, and resurrection of Christ. Introversion (*Umkehr*) here assumes importance as the chief characteristic. The spirit assumes an attitude of hostility toward, and over-comes, its own immediacy and finitude, and through thus ren-dering itself free it attains to its infinity, and absolute inde-pendence in its own sphere.

2. Secondly, this independence passes out of the abstract divine of the spirit, and also leaves aside the elevation of finite man to God, and passes into the affairs of the secular world. Here at once it is the individual (*Subjekt*), as such, that has become affirmative for itself, and has for the substance of its consciousness, as also for the interest of its existence, the vir-tues of this affirmative individuality, namely, honor, love, fidelity, and valor—that is, the aims and duties which belong to Romantic Knighthood.

3. The content and form of the third division may be summed up, in general, as *Formal Independence of Character*. If, in-deed, personality is so far developed that spiritual independ-ence has come to be its essential interest, then there comes, also, to be a special content, with which personality identifies itself as with its own, and shares with it the same independence, which, however, can only be of a formal type, since it does not consist in the substantiality of its life, as is the case in the circle of religious truth, properly speaking. But, on the other hand, the form of outer circumstances and situations, and of the development of events, is indeed that of freedom, the result of which is a reckless abandonment to a life of capricious adventures. We thus find the termination of the Romantic, in general, to consist in the accidentality both of the external and of the internal, and with this termination the two elements fall asunder. With this we emerge from the sphere of art

altogether. It thus appears that the necessity which urges consciousness on to the attainment of a complete comprehension of the truth demands higher forms than Art is able in anywise to produce.

1. After the above introductory remarks, it is now time to pass to the study of our object-matter.* But we are still in the introduction, and an introduction cannot do more than lay down, for the sake of explanation, the general sketch of the entire course which will be followed by our subsequent scientific considerations. As, however, we have spoken of art as proceeding from the absolute Idea, and have even assigned as its end the sensuous representation of the absolute itself, we shall have to conduct this review in a way to show, at least in general, how the particular divisions of the subject spring from the conception of artistic beauty as the representation of the absolute. Therefore we must attempt to awaken a very general idea of this conception itself.

It has already been said that the content of art is the Idea, and that its form lies in the plastic use of images accessible to sense. These two sides art has to reconcile into a full and united totality. The *first* attribution which this involves is the requirement that the content, which is to be offered to artistic representation, shall show itself to be in its nature worthy of such representation. Otherwise we only obtain a bad combination, whereby a content that will not submit to plasticity and to external presentation, if forced into that form, and a matter which is in its nature prosaic is expected to find an appropriate mode of manifestation in the form antagonistic to its nature.

The *second* requirement, which is derivable from this first, demands of the content of art that it should not be anything abstract in itself. This does not mean that it must be concrete

---

* Here follows the section translated by Bosanquet. The footnotes in this section are Bosanquet's own.—Ed.

as the sensuous is concrete in contrast to everything spiritual
and intellectual, these being taken as in themselves simple and
abstract. For everything that has genuine truth in the mind
as well as in nature is concrete in itself, and has, in spite of its
universality, nevertheless, both subjectivity and particularity
within it. If we say, e.g., of God that he is simply *One*, the
supreme Being as such, we have only enunciated a lifeless abstraction of the irrational understanding. Such a God, as he
himself is not apprehended in his concrete truth, can afford no
material for art, least of all for plastic art. Hence the Jews
and the Turks have not been able to represent their God, who
does not even amount to such an abstraction of the understanding, in the positive way in which Christians have done so.
For God in Christianity is conceived in His truth, and therefore, as in Himself thoroughly concrete, as a person, as a subject,* and more closely determined, as mind or spirit. What He
is as spirit unfolds itself to the religious apprehension as the
Trinity of Persons, which at the same time in relation with
itself is *One*. Here is essentiality, universality, and particularity,
together with their reconciled unity; and it is only such unity
that constitutes the concrete. Now, as a content in order to
possess truth at all must be of this concrete nature, art demands
the same concreteness, because a mere abstract universal has
not in itself the vocation to advance to particularity and phenomenal manifestation and to unity with itself therein.

If a true and therefore concrete content is to have corresponding to it a sensuous form and modeling, this sensuous

---

* It is natural for a reader to ask in *what* person or subject God is conceived to have reality. It appears certain to me that Hegel, when he
writes thus, is referring to the self-consciousness of individual human
beings as constituting, and reflecting on, an ideal unity between them.
This may seem to put a non-natural meaning on the term "person" or
"subject," as if the common element of a number of intelligences could
be a single person. It is obvious that the question hinges on the degree
in which a unity that is not sensuous but ideal can be effective and
actual. I can only say here, that the more we consider the nature of
ideal unity the higher we shall rate its capabilities.

form must, in the third place, be no less emphatically something individual, wholly concrete in itself, and one. The character of concreteness as belonging to both elements of art, to the content as to the representation, is precisely the point in which both may coincide and correspond to one another; as, for instance, the natural shape of the human body is such a sensuous concrete as is capable of representing spirit, which is concrete in itself, and of displaying itself in conformity therewith. Therefore we ought to abandon the idea that it is a mere matter of accident that an actual phenomenon of the external world is chosen to furnish a shape thus conformable to truth. Art does not appropriate this form either because it simply finds it existing or because there is no other. The concrete content itself involves the element of external and actual, we may say indeed of sensible manifestation. But in compensation this sensuous concrete, in which a content essentially belonging to mind expresses itself, is in its own nature addressed to the inward being; its external element of shape, whereby the content is made perceptible and imaginable, has the aim of existing purely for the heart and mind. This is the only reason for which content and artistic shape are fashioned in conformity with each other. The *mere* sensuous concrete, external nature as such, has not this purpose for its exclusive ground of origin. The birds' variegated plumage shines unseen, and their song dies away unheard, the *Cereus** which blossoms only for a night withers without having been admired in the wilds of southern forests, and these forests, jungles of the most beautiful and luxuriant vegetation, with the most odorous and aromatic perfumes, perish and decay no less unenjoyed. The work of art has not such a naïve self-centered being, but is essentially a question, an address to the responsive heart, an appeal to affections and to minds.

Although the artistic bestowal of sensuous form is in this

---

* *Fackeldistel*—"Torch thistle," a plant of the genus *Cereus*. Nat. Order *Cactaceoe*.

respect not accidental, yet on the other hand it is not the highest mode of apprehending the spiritually concrete. Thought is a higher mode than representation by means of the sensuous concrete. Although in a relative sense abstract, yet it must not be one-sided but concrete thinking, in order to be true and rational. Whether a given content has sensuous artistic representation for its adequate form, or in virtue of its nature essentially demands a higher and more spiritual embodiment, is a distinction that displays itself at once, if, for instance, we compare the Greek gods with God as conceived according to Christian ideas. The Greek god is not abstract but individual, and is closely akin to the natural human shape; the Christian God is equally a concrete personality, but in the mode of pure spiritual existence, and is to be known as *mind* and in mind.* His medium of existence is therefore essentially inward knowledge and not external natural form, by means of which He can only be represented imperfectly, and not in the whole depth of His idea.

But inasmuch as the task of art is to represent the idea to direct perception in sensuous shape, and not in the form of thought or of pure spirituality as such, and seeing that this work of representation has its value and dignity in the correspondence and the unity of the two sides, i.e., of the Idea and its plastic embodiment, it follows that the level and excellency of art in attaining a realization adequate to its idea,† must depend upon the grade of inwardness and unity with which Idea and Shape display themselves as fused into one.

Thus the higher truth is spiritual being that has attained a shape adequate to the conception of spirit. This is what furnishes the principle of division for the science of art. For before the mind can attain the true notion of its absolute essence, it has to traverse a course of stages whose ground is in this idea itself; and to this evolution of the content with which it sup-

---

* Or "as spirit and in spirit."
† The idea of art

plies itself, there corresponds an evolution, immediately connected therewith, of the plastic forms of art, under the shape of which the mind as artist presents to itself the consciousness of itself.

This evolution within the art-spirit has again in its own nature two sides. In the *first* place the development itself is a spiritual * and universal one, in so far as the graduated series of definite *conceptions of the world* as the definite but comprehensive consciousness of nature, man and God, gives itself artistic shape; and, in the *second* place, this *universal* development of art is obliged to provide itself with external existence and sensuous form, and the definite modes of the sensuous art-existence are themselves a totality of necessary distinctions in the realm of art—which are the *several arts*. It is true, indeed, that the necessary kinds of artistic representation are on the one hand *qua* spiritual of a very general nature, and not restricted to any one material †; while sensuous existence contains manifold varieties of matter. But as this latter, like the mind, has the Idea potentially for its inner soul, it follows from this that particular sensuous materials have a close affinity and secret accord with the spiritual distinctions and types of art presentation.

In its completeness, however, our science divides itself into three principal portions.

First, we obtain a *general part.* It has for its content and

---

* The two evolutions are, speaking roughly, (i.) that of the subject-matter; (ii.) that of the particular mode of art: (i.) e.g., you have Egyptian, Greek, Christian religion, etc., with the corresponding views and sentiments, each in its own relation to art; (ii.) you have, as a cross division to the former, the several arts—sculpture, music, poetry-etc., each having its special ground and warrant.

† He is asking himself why sound or paint, etc., should correspond to one type of art as theoretically defined—this being intellectual, not sensuous, at root—and answers that these media *qua* natural objects have, though more latent than in works of art, an import and purpose of their own, which reveals itself in their suitability to particular forms of art.

object the universal Idea of artistic beauty—this beauty being conceived as the Ideal—together with the nearer relation of the latter both to nature and to subjective artistic production.

Secondly, there develops itself out of the idea of artistic beauty a *particular* part, in as far as the essential differences which this idea contains in itself evolve themselves into a scale of *particular* plastic* forms.

In the *third* place there results a *final* part, which has for its subject the individualization of artistic beauty, that consists in the advance of art to the sensuous realization of its shapes and its self-completion as a system of the several arts and their genera and species.

2. With respect to the first part, we must begin by recalling to mind, in order to make the sequel intelligible, that the Idea *qua* the beautiful in art is not the Idea as such, in the mode in which a metaphysical logic apprehends it as the absolute, but the Idea as developed into concrete form fit for reality, and as having entered into immediate and adequate unity with this reality. For the *Idea* as such, although it is the essentially and actually true, is yet the truth only in its generality which has not yet taken objective shape; but the Idea as the *beautiful in art* is at once the Idea when specially determined as in its essence individual reality, and also an individual shape of reality essentially destined to embody and reveal the Idea. This amounts to enunciating the requirement that the Idea, and its plastic mold as concrete reality, are to be made completely adequate to one another. When reduced to such form the Idea, as a reality molded in conformity with the conception of the Idea, is the *Ideal*. The problem of this conformity might, to begin with, be understood in the sense that any Idea would serve, so long as the actual shape, it did not matter what shape,

---

* *"Gestaltungsformen."* I use "plastic" all through in a pregnant sense, as one speaks of plastic fancy, etc.; meaning ideally determinate, and fit for translating into pictures, poetry, etc. These "plastic forms" are the various modifications of the subject-matter of art.

represented this particular Idea and no other. But if so, the required truth of the Ideal is confounded with mere correctness, which consists in the expression of any meaning whatever in appropriate fashion so that its import may be readily recognized in the shape created. The Ideal is not to be thus understood. Any content whatever may attain to being represented quite adequately, judged by the standard of its own nature, but it does not therefore gain the right to claim the artistic beauty of the Ideal. Compared indeed with ideal beauty, even the presentation will in such a case appear defective. From this point of view we must remark to begin with, what cannot be proved till later, that the defects of a work of art are not to be regarded simply as always due, for instance, to individual unskillfulness. *Defectiveness of form* arises from *defectiveness of content*. So, for example, the Chinese, Indians, and Egyptians in their artistic shapes, their forms of deities, and their idols, never got beyond a formless phase, or one of a vicious and false definiteness of form, and were unable to attain genuine beauty; because their mythological ideas, the content and thought of their works of art, were as yet indeterminate in themselves, or of a vicious determinateness, and did not consist in the content that is absolute in itself. The more that works of art excel in true beauty of presentation, the more profound is the inner truth of their content and thought. And in dealing with this point, we have not to think merely perhaps of the greater or lesser skill with which the natural forms as given in external reality are apprehended and imitated. For in certain stages of art-consciousness and of representation, the distortion and disfigurement of natural structures is not unintentional technical inexpertness and want of skill, but intentional alteration, which emanates from the content that is in consciousness, and is required thereby. Thus, from this point of view, there is such a thing as imperfect art, which may be quite perfect, both technically and in other respects, *in its determinate* sphere, yet reveals itself to be defective when compared with the conception of art as such, and with the Ideal. Only in the highest art are the Idea and the representation genuinely adequate to one another, in the sense that the outward shape given to the Idea is in itself essentially and actually the true shape, because the content of the Idea, which that shape expresses, is itself the true and real content. It is a corollary from this, as we indicated above, that the Idea must be defined in and through itself as concrete totality, and thereby possess in itself the principle and standard of its particularization and determination in external appearance. For example, the Christian imagination will be able to represent God only in human form and with man's intellectual expression, because it is herein that God Himself is completely known in Himself as mind. Determinateness is, as it were, the bridge to phenomenal existence. Where this determinateness is not totality derived from the Idea itself, where the Idea is not conceived as self-determining and self-particularizing, the Idea remains abstract and has its determinateness, and therefore the principle that dictates its particular and exclusively appropriate mode of presentation, not in itself but external to it. Therefore, the Idea when still abstract has even its shape external, and not dictated by itself. The Idea, however, which is concrete in itself bears the principle of its mode of manifestation within itself, and is by that means the free process of giving shape to itself. Thus it is only the truly concrete Idea that can generate the true shape, and this correspondence of the two is the Ideal.

3. Now because the Idea is in this fashion concrete unity, it follows that this unity can enter into the art-consciousness only by the expansion and reconciliation of the particularities of the Idea, and it is through this evolution that artistic beauty comes to possess a *totality of particular stages and forms*. Therefore, after we have studied the beauty of art in itself and on its own merits, we must see how beauty as a whole breaks up into its particular determinations. This gives, as our

second part, the doctrine of the types of art. These forms find their genesis in the different modes of grasping the Idea as artistic content, whereby is conditioned a difference of the form in which it manifests itself. Hence the types of art are nothing but the different relations of content and shape, relations which emanate from the Idea itself, and furnish thereby the true basis of division for this sphere. For the principle of division must always be contained in *that* conception whose particularization and division is in question.

We have here to consider *three* relations of the Idea to its outward shaping.*

a. First, the Idea gives rise to the beginning of Art when, being itself still in its indistinctness and obscurity, or in vicious untrue determinateness, it is made the import of artistic creations. As indeterminate it does not yet possess in itself that individuality which the Ideal demands; its abstractness and one-sidedness leave its shape to be outwardly bizarre and defective. The first form of art is therefore rather a mere search after plastic portrayal than a capacity of genuine representation. The Idea has not yet found the true form even within itself, and therefore continues to be merely the struggle and aspiration thereafter. In general terms we may call this form the *Symbolic* form of art. In it the abstract Idea has its outward shape external to itself † in natural sensuous matter, with which the process of shaping begins, and from which, *qua* outward expression, it is inseparable.

Natural objects are thus primarily left unaltered, and yet at the same time invested with the substantial Idea as their significance, so that they receive the vocation of expressing it, and

---

* *"Gestaltung."* I do not think this means the process of shaping, but the shapes taken collectively.

† Not in a separate ideal shape devoted to it. He means that man takes a stick or stone as representation or symbol of the divine, and as there is no real connection between divinity and the stone, it may either be left untouched and unshaped, or be hewn into any bizarre or arbitrary shape that comes to hand: see next paragraph.

claim to be interpreted as though the Idea itself were present in them. At the root of this is the fact that natural objects have in them an aspect in which they are capable of representing a universal meaning. But as an adequate correspondence is not yet possible, this reference can only concern *an abstract attribute,* as when a lion is used to mean strength.

On the other hand, this abstractness of the relation brings to consciousness no less strongly the foreignness of the Idea to natural phenomena; and the Idea, having no other reality to express it, expatiates in all these shapes, seeks itself in them in all their unrest and disproportion, but nevertheless does not find them adequate to itself. Then it proceeds to exaggerate the natural shapes and the phenomena of reality into indefiniteness and disproportion, to intoxicate itself in them, to seethe and ferment in them, to do violence to them, to distort and explode them into unnatural shapes, and strives by the variety, hugeness, and splendor of the forms employed * to exalt the phenomenon to the level of the Idea. For the Idea is here still more or less indeterminate and non-plastic, but the natural objects are in their shape thoroughly determinate.

Hence, in view of the unsuitability of the two elements to each other, the relation of the Idea to objective reality becomes a *negative* one, for the former, as in its nature inward, is unsatisfied with such an externality, and as being its inner universal substance† persists in exaltation or *Sublimity* beyond and above all this inadequate abundance of shapes. In virtue of this sublimity the natural phenomena and the human shapes and incidents are accepted, and left as they were, though

---

* This description is probably directed, in the first place, to the Indian representation of deities, and would apply to those of many barbaric religions. But its truth may be very simply verified in daily observation of the first attempts of the uneducated at plastic representation of their ideas, where costliness, ingenuity, labor or size take the place of beauty.
† An idea or purpose which gives these partial and defective representations all the meaning they have, although they are incapable of really expressing it.

at the same time understood to be inadequate to their significance, which is exalted far above every earthly content.

These aspects may be pronounced in general terms to constitute the character of the primitive artistic pantheism of the East, which either charges even the meanest objects with the absolute import, or again coerces nature with violence into the expression of its view. By this means it becomes bizarre, grotesque, and tasteless, or turns the infinite but abstract freedom of the substantive Idea disdainfully against all phenomenal being as null and evanescent. By such means the import cannot be completely embodied in the expression, and in spite of all aspiration and endeavor the reciprocal inadequacy of shape and Idea remains insuperable. This may be taken as the first form of art—symbolic art with its aspiration, its disquiet,* its mystery and its sublimity.

b. In the second form of art, which we propose to call "Classical," the double defect of symbolic art is canceled. The plastic shape of symbolic art is imperfect, because, in the first place, the Idea in it only enters into consciousness in *abstract* determinateness or indeterminateness, and, in the second place, this must always make the conformity of shape to import defective, and in its turn merely abstract. The classical form of art is the solution of this double difficulty; it is the free and adequate embodiment of the Idea in the shape that, according to its conception, is peculiarly appropriate to the Idea itself. With it, therefore, the Idea is capable of entering into free and complete accord. Hence, the classical type of art is the first to afford the production and intuition of the completed Ideal, and to establish it as a realized fact.

The conformity, however, of notion and reality in classical art must not be taken in the purely *formal* sense of the agreement of a content with the external shape given to it, any more than this could be the case with the Ideal itself. Other-

* *"Gährung,"* literally "fermentation."

wise every copy from nature, and every type of countenance, every landscape, flower, or scene, etc., which forms the purport of any representation, would be at once made classical by the agreement which it displays between form and content. On the contrary, in classical art the peculiarity of the content consists in being itself concrete idea, and, as such, the concrete spiritual; for only the spiritual is the truly inner self. To suit such a content, then, we must search out that in Nature which on its own merits belongs to the essence and actuality of the mind. It must be the absolute* notion that *invented* the shape appropriate to concrete mind, so that the *subjective* notion—in this case the spirit of art—has merely *found* it, and brought it, as an existence possessing natural shape, into accord with free individual spirituality.† This shape, with which the Idea as spiritual—as individually determinate spirituality—invests itself when manifested as a temporal phenomenon, is *the human form.* Personification and anthropomorphism have often been decried as a degradation of the spiritual; but art, in as far as its end is to bring before perception the spiritual in sensuous form, must advance to such anthropomorphism, as it is only in its proper body that mind is adequately revealed to sense. The migration of souls is in this respect a false abstraction,‡ and physiology ought to have made it one of its axioms that life had necessarily in its evolution to attain to the human shape, as the sole sensuous phenomenon that is appropriate to mind. The human form is employed in the classical type of art not as mere sensuous existence, but exclusively as the existence and physical form corresponding to mind, and is therefore exempt from all the deficiencies of what is merely sensuous, and from

---

* "*Der ursprüngliche Begriff,*" literally "the original notion."

† God or the Universe *invented* man to be the expression of mind; art *finds* him, and adapts his shape to the artistic embodiment of mind as concentrated in individual instances.

‡ Because it represents the soul as independent of an appropriate body— the human soul as capable of existing in a beast's body.

the contingent finiteness of phenomenal existence. The outer shape must be thus purified in order to express in itself a content adequate to itself; and again, if the conformity of import and content is to be complete, the spiritual meaning which is the content must be of a particular kind. It must, that is to say, be qualified to express itself completely in the physical form of man, without projecting into another world beyond the scope of such an expression in sensuous and bodily terms. This condition has the effect that Mind is by it at once specified as a particular case of mind, as human mind, and not as simply absolute and eternal, inasmuch as mind in this latter sense is incapable of proclaiming and expressing itself otherwise than as intellectual being.*

Out of this latter point arises, in its turn, the defect which brings about the dissolution of classical art, and demands a transition into a third and higher form, viz., into the *romantic* form of art.

c. The romantic form of art destroys the completed union of the Idea and its reality, and recurs, though in a higher phase, to that difference and antagonism of two aspects which was left unvanquished by symbolic art. The classical type attained the highest excellence, of which the sensuous embodiment of art is capable; and if it is in any way defective, the defect is in art as a whole, i.e., in the limitation of its sphere. This limitation consists in the fact that art as such takes for its object Mind—the conception of which is *infinite* concrete universality—in the shape of *sensuous* concreteness, and in the classical phase sets up the perfect amalgamation of spiritual and sensuous existence as a Conformity of the two. Now, as a matter of fact, in such an amalgamation Mind cannot be represented

---

* *"Geistigkeit."* "The nature of thought, mind or spirit." It cannot be here rendered by mind or spirit, because these words make us think of an isolated individual, *a* mind or soul, and neglect the common spiritual or intellectual nature, which is referred to by the author.

according to its true notion. For mind is the infinite subjectivity of the Idea, which, as absolute inwardness,* is not capable of finding free expansion in its true nature on condition of remaining transposed into a bodily medium as the existence appropriate to it.

As *an escape from such a condition* the romantic form of art in its turn dissolves the inseparable unity of the classical phase, because it has won a significance which goes beyond the classical form of art and its mode of expression.† This significance —if we may recall familiar ideas—coincides with what Christianity declares to be true of God as Spirit, in contradistinction to the Greek faith in gods which forms the essential and appropriate content for classical art. In Greek art the concrete import is potentially, but not explicitly, the unity of the human and divine nature; a unity which, just because it is purely *immediate‡* and *not explicit,* is capable of adequate manifestation in an immediate and sensuous mode. The Greek god is the object of naïve intuition and sensuous imagination. His shape is, therefore, the bodily shape of man. The circle of his power and of his being is individual and individually limited. In relation with the subject, he is, therefore, an essence and a power with which the subject's inner being is merely in latent unity, not itself possessing this unity as inward subjective knowledge. Now the higher stage is the *knowledge* of this *latent* unity, which as latent is the import of the classical form of art, and capable of perfect representation in bodily shape. The elevation of the latent or potential into self-conscious knowledge produces an enormous difference. It is the infinite difference which, e.g., separates man as such from the animals. Man is animal, but even in his animal functions he is not confined

---

* It is the essence of mind or thought not to have its parts outside one another. The so-called terms of a judgment are a good instance of parts in thought which are inward to each other.

† Compare Browning's "Old Pictures in Florence."

‡ In the form of feeling and imagination—not reflected upon.

within the latent and potential as the animal is, but becomes conscious of them, learns to know them, and raises them—as, for instance, the process of digestion—into self-conscious science. By this means Man breaks the boundary of merely potential and immediate consciousness, so that just for the reason that he knows himself to be animal, he ceases to be animal, and, as *mind*, attains to self-knowledge.

If in the above fashion the unity of the human and divine nature, which in the former phase was potential, is raised from an *immediate* to a *conscious* unity, it follows that the true medium for the reality of this content is no longer the sensuous immediate existence of the spiritual, the human bodily shape, but *self-conscious inward intelligence.** Now, Christianity brings God before our intelligence *as spirit,* or mind— not as particularized individual spirit, but as absolute, in *spirit* and in truth. And for this reason Christianity retires from the sensuousness of imagination into intellectual inwardness, and makes this, not bodily shape, the medium and actual existence of its significance. So, too, the unity of the human and divine nature is a conscious unity, only to be realized by *spiritual* knowledge and in *spirit.* Thus the new content, won by this unity, is not inseparable from sensuous representation, as if that were adequate to it, but is freed from this immediate existence, which has to be posited as negative, absorbed, and reflected into the spiritual unity. In this way, romantic art must be considered as art transcending itself, while remaining within the artistic sphere and in artistic form.

Therefore, in short, we may abide by the statement that in this third stage the object (of art) is *free,* concrete intellectual being, which has the function of revealing itself as spiritual existence for the inward world of spirit. In conformity with such an object-matter, art cannot work for sensuous perception. It must address itself to the inward mind, which coalesces with

---

* *"Innerlichkeit,"* lit. "inwardness."

Its object simply and as though this were itself, to the subjective inwardness, to the heart, the feeling, which, being spiritual, aspires to freedom within itself, and seeks and finds its reconciliation only in the spirit within. It is this *inner* world that forms the content of the romantic, and must therefore find its representation as such inward feeling, and in the show or presentation of such feeling. The world of inwardness celebrates its triumph over the outer world, and actually in the sphere of the outer and in its medium manifests this its victory, owing to which the sensuous appearance sinks into worthlessness.

But, on the other hand, this [romantic] type of Art, like every other, needs an external vehicle of expression. Now the spiritual has withdrawn into itself out of the external and its immediate oneness therewith. For this reason, the sensuous externality of concrete form is accepted and represented, as in Symbolic art, as something transient and fugitive. And the same measure is dealt to the subjective finite mind and will, even including the peculiarity or caprice of the individual, of character, action, etc., or of incident and plot. The aspect of external existence is committed to contingency, and left at the mercy of freaks of imagination, whose caprice is no more likely to mirror what is given *as* it is given, than to throw the shapes of the outer world into chance medley, or distort them into grotesqueness. For this external element no longer has its notion and significance, as in classical art, in its own sphere, and in its own medium. It has come to find them in the feelings, the display of which is *in themselves* instead of being in the external and *its* form of reality, and which have the power to preserve or to regain their state of reconciliation with themselves, in every accident, in every unessential circumstance that takes independent shape, in all misfortune and grief, and even in crime.

Owing to this, the characteristics of symbolic art, in difference, discrepancy, and severance of Idea and plastic shape, are here reproduced, but with an essential difference. In the sphere of the romantic, the Idea, whose defectiveness in the case of the symbol produced the defect of external shape, has to reveal itself in the medium of spirit and feelings as perfected in itself. And it is because of this higher perfection that it withdraws itself from any adequate union with the external element, inasmuch as it can seek and achieve its true reality and revelation nowhere but in itself.

This we may take as in the abstract the character of the symbolic, classical, and romantic forms of art, which represent the three relations of the Idea to its embodiment in the sphere of art. They consist in the aspiration after, and the attainment and transcendence of the Ideal as the true Idea of beauty.

4. The third part of our subject, in contradistinction to the two just described, presupposes the conception of the Ideal, and the general types of art, inasmuch as it simply consists of their realization in particular sensuous media. Hence we have no longer to do with the inner development of artistic beauty in conformity with its general fundamental principles. What we have to study is how these principles pass into actual exist- ence, how they distinguish themselves in their external aspect, and how they give actuality to every element contained in the idea of beauty, separately and by itself *as a work of art,* and not merely as a general type. Now, what art transfers into external existence are the differences proper to the idea of beauty and immanent therein. Therefore, the general types of art must reveal themselves in this third part, as before, in the character of the fundamental principle that determines the arrangement and definition of the *several arts;* in other words, the species of art contain in themselves the same essential modifications as those with which we become acquainted as the general types of art. External objectivity, however, to which these forms are introduced through the medium of a sensuous and therefore *particular* material, affects these types in the way of making them *separate* into independent and so particular

forms embodying their realization. For each type finds its definite character in some one definite external material, and its adequate actuality in the mode of portrayal which that prescribes. But, moreover, these types of art, being for all their determinateness, its *universal* forms, break the bounds of *particular* realization by a determinate form of art, and achieve existence in other arts as well, although in subordinate fashion. Therefore, the particular arts belong each of them specifically to *one* of the general types of art, and constitute *its adequate* external actuality; and also they represent, each of them after its own mode of external plasticity, the totality of the types of art.*

Then, speaking generally, we are dealing in this third principal division with the beautiful of art, as it unfolds itself in the several arts and in their creations into a *world* of actualized beauty. The content of this world is the beautiful, and the true beautiful, as we saw, is spiritual being in concrete shape, the Ideal; or, more closely looked at, the absolute mind, and the truth itself. This region, that of divine truth artistically represented to perception and to feeling, forms the center of the whole world of art. It is the independent, free, and divine plasticity, which has thoroughly mastered the external elements of form and of medium, and wears them simply as a means to manifestation of itself. Still, as the beautiful unfolds itself in this region in the character of *objective* reality, and in so doing distinguishes within itself its individual aspects and elements, permitting them independent particularity, it follows that this center erects its extremes, realized in their peculiar actuality, into its own antitheses. Thus one of these extremes comes to consist in an objectivity as yet devoid of

---

* Thus, e.g., Sculpture is *the* art which corresponds *par excellence* to the general type called Classical Art; but there is *a* Symbolic kind of sculpture, and I suppose *a* Romantic or modern kind of sculpture, although neither of these types is exactly fitted to the capabilities of Sculpture.

mind, in the merely natural vesture of God. At this point the external element takes plastic shape as something that has its spiritual aim and content, not in itself, but in another.*

The other extreme is the divine as inward, as something known, as the variously particularized *subjective* existence of the Deity; it is the truth as operative and vital in sense, heart, and mind of individual subjects, not persisting in the mold of its external shapes, but as having returned into subjective, individual inwardness. In such a mode, the Divine is at the same time distinguished from its first manifestation as Deity, and passes thereby into the diversity of particulars which belongs to all subjective knowledge—emotion, perception, and feeling. In the analogous province of religion, with which art at its highest stage is immediately connected, we conceive this same difference as follows. *First,* we think of the earthly natural life in its finiteness as standing on one side; but, then, *secondly,* consciousness makes God its object, in which the distinction of objectivity and subjectivity is done away. And at last, *thirdly,* we advance from God as such to the devotion of the community, that is, to God as living and present in the subjective consciousness. Just so these three chief modifications present themselves in the world of art in independent development.

a. The *first* of the particular arts with which, according to their fundamental principle, we have to begin, is architecture considered as a fine art.† Its task lies in so manipulating external inorganic nature that it becomes cognate to mind, as an artistic outer world. The material of architecture is matter itself in its immediate externality as a heavy mass subject to mechanical laws, and its forms do not depart from the forms of inorganic nature, but are merely set in order in conformity with relations of the abstract understanding, i.e., with relations of symmetry. In this material and in such forms, the ideal as concrete spirituality does not admit of being realized. Hence

---

* Architecture as relative to the purposes of life and of religion.

† *"Die schöne Architectur."*

the reality which is represented in them remains contrasted with the Idea, as something external which it has not penetrated, or has penetrated only to establish an abstract relation. For these reasons, the fundamental type of the fine art of building is the *symbolical* form of art. It is architecture that pioneers the way for the adequate realization of the God, and in this its service bestows hard toil upon existing nature, in order to disentangle it from the jungle of finitude and the abortiveness of chance. By this means it levels a space for the God, gives form to his external surroundings, and builds him his temple as a fit place for concentration of spirit, and for its direction to the mind's absolute objects. It raises an enclosure round the assembly of those gathered together, as a defense against the threatening of the storm, against rain, the hurricane, and wild beasts, and reveals the will to assemble, although externally, yet in conformity with principles of art. With such import as this it has power to inspire its material and its forms more or less effectively, as the determinate character of the content on behalf of which it sets to work is more or less significant, more concrete or more abstract, more profound in sounding its own depths, or more dim and more superficial. So much, indeed, may architecture attempt in this respect as even to create an adequate artistic existence for such an import in its shapes and in its material. But in such a case it has already overstepped its own boundary, and is leaning to sculpture, the phase above it. For the limit of architecture lies precisely in this point, that it retains the spiritual as an inward existence over against the external forms of the art, and consequently must refer to what has soul only as to something other than its own creations.

b. Architecture, however, as we have seen, has purified the external world, and endowed it with symmetrical order and with affinity to mind; and the temple of the God, the house of his community, stands ready. Into this temple, then, in the *second* place, the God enters in the lightning-flash of individuality, which strikes and permeates the inert mass, while the infinite* and no longer merely symmetrical form belonging to mind itself concentrates and gives shape to the corresponding bodily existence. This is the task of *Sculpture*. In as far as in this art the spiritual inward being which architecture can but indicate makes itself at home in the sensuous shape and its external matter, and in as far as these two sides are so adapted to one another that neither is predominant, sculpture must be assigned the *classical form of art* as its fundamental type. For this reason the sensuous element itself has here no expression which could not be that of the spiritual element, just as, conversely, sculpture can represent no spiritual content which does not admit throughout of being adequately presented to perception in bodily form. Sculpture should place the spirit before us in its bodily form and in immediate unity therewith at rest and in peace; and the form should be animated by the content of spiritual individuality. And so the external sensuous matter is here no longer manipulated, either in conformity with its mechanical quality alone, as a mass possessing weight, nor in shapes belonging to the inorganic world, nor as indifferent to color, etc.; but it is wrought in ideal forms of the human figure, and, it must be remarked, in all three spatial dimensions.

In this last respect we must claim for sculpture, that it is in it that the inward and spiritual are first revealed in their eternal repose and essential self-completeness. To such repose and unity with itself there can correspond only that external shape which itself maintains its unity and repose. And this is fulfilled by shape in its abstract spatiality. The spirit which sculpture represents is that which is solid in itself, not broken up in the play of trivialities and of passions; and hence its

---

* In the sense "self-complete," "not primarily regarded as explained by anything outside," like a machine or an animal contrasted with a wheel or a limb, which latter are finite, because they demand explanation and supplementation from without, i.e., necessarily draw attention to their own limit.

external form too is not abandoned to any manifold phases of appearance, but appears under this one aspect only, as the abstraction of space in the whole of its dimensions.

c. Now, after architecture has erected the temple, and the hand of sculpture has supplied it with the statue of the God, then, in the third place, this god present to sense is confronted in the spacious halls of his house by the *community*. The community is the spiritual reflection into itself of such sensuous existence, and is the animating subjectivity and inner life which brings about the result that the determining principle for the content of art, as well as for the medium which represents it in outward form, comes to be particularization (dispersion into various shapes, attributes, incidents, etc.), individualization, and the subjectivity which they require.* The solid unity which the God has in sculpture breaks up into the multitudinous inner lives of individuals, whose unity is not sensuous, but purely ideal.†

It is only in this stage that God Himself comes to be really and truly spirit—the spirit in His (God's) community; for He here begins to be a to-and-fro, an alternation between His unity within himself and his realization in the individual's knowledge and in its separate being, as also in the common nature and union of the multitude. In the community, God is released from the abstractness of unexpanded self-identity, as well as from the simple absorption in a bodily medium, by which sculpture represents Him. And He is thus exalted into spiritual

---

* The terms used in the text explain themselves if we compare, e.g., a Teniers with a Greek statue, or again, say, a Turner with the same. "Subjectivity" means that the work of art appeals to our ordinary feelings, experiences, etc. Music and poetry are still stronger cases than painting, according to the theory. Poetry especially can deal with *everything*.

† The unity of the individuals forming a church or nation is not visible, but exists in common sentiments, purposes, etc., and in the recognition of their community.

existence and into knowledge, into the reflected * appearance which essentially displays itself as inward and as subjectivity. Therefore the higher content is now the spiritual nature, and that in its absolute shape. But the dispersion of which we have spoken reveals this at the same time as particular spiritual being, and as individual character. Now, what manifests itself in this phase as the main thing is not the serene quiescence of the God in Himself, but appearance as such, being which is *for* another, self-manifestation. And hence, in the phase we have reached, all the most manifold subjectivity in its living movement and operation—as human passion, action, and incident, and, in general, the wide realm of human feeling, will, and its negation—is for its own sake the object of artistic representation. In conformity with this content, the sensuous element of art has at once to show itself as made particular in itself and as adapted to subjective inwardness. Media that fulfill this requirement we have in color, in musical sound, and finally in sound as the mere indication of inward perceptions and ideas; and as modes of realizing the import in question by help of these media we obtain painting, music, and poetry. In this region the sensuous medium displays itself as subdivided in its own being and universally set down as ideal.†

---

* An expression constantly applied to consciousness, because it can look at itself.

> " 'Tell me, good Brutus, can you see your face?'
> 'No, Cassius; for the eye sees not itself
> But by reflection, by some other things.' "
>   *Julius Caesar*

† Posited or laid down to be ideal; almost = pronounced or made *to be* in the sense of *not being*; e.g., musical sound is "ideal" as existing, *qua* work of art, in memory only, the moment in which it is actually heard being fugitive; a picture, in respect of the third dimension, which has to be read into it; and poetry is almost wholly ideal, i.e., uses hardly any sensuous element, but appeals almost entirely to what exists *in the mind*. "Subdivided," *"Besondert,"* like *"particularisirt"* above; because of the variety and diversity present in the mere material of colors, musical sounds, and ideas.

Thus it has the highest degree of conformity with the content
of art, which, as such, is spiritual, and the connection of intelligible import and sensuous medium develops into closer in-
timacy than was possible in the case of architecture and sculpture. The unity attained, however, is a more inward unity, the
weight of which is thrown wholly on the subjective side, and
which, in as far as form and content are compelled to particu-
larize themselves and give themselves merely ideal existence,
can only come to pass at the expense of the objective universality of the content and also of its amalgamation with the
immediately sensuous element.* The arts, then, of which form
and content exalt themselves to ideality, abandon the character of symbolic architecture and the classical ideal of sculpture, and therefore borrow their type from the romantic form
of art, whose mode of plasticity they are most adequately
adapted to express. And they constitute a *totality* of arts, because the romantic type is the most concrete in itself.†

(1) The articulation of this *third sphere* of the individual
arts may be determined as follows. The *first* art in it, which
comes next to sculpture, is painting. It employs as a medium
for its content and for the plastic embodiment of that content
visibility as such in as far as it is specialized in its own nature,
i.e., as developed into color. It is true that the material employed in architecture and sculpture is also visible and colored;
but it is not, as in painting, visibility as such, not the simple
light which, differentiating itself in virtue of its contrast with

* Again, the subject of a Turner or Teniers is not objectively universal,
in the simplest sense; not something that is actually and literally the
same everywhere and for everyone. And both painting and music
(immediately sensuous elements) are less completely amalgamated with
the ideal, represent it less solidly and thoroughly than the statue, in so
far as the ideal is itself external or plastic.

† The greater affinity of Romantic art with the movement and variety of
the modern spirit displays itself not only in the greater flexibility of
painting, music, or poetry, as compared with architecture and sculpture,
but in the fact that the Romantic type contains these three arts at
least, while the Symbolic and Classical types had only one art each.

darkness, and in combination with the latter, gives rise to color.* This quality of visibility, made subjective in itself and treated as ideal, needs neither, like architecture, the abstractly mechanical attribute of mass as operative in the properties of heavy matter, nor, like sculpture, the complete sensuous attributes of space, even though concentrated into organic shapes. The visibility and the rendering visible which belong to painting have their differences in a more ideal form, in the several kinds of color, and they liberate art from the sensuous completeness in space which attaches to material things, by restricting themselves to a plane surface.

On the other hand, the content also attains the most comprehensive specification. Whatever can find room in the human heart, as feeling, idea, and purpose; whatever it is capable of shaping into act—all this diversity of material is capable of entering into the varied content of painting. The whole realm of particular existence, from the highest embodiment of mind down to the most isolated object of nature, finds a place here. For it is possible even for finite nature,† in its particular scenes and phenomena, to make its appearance in the realm of art, if only some allusion to an element of mind endows it with affinity to thought and feeling.

(2) The *second* art in which the romantic type realizes itself is contrasted with painting, and is music. Its medium, though still sensuous, yet develops into still more thorough subjectivity and particularization. Music, too, treats the sensuous as ideal, and does so by negating,‡ and idealizing into

---

* This is drawn from Goethe's doctrine of color, which Hegel unfortunately adopted in opposition to Newton's theory.

† He means landscape, principally.

‡ *"Aufheben,"* used pregnantly by Hegel to mean *both* "cancel," "annul," *and* "preserve," "fix in mind," "idealize." The use of this word is a cardinal point of his dialectic. See "Wiss. der Logik.," i. 104. I know of no equivalent but "put by," provincial Scotch "put past." The negation of space is an attribute of music. The parts of a chord are no more in space than are the parts of a judgment. Hegel expresses this by saying that music idealizes space and concentrates it into a point.

the individual isolation of a single point, the indifferent externality* of space, whose complete semblance is accepted and imitated by painting. The single point, *qua* such a negativity (excluding space) is in itself a concrete and active process of positive negation within the attributes of matter, in the shape of a motion and tremor of the material body within itself and in its relation to itself. Such an inchoate ideality of matter,† which appears no longer as under the form of space, but as temporal ideality,‡ is sound, the sensuous set down as negated, with its abstract visibility converted into audibility, inasmuch as sound, so to speak, liberates the ideal content from its immersion in matter. This earliest inwardness of matter and inspiration of soul into it furnishes the medium for the mental inwardness—itself as yet indefinite—and for the soul ¶ into which mind concentrates itself; and finds utterance in its tones for the heart with its whole gamut of feelings and passions. Thus music forms the center of the romantic arts, just as sculpture represents the central point between architecture and the arts of romantic subjectivity. Thus, too, it forms the point of transition between abstract spatial sensuousness, such as painting employs, and the abstract spirituality of poetry. Music has within itself, like architecture, a relation of quantity conformable to the understanding, as the antithesis to emotion and inwardness; and has also as its basis a solid conformity to law on the part of the tones, of their conjunction, and of their succession.

(3) As regards the *third* and most spiritual mode of repre-

---

* The parts of space, though external to each other, are not distinguished by qualitative peculiarities.

† "Ideality of matter": the distinctively material attribute of a sonorous body, its extension, only appears in its sound indirectly, or inferentially, by modifying the nature of the sound. It is, therefore, "idealized."

‡ Succession in time is a degree more "ideal" than coexistence in space, because it exists solely in the medium of memory.

¶ "Seele": mind on its individual side, as a particular feeling subject. "Geist" is rather mind as the common nature of intelligence. Thus in feeling and self-feeling, mind is said to concentrate itself into a soul.

sentation of the romantic art-type, we must look for it in *poetry*. Its characteristic peculiarity lies in the power with which it subjects to the mind and to its ideas the sensuous element from which music and painting in their degree began to liberate art. For sound, the only external matter which poetry retains, is in it no longer the feeling of the sonorous itself, but is a *sign*, which by itself is void of import. And it is a sign of the idea which has become concrete in itself, and not merely of indefinite feeling and of its *nuances* and grades. This is how sound develops into the *Word*, as voice articulate in itself, whose import it is to indicate ideas and notions. The merely negative point up to which music has developed now makes its appearance as the completely concrete point, the point which is mind, the self-conscious individual, which, producing out of itself the infinite space of its ideas, unites it with the temporal character of sound. Yet this sensuous element, which in music was still immediately one with inward feeling, is in poetry separated from the content of consciousness. In poetry the mind determines this content for its own sake, and apart from all else, into the shape of ideas, and though it employs sound to express them, yet treats it solely as a symbol without value or import. Thus considered, sound may just as well be reduced to a mere letter, for the audible, like the visible, is thus depressed into a mere indication of mind.* For this reason the proper medium of poetical repre-

---

* Hegel seems to accept this view. Was he insensible to sound in poetry? Some very grotesque verses of his, preserved in his biography, go to show that his ear was not sensitive. Yet his critical estimate of poetry is usually just. Shakespeare and Sophocles were probably his favorites. And, as a matter of proportion, what he here says is true. It must be remembered that the beauty of sound in poetry is to a great extent indirect, being supplied by the passion or emotion which the ideas symbolized by the sounds arouse. The beauty of poetical sound in itself *is* very likely less than often supposed. It must have the capacity for receiving passionate expression; but that is not the same as the sensuous beauty of a note or a color. If the words used in a noble poem were divested of all meaning, they would lose much, though not all, of the beauty of their sound.

sentation is the poetical imagination and intellectual portrayal itself. And as this element is common to all types of art, it follows that poetry runs through them all and develops itself independently in each. Poetry is the universal art of the mind which has become free in its own nature, and which is not tied to find its realization in external sensuous matter, but expatiates exclusively in the inner space and inner time of the ideas and feelings. Yet just in this its highest phase art ends by transcending itself, inasmuch as it abandons the medium of a harmonious embodiment of mind in sensuous form, and passes from the poetry of imagination into the prose of thought.

5. Such we may take to be the articulated totality of the particular arts, viz., the external art of architecture, the objective art of sculpture, and the subjective art of painting, music and poetry. Many other classifications have been attempted, for a work of art presents so many aspects, that, as has often been the case, first one and then another is made the basis of classification. For instance, one might take the sensuous medium. Thus architecture is treated as crystallization; sculpture, as the organic modeling of the material in its sensuous and spatial totality; painting, as the colored surface and line; while in music, space, as such, passes into the point of time possessed of content within itself, until finally the external medium is in poetry depressed into complete insignificance. Or, again, these differences have been considered with reference to their purely abstract attributes of space and time. Such abstract peculiarities of works of art may, like their material medium, be consistently explored in their characteristic traits; but they cannot be worked out as the ultimate and fundamental law, because any such aspect itself derives its origin from a higher principle, and must therefore be subordinate thereto.

This higher principle we have found in the types of art—symbolic, classical, and romantic—which are the universal stages or elements* of the Idea of beauty itself. For *symbolic art* attains its most adequate reality and most complete application in *architecture,* in which it holds sway in the full import of its notion, and is not yet degraded to be, as it were, the inorganic nature dealt with by another art. The *classical* type of art, on the other hand, finds adequate realization in sculpture, while it treats architecture only as furnishing an enclosure in which it is to operate, and has not acquired the power of developing painting and music as absolute forms for its content. The *romantic* type of art, finally, takes possession of painting and music, and in like manner of poetic representation, as substantive and unconditionally adequate modes of utterance. Poetry, however, is conformable to all types of the beautiful, and extends over them all, because the artistic imagination is its proper medium, and imagination is essential to every product that belongs to the beautiful, whatever its type may be.

And, therefore, what the particular arts realize in individual works of art, are according to their abstract conception simply the universal types which constitute the self-unfolding Idea of beauty. It is as the external realization of this Idea that the wide Pantheon of art is being erected, whose architect and builder is the spirit of beauty as it awakens to self-knowledge, and to complete which the history of the world will need its evolution of ages.

---

* "Stages or elements." *"Momente,"* Hegel's technical phrase for the stages which form the essential parts or factors of any idea. They make their appearance successively, but the earlier are implied and retained in the later.

Selections from

THE PHENOMENOLOGY OF THE SPIRIT

Translated by J. B. Baillie*
Revised by C. J. Friedrich

* Reprinted with the permission of George Allen and Unwin Ltd

Note

The following selections from Hegel's *Phenomenology*, while based upon Sir James Baillie's well-known translation of more than fifty years ago, have been adapted to bring them into line with the terminology of the rest of the selections as much as possible. Also in various places it seemed possible to convey the meaning somewhat more clearly and precisely. Just why Sir James should have employed certain terms, such as notion for *Begriff* and self-existence for *Fürsichsein* can be learned from his other writings; why *Herr* and *Knecht* should be rendered as lord and bondsman, rather than master and servant (the obvious meaning) escapes me.

It is hoped that the headings will indicate which sections have been used, since they are found in the various editions of the *Phaenomenologie*. We have inserted in square brackets the sub-headings which Hegel's most recent and most learned editor, Georg Lasson, added to help the reader through the complexities of the text; we have also retained a few of Lasson's notes, putting them into square brackets. Here and there, we have cut passages which seemed prolix and repetitive or duplicated matters discussed more fully in another selection.

Independence and Dependence of Self-consciousness

Master and Servant

SELF-CONSCIOUSNESS EXISTS IN ITSELF AND FOR ITSELF, IN THAT, and by the fact that it exists for another self-consciousness; that is to say, it *is* only by being acknowledged or "recognized." The conception of this its unity in its duplication, of infinitude realizing itself in self-consciousness, has many sides to it and encloses within it elements of varied significance. Thus its moments must on the one hand be strictly kept apart in detailed distinctiveness, and, on the other, in this distinction must, at the same time, also be taken as not distinguished, or must always be accepted and understood in their opposite sense. This double meaning of what is distinguished lies in the nature of self-consciousness: of its being infinite, or directly the opposite of the determinateness in which it is fixed. The detailed exposition of the notion of this spiritual unity in its duplication will bring before us the process of Recognition.

1. [The double self-consciousness.]

Self-consciousness has before it another self-consciousness; it has come outside itself. This has a double significance. First, it has lost its own self, since it finds itself as an *other* being; secondly, it has thereby sublimated that other, for it does not regard the other as essentially real, but sees its own self in the other.

It must suspend this its other self. To do so is to suspend and preserve that first double meaning, and is therefore a second double meaning. First, it must set itself to suspend the other independent being, in order thereby to become certain of itself as true being; secondly, it thereupon proceeds to suspend its own self, for this other is itself.

This suspension in a double sense of its otherness in a double sense is at the same time a return in a double sense into itself. For, firstly, through suspension, it gets back itself, because it becomes one with itself again through the canceling of its otherness; but secondly, it likewise gives otherness back again to the other self-consciousness, for it was aware of being in the other, it cancels this its own being in the other and thus lets the other again go free.

This process of self-consciousness in relation to another self-consciousness has in this manner been represented as the action of one alone. But this action on the part of the one has itself the double significance of being at once its own action and the action of that other as well. For the other is likewise independent, shut up within itself, and there is nothing in it which is not there through itself. The first does not have the object before it in the way that object primarily exists for desire, but as an object existing independently for itself, over which therefore it has no power to do anything for its own behoof, if that object does not *per se* do what the first does to it. The process then is absolutely the double process of both self-consciousness. Each sees the other do the same as itself; each itself does what it demands on the part of the other, and for that reason does what it does, only so far as the other does the same. Action from one side only would be useless, because what is to happen can only be brought about by means of both.

The action has then a *double meaning* not only in the sense that it is an act done to itself as well to the other, but also inasmuch as it is in its undivided entirety the act of the one as well as of the other.

In this movement we see the process repeated which came before us as the play of forces; in the present case, however, it is found in consciousness. What in the former had effect only for us (contemplating experience), holds here for the terms themselves. The middle term is self-consciousness which breaks itself up into the extremes; and each extreme is this interchange of its own determinateness, and complete transition into the opposite. While *qua* consciousness, it no doubt comes outside itself, still, in being outside itself it is at the same time restrained within itself, it exists for itself, and its self-externalization is for consciousness. *Consciousness* finds that it immediately is and is not another consciousness, as also that this other is for itself only when it cancels itself as existing for itself, and has self-existence only in the self-existence of the other. Each is the mediating term to the other, through which each mediates and unites itself with itself; and each is to itself and to the other an immediate self-existing reality, which, at the same time, exists thus for itself only through this mediation. They recognize themselves as mutually recognizing one another.

This pure conception of recognition, of duplication of self-consciousness within its unity, we must now consider in the way its process appears for self-consciousness. It will, in the first place, present the aspect of the disparity of the two, or the break-up of the middle term into the extremes, which *qua* extremes, are opposed to one another, and of which one is merely recognized, while the other only recognizes.

2. [The conflict of the opposed self-consciousnesses.]

Self-consciousness is primarily simple being-by-itself, self-identity by exclusion of every other from itself. It takes its essential nature and absolute object to be Ego; and in this immediacy, in this bare fact of its self-existence, it is individual. That which for it is the other stands as unessential object, as object with the impress and character of negation. But the other is also a self-consciousness; an individual makes its appearance in antithesis to an individual. Appearing thus in their immediacy, they are for each other in the manner of ordinary objects. They are independent individual forms, modes of consciousness that have not risen above the bare level of life (for the existent object here has been determined as life). They are, moreover, forms of consciousness which have not yet accomplished for one another the process of absolute abstraction, of uprooting all immediate existence, and of being merely the bare, negative fact of self-identical consciousness; or, in other words, have not yet revealed themselves to each other as existing purely for themselves, i.e., as self-consciousness. Each is indeed certain of its own self, but not of the other, and hence its own certainty of itself is still without truth. For its truth would be merely that its own individual existence for itself would be shown to it to be an independent object, or, which is the same thing, that the object would be exhibited as this pure certainty of itself. By the notion of recognition, however, this is not possible, except in the form that as the other is for it, so it is for the other; each in its self through its own action and again through the action of the other achieves this pure abstraction of existence for self.

The presentation of itself, however, as pure abstraction of self-consciousness consists in showing itself as a pure negation of its objective form, or in showing that it is fettered to no determinate existence, that it is not bound at all by the particularity everywhere characteristic of existence as such, and is *not* tied up with life. The process of bringing all this out involves a twofold action—action on the part of the other, and action on the part of itself. In so far as it is the other's action, each aims at the destruction and death of the other. But in this there is implicated also the second kind of action, self-activity; for each implies that it risks its own life. The relation of both self-consciousnesses is in this way so constituted that they prove themselves and each other through a life-and-death struggle. They must enter into this struggle, for they must bring their certainty of themselves, the certainty of being for themselves, to the level of objective truth, and make this a fact both in the case of the other and in their own case as well. And it is solely by risking life, that freedom is obtained; only thus is it tried and proved that the essential nature of self-consciousness is not bare existence, is not the merely immediate form in which it at first makes its appearance, is not its mere absorption in the expanse of life. Rather it is thereby guaranteed that there is nothing present but what might be taken as a vanishing moment—that self-consciousness is merely pure self-existence, being-for-self. The individual, who has not staked his life, may, no doubt, be recognized as a person; but he has not attained the truth of this recognition as an independent self-consciousness. In the same way each must aim at the death of the other, as it risks its own life thereby; for that other is to it of no more worth than itself; the other's reality is presented to the former as an external other, as outside itself; it must cancel that externality. The other is a purely existent consciousness and entangled in manifold ways; it must regard its otherness as pure existence for itself or as absolute negation.

This trying and testing, however, by a struggle to the death, cancels both the truth which was to result from it, and therewith the certainty of self altogether. For just as life is the natural "position" of consciousness, independence without absolute negativity, so death is the natural "negation" of consciousness, negation without independence, which thus remains without the requisite significance of actual recognition. Through death, doubtless, there has arisen the certainty that both did stake their life, and held it lightly both in their own case and in the case of the other; but that is not for those who underwent this struggle. They cancel their consciousness which had its place in this alien element of natural existence; in other words, they cancel themselves and are sublated, as terms or extremes seeking to have existence on their own account. But along with this there vanishes from the play of change, the essential moment, viz., that of breaking up into extremes with opposite characteristics; and the middle term collapses into a lifeless unity which is broken up into lifeless extremes, merely existent and not opposed. And the two do not mutually give and receive one another back from each other through consciousness; they let one another go quite indifferently, like things. Their act is abstract negation, not the negation characteristic of consciousness, which cancels in such a way that it preserves and maintains what is sublated, and thereby survives its being sublated.

In this experience self-consciousness becomes aware that *life* is as essential to it as pure self-consciousness. In immediate self-consciousness the simple ego is absolute object, which, however, is for us or in itself absolute mediation, and has as its essential moment substantial and solid independence. The dissolution of that simple unity is the result of the first experience; through this there is posited a pure self-consciousness, and a consciousness which is not purely for itself, but for another, i.e., as an existent consciousness, consciousness in the form and shape of thinghood. Both moments are essential, since, in the first instance, they are unlike and opposed, and their reflection into unity has not yet come to light, they stand as two opposed forms or modes of consciousness. The one is independent whose essential nature is to be for itself, the other is dependent whose essence is life or existence for another. The former is the Master, or Lord, the latter the Bondsman.

3. [Master and Servant. (a) Rule of the master.]

The master is the consciousness that exists *for itself*; but no longer merely the general notion of existence for the self. Rather, it is consciousness which, while existing on its own account, is mediated with itself through another consciousness, viz., bound up with an independent being or with thinghood in general. The master brings himself into relation to both these moments, to a thing as such, the object of desire, and to the consciousness whose essential character is thinghood, and since the master, *qua* notion of self-consciousness, is (a) an immediate relation of self-existence, but is now moreover at the same time (b) mediation, or a being-for-self which is for itself only through an other—he (the master) stands in relation (a) immediately to both, (b) mediately to each through the other. The master relates himself to the servant mediately through independent existence, for that is precisely what keeps the servant in bond; it is his chain, from which he could not, in the struggle, get away, and for that reason he proves himself dependent, shows that his independence consists in his being a thing. The master, however, is the power controlling this state of existence, for he has shown in the struggle that he holds existence to be merely something negative. Since he is the power dominating the negative nature of existence, while this existence again is the power controlling the other (the servant), the master holds, as a consequence, this other in subordination. In the same way the master relates himself to the thing mediately through the servant. The servant being a self-consciousness in the broad sense, also takes up a negative attitude to things and cancels them; but the thing is, at the same time, independent for him, and, in consequence, he cannot, with all his negating, get so far as to annihilate it outright and be done with it; that is to say, he merely works on it. To the master, on the other hand, by means of this mediating process, belongs the immediate relation, in the sense of the pure negation of it; in other words he gets the enjoyment. What mere desire did not attain, he now succeeds in attaining, viz., to have done with the thing, and find satisfaction in enjoyment. Desire alone did not get the length of this, because of the independence of the thing. The master, however, who has interposed the servant between it and himself, thereby relates himself merely to the dependence of the thing, and enjoys it without qualification and without reserve. The aspect of its independence he leaves to the servant, who labors upon it.

In these two moments, the master gets his recognition through another consciousness, for in them the latter affirms itself as unessential, both by working upon the thing, and, on the other hand, by the fact of being dependent on a determinate existence; in neither case can this other get the mastery over existence, and succeed in absolutely negating it. We have thus here this moment of recognition, viz., that the other consciousness cancels itself as self-existent, and *ipso facto,* itself does what the first does to it. In the same way we have the other moment, that this action on the part of the second is the action proper of the first; for what is done by the servant is properly an action on the part of the master. The latter exists only for himself, that is his essential nature; he is the negative power without qualification, a power to which the thing is nothing, and his is thus the absolutely essential action in this situation, while the servant's is not so, his is an unessential activity. But for recognition proper there is needed the moment that what the master does to the other he should also do to himself, and what the servant does to himself, he should do to the other also. On that account a form of recognition has arisen that is one-sided and unequal.

In all this, the unessential consciousness is, for the master, the object which embodies the truth of his certainty of himself. But it is evident that this object does not correspond to its notion; for, just where the master has effectively achieved rule, he really finds that something has come about quite different from an independent consciousness. It is not an independent, but rather a dependent consciousness that he has achieved. He is thus not assured of self-existence as his truth; he finds that his truth is rather the unessential consciousness, and the fortuitous unessential action of that consciousness.

The truth of the independent consciousness is accordingly the consciousness of the servant. This doubtless appears in the first instance outside it, and not as the truth of self-consciousness. But just as the position of master showed its essential nature to be the reverse of what it wants to be, so, too, the position of servant will, when completed, pass into the opposite of what it immediately is: being a consciousness repressed within itself, it will enter into itself, and change around into real and true independence.

[(b) Anxiety.]

We have seen what the position of servant is only in relation to that of the master. But it is a self-consciousness, and we have now to consider what it is, in this regard, in and for itself. In the first instance, the master is taken to be the essential reality for the state of the servant; hence, for it, the truth is the independent consciousness existing for itself, although this truth is not yet taken as inherent in the servant's position itself. Still, it does in fact contain within itself this truth of pure negativity and self-existence, because it has experienced this reality within it. For this self-consciousness was not in peril and fear for this element or that, nor for this or that moment of time, it was afraid for its entire being; it felt the fear of death, it was in mortal terror of its sovereign master. It has been through that experience melted to its inmost soul, has trembled throughout its every fiber, the stable foundations of its whole being have quaked within it. This complete perturbation of its entire substance, this absolute dissolution of all its stability into fluent continuity, is, however, the simple, ultimate nature of self-consciousness, absolute negativity, pure self-referent existence, which consequently is involved in this type of consciousness. This moment of pure self-existence is moreover a fact for it; for in the master this moment is consciously his object. Further, this servant's consciousness is not only this total dissolution in a general way; in serving and toiling, the servant actually carries this out. By serving he cancels in every particular moment his dependence on and attachment to natural existence, and by his work removes this existence.

[(c) Shaping and fashioning.]

The feeling of absolute power, however, realized both in general and in the particular form of service, is only dissolution implicitly, and albeit the fear of his master is the beginning of wisdom, consciousness is not therein aware of being self-existent. Through work and labor, however, this consciousness of the servant comes to itself. In the moment which corresponds to desire in the case of the master's consciousness, the aspect of the non-essential relation to the thing seemed to fall to the lot of the servant, since the thing there retained its independence. Desire has reserved to itself the pure negating of the object and thereby unalloyed feeling of self. This satisfaction, however, just for that reason is itself only a state of evanescence, for it lacks objectivity or subsistence. Labor, on the other hand, is desire restrained and checked, evanescence delayed and postponed; in other words, labor shapes and fashions the thing. The negative relation to the object passes into the *form* of the object, into something that is permanent and remains; because it is just for the laborer that the object has independence. This negative mediating agency, this activity giving shape and form, is at the same time the individual existence, the pure self-existence of that consciousness, which now in the work it does is externalized and passes into the condition of permanence. The consciousness that toils and serves accordingly comes by this means to view that independent being as its self.

But again, shaping or forming the object has not only the positive significance that the servant becomes thereby aware of himself as factually and objectively self-existent; this type of consciousness has also a negative import, in contrast with its first aspect, the element of fear. For in shaping the thing it only becomes aware of its own proper negativity, its existence on its own account, as an object, through the fact that it cancels the actual form confronting it. But this objective negative element is precisely the alien, external reality, before which it trembled. Now, however, it destroys this extraneous alien negative, affirms and sets itself up as a negative in the element of permanence, and thereby becomes aware of being objectively for itself. In the master, this self-existence is felt to be an other, is only external; in fear, the self-existence is present implicitly; in fashioning the thing, self-existence comes to be felt explicitly as its own proper being, and it attains the consciousness that itself exists in its own right and on its own account (*an und fuer sich*). By the fact that the form is objectified, it does not become something other than the consciousness molding the thing through work; for just that form is his pure self-existence, which therein becomes truly realized. Thus precisely in labor where there seemed to be merely some outsider's mind and ideas involved, the servant becomes aware, through this rediscovery of himself by himself, of having and being a "mind of his own."

For this reflection of self into self the two moments, fear and service in general, as also that of formative activity, are necessary: and at the same time both must exist in a universal manner. Without the discipline of service and obedience, fear remains formal and does not spread over the whole known reality of existence. Without the formative activity shaping the thing, fear remains inward and mute, and consciousness does not become objective for itself. Should consciousness shape and form the thing without the initial state of absolute fear, then it has merely a vain and futile "mind of its own"; for its form or negativity is not negativity *per se*, and hence its formative activity cannot furnish the consciousness of itself as essentially real. If it has endured not absolute fear, but merely some slight anxiety, the negative reality has remained external to it, its substance has not been through and through infected thereby. Since the entire content of its natural consciousness has not tottered and been shaken, it is still inherently a determinate mode of being; having a "mind of its own" (*der eigene sinn*) is simply stubbornness (*Eigensinn*), a type of freedom which does not get beyond the attitude of the servant. The less the pure form can become its essential nature, the less is that form, as overspreading and controlling particulars, a universal formative activity, an absolute conception; it is rather a piece of cleverness which has power within a certain range, but does not wield universal power and dominate the entire objective reality.

The Spirit

REASON is spirit, when its certainty of being all reality has been raised to the level of truth, and reason is consciously aware of itself as its own world, and of the world as itself. The development of spirit was indicated in the immediately preceding movement of mind, where the object of consciousness, the category pure and simple, rose to be the notion of reason. When reason "observes" this pure unity of ego and existence, the unity of subjectivity and objectivity, of for-itself-ness and in-itself-ness this unity is immanent, has the character of implicitness or of being; and consciousness of reason finds itself. But the true nature of "observation" is rather the transcendence of this instinct of finding its object lying directly at hand, and passing beyond this unconscious state of existence. The directly perceived (*angeschaut*) category, the thing simply "found," enters consciousness as the self-existence of the ego—an ego which now knows itself in the objective reality, and knows itself there as the self. But this feature of the category, viz., of being for-itself as opposed to being immanent within itself, is equally one-sided, and a moment that cancels itself. The category therefore gets for consciousness the character which it possesses in its universal truth—it is self-contained essential reality (*an und fuersich seiendes Wesen*). This character, still abstract, which constitutes the nature of absolute fact, of "fact itself," is to begin with "spiritual reality" (*das geistige Wesen*); and its mode of consciousness is here a formal knowledge of that reality, a knowledge which is occupied with the varied and manifold content thereof. This consciousness is still, in point of fact, a particular individual distinct from the general substance, and either prescribes arbitrary laws or pretends to possess within its own knowledge as such the laws as they absolutely are (*an und fuer sich*), and takes itself to be the power that passes judgment on them. Or again, looked at from the side of the substance, this is seen to be the self-contained and self-sufficient spiritual reality, which is not yet a consciousness of its own self. The self-contained and self-sufficient reality, however, which is at once aware of being actual in the form of consciousness and presents itself to itself, is Spirit.

Its essential spiritual being (*Wesen*) has been above designated as the ethical substance; spirit, however, is concrete ethical actuality (*Wirklichkeit*). Spirit is the self of the actual consciousness, to which spirit stands opposed, or rather which appears over against itself, as an objective actual world that has lost, however, all sense of strangeness for the self, just as the self has lost all sense of having a dependent or independent existence by itself, cut off and separated from that world. Being substance and universal self-identical permanent essence (*Wesen*), spirit is the immovable irreducible basis and the starting point for the action of all and every one; it is their purpose and their goal, because the ideally implicit nature (*Ansich*) of all self-consciousnesses. This substance is likewise the universal product, wrought and created by the action of each and all, and giving them unity and likeness and identity of meaning; for it is being-by-itself (*Fuersichsein*), the self, action. When considered as substance, spirit is unbending righteous self-sameness, self-identity; but when considered as being-by-itself (*Fuersichsein*), its continuity is resolved into discrete elements, it is the self-sacrificing soul of goodness, the benevolent essential nature, in which each fulfills his own special work, rends the continuum of the universal substance, and takes his own share of it. This resolution of the essence into individual forms is just the aspect of the separate action and the separate self of all the several individuals; it is the moving soul of the ethical substance, the resultant universal spiritual being. Just because this substance is a being resolved in the self, it is not a lifeless essence, but real and alive.

Spirit is thus the self-supporting absolutely real ultimate being (*Wesen*). All the previous modes of consciousness are abstractions from it: they are constituted by the fact that spirit analyzes itself, distinguishes its moments, and halts at each individual mode in turn. The isolating of such moments presupposes spirit itself and requires spirit for its subsistence; in other words, this isolation of modes only exists within spirit, which is existence. Taken in isolation they appear as if they existed as they stand. But their advance and return upon their real ground and essential being showed that they are merely moments or vanishing quantities; and this essential being is precisely this movement and resolution of these moments. Here, where spirit, the reflection of these moments into itself, has become established, our reflection may briefly recall them in this connection: they were consciousness, self-consciousness, and reason. Spirit is thus Consciousness in general, which contains sense-experience, perception and understanding, so far as in analyzing its own self it holds fast by the moment of being a reality objective to itself, and by abstraction eliminates the fact that this reality is its own self objectified, its own self-existence. When again it holds fast by the other abstract moment produced by analysis, the fact that its object is its own self become objective to itself, is its self-existence, and thus is Self-consciousness. But as immediate consciousness of its inherent and its explicit being, of its immanent self and its objective self, as the unity of consciousness and self-consciousness, it is that type of consciousness which has Reason: it is the consciousness which, as the word "have" indicates, has the object in a form which is implicitly and inherently rational, or is categorized, but in such a way that the object is not yet taken by the consciousness in question to have the value of a category. Spirit here is that consciousness from the immediately preceding consideration of which we have arrived at the present stage. Finally, when this reason, which spirit "has," is seen by spirit to be reason which actually is, that is, to be reason which is actual in spirit and is its world, then spirit has come to its truth; it is spirit, the essential nature of ethical life actually existent.

Spirit, so far as it is the immediate truth, is the ethical life of a nation—the individual, which is a world. It has to advance to the consciousness of what it is immediately; it has to abandon and transcend the beautiful simplicity of ethical life, and get to a knowledge of itself by passing through a series of stages and forms. The distinction between these and those that have gone before consists in their being real spiritual individualities (*Geister*), actualities proper, and instead of being forms of consciousness, they are forms of a world.

The living ethical world is spirit in its truth. As it first comes to an abstract knowledge of its essential nature, ethical life (*Sittlichkeit*) vanishes into the formal generality of right and law (*Recht*). Spirit, being now divided against itself, traces one of its worlds in the element of its objectivity as in a hard reality; this is the realm of culture and civilization; while over against this in the element of thought is traced the world of faith, the realm of essence (*Wesen*). Both worlds, however, when in the grip of the conception—when grasped by the spirit, which, after this loss of its self reflects upon itself—are thrown into confusion and revolutionized through insight (*Einsicht*) and its general diffusion, known as the "Enlightenment" (*Aufklaerung*). And the realm which had thus been divided and expanded into the "present" and the "beyond," into the "here" and the "hereafter," turns back into self-consciousness. This self-consciousness, again, taking now the form of morality (the inner moral life) apprehends itself as the essential truth, and the real essence as its actual self: no longer puts its world and its ground and basis outside itself, but lets everything fade into itself, and in the form of conscience (*Gewissen*) is spirit sure and certain (*gewiss*) of itself.

The ethical world, the world rent asunder into the "here" and the "hereafter" and the moral point of view (*moralische*

Weltanschauung) are, then, individual forms of spirit (*Geister*) whose process and whose return into the self of spirit, a self simple and being by itself (*fuer sich seiend*), will be developed. When these attain their goal and final result, the actual self-consciousness of absolute spirit will make its appearance.

The Objective Spirit—The Ethical Order

The spirit, in its simple truth, is consciousness, and breaks asunder its elements from one another. An act divides spirit into spiritual substance on the one side, and consciousness of the substance on the other; and divides the substance as well as consciousness. The substance as general nature and end contrasts with itself as particularized reality. The middle or mediating term, infinite in character, is self-consciousness, which, being implicitly the unity of itself and that substance, becomes so, now, explicitly (*fuer sich*), unites the general nature and its particular realization, raises the latter to the former and becomes ethical action: and, on the other hand, brings the former down to the latter and carries out the purpose, the substance presented merely in thought. In this way it brings to light the unity of its self and the substance, and produces this unity in the form of a "work" done, and thus as actual reality (*Wirklichkeit*).

When consciousness breaks up into these elements, the simple substance has in part preserved the attitude of opposition to self-consciousness; in part it thereby manifests in itself the very nature of consciousness, which consists in distinguishing its own content within itself—manifests a world articulated into separate areas. The substance is thus an ethical being split up into distinct elemental forms, a human and a divine law. In the same way, the self-consciousness appearing over against the substance assigns itself, in virtue of its inner nature, to one of these powers, and, as involving knowledge, gets broken up into ignorance of what it is doing on the one hand, and knowledge of this on the other, a knowledge which for that reason proves a deception. It learns, therefore, through its own act at once the contradictory nature of those powers into which the inner substance divided itself, and their mutual overthrow, as well as the contradiction between its knowledge of the ethical character of its act and what is truly and essentially ethical, and so finds its own destruction. In point of fact, however, the ethical substance has by this process become actual concrete self-consciousness: in other words this particular self has become self-sufficient and self-dependent (*An und Fuersichseiend*), but precisely therein the ethical order has perished.

The Ethical World: Law Human and Divine: Man and Woman

1. [People or nation and family. The law of the day and the right of the shadows.]

The simple substance of spirit, being consciousness, divides itself into parts. In other words, just as consciousness of abstract sensuous existence passes over into perception, immediate certainty of real ethical existence dies; and just as for sense perception bare "being" becomes a "thing" with many properties, so for ethical perception a given act becomes a reality involving many ethical relations. For the former, again, the unnecessary plurality of properties concentrates itself into the form of an essential opposition between individual and universal; and still more for the latter, which is consciousness purified and substantial, the plurality of ethical aspects is reduced to and assumes a twofold form, that of a law of individuality and a law of universality. Each of these areas or "masses" of the substance remains, however, spirit in its entirety. If in sense-perception "things" have no other substantial reality than the two determinations of individual and universal, these determinations express, in the present instance, merely the superficial opposition of both sides to one another.

[a. Human Law.]

Individuality, in the case of the being we are here consider-ing, has the significance of self-consciousness in general, not of any particular consciousness we care to take. The ethical substance is, thus, in this determination actual concrete sub-stance, absolute spirit realized in the plurality of distinct con-sciousnesses definitely existing. It (this spirit) is the community which, as we entered the stage of the practical embodiment of reason in general, came before us as the absolute and ultimate reality, and which here comes objectively before itself in its true nature as a conscious ethical being and as the essential reality, for that mode of consciousness we are now dealing with. It is spirit which is for itself, since it maintains itself by being reflected in the minds of the component individuals; and which is in itself or substance, since it preserves them within itself. As an actual substance, that spirit is a nation (*Volk*); as a concrete consciousness, it is the citizens of a nation. This consciousness has its essential being in simple spirit, and is certain of itself in the actual realization of this spirit, in the entire nation; it has its truth there directly, not therefore in something unreal, but in a spirit which exists and makes itself felt.

This spirit can be named human law, because it has its being essentially in the form of self-conscious actuality. In the form of universality, that spirit is law known to everybody, familiar and recognized, and is everyday, present custom (*Sitte*); in the form of particularity it is the concrete certainty of itself in any and every individual; and the certainty of itself as a single individuality is that spirit in the form of government. Its true and complete nature is seen in its authoritative validity openly and unmistakably manifested, an existence which takes the form of unconstrained independent objective fact, and is im-mediately apprehended with conscious certainty in this form.

[b. The Divine Law.]

Over against this power and publicity of the ethical secular human order there appears, however, another power, the divine law. For the ethical power of the state, being the movement of self-conscious action, finds its opposition in the simple immediate essential being of the moral order; as actual concrete universality, it is a force exerted against the independence of the individual; and, as actuality in general, it finds inherent in that essential being something other than the power of the state.

We mentioned before that each of the opposite ways in which the ethical substance exists contains that substance in its entirety, and contains all aspects of its contents. If, then, the community is that substance in the form of self-consciously realized action, the other side has the form of immediate or directly existent substance. The latter is thus, on the one hand, the inner conception (*Begriff*) or universal possibility of the ethical order in general, but, on the other hand, contains within it also the aspect of self-consciousness. This aspect which expresses the ethical order in this element of immediacy or mere being, which, in other words, is an immediate consciousness of self (both as regards its essence and its particular such-ness) in an "other," and hence, is a natural ethical community; this community is the family. The family, as the inner indwelling principle of social relations operating in an unconscious way, stands opposed to its own actuality when explicitly conscious; as the basis of the actuality of a nation, it stands in contrast to the nation itself; as the immediate ethical existence, it stands over against the ethical order which shapes and preserves itself by work for universal ends; the Penates of the family stand in contrast to the universal spirit.

Although the ethical existence of the family has the character of immediacy, it is within itself an ethical entity, but not so far as it is the natural relation of its component members, or so far as their connection is one immediately holding between individual concrete beings. For the ethical element is intrinsically universal, and this relation established by nature is essentially just as much a spiritual fact, and is only ethical by being spiritual. Let us see wherein its peculiar ethical character consists.

In the first place, because the ethical element is the intrinsically universal element, the ethical relation between the members of the family is not that of sentiment or the relationship of love. The ethical element in this case seems bound to be placed in the relation of the individual member of the family to the entire family as the real substance, so that the purpose of his action and the content of his actuality are taken from this substance, are derived solely from the family life. But the conscious purpose which dominates the action of this whole, so far as that purpose concerns that whole, is itself the individual member. The procuring and maintaining of power and wealth turn, in part, merely on needs and wants, and are a matter that has to do with desire; in part, they become in their higher aspect something which is merely of mediate significance. This aspect does not fall within the family itself, but concerns what is truly universal, the community; it acts rather in a negative way on the family, and consists in setting the individual outside the family, in subduing his merely natural existence and his mere particularity and so drawing him on toward virtue, toward living in and for the whole.

The positive purpose peculiar to the family is the individual as such. Now in order that this relationship may be ethical, neither the individual who does an act nor he to whom the act refers, must show any trace of contingency such as obtains in rendering some particular help or service. The content of the ethical act must be substantial in character, or must be entire and general; hence it can only stand in relation to the entire individual, to the individual as a general being. And this, again, must not be taken as if it were merely in idea that an act of service furthered his entire happiness, whereas the service, taken as an immediate or concrete act, only does something particular in regard to him. Nor must we think that the service really takes him as its object, and deals with him as a whole, in a series of efforts, as if it were a process of education, and produces him as a kind of work, where apart from the purpose, which operates in a negative way on the family, the real act has merely a limited content. Finally, just as little should we take it that the service rendered is a help in time of need, by which in truth the entire individual is saved; for it is itself an entirely casual act which can as well be as not be, the occasion of which is an ordinary actuality. The act, then, which embraces the entire existence of the blood relation, does not concern the citizen, for he does not belong to the family, nor does it deal with one who is going to be a citizen and so will cease to have the significance of a mere particular individual; it has as its object and content this specific individual belonging to the family, takes him as a general being, divested of his sensuous, or particular reality. The act no longer concerns the living but the dead, one who has passed through the long sequence of his broken and diversified existence and gathered up his being into its one completed embodiment, who has lifted himself out of the unrest of a life of chance and change into the peace of simple generality. Because it is only as citizen that he is real and substantial, the individual, when not a citizen, and belonging to the family, is merely an unreal insubstantial shadow.

[c. The rights of the individual.]

This condition of generality, which the individual as such reaches, is mere being, death; it is the immediate issue of a natural process, and is not the action of a conscious mind. The duty of the member of a family is on that account to attach this aspect too, in order that this last phase of being also (this general being) may not belong to nature alone, and remain something irrational, but may be something actually done, and the right of consciousness be asserted in it. Or rather the significance of the act is that, because in truth the peace and general existence of a self-conscious being does not belong to nature, the apparent claim which nature has made to act in this way, may be given up and the truth reinstated.

What nature did in the individual's case concerns the aspect in which his process of becoming something general is manifested as the movement of an existent. It takes effect no doubt within the ethical community, and has this in view as its purpose: death is the fulfillment and final task which the individual as such undertakes on its behalf. . . .

Because the ethical order is spirit in its immediate truth, those aspects into which its conscious life breaks up fall also into this form of immediacy; and the individual's particularity passes over into this abstract negativity, which, being in itself without consolation or reconciliation, must receive them essentially through a concrete and external act.

Blood-relationship therefore supplements the abstract natural process by adding to it the process of consciousness, by interrupting the work of nature, and rescuing the blood-relation from destruction; or better, because destruction, the passing into mere being, is necessary, it takes upon itself the act of destruction.

Through this it comes about that the general being, the sphere of death, is also something which has returned into itself, something self-existent; the powerless bare particular unity is raised to general individuality. The dead individual, by his having detached and liberated his being from his action or his negative unity, is an empty particular, merely existing passively for some other, at the mercy of every lower irrational organic agency, and the (chemical, physical) forces of abstract material elements, both of which are now stronger than himself, the former on account of the life which they have, the latter on account of their negative nature. The family preserves the dead from this dishonoring by . . . unconscious organic processes and by abstract elements, puts its own action in place of theirs, and weds the relative to the bosom of the earth, the elemental individuality that does not pass away. Thereby the family makes the dead a member of a community which prevails over and holds under control the powers of the particular material elements and the lower living creatures, which sought to have their way with the dead and destroy him.

This last duty thus accomplishes the complete divine law, or constitutes the positive ethical act toward the given individual. Every other relation toward him which does not remain at the level of love, but is ethical, belongs to human law, and has the negative significance of lifting the individual above the confinement within the natural community to which he belongs as a concrete individual. But, now, though human right has for its content and power the actual ethical substance consciously aware of itself, the entire nation, while divine right and law derive theirs from the particular individual who is beyond the actual yet he is still not without power. His power lies in the purely abstract, the shadowy individual, which seizes upon the individuality that cuts itself loose from the element and constitutes the self-conscious reality of the nation, and draws it back into the pure abstraction which is the essential nature of the shadowy individual, while at the same time the latter is its ultimate ground as well. How this power is made explicit in the nation itself will come out more fully as we proceed.

2. [The process or movement in both laws.]

Now in the one law as in the other there are differences and stages. For since these laws involve the element of consciousness in both cases, distinction is developed within themselves: and this is just what constitutes the peculiar process of their life. The consideration of these differences brings out the way they operate, and the kind of self-consciousness at work in both the essential being (*Wesen*) of the ethical world, as also their connection and transition into one another.

[a. Government, war power.]

The community, the higher law whose validity is open to the light of day, makes its concrete activity felt in government; for in government it is an individual whole. Government is concrete actual spirit reflected into itself, the self pure and simple of the entire ethical substance. This simple force allows, indeed, the community to unfold and expand into its component members, and to give each part subsistence and self-existence of its own (*Fuersichsein*). Spirit finds in this way its realization or its objective existence, and the family is the medium in which this realization takes effect. But spirit is at the same time the force of the whole, combining these parts again within the unity which negates them, giving them the feeling of their lack of independence, and keeping them aware that their life only lies in the whole. The community may thus, on the one hand, organize itself into the systems of property and of personal independence, of personal right and right in things; and, on the other hand, articulate the various ways of working for what in the first instance are particular ends—those of gain and enjoyment—into their own special guilds and associations, and may thus make them independent. The spirit of universal assemblage and association is the single and simple principle, and the negative essential factor at work in the segregation and isolation of these systems. In order not to get them rooted and settled in this isolation and thus break up the whole into fragments and let the common spirit evaporate, government has from time to time to shake them to the very center by war. By this means it confounds the order that has been established and arranged, and violates that right to independence, while the individuals . . . are made, by the task thus imposed on them by government, to feel the power of their lord and master, death. By thus breaking up the form of fixed stability, spirit guards the ethical order from sinking into merely natural existence, preserves the self of which it is conscious, and raises that self to the level of freedom and its own powers. The negative essential being shows itself to be the might proper of the community and the force it has for self-maintenance. The community therefore finds the true principle and corroboration of its power in the inner nature of divine law, and in the kingdom of the world beyond.

[b. The ethical relation of man and woman as brother and sister.]

The divine law which holds sway in the family has also on its side distinctions within itself, the relations among which make up the living process of its realization. Amongst the three relationships, however, of husband and wife, parents and children, brothers and sisters, the relationship of husband and wife is to begin with the primary and immediate form in which one consciousness recognizes itself in another, and in which each finds reciprocal recognition. Being natural self-knowledge, knowledge of self on the basis of nature, and not on that of ethical life, it merely represents and typifies in a figure the life of spirit, and is not spirit itself actually realized. This figurative representation, however, gets its realization in an other than it is. This relationship, therefore, finds itself realized not in itself as such, but in the child—an other, in whose coming into being that relationship consists, and with which it passes away. And this change from one generation onward to another is permanent in and as the life of a nation.

The reverent devotion of husband and wife toward one another is thus mixed up with a natural relation and with feeling, and their relationship is not inherently complete; similarly, too, the second relationship, the reverent devotion of parents and children to one another. The devotion of parents toward their children is affected and disturbed just by its being consciously realized in what is external to themselves (viz., the children), and by seeing them become something on their own account without this returning to the parents: independent existence on the part of the children remains a foreign reality, a reality all their own. The devotion of children, again, toward their parents is conversely affected by their coming into being from, or having their essential nature in, what is external to themselves (viz., the parents) and passes away; and by their attaining independent existence and a self-consciousness of their own solely through separation from the source whence they came —a separation in which the spring gets exhausted.

Both these relationships are constituted by and hold within the transience and the dissimilarity of the two sides which are assigned to them.

An unmixed intransitive form of relationship, however, holds between brother and sister. They are the same blood, which, however, in them has entered into a condition of stable equilibrium. They therefore stand in no such natural relation as husband and wife, they do not desire one another; nor have they given to one another, nor received from one another, this independence of individual being; they are free individualities with respect to each other. The feminine element, therefore, in the form of the sister, foreshadows most completely the nature of ethical being (sittliches Wesen). She does not become conscious of it, and does not actualize it, because the law of the family is her inherent implicit inward nature, which does not lie open to the daylight of consciousness, but remains inner feeling and the divine element exempt from actuality. The life of woman is attached to these household divinities (Penates), and sees in them both her universal substance, and her particular individuality, yet so views them that this relation of her particular being to them is at the same time not the natural one of pleasure.

As a daughter, the woman must now see her parents pass

away with natural emotion and yet with ethical resignation, for it is only at the cost of this condition that she can come to that individual existence of which she is capable. She thus cannot see her independent existence positively attained in her relation to her parents. The relationships of mother and wife, however, are individualized partly in the form of something natural, which brings pleasure; partly in the form of something negative which finds simply its own evanescence in those relationships; partly again the individualization is just on that account something contingent, which can be replaced by another particular individuality. In a household of the ethical kind, a woman's relationships are not based on a reference to this particular husband, this particular child, but to a husband, to children in general—not to feeling, but to the general. The distinction between her ethical life (*Sittlichkeit*), (while it determines her particular existence and brings her pleasure), and that of her husband consists just in this, that it has always a directly general significance for her, and is quite alien to the impulsive condition of mere particular desire. On the other hand, in the husband these two aspects get separated; and since he possesses, as a citizen, the self-conscious power belonging to the general life of the community, the life of the social whole, he acquires thereby the rights of desire, and keeps himself at the same time in detachment from it. So far, then, as particularity is implicated in this relationship in the case of the wife, her ethical life is not purely ethical; so far, however, as it is ethical, the particularity is a matter of indifference, and the wife is without the moment of knowing herself as this particular self in and through an other.

The brother, however, is in the eyes of the sister a being whose nature is unperturbed by desire and is ethically like her own; her recognition in him is pure and not mixed with any sexual relation. The indifference characteristic of particular existence, and the ethical contingency arising from it, are, therefore, not present in this relationship. Instead, the moment of individual selfhood, recognizing and being recognized, can here assert its right, because it is bound up with the balance and equilibrium resulting from their being of the same blood, and from their being related in a way that involves no mutual desire. The loss of a brother is thus irreparable to the sister, and her duty toward him is the highest.

[c. The passing of the two aspects, of divine and human law, into each other.]

This relationship at the same time is the limit, at which the circumscribed life of the family is broken up, and passes beyond itself. The brother is the member of the family in whom its spirit becomes individualized, and enabled thereby to turn toward another sphere, toward what is other than and external to itself, and pass over into consciousness of more general problems. The brother leaves this immediate, rudimentary, and, therefore, strictly speaking, negative ethical life of the family, in order to acquire and produce the concrete ethical order which is conscious of itself.

He passes from the divine law, within whose realm he lived, over to the human law. The sister, however, becomes, or the wife remains, the director of the home and the preserver of the divine law. In this way both the sexes overcome their merely natural being, and become ethically significant, as diverse forms dividing between them the different aspects which the ethical substance possesses. Both these universal factors of the ethical world have their specific individuality in naturally distinct self-consciousnesses, for the reason that the spirit at work in the ethical order is the immediate unity of the substance (of ethical life) with self-consciousness—an immediacy which thus appears as the existence of a natural difference, at once as regards its aspect of reality and of difference. It is that aspect which, in the conception of spiritual reality, came to light as "original determinate nature," when we were dealing with the stage of "individuality which is real to itself." This aspect loses the indeterminateness which it still has there, and the contingent diversity of "constitution" and "capacities." It is now the specific opposition of the two sexes, whose natural character acquires at the same time the significance of their respective ethical determinations.

The distinction of the sexes and of their ethical being remains all the same within the unity of the ethical substance, and its operation is just the constant process of that substance. The husband is sent forth by the spirit of the family into the life of the community, and finds there his self-conscious reality. Just as the family thereby finds in the community its general substance and subsistence, so conversely the community finds in the family the formal element of its own realization, and in the divine law its power and confirmation. Neither of the two is alone self-complete. Human law as a living and active principle proceeds from the divine, the law holding on earth from that of the world beyond, the conscious from the unconscious, mediation from immediacy; and this law also returns to where it came from. The power of the world beyond, on the other hand, finds its realization upon earth; it comes through consciousness to have existence and efficacy.

3. [The ethical world as totality or infinitude.]

[After summing up the preceding analysis, Hegel continues:]

The whole is a stable equilibrium of all the parts, and each part a spirit in its native element, a spirit which does not seek its satisfaction beyond itself, but has the satisfaction within itself for the reason that itself is in this balanced equipoise with the whole. This condition of stable equilibrium can, of course, only be living by inequality arising within it, and being brought back again to equipoise by righteousness and justice. Justice, however, is neither an alien being somewhere remote from the present, nor the actual behavior of mutual malice, treachery, ingratitude, etc. (unworthy of the name of justice). . . . On the contrary, being justice in human law, it brings back to the whole, to the general life of society, what has separately broken away from the harmony and equilibrium of the whole: the independent classes and individuals. In this way justice is the government of the nation, and is its all-pervading essential life in a consciously present individual form, and is the personal self-conscious will of all.

That justice, however, which restores to equilibrium the general when getting the mastery over the particular individual, is similarly the simple single spirit of the individual who has suffered wrong; it is not broken up into the two elements, one who has suffered wrong, and a remote being. The individual himself is the power of the world beyond, and that reality is his "fury," wreaking vengeance upon him. For his individuality, his blood, still lives in the house, his substance has a lasting actuality. The wrong, which can be brought upon the individual in the realm of the ethical world, consists merely in this, that a bare something by chance happens to him. The power which perpetrates on the conscious individual this wrong of making him into a mere thing, is "nature." . . . And the particular individual, in wiping out the wrong suffered, turns not against the community, for he has not suffered at its hands. . . .

The ethical realm remains in this way permanently a world without blot or stain, a world untainted by any internal dissension. So, too, its process is an untroubled transition from one of its powers to the other, in such a way that each preserves and produces the other. We see it no doubt divided into two ultimate elements and their realization; but their opposition is rather the confirming and substantiation of one through the other; and where they directly come in contact and affect each other as actual factors, their mediating common element straightway permeates and suffuses the one with the other. The one extreme, universal spirit conscious of itself, becomes, through the individuality of man, linked together with its other extreme, its force and its element, with unconscious spirit. On the other hand, divine law is individualized, the unconscious spirit of the particular individual finds its existence, in woman, through the mediation of whom the spirit of the individual comes out of its unrealizedness into actuality, out of the state of unknowing and unknown, and rises into the conscious realm of universal spirit. The union of man with woman constitutes the operative mediating agency for the whole, and constitutes the element which, while separated into the extremes of divine and human law, is, at the same time, their immediate union. This union, again, turns both those first mediate conclusions into one and the same synthesis, and unites into one process the twofold movement in opposite directions—one from reality to unreality, the downward movement of human law, organized into independent members, to the danger and trial of death—the other, from unreality to reality, the upward movement of the law of the world beyond to the daylight of conscious existence. Of these movements the former falls to man, the latter to woman.

Spirit Estranged from Itself: Culture (Bildung)

The ethical substance preserved and kept opposition enclosed within its simple conscious life; and this consciousness was in immediate unity with its own essential nature. That nature has therefore the simple characteristic of something merely existing for the consciousness which is directed immediately upon it, and whose custom (Sitte) it is. Consciousness does not stand for a particular excluding self, nor does the substance mean for it an existence shut out from it, with which it would have to establish its identity only through estranging itself, and yet at the same time have to produce that estrangement. But that mind, whose self is absolutely insular, absolutely discrete, finds its content over against itself in the form of a reality that is just as impenetrable as itself, and the world here gets the characteristic of being something external, negative to self-consciousness. Yet this world is a spiritual reality; it is essentially the fusion of individuality with being. Thus its existence is the work of self-consciousness, but likewise an actuality immediately present and alien to it, which has a peculiar being of its own, and in which it does not know itself. This reality is the external element and the free content of the sphere of law and right. But this external reality, which the master of the world of law and right takes control of, is not merely this elementary irreducible entity casually lying before the self; it is his work, but not in a positive sense, rather negatively so. It preserves its existence by self-consciousness of its own accord relinquishing itself and giving up its essential nature, the condition which, in that waste and ruin which prevail in the sphere of law and right, the external force of elements let loose seems to bring upon self-consciousness. These elements by themselves are sheer ruin and destruction, and cause their own overthrow. This overthrow, however, this their negative nature, is just the self; it is their subject, their action, and their process. Such process and activity again, through which the substance becomes actual, are the alienation of personality, for the immediate self, i.e., the self without estrangement and holding good as it stands, is without substantial content, and at the mercy of these raging elements. Its substance is thus just its relinquishment, and the relinquishment is the substance, i.e., the spiritual powers forming themselves into a coherent world, and thereby securing their subsistence.

The substance in this way is spirit, self-conscious unity of the self and the essential nature; but both also take each other to mean and to imply alienation. Spirit is consciousness of an objective reality which exists independently on its own account. Over against this consciousness stands, however, that unity of the self with the essential nature, consciousness pure and simple over against actual consciousness. On the one side actual self-consciousness by its self-relinquishment passes over into the real world, and the latter back again into the former. On the other side, however, this very actuality, both person and objectivity, is suspended and superseded; they are purely universal. This its alienation is pure consciousness, or the essential nature. The present has at once its opposite in its beyond, which consists in its thinking and its being thought; just as this again has its opposite in what is here in the present, which is its actuality alienated from it.

Spirit in this case, therefore, constructs not merely one world, but a twofold world, divided and self-opposed. The world of the ethical spirit is its own proper present; and hence every power it possesses is found in this unity of the present, and in so far as each separates itself from the other, each is still in equilibrium with the whole. Nothing has the significance of a negative of self-consciousness; even the spirit of the departed is in the life-blood of his relative, is present in the self of the family, and the general power of government is the will, the self of the nation. Here, however, what is present means merely objective actuality, which has its consciousness in the beyond; each particular moment, as an essential entity, receives this, and thereby actuality from an other, and so far as it is actual, its essential being is something other than its own actuality. Nothing has a spirit self-established and indwelling within it; rather each is outside itself in what is alien to it. The equilibrium of the whole is not the unity which abides by itself, nor its inwardly secured tranquillity, but rests on the alienation of its opposite. The whole is, therefore, like each particular moment, a self-estranged reality. It breaks up into two spheres: in one kingdom self-consciousness is actually both the self and its object, and in another we have the kingdom of pure consciousness, which, being beyond the former, has no actual present, but exists for faith, is a matter of belief.

Now just as the ethical world passes from the separation of divine and human law, with its various forms, and its consciousness gets away from the division into knowledge and the absence of knowledge, and returns into the principle which is its destiny, into the self which is the power to destroy and negate this opposition, so, too, both these kingdoms of self-alienated spirit will return into the self. But while the former was the first self, holding good directly, the particular person, this second, which returns into itself from its self-relinquishment, will be the universal self, the consciousness grasping the conception; and these spiritual worlds, all of whose moments insist on being a fixed reality and an unspiritual subsistence, will be dissolved in the light of pure Insight. This insight, being the self getting hold of itself, completes the stage of culture. It takes up nothing but the self, and everything as the self, i.e., it comprehends everything, extinguishes all objectiveness, and converts everything implicit into something explicit, everything which has a being in itself into what is for itself. When turned against belief, against faith, as the far-away region of inner being lying in the distant beyond, it is enlightenment (*Aufklaerung*). This enlightenment also terminates self-estrangement . . . in this region to which spirit in self-alienation turns to seek its safety . . . there it becomes conscious of a peace adequate to itself. Enlightenment upsets the household arrangements, which spirit carries out in the house of faith, by bringing in the goods and furnishings belonging to the world of the Here and Now, a world which that spirit cannot refuse to accept as its own property, for its conscious life likewise belongs to that world. In this negative task pure insight realizes itself at the same time, and brings to light its own proper object, the "unknowable absolute Being" and utility. Since in this way actuality has lost all substantiality, and there is nothing more implicit in it, the kingdom of faith is overthrown, as is also that of the real world; and this revolution brings about absolute freedom, the stage at which the spirit formerly . . . has gone back completely into itself, leaves behind this sphere of culture, and passes over into another region, the land of the inner or subjective moral consciousness.

A. The World of Spirit Estranged from Itself

The sphere of spirit at this stage breaks up into two regions. The one is the world of actual reality or of its self-estrangement; the other is constructed and set up in the ether of pure consciousness, and is exalted above the first. This second world, being constructed in opposition and contrast to that estrangement, is just on that account not free from it; on the contrary, it is only another form of that very estrangement, which consists precisely in having a conscious existence in two sorts of worlds, and embraces both. Hence it is not self-consciousness of absolute being in and for itself, not religion, which is here dealt with: it is belief, faith, in so far as faith is a flight from the actual world, and thus is not an experience in and by itself. Such flight from the realm of the present is, therefore, directly in its very nature a dual state of mind. Pure consciousness is the sphere into which spirit rises: but it is not only the element of faith, but of the conception as well. Consequently both appear on the scene together at the same time, and the latter comes before us only in antithesis to the former.

(I.) Culture and Its Sphere of Objective Reality

The spirit of this world is spiritual essence permeated by a self-consciousness which knows itself to be directly present as a self-existent particular, and has that essence as its objective actuality over against itself. But the existence of this world, as also the actuality of self-consciousness, depends on the process that self-consciousness divests itself of its personality, by so doing creates its world, and treats it as something alien and external, of which it must now take possession. But the renunciation of its self-existence is itself the creation of objective actuality, and in doing this, therefore, self-consciousness *ipso facto* makes itself master of this world.

To put the matter otherwise, self-consciousness is only something definite, it only has real existence, so far as it alienates itself from itself. By doing so, it puts itself in the position of something universal, and this its universality actualizes it, establishes it objectively, makes it valid. This equality of the self with all selves is, therefore, not the equality that was found in the case of right; self-consciousness does not here, as there, get immediate recognition and acknowledgment merely because it is; on the contrary, its claim to be rests on its having made itself, by that mediating process of self-alienation, conform to what is universal. The spiritless formal universality which characterizes the sphere of right takes up every natural form of character as well as of existence, and sanctions and establishes them. The universality which holds good here, however, is one that has undergone development, and for that reason it is concrete and actual.

1. [Culture as the estrangement of natural existence.]
   [a. The good and the bad; power and wealth.]

The means, then, whereby an individual gets objective validity and concrete actuality here is the formative process of culture. The alienation on the part of spirit from its natural existence is here the individual's true and original nature, his very substance. The relinquishment of this natural state is, therefore, both his purpose and his mode of existence; it is at the same time the mediating process, the transition of the thought-constituted substance to concrete actuality, as well as, conversely, the transition of determinate individuality to its essential constitution. This individuality molds itself by culture to what it inherently is, and only by so doing is it then something *per se* and possessed of concrete existence. The extent of its culture is the measure of its reality and its power. Although the self, as this particular self, knows itself here to be real, yet its concrete realization consists solely in canceling and transcending the natural self. The original determinateness of its nature is, therefore, reduced to a matter of quantity, to a greater or less energy of will, a non-essential principle of distinction. But purpose and content of the self belong to the universal substance alone, and can only be something universal. The specific particularity of a given nature, which becomes purpose and content, is something powerless and unreal: it is a "kind of being" which exerts itself foolishly and in vain to attain embodiment: it is the contradiction of giving reality to the bare particular, while reality is, *ipso facto*, something universal. If, therefore, individuality is falsely held to consist in particularity of nature and character then the real world contains no individualities and characters; individuals are all alike for one another; the presumed individuality in that case is thus only the existence referred to which has no permanent place in this world where only renunciation of self, and, therefore, only universality achieve actual reality. What is referred to passes, therefore, simply for what it is, for a kind of being. . . .

That which, in reference to the particular individual, appears as his culture, is the essential aspect of spiritual substances as such, that is, the direct transition of its ideal, thought-constituted, universality into actual reality; or otherwise put, culture is the single soul of this substance, in virtue of which the essentially inherent (*Ansich*) becomes something explicitly acknowledged, and assumes definite objective existence. The process by which an individuality cultivates itself is, therefore, *ipso facto*, the development of individuality as universal objective being; that is to say, it is the development of the actual world. This world, although it has come into being by means of individuality, is in the eyes of self-consciousness something that is alienated . . . and, for self-consciousness, takes on the form of a fixed, undisturbed reality. But at the same time self-consciousness is sure this is its own substance, and proceeds to take it under control. This power over its substance it acquires by culture, which, looked at from this aspect, appears as self-consciousness making itself conform to reality, and doing so to the extent permitted by the energy of its original character and talents. What seems here to be the individual's power and force, bringing the substance under it, and thereby doing away with that substance, is the same thing as the actualization of the substance. For the power of the individual consists in conforming itself to that substance, i.e., in emptying itself of its own self, and thus establishing itself as the objectively existing substance. Its culture and its own reality are, therefore, the process of making the substance itself actual and concrete.

The self is conscious of being actual only as a suspended one. The self does not here constitute the unity of consciousness of self and object; rather this object is negative as regards the self. By means of the self as inner soul of the process, the substance is so molded and worked up in its various aspects that one opposite puts life into the other, each opposite, by its alienation from the other, gives the other stability, and similarly gets stability from the other. At the same time, each aspect has its own definite nature, in the sense of having an insuperable worth and significance; and has a fixed reality as against the other. The process of thought fixes this distinction in the most general manner possible, by means of the absolute opposition of "good" and "bad," which are poles asunder, and can in no way become one and the same. But the very soul of what is thus fixed consists in its immediate transition to its opposite; its existence lies really in transmuting each determinate element into its opposite; and it is only this alienation that constitutes the essential nature and the preservation of the whole. We must now consider this process by which the aspects are thus made actual and give each other life; the alienation will be found to alienate itself, and the whole thereby will take all its contents back into the ultimate conception it implies.

At the outset we must deal with the substance pure and simple in its immediate aspect as an organization of its aspects; they exist there, but are inactive; their soul is wanting. The inner essential nature, the simple life of spirit that pervades self-conscious reality, is resolved, spread out into similar general areas or masses, spiritual masses in this case, and appears as an entire organized world. In the first area or mass it is the inherently universal spiritual being, self-identical; in the second it is self-existent being, it has become inherently self-discordant, sacrificing itself, abandoning itself; the third which takes the form of self-consciousness is a subject, and possesses in its very nature the fiery force of dissolution. In the first case it is conscious of itself, as immanent and implicit, as existing *per se;* in the second it finds independence, existence by itself, developed and carried out by means of the sacrifice of what is general. But spirit itself is the self-containedness and self-completeness of the whole, which splits up into substance as constantly enduring and substance engaged in self-sacrifice, and which at the same time resumes substance again into its own unity; a whole which is at once a flame of fire bursting out and consuming the substance, as well as the abiding form of the substance consumed. We can see that the areas of spiritual reality here referred to correspond to the community and the family in the ethical world, without, however, possessing the native familiarity of spirit which the latter have. On the other hand, if destiny is alien to this spirit, self-consciousness is and knows itself here to be the real power underlying them. We have now to consider these separate members, in the first instance as regards the way they are presented as thoughts, as essential inherent entities falling within pure consciousness, and also secondly as regards the way they appear as objective realities in concrete conscious life.

In that form of simple being, the first is the Good, the self-identical, immediate, unchanging, and primal nature of every consciousness, the independent spiritual power inherent in its essence, alongside which the activity of the mere self-existent consciousness is only by-play. The other is the passive spiritual being, the general so far as it parts with its own claims, and lets individuals get in it the consciousness of their particular existence; it is a state of nothingness, a being that is null and void, the Bad. This absolute break-up of the real into these disjointed members is itself a permanent condition; while the first member is the foundation, starting point, and result of individuals, which are there purely universal, the second member, on the other hand, is a being partly sacrificing itself for another, and, on that very account, is partly their incessant return to the self as individual, and their constant development of a separate being of their own.

But these simple thoughts of Good and Bad are similarly and immediately alienated from one another; they are actual, and in actual consciousness appear as objective aspects. Thus the first being is the power of the state, the second is wealth. The power of the state is the simple spiritual substance, as well as the achievement of all, the absolutely accomplished fact, wherein individuals find their essential nature expressed, and where their particular existence is simply and solely a consciousness of their own general significance. It is likewise the achievement and simple result from which the sense of its having been their doing has vanished: it stands as the absolute basis of all their action, where all their action securely subsists. This simple pervading substance of their life, owing to its thus determining their unalterable self-identity, has the nature of objective being, and hence only stands in relation to and exists for "another." It is thus, *ipso facto,* inherently the opposite of itself, namely, wealth. Although wealth is something passive, is nothingness, it is likewise a general spiritual entity, the continuously created result of the labor and action of all, just as it is again dissipated into the enjoyment of all. In enjoyment each individuality no doubt becomes aware of self-existence, aware of itself as particular; but this enjoyment is itself the result of general action, just as, reciprocally, wealth calls forth general labor, and produces enjoyment for all. The actual has through and through the spiritual significance of being also general. Each individual doubtless thinks he is acting in his own interests when getting this enjoyment; for this is the aspect in which he gets the sense of being something on his own account, and for that reason he does not take it to be something spiritual. Yet looked at even in external fashion, it becomes manifest that in his own enjoyment each gives enjoyment to all, in his own labor each works for all as well as for himself, and all for him. His self-existence is, therefore, inherently of general significance, and self-interest is merely something intended, a point of reference that cannot succeed in making concrete and actual what it intends, namely, to do something which does not further the good of all.

[b. The judgment of self-consciousness; the noble and the base consciousness.]

In these two spiritual potencies self-consciousness finds its own substance, content, and purpose; it sees there its twofold nature; in one it sees what it is inherently in itself, in the other what it is explicitly for itself. At the same time as spirit, it is the negative unity, uniting the subsistence of these potencies with the separation of individuality from the universal, or that of reality from the self. Dominion (power) and wealth are, therefore, confronting the individual as objects he is aware of, i.e., as objects from which he knows himself to be detached and between which he thinks he can choose, or even decline to choose altogether. In the form of this free and pure consciousness the individual confronts the essential reality as one which is merely there for him. He then has the reality as essential reality within itself. In this bare consciousness the aspects of the substance are taken to be not power and wealth, but the thoughts of Good and Bad. But further, self-consciousness is a relation of his pure consciousness to his actual consciousness, of what is thought to the objective being; it is essentially judgment. What is Good and what is Bad has already been brought out in the case of the two aspects of actual reality by determining what the aspects primarily are; the one is power (of the state), the other wealth. But this first judgment, this first distinction as to content, cannot be looked at as a "spiritual" judgment; for in that first judgment the one side has been characterized as only the inherently existing or positive, and the other side as only the explicit self-existent and negative. But as spiritual qualities, each permeates and pervades both aspects; and thus their nature is not exhausted in those specific characteristics (positive and negative). The self-consciousness that has to do with them is self-complete, is in itself and for itself. It must, therefore, relate itself to each in that twofold form in which they appear; and by so doing, this nature of theirs, which consists in being self-estranged determinations, will come to light.

Now self-consciousness takes that object to be good, and to exist *per se*, in which it finds itself; and that to be bad when it finds the opposite of itself there. Goodness means its identity with objective reality, badness their disparity. At the same time what is for it good and bad, is *per se* good and bad; because it is just that in which these two aspects—of being *per se*, and of being for it—are the same; it is the real indwelling soul of the objective facts, and the judgment is the evidence of its power within them, a power which makes them into what they are in themselves. What they are when spirit is actively related to them, their identity or non-identity with spirit—that is their real nature and the test of their true meaning, and not how they are identical or diverse taken immediately in themselves apart from spirit, i.e., not their inherent being and self-existence *in abstracto*. The active relation of spirit to these aspects—which are first put forward as objects to it and thereafter pass by its action into what is essential and inherent—becomes at the same time their reflection into themselves, in virtue of which they obtain actual spiritual existence, and their spiritual meaning comes to light. But as their first immediate characteristic is distinct from the

relation of spirit to them, the third determinate aspect—their
own proper spirit—is also distinguished from the second aspect.
Their second inherent nature, their essentiality which comes
to light through the relation of spirit to them, must in the first
instance turn out different from the immediate inherent nature;
for indeed this mediating process of spiritual activity puts in
motion the immediate characteristic, and turns it into something else.

As a result of this process, the self-contained conscious mind
doubtless finds now in the power of the state its reality pure
and simple, and its subsistence; but it does not find its individuality as such; it finds its inherent and essential being, but
not what it is for itself. Rather, it finds there its action as individual action rejected and denied, and subdued into obedience. The individual thus recoils before this power and turns
back into himself; it is the reality that suppresses him, and is
the bad. For instead of being identical with him, that with
which he is at one, it is something utterly in discordance with
individuality. In contrast with this, wealth and riches are the
good; they tend to the general enjoyment, they are there simply
to be disposed of, and they ensure for everyone the consciousness of his particular self. Wealth means in its very
nature general beneficence: if it refuses any benefit in a given
case, and does not gratify every need, this is merely an accident
which does not detract from its universal and necessary nature
of imparting to every individual his share and being a thou-
sand-handed benefactor.

The conceptions good and bad thus receive here a content
the opposite of which they had before.

These two ways of judging find each of them an identity
and a disagreement. In the first case consciousness finds the
power of the state out of agreement with it, and the enjoyment
that came from wealth in accord with it; while in the second
case the reverse holds good. There is a twofold attainment of
identity and a twofold form of disagreement: there is an op-

posite relation established toward both the essential realities. We must pass judgment on these different ways of judging as such; to this end we have to apply the criterion already mentioned. The conscious relation where identity or agreement is found is, according to this standard, the good; that where want of agreement obtains, the bad. These two types of relation must henceforth be regarded as modes or forms of conscious existence. Conscious life, through taking up a different kind of relation, thereby becomes itself characterized as different, comes to be itself good or bad. It is not simply distinct in virtue of the fact that it took as its constitutive principle either existence for itself, or mere being in itself; for both are equally essential aspects of its life: that dual way of judging, above discussed, presented those principles as separated, and contained, therefore, merely abstract ways of judging. Concrete actual conscious life has within it both principles, and the distinction between them falls solely within its own nature, viz., inside the relation of itself to the actually real.

This relation takes opposite forms; in the one there is an active attitude toward political power and wealth as to something with which it is in accord, in the other it is related to these realities as to something with which it is at variance. A conscious life which finds itself at one with them has the attribute of nobility. In the case of the public authority of the state, it beholds what is in accord with itself and sees that it has there its own nature pure and simple and the region for the exercise of its own powers, and takes up the position of open willing and obedient service in its interests, as well as that of inner reverence toward it. In the same way in the sphere of wealth, it sees that wealth secures for it the consciousness of self-existence, of realizing the other essential aspect of its nature: hence it looks upon wealth likewise as something essential in relation to itself, acknowledges it as something from which the enjoyment comes as from a benefactor, and considers itself under a debt of obligation.

The conscious life involved in the other relation, that of disagreement, has the attribute of baseness. It remains at variance with both those essential elements. It looks upon the authoritative power of the state as a chain, as something suppressing its separate existence for its own sake, and hence hates the ruler, obeys only with secret malice, and stands ever ready to burst out in rebellion. It sees, too, in wealth, by which it attains to the enjoyment of its own independent existence, merely something discordant, or out of harmony with its permanent nature; since through wealth it only gets a sense of its particular isolated existence and a consciousness of passing enjoyment, this type of mind loves wealth, but despises it, and, with the disappearance of enjoyment, of what is inherently evanescent, regards its relation to the man of wealth as having ceased too.

[c. The service and counsel.]

The noble type of consciousness, then, finds itself in its judgment related to political power, in the sense that this power is indeed not a self as yet but at first is a general substance; in it this form of mind feels its own essential nature to exist as it is conscious of its own purpose and absolute content. By taking up a positive relation to this substance, it assumes a negative attitude toward its own special purposes, its particular content and individual existence, and lets them disappear. This type of mind implies the heroism of service; the virtue which sacrifices individual being to the general, and thereby brings this into existence. It is the type of personality which renounces possession and enjoyment, acts for the existent power, and is thus real.

Through this process the general good becomes united and bound up with existence in general, just as the individual consciousness makes itself by this renunciation essentially general. That from which this consciousness alienates itself by submitting to serve is its consciousness immersed in mere existence: but the being alienated from itself is the inherent nature. By thus shaping its life in accord with what is general, it acquires a reverence for itself, and gets reverence from others. The power of the state, however, which to start with was merely general in thought, the inherent nature, becomes through this very process general in fact, becomes actual power. It is actually so only by getting that actual obedience which it obtains through self-consciousness judging it to be the essential reality, and through the self freely surrendering to it. The result of this action, binding the essential reality and the self indissolubly together, is to produce a twofold actual reality —a self that has truly actual reality, and a political power which is true and hence valid.

Owing to this alienation implied in the idea of sacrifice, political power, however, is not yet a self-consciousness that knows itself as power of the state. It is merely the law of the state, its inherent principle, that is accepted; political power has as yet no particular will. For as yet the self-consciousness rendering service has not alienated its pure selfhood, and made it an animating influence in the exercise of political power; the serving attitude merely gives the state its bare being, sacrifices merely its existence to the state, not its essential nature. This type of self-consciousness passes thus for something that is in conformity with the essential nature, and is acknowledged and accepted because of its inherent reality. The others find their essential nature operative in it, but not their independent existence—find their thinking, their pure consciousness fulfilled, but not their specific individuality. It has a value, therefore, in their thoughts, and is honored accordingly. Such a type is the haughty vassal; he is active in the interests of the state, so far as the state is not the personal will of a monarch, but an essential will. . . . The language he would use, were he to have a direct relation to the personal will of the state, which thus far has not arisen, would take the form of "counsel" imparted in the interests of what is the best for all.

Public power has, therefore, at this stage no will yet to use the advice, and does not decide between the different opinions as to what is generally the best. It is not yet governmental control, and on that account is in truth not yet real state power. Individual self-existence, the possession of an individual will that is not yet surrendered as will, is the inner centrifugal spiritual principle of the various classes and estates, a spirit which keeps for its own behoof what suits it best, in spite of its words about the general good, and this claptrap about what is the general good tends to be made a substitute for action bringing it about. . . .

This contradiction, which has to be eliminated, this discordance and opposition between the independence of the individual conscious life and the general interest fostered by the state's authority, contains at the same time another aspect. That sacrifice, that renunciation of existence, when it is complete, as it is in death, is one that does not revert to the conscious life that makes the sacrifice. The fact is, this conscious life does not survive the renunciation and exist in and by itself; it merely passes away in the unreconciled opposition. Therefore, that alone is true sacrifice in which the individuality gives itself up as completely as in the case of death, but all the while preserves itself in the renunciation. It comes thereby to be actually what it is implicitly—the identical unity of self with its opposed self.

2. [Language as the actual reality of the estrangement or of the culture.]

This estrangement, however, takes place in language, in words alone, and language assumes here its peculiar role. Both in the sphere of general ethics (*Sittlichkeit*), where language conveys laws and commands, and in the sphere of actual life, where it appears as conveying advice, the content of what it expresses is the essential reality, and language is the form of that essential content. Here, however, it takes the form in which as language it exists to be its content, and possesses authority, as spoken word; it is the power of utterance as utterance which, just in speaking, performs what has to be performed. For it is the existence of a pure self as self; in speech the particular self-existent self-consciousness comes as such into existence, so that its particular individuality is something for others. . . . Language contains the ego in its purity; it alone expresses the "I," as self. Its existence in this case is, as existence, a form of objectivity which has in it the true nature of existence. The ego is this particular ego, but at the same time it is general; its appearing is *ipso facto* and at once the relinquishing and disappearing of this particular ego, and in consequence its remaining all the while general. The "I" that expresses itself is apprehended as an ego; it is a kind of infection as a result of which it establishes at once a unity with those who are aware of it, a spark that kindles a general consciousness of self. That it is perceived as a fact by others means *eo ipso* that its existence is itself dying away: this its otherness is taken back into itself; and its existence lies just in this, that, *qua* self-conscious now, as it exists, it has no subsistence and that it subsists just through its disappearance. This disappearance is, therefore, itself *ipso facto* its continuance; it is its own cognition of itself, and its knowing itself as something that has passed into another self that has been perceived and apprehended and is universal. . . .

[Hegel goes on to elaborate this position in terms of "unity" in its "opposites," thus adumbrating the dialectics of the spirit of language. He then returns to the main theme:]

Both extremes, the power of the state and the noble consciousness, are disintegrated by this latter (the spirit of language). The state's power is disintegrated into the abstract universal which is obeyed, and the will being by itself, which, however, does not yet belong to the state itself. The noble consciousness is disintegrated into the obedience of the suspended existence, or into the inherent self-respect and honor, and into a self which is not as yet suspended as pure being by itself, that is, into the will which still remains in reserve. These two aspects into which both extremes are purified, and which, therefore, are aspects of language, are the abstract and the general, which is called the general good, and the pure self which by rendering service abrogated the consciousness which is absorbed in the manifold variety of existence. Both in conception are the same; for pure self is just the abstract and the general, and hence their unity is posited as their mediating term. But the self is, to begin with, actual only in consciousness as one extreme, while the inherent nature (*Ansich*) is actualized in the power of the state as the other extreme. What is lacking to consciousness is that the state's power should be transferred to it, not merely in the form of honor but in reality; what is lacking to the state's authority is that it is obeyed not merely as a so-called general good, but as will, in other words, that the state's power is itself the deciding self. The unity of the conception in which the state's power remains, and to which consciousness has been refined, becomes real in this mediating process and this mediating process exists as language. All the same, the aspects of this unity are not yet present in the form of two selves as selves; for the state's power is yet to be spiritualized into a self. This language is, therefore, not yet the spirit which completely knows and expresses itself.

[a. Flattery.]

The noble consciousness, because the extreme form of the self, appears in the creating of language by which the separate aspects are formed into animated wholes. The heroism of silent service passes into the heroism of flattery. This reflection of service in express language constitutes the self-conscious self-disintegrating middle (term), and reflects back into itself not only its own special extreme, but reflects the extreme of general power back into this self too, and makes that power, which is at first implicit, into an independent self-existence, and gives it the individualistic form of self-consciousness. Through this process the indwelling spirit of this power of the state comes into existence—that of an unlimited monarch. It is unlimited; the language of flattery raises power into its purified generality; this aspect as the product of language, of existence purged to become spirit, is a purified form of self-identity. It is a monarch; for flattering language likewise puts individuality on its pinnacle; what noble consciousness divests itself of regarding this aspect of pure spiritual unity is the pure essential nature of its thought, its ego itself. Flattery elevates the particularity (of its ego), which otherwise is only imagined into its pure existence by giving the monarch his proper name. For it is in the name alone that the distinction of the individual from everyone else is not imagined but is made actually real by all. By having a name the individual passes for a pure individual not merely in his own consciousness of himself, but in the consciousness of all. By his name, then, the monarch becomes absolutely detached from everyone, exclusive and solitary, and in virtue of it is unique as an atom that cannot commute any part of its essential nature, and has nothing like itself. This name is thus the reflection into itself, or it is the actual reality which the general power has inherently in itself: through the name the power is the monarch.* Conversely he, this particular individual, thereby knows himself, this individual self, to be the general power, knows that the nobles not only are ready and prepared for the service of the state, but are grouped as an ornamental setting around the throne, and that they are forever telling him who sits on it what he is.

The language of their praise is in this way the spirit that

* Cf., "L'état c'est moi."

unites together the two extremes in the state's power itself. This language reflects in itself the abstract power and gives to it the aspect peculiar to the other extreme, an isolated self of its own, willing and deciding on its own account, and consequently gives it self-conscious existence. Or again, by that means this self-conscious particular being comes to be aware of itself for certain as the supreme authority. This power is the central focal self into which, through relinquishing their own inner certainty of self, the many separate centers of selfhood are fused together into one.

Since, however, this proper spirit of the state and its power subsists by getting its realization and its nourishment from the homage of action and thought rendered by the nobility, it is a form of independence . . . The noble, the extreme form of being by itself, receives the other extreme of actual generality in return for the generality of thought which it has relinquished. The power of the state has passed over to the noble consciousness. Through this noble consciousness the state's power becomes truly active; through its essential nature political power ceases to be the inert being it appeared to be as the extreme of abstract being-by-itself.

Looked at by itself, the state's power reflected back into itself, or becoming spiritual, means nothing else than that it has come to be an aspect of self-conscious life, i.e., exists only by being superseded. Consequently it is now the real in the sense of something whose spiritual meaning lies in being sacrificed and squandered; it exists in the sense of wealth. It continues, no doubt, to subsist at the same time as a form of reality as contrasted with wealth, into which in principle it is forever passing; but it is a reality whose inherent principle (conception) is this very movement of passing over, owing to the service and the reverence rendered to it, and by which it arises, into its opposite, into the relinquishing of its power. Thus from its point of view (*Fuersich*), the special and peculiar self, which constitutes its will, becomes, by the self-abasement of the noble consciousness, the general being that renounces itself, becomes completely an isolated particular, a mere accident, which is the prey of every stronger will. What remains to it of the generally acknowledged and incommunicable independence is the empty name.

While, then, the noble consciousness is determined as the something which in the same way is related to the general power, its true nature lies rather in retaining its own separateness of being when rendering its service, but, in what is properly the abnegation of its personality, its true being lies in actually suspending and tearing apart the general substance. Its spirit is the attitude of thoroughgoing discordance (inequality): on one side it retains its own will in the honor it receives, on the other hand, it gives up its will: in part it alienates its inner nature from itself, and arrives at the extreme of discordance with itself, in part it subdues the general substance to itself, and puts this entirely at variance with itself. It is obvious that, as a result, its own specific nature, which kept it distinct from the so-called base type of mind, disappears, and with that this latter type of mind too. The base type has gained its end, that of subordinating the general power to self-centered isolation of the self.

Endowed in this way with general power, self-consciousness exists in the form of general beneficence: or, from another point of view, general power is wealth that again is itself an object for consciousness. For wealth is here taken to be the general put in subjection, which, however, through this first transcendence, is not yet absolutely returned into the self. Self has not as yet its self as such for object, but the universal essential reality in a state of suspension. Since this object has first come into being, the relation of consciousness toward it is immediate, and consciousness has thus not yet set forth its lack of congruity with this object: we have here the noble consciousness preserving its own self-centered existence in the general that has become non-essential, and hence acknowledging the object and feeling grateful to its benefactor.

Wealth has within it from the first the aspect of being-by-itself. It is not the selfless general being, like state-power, or the unconstrained simplicity of the natural life of spirit; it is the state's power as holding its own by an effort of the will in opposition to a will that wants to get the mastery over wealth and get enjoyment out of it. But since wealth has merely the form of being essential, this one-sided self-existent life—which has no being in itself, which is rather the suspension of inherent being—is the return of the individual into himself to find no essential reality in his enjoyment. It thus itself needs to be given animation; and its reflective process of bringing this about consists in its becoming something real in itself as well as for itself, instead of being merely for itself; wealth, which is the suspended essential reality, has to become the essentially real. In this way it preserves its own spiritual principle in itself.

It will be sufficient here to describe the content of this process since we have already explained at length its form. The noble consciousness, then, stands here in relation not to the object in the general sense of something essential; what is alien to it is being-by-itself. It finds itself face to face with its own self as such in a state of alienation, as an objective solid actuality which it has to take from the hands of another self-centered being, another equally fixed and solid entity. Its object is being-by-itself; i.e., its own being: but by being an object it is at the same time *ipso facto* an alien reality, which is a self-centered being on its own account, has a will of its own; i.e., it sees its self under the impact of an alien will on which it depends for the concession of its self.

From each particular aspect self-consciousness can abstract, and for that reason, even when under an obligation to one of these aspects, retains the recognition and inherent validity of self-consciousness as an independent reality. Here, however, it finds that, as regards its own ego, its own proper and peculiar actuality, it is outside itself and belongs to an other, finds its personality as such dependent on the chance personality of an other, on the accident of a moment, of an arbitrary caprice, or some other sort of irrelevant circumstance.

In the sphere of law and right, what lies in the power of the objective being appears as an incidental content, from which it is possible to make abstraction; and the governing power does not affect the self as such; rather this self is recognized. But here the self sees its self-certainty as such to be the most unreal thing of all, finds its pure personality to be absolutely without the character of personality. The sense of its gratitude is, therefore, a state in which it feels profoundly this condition of being utterly outcast, and feels also the deepest revolt as well. Since the pure ego sees itself outside self, and torn asunder, everything that gives continuity and generality, everything that bears the name of law, good, and right, is thereby torn to pieces at the same time, and goes to wrack and ruin: all identity and concord break up, for what holds sway is the purest discord and disunion, what was absolutely essential is absolutely unessential, what has a being on its own account has its being outside itself: the pure ego itself is completely disintegrated.

Thus since this consciousness receives back from the sphere of wealth the objective form of being a separate being-by-itself, and suspends that objective character, it is in principle not only, like the preceding reflection, not completed, but is consciously unsatisfied: the reflection, since the self receives itself as an objective fact, is the immediate contradiction that has taken root in the pure ego as such. As a self, however, it at the same time immediately rises above this contradiction; it is absolutely elastic, and again suspends this suspension of itself, repudiates this repudiation of itself, wherein its being-by-itself is made to be something alien to it, revolts against this acceptance of itself and in the very reception of itself is by itself.

[b. The language of disjointedness and disintegration (*Zerrissenheit*).]

Since, then, this type of consciousness is bound up with this condition of utter disintegration, the distinction constituting its spiritual nature—that of being noble as contrasted with the base—is gone and both are the same.

The spirit of a wealth that does good may, further, be distinguished from the spirit of the consciousness which receives such a benefit, and deserves special consideration.

The spirit animating wealth had an unreal insubstantial being-by-itself; wealth was something to be given up. By being communicated it passes into something in and of itself; since it fulfills its nature in sacrificing itself, it suspends the aspect of particularity, of merely seeking enjoyment for one's own particular self, and, being thus suspended as a particular, the spirit (of wealth) becomes a general being.

What it imparts, what it gives to others, is being-by-itself. It does not hand itself over, however, as a natural selfless object, as the frankly and freely offered condition of unconscious life, but as something self-conscious, as a reality keeping hold of itself: it is not like the power of an inorganic element which is felt by the consciousness receiving its force to be inherently transitory; it is the power over the self, a power aware that it is independent and voluntary, and knowing at the same time that what it dispenses becomes the self of someone else.

Wealth thus shares baseness with its clientele; but in place of revolt appears arrogance. For in one aspect it knows, as well as the self it benefits, that its being-by-itself is a matter of accident; but itself is the accident in whose power personality is placed. In this mood of arrogance—which thinks it has secured through a dole an alien ego-nature, and thereby brought its inmost being into submission—it overlooks the secret rebellion of the other self: it overlooks the fact of all bonds being completely cast aside, overlooks this pure disintegration, in which, the self-identity of what exists for its own sake having become sheer internal discordance, all oneness and concord, all subsistence is rent asunder, and in which in consequence the thoughts and intentions of the benefactor are the first to be shattered. It stands directly in front of this abyss, cleaving it to the innermost, this bottomless pit, where every solid base and stay have vanished: and in the depths it sees nothing but a common thing, a display of whims on its part, a chance result of its own caprice. Its spirit consists in quite unreal opining, in being superficially forsaken of all true spirit.

Just as self-consciousness had its own language in dealing with the state's power, in other words, just as spirit took the form of expressly and actually mediating between these two extremes, self-consciousness has also a mode of speech in dealing with wealth; but still more when in revolt does it adopt a language of its own. The form of utterance which gives to wealth the sense of its own essential significance, and thereby makes it master of itself, is likewise the language of flattery, but of ignoble flattery; for what it gives out to be essential reality, it knows to be a reality without an inherent nature of its own, to be something at the mercy of another. The language of flattery, however, as already remarked, is that of a one-sided spirit. To be sure, its constituent elements are, on the one hand, a self molded by service into a shape where it is reduced to bare existence, and, on the other, the inherent reality of the power dominating the self. Yet the pure conception, in which the mere self and the inherent reality (Ansich), that pure ego and this pure reality or thought, are one and the same thing—this conceptual unity of the two aspects between which reciprocity takes effect, is not consciously felt when this language is used. The object is consciously still the inherent reality in opposition to the self; in other words, the object is not for consciousness at the same time its own proper self as such.

The language of world-weariness (*Zerrissenheit-Weltschmerz*), wherein spiritual life is rent asunder, is, however, the perfect form of utterance for this entire stage of spiritual culture and development, the formative process of molding self-consciousness (*Bildung*), and expresses the spirit in which it most truly exists. This self-consciousness, which finds befitting the rebellion that repudiates its own repudiation, is *eo ipso* absolute self-identity in absolute weariness, the pure activity of mediating pure self-consciousness with itself. It is the oneness expressed in the identical judgment, where one and the same personality is subject as well as predicate. But this identical judgment is at the same time the infinite judgment; for this personality is absolutely split in two, and subject and predicate are entities utterly indifferent one to the other, which have nothing to do with each other, with no necessary unity, so much so that each has the power of an independent personality of its own. What exists as a self on its own account has for its object its own self-existence, which is object in the sense of an absolute other, and yet at the same time directly in the form of itself—itself in the sense of another, not as if this had another content, for the content is the same self in the form of an absolute opposite, with an existence completely all its own and indifferent.

We have, then, here the spirit of this real world of formative culture, conscious of its own nature as it truly is, and conscious of its ultimate and essential conception.

This type of spiritual life is the absolute and universal inversion of reality and thought, their entire estrangement the one from the other; it is pure culture. What is experienced in this sphere is that neither the concrete realities, political power and wealth, nor their determinate conceptions, good and bad, nor the consciousness of good and bad, the noble and the base consciousness, possesses real truth; it is found that all these aspects are inverted and transmuted the one into the other, and each is the opposite of itself.

The general power, which is the substance, since it gains a spiritual nature peculiarly its own through the principle of individuality accepts the possession of a self of its own merely as a name by which it is described, and, even in being actual power, is really so powerless as to have to sacrifice itself. But this selfless reality given over to another, this self that is turned into a thing, is in fact the return of the reality into itself; it is a being-by-itself that is there for its own sake, the existential form of spirit.

The principles belonging to these realities, the thoughts of good and bad, are similarly transmuted and reversed in this process; what is characterized as good is bad, and vice versa. The consciousness of each of these aspects by itself, the conscious types judged as noble and base—these are rather in their real truth similarly the reverse of what these specific forms should be; nobility is base and repudiated, just as what is repudiated as base turns into the nobleness that characterizes the most highly developed form of free self-consciousness.

Looked at formally, everything is likewise in its external aspects the reverse of what it is internally for itself; and again it is not really and in truth what it is for itself, but something else than it wants to be; being-by-itself on its own account is, strictly speaking, the loss of self, and alienation of self is really self-preservation.

The state of things brought about here, then, is that all aspects execute justice on one another all around, each is just as much in a condition of inherent alienation as it fancies itself in its opposite, and in this way reverses its nature.

Spirit truly objective, however, is just this unity of absolutely separate aspects, and in fact comes into existence as the common ground, the mediating agency, just through the independent reality of these selfless extremes. Its very existence lies in general talk and depreciatory judgment rending and tearing everything, before which all those aspects are broken up that are meant to signify something real and to stand for actual members of the whole, and which at the same time plays with itself this game of self-dissolution. This judging and talking is, therefore, the real truth, which cannot be got over, while it overpowers everything—it is that which in this real world comes to find there its spirit expressed, or gets to be spoken of with spirit and finds said of it what it is.

The honest consciousness takes each aspect as a permanent and essential fact, and is an uncultivated unreflective condition, which does not think and does not know that it is just doing the very inverse. The distraught and world-weary consciousness is, however, aware of inversion; it is, in fact, a condition of absolute inversion: the concept predominates there, brings together into a single unity the thoughts that lie far apart in the case of the honest consciousness, and the language clothing its meaning is, therefore, full of esprit and wit (*Geistreich*).

[c. The vanity of culture.]

The content uttered by spirit and uttered about itself is, then, the inversion and perversion of all conceptions and realities, a universal deception of itself and of others. The shamelessness manifested in stating this deceit is just on that account the greatest truth. This style of speech is the madness of the musician "who piled and mixed up together some thirty airs, Italian, French, tragic, comic, of all sorts and kinds; now, in a deep undertone, he descended to the depths of hell, then, contracting his throat to a high, piping falsetto, he rent the vault of the skies, raving and soothing, haughtily imperious and mockingly jeering by turns." * The placid consciousness that in simple honesty of heart takes the music of the good and true to consist in harmony of sound and uniformity of tone,

---

* Quoted again from Diderot's *Le Neveu de Rameau;* what follows is built around the discussion therein.

i.e., in a melodious chord, regards this style of expression as a "fickle fantasy of wisdom and folly, a mêlée of so much skill and low cunning, composed of ideas as likely to be right as wrong, with as complete a perversion of sentiment, with as much consummate shamefulness in it, as absolute frankness, candor, and truth. It is not able to refrain from bringing out the sound of every note, and running up and down the whole gamut of feeling, from the depths of contempt and repudiation to the highest pitch of admiration and stirring emotion. A vein of the ridiculous will be diffused through the latter, which takes away from their nature"; the former will find in their very candor a strain of atoning reconciliation. will find in their shuddering depths the all-powerful qualities which give spirit a self.

If we consider, by way of contrast to the mode of expression of this confusion (which is nonetheless clear to itself), the language adopted by that simple, placid consciousness of the good and the true, we find that it can only speak in mono-syllables when face to face with the frank and self-conscious eloquence of the mind developed under the influence of cul-ture; for it can say nothing to the latter that the latter does not know and say. If it gets beyond speaking in monosyllables then it says the same thing that the cultivated mind expresses, but in doing so commits, in addition, the folly of imagining that it is saying something new, something different. Its very syllables, "disgraceful," "base," are this folly already, for the other says them of itself.

If the simple consciousness substitutes for this thought with-out spirit the concrete reality of what is excellent, by producing an example of what is excellent, whether in the form of a fictitious case or a true story, and thus shows it to be not an empty name, but an actual fact, then the general reality of wrong action stands in sharp contrast to the entire real world, where that example constitutes merely something quite iso-lated and particular. merely an *espèce*, a sort of thing. And to represent the existence of the good and the noble as an isolated particular anecdote, whether fictitious or true, is the bitterest thing that can be said about it.

Finally, should the simple consciousness require this entire sphere of perversion to be dissolved and broken up, it cannot ask the individual to withdraw out of it, for even Diogenes in his tub (with his pretense of withdrawal) is under the impact of that perversion; and to ask this of the particular individual is to ask him to do precisely what is taken to be bad, viz., to treat the self as particular. But if the demand to withdraw is directed at the general individual, it cannot mean that reason must again give up the culture and development of spiritual conscious life which has been reached, that reason should let the extensive riches of its aspects of development sink back into the naïveté of natural emotion, and revert to and approximate the wild condition of the animal consciousness, which is also called the natural state of innocence. On the contrary, the demand for this dissolution when addressed to the spirit realized in culture can only mean that it must as spirit return out of its confusion into itself, and win for itself a still higher level of conscious life.

In point of fact, however, spirit has already accomplished this result. To be conscious of its own distraught and torn condition and to express itself accordingly—this is to pour scornful laughter on its existence, on the confusion pervading the whole and on itself as well: it is at the same time this whole confusion dying away and yet apprehending itself to be doing so. This self-apprehending vanity of all reality and of every definite principle reflects the real world into itself in a twofold form: in the particular self of consciousness as a particular, and in the pure universality of consciousness, in thought. According to the one aspect, mind thus come to itself has directed its gaze into the world of actual reality, and makes that reality its own purpose and its immediate content: from the other side, its gaze is in part turned solely on itself and against that world of reality, in part turned away from it toward heaven, and its object is the region beyond the world.

In respect of that return into self the vanity of all things is its own peculiar vanity, it is itself vain. It is the self existing by and for itself, a self that knows not only how to sum up and chatter about everything, but with esprit and wit to set forth the contradiction that lies at the heart of the all so solid-seeming reality, and the fixed determinations which judgment sets up; and that contradiction is their real truth. Looked at formally it finds everything alienated from itself, being-by-itself is cut off from being in itself (*Ansich*), what is intended and the purpose are separated from real truth, and from both again existence for another, what is ostensibly put forward is cut off from the proper meaning, the real fact, the true intention.

The self existing by-and-for-itself thus knows exactly how to put each moment in antithesis to every other, knows in short how to express correctly the perversion that dominates all of them: it knows better than each what each is, no matter how it is constituted. Since it apprehends what is substantial from the side of that disunion and contradiction of elements combined within its nature, but not from the side of this unity itself, it understands very well how to pass judgment on this substantial reality, but has lost the capacity of truly grasping it.

This vanity needs at the same time the vanity of all things, in order to get from them consciousness of itself; it therefore itself creates this vanity, and is the soul that supports it. Political power and wealth are the supreme purposes of its strenuous exertion, it is aware that through renunciation and sacrifice it is molded into general shape, that it attains universality, and in possessing universality finds general recognition and acceptance: political power and wealth are the real and actually acknowledged sources of power. But its thus gaining acceptance is itself vain, and just by the fact that it gets the mastery over them it knows them to be not real by themselves, knows rather itself to be the power within them, and them to be vain and empty. That in possessing them it thus itself is able to stand apart from and outside them—this is what it expresses in language that is full of spirit; and to express this is, therefore, its supreme interest, and the true meaning of the whole process. In such utterance this self—in the form of a pure self not associated with or bound by determinations derived either from reality or thought—comes consciously to be a spiritual entity having a truly universal significance and value. It is the condition in which the nature of all relationships is rent asunder, and it is the conscious rending of them all. But only by self-consciousness being roused to revolt does it know its own peculiar torn and shattered condition; and in its knowing this it has in fact risen above that condition. In that state of self-conscious vanity all substantial content comes to have a negative significance, which can no longer be taken in a positive sense. The positive object is merely the pure ego itself; and the consciousness that is rent asunder is inherently and essentially this pure self-identity of self-consciousness returned to itself.

Religion

In the forms of experience hitherto dealt with—which are distinguished broadly as consciousness, self-consciousness, reason, spirit, and religion—the consciousness of absolute being in general has also made its appearance. But that was from the point of view only of consciousness, when it is conscious of the absolute being. Absolute being, however, in its own distinctive nature, the self-consciousness of spirit, has not appeared in those forms.

Even at the plane of consciousness, when it is mere intellect, there is a consciousness of the supersensuous, of the inner aspect of objective existence. But the supersensuous, the eternal, or whatever we care to call it, is devoid of selfhood. It is merely, to begin with, something universal, which is still a long way from being spirit knowing itself as spirit.

Then there was self-consciousness, which came to its final

shape in the "unhappy consciousness"; that was merely the pain
and sorrow of spirit wrestling to become objectified once more,
but not succeeding. The unity of the individual self-consciousness with its unchangeable essence, which is what this stage
arrives at, remains, in consequence, a "beyond."

The immediate existence of reason, which we found arising
out of that state of sorrow, and the special forms which reason
assumes have no religion because the self-consciousness in
these forms knows itself or looks for itself in the direct and
immediate present.

On the other hand, in the world of ethics, we met with a
type of religion, the religion of the nether world. This is
belief in the fearful and unknown darkness of Fate, and in
the Eumenides of the spirit of the departed: the former being
pure negation taking the form of universality, the latter the
same negation but in the form of particularity. The absolute
being is, then, in the latter shape no doubt the self and is present, as there is no other way for the self to be except present.
But the particular self is the particular shadow, which keeps
the universal element, Fate, separated from itself. It is indeed
a shadow, a superseded particular, and so a general self. But
that negative meaning has not yet turned into this latter positive significance, and hence the superseded self still means
specifically this particular being, this unsubstantial reality. Fate,
however, without the self remains the darkness of night without consciousness, which never comes to draw distinctions
within itself, and never attains the clearness of self-knowledge.

This belief in a necessity that produces nothingness, this
belief in the nether world, becomes belief in Heaven, because
the self which has departed must be united with its universal
nature, must unfold what it contains in terms of this universality, and thus become clear to itself. This kingdom of belief,
however, we saw unfold its content merely in the element of
reflective thought (*Denken*), without a true conception; and
we saw it, on that account, perish in its final fate, that in the

religion of enlightenment. Here in this type of religion, the supersensuous beyond, which we found in the intellect, is reinstated again, but in such a way that self-consciousness rests and feels satisfied in the mundane present, not in the "beyond," and thinks of the supersensuous beyond, void and empty, unknowable, and free of all terrors, neither as a self nor as power and might.

In the religion of morality this much is reconstructed, that absolute being has a positive content; but that content is bound up with the negative characteristic of the enlightenment. The content is an objective being, which is at the same time taken back into the self, and remains there enclosed, and is a content with internal distinctions, while its parts are just as immediately negated as they are posited. The final destiny, however, which absorbs this contradictory process, is the self conscious of itself as the controlling necessity or fate (*Schicksal*) of what is essential and actual.

The spirit knowing itself is in religion primarily and immediately its own pure self-consciousness. Those modes of it above considered—"objective spirit," "spirit estranged from itself" and "spirit certain of itself"—together constitute what the spirit is in its condition of consciousness, the state in which, being objectively opposed to its own world, it does not therein apprehend and consciously possess itself. But in conscience it brings itself as well as its objective world as a whole into subjection, as also its idea (*Vorstellung*) and its various specific conceptions (*Begriffe*); it is now self-consciousness at home with itself. Here spirit, represented as an object, has the significance for itself of being universal spirit which contains within itself all that is ultimate and essential and all that is concrete and actual; yet is not in the form of freely subsisting actuality, or of the detached independence of external nature. It has a shape, no doubt, the form of objective being, in that it is the object of its own consciousness; but because this being is put forward in religion with the essential character of being self-consciousness, the form or shape assumed is one perfectly transparent to itself; and the reality which the spirit contains is enclosed in it, or suspended in it, just in the same way as when we speak of "all reality"; it is the universal reality in the sense of a product of thought.

Since, then, in religion, the peculiar characteristic of what is properly consciousness of spirit does not have the form of de-tached and external otherness, the existence of spirit is distinct from its self-consciousness, and its actual reality proper falls outside religion. There is no doubt one spirit in both, but its consciousness does not embrace both together; and religion appears as a part of existence, of acting, and of striving, whose other part is the life within its own actual world. As we now know that spirit in its own world is the same as spirit conscious of itself as spirit, i.e., spirit in the sphere of religion, the perfection of religion consists in the two forms becoming identical with one another; not merely in its reality being grasped and embraced by religion, but conversely; it, as spirit conscious of itself, becomes actual to itself, and real object of its own consciousness. . . .

While, therefore, religion is the completion of the life of spirit, its final and complete expression, into which, as being their ground, its individual phases, consciousness, self-consciousness, reason, and spirit, return and have returned, they, at the same time, together constitute the objectively existing realization of spirit in its totality; as such spirit is real only as the moving process of these aspects which it possesses, a process of distinguishing them and returning back into itself. In the process of these general phases is contained the development of religion generally. Since, however, each of these attributes was set forth and presented, not only in the way it in general determines itself, but as it is in and for itself, i.e., as, within its own being, running its course as a distinct whole, there has thus been presented not merely the development of religion generally; those independently complete processes pursued by the individual phases and stages of spirit contain at the same time the determinate forms of religion itself. Spirit in its entirety, spirit in religion, is once more the process from its immediacy to the attainment of a knowledge of what it implicitly or immediately is; it is the process of attaining the state where the shape and form, in which it appears as an object for its own consciousness, will be perfectly identical with and adequate to its essential nature, and where it will behold itself as it is.

In this development of religion, then, spirit itself assumes definite forms, which constitute the distinctions involved in this process; and at the same time a determinate or specific form of religion has likewise an actual spirit of a specific character. Thus, if consciousness, self-consciousness, reason, and spirit belong to self-knowing spirit in general, in a similar way the specific patterns which self-knowing spirit assumes appropriate and adopt the distinctive forms which were specially developed in the case of each of the stages—consciousness, self-consciousness, reason, and spirit. The determinate pattern, assumed in a given case by religion, appropriates, from among the forms belonging to each of its moments, the one adapted to it, and makes this its actual spirit. This one determinate attitude of religion pervades and permeates all aspects of its actual existence, and stamps them with this common feature.

In this way the arrangement now assumed by the forms and patterns which have thus far appeared is different from the way they appeared in their own order. On this point we may note shortly at the outset what is of chief importance. In the series we considered, each phase, exhaustively elaborating its entire content, evolved and formed itself into a single whole within its own peculiar principle. And knowledge was the inner depth, or the spirit, wherein the elements, having no subsistence of their own, possessed their substance. This substance, however, has now at length made its appearance; it is the deep life of spirit certain of itself; it does not allow the principle belonging to each individual form to get isolated, and become a whole within itself: rather it collects all these aspects into its own content, keeps them together, and advances within this total wealth of its concrete actual spirit; while all its particular aspects take into themselves and receive together in common the like determinate character of the whole. This spirit which is certain of itself, and the process it goes through is the true reality, the independent self-subsistence, which belongs to each individuality. . . .

The distinction made between the actual spirit and the spirit which knows itself as spirit, or between itself as consciousness and as self-consciousness, is suspended (and preserved) in the spirit which knows itself in its real truth. Its consciousness and its self-consciousness are harmonized. But at first, merely the conception of religion is established. In this the essential element is self-consciousness, which is conscious of being all truth, and which contains all reality within that truth. This self-consciousness, being consciousness (and so aware of an object), has itself for its object. . . .

The configuration which the spirit adopts when it is the object of its own consciousness remains filled with the certainty of spirit, and this self-certainty constitutes its substance. Through this content, the degrading of the object to being merely an object, to the form of something that negates self-consciousness, disappears. The immediate unity of spirit with itself is the fundamental basis, or the pure consciousness, inside which consciousness breaks up into its constituent elements. In this way, enclosed within its pure self-consciousness, spirit does not exist in religion as the creator of nature in general; rather what it produces in the course of this process are its forms and patterns as spirits, which together constitute all that it can reveal when it is completely manifested. And this process itself is the development of its perfect and complete actual reality through the individual aspects thereof, *i.e.*, through its imperfect modes of realization.

The first realization (*Wirklichkeit*) of the spirit is the conception of religion itself, religion as immediate and thus natural religion. Here spirit knows itself as its object in a "natural" or immediate shape. The second realization, is, however, necessarily that of knowing itself in the form of superseded natural existence. This is the religion of art or productive activity. For the configuration it adopts is raised to the form of the self through the productive activity of consciousness, by which this consciousness beholds in its object its own action, i.e., sees the self. The third realization, finally, suspends the one-sidedness of the first two: the self is as much an immediate self as the immediacy is a self. If spirit in the first phase is in the form of consciousness, and in the second in that of self-consciousness, it is in the third in the form of the unity of both; it has then the form of what is completely self-contained (*An- und Fuersichseins*); and since it is thus presented as it is in and for itself, this is the sphere of Revealed Religion. . . .

Natural Religion

Spirit knowing spirit is consciousness of itself; and is to itself in the form of an object. . . . It is by the determinate character of this form, in which spirit knows itself, that one religion is distinguished from another. But we have at the same time to note that the systematic exposition of this knowledge about itself, in terms of this particular specific character, does not as a fact exhaust the whole meaning of a given actual religion. The series of different religions, which will come before us, just as much sets forth again merely the different aspects of a single religion, and indeed of every particular religion, and the ideas, the conscious processes, which seem to mark off one concrete religion from another, make their appearance in each of them as well. All the same the diversity must also be seen as a diversity of religion. For while spirit lives in the distinction of its consciousness and its self-consciousness, the process it goes through finds its goal in the suspension of this fundamental distinction and in giving the form of self-consciousness to the given pattern which is object of consciousness. . . .

The truth of the faith in a given determination of the religious spirit shows itself in this, that the actual spirit is constituted after the same manner as the form in which spirit beholds itself in religion; thus, e.g., the incarnation of God, which is found in Eastern religion, has no truth, because the concrete actual spirit of this religion is without the reconciliation which this principle implies.

This is not the place to return from the totality of specific determinations back to the particular determination, and show in what form the plenitude of all the others is contained within it and within its particular form of religion. The higher form, when put back under a lower, is deprived of its significance for self-conscious spirit belongs to spirit merely in a superficial way, and is for it at the level of an idea. The higher form has to be considered in its own peculiar religion, and is certified and approved by its actual spirit.

God as Light

[The Parsee Religion]

Spirit, as the absolute Being, which is self-consciousness, or the self-conscious absolute Being, which is all truth and knows all reality as itself, is, to begin with, merely its conception in contrast to the reality which it acquires in the process of its conscious activity. And this conception is, as contrasted with the clear daylight of that explicit development, the darkness and night of its inner life; in contrast to the existence of its various moments as independent configurations, this conception is the creative secret of its birth. This secret has its revelation within itself; for existence has its necessary place in this conception, because this conception is spirit knowing itself, and thus possesses in its own nature the moment of being consciousness and of presenting itself objectively. We have here the pure ego, which, in externalizing itself, in seeing itself as a universal object, has the certainty of its self; in other words, this object is, for the ego, the fusion of all thought and all reality.

When the first and immediate cleavage is made within the self-knowing absolute spirit, its form assumes that character which belongs to immediate consciousness or to sense-certainty. It beholds itself in the form of being; but not being in the sense of what is without spirit, containing only the contingent qualities of sensation, the kind of being that belongs solely to sense-certainty. Its being is filled with the content of spirit. It also includes within it the form which we found in the case of immediate self-consciousness, the form of lord and master with reference to the self-consciousness of spirit which retreats from its object.

This existence, having as its content the conception of spirit, is, then, the mode of spirit in relation simply to itself—the form of having no special form at all. In virtue of this characteristic, this mode is the pure all-containing, all-suffusing light as it rises, which preserves itself in its formless indeterminate substantiality. Its counterpart, its otherness, is the equally simple negative: darkness. The processes of its own alienation, its creations in the unresisting element of its counterpart, are bursts of light. At the same time in their ultimate simplicity they are its way of becoming something for itself, its return from its objective existence, streams of fire consuming all configurations. The distinction, which it gives itself, no doubt thrives abundantly on the substance of existence, and grows into and assumes the diverse forms of nature. But the essential simplicity of its thought rambles and roves about inconstant and inconsistent, enlarges its bounds to measureless extent, and its beauty heightened to splendor is lost in its sublimity.

The content, which this state of mere being involves, its perceptive activity, is, therefore, an unreal byplay on this substance which merely rises, without descending into itself to become subject and secure firmly its distinctions through the self. Its determinations are merely attributes, which do not succeed in attaining independence; they remain merely names of the One, called by many names. This One is clothed with the manifold powers of existence and with the shapes of reality, as with a soulless, selfless ornament; they are merely messengers of its mighty power, claiming no will of their own, visions of its glory, voices in its praise.

This revel of heaving life must, however, assume the character of distinctive self-existence, and give enduring subsistence to its fleeting forms. Immediate being, in which it places itself over against its own consciousness, is itself the negative destructive agency which dissolves its distinctions. It is thus in truth the Self; and spirit therefore passes on to know itself in the form of self. Pure light scatters its simplicity as an infinity of separate forms, and presents itself as an offering to self-existence, that the individual may be sustained in its substance.

Plants and Animals as Objects of Religion

[Primarily the Religions of India]

Self-conscious spirit, passing away from abstract, formless essence and going into itself, or, in other words, having raised its immediacy to the level of the self, makes its simple unity assume the character of a manifold of entities existing by themselves; this is the religion of spiritual sense-perception. Here spirit breaks up into an innumerable plurality of weaker and stronger, richer and poorer spirits. This Pantheism, which, to begin with, consists in the quiescent stability of these spiritual atoms, passes into a process of active internal hostility. The innocence, which characterizes the flower and plant religions, and which is merely the selfless idea of Self, gives way to the seriousness of struggling, warring life, to the guilt of animal religions; the quiescence and impotence of merely contemplative individuality pass into destructive being-by-itself.

It is of no avail to have removed the lifelessness of abstraction from the things of perception, and to have raised them to the level of realities of spiritual perception: the animation of this spiritual kingdom has death at the heart of it, owing to the fact of determinateness and the inherent negative quality, which invades and trenches upon their innocent and harmless indifference to one another. Owing to this determinateness and negative quality, the dispersion of passive plant-forms into manifold entities becomes a hostile process, in which the hatred stirred up by their independent being rages and consumes.

The actual self-consciousness at work in this dispersed and disintegrated spirit takes the form of a multitude of individualized mutually antipathetic folk-spirits, who fight and hate each other to the death, and consciously accept certain specific forms of animals as their essential reality, their god: for they are nothing else than spirits of animals, their animal life separate and cut off from one another, and with no universality consciously present in them.

The characteristic of purely negative independent being, however, consumes itself in this active hatred toward one another; and through this process, involved in its very principle, spirit enters into another shape. Independent being-by-itself suspended and abolished is the form of the object, a form which is produced by the self, i.e., the self that becomes a "thing." The agent at work, therefore, retains the upper hand over these animal spirits merely tearing each other to pieces; and his action is not merely negative, but composed and creative. The consciousness of spirit is, thus, now the process which is above and beyond the immediate inherent (universal) nature; it suspends as well the abstract being-by-itself in isolation. Since the implicit inherent nature is relegated, through opposition, to the level of a specific character, it is no longer the proper form of the absolute spirit, but a reality which its consciousness finds confronting itself as an ordinary existence, and therefore suspends; at the same time this consciousness is not merely this negative being-by-itself which suspends but it produces its own objective idea of itself—being-by-itself put forth in the form of an object. This production is, all the same, not yet perfect; it is a conditioned activity, the forming of a given material.

The Artificer

[Egyptian Religions]

Spirit, then, here takes the form of the artificer, and its action, when producing itself as object, but without having as yet understood the thought of itself, is an instinctive kind of working, like bees building their cells.

The first form, because immediate, is the abstract one of the intellect and the work accomplished is not yet in itself filled with the spirit. The crystals of Pyramids and Obelisks, simple combinations of straight lines with even surfaces and equal relations of parts in which incommensurability of curvature is set aside—these are the works produced in strict geometrical form by this artificer. Owing to the purely abstract intelligible nature of the form, it is not in itself the true significance of the form; it is not the spiritual self. Thus, either the works produced only receive spirit into them as an alien, departed spirit, one that has forsaken its living suffusion and permeation with reality, and, being itself dead, enters into these lifeless crystals; or they take up an external relation to spirit as something which is itself external and not there as spirit, they are related to it as to the rising light, which throws its significance on them.

The separation of elements from which spirit as artificer starts, the separation of the implicit essential nature, which becomes the material it works upon, and independent being-by-itself, which is the aspect of self-consciousness at work—this division has become objective in the result achieved. Its further endeavor has to be directed to suspending this separation of soul and body; it must strive to clothe and give embodied shape to soul in itself, and endow the body with soul. The two aspects, since they are brought closer to one another, bear toward each other, in this condition, the character of ideally imagined spirit and of enveloping shell. Spirit's oneness with itself contains this opposition of individuality and universality. Since the aspects of a work produced come nearer to each other by performance of it, it also results therefrom that the work gets nearer to the self-consciousness performing it, and that the latter attains in the work knowledge of itself as it truly is. In this way, however, the work merely constitutes, to begin with, the abstract side of the activity of spirit, which does not yet perceive the content of this activity within itself but in its work, which is a "thing." The artificer as such, spirit in its entirety, has not yet appeared; the artificer is still the inner, hidden essence, which is present as a whole, but broken up into active self-consciousness and the object it has produced.

The surrounding habitation, external reality, which to begin with is raised merely to the abstract form of the intellect, is worked up by the artificer and made into a more animated form. The artificer employs plant life for this purpose, which is no longer sacred, as was previously the case in inactive impotent pantheism; rather, the artificer, who holds himself to be the self-existent reality, takes that plant life as something to be used and degrades it to an external aspect, to the level of an ornament. But it is not turned to use without some alteration: for the worker producing the self-conscious form destroys at the same time the transitoriness, inherently characteristic of the immediate existence of this life, and brings its organic forms nearer to the more exact and more universal forms of thought. The organic form, which, left to itself, grows and thrives in particularity, being on its side subjugated by the form of thought, elevates in turn these straight-lined and level figures into more animated roundedness, a blending which becomes the root of free architecture.

This dwelling [the aspect of the universal element or inorganic nature of the spirit] also includes within it now a form of individuality, which brings nearer to actuality the spirit that was formerly separated from existence and was external or internal thereto, and thus makes the work to accord more with active self-consciousness. The worker lays hold, first of all, on the form of being-by-itself in general, on the forms of animal life. That he is no longer directly aware of himself in animal life, he shows by the fact that in reference to this he constitutes himself the productive force, and knows himself in it as being his own work, whereby the productive force at the same time is one which is superseded and becomes the hieroglyphic symbol of another meaning, the hieroglyph of a thought. Hence also this force is no longer solely and entirely used by the worker, but becomes blended with the figure embodying thought, with the human form. Still, the work lacks the form and existence where the self as self appears: it also fails to express in its very nature that it includes within itself an inner meaning; it lacks language, the element in which the sense and meaning contained are actually present. The work done, therefore, even when quite purified of the animal aspect, and bearing the form and shape of self-consciousness alone, is still the silent soundless form, which needs the rays of the rising sun in order to have a sound which, when produced by light, is even then merely noise and not speech, shows merely an outer self, not the inner self.

Contrasted with this outer self of the figure, stands the other form, which indicates that it has in it an inner being. Nature, turning back into its essential being, degrades its multiplicity of life, ever individualizing itself and confounding itself in its own process, to the level of an external encasing shell, which is the covering for the inner being. And still this inner being is primarily mere darkness, the unmoved, the black formless stone.

Both representations contain inwardness and mere existence, the two aspects of spirit: and both kinds of manifestation contain both aspects at once in a relation of opposition, the self both as something inward and as something outward. Both have to be united. The soul of the statue in human form does not yet come out of the inner being, is not yet speech, objective existence of the self which is inherently internal. And the inner being of multiform existence is still without voice or sound, still draws no distinctions within itself, and is still separated from its outer being, to which all distinctions belong. The artificer, therefore, combines both by blending the forms of nature and self-consciousness; and these ambiguous beings, a riddle to themselves, the conscious struggling with what has no consciousness, the simple inner with the multiform outer, the darkness of thought mated with clearness of expression, these burst into the language of a wisdom that is darkly deep and difficult to understand.

With the production of this work, the instinctive method of working ceases, which, in contrast to self-consciousness, produced a work devoid of consciousness, for here the activity of the artificer, which constitutes self-consciousness, comes face to face with an inner being equally self-conscious and giving itself expression. He has therein raised himself by his work up to the point where his conscious life breaks asunder, where spirit greets spirit. In this unity of self-conscious spirit with itself, so far as it is aware of being embodiment and object of its own consciousness, its blending and mingling with the unconscious condition of immediate forms of nature become purified. These monsters in form and shape, word and deed, are resolved and dissolved into a shape which is spiritual—an outer which has entered into itself, an inner which expresses itself out of itself and in itself, they pass into thought, which brings forth itself, preserves the shape and form suited to thought, and is transparent existence. The spirit is an artist.

Religion in the Form of Art

[Greek Religion]*

Spirit has raised the shape in which it is object for its own consciousness into the form of consciousness itself; and spirit sets such a form before itself. The artificer has given up the external synthesizing activity, that blending of the heterogeneous forms of thought and nature. When the configuration has gained the form of self-conscious activity, the artificer has become a spiritual workman.

If we next ask, what the actual spirit is, which finds in the religion of art the consciousness of its absolute, it turns out that this is the ethical or objective spirit. This spirit is not merely the general substance of all individuals; but when this substance is said to have, as an objective fact for actual consciousness, the form of consciousness, this amounts to saying that the substance, which is individualized, is known by the individuals within it as their proper essence and their own achievement. It is for them neither the Light of the World, in whose unity the being-by-itself of self-consciousness is contained only negatively, only transitorily, and beholds the lord and master of its reality; nor is it the restless waste and destruction of hostile nations; nor their subjection to "castes," which together constitute the semblance of organization of a completed whole, where, however, the general freedom of the individuals is wanting. Rather this spirit is that of a free nation, in which the ethical order constitutes the common substance

* This section is abbreviated, because of duplications with the section on Greece in the *Philosophy of History*, above, p. 53 ff. See also the *Aesthetics*, above, p. 377.

of all, whose reality and existence each and everyone knows to be his own will and his own deed.

The religion of the ethical spirit, however, raises it above its actual realization, and is the return from its objectivity into pure knowledge of itself. Since an ethically constituted nation lives in direct unity with its own substance, and does not contain the principle of pure individualism of self-consciousness, the religion characteristic of its sphere first appears in complete form apart from its stable security. . . .

The complete fulfillment of the ethical life in free self-consciousness and the destiny (*Schicksal*) of the ethical world are therefore found when individuality has entered into itself; the condition is one of absolute carelessness on the part of the ethical spirit; it has dissipated and resolved into itself all the firmly established distinctions constituting its own stability, and the separate components of its own articulated organization, and, being perfectly sure of itself, has attained to boundless cheerfulness of heart and the freest enjoyment of itself. This simple certainty of spirit within itself suffers from equivocation; it is quiet stability and solid truth, as well as absolute unrest, and the disappearance of the ethical order. It turns, however, into the latter; for the truth of the ethical spirit lies primarily just in this substantial objectivity and trust, in which the self does not think of itself as a free individual, and where the self, therefore, in this inner subjectivity of becoming a free self, perishes. Since then its trust is broken, and the substance of the nation cracked, the spirit, which was the connecting medium of the unstable extremes, has now come forward as an extreme, that of self-consciousness taking itself to be essential and ultimate. This is the spirit certain within itself, which mourns over the loss of its world, and now produces out of the abstraction of self its own essential being, raised above actual reality.

At such an epoch art in absolute form appears. . . .

The Abstract Work of Art

The first work of art is, because immediate, abstract and particular. On its own side it has to move away from this immediate and objective phase toward self-consciousness, while, on the other side, the latter for itself endeavors in the ritual to do away with the distinction, although it at first gave itself this distinction against its own spirit, and by so doing to produce a work of art inherently endowed with life.

1. [The Statues of the Gods.]

The first way in which the artistic spirit keeps its form and active consciousness, as far as possible removed from each other, is immediate in character; the form assumed is there as a "thing" in general. It breaks up into the distinction of particularity, which contains the form of the self, and universality, which represents the inorganic elements in reference to the form adopted, and is its environment and habitation. This form obtains its pure form, the form belonging to spirit, by the whole being raised into the sphere of the pure conception. It is not the crystal, belonging as we saw to the level of the intellect, a form which housed and covered a lifeless element, or is shone upon externally by a soul. Nor, again, is it that commingling of the forms of nature and thought, which first arose in connection with plants, thought's activity here being still an imitation. Rather the conception strips off the remnants of root, branches and leaves, still clinging to the forms, purifies the forms and makes them into figures in which the crystal's straight lines and surfaces are raised into incommensurable relations, so that the animation of the organic is taken up into the abstract form of the intellect, and at the same time, its essential nature—incommensurability—is preserved for the mind.

The indwelling god, however, is the black stone extracted

from the animal encasement, and suffused with the light of consciousness. The human form strips off the animal character with which it was mixed up. The animal form is for the god merely an accidental vestment; the animal appears alongside its true form, and has no longer a value on its own account, but has sunk into being a significant sign of something else, has become a mere symbol. By that very fact, the form assumed by the god in itself casts off even the need for the natural conditions of animal existence, and hints at the internal arrangements of organic life melted down into the surface of the form, and pertaining only to this surface.

The essence of the god, however, is the unity of the general existence here-and-now of nature and of the self-conscious spirit, which in its actuality appears confronting the former. At the same time, being in the first instance a particular form, its existence here-and-now is one of the elements of nature, just as its self-conscious actuality is a particular national spirit. But the former is, in this unity, that element reflected back into spirit, nature made transparent by thoughts and united with self-conscious life. The form of the gods retains, therefore, within it its natural element as something suspended, as a shadowy, obscure memory. The utter chaos and confused struggle amongst the elements existing free and detached from each other, the non-ethical disordered realm of Titans, is vanquished and banished to the outskirts of a reality which has become clear, to the misty boundaries of a world which finds itself in the sphere of the spirit and is at peace. These ancient gods, first-born children of the union of Light with Darkness, Heaven, Earth, Ocean, Sun, Earth's aimless typhonic Fire, and so on, are supplanted by figures which do but darkly recall those earlier titans, and which are no longer things of nature, but spirits clarified by the ethical life of self-conscious nations.

This simple form has thus destroyed within itself the restless endless isolation, and has gathered it up into quiet individuality. This isolation (*Vereingelung*) we find both in the life of nature, which is necessary only as a universal essence, but is contingent in its actual existence and process; and also in the life of a nation, which, though scattered and broken into particular spheres of action and into individual centers of self-consciousness, has an existence rich in action and meaning. Hence the condition of unrest stands contrasted with this simple form; confronting quiescent individuality, the essential reality, stands self-consciousness, which, being its source and origin, has nothing left over for itself except to be pure activity. What belongs to the substance, the artist gave entirely along with his work; to himself, however, as a specific individuality there belongs in his work no actual reality. He could only have conferred completeness on it by relinquishing his particular nature, divesting himself of his own being, and rising to the abstraction of pure action. . . .

The artist finds out, then, in his work, that he did not produce a reality like himself. No doubt there comes back to him from his work a consciousness in the sense that an admiring multitude honors it as the spirit, which is their own true nature. But this way of animating or spiritualizing his work, since it renders him his self-consciousness merely in the form of admiration, is rather a confession that the work is not animated in the same manner as the artist. Since the work comes back to him in the form of gladness in general, he does not find in it the pain of his self-discipline and the pain of production, nor the exertion and strain of his own toil. People may, moreover, judge the work, or bring him offerings and gifts, or endue it with their consciousness in whatever way they like; if they with their knowledge set themselves over it, he knows how much more his act is than what they understand and say; if they put themselves beneath it, and recognize in it their own dominating essential reality, he knows himself as the master of this.

2. [The Hymnos.]

The work of art hence requires another element for its existence; God requires another way of going forth than this, in which, out of the depths of his creative night, he drops into the opposite, into externality, to the character of a "thing" with no self-consciousness. This higher element is that of language—a way of existing which is directly self-conscious existence. When individual self-consciousness exists in that way, it is at the same time directly a form of universal communication; complete isolation of independent self-existent selves is at once fluent continuity and universally communicated unity of the many selves; it is the soul existing as soul. The god, then, who takes language as his medium of embodiment, fosters the work of art inherently spiritualized, endowed with a soul, a work which directly in its existence contains the pure activity which was apart from and in contrast to the god when existing as a "thing." In other words, self-consciousness, when its essential being becomes objective, remains in direct relation with itself. It is, when thus at home with itself in its essential nature, pure thought or devotion, whose inwardness achieves at the same time expression in the hymn. The hymn retains the individuality of self-consciousness. . . . Devotion, kindled in everyone, is a spiritual stream which in all the manifold self-conscious units is conscious of itself as one and the same function in all alike and a simple state of being. Spirit, being this universal self-consciousness of everyone, holds in a single unity its pure inwardness as well as its objective existence for others and the independent self-existence of the individual units.

This kind of language is distinct from another one through which God speaks, which is not that of universal self-consciousness. The oracle, both in the case of the god of the religions of art as well as of the preceding religions, is the necessary and the first form of divine utterance. For its very principle implies that God is at once the essence of nature and of spirit and hence has not merely natural but spiritual existence as well. In so far as this moment is implied primarily in its principle and is not yet realized in religion, the language used is, for the religious self-consciousness, the speech of an alien and external self-consciousness. . . .

As the universal truth, revealed by the "Light" of the world, is here returned into what is within or what is beneath, and has thus got rid of the form of contingent appearance; so, too, on the other hand, in the religion of art, because God's figure has taken on consciousness and hence particularity in general, the peculiar utterance of God, who is the spirit of an ethically constituted nation, is the oracle, which knows its special circumstances and situation, and announces what is serviceable to its interests. Reflective thought, however, satisfied itself as to the universal truths enunciated, because these are known as the essential implicit reality of the nation's life; and the utterance of them is thus for such reflection no longer a strange and alien speech, but is its very own. Just as that wise man of old [Socrates] searched in his own thought for what was worthy and good, but left it to his "Diamon" to find out and decide the petty contingent content of what he wanted to know, whether it was good for him to keep company with this or that person, or good for one of his friends to go on a journey, and suchlike unimportant things; in the same way the general consciousness derives knowledge about the contingent from birds, or trees, or fermenting earth, the steam from which deprives the self-conscious mind of its powers of discrimination. For what is accidental is something undiscerned, undiscriminated, and extraneous; and hence the ethical consciousness lets itself, as if by a throw of the dice, settle the matter in a manner that is similarly undiscriminating and extraneous.

The true self-conscious existence, which spirit receives in the form of speech, which is not the utterance of extraneous and so accidental, i.e., not universal, self-consciousness, is the work of art which we met with before. It stands in contrast to the statue, which has the character of a "thing." As the statue is existence in a state of rest, the other is existence in a state of transience. In the case of the former, objectivity is set free and dispenses with the immediate presence of the self proper; in the latter, on the other hand, objectivity is too much bound up with the self, attains insufficiently to definite embodiment, and is, like time, no longer there just as soon as it is there.

The religious cult constitutes the process of the two sides—a process in which the divine embodiment in motion within the pure feeling-element of self-consciousness and its embodiment at rest in the element of thinghood, reciprocally abandon the different character each possesses, and the unity, which is the underlying principle of their being, becomes an existing fact. Here in the cult, the self gives itself a consciousness of the Divine Being descending from its remoteness into it, and this Divine Being, which was formerly the unreal and merely objective, thereby receives the proper actuality of self-conciousness.

This principle of the cult is essentially contained and present already in the flow of the melody of the hymn. These hymns of devotion are the way the self obtains immediate pure satisfaction through and within itself. It is the soul purified, which, in the purity it thus attains, is immediately and only absolute being, and is one with absolute being. The soul, because of its abstract character, is not consciousness distinguishing its object from itself, and is thus merely the night of its existence and the place prepared for its form. The abstract cult, therefore, raises the self into being this pure divine element. The soul brings about the attainment of this purity in a conscious way. Still it is not yet the self, which has descended to the depths of its being, and knows itself as evil. It is something that merely is, a soul, which cleanses its exterior with the washing of water, and robes it in white, while its

innermost traverses the path set before itself of labor, punishment, and reward, the way of spiritual discipline, of altogether
relinquishing its particularity—the road by which it reaches
the mansions and the fellowship of the blest.

This ceremonial cult is, in its first form, merely in secret,
i.e., is merely a performance accomplished subjectively in
idea, and unrealized. It has to become a real act, for an unreal
act is a contradiction in terms. Consciousness proper, thereby,
rises to the level of its pure self-consciousness. The essential
being has in it the significance of a free object; through the
actual cult this object turns back to the self; and in so far as,
in pure consciousness, it has the significance of absolute being
dwelling in its purity beyond actual reality, this being descends,
through this mediating process of the cult, from its universality
into individual form, and thus combines and unites with actual
reality.

The way the two sides make their appearance in the act is
of such a character that the self-conscious aspect, so far as it
is actual consciousness, finds the absolute being manifesting
itself as actual nature. On the one hand, nature belongs to
self-consciousness as its possession and property, and stands
for what has no existence *per se*. On the other hand, nature
is its proper immediate reality and particularity, which is
equally regarded as not truly real and essential, and is abrogated. At the same time, that external nature has the opposite
significance for its pure consciousness—viz., the significance of
being the inherently real, for which the self sacrifices its own
(relative) unreality, just as, conversely, the self sacrifices the
unessential aspect of nature to itself. The act is thereby a
spiritual movement, because it is this double-sided process of
canceling the abstraction of absolute being (in the way devotion determines the object), and making it something concrete
and actual, and, on the other hand, of canceling the actual
(in the way the agent determines the object and the self acting), and raising it into universality.

The practice of religious cult begins, therefore, with the pure and simple "offering up" or "surrender" of a possession, which the owner apparently considers quite useless for himself and spills on the ground or lets rise up in smoke. By so doing he renounces before the ultimate being of his pure consciousness all possession and right of property and enjoyment thereof; renounces personality and the reversion of his action to his self; and instead, reflects the act into the universal, into the absolute being rather than into himself. Conversely, however, the objective ultimate being too is annihilated in that very process. The animal offered up is the symbol of a god; the fruits consumed are the actual living Ceres and Bacchus. In the former die the powers of the upper law (the Olympians) which has blood and actual life, in the latter the powers of the lower law (the Furies) which possesses in bloodless form secret and crafty power.

The sacrifice of the divine substance, so far as it is active, belongs to the side of self-consciousness. That this concrete act may be possible, the absolute being must have from the start implicitly sacrificed itself. This it has done in the fact that it has given itself definite existence and made itself an individual animal and fruit of the earth. The self actively sacrificing demonstrates in actual existence, and sets before its own consciousness, this already implicitly completed self-renunciation on the part of absolute being; and replaces that immediate reality, which absolute being has, by the higher, viz., that of the self making the sacrifice. For the unity which has arisen, and which is the outcome of transcending the particularity and separation of the two sides, is not merely negative destructive fate, but has a positive significance. It is merely for the abstract being of the netherworld that the sacrifice offered to it is wholly surrendered and devoted; and, in consequence, it is only for that being that the reflection of personal possession and individual self-existence back into the Universal is marked distinct from the self as such. At the same time, however, this is only a trifling part; and the other act of sacrifice is merely the destruction of what cannot be used, and is really the preparation of the offered substance for a meal, the feast that cheats the act out of its negative significance. The person making the offering at that first sacrifice reserves the greatest share for his own enjoyment; and reserves from the latter sacrifice what is useful for the same purpose. This enjoyment is the negative power which supersedes the absolute being as well as the unity; and this enjoyment is, at the same time, the positive actual reality in which the objective existence of absolute being is transmuted into self-conscious existence, and the self has consciousness of its unity with its absolute.

This cult, for the rest, is indeed an actual act, although its meaning lies for the most part only in devotion. What pertains to devotion is not objectively produced, just as the result when confined to the feeling of enjoyment is robbed of its external existence. The cult, therefore, goes further, and replaces this defect, in the first instance by giving its devotion an objective subsistence, since the cult is the common task—or the individual task for each and all to do—which produces for the honor and glory of God a house for Him to dwell in and adornment for His presence. By so doing the external objectivity of statuary is partly canceled; for by thus dedicating his gifts and his labors the worker makes God well disposed toward him and looks on his self as attached and appertaining to God. Furthermore, this course of action is not the individual labor of the artist; this particularity is dissolved in universality. But it is not only the honor of God which is brought about, and the blessing of His countenance and favor is not only shed in idea and imagination on the worker; the work has also a meaning the reverse of the first which was that of self-renunciation and of honor done to what is alien and external. The halls and dwellings of God are for the use of man, the treasures preserved there are in time of need his own; the honor which God enjoys in his decorative adornment, is the honor and glory of a refined artistic and high-spirited nation. At the festival season, the people adorn their own dwellings, their own garments, and their establishments too with the furnishings of elegance and grace. In this manner they receive a return for their gifts from a responsive and grateful God; and receive the proofs of His favor—wherewith the nation became bound to the God because of the work done for Him—not as a hope and a deferred realization but rather, in testifying to His honor and in presenting gifts, the nation finds directly and at once the enjoyment of its own wealth and adornment.

The Living Work of Art

That nation which approaches its god in the cult of the religion of art is an ethically constituted nation, knowing its state and the acts of the state to be the will and achievement of its own activity. This universal spirit, confronting the self-conscious nation, is consequently not the "Light" of the world, which, being selfless, does not contain the certainty of the individual selves, but is only their universal ultimate being and the dominating imperious power, wherein they disappear. The religious cult of this simple unembodied ultimate being gives back, therefore, to its votaries in the main merely this: that they are the nation of their god. It secures for them merely their stable subsistence, and their bare substance as a whole; it does not secure for them their actual self; this is indeed rejected. For they revere their god as the empty profound, not as spirit. The cult of the religion of art, on the other hand, dispenses with that abstract simplicity of the absolute being, and therefore with its "profundity." But that being, which is directly at one with the self, is inherently spirit and comprehending truth, although not yet known explicitly, in other words it does not know the "depths" of its nature. Because this absolute, then, implies the self, consciousness finds itself at home with it when it appears; and, in the cult, this consciousness receives not merely the general title to its own subsistence, but also its self-conscious existence within it: just as, conversely, in a despised and outcast nation whose mere substance is acknowledged, the absolute being has not a selfless reality, but the nation whose self is acknowledged as living in its substance.

From the ceremonial cult, then, self-consciousness that is at peace and satisfied in its ultimate being turns away, as also does the god that has entered into self-consciousness as into its place of habitation. This place is, by itself, the night of mere "substance," or its pure individuality; but no longer the strained and striving individuality of the artist, which has not yet reconciled itself with its essential being that gradually becomes objective; it is substance satisfied, having its "pathos" within it and being in want of nothing, because it comes back from mere beholding, from objectivity which is suspended and superseded. . . .

What has thus, through the cult, been revealed to self-conscious spirit within itself, is simple absolute being; and this has been revealed partly as the movement of stepping out of its night of concealment into the level of consciousness, to be there its silently nurturing substance; partly as the process of losing itself again in nether darkness, in the self, and of lingering above merely with the silent yearning of motherhood. The more conspicuous moving impulse, however, is the many-named "Light" of the East and its tumult of heaving life, which, having likewise abandoned its abstract state of being, has first embodied itself in the objective existence of the fruits of the earth, and then, surrendering itself to self-consciousness, attained there to its proper realization; and now it curvets and careers about in the guise of a crowd of excited, fervid women, the unrestrained revel of nature in self-conscious form.

However, it is still only absolute spirit in the sense of this simple abstract being, not as spirit as such, that is discovered to consciousness: i.e., it is merely immediate spirit, the spirit of nature. Its self-conscious life is therefore merely the mystery of the bread and the wine, of Ceres and Bacchus, not of the other, the strictly higher, gods of Olympus, whose individuality includes, as an essential aspect, self-consciousness as such. Spirit has not yet as a self-conscious spirit offered itself up to it, and the mystery of bread and wine is not yet the mystery of flesh and blood.

This unstable revel of the gods must come to rest as an object, and the enthusiasm, which did not reach consciousness, must produce a work which confronts it as the statue stands over against the enthusiasm of the artist in the previous case— a work too that is equally complete and finished, yet not as an inherently lifeless but as a living self. Such a cult is the festival which man makes in his own honor, though not imparting to a cult of that kind the significance of the absolute being; for it is the ultimate being that is first revealed to him, not yet spirit—not as a being that essentially takes on human form, namely Jesus Christ. But this cult provides the basis for this revelation, and lays out its moments individually and separately. Thus we here get the abstract moment of the living embodiment of ultimate being, just as formerly we had the unity of both in the state of unconstrained emotional fervency. In the place of the statue man thus puts himself as the form elaborated and molded for perfectly free movement, just as the statue is the perfectly free state of quiescence. If every individual knows how to play the part at least of a torch-bearer, one of them comes prominently forward who is the very embodiment of the movement, the smooth elaboration, the fluent energy and force of all the members. He is a lively and living work of art, which matches strength with its beauty; and to him is given, as a reward for his force and energy, the adornment, with which the statue was decorated, and the honor of being, amongst his own nation, instead of a god in stone, the highest bodily representation of what the essential being of the nation is. . . .

The perfect element in which the inwardness is as external as the externality is inward is once again language. But it is neither the language of the oracle, entirely contingent in its content and altogether individual in character; nor is it the emotional hymn sung in praise of only an individual god; nor is it the meaningless stammer of delirious bacchantic revelry. It has achieved its clear and general content and meaning. . . . Spirit has laid aside the particular impressions, the special overtones of that nature which it, as the actual spirit of the people, includes. Such a people, therefore, is no longer conscious in this spirit of its particular character, but rather of having laid this aside, and of the universality of its human existence.

The Spiritual Work of Art

The spirits of different peoples, which find their being in the form of some particular animal, coalesce into one single spirit. Thus it is that the separate artistically beautiful folk spirits combine to form a Pantheon, the element and habitation of which is language. The pure beholding of itself as general human nature takes, when the folk spirit is actualized, this form: the folk spirit combines with the others (which together with it constitute, through nature and natural conditions, one nation, in a common undertaking, and for this task builds up a collective people (Gesamtvolk), and, with that, a collective heaven. This generality, to which spirit attains in its existence here-and-now, is, nevertheless, merely its first generality, which, to begin with, starts from the individuality of ethical life, has not yet overcome its immediacy, has not yet built up a single state out of these separate folk elements. The ethical life of an actual national spirit rests partly on the simple confiding trust of individuals in the whole of their people, partly in the direct share which all, in spite of differences of position, take in the decisions and acts of its government. . . .

1. [The epic. (a) Its ethical world.]

The assembly of folk spirits constitutes a circle of configurations, which now embraces the whole of nature, as well as the whole ethical world. . . . The element in which these imagined ideas exist, language, is the earliest language, the epic as such, which contains the general content, at any rate general in the sense of completeness of the world presented, though not in the sense of generality of thought. The minstrel is the individual and actual spirit from whom, as a subject of this world, the epic is produced, and by whom it is carried out. His "pathos" is not the deafening powers of nature, but Mnemosyne, Recollection, a gradually evolved inwardness, the memory of an essential of being once directly present. He is the organ and instrument whose content is passing away; it is not his own self which is of any account, but his muse, his universal song. What, however, is present in fact, is the conclusion whereby the one extreme of universality, the world of the gods, is connected with individuality, the minstrel, through the middle term of particularity. The middle term is the people and its heroes, who are individual men like the minstrel, but only ideally presented, and thereby at the same time universal like the free extreme of universality, the gods.

[b. Men and the gods.]

In this epic, then, what is inherently established in the cult, the relation of the divine to the human, is set forth and displayed as a whole to consciousness. The content is an "act" of the essential being [as it is] conscious of itself. Acting disturbs the peace of the substance, and awakens the essential being; and by so doing its simple unity is divided into parts, and opened up into the manifold world of natural powers and ethical forces. The act is the violation of the peaceful earth;

it is the trench which, animated by the blood of the living, calls forth the spirits of the departed, who are thirsting for life, and who receive it in the action of self-consciousness. . . .

The universal powers assume the form of individual beings, and thus have in them the principle of action; when they effect anything, therefore, this seems to proceed as entirely from them and to be as free as in the case of men. Hence both gods and men have done one and the same thing. The seriousness with which those divine powers go to work is ridiculously superfluous, since they are in point of fact the moving force of the individualities engaged in the acts; while the strain and toil of the latter again is an equally useless effort, since the former direct and manage everything.

The over-zealous mortal creatures, who are as nothing, are at the same time the mighty self that brings into subjection universal beings, violates the gods, and procures for them actual reality and an interest in acting. Just as, conversely, these powerless gods, these impotent universal beings, which procure their sustenance from the gifts of men, and, through men, first get something to do, are the natural inner principle and the substance of all events, as also the ethical material, and the "pathos" of action. If their elementary natures first achieve actual reality and a sphere of effectual operation through the free self of individuality, it is equally true that they are the universal something, which withdraws from and avoids this connection, remains unrestricted and unconstrained in its own character, and, by the inexhaustible elasticity of its unity, extinguishes the atomic singleness of the individual acting and his various aspects, preserves itself in its purity, and dissolves all that is individual in the current of its own continuity.

[c. The gods by themselves.]

Just as the gods get involved in this contradictory relation with the antithetic nature having the form of self, in the same way their universality comes into conflict with their own specific character and the relation in which it stands to others. They are the eternal, beautiful individuals, who, resting in their own being here and now, are removed from the changes of time and alien forces. But they are at the same time determinate elements, particular gods, and thus stand in relation to others. But that relation to others, which, in virtue of the opposition it involves, is one of strife, is a comic self-forgetfulness of their eternal nature. The determinateness they possess is rooted in the divine subsistence, and, in its specific limitation, has the independence of the whole individuality; owing to this, their characters at once lose the sharpness of their distinctive peculiarity, and in their ambiguity blend together.

One purpose of their activity and their activity itself, being directed against an "other" and so against an invincible divine force, are a contingent and futile piece of bravado, which passes away at once, and transforms the pretense of seriousness in the act into a harmless, self-confident piece of sport with no result and no issue. . . .

The content of the world of idealizing imagination carries on its movement in the center, unrestrained and by itself, gathering around the individuality of some hero, who, however, feels the strength and splendor of his life broken, and mourns the early death he sees ahead of him. For the actual individuality, firmly fixed in itself, is isolated and excluded to the utmost point, and severed into its elements, which have not yet found each other and become united. The one separate element, the abstract unreal something, is necessity which does not share the life of the center just as little as does the other, the concrete real individual, the minstrel, who keeps himself outside it, and disappears in what he ideally represents. Both extremes must get nearer the content; the one, necessity, has to get filled with it, the other, the language of the minstrel, must have a share in it. And the content formerly left to itself must preserve in it the certainty and the fixed character of the negative.

2. [Tragedy.]

This higher language, that of tragedy, gathers and keeps more closely together the dispersed and disintegrated aspects of the inner essential world and the world of action. The substance of the divine separates in accordance with the nature of the conception, into its several configurations, and their movement is likewise in conformity with that conception. In regard to form, the language here ceases to be narrative, because it enters into the content, just as the content ceases to be merely one that is ideally represented. The hero is himself the spokesman, and the representation given brings before the audience, who are also spectators, self-conscious human beings, who know their own rights and purposes, the power and the will belonging to their specific nature, and who know how to state them. They are artists who do not express with unconscious naïveté and naturalness the merely external aspect of what they begin and what they decide upon, as is the case in the language accompanying ordinary action in actual life; they make the very inner being external, they prove the righteousness of their action, and the "pathos" controlling them is soberly asserted and definitely expressed in its universal individuality, free from all accident of circumstance and the particular peculiarities of personalities. Lastly, it is in actual human beings that these characters achieve existence here and now, human beings who impersonate heroes, and represent them in actual speech, not in the form of a narrative, but speaking in their own person. Just as it is essential for a statue to be made by human hands, so is the actor essential to his mask.

[a. The individuality of the chorus, the heroes, the divine
powers.]

The general ground, on which the movement of these
figures, begot by the conception, takes place, is the consciousness of the first form of language, where the content is ideally
presented, and its detail spread out without reference to the
self. It is the common people in general, whose wisdom finds
expression in the Chorus of the Elders; in the powerlessness
of this chorus the generality finds its representative, because
the common people itself compose merely the positive and
passive material for the individuality of the government confronting it. Lacking the power to negate and oppose, it is
unable to hold together and keep within bounds the riches
and varied fullness of divine life; it allows each individual
moment to go off its own way, and in its reverential hymns
praises each individual aspect as an independent god, now
this god and now again another. Where, however, the chorus
detects the seriousness of the conception, and perceives how
the conception proceeds to deal with these figures, shattering
them as it goes along; and where it comes to see how badly
its praised and honored gods come off when they venture on
the ground where the conception holds sway; there it is not
itself the negative power actively setting to work, but keeps
itself within the abstract selfless thought of such power, con-
fines itself to the consciousness of an alien and external
destiny, and produces the empty wish to relax, and feeble
ineffective talk intended to appease. In its terror before the
higher powers, which are the immediate arms of the substance,
in its terror before their struggle with one another, and before
the simple and uniform action of that necessity, which crushes
them as well as the living beings bound up with them; in its
compassion for these living beings, whom it knows at once to
be the same with itself, the chorus is conscious of nothing but

inactive horror of this whole process, conscious of equally helpless pity, and [recommends], in fine, the empty peace of surrender to necessity, whose work is apprehended neither as the necessary act of character, nor as the action of the absolute being itself. . . .

The content and movement of spirit, which is object of itself here, have been already considered as the nature and realization of the substance of ethical life. In its religion spirit attains to consciousness in its purer form and its simpler mode of embodiment. If, then, the ethical substance through its very conception became divided, as regards its content, into two powers, which were defined as divine and human law, as law of the nether world and law of the upper world—the one relating to the family, the other to the power of the state—the first bearing the impress and character of woman, the other that of man, then in the same way, the previously multiform circle of gods, with its wavering and unsteady characteristics, is reduced to these powers, which thus are brought closer to individuality proper. For the previous dispersion of the whole into manifold abstract forces, which appear substantiated, is the dissolution of the subject which comprehends them merely as aspects in its self; and individuality is therefore only the superficial form of those entities. Conversely, a further distinction of characters than that just named is to be attributed to contingent and inherently external personality.

[b. The double meaning of individuality.]

At the same time, the essential nature is divided in its form, i.e., with respect to knowledge. Spirit when acting, confronts, as consciousness, the object toward which its activity is directed, and which, in consequence, is determined as the negative of the knowing agent. The agent finds himself thereby in the contradiction of knowing and not knowing. He takes his purpose from his own character, and knows it to be the ethical essence; but owing to the determinateness of his character, he knows merely the one power of substance; the other remains for him concealed. The objectively present reality, therefore, is one thing in itself, and another for consciousness. The higher and lower right come to signify in this connection the power that knows and reveals itself to consciousness, and the power concealing itself and lurking in the background. The one is the aspect of light, the god of the oracle, who as regards his natural aspect (light) has sprung from the all-illuminating Sun, knows all and reveals all, Phoebus, and Zeus who is his Father. But the commands of this truth-speaking god, and his proclamations of what is, are really deceptive and fallacious. For this knowledge is, in its very conception, directly ignorance (*Nichtwissen*), because consciousness when acting is inherently this contradiction. He who had the power to unlock the riddle of the sphinx [*Oedipus*] and he too who trusted with childlike confidence [*Orestes*] are, therefore, both sent to destruction through what the god reveals to them. The priestess, through whose mouth the gracious god speaks, is in nothing different from the equivocal sisters of fate [the witches in *Macbeth*], who drive their victim to crime by their promises, and who, by the double-tongued, equivocal character of what they give out as a certainty, deceive the King when he relies upon the manifest and obvious meaning of what they say. There is a type of consciousness that is purer than that which believes in witches, and more discriminating, more thorough and more solid than the former which puts its trust in the priestess and the gracious god. This type of consciousness, therefore, lets its revenge wait for the revelation which the spirit of its father makes about the crime that did him to death, and institutes other proofs in addition—for the reason that the spirit giving the revelation might possibly be the devil [*Hamlet*]. . . .

[The following sections elaborate this problem.]

[c. The end of individuality.]

Consciousness disclosed this contradiction by action, through doing something. Acting in accordance with the knowledge revealed, it found out the deceptiveness of that knowledge, and being committed, in view of the inner meaning, to one of the attributes of substance, it did violence to the other and thereby gave the latter a right against itself. When following the god who knows and reveals himself, consciousness really seized hold of what is not revealed, and thereafter had to atone for having trusted the knowledge, whose equivocal character (since this is its very nature) should have been known to it, as a warning. The frenzy of the priestess, the inhuman shape of the witches, the voices of trees and birds, dreams, and so on, are not ways in which truth appears; they are admonitory signs of deception, of want of discernment, of the individual and accidental character of knowledge. Or, what amounts to the same thing, the opposed power, which consciousness has violated, is present as express law and authentic right, whether law of the family or law of the state; while consciousness, on the other hand, pursued its own proper knowledge, and hid from itself what was revealed. The truth, however, of the opposing powers of content and consciousness is, in the last analysis, that both are equally right, and, hence, in their opposition (which comes about through action) are equally wrong. The process of action proves their unity in the mutual overthrow of both powers and the self-conscious characters. The reconciliation of the opposition with itself is the Lethe of the nether world through death or the Lethe of the upper world through acquittal, not from guilt (for consciousness cannot deny its guilt, because the act was done), but from the crime, and of the atoning consolation and peace of soul which such acquittal gives. Both bring forgetfulness, the disappearance of the reality and action of the powers of the substance, its component individualities, and of the powers of the abstract thought of good and evil. For neither of them by itself is the real essence; this consists in the undisturbed calm of the whole within itself, the immovable unity of Fate, the quiescent existence and hence want of activity and vitality in the family and government, and the equal honor and consequent indifferent unreality of Apollo and Furies, and the return of their spiritual life and activity into Zeus solely and simply.

This destiny completes the depopulation of heaven, of that unthinking mixture of individuality and ultimate being, a blending whereby the action of this absolute being appears as something incoherent, inconsistent, contingent, unworthy of itself; for individuality, when attaching in a merely superficial way to absolute being, is unessential. The expulsion of such unreal insubstantial ideas, which was demanded by the philosophers of antiquity, thus already had its beginning in tragedy in general, through the fact that the division of the substance is controlled by the conception, and hence individuality is the essential individuality, and the specific determinations are absolute characters. The self-consciousness represented in tragedy knows and acknowledges on that account only one highest power, Zeus. This Zeus is known and acknowledged only as the power of the state or of the hearth and home, and, in accordance with the contradictions in knowledge, merely as the father of the particular knowledge assuming a definite shape; he is the Zeus acknowledged in the taking of oaths, the Zeus of the Furies, the Zeus of what is universal, of the inner being which remains concealed. The further aspects derived from the conception and dispersed in the imagination (*Vorstellung*)—aspects which the chorus acknowledges, one after the other, are, on the other hand, not the "pathos" of the hero; they sink to the level of passions in the hero, to the level of accidental, unessential moments, which the impersonal chorus no doubt praises, but which are not capable of constituting the character of heroes, nor of being expressed and regarded by them as their real nature. . . .

The self-consciousness of the heroes must step forth from its mask and be represented as it knows itself to be the fate both of the gods of the chorus and of the absolute powers themselves, and as it is no longer separated from the chorus, the general consciousness.

3. [The Comedy.]

Comedy has, first of all, the aspect that actual self-consciousness represents itself as the Fate of the gods. These elemental beings are, as general aspects, no definite self, and are not actually real. They are, indeed, endowed with a form of individuality, but this is in their case merely put on, and does not really and truly suit them. The actual self has no such abstract aspect for its substance and content. The subject, therefore, is raised above such an aspect which is a particular quality, and when clothed with this mask expresses the irony of such a quality trying to be something on its own account. The pretensions of the general essence are betrayed by being attributed to an actual self; it is seen to be caught in an actual reality, and lets the mask drop, as it wants to be something good. The self, appearing here in its significance as something actual, plays with the mask which it once puts on, in order to be its own person; but it breaks away from this seeming and pretense just as quickly again, and comes out in its own nakedness and usual character, which it shows not to be distinct from the proper self, the actor, nor again from the onlooker.

This general dissolution, which the formally embodied essential nature as a whole undergoes when it assumes individuality, becomes in its content more serious, and hence more petulant and bitter, in so far as the content possesses its more serious and necessary meaning. The divine substance combines the meaning of natural and ethical essentiality.

[a. The essence of natural existence.]

As regards the natural element, actual self-consciousness shows, in the very fact of applying elements of nature for its adornment, for its abode and so on, and again in feasting on its own offering, that it itself is the Fate to which the secret is disclosed, as to what is the meaning of the independent substantiality of nature. In the mystery of bread and wine it makes its very own this self-subsistence of nature together with the significance of inner reality; and in comedy it is conscious of the irony of this meaning.

So far, again, as this meaning contains the essence of ethical reality, it is partly the people in its two aspects of the state, or Demos proper, and individual family life; partly, however, it is self-conscious pure knowledge, or rational thought of the universal. Demos, the general mass, which knows itself as master and governor, and is also aware of having the insight and intelligence which demand respect, compels and fools itself through the particularity of its actual life, and exhibits the laughable contrast between its own opinion of itself and its immediate existence, between its necessity and contingency, its generality and its vulgarity. If the principle of its individual existence, cut off from the general, comes on the scene in the proper form of actual reality and openly usurps and administers the commonwealth, to which it is a secret harm and detriment [*Knights* of Aristophanes], then immediately there is disclosed the contrast between the general in the sense of an abstract theory, and that with which practice is concerned; the entire emancipation of the ends and aims of the mere individual from the general order, and the scorn the mere individual shows for such order.

[b. The unreality of the abstract individuality of the gods.]

Rational thinking removes contingency of form from the divine being; and, in opposition to the uncritical wisdom of the chorus—a wisdom, expressing all sorts of ethical maxims and stamping with validity and authority a multitude of laws and specific conceptions of duty and right—rational thought elevates these to the simple ideas of the beautiful and the good. The process or movement of this abstraction is the consciousness of the dialectic involved in these maxims and laws themselves, and hence the consciousness of the disappearance of that absolute validity with which they previously appeared. Since the contingent character and superficial individuality which mere presentation lent to the divine beings, vanish, they are left, as regards their natural aspect, with merely the nakedness of their immediate existence; they are clouds, a passing vapor, like those images [*The Clouds* of Aristophanes]. Having passed in accordance with their essential character, as determined by thought, into the simple thoughts of the beautiful and the good, these latter allow themselves to be filled with every kind of content. The force of dialectic knowledge puts determinate laws and maxims of action at the mercy of the pleasure and carelessness of youth, led astray thereby, and gives weapons of deception into the hands of solicitous and apprehensive old age, restricted in its interests to the individual details of life. The pure thoughts of the beautiful and the good thus produce a comic spectacle: through their being set free from opinion, which contains both their determinateness in the sense of content and also their absolute determinateness, the firm hold of consciousness upon them, they become empty, and, on that very account, the sport of the private opinion and caprice of any chance individuality.

[c. The self, certain of itself as an absolute being.]

Here, then, Fate, formerly without consciousness, consisting in mere rest and forgetfulness, and separated from self-consciousness, is united with self-consciousness. The individual self is the negative force through which and in which the gods, as also their aspects, nature as existent fact and the thoughts of their determinate characters, pass away and disappear. At the same time, the individual self is not the mere vacuity of something disappearing, but it preserves itself in this very nothingness, holds to itself and is the sole and only reality. The religion of art is fulfilled and consummated in it, and is come full circle. Through the fact that it is the individual consciousness in its certainty of self which is shown to be this absolute power, this latter has lost the form of something imagined (*vorgestellt*), separated from and alien to consciousness in general—as were the statue and also the living embodiment of beauty or the content of the epic and the powers and persons of tragedy. Nor again is the unity the unconscious unity of the cult and the mysteries; rather the self proper of the actor coincides with the part he impersonates, just as the onlooker is perfectly at home in what is represented before him, and sees himself playing in the drama before him. What this self-consciousness beholds is that that which assumes the form of essentiality as against self-consciousness is resolved and dissolved within its thought, its existence and action, and is quite at its mercy. It is the return of everything universal into certainty of self, a certainty which, in consequence, is this complete loss of substantial reality on the part of what is alien and external. Such certainty is a state of spiritual good health and of self-abandonment thereto, on the part of consciousness, in a way that, outside this kind of comedy, is not to be found anywhere.

Revealed Religion

[Christianity]

Through the religion of art spirit has passed from the form of substance into that of subject; for art produces its figure and form, and imbues it with the nature of action or establishes in it the self-consciousness which merely disappears in the awesome substance and in the attitude of simple trust does not itself comprehend itself. This incarnation in human form of the divine being begins with the statue, which has in it only the outward shape of the self, while the inner life thereof, its activity, falls outside it. In the case of the cult, however, both aspects have become one; in the outcome of the religion of art this unity being completely attained has at the same time also passed over to the extreme of self; in the type of spirit, which becomes perfectly certain of itself in the individual existence of consciousness, all essential content is submerged. The proposition, which gives this lighthearted action expression, runs thus: "The self is the absolute being." The being which was substance, and in which the self was the accidental element, has dropped to the level of a predicate; and in this self-consciousness, over against which nothing appears in the form of objective being, spirit has lost its aspect of consciousness.

1. [The assumptions underlying the conception of revealed religion.]

This statement, "The self is absolute being," belongs, as is evident on the face of it, to the non-religious, the concrete actual spirit; and we have to recall what the form of it is which gives expression to it. This form will contain at once the movement of that spirit and its conversion, which lowers the self to the note of a predicate and raises substance into subject. This we must understand to take place in such a way that the converse statement does not *per se,* or for us, make substance into subject, or, what is the same thing, does not reinstate substance again so that the consciousness of spirit is carried back to its commencement in natural religion; but rather in such a way that this conversion is brought about for and through self-consciousness itself. Since this latter consciously gives itself up, it is preserved and maintained in thus relinquishing itself, and remains the subject of the substance; but as being likewise self-relinquished, it has at the same time the consciousness of this substance. In other words, since by thus offering itself up, it produces substance as subject, this subject remains its own very self. If, then, we take the two propositions we can say that, in the first the subject merely disappears in substantiality, and in the second the substance is merely a predicate, and both sides are thus present in each with contrary inequality of value —the result hereby effected is that the union and transfusion of both natures (subject and substance) become apparent. In this union both, with equal value and worth, are at once essential and also merely moments. Hence it is that spirit is equally consciousness of itself as its objective substance, as well as simple self-contained self-consciousness. The religion of art belongs to the spirit animating the ethical sphere, the spirit which we formerly saw sink and disappear in the condition of right, i.e., in the proposition: "The self as such, the abstract person, is absolute being." In ethical life the self is absorbed in the spirit of its people, it is universality filled to the full. Simple abstract individuality, however, rises out of this content, and its lightheartedness clarifies and rarefies it till it becomes a "person" and attains the abstract universality of right. Here the substantial reality of the ethical spirit is lost, the abstract insubstantial spirits of national individuals are gathered together into a pantheon; not into an imagined pantheon whose impotent form lets each alone to do as it likes, but into the pantheon of abstract universality, of pure thought, which disembodies them, and bestows on the spiritless self, on the individual person, complete existence on its own account.

But this self, through its being empty, has let the content go; this consciousness is being merely within itself. Its own very existence, the legal recognition of the person, is an unfulfilled empty abstraction. It thus really possesses merely the thought of itself; in other words, as it there exists and knows itself as object, it is something unreal. Consequently, it is merely stoic

Independence, the independence of thought; and this finds, by passing through the process of skepticism, its ultimate truth in that form we called the "unhappy self-consciousness."

This self knows how the case stands with the actual claims to validity which the abstract person puts forward, as also with the validity of these claims in pure thought [in Stoicism]. It knows that a vindication of such claims means really being altogether lost; it is just this loss become conscious of itself, and is the surrender and relinquishment of its knowledge about itself. We see that this "unhappy consciousness" constitutes the counterpart and the complement of the perfectly happy consciousness, that of comedy. All divine reality goes back into this latter type of consciousness; it means, in other words, the complete relinquishment and emptying of substance. The former, on the contrary, is conversely the tragic fate that befalls certainty of self which aims at being absolute, at being self-sufficient. It is consciousness of the loss of everything of significance in this certainty of itself, and of the loss even of this knowledge or certainty of self, the loss of its substance as well as of self; it is the bitter pain which finds expression in the cruel words, "God is dead."

In the state of right and law, then, the ethical world has vanished, and its type of religion has passed away in the mood of comedy. The "unhappy consciousness" is just the knowledge of all this loss. It has lost both the worth and dignity it attached to its immediate personality as well as that attaching to its personality when reflected in the medium of thought. Trust in the eternal laws of the gods is silenced, just as the oracles are dumb, whose work it was to know what was right in particular cases. The statues set up are now corpses in stone from whom the animating soul has flown, while the hymns of praise are words from which all belief has gone. The tables of the gods are bereft of spiritual food and drink, and from his games and festivals man no more receives the joyful sense of his unity with the divine being. The works of the muse lack the force and energy of the spirit which derived the certainty and assurance of itself just from the crushing ruin of gods and men. They are themselves now just what they are for us—beautiful fruit broken off the tree; a kindly fate has passed on those works to us, as a maiden might offer such fruit off a tree. It is not their actual life as they exist, that is given us, not the tree that bore them, not the earth, and the elements, which constituted their substance, nor the climate that determined their constitutive character, nor the change of seasons which controlled the process of their growth. So too it is not their living world that fate preserves and gives us with those works of ancient art, nor the spring and summer of that ethical life in which they bloomed and ripened, but the veiled remembrance alone of all this reality. Our action, therefore, when we enjoy them is not that of worship, through which our conscious life might attain its complete truth and be satisfied to the full: our action is external; it consists in wiping off some drop of rain or speck of dust from these fruits, and in place of the inner elements composing the reality of the ethical life, a reality that environed, created and inspired these works, we erect in prolix detail the scaffolding of the dead element of their outward existence—language, historical circumstances, etc. All this we do, not in order to enter into their very life, but only to imagine them within ourselves. But just as the maiden who hands us the plucked fruit is more than the nature which presented them in the first instance—the nature which provided all—tree, air, light and so on—since in a higher way she gathers all this together into the light of her self-conscious eye, and her gesture in offering the gifts; so too the spirit of the fate, which presents us with those works of art, is more than the ethical life realized in that people. For it is the making inward of the spirit, in the form of conscious memory (*Erinnerung*), which in them was manifested in an outward external way—it is the spirit of the tragic fate which collects all those individual gods and attributes of the substance into one Pantheon, into the spirit which is itself conscious of itself as spirit.

[Hegel here sketches the cycle of art creations, given in his *Aesthetics*. See above, pp. 341–42.]

All the conditions for the production of the spirit are present, and this totality of its conditions constitutes the development of it, its conception, or the inherent production of it.

2. [The simple content of absolute religion: the actual reality of God becoming man.]

Spirit has two sides, which are above represented as the two converse statements: one is that substance empties itself of itself, and becomes self-consciousness; the other is the converse, that self-consciousness empties itself of itself and makes itself into the form of a "thing," or makes itself a universal self. Both sides have in this way met each other, and, in consequence, their true union has arisen. The relinquishment or "kenosis" on the part of the substance, its becoming self-consciousness, expresses the transition into the opposite, the unconscious transition of necessity, in other words, that it is implicitly self-consciousness. Conversely, the emptying of self-consciousness expresses this, that implicitly it is universal being, or, because the self is pure self-existence, which is at home with itself in its opposite, it means that the substance is self-consciousness explicitly for the self, and, just on that account, is spirit. Of this spirit, which has left the form of substance behind, and enters existence in the shape of self-consciousness, we may say, therefore, if we wish to use terms drawn from the process of natural generation, that it has a real mother but a potential or an implicit father. For actual reality, or self-consciousness, and implicit being in the sense of substance, are its two moments; and by the reciprocity of their kenosis, each relinquishing or "emptying" itself of itself and becoming the other, spirit thus comes into existence as their unity.

[a. The immediate existence of the divine self-consciousness.]

In so far as self-consciousness in a one-sided way understands only its own relinquishment, although its object is thus for it at once both existence and self and it knows all existence to be spiritual in nature, yet true spirit has not become thereby objective for it. For, so far, being in general or substance, would not necessarily from its side be also emptied of itself, and become self-consciousness. In that case, then, all existence is spiritual reality merely from the standpoint of consciousness, not inherently in itself. Spirit in this way has merely a fictitious or imaginary existence. This fanciful imagination is fantastic extravagance of mind, which introduces into nature as well as history, the world and the mythical ideas of early religions, another inner esoteric meaning different from what they, on the face of them, bear directly to consciousness, and, in particular, in the case of religions, another meaning than the self-consciousness, whose religions they were, could find and admit to be there. But this meaning is one that is borrowed, a garment, which does not cover the nakedness of the outer appearance, and secures no belief and respect; it is no more than murky darkness and a peculiar crazy twist of consciousness.

If then this meaning of the objective is not to be bare fancy and imagination, it must be inherent and essential (*an sich*), i.e., must at once arise in consciousness as springing from the very notion, and must come forward in its necessity. It is thus that self-knowing spirit has arisen; it has arisen by means of its necessary process through the knowledge of immediate consciousness, i.e., of consciousness of the immediately existing object. This conception, which, being immediate, had also for consciousness the form of immediacy, has in the second place taken on the form of self-consciousness essentially and inherently, i.e., by just the same necessity of the conception by which being or immediacy, the abstract object of sense-consciousness, renounces itself and becomes, for consciousness, the ego. The immediate entity (*Ansich*), or objectively existent necessity, is, however, different from the subjective thinking entity, or the knowledge of necessity—a distinction which, at the same time, does not lie outside the conception, for the simple unity of the conception is itself immediate being. The conception is at once what empties or relinquishes itself, or the explicit unfolding of directly beheld (*angeschaut*) necessity, and is also at home with itself in that necessity, knows it and comprehends it. The immediate inherent nature of spirit, which takes on the form of self-consciousness, means nothing else than that the concrete actual world spirit has reached this knowledge of itself. It is then too that this knowledge first enters its consciousness, and enters it as truth. How that came about has already been explained.

That absolute spirit has taken on the form of self-consciousness inherently and necessarily, and has done so too as a conscious fact, this position appears now as the belief of the world, the belief that spirit exists in fact as a definite self-consciousness, i.e., as an actual human being, that spirit is an object for immediate experience, that the believing mind sees, feels, and hears this divinity. Taken thus it is not an imagination, not a fancy; it is actual in the believer. Consciousness in that case does not set out from its own inner life, does not start from thought, and enclose the thought of God along with existence; rather it sets out from immediate present existence, and finds God there.

The moment of immediate existence is present as an element in the conception, and present in such a way that the religious spirit, on the return of all ultimate reality into consciousness, has become the simple positive self, just as the actual spirit as such, in the case of the "unhappy consciousness," was just this simple self-conscious negativity. The self of the definitely existent spirit has in that way the form of complete immediacy. It is neither set up as something thought, or imaginatively represented, nor as something produced, as is the case with the immediate self both in natural religion, and in religion as art. Rather, this concrete God is beheld sensuously and immediately as a self, as a real individual human being; only so is it a self-sciousness.

[b. The completion of the conception of the highest being in the identity of abstraction and the immediacy in the individual self.]

This incarnation of the divine being, its having essentially and directly the form of self-consciousness, is the simple content of absolute religion. Here the divine being is known as spirit; this religion is the divine being's consciousness concerning itself that it is spirit. For spirit is knowledge of itself in its state of self-alienation, the absolute reality, which is the process of retaining its harmony and identity with itself in its otherness. This, however, is substance, so far as in its accidents substance at the same time turns back into itself; and does so, not as being indifferent toward something unessential and, consequently, finding itself in some alien element, but as being there within itself, i.e., so far as it is subject or self.

In this form of religion the divine being is, on that account, revealed. Its being revealed obviously consists in this, that what it is, is consciously known. It is, however, known just in its being known as spirit, as a being which is essentially self-consciousness.

There is something in the object always concealed from consciousness when the object is for consciousness an "other," something alien and extraneous, and when consciousness does not know the object as its self. This concealment, this secrecy, ceases when the absolute being as spirit is object of consciousness. For here in its relation to consciousness the object is in the form of self; i.e., consciousness at once and immediately knows itself there, or is manifest, revealed, to itself in the object. Its self is manifest to itself merely in its own certainty of self; the object it has is the self; the self, however, is nothing alien and extraneous, but inseparable unity with itself, the immediate universal. It is the pure conception, pure thought, or self-existence, being-for-and-by-itself, which is immediate being, and, therewith, being-for-another, and, as this being-for-another, is immediately turned back into itself and is at home with itself (*bei sich*). It is thus the truly and solely revealed. The good, the righteous, the holy, creator of heaven and earth, etc.—all these are predicates of a subject, universal moments, which depend on this central point, and only are when consciousness goes back into thought.

As long as it is they that are known, their ground and essential being, the subject itself is not yet revealed; and in the same way the specific determinations of the universal are not this universal itself. The subject itself, and consequently this pure universal too, is, however, revealed as self; for this self is just this inner being reflected into itself, the inner being which is immediately given and is the proper certainty of that (other) self, for which it is object. To be in its conception that which reveals and is revealed, this is, then, the true form of spirit; and moreover, this form, its conception, is alone its very essence and its substance. The spirit is known as self-consciousness, and to this self-consciousness it is directly revealed, for it is this self-consciousness itself. The divine nature is the same as the human, and it is this unity which is beheld (*angeschaut*).

Here, then, we find as a fact that consciousness, or the general form in which being is aware of being, the figure which being adopts, is identical with its self-consciousness. This figure is itself a self-consciousness; it is thus at the same time an existent object; and this existence possesses equally directly the significance of pure thought, of absolute being.

The absolute being existing as a concrete actual self-consciousness, seems to have descended from its eternal pure simplicity; but in fact it has, in so doing, attained for the first time its highest nature, its supreme reach of being. For when the notion of being has reached its simple purity of nature, it is then both the absolute abstraction, which is pure thought and hence the pure singleness of self, and immediacy or objective being, on account of its pure simplicity.

What is called sense-consciousness is also just this pure abstraction; it is this kind of thought for which being is the immediate. The lowest is thus at the same time the highest; the revelation which has appeared entirely on the surface is just therein the deepest that can be made. That the supreme being is seen, heard, etc., as an existent self-consciousness—this is, in very truth, the culmination and consummation of its conception. And through this consummation, the divine being is given to sense, exists immediately, in its character as divine being.

[c. Speculative knowledge as the image of the community in
    absolute religion.]

This immediate existence is at the same time not solely and simply immediate consciousness; it is religious consciousness. This immediacy means not only an existent self-consciousness, but also the purely thought-constituted or absolute being; and these meanings are inseparable. What we are conscious of in our conception, namely, that objective being is ultimate essence, is the same as what the religious consciousness is aware of. This unity of being and essence, of thought which is immediately existence, is immediate knowledge on the part of this religious consciousness just as it is the inner thought or the mediated reflective knowledge of this consciousness. For this unity of being and thought is self-conscious and actually exists; in other words, the thought-constituted unity has at the same time this concrete shape of what it is. God, then, is here revealed as He is. He actually exists as He is in Himself. He is real as Spirit.

God is attainable in pure speculative knowledge alone, and only is in that knowledge, and is merely that knowledge itself, for He is spirit; and this speculative knowledge is the knowledge furnished by revealed religion. That knowledge knows God to be thought, or pure essence; and knows this thought as actual being and as real existence, and existence as the negativity, the reflection of itself, hence as self, a particular "this," and a universal self. It is just this that revealed religion knows.

The hopes and expectations of preceding ages pressed forward to, and were solely directed toward this revelation, the vision of what absolute being is, and the discovery of themselves therein. This joy, the joy of seeing itself in absolute being, becomes realized in self-consciousness, and seizes the whole world. For the absolute is spirit; it is the simple movement of those pure abstract aspects, which expresses just this, that ultimate reality is then at once known as spirit when it is seen and beheld as immediate self-consciousness.

This conception of spirit knowing itself to be spirit is still the immediate conception; it is not yet developed. The ultimate being is spirit; in other words, it has appeared, it is revealed. This first revelation is itself immediate; but the immediacy is likewise thought, or pure mediation, and must therefore exhibit and set forth this moment in the sphere of immediacy as such.

Looking at this more precisely, spirit, when self-consciousness is immediate, is a particular "this"; it is an individual self-consciousness set up in contrast to the universal self-consciousness. It is a single, a repelling and excluding unit, which appears to that consciousness for which it exists in the impervious form of a sensuous "other," an unreduced opposite in the sphere of sense. This other does not yet know spirit to be its own; in other words, spirit, in its form as an individual self, does not yet exist as an equally universal self, as all self. Or again, the shape it assumes has not as yet the form of the conception, i.e., of the universal self, of the self which in its immediate actual reality is at once suspended, is thought, universality, without losing its reality in this universality.

The next and similarly immediate form of this universality is, however, not at once the form of thought itself, of the conception as conception; it is the universality of actual reality, it is the "allness," (*Allheit*) the collective totality, of the selves, and is the elevation of existence into the sphere of presentative or figurative thought (*Vorstellung*); just as in general, to take a concrete example, the "this" of sense, when suspended, is first of all the "thing" of "perception," and is not yet the "universal" of the intellect or mind.

This individual human being, then, which absolute being is revealed to be, goes in its own case as an individual through the process found in sense existence. He is the immediately present God; in consequence His being passes over into His having been. Consciousness, for which God is thus sensuously present, ceases to see Him, to hear Him: it has seen Him, it has heard Him. And it is by the mere fact that it has seen and heard Him, that it first becomes itself spiritual consciousness; or, in other words, He has now arisen in the life of spirit, as He formerly rose before consciousness as an object existing in the sphere of sense. For, a consciousness which sees and hears Him by sense, is one which is itself merely an immediate consciousness, which has not suspended the disparateness of objectivity, has not withdrawn it into pure thought, but accepts this objectively presented individual, and not itself, as spirit. In the disappearance of the immediate existence of what is known to be absolute being, immediacy preserves its negative moment. Spirit remains the immediate self of actual reality, but in the form of the universal self-consciousness of a religious community, a self-consciousness which rests in its own proper substance, just as in it this substance is universal subject: it is not the individual subject by himself, but the individual along with the consciousness of the community, and what he is for this community is the complete whole of the individual spirit.

The terms "past" and "distance" are, however, merely the imperfect form in which the immediateness gets mediated or made universal; this is merely dipped superficially in the element of thought, is kept there as a sensuous mode of immediacy, and not made one with the nature of thought itself. It is lifted out of sense merely into the region of imagination, for this is the synthetic connection of sensuous immediacy and its universality or thought.

Imaginative presentation constitutes the characteristic form in which spirit is conscious of itself in this its religious community. This form is not yet the self-consciousness of spirit which has reached its conception as conception; the mediating process is still incomplete. In this connection of being and thought, then, there is a defect; spiritual life is still encumbered with an unreconciled separation into a "hither" and a "yonder," a "here" and a "beyond." The content is the true content; but all its aspects, when merely imagined, have the character, not of being conceptually comprehended, but of appearing as completely independent aspects, externally related to one another.

In order that the true content may also preserve its true form when before consciousness, the latter must necessarily pass to a higher plane of mental development, where the absolute substance is not intuitively apprehended but conceptually comprehended and where consciousness is for itself brought to the level of its self-consciousness; in the way this has already taken place objectively or for us (who have analyzed the process of experience).

We have to consider this content as it exists in its consciousness. Absolute spirit is content; that is how it exists in the form of its truth. But its truth consists not merely in being the substance or the inherent reality of the religious community; nor again in coming out of this inwardness into the objective quality of something imagined; but in becoming concrete actual self, reflecting itself into self, and being a subject. This, then, is the movement or process which Spirit realizes in its community; this is its life. What this self-revealing spirit is in and by itself, is therefore not brought out by the rich and full content of its life being, so to say, untwined and reduced to its original and primitive strands, to the ideas, for instance, of the first imperfect religious community, or worse still, to what the actual human being incarnating the divine spirit has spoken. This reversion to the original and elementary is based on the instinct to get at the conception; but it confuses the origin, in the sense of the immediate existence of the first historical appearance, with the pure simplicity of the conception. By thus impoverishing the life of spirit, by eliminating the idea of the community and its action with regard to its idea, there arises, therefore, not the conception, but bare externality and particularity, the historical manner in which spirit once upon a time appeared, the unintelligent recollection of a historical figure and its past.

3. [Development of the concept of absolute religion.]

Spirit is content of its consciousness to begin with in the form of pure substance; in other words, it is content of its pure consciousness. This element of thought is the process of descending into existence, the sphere of particularity. The middle term between these two is their synthetic connection, the consciousness of passing into otherness, the process of imagining as such. The third stage is the return from imagination or presentation in idea and from that otherness; in other words, it is the element of self-consciousness itself.

These three movements constitute the life of spirit. Its resolution into separate parts, when it enters the form of imagination, consists in its taking on a determinate mode of being; this determinateness, however, is nothing but one of its aspects or phases. Its detailed process thus consists in spreading its nature over its various phases, entering every one, each being an element in its composition: and since each of these spheres is self-complete, this reflection into itself is at the same time the transition into another sphere of its being. The imagination or representation (*Vorstellung*) constitutes the middle term between pure thought and self-consciousness as such, and is merely one of the determinate forms. At the same time how-ever, as has been shown, the character belonging to such imagi-nation, that of being a "synthetic connection," is spread over all these elements and is their common characteristic.

The content itself, which we have to consider, has partly been met with already, as the idea or presentation of the "un-happy" and the "believing" types of consciousness. In the case of the "unhappy" consciousness, however, the peculiarity lies in the content being produced from consciousness and long-ingly desired, wherein the spirit can never be satisfied nor find rest because the content is not yet its own content inherently and essentially, or in the sense of being its substance. In the case of the "believing" consciousness, again, this content has been regarded as the impersonal being of the world, as the essentially objective content of the imagining, a pictorial think-ing that seeks to escape the actual world altogether, and con-sequently has not the certainty of self-consciousness, a certainty which is cut off from it, partly as being conceit of knowledge, partly as being pure insight. The consciousness of the religious community, on the other hand, possesses the content as its sub-stance, just as the content is the certainty the community has of its own spiritual life.

Spirit, represented at first as substance in the element of pure thought, is, thus, primarily the eternal being, simple, self-identi-cal, which does not, however, have this abstract meaning of being, but the meaning of absolute spirit.

[There follow here metaphysical paraphrasings of Hegel's view of Christian dogmas, such as the Trinity, Jesus as the son of God, the world, of good and evil (original sin), of atonement, salvation and reconciliation, culminating in a section on "the spirit in its ful-fillment, the realm of the spirit." Here the previously expressed thoughts are elaborated, culminating in some revealing passages of religious sentiment:]

. . . Just as the individual divine man [Jesus] has a father who is in Himself (*ansichseiend*) and only an actual mother, so the general divine man, the community, has its own action and thought for its father, but as its mother the eternal love which it only feels, but does not behold in its consciousness as an actual immediate object. The community's reconciliation is therefore in their (the members') heart, but at odds with their consciousness. . . . For the self-consciousness this immediate present does not yet have spiritual meaning. The spirit of the community is thus in its immediate consciousness separated from its religious consciousness. . . .

[The next chapter, entitled "Absolute Knowledge," contains a preliminary résumé of the ideas Hegel more fully developed in his *Logic*.]

POLITICAL ESSAYS

A. *The Internal Affairs of Württemberg* (1798)
B. *The Constitution of Germany* (1802)
C. *Concerning the English Reform Bill* (1832)

Translated by C.J.F.

CONCERNING THE MOST RECENT INTERNAL AFFAIRS IN WÜRTTEMBERG, AND MORE ESPECIALLY THE SHORTCOMINGS OF THE CONSTITUTION OF CITY MAGISTRATES (Fragment)

IT IS TIME THAT THE PEOPLE OF WÜRTTEMBERG STOPPED wavering between fear and hope, stopped expecting something and being disappointed. I would not want to say that it is also time that each who, regarding the possible change of things or their continuance desires only his limited advantage or the profit of his class, or consults only his vanity, gave up these meager desires, these small cares, and considered only the care for the general [good]. But for men of better desires, of purer concern, it is time to confront their uncertain will with those parts of the constitution which are based upon injustice, and to concentrate their efforts upon the necessary change of these parts.

The quiet contentment with what is, the despondency, the patient acceptance of an all-powerful fate has been transformed into expectancy, and into courage for something different. The image of better, more just times has vividly entered the souls of men, and a nostalgia, a longing for a purer, a freer state has begun to agitate all minds and has divided them from reality. The drive to break through the weak barriers has raised man's hope by each event, by each ray, even by crimes. From where could the Württemberger expect more just help than from the diet of their estates? As to the delay in the satisfaction of these hopes—time can only purify these longings, can separate the pure from the impure, but time will reinforce the drive for something that will meet the general desire; at each delay the longing will only eat more deeply into the hearts; it is no accidental fraud which passes. Perhaps one could call it the paroxysm of a fever, but it ends only in death or by sweating out the sick matter. It is an effort of the healthy parts to drive out the evil.

The feeling is general and deep that the governmental structure as it still exists is untenable. The anxiety is very general that it will collapse and will hurt everyone in its fall. Should fear, as a result of this belief, be allowed to become so strong that it is left to good luck what is overturned, what maintained, what to stand and what to fall? Should one not want to abandon what cannot be maintained? To investigate unexcitedly what is untenable? Justice is the only measuring rod for such an evaluation. The courage to apply justice is the only power which can remove what is shaky with honor and stolidity and produce a secure state.

How blind are those who believe that institutions, constitutions, laws which do not longer correspond to the mores, the needs, the opinion of people, from which the spirit has fled, could continue to exist, that forms which neither mind nor feeling is any longer interested in are strong enough to provide the bond for a people!

All attempts to get back confidence for parts of a constitution the faith in which has been lost by big words and tricks, to cover the grave digger with nice words, not only bring shame upon the clever inventors, but prepare a more terrible explosion. In such an outburst revenge becomes associated with the desire for reform, and in which the long-deceived and suppressed mass metes out punishment to such fraudulence.

When a change is to take place, something must be changed. So trivial a truth must be stated because the anxiety which is compelled ought to be distinguished from the courage which decides. Men driven by fear may sense the necessity of a change and even admit it, but when a start is to be made, they are weak and want to keep everything they possess, like a wastrel who ought to cut down his expenses, but who finds every article essential which might be eliminated, and who therefore refuses to give up anything until finally the essential is taken with the unessential. No Germans should show such weakness; on the basis of cool conviction that a change is necessary, they must not be afraid to investigate in detail, and if any injustices are found, he who suffers it should demand its removal, and he who possesses unjustly must sacrifice it voluntarily.

This strength to rise above one's little interest and be just is as much presupposed in what follows as is the sincerity really to want it and not merely to pretend. Too often a reservation is hidden behind the eager concern for the general welfare: as long as it coincides with our own interest. Such eagerness to consent to proposed reforms gets scared as soon as a demand is made upon it.

Far from this hypocrisy, each estate, each individual ought to start with itself, before making demands upon others or seeking the cause of trouble elsewhere, weigh its situation, its privileges, and if it should find itself in the possession of unequal privileges, it ought to strive to achieve a balance with the rest. . . .

[Here the fragment ends. We know that the rather forceful critique which followed (and of which a brief extract has been preserved in R. Haym, *Hegel und seine Zeit,* 1857, pp. 483–85) seemed sufficiently risky to Hegel's friends to urge him not to publish it. It castigated, presumably, the old estate representation and called for a decent, effective government according to law. That, at any rate, is the tenor of the critique of the *Constitution of Germany* from which the next extract is taken. Hegel wrote later, when he was professor at Heidelberg, a long critical analysis of the negotiations of the Württemberg Diet in 1815 and 1816 in which constitutional reform was debated. Since he took the side of the monarchical proposals, he was sharply criticized by some of his friends who stood for the "good old law." Hegel took the position that "Time has brought for Württemberg a new task and a demand for its solution, the task of building a state of the territories belonging to it." Noting that "the nonsense of the institution which was called German Reich," but which more properly might be called anarchy had found its deserved and shameful end, Hegel insists that the royal dignity of its prince brought with it sovereignty and the position of a state—one of the real German realms (*Reichc*) which have taken the place of the "non-thing" which had had the name of a *Reich*. In terms of both logic and history, Hegel had the better of the argument.]

THE CONSTITUTION OF GERMANY

GERMANY IS NO LONGER A STATE. THE OLDER CONSTITUTIONAL lawyers who, in treating German constitutional law, had tried to fix a concept of the German constitution could not agree, until the more recent ones gave up the attempt. . . . There is no longer any argument about which concept of a constitution the German one belongs to. What cannot be understood, does not exist. If Germany were to be a state, this dissolution would have to be called anarchy, but parts of it have reconstituted themselves as states which retain in memory of a former bond a semblance of association. . . .

The health of a state manifests itself generally not in the quietness of peace but in the commotion of war. Peace is a state of enjoyment and activity in isolation, when the government is a wise paternalism, which demands from the subjects only what is customary. In war, the strength of the cohesion of all with the whole is demonstrated, how much the state can demand of them and how much that is worth which all may be willing to do for it out of their own initiative and sentiment.

Thus Germany has experienced in its war with the French Republic how it is no longer a state . . . the tangible results of this war are the loss of some of the most beautiful German regions and several millions of its inhabitants [the French had annexed the left bank of the Rhine in the Treaty of Luneville, 1802], a great burden of debt . . . and several states losing their quality as states. . . .

But he who would try to learn what happens in Germany merely by studying constitutional law would greatly err. For the dissolution of a state is to be recognized primarily by everything going differently than the laws provide. Because of these notions, the Germans appear so insincere; they appear not to admit anything to be what it is; they remain loyal to their concepts, to law and the laws, but events do not correspond to them. The notion which includes the others is that Germany is still a state because it once was a state and the forms remain from which life has fled.

The organization of this body which is called the German political constitution was formed under very different living conditions than afterwards or now prevail. The justice and the violence, the wisdom and the courage of past times, the honor and the blood, the well-being and the needs of long-dead generations and of their mores and conditions are expressed in the forms of this body politic. The passage of time and the configurations which have developed have severed the destiny of that age and the present one. The structure wherein that destiny dwelt is no longer supported by the destiny of the present generation; it stands . . . isloated from the spirit of the world. If those laws have lost their old life, the present vital concerns have not known how to shape themselves into laws . . . the whole is dissolved, the state no longer exists.

This form of German constitutional law is profoundly linked to what has made the Germans most famous, namely their sense of freedom. This instinct of freedom has prevented the Germans, after each other European nation has subjected itself to the rule of a common political authority (*geme in-schaftliche Staatsgewalt*) from doing the same. The obstinacy of the German character has not yielded to the point where the separate parts would sacrifice their particular interests for the whole society, where all would be united in one general body and where freedom might be achieved in common with free subjection to the supreme political authority.

The supreme political authority was originally, among European nations, a general power of which each had a kind of free and personal share. The Germans have refused to transform this free personal share which was dependent upon arbitrary force into the free share, not dependent upon arbitrary force which consists of the general enforcement of laws. Their condition even lately is that of a state of arbitrariness, not contrary, but without law.

The later situation follows from the earlier one where the nation, without being a state, constituted a people. During that time of the old German freedom, the individual depended upon himself in life and activity. He had his honor and his fortune, depending upon himself, not upon a class. He belonged to the whole as a result of mores, religion, an invisible living spirit and a few major interests. For the rest, he did not allow himself to be restricted by the whole.

From this self-centered activity, which alone was called freedom, spheres of power of others formed according to accident and force of character, without regard to any general interest and little restricted by what one calls political authority (Staatsgewalt); such authority hardly existed as a check to the individual. . . . The parts of general political authority were attached to a manifold of mutually exclusive properties, real estates which were distributed without rhyme or reason and were independent of the state. This manifold property formed no system of rights, but a collection without principle* . . . Political power and privilege are not governmental offices which are calculated in relation to the organization of the whole, the contributions and duties of the individual are not determined in relation to the needs of the whole, but each member of the political hierarchy, each princely house, each estate, each town, each guild, etc., everyone who has right or duties in relation to the state, has himself acquired them. The state has in view of this reduction of its power nothing else to do but to confirm that its power has been torn away. If thus the state loses all authority and yet the possessions of the parts depend upon its power, these possessions necessarily must become very unstable, since they have no other support, which is equal to zero.

---

* Hegel here gives vent to his intense dislike for feudalism as a system of political organization. He goes on to elaborate its persistence in Germany.

The principles of German public law can therefore not be deduced from the concept of the state or from that of a specific constitution, like that of a monarchy. German constitutional law is not a science according to principles, but a collection of the most diverse public rights acquired like private ones. Legislative, judicial, ecclesiastical, military powers are intermingled, divided and conjoined in the most irregular way and in the most varied amounts, just as if they were private property.

By resolutions of the diets, peace treaties, electoral agreements, family contracts, judicial decisions, etc., the political property of each member of the German body politic is most carefully determined. The most insignificant detail, such as titles, order of precedence in walking and sitting, color of furniture have consumed years of work.* . . . The German Reich is like the Reich of nature in its productions, unfathomable in big things, inexhaustible in small matters. It is this side of the situation which fills the insiders acquainted with these infinite details of right and privilege with that awe in face of the venerableness of the German body politic and with that admiration for such a system of the most elaborate justice.†

This sort of justice maintains every part as separate from the state, and hence the necessary demands of the state upon its members are in complete conflict. A state demands a general center, a monarch and representatives (*Stände*) in which the several powers, such as foreign relations, war, finances, are united. Such a center must also possess the necessary power for directing [such matters], to enforce its decisions and to maintain the several parts in subjection. . . . The German political structure on the other hand is nothing but the sum of the rights

---

* Hegel here refers to the notorious picayune concerns of the Imperial Diet after the Treaty of Westphalia had turned it into a shadow of its former self.

† These ironical remarks refer to such writers, as Justus Möser, who in Hegel's time had surrounded the traditionalism of German political life with the halo of romantic awe (the enchantment of the ruin!).

and privileges which the several parts have taken from the whole. . . .

[Hegel then reiterates how constitutional lawyers will, against all practical requirements, prove how these privileges exist by right and law, and if the general confusion leads to defeat in war, as it recurrently has, these lawyers will prove that that too is according to law.]

For the legal system of the German state there is perhaps no more suitable inscription than: *Fiat justitia, pereat Germania!*

It is if not a reasonable still in a sense a noble trait of German character that the law as such, whatever its basis and consequences, is sacred for the German. If Germany, as seems probable, perishes as an individual, independent state, and if the German nation likewise, it is some consolation to discover the awe in face of the law among the destructive spirits.

The view we have just sketched of the political situation and the constitutional law of Germany would hold, if Germany is looked upon as a state; her political situation would have to be considered a legal anarchy. . . . However, if one looks upon Germany not as a united political whole, but as a number of independent and essentially sovereign states, matters make more sense. If one objects that Germany is a "Reich," a body politic, it is subject to one common head of the Reich, it still is one Reich association, the answer is that an inquiry which tries to comprehend has no concern with such titles.

[Hegel gives further illustrations of the manner in which formal law tries to escape from the obvious conclusions by verbal tricks and playing upon the word Reich, as if that were a solution.]

Scientifically and historically speaking, such terms ought to be avoided since they mean nothing. In view of the obstinacy of German character and its insistence upon its own will, it may be the best means, though, to find some general term which satisfies both parties and which leaves both in possession of what they want.

If the Germans have deluded themselves for centuries with such general terms, scientific reflection must determine the concept of the state and the extent of power required for it. It will then appear that Germany cannot really be called a state.

Concept of the State

A group of human beings can only call itself a state, if it joined together for the common defense of the entirety of its property. It is a matter of course, yet it is necessary to remark that such a union has not only the intention of defending itself, but that it also does in fact defend itself, regardless of what might be its power or success, by really fighting back. For no one will be able to deny that Germany is united for its defense by laws and words. Property and its defense through political union are matters which relate entirely to reality.

To repeat, so that a multitude form a state, it is necessary that it establish a common defense and political authority. It is irrelevant what may be the particular constitution . . . We must distinguish that which is necessary so that a multitude be a state and a common power, and that which is merely a particular form of this power . . .

This distinction has a very important aspect for the inner peace of states, the security of governments and the freedom of peoples. For if the general political authority demands of the individual only what is necessary, and limits itself to those tasks which ensure that it receives this essential share, it can let the living freedom and the initiative of the citizens alone and grant it a wide scope in which to play. As a result political authority which is concentrated in the government as its center will not be looked upon with suspicion by the individual . . .

[Hegel then elaborates his thought that specific constitutional provisions are not essential for the establishment of a state; hence the rich variety of associational and local government, as it exists in

Germany, does not seem to him objectionable, provided the essential central power is organized and maintained.]

In regard to particular civil law and judicial administration the sameness of laws and of judicial practice would not make a state out of Europe, any more than would the sameness of weights, measures or coins, nor would their difference destroy the unity of the state. If the concept of the state did not show that the more detailed determination of legal relations among individuals does not touch the state's political power, the example of virtually all European states would demonstrate it; for the most powerful of the true states have very divergent laws. France had, before the revolution, such a manifold law that besides the Roman law which was in force in many provinces, there prevailed also Burgundian, Breton, etc., law and nearly every province, even every town had its special customary law; a French writer rightly remarked that a man traveling in France was changing his laws as often as his post horses.

It is also outside the concept of the state how much either particular estates or individual citizens participate in lawmaking, what is the nature of the courts, whether the office of judge is inherited or appointed by the highest authority or chosen by the citizens. . . . Equally independent of the state and however diversified may be the administration as such, the magistrates' institution, the privileges of towns and professions—all these matters are only relatively important for the state.

In all European states, there is an inequality of contributions of the different classes, their rights and duties. . . . Inequalities of wealth lead to inequalities of contribution to the state's expenses and far from hindering the state, the modern states depend upon it.

[Hegel then recites a long list of other inequalities which do not affect the basic question of whether a community is a state or not. He then proceeds. His sharp divergence from the typically romantic notions, as found in Burke, should be noted.]

In our times a very loose connection, or in fact none at all, may be found in mores, education and language; the identity of these, which at one time was a central pillar of a people's cohesion, may now also be reckoned an accidental aspect; their divergence does not prevent a multitude from constituting a state. Rome or Athens and every small modern state could not exist, if the many languages which are current in the Russian Empire were spoken there; the same holds true, if the mores were as different as they are in that empire—or even as different as they now are in every capital of a large country. The diversity of language and of dialects . . . the difference in mores and of education in the various classes . . . such heterogeneous elements can now in modern states be managed and kept together by the art of political organization. Even in religion wherein the innermost of man expresses itself—which enables the citizens to have confidence in and be sure of each other— I say even in this respect identity has been found unnecessary in modern states.

[After elaborating this thought, Hegel concludes:]

Just as the sameness of religion has not prevented wars among separate nations, so the lack of sameness of religion does not nowadays tear a state apart. Political authority has learned how to separate itself as pure constitutional law from religious authority and its law, and to acquire enough continuity to establish itself in such a way as no longer to need the church. The modern state has placed the church into the separation from itself which it originally had in the Roman state.

To be sure, political theories, which have in our time been put forward by self-appointed philosophers and humanitarians (*Menschheitsrechtlern*) and which have even been realized in vast political experiments, have subjected all that we have excluded from the immediate activity of the highest political authority, with the sole exception of language, mores and religion (admittedly the most important). All aspects of a nation's life are to be determined down to their most minute detail.

That the highest political authority must have the supervision, and prevent these various aspects from hindering the main action of the state is a matter of course. But it is a great advantage of the older states in Europe that they, after insuring what is necessary for the state, can leave plenty of room for the activity of the citizen in the fields of administration and adjudication, whether in regard to choosing the officials or in regard to current business and the handling of law and custom.

It is in view of the size of present states not possible to realize the ideal according to which each free man should participate in the deliberation and determination of general public policy. Political authority must be concentrated, be it as government for the executing, or for the determination thereof. If this center of authority is made secure in itself by the respect of the peoples and is sanctified in the person of the monarch as unchangeable . . . a political authority can leave without fear or jealousy to the subordinate systems and corporate bodies a great part of the relations which are produced in a society. It can leave to them their maintenance according to law, and each class, city, village, community, etc., can enjoy the freedom of doing and executing what lies within its sphere.

[After elaborating this idea of the compatibility of local self-government and corporate autonomy, Hegel recurs to his critique of contrary thought:]

In the new, partly developed theories it is the central prejudice that the state is a machine with a single spring which gives motion to the infinite remaining wheels. All institutions which constitute the nature of a society ought to stem from the highest political authority, to be regulated, commanded, supervised and directed.

The pedantic passion to determine everything in detail, the unfree jealousy which wants to order and administer everything oneself . . . this ignoble fussing over any self-activity of the citizens, even though it has no general relation to the state's authority, has been clothed in rational principles. Not a cent of ordinary expense which may be made for the poor in a country of 20 or 30 million ought to be spent without being commanded, controlled, inspected by the highest authority. Out of a concern for education, the appointment of every village teacher, the expenditure of every penny for a window glass in the school house, the appointment of every secretary or policeman, of every village judge is supposed to be the emanation of the highest political authority. In the whole state every bite should be taken from the soil which produced it to the mouth in a straight line which state and law and government have investigated, calculated, corrected and commanded.

This is not the place to develop more at length that the center of political authority, the government, should leave to the freedom of the citizens all that is not essential to its purpose, namely to organize and to maintain [the highest] authority and power which is necessary for external and internal security. Nothing should be more sacred [to a government] than to leave to the free action of the citizens all these matters and to protect it without regard to utility. For this freedom is sacred in itself.

[Hegel then proceeds to point out that in terms of utility, the local autonomy is supposed to create a financial disadvantage for the central authorities, robbing them of revenue, and to interfere with uniformity, while on the other side it creates satisfaction and an aliveness in the community. He combats the first two arguments by remarking that the central authorities do forego expenses as well as revenues, and the second by commenting that regimentation kills not only initiative, but also morale. He then concludes:]

The difference is enormous between a situation where the political authority so arranges things that everything it can count on is in its hands, but where it cannot count on anything else, and the situation where it can count also upon the free loyalty, the self-confidence and the initiative of the people: an all-powerful, unconquerable spirit which that bureaucratic hierarchy would chase away, because it only stays alive where the highest political authority leaves as much as possible to the self-help of the citizens. By contrast in a modern state, such as the French Republic, where everything is regulated from above, where nothing that has a general aspect is left to the administration and execution of that part of the people who are interested, a dull, stupid life will result from the pedantic approach to ruling; but how, only the future can tell. But what kind of life and what barrenness prevails in another state so regimented, namely the Prussian, strikes anyone who enters the first village, or who observes its complete lack of scientific or artistic genius, or who does not judge its strength by the ephemeral energy which a singular genius has been able to force upon it for a while.

We therefore consider that people happy to which the state leaves much freedom in the subordinated, general activities, and that political authority infinitely strong which will be supported by the free and untrammeled spirit of its people.

[Hegel hereafter proceeds to review the several aspects of government which he considers central, starting with the army which he insists must be unified, if Germany is to be a state; there follow the finances, a discussion of Germany's territorial losses, the organization of law, religion and the "estates"; after two sections on foreign policy, under the headings of "the states of Europe," and "the two German great powers," Hegel in the two concluding sections discusses (a) civic and professional freedom, and (b) the unification of Germany. We quote a few passages from these:]

It is clear that as a result of the ten years of struggle resulting from the French Revolution and the misery of a large part of Europe this much has been learned about basic concepts, that people have become resistant to blind cries of freedom. In this bloody game, the cloud of freedom has dissolved. The noise about freedom will no longer have effect, anarchy has been distinguished from freedom, and the deep conviction has become settled that a firm government is essential to freedom, equally deeply however, that the people must participate in legislation and in the most important affairs of state. The people have a guarantee for the fact that the government will act according to law, and that it will participate in the most important matters touching the general interest—this guarantee is the organization of a body which represents it.

Without such a representative body no freedom is any longer imaginable; all the vagueness and the emptiness of the shouting about freedom has been replaced by this provision. It is a principle of public opinion, a part of common sense. Most German states have such a representation . . .

This German freedom seeks protection for its interests from a state which rests upon this system . . . no war of Prussia can any longer be considered a German war for freedom by public opinion. The true, the persistent and now sharply defined interest in freedom can no longer find protection there.

[Hegel points out that Austria, on the other hand, has such representative institutions, but then recalls at length how in past history this true freedom has been jeopardized by the freedom for the "estates."]

The principle of the original German state which has spread from Germany over all of Europe was the principle of monarchy, a political power under a head for the conduct of general affairs, and with the participation of the people through representatives. The form has remained in the "Reichstag," but the substance has vanished. In the long vacillation of Europe between barbarity and culture, the German state has not succeeded in transforming itself—the state has dissolved. The Germans did not suceed in finding the mean between suppression and despotism—what they called universal monarchy —and complete dissolution.

[This thought is further elaborated in the paragraphs which follow. He despairs of arriving at a solution by negotiation and so turns to the ever-recurrent use of coercion.]

Even though all parts would gain, if Germany became one state, it should be remembered that such an event has never been the fruit of reflection, but only of force, even if it corresponded to the general development and the need were felt deeply and distinctly. The common multitude of the German people together with their local estates must be gathered into one mass by the force of a conqueror, they must be forced to consider themselves as belonging to Germany. Such a Theseus ought to have generosity and to give to the people whom he has created out of the little peoples a share in what concerns all. . . .

CONCERNING THE ENGLISH
REFORM BILL

THE PRESENT REFORM BILL BEFORE THE ENGLISH PARLIAMENT intends first of all to introduce justice and equity into the distribution of the share which the different classes and divisions of the people have in the election of members of Parliament, by establishing more order and symmetry in place of the present most bizarre, most deformed irregularities and inequalities. But the noble entrails, the vital principles of the constitution of Great Britain are at the same time being invaded. The more elevated views which have been expressed in the parliamentary debates shall be reviewed here. That the bill has encountered so much opposition, and the second reading only passed with one vote, cannot surprise one, since the powerful interests of the aristocracy which dominate the lower house are the very ones the bill attacks and seeks to reform.

The projected reform starts from the incontestable fact that the basis for determining the share which the several counties and communities of England should have in forming the Parliament has completely changed in the course of time. One of the most important opponents of the bill, Robert Peel, admits that it may be easy to discourse upon the anomalies and the absurdity of the English constitution, and these absurdities have been in all detail presented both in Parliament and in the press.

[Here follow the familiar facts about parliamentary corruption.]

Hardly ever a similar symptom of the political rottenness of a people can be shown. Montesquieu has declared virtue, the unselfish sense of duty toward the state, to be the principle of the democratic constitution. In the English constitution, the democratic element plays an important part through the participation of the people in the election of the members of the Commons—the statesmen who have the largest share in the power of deciding upon general matters. It is a nearly general opinion among historians that when private interest and dirty monetary advantage interfere in the election of the key men of the state, such a state of affairs must be considered a precursor to the loss of political freedom, of the collapse of its constitution and of the state itself. We Germans may observe that even though the former Reich constitution was a shapeless aggregate of particular interests, it was merely the outer bond of the German states, and that political life in these states never reached the degree of absurdity in relation to appointments and elections nor even less that rottenness permeating all classes of society.

[After elaborating his sharply critical views, Hegel completes this section by pointing out that far from strengthening the monarchical element, the proposed reform is expected further to weaken it. After reviewing a number of more detailed provisions with care, Hegel returns to the problem of the distribution of governmental powers which seems to him the really crucial issue.]

The peculiar feature of England that a power which is supposed to be subordinate and the members of which decide the general affairs of the state, though without instruction, responsibility or the quality of officials, brings it about that the monarchical power and the power of government are quite distinct from each other. To the monarchical power are attributed the main branches of supreme political power, foreign relations, peace and war, command of the army and appointment of the ministers, the officers, the ambassadors, etc. But since to Parliament is given the sovereign decision over the budget (including even the civil list), that is to say the decision over all the means for making war, having an army, ambassadors, etc., and a ministry can therefore only govern, i.e., exist, if it agrees with the opinions and the will of Parliament, the share of the monarch of governmental authority is illusory rather than real, and the substance is found in Parliament.

[After recalling Siéyès' ill-fated scheme for reproducing such a system on a republican basis, Hegel remarks that the true power to govern always coincides with the power to appoint the chief ministers.]

This power we see in England to be in the hands of Parliament; if in the several monarchical constitutions . . . the formal separation of the governmental power as the executive from a strictly legislative and judicial power is enunciated. The appointment of the ministry is still the center of the contest and struggle, even if this right is unconditionally attributed to the crown, and the so-called merely legislative power has achieved victory; under the newest French constitution, too, the government found itself soon forced to establish its headquarters in the Chamber of Deputies.

To this power of government invested in Parliament is related what the enemies of the reform put forward as arguments in favor of rotten boroughs, namely, that as a result of this fact which implies that many parliamentary seats depend upon a few individuals or families, the most eminent statesmen of England have found their way into Parliament and from there into the ministry.

[Hegel admits that private friendship may well have done this; yet he suggests that this belongs to the realm of accidents in which new advantages may counterbalance the loss of these old ones.]

Connected with this is another supposed consequence of greater importance to which the Duke of Wellington has drawn attention. He does not possess the reputation of an orator, because he lacks fluent, ostentatious loquacity which entertains by the hour by which so many members of Parliament have achieved great fame as orators. His discourses, the disjointed sentences of which he is criticized for, often contain viewpoints which hit the essence of the matter. He utters the concern, lest entirely new men will replace those now charged with attending to the public interest, and he asks whether the merchants who will constitute the majority of the electorate under the new bill, are the kind of people who should choose members of Parliament for the great council of the nation which decides about domestic and foreign affairs, about agriculture, colonies and manufactures. The Duke is speaking from his knowledge of the English Parliament in which a small number of talented men who devote themselves completely to political activity and the state's interest stand above a mass of incompetent and ignorant members who possess only the lacquer of common prejudices and such education as one gathers from conversation.

[After elaborating this thought, Hegel observes:]

Where the public service is not made dependent upon conditions such as scientific studies, public examinations, practical preparation, etc., an individual must join a class and a party; it must acquire importance within this group, and will be supported by its influence. There are only rare exceptions.

A main factor of the power of this sort of cohesion—the other bonds of it like family connections, politicking, speaking at dinners, etc., the endless correspondence carried on to all parts of the world, even the joint hanging around at country estates, races, and fox hunts need not be disturbed—namely, the disposition over many parliamentary seats, may indeed be greatly modified by the reform bill. This may well have the effect which the Duke mentions that many new individuals may take the place of those who now belong to the circle that concerns itself with the interest of the government of the state. But it may also have the advantage that the uniformity of maxims and prejudices which prevail in that class and constitute the common sense (*Verstand*) of Parliament may be disturbed.

[Hegel proceeds to develop this aspect of the matter quite fully, wisely recognizing that the new men may be often *hommes de principe* rather than *hommes d'état*. He also suggests that the distribution of power may be further changed. Not that the question of parliamentary supremacy would be at issue; for that has long been settled. But the effective power of Parliament may be exercised in a different way, since the opposition may change its character; instead of the near alikeness of the two parties, a sharper conflict may arise, and the parties may fight over other matters than who is to become minister. Alluding to the French situation, where the opposition is a matter of radical divergence of principle, more especially such abstract principles as freedom, equality, popular sovereignty and the like, Hegel points to a basic conflict or paradox:]

Obedience to law is admitted as necessary, but when demanded by the authorities who are, after all, human beings, such obedience seems to be opposed to freedom; the authority to command, and the difference between commanding and obeying is contrary to equality; a multitude of people can give itself the title of people, and with justification, for the people are this indefinite multitude; from it are distinguished the authorities and the officials, and they appear therefore to be without right, since they have stepped outside this equality and stand opposite the people which has the great advantage of being recognized as the sovereign will. These are the extreme of contradictions between which a nation is torn which has been seized by these formal categories. The members of the English Parliament and generally Englishmen have a more practical political sense and have a notion of what is involved in government and governing. Furthermore, the nature of their constitution is such that the government does not interfere in the particular spheres of social life, the administration of the counties, and towns, the affairs of church and education, and in other common concerns, such as road-building. This freer and more concrete condition of civic life may increase the probability that the formal principles of freedom will not be accepted by the class above the lower one—which latter is, however, very large in England and is most receptive to such formalism—though the opponents of the reform bill see it as threateningly near.

[Hegel concludes with a statement that if the contrary should prove to be the case, and yet the opposition not be able to prevail, they might be tempted to appeal to the people and to bring about a revolution, rather than a reform.]

NOTES FOR INTRODUCTION

[1] Karl Popper, *The Open Society and Its Enemies,* vol. II.

[2] Eric Weil, *Hegel et l'Etat* (1950). The estimate by Morris Cohen is found in his article on Hegel in the *Encyclopedia of the Social Sciences* (1932).

[3] Among the more important special works signalizing this rebirth in its political perspective, Franz Rosenzweig, *Hegel und der Staat* (1920), takes first place. Nicolai Hartmann's *Hegel* (1929) gives a sympathetic general estimate. Herbert Marcuse's *Hegels Ontologie und die Grundlagen einer Theorie der Geschichtlichkeit* (1931) elucidates the central importance of the problem of history for Hegel's work. The decisive work by which the revival of Hegel was initiated is Wilhelm Dilthey's work (see bibliography, p. 551).

[4] Besides the famous comment in the Preface to *Das Kapital,* see also the Introduction to his *Zur Kritik der politischen Oekonomie;* Lenin confirmed the judgment of Marx and suggested that Marx *"knüpft unmittelbar an Hegel an."* Compare for these interrelationships the work by Georg Lukacs, *Der Junge Hegel* (1948), especially pp. 446 ff. and 680 ff., who stresses the rationalist side of Hegel which leads into Marxism, as contrasted with what he considers the fascistic reinterpretation of Hegel initiated by Dilthey who stressed the irrational elements. J. Löwenstein, *Hegels Staatsidee* (1927), stresses rightly the unresolved conflict of the ideal and the real.

[5] Rudolf Haym, *Hegel und seine Zeit,* 2.ed. edited by Hans Rosenberg (1927), pp. 510 ff.

[6] F. C. S. Northrop, *The Meeting of East and West* (1947), pp. 211 ff.

[7] *Werke,* XIII, p. 420. The quotation of Lasson is found in his *Einleitung* to his edition of the *Phänomenologie* (1907), pp. lxxxi–ii. Regarding Plato's and Hegel's political philosophies, see the interesting study by M. B. Foster, *The Political Philosophies of Plato and Hegel* (1935).

[8] This point is the central theme of Marcuse's work (see above, note 3).

[9] Hans Urs von Balthasar, *Apokalypse der deutschen Seele,* vol. I, *Der Deutsche Idealismus,* p. 565.

[10] In his *Gesammelte Schriften,* vol. IV, pp. 1–187. The study was first presented to the Berlin Academy of Sciences in 1905, and published in the Proceedings for 1906. See for all this the Introduction by Richard Kroner to T. M. Knox's useful *Georg Wilhelm Friedrich Hegel—Early Theological Writings* (1948). Note also Johannes Hoffmeister's fine study *Hölderlin und Hegel* (1931).

[11] See for these writings Herman Nohl, *Hegels Theologische Jugendschriften* (1907); the second and third were translated by Knox and published in the book noted under note 10.

[12] These problems are central to Karl Popper's *The Open Society and Its Enemies* (new ed. 1950) who sharply points up the contrast. Unfortunately, Popper has followed in the footsteps of Schopenhauer and engages in invective, where rational argument would be more in keeping with his own position. His discussion of Hegel is a travesty of what needs to be said. Cf. for Kant, my *Inevitable Peace* (1948) and the Introduction to *The Philosophy of Kant* (1949).

[13] See his introduction to *Hegels Schriften zur Politik und Rechtsphilosophie* (1913), p. xi. Lasson there refers to Mayer-Moreau, *Hegels Sozialphilosophie* (1910), p. 75 ff., for further authority.

[14] See for this Theodor Steinbüchel, *Das Grundproblem der Hegelschen Philosophie,* esp. vol. I, "Die Entdeckung des Geistes" (1933).

[15] Cf. H. Trescher, *Montesquieus Einfluss auf die Philosophischen Grundlagen der Staatslehre Hegels,* in *Schmollers Jahrbücher* XLII.

[16] Rosenkranz suggests: "So plastic, so beautiful, so well-shaped, so devoid of all alien admixture and of ephemeral concessions Hegel never worked again." Op. cit., p. 207.

[17] See for this K. Rosenkranz, *Hegel als Deutscher Nationalphilosoph* (1870). The passage refers to a formulation by R. Haym, *Hegel und seine Zeit,* p. 243 (in the chapter on the *Phänomenologie*).

[18] Cf. M. Heidegger, "Hegels Begriff der Erfahrung" in *Holzwege* (1950) pp. 105–192.

[19] See *Phänomenologie des Geistes* (ed. Lasson) p. 74. The translation by Baillie (p. 104 of his edition) is quite misleading. Generally speaking the German word *"Dieses"* which lends itself to being used in the noun form, cannot when so used be rendered by the English "this" because it has no noun form. We have rendered it usually as a "particular something" for that gives Hegel's meaning of *Dieses* as a thing (or event, etc.) confronting us.

[20] See Kuno Fischer, *Hegels Leben, Werke und Lehre* (1901), p. 305.

[21] We are following Lasson who in his Introduction to the *Phänomenologie,* p. xciv, rightly insists, contrary to Rosenkranz and K. Fischer, that in dealing with the consciousness of actuality, Hegel means to deal with actuality itself, according to the principle of identity. But we object to Lasson's view that this confounding of the two represents "progress beyond Kant."

[22] *Phänomenologie* (ed. Lasson), pp. 29/30. Cf. also pp. 32/3.

[23] The problem is discussed by K. Fischer, op. cit. p. 310, but in such a way as to confuse the negating with the suspending; Fischer, too, seems doubtful about the third meaning when speaking of the triad of *negare, conservare* and *elevare.*

[24] See below, p. 163 ff, for further elaboration. The sentence quoted is translated from Johannes Hoffmeister's edition of Hegel's *Vorlesungen,* p. 148.

[25] The matter is touched upon, but not treated with the insight and penetration displayed elsewhere in their volume by A. L. Kroeber and Clyde Kluckhohn, *Culture—A Critical Review of Concepts and Defini-*

tions (1952). The relation of *Bildung,* a central concept of Hegel's approach to culture, and the fact that Hegel at crucial points actually refers to *Kultur,* are neglected, and that in turn leads the authors to fail to bring out the fact that the approach they are interested in, namely the interrelation of all cultural phenomena as part of one consistent whole, is first and foremost that of Hegel. He above all others gave it currency and provided it with a philosophical foundation. That this philosophical foundation, namely that all these manifestations are the expression of one spirit, may be objectionable to many today, does not alter the central fact of Hegel's recognizing the problem. And by the way, what philosophical explanation has since been offered by cultural anthropology for this alleged coherence and inner consistency of cultural wholes that is clearly more nearly right than Hegel's?

²⁶ Rosenkranz, op. cit., p. 201.

²⁷ Iwan Iljin, *Die Philosophie Hegels als Kontemplative Gotteslehre* (1946). This highly significant work is an abbreviation of an earlier and longer Russian one.

²⁸ *The Logic of Hegel,* transl. by W. Wallace (1892) pp. 93/4.

²⁹ This is the reason for including the later chapters of the *Phenomenology,* rather than the more diffuse material of his *Lectures on Religion,* in our selections. What is perhaps even more important a consideration is that they *are* lectures and on account of Hegel's way of lecturing are both diffuse and repetitive.

¹⁰ Rudolf Haym, *Hegel und seine Zeit* (1857) (ed. Rosenberg 1927) pp. 397 ff. Some of Haym's strictures apply more appropriately to Hegel's *Lectures on the Philosophy of Religion,* than they do to the *Phenomenology.* But in both Hegel insists upon the importance of the basic religious experience.

¹ *Lectures on the Philosophy of Religion* (transl. and edited by E. B. Speirs and J. Burdon Sanderson) (1895) vol. I, p. 33.

² Hegel's position has been related to, and at times been confused with that of Spinoza. A reading of Hegel's treatment of Spinoza in his *Geschichte der Philosophie* (1833) pp. 368/411 will prevent one from making this mistake. Specifically on the subject of pantheism, Hegel takes up the charge that Spinoza's pantheism meant atheism; he considers this charge both false and true. True, significantly, in this respect that Spinoza does not distinguish God from the world, from nature and human spirit which he says is God. Hegel adds: "Spinoza asserts that what is called world does not exist; it is only a form of God, and nothing in and by itself. . . . Spinozism is thus far removed from being atheism in the usual sense; but in the sense that God is not conceived as spirit, it is atheism. But in the same sense, many theologians are atheists when they call God merely the all-powerful, the highest being, etc. They do not want to know God . . . which is worse." These remarks show clearly the deep gulf that separates Spinoza's idealism from that of Hegel; it is, in Hegelian

terms, abstract and formal, instead of being concrete and substantive.

[33] Hegel himself at one time in his later years spoke of the *Phenomenology* as containing his exploratory trips or *"Entdeckungsreisen."*

[34] See below, p. 519. Note also the discussion in K. Fischer, p. 427, and the entire chapter XII, pp. 413 ff. ibid. For the letter, see Fischer, p. 46.

[35] Rosenkranz, op. cit. pp. 258–267.

[36] *Logik* (ed. Lasson) (1923) *Einleitung des Herausgebers* p. xvii.

[37] ibid., p. 36.

[38] Hegel's central term *Begriff* has been rendered by some careful students, e.g. Baillie, as notion; but while notion may be more comprehensive than concept, it gainsays the intended *logical* sharpness of Hegel's term. In the same connection, we might mention some of the difficulties encountered in rendering the German term *Anschauung,* usually translated as intuition. The matter is discussed in my Introduction to *The Philosophy of Kant,* in the Modern Library.

[39] See Nicolai Hartmann, *Die Philosophie des Deutschen Idealismus, II, Hegel* (1929), which contains the most penetrating recent discussion of Hegel's *Logic;* the reference is to p. 168.

[40] *Logik,* ed. Lasson, p. 67.

[41] ibid., p. 93.

[42] See Rosenkranz, op. cit. pp. 368–373. Cousin, a friend and collaborator of Royer-Collard, the liberal leader, popularized Hegel in Paris.

[43] Among recent treatments of Hegel's philosophy of right and law, mention should be made especially of Rosenzweig, Löwenstein and Eric Weil, mentioned above in notes 2–4. An interesting general sketch is contained in George Sabine's *History of Political Theory* (rec. ed. 1951). Perhaps the most authoritative, from a Hegelian viewpoint at least, is G. Lasson's Introduction to his edition of the *Rechtsphilosophie;* this edition is in important respects superior to the old edition contained in the *Werke* and should be supplemented further by Lasson's very interesting edition of Hegel's *Eigenhaendige Randbemerkungen zu seiner Rechtsphilosophie* (1930). We have used these for some critical control in the translation of the work, though following generally the established edition. Among older English treatments B. Bosanquet's *Philosophical Theory of the State,* chs. 9–10, and L. T. Hobhouse, *The Metaphysical Theory of the State* (1918) are still outstanding.

[44] Much popular writing is vitiated by this error, for example the comments on Hegel contained in Karl Popper's in many ways admirable *The Open Society and Its Enemies* (1950) ch. 12; it must be admitted, however, that many ardent Hegelians and Neo-Hegelians have contributed to this mistaken interpretation. And since Hegel's unusual terminology engenders such misunderstandings, it has contributed greatly to the "deification" of the existent state, so popular in Germany.

[45] Rosenkranz, op. cit. p. 303.

[46] The implications of this essay of William James are briefly discussed in my *Inevitable Peace* (1948) p. 203.

[47] Rosenkranz noted that Hegel's approach in some respects fell short of the existent degree of liberalism reached by the kingdom of Prussia at that time. I suspect that this was due to the influence of his rather conservative native Württemberg which although often praised for its "constitutionalism," its *gutes altes Recht* was actually at this time inclined toward an outmoded patriarchalism.

[47a] Richard Hooker, *The Laws of Ecclesiastical Polity*, I, V, 1.

[48] See Carl Becker, *Everyman His Own Historian* (1935), pp. 233 ff.

[49] There is a rapidly increasing literature on philosophy of history in English, highlighted by Toynbee, Collingwood, and most recently Richard McKeon whose *Freedom and History* (1952) is particularly relevant to a reassessment of Hegel. An important general perspective is offered in Raymond Aron's *Introduction à la philosophie de l'histoire* (1948).

[50] See *Die Vernünft an der Geschichte* (ed. Lasson), p. 200.

[51] See Marcuse, op. cit. passim. The fact that Hegel's view is one focused in terms of the "end of history" (*endgeschichtlich*) has been put into the center of his broad and very helpful analysis by Karl Löwith, *Von Hegel zu Nietzsche* esp. p. 44 ff. (1941).

[52] H. G. Hotho, *Vorstudien füer Leben und Kunst*, pp. 385 ff., as quoted in Fischer, op. cit., p. 215.

[53] *Briefe Hegels* (ed. Hoffmeister) vol. I, pp. 425/6. On Hegel's aesthetics, see B. Bosanquet's introduction to his translation of Hegel's own introduction to his aesthetics (see next note). Cf. also the recent *Hegels Aesthetik* (1928) by Walter Frost.

[54] Hegel, *Vorlesungen üeber Aesthetik, Werke* (XII–XIV), XII, p. 89.

[55] Many details can be gleaned from his letters for these years; see *Werke*, vol. XIX, second part.

[56] See Hegel, *Asthetik* (1838), vol. iii, p. 208.

[57] *Werke*, XIV, p. 580.

[58] W. T. Stace, *The Philosophy of Hegel* (1924) p. 31.

[59] The most detailed and passionately one-sided account of this matter is to be found in Georg Lukacs, op. cit. Cf. also Konrad Bekker, *Marx' philosophische Entwicklung und sein Verhäeltnis zu Hegel* (1940).

[60] Wayne A. R. Leys, *Ethics for Policy Decisions* (1952) p. 136. See the interesting summary in Morris Cohen's article on Hegel in the Encyclopedia of the Social Sciences.

[61] See T. S. Baer, *Max Weber's Methodology of Social Science: A Critique* (1952), Doctoral Dissertation at Harvard, as yet unprinted.

[62] B. Croce, *Ce qui est vivant et ce qui est mort de la Philosophie de Hegel* (French ed. by H. Buriot, 1910; orig. ed. in Italian 1906).

BIBLIOGRAPHY

Hegel's works were edited and published in the years after his death by a group of devoted students, including his son Karl Hegel; this edition was eventually republished by Glockner, with some changes. Unless special references are given, *Werke* in the *Notes* refers to this edition. However, a great many valuable critical editions were made of individual works of Hegel by Georg Lasson which were gathered into an edition of *Sämtliche Werke*, published by Felix Meiner; they are at present in the process of revision by Johannes Hoffmeister who already in 1936 edited the very valuable *Dokumente zu Hegels Entwicklung*.

A critical bibliography was included by B. Croce in his study of Hegel's philosophy. Hermann Glockner put every student of Hegel into his lasting debt by compiling a four-volume *Hegel-Lexikon* (publ. as vols. XXIII–XXVI of his edition of Hegel's work).

The following titles are merely suggestive, stressing the more recent work on Hegel which the editor has found especially useful. Other references are found in the notes above.

Antoni, Carlo, *Considerazioni su Hegel e Marx* (1946)

Baillie, J. B. *The Origin and Significance of Hegel's Logic—A General Introduction* (1901)

Bosanquet, B. *Introduction to Hegel's Philosophy of Fine Art* (1886) (note also his *Philosophical Theory of the State*, 1899)

Caird, E. *Hegel* (1883 and later)

Croce, Benedetto, *What Is Living and What Is Dead in Hegel's Philosophy* (1915 Engl. edition of Italian original of 1906)

Dilthey, Wilhelm, *Die Jugendgeschichte Hegels* (1905) (in *Gesammelte Schriften* Bd. IV, 1921)

Fischer, Kuno, *Hegels Leben, Werke und Lehre* (1901)

Foster, Michael B. *Die Geschichte als Schicksal des Geistes in der Hegelschen Philosophie* (1929)

Glockner, Herrmann, *Hegel* (2 vols., 1929)

551

Hartmann, Nicolai, *Die Philosophie des Deutschen Idealismus, II, Hegel* (1929)

Haym, R. *Hegel und seine Zeit* (1857) (reprinted with an interesting appendix by Rosenberg on the *"Geschichte der Hegelauffassung,"* 1927)

Hook, Sidney, *From Hegel to Marx* (1936)

Hyppolyte, Jean, *Genèse et Structure de la Phénoménologie de l'Espirit de Hegel* (1946)

Iljin, Iwan, *Die Philosophie Hegels als Kontemplative Gotteslehre* (1946)

Kojève, Alexandre, *Introduction à la Lecture de Hegel—Leçons sur la Phénoménologie de l'Esprit publ. par R. Queneau* (1947)

Kroner, Richard, *Von Kant bis Hegel* (2 vols., 1921–4) See also the same author's fine Introduction to G. W. F. Hegel—*Early Theological Writings* (ed. T. M. Knox) pp. 1–66 (1948)

Levy, H. *Die Hegelrenaissance* (1927)

Löwenstein, Julius, *Hegels Staatsidee—Ihr Doppelgesicht und ihr Einfluss im 19. Jahrhundert* (1927)

Löwith, Karl, *Von Hegel zu Nietzsche* (1941)

Lukacs, Georg, *Der Junge Hegel* (1948)

Marcuse, Herbert, *Reason and Revolution—Hegel and the Rise of Social Theory* (1941)

——— *Hegels Ontologie und die Grundlagen einer Theorie der Geschichtlichkeit* (1931)

McTaggart, John M. E. *Studies in the Hegelian Dialectic* (1922)

Moog, Willy, *Hegel und die Hegelsche Schule* (1930)

Rosenkranz, Karl, *Georg Wilhelm Friedrich Hegels Leben* (1844) (note also his *Hegel als Deutscher Nationalphilosoph,* 1870)

Rosenzweig, Franz, *Hegel und der Staat* (2 vols., 1920)

Steinbüchel, Theodor, *Das Grundproblem der Hegelschen Philosophie* (2 vols., 1933)

Schwarz, Justus, *Hegels Philosophische Entwicklung* (1938)

Stace, W. T. *The Philosophy of Hegel—A Systematic Exposition* (1924)

Weil, Eric, *Hegel et l'Etat* (1950)

MODERN LIBRARY GIANTS

A series of sturdily bound and handsomely printed, full-sized library editions of books formerly available only in expensive sets. These volumes contain from 600 to 1,400 pages each.

THE MODERN LIBRARY GIANTS REPRESENT A SELECTION OF THE WORLD'S GREATEST BOOKS

G68   PAINE, TOM: *Selected Work*
G86   PASTERNAK, BORIS: *Doctor Zhivago*
G5   PLUTARCH: *Lives* (The Dryden Translation)
G40   POE, EDGAR ALLAN: *Complete Tales and Poems*
G29   PRESCOTT, WILLIAM H.: *The Conquest of Mexico and The Conquest of Peru*
G62   PUSHKIN: *Poems, Prose and Plays*
G65   RABELAIS: *Complete Works*
G12   SCOTT, SIR WALTER: *The Most Popular Novels* (Quentin Durward, Ivanhoe & Kenilworth)
G4   SHELLEY & KEATS: *Complete Poems*
G32   SMITH, ADAM: *The Wealth of Nations*
G61   SPAETH, SIGMUND: *A Guide to Great Orchestral Music*
G92   SPENGLER, OSWALD: *The Decline of the West* (one volume)
G91   SPENSER, EDMUND: *Selected Poetry*
G75   STEVENSON, ROBERT LOUIS: *Selected Writings*
G53   SUE, EUGENE: *The Wandering Jew*
G42   TENNYSON: *The Poems and Plays*
G23   TOLSTOY, LEO: *Anna Karenina*—tr. revised
G1   TOLSTOY, LEO: *War and Peace*
G49   TWAIN, MARK: *Tom Sawyer* and *Huckleberry Finn*
G50   WHITMAN, WALT: *Leaves of Grass*
G83   WILSON, EDMUND: *The Shock of Recognition*

MISCELLANEOUS

G77   *An Anthology of Famous American Stories*
G54   *An Anthology of Famous British Stories*
G67   *Anthology of Famous English and American Poetry*
G81   *An Encyclopedia of Modern American Humor*
G47   *The English Philosophers from Bacon to Mill*
G16   *The European Philosophers from Descartes to Nietzsche*
G31   *Famous Science-Fiction Stories*
G85   *Great Ages and Ideas of the Jewish People*
G89   *Great Classical Myths*
G72   *Great Tales of Terror and the Supernatural*
G9   *Great Voices of the Reformation*
G87   *Medieval Epics*
G48   *The Metropolitan Opera Guide*
G46   *A New Anthology of Modern Poetry*
G69   *One Hundred and One Years' Entertainment*
G93   *Parodies: An Anthology from Chaucer to Beerbohm and After*
G90   *Philosophies of Art and Beauty: Readings in Aesthetics from Plato to Heidegger*
G21   *Sixteen Famous American Plays*
G63   *Sixteen Famous British Plays*
G71   *Sixteen Famous European Plays*
G45   *Stoic and Epicurean Philosophers*
G22   *Thirty Famous One-Act Plays*
G66   *Three Famous Murder Novels, Before the Fact,* FRANCIS ILES, *Trent's Last Case,* E. C. BENTLEY, *The House of the Arrow,* A. E. W. MASON
G10   *Twelve Famous Plays of the Restoration and Eighteenth Century* (1660–1820): Dryden, Congreve, Wycherley, Gay, etc.
G56   *The Wisdom of Catholicism*
G59   *The Wisdom of China and India*
G79   *The Wisdom of Israel*